BAMBOO

William Boyd is the author of nine novels, many of which have won prizes. *A Good Man in Africa* won the Whitbread Literary Award for Best First Novel; *An Ice-Cream War* won the John Llewellyn Rhys Memorial Prize and was shortlisted for the Booker Prize; *Brazzaville Beach* won the James Tait Black Memorial Prize; *The Blue Afternoon* was the winner of the *Los Angeles Times* Book Prize for Fiction; and most recently *Restless* won the 2006 Costa Novel Award. In addition, some thirteen of his screenplays have been filmed and in 1998 he both wrote and directed the feature film *The Trench*.

BY THE SAME AUTHOR

A Good Man in Africa

On the Yankee Station

An Ice-Cream War

Stars and Bars

School Ties

The New Confessions

Brazzaville Beach

The Blue Afternoon

The Destiny of Nathalie 'X'

Armadillo

Nat Tate: an American Artist

Any Human Heart

Fascination

Restless

The Dream Lover

Bamboo

WILLIAM BOYD

BLOOMSBURY

First published in 2005 by Hamish Hamilton
This paperback edition published 2008

Copyright © 2005 by William Boyd

The moral right of the author has been asserted

Bloomsbury Publishing Plc, 36 Soho Square, London W1D 3QY

A CIP catalogue record for this book is available from the British Library

ISBN 9 780 7475 9768 1

10 9 8 7 6 5 4 3 2 1

Printed in Great Britain by Clays Ltd, St Ives plc

All papers used by Bloomsbury Publishing are natural, recyclable products made
from wood grown in well-managed forests. The manufacturing processes
conform to the environmental regulations of the country of origin

www.williamboyd.co.uk

for Susan

'Plant one bamboo shoot – cut bamboo for the rest of your life'

Chinese proverb

Contents

Introduction

'Plant one bamboo shoot – cut bamboo for the rest of your life.' This Chinese saying seemed an apt epigraph for this enterprise and the bamboo shoot of the first properly published review that I wrote for the *New Review* in 1978 has, like the plant does itself, multiplied exponentially. Surveying the totality of my non-fiction writing over the last quarter of a century as it was gathered in for this volume has provoked several reactions: astonishment, curiosity, incredulity. When did I find the time to write these hundreds of thousands of words alongside the main business of my writing life: novels and screenplays?

In any event, here is a judicious selection, perhaps 40 per cent of the total, covering seven broad subjects: Life, Literature, Art, Africa, Film, Television and People and Places. The various articles, prefaces, profiles, reviews and introductions amount to a form of intellectual portrait, I suppose. These subjects, and their subdivisions, represent what interests me, infuriates me, obsesses me, fascinates me. It's one reason why, when the invitation to write comes from an editor, I find it so hard to say 'no'.

In fact I realize that I have been writing criticism for as long as, and in parallel with, my fiction. While I was at university in Glasgow I wrote a novel (unpublished) called *Is That All There Is?* and at the same time I edited the arts pages in the university newspaper, giving myself the plum jobs of film and theatre critic. When I went to Oxford to do a postgraduate degree I contributed articles to *Isis* (interviews with other writers, in the main) as I began to write fiction more seriously (there was another bottom-drawered novel) and started slowly but surely to publish short stories. None of these articles makes it into this collection however, even though there might be grounds for including it or others as intriguing juvenilia. One of the reasons for writing criticism that is often passed over in silence is that not only do you see your own name in print (very important for a young writer) but also you get paid (most of the time) and you receive a free book. So I thought it was fitting to begin the selection process with the first published review that I received money for. It was commissioned in 1978 by Craig

Raine, who was then books editor of the long-defunct *New Review* (and can be found on page 93). Interestingly enough, I have been writing sporadically for Craig in one form or another ever since, after the *New Review* at *Quarto* and more recently in *Areté*, and we were colleagues for a while on the *New Statesman* in the early eighties. I have had several similar editorial relationships over the period this compilation encompasses. As the editor has moved and changed jobs so have I tagged along. I think, amongst others, of Bill Buford at *Granta* and then the *New Yorker*, of Peter Stothard at *The Times* and now the *Times Literary Supplement*, of Mary Kay Wilmers at the *TLS* and then the *London Review of Books*, and of Rebecca Nicolson at the *Spectator*, the *Observer Magazine*, the *Sunday Telegraph* and finally at Short Books. Christopher Hawtree oversaw some of my earliest reviews in the *London Magazine* in the early eighties and was an invaluable and indefatigable help in bringing this collection together. I am very grateful to him. One of the bonuses of assembling these pieces is that it enables you to trace these literary song-lines in your output and your life. It's never quite so haphazard a journey as you think.

Faced with these hundreds of thousands of words I decided to impose a rough criterion of choice. I have tried mainly to include pieces that throw a light, sometimes strong and clear, sometimes oblique and occluded, on my novels, short stories and films. These pieces are often guileless anticipations of something I was going to write about; sometimes arguments with myself about subjects that were preoccupying me; and sometimes retrospective glances at aspects of our world about which my novelist's research had made me a temporary authority. Writing a novel, amongst all manner of other things, is also a form of self-education: *The Blue Afternoon* led me to early powered flight and surgery, *Brazzaville Beach* to primatology, *The New Confessions* to Jean-Jacques Rousseau and so on.

At the same time I have resisted the temptation to fiddle and tamper. What is true of all writers is true of me also: we have our particular quirks, tropes and tricks of the trade, our favourite words, metaphors and jokes, our regular *points de repère* (in my case, it seems, an abiding fondness for bringing in Wallace Stevens, Paul Klee, Anton Chekhov, T. S. Eliot and Pablo Picasso to back up my contentions). There seemed no purpose in removing the inevitable repetitions: they make their own valid point about the way I argue my case.

Another motive for writing all these pieces is that it has always seemed entirely normal. It never occurred to me that this might be a waste of energy and inspiration that might be better employed elsewhere: I always wanted to write articles and reviews from the beginning of my literary career. Isn't this what novelists do? I thought. Don't they write as much as they can, all the time? In hindsight this argument may seem naive but in one of these articles I advance the notion that this is perhaps a particularly British phenomenon. Certainly in the two other literary worlds I am familiar with – the USA and France – their novelists seem positively costive compared to ours – always excluding the prodigious John Updike, of course. It is as if the tireless energy of our great nineteenth-century exemplars – Dickens, Trollope, Thackeray – still inspires us, or has established a norm of writerly endeavour and output that – with a few notable exceptions – most British novelists (and many British poets, come to think of it) are happy to live with.

And yet there is an injunction to myself often to be found in the pages of my journal (something else I've been writing for twenty-five years): the cry of, 'NO MORE JOURNALISM!' And yet again, I seem incapable of following my own advice. The last piece that appears in this volume was written in December 2004. As I write this introduction, a month into 2005, I note that I have agreed to review a book for the *Times Literary Supplement*, produce a preface for some Katherine Mansfield stories and write a long article on films that feature Adolf Hitler. That bamboo shoot planted in 1978 has produced a bamboo grove that continues to expand, lush and densely green, spreading and thickening remorselessly.

WILLIAM BOYD, London, 2005

LIFE

I have gone on record claiming that I am not an autobiographical writer, that my fiction will provide no handy keys to unlock the door to my personal history. However, I have written autobiographically in my non-fiction, more than I had ever imagined, and particularly about my African childhood and my schooldays – a near-decade spent in a boarding school in the north of Scotland. But in putting this collection together I realized that, over the years, even more of my life had crept into my writings than I had thought. Therefore these pieces are assembled in rough chronological order – the chronology of my life rather than their writing: there are big gaps but, to my vague surprise, they cover a fair bit of the ground. I still believe I'll never attempt a bona fide autobiography or memoir. I suspect that these occasional scraps and gleanings will be all that it will amount to.

This section also introduces one of my favourite formal devices: the A–Z. I have used it with some regularity in my non-fiction (and it will be encountered later, several times) for the signal reason that it allows me to squeeze a quart into a pint pot or at least give the illusion of so doing. The strict logical progression of the alphabet paradoxically forces you to be arbitrary: you have to find something that fits a 'Q' or an 'X' or an 'O' or a 'V' even when nothing appears obvious or forthcoming. An A–Z of a given subject (a painter, a borough of London, an iconic writer) somehow seems more all-inclusive than a measured essay of exactly the same length. The necessary darting around, as you try to fit the letters to a relevant subject – makeshift invention requiring you to hammer a square peg into a round hole from time to time – inevitably assures a skewed, disparate and eccentric account that, when it works, produces a richer, more accurate portrait.

Memories of the Sausage Fly

The ant-lion builds its traps in sandy soil. It fashions – somehow – a geometrically perfect inverted cone. At the tip of the cone the ant-lion lurks, buried and invisible, waiting for any small insect to tumble in. When this occurs, the ant-lion at first makes no move. The walls of the cone are so smooth, the sand-grains they are composed of so fine, that only the largest insects can gain any purchase. As the smaller victims slither and scrabble on the steep sides of the cone, the ant-lion spits – or flicks – more sand at them, causing them to tumble down into the cone-tip where they are dragged beneath the sand and devoured.

The largest ant-lion cone I ever saw was about three inches deep; the predator itself half an inch long. I caught it underneath our house in Signals Road, Achimota, in what was then the Gold Coast. The house was built on six-foot concrete piles. Beneath it was sand, pocked with ant-lion traps. A lunar landscape of immaculate craters. Hundreds upon hundreds of ant-lions. A no man's land for any small crawling insect. Our particular ploy was to dig out a small ant-lion and drop it in the hole of a larger one.

I always think of ant-lions when I think of our house in Achimota. It is the first of our houses in Africa that I remember, though we had lived in two before that. At the time I was born we lived in a converted officers' mess, made of mud bricks and with a corrugated-iron roof. Achimota was about six miles from Accra and the coast. On the huge beaches, ten-foot breakers would cream in from the Atlantic. We weren't allowed on the surf beaches until we were older and could belly-surf, but there were rocky stretches with rock pools burgeoning with sub-marine life. Sitting in a rock pool, waist deep in blood-warm water, aged five. Life was good.

We moved away from Achimota to Legon, three miles further inland, to the new campus of the University of Ghana. We lived in a large U-shaped house, painted white with a red-tiled roof. There was a large stoep, big enough for thirty to gather on, that gave on to the enormous garden and a view of the surrounding countryside – grass-covered hills, clumps of small tough trees.

The insect I associate with the house in Legon is the velvet mite. These completely benign creatures were the size of a fingernail, a brilliant coruscating red, and did indeed seem to be covered in a sort of velvety fur. They were the only insects I've ever encountered that you could stroke. At certain times of the year, particularly after the rainy season, they proliferated, and the grass around our house hotched with them. My sisters and I used to ranch velvet mites, gathering them in their hundreds into makeshift twig corrals. There the mites would mill around aimlessly, square feet of shifting scarlet velvet, a boiling carpet of red.

We moved to Nigeria, to Ibadan, in 1963. Our house on the university campus there was long and straight. The garden was surrounded by a dense hibiscus and poinsettia hedge and was full of trees: frangipani, cotton trees and tall elegant casuarina pines. I would borrow our gardener's machete and chop at the frangipani trees. Bury the curved blade (made in Czechoslovakia) in the bole, which was soft and yielding. The tree bled a white milk that dripped all day. Later I bought my own machete for five shillings. It was useful for hacking things down. Ibadan is set in the middle of tropical rain forest, things grow at an enormous speed. I cut two poles and stuck them in the ground to support our badminton net. When I came back from school three months later they had turned into trees.

The insect I associate with our house in Ibadan is the sausage fly. It's not really a fly at all but some kind of bloated ant that grows wings and takes to the air after rain. The sausage fly is about an inch long, a hard shiny banger-brown, hence its name. In the evening, after it has rained, you shut all your windows. Wings unfold from the carapace of the sausage fly and they take to the air in droves. They are not very good in the air – it isn't their natural element – and it's as if they have only borrowed the wings for the day. They steer haphazardly for the nearest light. Inside the house you can hear them carom into the windows and wire mosquito-netting. Squadrons veer unsteadily around exterior lights. They only have their wings for an hour or so. The sausage flies touch down and their wings fall off. A lot of them die as a result of mid-air collisions, flying into walls and such like. The next morning the veranda is crunchy underfoot with their hard bodies, and brilliant fragile drifts of discarded wings lie in the corners. The surviving sausage flies have resumed their earthly existence and have crawled off somewhere to complete their life cycle.

My father went out to West Africa during the Second World War. He was in the Royal Army Medical Corps and was based in Lagos, Jos, in northern Nigeria (where they grow strawberries and new potatoes on the plateau all year round) and in the Gold Coast. We have a picture of him, very young and thin, sitting on a cane chair outside a grass hut some time in 1945. He came back to the Gold Coast in 1951 with my mother, planning to stay a few years only. He remained until 1977, until he was forced to leave because of ill-health. He had contracted a curious and rare disease called 'Q' fever. He had been a doctor working in Africa all his life and eventually Africa was literally the death of him.

His work began very early in the day. He would work through until two in the afternoon when he returned home for lunch. He would sleep until four and then go and play nine holes of golf. In the evening my mother would join him and their friends on the stoep of the golf club (drink was plentiful, very cheap and on credit). Perhaps there would be an impromptu supper-party later on. There was nothing frenetic or debauched in this social round – it was a far cry from Happy Valley – but in comparison to the life that most of these members of the professional middle class would have been living in Britain in the fifties it must have seemed paradisiacal.

They could lead this life because everyone had servants. My parents had only been in the Gold Coast a week when one morning they discovered a small old man sitting on the kitchen steps. He said his name was Kofi and he had heard they needed a cook. Kofi was our cook for the next eleven years. He and his family lived in a village some two miles away. In Legon our house had servants' quarters, a simple, not to say crude, concrete cottage a few yards from the main house. This was occupied by Kofi's son, Kwame, who was then in his twenties. He is now a major in a tank battalion in the Ghanaian Army. Kwame used to babysit for my parents. My sisters and I would often spend the evenings in his hot concrete room, eating the very peppery fried plantain that he would prepare on a small cast-iron charcoal brazier in the corner.

In Nigeria we had a cook and a houseboy, Johnson and Israel. Johnson was very old, his hair was greying, and he was very set in his ways. When I read Joyce Cary's *Mister Johnson* I always think of our old cook. Cary's Johnson is much younger but the two had much in common. Johnson had been married many times but had no children. This, he claimed, was the fault of the wives he had had and nothing to do with his potency. Just before we left Nigeria he got married again to a very young girl. She used to do our washing for us and when Johnson was away in the afternoons received visits from other men. Eventually she became pregnant and later had a baby girl. There never was a prouder father.

Johnson was very tall and lanky, Israel was extremely small and walked everywhere very fast. He was an Easterner, an Ibo, and during the Biafran War he joined the Biafran Army in order to get something to eat. One day he was given a rifle and five rounds of ammunition and was deployed in the bush to repel an attack by the Federal forces. He was always quite candid about what he did next. He took off his camouflage jacket (the only uniform he possessed) and buried it. Then he threw his rifle away and deserted.

Once, in some waiting-room, or at some station bookstall, I picked up a copy of *Scientific American*. On the cover was what looked like a picture of a badly made patchwork quilt, all greys, rusts and ochrous browns. I recognized it immediately as an aerial photograph of Ibadan town centre, without need of recourse to the theme of the issue – which was 'Town Planning in the Third World', or something equivalent. Ibadan is lodged as firmly in my mind as any of the other cities I've lived in. It is known, sometimes affectionately, as the largest village in Africa. It has a population of well over one million. Most of the buildings within its sprawling purlieus are made of mud and roofed with corrugated iron. The streets crumble away at the edges into large deep ditches and are permanently crammed with cars. From every house and shop, radio music blares. At night the buildings are lit with fluorescent tubes, predominantly green and blue. There is public transport but the most common way of getting about the city is in Volkswagen vans. When you see a VW coming you stick out your hand and it stops. You climb in (the sliding doors are removed) and give sixpence to a small boy who hangs on to the outside. The vans ply certain basic routes. When you want to get off you rap with your knuckles on the roof. The van stops at once.

I used to travel by this means from the university campus into town to the Recreation Club. Here you could play tennis, golf and squash, swim at the pool, eat snacks and drink at the bars. During school holidays it was a focal point for the children of expatriates. We would spend the entire day there. In the evening we would go to the cinema or go to a party. There were lots of parties. Parties in town, parties at the university, parties at the New Reservation, parties in Bodija. Teenage parties: the same boys, the same girls, records and beer, sometimes a punch made from illicit gin brewed on the banks of distant creeks and reputed to make you blind if you drank too much.

Excursions out of town were few and far between. Sometimes we would go fishing. Drive out a couple of hours into the jungle to find a slow brown river and spin for perch. Sometimes we went down to Lagos for a week to stay in rickety beach huts at Tarqua Bay. Fish off the breakwater, go sailing – dodging the merchant ships steaming into Lagos harbour; surf at the surfing beach, and at night sleep on camp beds in the open air, beneath the stars and a mosquito net. The Americans refer to the children of US Army personnel serving abroad as 'army brats' or 'air force brats'. There were times when we were 'colonial brats'. Lazy, self-regarding, pleasure-seeking and utterly incurious about the country we were living in.

That all changed with the Biafran War. I well remember the day of the military coup that precipitated the country into its civil war. I was due to fly back to Britain for the start of the school term. Johnson, our cook, laconically told me that I wouldn't be going. Why not? I asked. Because, he said, there's going to be a military coup on Monday. He was right.

When the war was on (1967–70) the tenor of life changed radically, largely because of the overwhelming presence of the Nigerian Army. From the minute you stepped off the plane at Ikeja airport armed soldiery became a constant feature of your day. Off-duty soldiers kept their guns with them: on buses, in bars, taking their kids for a walk.

One evening, driving along a quiet road with my father, we turned a corner and passed an oil drum with a plank leaning against it jutting a couple of feet into the road. It was only when we saw half a dozen soldiers spring from the trees with Kalashnikovs levelled that we real-ized it was a road block. We stopped abruptly and got out of the car. The guns were lowered and the car was searched. They were looking for currency smugglers, they said. The soldiers were young and edgy. They wore the odd bit of camouflage uniform supplemented by their own clothes, gym shoes, flannel trousers, an Hawaiian shirt. Their guns looked very old Warsaw Pact surplus – with numbers burned crudely into the stock. You looked at these guys, who had volunteered because of the free beer and cigarettes the Army provided, and wondered what was going on in the rebel heartland.

I haven't been back to Nigeria or any part of West Africa since 1973. I started writing about it in 1976 when I wrote an (unpublished) novel about the Biafran War. Subsequent efforts of hindsight and occasional nostalgia keep it very fresh in my mind. Particularly heavy rain, a warm and muggy night, the sound of crickets, a cold beer on a hot day, are always weighed up against their African equivalents and always found wanting. But it's the music of Nat King Cole that proves the most effective Proustian trigger.

It was one of my father's habits when he first got up in the morning almost immediately to put a record on a shiny walnut hi-fi he had shipped out from Britain. Invariably, the record he chose was by Nat King Cole, the first bars of which were greeted by loud groans from the rest of the family, but he paid no heed. He would stand in the middle of the main room, the sliding glass doors thrown wide open to catch the cool early-morning breeze and look out on the sunlit view as he sang along with Nat Cole. He always struck me in those moments as being a very happy man. Whenever I hear that distinctive dry voice I think of my father and of Africa in the early morning.

1984

Fly Away Home

York, Hermes, Argonaut, Stratocruiser, Super Constellation, Britannia, Boeing 707, VC10 . . . The story of my early encounters with England is a small history of aviation. I do not remember the York, a development of the Lancaster bomber, I believe, but in 1952 – the year I was born – my flying life began, in a Hermes. I was born in March in the Ridge Hospital in Accra, the capital of the Gold Coast. Four months later I was carried up the steps to the waiting Hermes to begin my first flight from my native land back to the place my parents came from. The Hermes followed the York on the first passenger services from the Gold Coast to London, making a series of short hops across the great protruding bulge of western Africa – Accra, Lagos, Kano, Tripoli – before crossing the Mediterranean to Madrid, Rome or Frankfurt and then on to London. The whole journey took seventeen hours.

I do remember the Argonaut quite well, however, a British version of the DC6, a four-engined prop plane that did not owe anything to World War Two precursors and was the first to make the trans-Sahara overfly routine (if one discounts the truly terrifying turbulence), and was thus able to cut the time of the West Africa to London trip substantially. We would land in Kano in northern Nigeria to refuel before setting off on the long leg over the desert to Tripoli. Kano airport was so fly-infested that the airport buildings were proofed with mosquito wire. Vultures perched on the control tower. We always crossed the Sahara at night (perhaps at the level the planes flew in those days the turbulence made it impassable when the sun was up?) and we would arrive at Tripoli as dawn broke. For this reason Tripoli airport always seemed dramatic and somewhat disturbing to me, as I recall: its hangars were colandered from World War Two shrapnel and in the pale light you could see cannibalized hulks of Italian bombers of the same era rusting mysteriously in the thin blond grass that fringed the runways. Beyond the perimeter fence camels grazed . . . There was still one more stop to be made in mainland Europe before we cruised over the English Channel to land at London airport – as Heathrow was always quaintly referred to in those days.

The Stratocruiser represented the ultimate in luxury. Twin-decked, with a glassy round bulbous nose, the plane tried to simulate the elegance of the Pullman cars in transcontinental express trains. Seats were arranged in fours, pairs facing each other. Above our heads was a reach-me-down bunk bed for children. On the lower deck was a small bar accessed by a tight spiral staircase, which I remember my parents descending for a cocktail before the meal was served – a side of roast beef on a silver trolley, the steward carving slices off it as if he were for all the world in the Savoy Grill and not twenty thousand feet above the dark wadis and sand seas of the endless Sahara.

All these aeroplanes and their successors – the Britannia, the VC10, and so on – were in the livery of BOAC – the British Overseas Airways Corporation – crisp white and navy blue and badged with the famous speedbird logo (now long vanished). As I grew older and became conscious of our annual trips back to Britain on leave, the planes, and by extension the company, came to represent the country by proxy, as if a little segment of Britain had been sent out to the colonies to fetch us back to the motherland. It was a kind of idealized metaphor, I suppose – the smart modern planes and their smart modern crew luring us on board with their smiles and their trays of boiled sweets – showing us what we had left behind, reminding us of our good fortune in being able to return.

My early experience of air travel instilled in me a love of flying, of airports and all the accoutrements of aviation which has not left me to this day. How could such an introduction to flight, at such an impressionable age, and with such magnificent ambassadors, not fail to entrance? As children our idea of a treat was to be driven from home to Accra airport to look at the BOAC plane. One runway, one uneven expanse of tarmac apron, a control tower, a few hangars, some low sheds doubling as immigration and customs, arrival and departure halls, Accra airport was modest and unassuming in the extreme. Across the road from the airport was the airport hotel, called The Lisbon for some forgotten reason, a single-storeyed wooden building with a wide veranda. On Saturday nights a highlife band would play and the more daring young expatriate couples would come there to dance. Like all airport hotels in Africa it effortlessly maintained a louche and faintly racy ambiance. We children would take our drinks – our Fantas and Cokes – and go and stand at the wood paling fence and stare at the silver giant, propellers stilled, parked on the tarmac. Fuel bowsers and generators hummed, linked trolleys bouncing with luggage trundled from the departure lounge, engineers and cleaners ran up and down the wheeled steps set against the doorways. Then came the crew, then came the long lines of passengers. Doors were closed, propellers turned, the plane was freed of its various appurtenances and it taxied to the end of the runway.

To see it lift off and climb into the dusty evening air was both exhilarating and melancholy, emotions perhaps not fully comprehended then but more easily analysed now. It has to be understood that in the fifties, certainly from an African perspective, these tremendous aeroplanes, and the world they both encompassed and conjured up, were for us a vision of immense and modern glamour and at the same time, like all people being left behind, we felt a sense of flatness and disappointment lingering as we returned to the car and were driven home, counting the weeks and months until it would be our turn to cross that cracked uneven piste towards the blue and white flying machine and be carried away by it also, cosseted and nourished, across the desert to Europe, to England, homeward.

As you mounted the steps towards the door, almost swooning with excitement, the first impression, aside from the stewardess (a figure of unearthly exoticism), was olfactory. The smell of the flyspray that was liberally pumped throughout the plane's interior prior to take off was both sweet and oddly choking. It was a smell replicated nowhere else in my range of nasal memory – part marzipan, part cough medicine, part liqueur, part candy, part liniment . . . I could not place it: our flysprays at home did not smell remotely the same. But whatever it was, whatever brand it was or compound of chemical meeting unnatural fabric in a confined space, the BOAC version was potent and palpable. It was always, for me at least, the first smell of England. It was a kind of Rubicon; as you stepped over the threshold and were directed down the aisle, your lungs were filled with this curious reek. You soon became used to it but it signalled that your journey home had truly begun.

And yet my real home was in West Africa, in the Gold Coast – which in 1957 became Ghana. Until my tenth year I only spent summers in Britain, almost always in Scotland. But my parental home was in Ghana, and so were my bedroom, my things, my school, my friends. Scotland was where my relatives lived, where we rented a house and my parents caught up with their families. We were always in transit, welcomed but always 'just visiting'. The real business of my life lay at the end of another plane journey in the reverse direction. And the comparative brevity of the annual leave never allowed us fully to integrate, to take things for granted, to become *au fait* with the latest fads and fashions. Little details remind me now of that sense of apartness. I felt ill at ease walking past school playgrounds, always stared at. Why wasn't this boy (me) at school? (one could sense the unspoken question). How were my sullenly curious coevals to know that African school holidays did not coincide with the British? If I had not detoured, I crossed the street, head down. I never felt comfortable with children of my age group, en masse. I remember my father too, a man of status and real importance on the university campus where he ran a hospital and health clinics responsible for 20,000 people, fumbling like a new immigrant with his unfamiliar change as he tried to buy a newspaper in Edinburgh. You could sense the newsagent's impatience building as my father picked and prodded hesitantly at a palmful of coins. I possessed also a vague embarrassment about my clothes. The shorts and sandals and shirts made from local tie-dyed cloth – which were wholly unexceptional in Ghana – seemed eccentric, not to say bizarre, in breezy St Andrews or the High Street in Peebles. I had no long trousers at all, and how I coveted my first pair of jeans – finally bought at the age of nine with an aunt in a department store in Birmingham – at last, knees covered, I might not stand out from the crowd. Needless to say I never felt like this in Africa, where I roamed about the countryside, cycled through the streets and boulevards of the enormous, sprawling campus, possessing the place so thoroughly, so intimately, that such unreflecting familiarity has never been reproduced, no matter where I have subsequently lived. I knew paths through the bush, short cuts through servants' quarters. I knew where the biggest mangoes grew, the best spot to catch pythons, what pie-dogs to avoid, how to eat fufu, who would sell you a single stick of chewing gum, what were the rules and penalties of a complicated game involving the spinning of hollow snail shells . . . My life in Africa up until the age of ten was a modest but genuine idyll and its basic elements will be familiar to anyone who has grown up in the tropics – the child, the white child, still possessed a form of tolerant *laisser passer* denied the adult. We were unnoticed, or barely noticed, everywhere – which, when freedom to come and go is all you ask, is the best and most sincere form of welcome.

And then June came round and the rainy season threatened and it was time to go on leave. BOAC would send one of its planes to fetch us and the strange and exciting process that led to our landfall in England would begin. Sunset in Kano, the lurching rollercoaster of the night flight across the Sahara, dawn in Tripoli, morning in Madrid or Rome – finally peering through clearing clouds at the green patchwork of English fields and the occasional wink of sunburst from a car's windscreen. London airport. More low wooden buildings. Lino and formica. Tall blue policemen. Pale pasty faces. Strange accents . . . And somewhere, deep inside me, the private hollow of fear and insecurity that all aliens (however legal) carry within them. My passport was British so why was I uneasy?

It all changed when I was sent to boarding school in Scotland, something that happened to all expatriate children, as inevitable as puberty. However, my routine was turned on its head, everything was reversed: now I flew to Africa in the holidays. My family, my home, my room, my things, my friends were all as they had always been but now I only saw them for two months of the year. But back in Britain I was beginning to understand the place; I was beginning to be assimilated; I had started to fit in.

I was barely four months old when I made that first flight in a Hermes from Africa to England in 1952. My parents took me up to Scotland to present me to my grandmothers and the rest of the family. For some reason my father went back early and my mother and I joined him some weeks later at the end of our leave. By curious chance, as we were waiting in London airport for our plane to be called, there was a photographer from the *Evening Standard* patrolling the departure lounge looking for a lighthearted filler, I suppose, a bit of human interest for a corner of a page, snapping babes in arms about to go on a long plane journey, still a rarish event in those days, no doubt. My mother has kept the cutting. In the picture one glum and tearful toddler sits morosely on her mother's knee. Opposite is me, aged six months, fizzing with energy, bald and beefy as a Buddha, beaming hugely, my mother's arm clamped around my middle trying to stop the thrashing and the squirming. 'Why is master William Andrew Murray Boyd so happy?' the caption asks. I could not answer then, but I can now – I was flying home.

1998

The Lion Griefs

I went to boarding school at the age of nine. This was not exceptional: when I arrived at my school in September 1961 I found boys of six and seven. One exceptionally tiny boy – tawny-skinned with crow-black, dead-straight hair (was he half-Chinese?) – was rumoured to be five, though he angrily denied it.

I was not unhappy to be going away to school. In West Africa, where my parents lived, all the children of expatriate Europeans were doing the same at around my age. It was entirely normal and for years we were gently prepared (a form of benign brain-washing, I suppose) for the day when we would be left to fend for ourselves. Neither of my parents had been to public school or boarding school and both were unfamiliar with where or how to introduce me into the system. In the end it was decided that I should go to the same school as had a son of close friends. They had heard good reports of it; it was not horrifically expensive; I had seemed to like the place when I had been interviewed one summer when we were back on leave and, as I was Scottish, it was an advantage that the school was in Scotland, albeit in the remote far north. This northerly aspect provided the school with a not entirely deserved reputation for a Spartan, no-frills style of education, its most obvious manifestation being a proclaimed fondness for cold showers and early morning runs and the odd fact that the boys wore shorts throughout their school career, regardless of the seasons and the weather, until they left, aged eighteen.

The main school was serviced by two prep schools: the junior for boys up to the age of ten and a senior for boys from ten to thirteen who then, if they passed an undemanding entrance exam, were claimed by the parent institution. It was to the junior school that I was driven that September afternoon by my mother, all the way from Edinburgh, to find the field in front of the school house filled with forty or fifty small boys, dressed in navy blue jerseys and shorts, running about, kicking balls, wrestling and generally horsing around. It seemed like fun and I was oblivious to my mother's brimming tears as she said goodbye. She told me later she had had to stop outside the school gates, had pulled the car in to the side of the road and wept for an hour.

The junior prep school was housed in a former shooting lodge called Wester Elchies (now sadly demolished), a rather magical-looking Scottish baronial building with turrets and castellation set in fair-sized grounds with its own home farm. There were extensive woods, a telescopeless observatory and a curling pond. Over the hill was an orphanage (we were terrified of the orphans – sinister yahoos to our over-privileged eyes) and not far away, in the valley below, the River Spey flowed where salmon were caught by our headmaster, a legendary fly-fisher.

I was introduced to my 'minder', a tall rather glamorous blond boy called Holland. Holland was rich (his father had a Rolls-Royce) and he had an older brother who played in a pop group. This was a stroke of luck for me as, with Holland's patronage, I was introduced to his 'set' and achieved almost instant acceptance into the relatively innocent, tribal world of a prep school.

We were not particularly cruel to each other at this stage of our scholarly life, cruelty (sometimes exceptionally vicious) came later, after puberty, at the main school. For the pre-adolescent there seems to me to be only one requirement for success at prep school and that is popularity. Academic and sporting achievements at that age are so ephemeral and inconsequential that they gain little kudos, and at Wester Elchies the only miserable boys I recall were the unpopular ones. They were unpopular because they looked peculiar: Webster had the aspect of a puppet or cartoon character – with thick, springy carrot-coloured hair and heavy black specs; Sedley had dark, bruised eyes and unusually dun, greasy skin. Sedley was genially and routinely persecuted because he cried so easily. All it took was three or four of us to gather round him making quacking duck-bill movements with our hands and chanting 'Baitey! Baitey! Baitey!' and Sedley would obligingly break down into incoherent and hysterical weeping fits. We found this very amusing and never tired of the game. It was gratuitous but not malevolent. I don't think life at prep school as I experienced it was ever malign. The school's regime was good-natured, on the whole, the staff kind and tolerant. Sex and power, the two elements in boarding school life that really corrupt, even to the extent that they can make people evil, were waiting for our older selves up ahead.

Life at an all-boy prep school, though unreal (as all monosexual societies must be, by definition), was still an extension of childhood, and consequently our ambitions and disappointments, our desires and our hatreds retained some quality of childhood innocence. Most of our carnal energies, for example, were expended in trying to see female members of staff in the nude or, second best, to find some way of peering up into the dark recesses of their skirts. I and many others nurtured simultaneous passions for Miss Grey, the art teacher, and Miss Cibber, the music teacher. Miss Grey was tall and languorous with glossy dark hair wound round her head in a loose Bloomsburyesque bun. Her clothes were rich-looking, romantically hued. Miss Cibber too was dark, almost swarthy in fact, with a sturdier more curvaceous figure. For a term she ousted Miss Grey from my fantasies as I found myself allotted to a dormitory outside one of the staff bathrooms which she used. There was an inch-wide crack between the bottom of the door and the floor through which, if you pressed your head to the cold linoleum of the corridor, you could obtain a partial view of the bathroom beyond. Miss Cibber's strong legs from the thigh down became very familiar. We kept praying she would drop a towel or her toothbrush and have to bend over. She excluded herself from all our affections when she was surprised one day in a passionate kiss with the English master – a dull, weak fellow, to our eyes – called Hearn.

We did not like Hearn and therefore could not like anyone who liked him. Our affections were extremely fickle. Miss Cibber was dropped and I returned my loyalty to Miss Grey.

Ah, Miss Grey, Miss Catriona Grey! Strange how passionate the pre-pubertal crush can be. She must have been very young, in her early twenties, I suppose, and, as I recall her face, I realize she was very pretty too. I was good at art and saw a lot of her and became something of a favourite. Because I was close to her it is with Miss Grey that I associate my first adult feelings of envy – a pure, elemental, resentment-driven emotion. Miss Grey's beauty was not just apparent to her acolytes in the art room: the headmaster, Mr Vaughan, was also susceptible.

I was impressed by Mr Vaughan: he was the first person whom I recognized – unconsciously – as 'sophisticated'. He drove an MG road-ster with leather straps holding down the bonnet. He wore suede shoes, he smoked a lot, Player's Navy Cut, and had a deep, raspy smoker's voice. I can recall his flat in the school house with real clarity. A dark blue carpet, loose cream lineny covers on the sofas, good pictures on the walls. He was, I now realize, genuinely urbane, a confirmed bach-elor, a throwback figure from John Buchan or Sapper who had taken up schoolmastering before the war in the way that young men did coming down from Varsity with a poor degree (think of Waugh and

Auden) and had been too lazy, or found the life too congenial, ever to move on. He was white-haired – in his fifties – and being headmaster of a small prep school in Banffshire was to be the pinnacle of his professional life. But he seemed perfectly content and he used regularly to invite Miss Grey (a fellow smoker) to share a cigarette with him at his table at the end of the midday meal.

I can conjure up the tableau now, and the green fog of envious bile through which I viewed it, as we filed out to go to our dormitories for the obligatory postprandial rest. Mr Vaughan would push his chair back so he could cross his legs and dangle one brown suede shoe. He smoked with a small flourish, his hand describing a generous arc, a flexing, cuff-shooting movement, as he brought the cigarette to his lips. Inhaling avidly, laughing, leaning forward to share a throaty smoky confidence with Miss Grey who, her body language tells me in hindsight, was not wholly at ease with Mr Vaughan's raffish innuendoes. Miss Grey stiffly upright, an arm crossed below her breasts, a palm supporting the elbow of the smoking hand, the cigarette more demurely, more delicately, puffed at – a social smoker, then, not with Mr Vaughan's nicotine craving. I can hear Mr Vaughan's barking laugh crossing the emptying dining room as we troop out, degenerating into a barking lung-tearing cough. I look back, hating him, wanting to kill him, to see Miss Grey leaning forward, helping him to a consoling glass of water.

What kind of person was I then, in my pre-teens? Memories are vivid and precise but I cannot summon up a retrospective self-consciousness. The world is a simpler more straightforward place when you are ten, eleven, twelve. It is adolescence, the burgeoning hormone-swarm in the body, that brings home real intimations of character and personality. I look at pictures of the fair-haired lad I was and gain no real access to the persona. The alternately carefree and moody fifteen-year-old, say – both precocious and deeply lazy – is far more familiar. And yet the pre-teen places and the people, the events and the adventures lurk in the memory bank pristine and available.

I was popular, thanks partly to Holland and his cronies, and I was tall and a fast runner – did not let the side down at rugby and cricket – but I realize I never made it into the first rank because I did not have a nickname. The real stars were called 'Ducky' or 'Fitzy' or plain 'Johnnie'. Once for a week or so a few boys took to calling me a Latinate 'Boydus' but it never caught on and soon died away, never to be resurrected. What made these boys so liked, what was the secret of their charm, so evident that even the staff addressed them by their nicknames? The answer, I think, is that they were unrelentingly cheerful. As they became teenagers they seemed almost visibly to fade away, without exception, puberty robbing them of their unfailingly sunny demeanours. But somehow at the age of ten or eleven an initial personality had developed, sufficient to make them the life and soul of the party, and this was enough to make them everybody's favourites. These boys were loved, admired and cherished, I am sure, by all of us without any jealousy. I remember when Johnnie's mother suddenly died the sense of collective grief in Elchies was palpable: his loss affected us all in a profound way that can only be explained by the role he played in our midst. Johnnie's loss was, of course, our loss too.

Indeed, within the small community of the prep school a kind of covert favouritism operates, rather as I imagine it does in a large family, with no real resentment being expressed by those excluded. For a while I was the beneficiary of such advancement when I became the favourite of the matron – I think as a result of having suffered a very bad dose of chickenpox – Mrs Herrick, a pallid but no-nonsense, vivacious woman, married to the Latin teacher (we called him 'Shirley' for some forgotten reason). Mrs Herrick was not the most powerful patron among the staff, but her benevolence did pay dividends.

Every morning – part of our Scottish heritage – we had porridge for breakfast. The school would gather in the assembly room before filing through to the dining room (a pre-fab wooden hall tacked on to the rear of the house). Mr Vaughan would declaim a prayer, read the day's notices and then Mrs Herrick would appear to select the sugar-server. This was one of the most coveted jobs in the school (our sweet ration was one Quality Street per day). The sugar-server's job was to place one dessertspoonful of brown Demerara sugar in the middle of each bowl of porridge. The key perk of the job was that one was permitted to sugar one's own bowl of porridge with boundless liberality. And, naturally, friends of the sugar-server benefited also. During my reign as Mrs Herrick's chosen one she would come into the assembly room each morning, scan the eager pleading faces of the boys and then, as if the result of spontaneous whim, select me. This went on for many weeks and nobody ever appeared to express surprise or complain at this manifest unfairness. I became rather smug and developed a sweet tooth that I have never really managed to neutralize.

My move to prep school from my school in Africa meant the first of several progressive steps that shifted me away from being an 'African' child to becoming a British one. The winter of 1961 was the first time I saw snow. As I remember it there had been a heavy fall in the night, some six inches or so, and we woke to the refulgent, muffled, eerie landscape that dense snowfall brings. For two of us – me and another boy who had been born and raised in Jamaica – this was a surreal lifetime first. Amazed, astonished, we stepped outside and picked the stuff up, tasted it, felt its cold numb our fingers, heard its crump beneath our feet. Other boys and staff, amused, looked out at us from the big library windows – two aborigines out of their element – as we struggled to come to terms with this new natural phenomenon that we had heard and read so much about but never experienced – stamping our feet, throwing handfuls into the air – before we were gently summoned back inside for breakfast.

Quite a number of us lived abroad and made the long plane journey home at holidays – to India, West and East Africa, Singapore, the Caribbean – to a world of sun and humidity, ocean beaches and palm trees. On our return we wore our exclusivity proudly in the shower room, our deep tans contrasting strongly with the pale pink bodies of our coevals, quite unconcerned to be known to the others as 'wogs'. This sort of cheery racism was quite common, even at prep school, but, as with many of the less admirable aspects of boarding school life, our prejudices and bigotries tended to become more extreme as we grew older. Any deviation from our self-ordained norms was more mercilessly pilloried – accents, deformities, perceived ugliness – anything strange or out of the ordinary was grist to the intolerance mill.

But at the junior prep school our energies and animosities revolved instead around the forts we built in the woods. This was a form of peer-group-creation, joining a gang combined with war-gaming, a kind of obsessive militaristic territoriality that dominated our free time. Who was in, who was out, whose loyalties had been transferred and so on. In the dense woods around the house we would build elaborate shacks, lean-tos and tree houses, erect earthworks and construct trip wires and booby traps. Membership of the most splendid forts was eagerly striven for. Certain substantial forts of the recent past had assumed almost legendary proportions. There had been one called 'Laramie' – but somehow Laramie had fallen into disrepair and all that remained of it was a jumble of roped-together logs in a clearing. Old hands would take new boys to the site and reminisce about its Ozymandian splendours.

One was elected into a fort either by patronage (Holland helped me into his) or by the possession of tools. In this way feeble or unpopular boys could gain admission into elites by offering the use of a hammer or drill or, in one enterprising case, by having his father send up supplies of six-inch nails at weekly intervals. The six-inch nail was the key currency – you could buy your way anywhere.

The move to the senior prep school, a few miles away on the other side of the Spey, marked an end to the Edenic pleasures of the Wester Elchies. The new house was grander and larger, with a great pillared portico, a stable block and generous formal terraces leading down to playing fields. It represented a larger society, too, and within it were played out early and inchoate strategies of power and responsibility, and with that development came a corresponding loss of innocence. Here were thirteen-year-olds in the first hot flush of adolescence, voices breaking, pimples sprouting, the first snouty stirrings of pubertal lust. The easy egalitarianism of the junior school ebbed away, the sense of being part of a large, unruly but essentially loving family was replaced by the divisions familiar to all closed societies. There was the public face of the school – sporty, academic, disciplined – and there was the inevitable private face, one that was created and shaped by the boys and ran like a cold, unseen, dangerous current beneath the placid surface.

At a prep school, however, the tacit acknowledgement of this fact – that the two distinct worlds coexist, one overt, one hidden – is never really established. The real world (the world of the boys, the hothouse society) never gets full purchase because there remain old elements of that unspoilt innocence of childhood in place – we were still children, after all, even though, at the end of our prep school careers, the embryo adult in each of us could be perceived taking shape.

I developed a curious relationship with one of the matrons. I can't remember her name but she was attractive, energetic and a little plump with reddish blonde hair and a nicely cynical, gently mocking way with her charges. I can see her face in my mind's eye, see her in her white coat serving spoonfuls of malt to the needy and malnourished, dispensing aspirins for imagined headaches. In our pre-teens the female members of staff played a far more important part in our lives than the males did. I can bring all these young women to mind instantly, have them fixed in my memory far more vividly than all but a few of the men. It was as if we unconsciously realized that here was the only likely source of any vaguely maternal affection – a smile, a pat on the back, a literal shoulder to cry on – which we all, even the most rambunctious and independent spirits, separated from our real mothers three months at a time, periodically craved.

Thinking back, I suppose that what happened was that this matron and I must have become friends, an odd state of affairs to arise between a thirteen-year-old boy and a young woman in her twenties, especially given the institutional roles imposed on us. Perhaps, quite simply, she was lonely. There is another side to prep school life which the schoolboy seldom considers, if at all – that of the solitary teacher in his or her room, little more than a bedsit, whiling away their off-duty hours. What did you do if you weren't married? I suppose there were occasional visits to a pub or a local restaurant (though the junior staff must have been paid a pittance); or you could hopefully attempt to find a soul-mate amongst your colleagues . . . And the social life of a staff common room need not necessarily be congenial, populated – as all common rooms are – by its share of bores and petty martinets, third-raters and sadsacks. This matron, however, seemed a more feisty and worldly char-acter and, inevitably, she did not stay long with us, no more than a term or two. I never thought anything particular about her announced depar-ture: she was popular with the boys and we were collectively sorry to see her go but, most unusually, before she left she came into my dormi-tory late at night to say goodbye and sat on my bed and talked for an hour or so. The other boys fell asleep or tried to eavesdrop but she sat close to me and we chatted in low voices. Chatted about what? I can't remember exactly – where she was going, I suppose. I recall something about her telling me she was sitting more exams, better qualifications leading to a better job. Did she kiss me farewell, squeeze my hand? I hope so. I never saw or heard from her again.

Otherwise the relations between staff and boys were by and large cordial and run-of-the-mill. With one exception. There was one young master, popular with the boys, who distinguished himself in our eyes by demonstrating a clear sense of his own sartorial style – a worn leather greatcoat, knitted ties, Chelsea boots – and who, we guessed, possessed a source of income separate from his school salary. He had his own car, something sporty, went abroad in the summer – there was generally a debonair and confident manner about him that we responded to. Then, one evening in my dormitory a junior boy returned from a late-night punishment lesson (malefactors copying out lines in a classroom) in tears. When quizzed by the dormitory leader he confessed that this particular master had 'fiddled' with him. The boys had been in dressing gowns and pyjamas; when this fellow approached the master – the invigilator of the punishment period – with his completed lines the man had slid his hand into the fly of the boy's pyjamas. The seniors of us in the dormitory – I was probably thirteen by then – consulted. We reported the matter to the head boy who decided he would have to tell the headmaster. We watched him go downstairs and knock on the door of the headmaster's study. In the morning the young master had gone, not a sign, not a trace of him left. A brief, bland announcement was made about his sudden departure, 'a family crisis' had called him away, and it was never spoken of further. We, as I recall, were not so much outraged by the molestation as by the breaching of convention: it was not so much the act itself but the collapse of general principles it betokened – principles of decorum and staff–pupil relationships rather than anything more highly moral – this sort of thing really wouldn't do. We were pompously pleased that he had been sent packing and no more fuss was made.

Sex was definitely in the air as I approached the end of my prep school years. I remember a very young under-matron – no more than seventeen or eighteen – supervising ablutions in the shower room, inspecting the fingernails of naked, hirsute, mature thirteen-year-olds and, as I waited my turn, I caught myself wondering if she found it a bit embarrassing, standing there fully clothed with fifty assorted sizes of cocks and balls on display. And I think she did. Sexually we were insatiably curious: more advanced boys were envied for their masturbatory prowess; there would be the odd thrilling torchlit striptease cabaret in the dormitories late at night, and some more daring souls crept into each other's beds for mutual stimulation, but their numbers were few and they were regarded as mild eccentrics rather than pariahs.

As the time came for our transition to the main school a certain tension became evident in those about to make the move, uneasy at the idea of exchanging a small pond for a much larger one in which we would be conspicuous minnows. There was a rite of passage that took place in the final week of our final term and which symbolically marked this impending alteration in our status. It was known as 'P.D.' and was a one-on-one solemn discussion with the headmaster about the facts of life.

The initials referred to 'Pandrops' – a name peculiar to Scotland, I believe, which was given to a brand of large round white peppermints.

These the headmaster would feed the boy throughout his faintly embarrassed disquisition in the strange belief that the peppermint would prevent
any unseemly arousal. Where he discovered this faith in the anaphro-
disiac properties of peppermint I have no idea, but anyway, there one
sat, dutifully sucking on a succession of mints, as he tediously ran us
through the familiar mechanics of procreation. At the end he would ask
peremptorily: 'Have you any questions?' This was what we were waiting
for, the tacit understanding being that the headmaster was duty-bound
to answer everything – everything – we wanted to know. Consequently
medical textbooks, dictionaries and novels were scoured in advance for
sexual arcana: 'Sir, what are the symptoms of tertiary syphilis?' 'How do
you do soixante-neuf, sir?' The aim was to make the P.D. session last as
long as possible, a fact which, rather than displaying the appalling extent
of one's ignorance, was instead perceived to convey the impression of
massive virility. There was a record for the longest P.D. – an awesome
interrogatory effort which had endured for most of an afternoon, was
abandoned and resumed after breakfast the next day – but no one in
my year lasted much more than an hour.

So I left the world of the prep school after four years and everything
changed, but my memories of that period of my life seem fixed and
anchored in my first year at Wester Elchies; perhaps because of my
coming from Africa everything about it was so strange and new and its
impact inevitably left deeper traces. Recollections of my first summer
there are particularly resonant because by then I had settled in, I had
explored my world and was at home in it. And, I suppose, I was happy.
It was a kind of idyll living in that remote and rather beautiful Scottish
estate, for all its strangeness. I remember on summer nights after supper
we would gather around the teachers sitting out on the grass tennis
court, lounging beneath the cedar tree (or was it beech, or have I just
planted it?), pestering them, chatting and playing, before the bell was
rung and we were summoned inside for prayers, then bed. A wash and
a teeth clean standing on the wooden duckboards in the washroom,
then into the cool dormitory high under the eaves of the house. Lights
out at 8.00, not that it made much difference, the thin curtains drawn
vainly against the sunny northern skies. In reality I couldn't have spent
more than a few dozen summer evenings at Elchies but it is that particular limpid northern atmosphere – the sun still stubbornly in the sky
but the shadows long and with the warmth just beginning to go – that
my memory most associates with the place and that time of my life.

The ambience is always conjured up by Auden's haunting poem, 'Summer Night', written – coincidentally – while he was teaching at a prep school in Scotland himself:

> That later we, though parted then,
> May still recall those evenings when
> Fear gave his watch no look;
> The lion griefs loped from the shade
> And on our knees their muzzles laid
> And Death put down his book.

1998

The Hothouse

I have known few large buildings as intimately as I knew my house at school; after all, I lived there, day in, day out, for five years. All public schoolboys can claim a similar familiarity, but in almost every case you will find there is no nostalgia for the building itself. Apart from my parental home I have never lived in any one house for longer than three years, but I remember the shabbiest and most transient student bedsits with more affection. It is not all that surprising: the living quarters of your average public schoolboy are at best functional and soulless, and at worst utterly disgusting. If Borstals or remand homes were maintained in similar conditions, there would be a public outcry. I recently visited several famous public schools, and nothing I saw there made me so depressed as the dormitories and the thought that for so many years I had slept so many nights in such dismal and depressing circumstances.

It is, I think, a retrospective revulsion. Adolescent boys are not much preoccupied with personal hygiene, let alone the care and maintenance of their living quarters. But now, when I recall the concrete and tile washrooms and lavatories, the pale-green dormitories with their crude wooden beds, I form a new respect for the resilience and fortitude of the adolescent spirit.

Not that the conditions we experienced at school were the worst I have seen. At one school that I visited in Scotland some of the studies were in a converted greenhouse, which the boys had lined with egg boxes in an attempt to provide some insulation. Older buildings in older schools give rise to prospects of damp and decay that are almost Dickensian in their extravagance; the dormitories look like wards in some Crimean war hospital.

Anyway, we were fortunate, if that is the right word, in that our house was newish and made of wood. It looked rather like an army barracks, a large, single-storey frame building, creosoted brown, with a tar-paper roof, constructed around a square, grassy courtyard. There were four very long terraced corridors with rooms off each side. One edge of the square expanded to contain a large locker room, towel and shower room and lavatories; one corner contained the housemaster's flat. We ate in a dining room a mile away in the main school, an old, rather attractive, stone manor house whose fine architectural proportions had suffered when a Second World War fire destroyed its mansard roof.

When I arrived at the school, aged thirteen, in 1965, everything about the house was functional and anonymous. The floor, throughout, was brown linoleum; the lampshades were white plastic. Curtains at dorm windows were made from the same drab material. Only in the studies was individual decoration permitted, but as this consisted almost entirely of pictures of women scissored from lingerie and swimwear advertisements, they too had a homogeneous air.

Prospective parents being shown round the house often found the unrelieved wallpapering of brassière and corset ads (interspersed with the odd film star or motor car) something of a shock, and from time to time the housemaster or the headmaster would initiate a clean-up campaign. Shortly after I arrived new regulations were issued. (1) Nudity was banned. Even the most decorous and coy picture from a girlie magazine (or nude mags, nude books, skin mags, as we called them) was not permitted: the pin-up must be clothed. (2) Only three pin-ups were allowed on the wall per person. (3) As a special concession, a fourth pin-up could be kept concealed in a drawer for furtive, private consultation. This is true.

It was vain legislation and constantly had to be reinforced. But as years went by attitudes relaxed, and by the time I left every boy's study looked like a Soho bookshop or soft-porn emporium. Indeed, in terms of fixtures and fittings the history of my house, and of all the other six houses in the school, was one of prettification and improvement. Carpets were introduced; studies were subdivided into cubicles or converted to study-dormitories; painting and wallpapering were encouraged. Taste, as might be expected, was execrable. I remember that in one of my studies we lowered the ceiling by two feet by tacking string to and fro from one wall to another and laying brightly coloured crêpe paper on top of the resulting web. In the five years I lived there the character of the house altered by stages from that of some sort of penal institution to that of a moderately prosperous South American shanty town.

Much of this home decorating was subsidized by profits from the house shop. This sold nothing apart from sweets, soft drinks and ice cream and did a roaring trade. It was considered completely normal, in the hour of free time between end of prep and lights out, for one person to consume, say, a litre of Coca-Cola, a packet of Jaffa Cakes and a packet of digestive biscuits, a Mars bar, a slab of chocolate, some packets of crisps, some strips of liquorice and a couple of dozen aniseed balls. Everybody, while his money lasted, seemed to eat constantly. As one rose through the ranks kettles were permitted and, along with them, 'brewing' privileges. By the end of my school career I was allowed a toaster. During an average day I might drink between twenty and thirty mugs of instant coffee and eat two large white sliced loaves of bread.

Apart from eating and drinking, the other memory I retain of living in the house was the noise. Certain periods of the day were radio hours. As if on command, dozens of radios and record players would start up. Very little classical music was played. In my era the sophisticated public schoolboy listened to Jimi Hendrix, the Grateful Dead and Cream.

We had a television (black-and-white) in the house common room. Its use was very restricted. Far and away the most popular programme was *Top of the Pops*. I am sure its producers have no idea of the profound influence and effect this programme had on a generation of public schoolboys. I do not know if it commands the same allegiance today, but I would wager that during the last five years of the 1960s 99 per cent of public schoolboys religiously watched the programme every week during term time. Everything stopped for *Top of the Pops*. In the entire school nothing moved. In our house sixty boys would somehow cram themselves into the common room to watch it on Thursday nights. And, pathetic as it may seem today, we didn't watch it so much for the music but for the girls in the studio audience. The programme was accompanied throughout by the grunts and groans, the whoops and sighs, of group passion. It was, I believe, in every public school in the land, a spontaneous, countrywide expression of terrible lust.

The house was large, but it felt curiously constricted. In the summer one could get outside, but during the winter there was nowhere else to go. Curiously, there was not much traffic between houses, except at senior level. Going into another house in the school was like going into another country, but with the added disadvantage that its inhabitants constantly drew attention to your strangeness. Few events were more unsettling than, as a junior boy, to have to deliver a message to a boy in another house. To be jeered at as an alien was the best you could expect; more often you would be set upon. We were members not so much of different houses as of different tribes. The houses all had different atmospheres, almost different ideologies. One house was corrupt, full of villains; one was full of eccentrics; one house was obsessively self-interested. My house, at least when I first joined it, was very hard.

We had had a succession of popular and ineffectual housemasters. There was no discipline. A new housemaster was strenuously trying to impose his authority. But when he retired to his flat at the end of the day the old regime established itself. The source of the problem was a group of boys in the sixteen-to-seventeen age bracket. They were 'bad' in the sense that they had no interest in promotion. In the evenings they terrorized juniors with a kind of candid ruthlessness that I still find chilling to recall. They would roam the junior studies, four or five of these roughs, and beat people up at random, extort money or food, rifle letters and lockers in search of diversion. One felt in a way rather like a medieval peasant during the Hundred Years War: one never knew when another marauding army might march by, randomly distributing death and destruction. It was comparatively short-lived, this period of capricious thuggery, but it provided me with a full catalogue of the resourceful cruelties of the adolescent mind. Later the attitude of the house changed to something altogether more genial, but I will always remember my years as a junior, even though I was relatively unscathed. W. H. Auden said he detested fascism because at public school he lived in a fascist state. It is rarely a constant state of affairs, but it is not difficult for private life in a boarding school temporarily to take on certain fascist characteristics. It is the sense of being a victim, or potential victim, that lingers on: the way a house can become at certain moments a place of genuine terror and fear; the way you sacrifice all principles in order to save your skin; the ease with which the ideology of the dominant group seduces you. This is, of course, the private, unadministered life of a boarding house, but in a crucial sense it is *the* reality of being a boarder in a boys' public school. Its opposite is what I call 'the prison governor's view of the prison'. That has a reality too, but it is for public and official consumption. The inmates experience something entirely different, vital and basic.

If you are lucky, everything changes at school as you grow older, stronger and more senior. Those few to whom this transformation and relaxation does not apply are the saddest products of the system. But for the majority the tenor of the daily round eventually establishes itself as tolerable. However, the last year or two at school, although the most privileged, can also be the most irritating. Most people experience this, and no doubt most people have their own reasons. On reflection, I wonder if my own vague disquiet was not to do with a subconscious reaction against the unrelenting absence of privacy that one experiences as the norm in a boarding school. Looking back at it now, years later, I realize that of my nine years at boarding school I actually spent three years on holiday and a full six at school. So for those six years, for example, I usually bathed and showered in the company of eight or a dozen other people; I relieved myself in what was effectively a public lavatory; I dressed and undressed, to order, in a crowded locker room; and, except for my final year, I slept in a room that never had fewer than four people in it and on occasions had fourteen. As a way of life – I am trying to be objective about it – this seems to me to be positively bizarre, not to say noisome and rebarbative. Five years in the same house is not only five years of crowding personalities; it is also five years of enforced proximity to the bodies that accommodate those personalities. The house was not a place for the fastidious.

Few people ever wield power as absolute as that possessed by a public-school prefect. Perhaps if you are an officer in the army, it may be similar, but really I feel it is more akin to something you might encounter in a feudal or totalitarian society, in so far as your power is subject to your whim. Boys may not be allowed to administer corporal punishment, but apart from that the head of house at a public school can – or certainly could – exercise a degree of control over the sixty boys in his charge that, day by day, could be said to be greater even than that of the housemaster.

The power operates on two basic levels. First, you can order people to do things: to shave, to repolish their shoes, to comb their hair, to have their hair cut, to run instead of walk and so on. On the second level you can deprive them of things: their freedom (by enforcing detention), their pleasures (you can forbid them to watch TV or ride a bicycle, reduce their pocket money, confiscate their possessions). A prefect may not be able to beat anybody, but if he works at it, and if the transgressions persist, he could probably have a boy beaten. Conceivably, if the circumstances were right, he could get a boy expelled. It is perhaps sufficient to say that, if he feels like it, a head of house can make the life of anybody in his house absolute hell.

I ended my school career as a head of house – we called them 'house helpers'. I was not very officious, perhaps lethargic might be more apt, but I don't ever expect to re-encounter that curious sensation of strolling through the house at night while everyone else was working at prep, master of my own territory, knowing that I could go anywhere, search anywhere, order people to do my bidding. It is, for those inclined to exult in it, a heady experience – perhaps not the sort of thing an eighteen-year-old should indulge in.

The occasion when one's power, as it were, stared one in the face was over the issue of haircuts. In those days all young males had long hair, and one of the stigmata of being a public schoolboy was the fact that your hair was so short. Consequently, everyone endeavoured to grow their hair as long as possible. The longer your hair, the more 'cool' you were. Haircut nights saw the head of house, clipboard in hand, patrolling the studies. His word was law – there was no higher court of appeal. Real dread was in the atmosphere. A local barber visited the house once a fortnight. He had to have heads to cut, a minimum of half a dozen. Who would be chosen? To enter a study was an eerie experience; one might have come to claim hostages or to issue a decimation order. At that moment the power one wielded was palpable.

A side-effect of power was adulation. They were not always concomitant, but one usually went with the other. By the reduced standards that operate within any enclosed or confined community it was possible to reach a level of fame or renown similar to that enjoyed by film actors or pop stars in the wider world. These folk heroes had their own fans, even their own imitators. I am glad to say that at my school prowess at games was not the sole route to celebrityhood. It was the age of student rebellion and we had our own existential heroes. I remember a couple of them vividly. There was Burns, taciturn and poetic. His influence was widespread and was responsible for an improbable Ezra Pound craze that swept the school. Against type, he decided rugby was permissible and secured a place in the First XV. But somehow he managed to play his rugby in a dissident, rebellious manner too – brooding, never shouting, socks always round his ankles – so it did not diminish his *réclame*. Patmore's hero was Oscar Wilde. He always wore his duffel coat like a cloak and parted his hair in the middle. He would saunter around, carrying a daffodil, with half a dozen acolytes at his heels. I do not know what has become of these two, but from time to time I do encounter other erstwhile superheroes and am always astonished at how bland and ordinary they are, and wonder from where they derived their early renown. The sad thing for these people is that adult life can never duplicate the fabulous triumphs of their schooldays – they peak at age seventeen or eighteen and it is all a long slide down from then on. They are the great reminiscers.

At my school promotion did not bring any great increase in privileges. Everyone wore the same uniform and rank was demarcated only by a silk flash on the left-hand side of the regulation school jersey. A house helper usually got a single study bedroom, and the prefects ('colour bearers') enjoyed a more lax routine. Baths were a great luxury. We had two to serve sixty boys, and a house helper's privilege was to order any boy out of a bath and take it as his own. There was always a huge waiting list, and because of the time involved the water was never changed. As a junior I would often step into a tepid bath in which the water was absolutely opaque from the grime of its seventeen or so previous occupants. As I grew more senior so my baths grew clearer. My one decadent luxury as head of house was to order the bell-ringer (the boy who woke up the rest of the house) to run me a bath in the morning. It would wait there – unused, steaming, limpid – until I came down to the shower room to claim it.

My own progress to this exalted position was straightforward. I moved up through the various ranks to colour bearer, and there I would have stayed had not the head of my house been promoted to head boy and I was pushed up to fill the vacant role. I do not think, from the official point of view, that I was a very good head of house – I was too lazy to put myself about in the accepted way. My two interests at that stage of my school career were sport and painting, and they, rather than official duties, claimed most of my energies. I was demoted to colour bearer for a term for staying out one night during a tennis tour in Edinburgh. An energetic Canadian took over for the interregnum (I was reinstated the next term) and ran the house far more efficiently than I. Fortunately, I was not obliged to move out of my study, so – apart from a certain notoriety – the punishment affected me not at all.

Our school was in Scotland, was in almost every respect a Scottish public school, and yet a strong Scottish accent was a real stigma. Indeed, any regional accent was parodied mercilessly. When people spoke with a strong Scottish accent we would make harsh retching sounds in the base of our throats or emit loose-jawed idiot burblings. Anyone with a Midlands or north of England accent heard nothing but a barrage of 'Eee bah goom' and 'Trooble at t' mill'. We all found the mocking of accents endlessly amusing. This was part snobbery, part self-defence. All public schoolboys have an intensely adversarial relationship with the local population, especially with the local youths. To us the locals were 'yobs', 'oiks', 'plebs', 'proles', 'peasants' and 'yokels'. It now seems to me astonishing to recall the patrician venom we would express, like aristocrats faced with imminent revolution – a curious mixture of contempt, fear, guilt and jealousy. They lived, after all, in the real world beyond the school grounds, and however superior we congratulated ourselves on being, there was no escaping the fact that they were freer than we were – and that grated. I am sure that we in our turn were looked on as revolting, arrogant, nasty snobs. By no means a harsh judgement.

We longed to get out of school, but the outside world was both a lure and a taunt. It possessed everything that school denied us and at the same time was a constant reminder of the constraints and abnormalities of the society in which we were confined. Strenuous attempts were made to escape to it.

The easiest way to get there was to be selected for a school team. Because the school was situated so far north a considerable amount of travelling was involved in order to find reputable opponents. Rugby and hockey would take you to Inverness or Aberdeen two or three times a term, and often there were matches in Dundee, Glasgow and Edinburgh. Edinburgh occupied a place in our imaginations rather as Berlin did for poets in the 1930s. It seemed to our impoverished eyes unfailingly sinful and glamorous. To be selected for a rugby tour to Edinburgh meant happy hours in Thistle Street pubs rather than eager sporting challenges.

For the outside world meant alcohol rather than girls. Our stays were usually far too short and too well chaperoned to meet the opposite sex, but there always seemed to be a chance to get drunk. I remember a match in Dundee. A friend, who had left school a term earlier and had gone to Edinburgh Art School, caught the train to Dundee with two hefty overnight bags clinking with booze. After the match we had about forty minutes to drink the lot. The favourite tipple was neat gin washed down with a tot of Rose's Lime Cordial.

Once in the outside world, we tended to band together. This was because we were conspicuous in our uniforms (the authorities had introduced blazer and flannels for exeats to spare our blushes over shorts and knee-socks) but also because we were somehow fearful and on edge. The outside world was a welcome source of contraband – pornography, drink, cigarettes – and also, in a sense, fair game. When boys went into towns the shoplifting rate rose alarmingly. In the local Woolworth's two store detectives used to follow one particular boy around. He was the most accomplished kleptomaniac and used to take orders for his Saturday visits. We exulted in our delinquency and bandied legends of epic thefts: a souvenir shop in the Highlands left almost empty when a busload of boys cleaned it out; a boy who dug up copper wires on a nearby RAF station, at one stage blacking out the control tower when he sank his axe into a crucial cable. We would return gleefully to the safety of school, clutching our booty. And yet within the school itself theft was regarded as the most serious and antisocial of crimes – any thief could expect years of excoriation. Two worlds, two sets of standards.

Because of the isolation of the school we did not participate in the life of the local community in any significant way. We were too far away from most boys' homes to make any half-term break practicable. It was not difficult to pass an entire three-month term without ever leaving the school grounds. As one grew older this unnatural segregation became more irksome. My abiding memory of my final two or three years is of a sense of life going on elsewhere. I felt as if I were experiencing a form of internal exile. A few away matches with teams only seemed to sharpen the sensation of missing out, of being bypassed.

The school grounds were capacious, the houses scattered randomly about the estate. I had a friend in a house so far away – over two miles – that I could rarely be bothered to visit him. The scale made it logistically difficult to creep out at night. I believe this is something that happens in most public schools. Here, escape is indulged in for its own sake, not as a means to some illicit end. In our case, and to reduce the risk of discovery, the nearest safe town was eight miles away. To drop from a dormitory window, change into civilian clothes, cycle the eight miles in order to snatch a pint of beer before closing time, then cycle back, was too arduous to make it worth while.

The summer was always better. We were very near the coast, and it was not difficult to spend a fragrant afternoon hidden among the gorse on the endless sand dunes, replenished with food and drink bought from stores at nearby caravan sites. Summer meant tennis too. The school tennis team was a member of a league that operated among tennis clubs in that area of the north-east. We would play against clubs in places like Inverness, Forres and Fochabers. The great advantage was that these games were played mid-week, in the evening. There was something unreal about these matches. The six of us in the team would get into a minibus at about half-past five on a Wednesday or Thursday evening and be driven to a small county town. There we would be dropped at the local tennis club. The matches were so regular that often no master accompanied us. For some reason – perhaps it was to do with the nature of the league – we often played against mixed doubles, sometimes against women's teams. Here, at last, was life as most people led it. I have the most idyllic recollections of these warm summer evenings: long shadows cast across the red clay courts, the sonorous 'pock, pock' of the balls in the air, the punctilious courtesy of our game ('I'm not sure if that was out – play a let!'), a few idle spectators – two girls, a dog, a ruddy man with a pipe. And then, afterwards, in the small clubhouse, with the glowing, perspiring wives of dentists and solicitors, all of us still in our dusty tennis whites, drinking half-pints of ginger-beer shandy, chatting, laughing in the palpitating dusk. There was, at least to us boys, a tender, bourgeois eroticism about these encounters, which was much analysed on the bus ride back to school. We often got back late, well after ten, with the school in bed, all curtains drawn vainly against the sunny northern evenings. We felt immensely proud of our exclusivity and were the source of great envy. Although I was a very keen sportsman at school, I find it quite easy to understand why tennis is the only game I play today.

The two main vices were drinking and smoking. Drugs were taken too, mainly marijuana, but were not anything like as prevalent as they are today. Smoking was completely banned, drinking almost so. A senior boy might get a glass of sweet sherry or a half-pint of beer off his housemaster if he was very lucky. These drinking restrictions must seem positively antediluvian to today's public schoolboy. I recently sat down to dinner with a housemaster at one of our grandest schools, and the three boys who were invited seemed to drink as much wine as they wanted.

The underworld life of the school, then, was concerned almost exclusively with trying to procure and consume alcohol and tobacco without getting caught. Smoking was the most common. I would say that 95 per cent of boys smoked at some stage of their school career, regardless of rank and position. Like any law that is consistently broken by a majority, it became impossible to enforce. Most colour bearers – who probably smoked themselves – turned a blind eye. All they asked for was a degree of discretion. I remember my study overlooked a road that led to a nearby wood. Every night after prep I could see the hardened smokers, in all weathers, in all seasons, trudging off for a 'drag in the woods'. From time to time I'd ask them where they were going, to get the reply, 'For a walk.' There was nothing illegal about going for a walk. You could always tell the smokers because they chewed gum and reeked of Brut aftershave – a brand unanimously endorsed by schoolboys of my era for its wholly effective smoke-obliterating pungency.

Smoking was cheap, fast and easy to hide. Drinking, possessing none of these attributes, was consequently less frequently indulged in. Usually it took place outside the school grounds. Journeys to and from school at the beginning and end of term were drunken binges. Dances, school celebrations, open days and the like were also opportunities for excess. We tended to prefer neat spirits for speed of effect. I remember after one school dance a friend of mine drank half a bottle of gin. Apart from a euphoric light in his eye he seemed fine when he sneaked back to his dormitory. He was caught the next morning when he woke up in a rank and befouled bed to discover that at some time in the night, without his realizing it, he had not only pissed and shat himself but had also vomited all over his pillow.

There was a certain illicit trade in sex magazines. Scandinavian magazines that showed pubic hair were particularly prized and could be sold for high prices. One enterprising boy who ran the school film society for a term was sent blurry but lurid catalogues from blue-film makers which, as far as we were concerned, were the last word in shocking explicitness. Certain novels were censored: *Lady Chatterley's Lover*, *The Ginger Man*, *Last Exit to Brooklyn*. But what was permitted varied from house to house. As a fifteen-year-old I once got into fearful trouble with my housemaster because he discovered me reading Harold Robbins's *The Adventurers*. It was confiscated on the spot. When I boldly asked for it to be returned on the last day of term I was told it had been destroyed.

Apart from thieving, the only genuinely illegal act that occurred with any regularity was joyriding. In my house two boys used frequently to take the assistant housemaster's car out late at night. They would disconnect the mileometer and drive through the dark countryside for an hour or two. The owner of the car never noticed. This was an act of real daring, not to say foolhardiness; the consequences of being caught or of having an accident would have reverberated beyond the school – and yet it was not a rare event. All manner of cars were parked around the school buildings overnight. People would use them. The penalty for this crime would have been instant expulsion, but the staff, I am sure, never suspected that it went on. People could be expelled for theft, sex (homo or hetero) and consistent smoking or drinking or the taking of drugs. Few boys were expelled while I was at school: two went for having sex with school maids (the maids were sacked too); a small clique of drug-takers departed and a few heavy smokers. Boys often left of their own accord. Occasionally there would be 'scandals' that made the newspapers – boys vandalized a girl's flat on a rugby tour once, I recall – and also demanded the ultimate penalty. The boy who blacked out the RAF station also made the local newspapers. He was a simple, pale, gangly soul called Clough. He had made hundreds of pounds selling copper and lead pilfered from the air base to local scrap-metal merchants. The school, although properly outraged, had, I think, a sneaking regard for his entrepreneurial drive. His father, who did not want him at home, came up to plead for leniency with the headmaster. Clough's punishment was to dig up all the tree stumps on the estate, a task that occupied all his free time for about two terms.

Swearing was a minor crime too, naturally. It is perhaps worth emphasizing, for anyone who doubts it, that the language of a public school is as bad as that of any army barracks. We employed all the usual four-letter oaths with unreflecting abandon. There were not many nonce words or neologisms in our private language at school for some reason. Perhaps because the school had been founded only some decades before, traditions had yet to establish themselves. At prep school it was pure Jennings and Darbishire – 'Vanes', 'Quis?' 'Ego!', 'Stale news', 'Cave', etc., etc. One exchange that I have never encountered elsewhere I record here for those interested in the folkloric side of public-school life. If you farted ('buffed'), everyone was allowed to punch you. However, if you said, 'Safeties', before you were discovered, you could foul the air unpunished.

We were obsessed with sex. I know this is true of all adolescent experience, but when I think now of the energy and relentless focus of our interminable discussions about the subject a sort of retrospective lassitude descends upon me, as well as a retrospective anger. *Of course* we talked about sex – we lived in a freakish, monosexual society. There was a parallel world out there in which the two sexes mingled and interacted and to which entry was denied us. No wonder our curiosity was so febrile and intense – and so destructive. The sexual apartheid to which we were subjected all those years utterly warped our attitudes and precluded us from thinking about girls and women in any way but the most prurient and lubricious. The female sex was judged by one criterion – fanciable or non-fanciable, to put it rather more delicately than we did.

Endless conversation, speculation, fantasizing, poring over sex magazines, fervid masturbation . . . there is something soul-destroyingly monotonous about that facet of public-school life, and one looks back with genuine sadness and weariness at the thought of so much wasted time. But there it was, and at the time it was the favourite hobby. We made the best of our opportunities. Every girl and woman who set foot on the school grounds was subject to the most probing scrutiny – housemasters' wives, innocent secretaries, fond mothers and guileless sisters visiting the school were evaluated with ruthless purpose.

However, the people who bore the brunt of our lewd interest were the maids. These were local girls, I think, and were hired – so public-school rumour famously has it – solely on the grounds of their ugliness. It made little difference. Their encounters with the boys, three times a day at meals, were characterized by a one-sided traffic of sexual banter of the vilest and coarsest sort. Given the opportunity, more daring boys actually molested them – squeezing, pinching, feeling. The girls were remarkably tolerant. I never heard of any boy disciplined as a result of a complaint made by one of them. I think our attitudes to them brought out the very worst in our natures: it was male lust at its most dog-like and contemptuous, tarnished further by a brand of wilful class disdain and mockery that was almost dehumanizing. I dare say any male sodality – rugby team, army platoon, group of Pall Mall clubmen – can descend to this level for a while, but what is depressing and degrading about the male boarding school is the unrelieved constancy of the tone, year in, year out, for at least five years. It must have some effect.

There was also, it is true, a brand of passionate romanticism about our sexual curiosity that was slightly more amusing. Nobody ever admitted to being a virgin. By tacit consent conversation about the great day was always rather vague and woolly – it was just taken as read that everybody was, well, pretty experienced. There was one boy who made the mistake of confessing, at the age of seventeen, that he had still to lose his virginity. He became a laughing stock in the house. Little boys of fourteen would howl, 'Virgin! Virgin!' at him. He came back the next term claiming to have lost it in the holidays, but it was too late. His greatest mistake was to have admitted it – the only honest man among shameless liars. And it was easy to lie – no one could prove that you were not the satyr you claimed to be, come the holidays. It was quite important, however, to live up to your reputation on the rare occasion when the company was mixed. Many a self-appointed stud came to grief at school dances, for example.

There was also the problem of letters. If you boasted of having a girlfriend, some evidence needed to be furnished: a photograph at the very least or passionate letters. We liked our letters from our girlfriends to be as conspicuously feminine as possible – coloured paper and envelopes with deckle edges and illustrations and drenched in scent. Post was distributed after lunch in the common room. A letter was inhaled, fondled, groaned and swooned over – exhibit 'A' in the defence of your virility.

One boy, a jolly, rowdy person called Dunbar, used to exchange clippings of pubic hair with his girlfriend. In the dormitory the little tufts would be passed round like holy relics. We begged him to go further – the girl was French after all. At our crass prompting he finally did what we required. Together we composed a touching letter requesting a photograph in the nude. The girl was deeply offended, and the relationship shortly fizzled out.

Some boys, though, had exceptional good fortune. A friend of mine 'got off' with the headmaster's au pair, a pleasant Norwegian girl called Ingrid – a fabulously exotic creature to us. Another had an affair with his housemaster's daughter, provoking fraught dilemmas of divided loyalty. The rest of us had to rely on rare opportunities provided by school dances or the biennial Gilbert and Sullivan, when the girls were bussed in to play the female chorus.

The school dance was little more than a meat market. By the time the girls arrived all the boys were well-fortified with alcohol. At the first slow number they pounced. The occasion degraded everybody. The Gilbert and Sullivans were more fun and more decorum reigned. We were meant to be rehearsing, and we saw the girls quite regularly over a period of a month. Courtship rituals were rather primly observed, and the alliances that were struck up remained for a good while on a rather chaste level – one was often invited to the girl's house for tea on Sunday afternoons to meet her parents, for example. This more sustained contact usually provoked the dormant, romantic side of our nature, and many of us fell deeply in love as a consolation for being denied any physical release. That came, eventually, usually as the dates of the performances approached, a sense of time running out – as with soldiers due to return to the front – affecting both boy and girl. These wistful encounters were not so shaming. They were like any adolescent affair – cute, thrilling, melancholic – a brief foray into real life. They ended after the show as the barriers of the single-sex boarding school were reimposed. The only real victim was the Gilbert and Sullivan, in my memory always appalling, for the simple reason that none of the chorus had joined for the singing.

Every boy who leaves his boarding school has been shaped and formed, like it or not, by his years in that hothouse society. Of course, each individual will be affected to a different degree, but the only effective way of resisting the legacy is to get out early. My generation of schoolboys (class of 1970) was entirely typical not only of every other school but also of the generations that preceded us. We left school as unreflecting snobs – we had a very acute perception of 'us' and of 'them'. 'They' were all the yobs, oiks, lefties and deviants who hadn't been to public school. We were also racist, in a robust, cheery, easy-going manner, as the blacks and Arabs at school could testify. 'Wog' was the commonest of nicknames and, to us, devoid of pejorative intent. We thought of women quite simply as sexual objects. We were politically naive – which is to say, knee-jerk Tories of the old squirearchical model. We had our moody rebels, true, but they were influenced by Bob Dylan and Jack Kerouac rather than by any political faith. I knew only one boy at school who claimed to vote Labour – we thought him a ludicrous *poseur* at best, a patent moron at worst. Although most of us had done 'A' levels, and the more successful were trying to get into university, we were afflicted with a brand of philistinism that manifested itself as a grave suspicion of 'pseuds' or anyone who was too intellectual by half. Also many years of group loyalty, to the school, the house, the team, the power elite, had engendered a mistrust of the individual – indeed, 'individualist' was often employed as a term of abuse. The maverick, the odd one out, the not easily assimilable, were to be regarded with caution. Not the best set of values with which to rejoin the world in the last quarter of the twentieth century.

So what happened? I think that, usually, the shock of encountering real life stimulated a hasty course of unlearning. Most public schoolboys have to start a stringent programme of re-education almost as soon as the school gates close behind them. This assumes, of course, that the society in which you are compelled to mix operates under different codes. There are still many walks of life in contemporary Britain where the transition from schoolboy to adult is imperceptible – the attitudes that served you well at eighteen will see you nicely through to retirement.

When I left school I went to live on my own in France for a year. The signal inadequacies of my education swiftly presented themselves to me, and I suppose it was then that I began to look back on the strange institution in which I had spent half my life and to wonder at it.

I often found the focus of my thoughts coming round to one boy, a little younger than me, who had been in my house. This person, a sallow, weak boy called Gibbon, had been hated by everybody, myself included. I have no idea why; he was just very unpopular. He was never really persecuted, just spurned. Sometimes a gang would descend on him, demolish his desk, push him around, but most of the time the punishment was verbal. He was a whipping-boy for the house. He appeared to take it in reasonable spirit, was not abjectly miserable, and so there seemed no real cause to change attitudes. He had no friends and walked everywhere by himself. He was so disdained that even other unpopular boys in the house would not associate with him in case the taint was contagious.

My own school career was, in a banal way, a successful one, comparatively untroubled and orthodox, but I kept wondering what it had been like for Gibbon during his five years. When he went home in the holidays and his parents asked him how he was getting on at school, what did he say? And, more important, what effect would those five years have on him as an adult? Would he shrug them off? Struggle on regardless? Carry them like a yoke? When I looked at my contemporaries, boys who had had a far easier time, and saw them, years later, still living in the heavy shadow of their school days, still wrestling with aspects of their personalities that were somehow corrupted, undeveloped or warped, I doubted, somehow, that old Gibbon would be the breeziest and most carefree of fellows.

1985

The First World War

It was a piece of metal, dark grey, about three inches by one inch, with curious scalloped edges which resembled the crude working of a stone-age tool. In fact it was a chunk of German shell casing which, one night in October 1917, in no man's land, during the third Battle of Ypres, hit my grandfather – William Boyd – full in the back.

I have held that piece of shrapnel in my hand but I never had the chance to ask my grandfather – who survived this incident and the war – what it was like, because he died in 1952 when I was a week old. I never had the chance to ask him what was going through his mind during that wiring party (he was a sergeant in the Royal Engineers) as he unspooled fresh rolls of barbed wire in front of the British trenches, freezing motionless as the starshells came over from the German lines. Perhaps he heard the unmistakable noise of incoming artillery – he had been two years on the Western Front by 1917 – and wondered, as everybody must have done, if this time his number might be up.

When he came to, when he realized he was only wounded – not about to die, not hideously maimed – perhaps he thought of his brother, Sandy, who had also been wounded, a year previously, in August 1916, during the Battle of the Somme. The Boyd brothers were both sergeants, but Sandy was in the Australian Army – the Australian Imperial Force – having emigrated to Australia in 1914, only to be sent back to Europe two years later to fight for the Empire. Sandy's wounds earned him a medal – the DCM – as he had received them rallying his company in the face of a German counterattack at Mouquet Farm, organizing the remains of the company (all the officers were killed and wounded) and leading them out of harm's way. Sandy was shipped back to Australia to convalesce and was duly presented with his medal by the Governor General at a parade in a park in Melbourne. The two brothers never saw each other again – Sandy died of a heart attack in 1940.

What united them, and what united huge numbers of their generation, was the unique and terrible experience of the Great War. It wasn't actually very long ago, the First World War, just over eighty years, yet it seems to be preserved in our contemporary memories – as the twentieth century slips into the twenty-first – as something almost ancient, a mythic tale of bygone times. Those monochrome or sepia images still have the power to haunt and move, but I think we forget just how proximate they are and how the events they reflect have shaped and still shape our own times.

I remember, as a child, hearing stories about my grandfather's and my great-uncle's war experiences as I weighed in my hand the piece of shrapnel that finally got my grandfather out of the trenches. He was lucky, incredibly lucky, hindsight tells us, just as his brother Sandy was lucky – the only physical reminder of their respective ordeals was patches of fading scar tissue – though no one can really evaluate what the psychological wear and tear would have been; memories and images that would undoubtedly prove a more enduring legacy of their experience of battle. And perhaps my generation is the last one to feel any real closeness to those world-shattering events of 1914–18. It was oddly destabilizing, as I tried to track down an early photograph of my grandfather the other day, to hear one of my uncles referring to him casually as 'Dad'. Indeed, had William Boyd senior lived a few years longer (he was only sixty-two when he died) I might have had my own memories of that stout, mustachioed figure I have seen in family photographs. Not merely my grandfather, after all, but a man who managed to survive two years in the trenches.

I think it is that closeness, that familial proximity, that provoked my own abiding interest in the Great War. For me, fundamentally, it is the unknowingness, the unimaginability of that conflict that triggers the imagination. We have the newsreel images and the photographs, we have the memoirs, the regimental histories, the poetry and so on, but despite all this evidence the questions always remained only partially answered: what was it *really* like?

I can't speak for other novelists who have taken the Great War as their subject but sometimes the best way to arrive at the truth is to lie – to invent, to fictionalize. The curious alchemy of art – rather than the diligent assembling of documentary fact – can be a swifter and more potent route to understanding and empathy than the most detailed photographs or the most compendious documentation. You have to do your homework, sure – authenticity has to be striven for – but in the end it is the fecundity and idiosyncrasy of the novelist's imagination that will make the thing work – or not.

I first wrote about the First World War in my 1982 novel *An Ice-Cream War*. This was a forgotten corner of the Great War, an interminable struggle between the British and German colonies in East Africa (mirroring the larger one in Europe) – a surreal but bloody little affair that resembled the counterinsurgency conflicts of the sixties and seventies more than the traditional image of huge, immobile armies facing each other across 600 miles of trenches.

I turned to the Western Front proper in my novel *The New Confessions*, which was published in 1987. Here I tackled the battle where my grandfather had been wounded, the third Battle of Ypres, or Passchendaele, as it is more popularly known. In the course of my research I spent weeks in the Imperial War Museum in London, watching contemporary newsreel pictures.

For obvious reasons, most of the sequences were filmed well behind the lines – endless shots of Tommies marching through French villages, artillery blasting away at distant targets and so on. There was very little that was what you might call authentic front-line footage. It was dangerous in those trenches, after all, and the photographers wisely kept their distance. Yet many of the images that are routinely screened on our televisions around Armistice Day are patent fakes – 'action' staged in training camps with soldiers playing dead. The real stuff, when you can find it, is unmistakable, but it is rare – and of course it is mute.

One day, by chance, I ordered up a sequence about a burial party, just a few minutes long, of young soldiers lugging in dead bodies after a battle and dumping them by temporary graves. The misery and nauseated dread on the faces of the living is highly distressing and, just for a moment, because the cameraman was there, I was vouchsafed a tiny glimpse of the reality of what these young men, these boys, were going through.

It was during those weeks of watching miles and miles of newsreel that the idea of making *The Trench* was born. We forget that the First World War took place in glorious Technicolor, so familiar are we with its monochrome version. We forget also that those smiling faces, chatting, brewing up, puffing on their Woodbines, also spoke. The silence – and the sepia – distance the event from us profoundly, and it seemed to me one of the great values of making a film about the trench experience of the First World War at the end of the twentieth century would be that, at the very least, we would see it and hear it approximately as it must have been.

And perhaps, more importantly, it would be of some significance, as we leave the century behind, to attempt once again to come to terms with one of its defining events. It can be argued, with some conviction, that the twentieth century actually began in 1914, not 1900. Or, even more pertinently, that it began on 1 July 1916 at 7.30 in the morning as the barrage lifted and the first waves of Kitchener's Army left their trenches and walked across the dense untended meadows of the Somme valley, the misty morning sun beating down upon them, to their sudden, messy deaths.

Philip Larkin's great poem 'MCMXIV' contains the mordantly resonant line, 'Never such innocence again' – but the innocence that the hundreds of thousands of eager volunteers possessed in 1914 remained intact until the hideous debacle of the Somme in 1916. Sixty thousand were killed and wounded that first day – the bloodiest day of slaughter in the history of the British Army; perhaps even the bloodiest day of slaughter in any battle between armies, ever.

In the event, whether the world would have changed anyway, the battle usefully marks the great watershed. Without the disaster of the Somme the allies might well have brokered a peace with the Germans in 1916. But the terrible carnage of the Somme (400,000 British casualties, 175,000 French, 600,000 German) meant that the war had to be fought on, and fought on to be won. The cost of the war continuing for another two years – in every dimension (lives, damage, money) – exceeded everything that the first two years had balefully notched up. And as for the war itself, after 1918, nothing in the Western world could ever be the same again – socially, economically, sexually, politically, geo-politically, culturally – the twentieth century was full-throatedly under way.

This may explain why in the past two decades British novelists, at least, may have felt like re-exploring those turbulent four years. But I have a feeling that what may be whizzing about in the zeitgeist doesn't necessarily produce good art: good journalism, yes, good non-fiction, undoubtedly, but most novelists are drawn to a subject by the small scale, rather than the large. (How can you write a novel about the deaths of 9,000,000 people over a period of fifty-two months?)

The writer – the film-maker, the playwright – is drawn to a subject, I believe, by character and story, by their potential and by the imaginative possibilities of elaborating on them. One needs only to glance at any portrait or snapshot of the soldiers of the Great War to sense in yourself that burgeoning curiosity, to set those same questions running – who are you? Who did you leave behind? How frightened were you? Did you think you would die? How would I have coped if it had been me instead of them? And so on – the answers to which provide the foundations upon which the fiction will rise.

The Trench is my attempt to provide the answers to those questions. It is not a film about conflict – the Battle of the Somme only begins at the end – but about waiting to go into battle and the pressures of that wait – two days, with the clock clicking remorselessly down – on very young men.

For the novelist, writing a film, let alone directing one, represents a great social opportunity: suddenly from being in a state of creative solitude you are a member of an exclusive club that numbers 100 or so members. And, as a corollary, the novelist discovers that the one great advantage of making a film, rather than sitting alone in your room, is that your overwhelming desire to 'get it right' – to make it as authentic and true-to-life as is feasibly possible – is one that you share with all these fellow workers.

I looked on it as a good omen, just before we started filming, when a package arrived through the post. One of my uncles had unearthed a whole mass of material about his uncle, my great-uncle, Sandy. For the first time I saw a photograph of him, learned a little of his life before and after the war. He was a teetotaller and by coincidence I had written the part of the sergeant in my film as a teetotaller also.

The fact that he had fought and been injured at the Somme was also a curious benediction on our enterprise, it seemed, and Mouquet Farm, where he had been wounded, was in the same sector of the battle front where I had placed my notional platoon. Great-uncle Sandy looked very much like my late father (after whom he had been named) and, as we worked on through the film, if there was any ghostly presence haunting our trenches (and they were spookily evocative, especially in the early morning before the lights were switched on), I imagined it as being that of Sergeant Alexander Boyd, DCM.

I look at his face, as I have looked at countless other faces of soldiers of the Great War, and wonder what kind of a person he was and what his experience must have been like. We say, casually, that life in the trenches of the Western Front must have been 'unimaginable' but the challenge of art, surely, is to try to imagine it, to set the imagination free and to try to bring that bizarre, terrifying, boring, filthy world to life.

In the citation that accompanied uncle Sandy's DCM it says, 'when all the officers became casualties, he took charge, and extricated his company with great skill. He set a fine example of coolness and determination.' The bland vocabulary of military bureaucracy is literally meaningless. A padre wrote from a military hospital to Sandy's mother. 'I visited your dear boy this afternoon. He has several wounds, but none of them of a severe character. The doctors and nurses have good hopes of his recovery.'

Again, a dead wall of decorum and cliché. From what little I know of him and the ups and downs of his postwar life, he seems to have been a doggedly principled, determined, simple sort of person. There are passionate letters after his death to his mother from a woman who loved him and bore his child saying what a kind and good man he was. What stories lie there? The imagination starts working again, questions form, possible answers spring to mind.

Who was this young Scotsman who left his native country to travel across the globe only to be sent back to Europe to fight in the meadows of northern France? Close to home, but so far away. And a brother serving too, perhaps not far off. The questions form, but I think I'll leave them unanswered; I've done my own time in the trenches, now, in a novel and a film, and I don't think I'll be going back there again.

1999

Oxford

Saturday afternoon. Summer. Oxford, 1980. In Bonn Square – a patch of grass with a few trees that faces the Westgate shopping centre – there is a war memorial commemorating some remote colonial campaign at the tail end of the nineteenth century. On one side of the stunted obelisk there is an inscription: 'Killed by mutineers in Uganda, Brevet Major A. B. Thruston.' Beneath it, on the three steps at the base of the obelisk, loll a pride of fourteen-year-old skinheads, boys and girls, their cap-sleeved T-shirts revealing pale arms bruised with self-inflicted tattoos (biro ink and a safety pin). Three of them, like aged barflies, raise inflated plastic bags to their noses and leisurely inhale the fumes from the glue that congeals in the bottom. One fat boy, his face unnaturally red and shiny from the chemicals, rolls his eyes in simulated gourmet delight. You can practically see the damage being wreaked on his numb fist of a brain.

A few yards away around the maw of the shopping centre a group of sandalled young Christians sing modish hymns to the beat of a guitar and tambourine. Bearded, glossy-haired Iranian students chatter and gesticulate. Shirt-sleeved coppers stroll through the harassed mobs in Queen Street and Cornmarket. Three hundred French and Italian schoolkids assemble noisily at the foot of Carfax Tower. Coaches clog the bus station and bulk in every side street. The pavements are dark and sticky from the residue of ice-cream cones and abandoned lollies; waxpaper wrappers and polyurethane hamburger cartons form brittle drifts in shop doorways. Every step seems to connect with an empty Coke can. The city reels in a hot, jammed stupor, stunned by the heat and the perspiring shifting populace thronging its streets.

And yet . . . And yet the colleges somehow preserve their peace, effort-lessly – it seems – maintaining a world that Brevet Major A. B. Thruston would have no difficulty in recognizing. The college lawns are cropped like cricket squares, unbadged by weed or daisy; someone practising the piano in an upstairs music room runs off an appropriate arpeggio. Everywhere there is new, spanking clean sandstone. The colleges receive their regular face lift like placid Palm Beach crones. The rechiselled cornices and gargoyles are suddenly in sharp focus again, as if a lens has been twitched by an alert projectionist.

It is all, in fact, unsettlingly like an elaborate show. On my first visit to New York, within fifteen minutes of my arrival, I passed Woody Allen and Diane Keaton sauntering and chuckling down Park Avenue as if doing a retake for *Annie Hall*. I found this curiously sinister because it's exactly what the mythology of Manhattan makes you inclined to expect – before you get there. Oxford imposes a similar doubt. The University buildings, the colleges, are so close to their imagined forms that I felt I was being inveigled into some unwitting cameo role in a monstrous cinematic project. It affects everybody in this way, as the undergraduates so readily demonstrate with their arch self-consciousness and *Brideshead Revisited* pretensions. These antics – the braying voices, the paraded neuroses – are harmless irritants on the whole, but the perfection of the backdrop now seems to me to be Oxford's greatest attraction and – for its inhabitants in the University – its most insidious and damaging influence.

I came to Oxford five years ago to write a PhD thesis on Shelley. I had just got married and we lived in a large but inconveniently designed college flat on the Woodstock Road. It was inconvenient because the occupants of the upstairs flat could only reach their front door via our hall so we – perforce – got to know them quite well. Our neighbours over the next three years were a taciturn ginger-bearded chemist and his clog-wearing wife and, after them, a couple of timid American organ scholars. This couple, whose demeanour gave new resonance to the epithet 'mild-mannered', treated their flat with all the respect of H-block inmates and managed in the course of a year to wreak more damage on their abode than the most anarchic squat. As the rubbish began to tumble off the landing and creep down the stairs we began to feel like participants in a J. G. Ballard novel and hastily moved out.

We now live half a mile up the road – in a flat above a dentist's with no noise and no neighbours – but still in north Oxford. The houses around are large, Victorian and brick. Their walls are freighted with ivy and wisteria, the gardens are long and capacious, there are lots of trees. There is a smug air of self-satisfaction about this particular suburb, as if we all sense our luck in being able to live here. It used to be a kind of dons' ghetto and most of the houses, some of them enormous, were built in the last half of the last century when the colleges first allowed their Fellows to marry. The larger houses in north Oxford hover around £100,000 and today's Fellows, if they can afford a house at all – in many respects Oxford is more expensive than most districts in London – live in tiny terraced boxes in west Oxford – Jericho, Hinksey – or off the Cowley or Iffley roads to the south. West Oxford is undergoing radical class-surgery as its incredulous lower-income-group inhabitants sell-out for sums that must have seemed beyond their wildest dreams to the young academics, University Press editors and the 'new' middle-class professionals: designers of every shape and hue, folk-art manufacturers (original wooden toys, pine-furniture restorers, personalized roller-blind creators, etc.), management consultants and the like. Every third house these days has the obligatory skip parked outside as interior walls are battered out, old fireplaces revealed and basements are renovated. Now, tiny two-up, two-downs fetch prices in the mid twenty-thousands. The walls are so thin you can hear your neighbour cleaning his teeth.

East Oxford – Old Marston excepted – is bland and unremarkably modern in character. To the south lie Cowley and the British Leyland works.

Auden's poem on the city perfectly captures the spirit of the place, the

> Stones in those towers . . . utterly
> Satisfied with their weight.

And, in the next verse, fixes Cowley in so far as it impinges on the minds of the University's population:

> Outside, some factories, then a whole green county.

'Some factories', a meagre parenthesis for such a significant portion of the city and whose inhabitants probably supply 90 per cent of the 'town' in the famous Oxford polarity. Indeed town and gown seem as irredeemably divided as ever, almost as if some secret treaty has been signed, sectioning the city into discrete no-go areas almost as effectively as Derry. The Broad, St Giles and the Turl remain sedate and studenty on the most frantic Bank Holiday, while Cornmarket and Queen Street bulge with shoppers and garish consumerism.

Yet Cowley has developed its own character regardless, and the Cowley Road is probably the most heterodox and interesting thoroughfare – from a sociological point of view – that the city possesses. Its punks, rude boys and rastamen populate the edges of the University's hallowed precincts and occasional epidemics of 'student-bashing' provide more potent reminders of the 'town's' virile existence. And, nowadays, from the lawns of Garsington you can see the BL gasometer heavy on the horizon.

In the street where I live the graffiti on the walls says 'Ordine Nuovo', 'PCI' and 'Autonomia Operaia' – the lunatic extremes of Italian politics come to north Oxford. This year has definitely belonged to Italy, edging out France in Oxford's huge floating population of language students. Near my flat there's a school which runs summer courses for foreign students and from the window of the room where I work I can see them trooping up and down the street – vivid, lissom teenagers, smoking and lounging, the boys crass and arrogant, the girls sticking together, arms linked, eyes full of suspicion, or else dragging their feet, carrying their bordeom like rucksacks.

Every Friday the school runs a discotheque and for an hour or so in the evening an astonishing transformation occurs in the nearby side streets. The disco throbs away in the gym and all the boys disappear – waiting inside, I assume. Hesitantly, the girls gather in the quiet roads in small groups, affecting indifference, but undoubtedly lured by the occasion. The T-shirts, running shoes and jeans have been abandoned for jump-suits, lurid boob-tubes, high heels and make-up. There is little conversation, just an elaborate nonchalance as they gather, and an astonishing frisson of pubertal sexual tension charging the air. And then, as if on some silent signal, they are gone, and the gymnasium booms to the music. I've no idea what happens at the disco; I assume, like all adolescent experiences, that it's nothing like as exciting as the anticipation. It goes on well into the night and sometimes I ring up to complain about the noise.

When I first came to Oxford I was – as I think everyone is when they arrive – in awe of the place and its occupants. Starting a thesis proved harder than I thought and like most baffled post-graduates convinced myself things were going well by drawing up reading lists of staggering erudition and irrelevancy. Cautiously peering round the upper reading room in the Bodleian it seemed to me that everyone else there knew exactly what they were doing. Most of my companions seemed tense, humourless types, immersed in their work with a kind of obsessive ascetic fervour which was not a little depressing. Still, in the endless summer of 1976 it wasn't too hard to forget them and the frontiers of scholarship I was meant to be pushing back. The daily heat was as heavy as a glass door and the quadrangle lawns were parched and ochrous. I saw *A Midsummer Night's Dream* in St John's College gardens, cycled about in my shirtsleeves, went punting. The Emperors' Heads around the Sheldonian were renewed, Magdalen Tower hadn't yet assumed its mantle of scaffolding and the excellent Browns Restaurant had opened on the Woodstock Road to wild acclaim as the queues of Oxford's bright young things testified.

Steadily, remorselessly, I got to know more and more about Percy Bysshe Shelley and the first faltering chapters of my thesis were set down and a fascination with my subject began to grow. I came some way towards understanding the blinkered vigour of those scribbling away around me. I also got to know Shelley a lot better than I ever expected when I discovered a hitherto unremarked and unpublished piece of Shelley marginalia. Sandwiched between some speculations on Democritus' age and a rough draft of 'The Colliseum' in an uncatalogued folder of loose holograph sheets I came across a curious sketch, the significance of which was not immediately apparent. I turned the folder upside down and there it was: a page-sized phallus drawn with all the attention to detail of a bog-door graffitist. Such are the more arcane insights scholarship provides.

It wasn't until I came to Oxford that I met my first real writers, though none of them actually lived in the place. I did some work for *Isis* in my first year and in the course of this had the good fortune to meet and interview Gore Vidal, Martin Amis and Frederic Raphael. All were genial and encouraging, and thus encouraged I entered a short story for an *Isis* competition judged by Iris Murdoch and John Bayley. I came third. The next year I entered another – this time judged by Roald Dahl – and came second. I wisely didn't go in for a third, thinking the upward progression in itself a sufficient sign. I started sending stories into magazines. I felt that my big break had come – and that first truly public acceptance is a vital confidence booster – when *London Magazine* agreed to take a story for its summer double issue. That was in 1978.

A lot of writers live in and around Oxford, quite a few of them novelists – Iris Murdoch, A. N. Wilson, Susan Hill, Brian Aldiss and John Wain, for instance. There are probably many more but I don't know of them. Novelists, it seems to me, keep themselves very much to themselves and exhibit none of the solidarity and establish none of the social relationships that the poets do. There are many more poets in Oxford than novelists, and most people who do any form of imaginative writing here write poetry, I would say. Indeed, all the writers I know or am acquainted with in Oxford are poets. And of all the writing forms it is the one currently flourishing here. Several highly regarded poets live in the city or teach at the University and the 'poetry scene', such as it is, appears fairly active – lots of readings, a successful festival, encouragement for young writers and so on.

I have done all my writing in Oxford. My first novel and my story collection were written here, and, so it seems, my second novel will be too. But none of them has been about, or set in the city. Just why this should be so, I'm not exactly sure, because generally the place has a strong inspirational effect on writers. It's not so much a question of prudence but is rather, I think, a lack of curiosity. Perhaps it's also because when I started to write the rush of blood to the head that Oxford supplies had more or less spent itself. And again, the things that make Oxford special – its attractions and advantages – are so self-evident, have been so frequently described, eulogized and written up in all manner of ways that it doesn't take all that long for Oxford to seem terribly familiar. It's the Manhattan syndrome again: everything you expect of the place is here, right down to the last cliché. A deadening air of predictability settles over the city. Some views and buildings retain the occasional power to enchant, but – with rare exceptions – most of the people you meet about its streets can be categorized with a frightening swiftness, to such an extent that latterly what have come to engage my attention more and more are the exceptions to its magic lantern image. There are the glue-sniffers in Bonn Square; there's the Madam who controls the tarts in Jericho, the witty nutters patrolling the coffee bars cadging money off terrified tourists ('If I wasn't mad,' I heard one bellow at a horrified couple, 'how would you know you were normal, eh?'); and the thirteen shabby drunks I once saw – including a gap-toothed young woman – passing round a sherry bottle in unconscious parody on the Radcliffe Camera lawn . . .

*

Two or three months ago I was walking down Brasenose Lane – the alley that cuts between Turl Street and Radcliffe Square. There's nothing special about this featureless passageway. At the Turl Street end people park motorbikes in it and your hair is likely to be ruffled by gusts of Mazola-laden air from the Exeter College kitchen extractor fans. A bit further down it gets cool and dark where it's bounded on one side by the high walls of Exeter's garden and on the other by Brasenose and is overhung by thick plane and chestnut trees. I quite like Brasenose Lane, it's badly lit and at night can be quite spooky and evocative. During the day it acts as a kind of shadowy prelude to the more evident splendours of the Radcliffe Camera, the Bodleian, All Souls and the University Church which confront you at the end of your gentle descent from the Turl. On this occasion I was about halfway down when I spotted three soggy heaps huddled together at the foot of the Exeter garden wall. They were three derelict drunks – Oxford has a sizeable population – sleeping off their midday soak into oblivion, cider and sherry bottles scattered about like shell cases round a gun emplacement. One of them saw me coming, hauled himself to his feet and lurched towards me. 'Hey. Hey, peace man,' he yelled, weaving up, an exceedingly filthy Scottish hippie, bombed out of his skull, about twenty-four or twenty-five. 'Hey, man,' he breathed. 'Ah've written a pome. Wantae read it?'

That's what annoys me about Oxford, I suppose. Even the drunks have pretensions.

In the end one has to say that few places and few communities can be so entrenched in their own ideal projections as Oxford. In *Journey Without Maps* Graham Greene remarks that

When on rare occasions beauty and magnificence do coincide, one gets a sense of theatre or the films, it is 'too good to be true'. I find myself torn between two beliefs: the belief that life should be better than it is and the belief that when it is better it is really worse.

Auden sensed something very similar about Oxford, I think. Those 'Stones . . . utterly satisfied . . .', and its population,

> Mineral and creature, so deeply in love with themselves
> Their sin of accidie excludes all others

We exclude all others at our peril. Perhaps what unsettles me about living in Oxford is the feeling I receive that its inhabitants, or more specifically, the academic community amongst whom I work, sense and savour the beauty and magnificence but, ultimately, don't make the vital final qualification, and are content enough to live on with the sin. Perhaps it's time to leave.

1980

Being Translated

'Goodbye. I your new translator am.' The old joke about encountering your translator for the first time is both irrelevant and, curiously enough, often eerily correct. I remember meeting one of my translators at a British Council do somewhere abroad and he was virtually monoglot. We stood in a corner trying to talk to each other about whatever novel of mine he was currently translating and I could barely understand a word he said, so thick was his accent and wayward his syntax. Yet he was regarded as one of the country's finest translators and by all accounts had done my novels proud. Of course, what is most important in a translator is not his facility in *your* language but in his or her own. Also, I suspect that, initially, few authors worry a great deal about accuracy or style. The thrill of being translated is simply having a new copy of that familiar old book; of seeing that title transformed into something quite bizarre. Indeed, different alphabets do even more to satisfy this particular urge: Japanese, Hebrew and Greek versions can be relished and savoured quite uncomplicatedly.

However, as you get closer to home, I have to admit, worries start to intrude. My novels have been translated into twenty languages. I suppose that in at least half of the cases I have had absolutely no communication with the translator. And perhaps this is just as well: you can then repose all your trust in the professionalism of your publisher, confident that he would not employ someone merely desperate for cash. But once the translator makes contact your sanguinity can be all too easily undermined. My Norwegian translator, for example, actually concluded one of his letters to me thus: 'Hey listen, man, if you're ever in Oslo and short of bread you can crash in my pad anytime.' After I stopped laughing I started frowning. If this was his idea of English, how was his Norwegian? I conjured up images of a superannuated hippie sitting cross-legged on a mattress in an Oslo squat blithely grabbing at the wrong end of every textual stick in my novel. Luckily we fell out shortly after that. He berated me with some vigour over what he regarded as my thoughtlessness, not to say selfishness, in writing a novel as long as *The New Confessions*.

One of the first languages my novels were translated into was Dutch. Now, I cannot speak or read Dutch, my translator never made contact and, duly, the novels appeared. Because every Dutch person I had ever met spoke perfect English this was one set of translations that I never wondered about. But then, when *A Good Man in Africa*, *An Ice-Cream War* and *Stars and Bars* had been translated into, respectively, *Gewoon een Beste Kerel*, *Gewoon een Oorlogie* and *Sterren, Strepen en een Gewoon Englesman*, I began to worry. What was this '*Gewoon*' business, for Heaven's sake? Did they think I was writing some kind of serial novel? To this day I've never dared ask.

Most of the time one hopes earnestly for the best, trusts to luck and tries to suppress those horrible suspicions. That Bulgarian edition of *A Good Man in Africa* with a naked black lady spread-eagled across the endpapers . . . Someone completely mystified by the expression 'Tallyho!' and asking for an explanation . . . what, no dictionary to hand? And if 'Tallyho!' was such a poser what in God's name did he make of 'Haughmagandie'? So why wasn't he asking about it? And so on. But these instances are rare. On the whole I have exceptionally good relations with my translators and in the case of my French translator, Christiane Besse, I have a co-worker whose diligence and attention to detail are second to none. And in French, at least, the rewards of the new text can be appreciated. When one reads, for example, sentences like, 'Le lendemain matin, la véranda craque sous les pas, couverte comme elle l'est de leurs cadavres coriaces. Des lambeaux délicats et chatoyants d'ailes abandonnées gisent dans les coins,' the frisson of surprise and pleasure is genuine and acute and one realizes that a different language need not imply a loss and diminution of effect and how even a scrupulous literality can be transformed by the skill and art of a real expert.

1986

London

London is too big, too sprawling and attenuated, to be encompassed or defined, to be fixed on the page in one or many identities. The city spreads itself out generously, expanding north, south, east and west from its brown river looping lazily through its shallow limestone valley. I live near its centre, a hundred metres from the Thames in Chelsea. I have friends who live in Hampstead and Crouch End to the north, Barnes and Richmond to the west, Streatham and Tooting Bec in the south, Greenwich and the Isle of Dogs in the east, but they feel so far away, as if they were inhabitants of other towns, in other counties. If I were to visit them, for example, for lunch or dinner, I would think nothing of allotting an hour or more for the journey, or even longer, depending on the time of day. These are vast distances for a city dweller and they affect our perceptions of the place radically. To a very real extent it is quicker for me to go to Oxford than it is to Stoke Newington in north London, easier to travel to Cambridge than visit a colleague who works on a newspaper in Wapping in the city's east end. Oxford and Cambridge, provincial towns a hundred kilometres away, feel more accessible than districts of the city I inhabit. What does that tell me about London? What kind of Londoner does that make me? And I am not alone. No matter where you live in the city the same sense of isolation, the same alienation from other areas of the place affect you. We live so close and yet we feel so far apart, with such a long journey to make from district to district. And with these fraught trajectories across the city it is no wonder that we draw in on ourselves, create zones and parameters, homelands and reservations, beyond which we are reluctant to go. If Los Angeles can be defined as ninety suburbs in search of a city the same can be said of London too. There is no one London, there is no one place, one entity, it is a congregation, a plurality, the sum of its many and disparate parts.

Broadly speaking, the city is made up of two dozen or so villages, each geographically distinct and each with its own character. When I spread a map of London in front of me and look at those areas I know well, where I regularly frequent and visit, I am astonished at how much

of the place is still *terra incognita*. I live in Chelsea, I know the neighbouring 'villages' of Fulham, South Kensington and Knightsbridge well,
very well indeed. A little further beyond and things begin to grow
hazy: Hammersmith and Belgravia, Pimlico and Westminster, Notting
Hill and Bayswater, Mayfair and Bloomsbury are familiar but I can
easily get lost in them. I look at the map and I see I have barely strayed
beyond London's south-west quadrant. To the south, just across the
bridges over the river, lie Battersea, Wandsworth and Clapham – barely
explored. To the north, north of Regent's Park, lie places that are wholly
alien and strange. From time to time my work takes me to Camden
Town. And beyond Regent's Park, north of the great railway termini
of Euston, St Pancras and King's Cross, I feel I cross an invisible
boundary. Here in north London the buildings look darker, sootier, in
less good repair. The streets seem more narrow, the people scruffier,
the pavements littered and soiled. Yet I have travelled barely two miles
from my home. It is not so much that I have crossed a topographical
frontier, it is more of a psychological barrier that separates me from
these other areas. I *feel* different here in north London, just as I do in
the east or south of the river, and because I feel different everything
about these places – the buildings, the denizens, the atmosphere – is
subtly altered as well.

So we cling to our familiar territories and venture forth with a bizarre
reluctance. Everyone judges the other districts of London in unconscious comparison with their own. I have no desire to live anywhere
else in the city so for me 'London' is to a significant degree Chelsea
and its immediate environs. I don't drive either so my local streets possess
a familiarity denied the motorist. I walk for miles through south-west
London, in ever widening loops that take me to regular points of reference – bookshops, cafes, restaurants, cinemas, auction houses, newsagents.
Here they make the best cappuccinos in town; here I can buy a complete
copy of the Sunday edition of *The New York Times* on a Monday; here
I can sit and read in a garden by a fountain. My portion of the city is
exhaustively mapped, it is known intimately, but its grid references remain
private and subjective.

Chelsea, of course, is a famous place and has been a haunt of artists
and writers for two hundred years: Carlyle, Oscar Wilde, George Eliot,
Whistler, Rossetti, Henry James, Swinburne, Henry Moore, Francis Bacon
. . . From my bedroom window I can see the spire of the church Dickens
was married in. In a house in the little square around the corner Mark

Twain stayed, and so on. It is a district of narrow streets and stuccoed houses, of secret tree-filled squares and back-street pubs, of Georgian terraces and Victorian public buildings, all loosely held together by the winding ribbon that is the King's Road. Cyril Connolly (1903–74), writer, critic and bon viveur, in many ways the quintessential Chelsea dweller, developed a potent nostalgia for the place. He called it 'that leafy tranquil cultivated *spielraum* where I worked and wandered'. It is an enchanted place and there is a quality about the light too that appears different: perhaps it is the gleaming stucco that reflects back with extra force what little sun we receive in London, or perhaps it is the river – so close, but always out of sight – the air above and around it washed twice a day by its tidal ebb and flow, a conduit of freshness running through the grime of the city.

So much else of London suffers by comparison with Chelsea (or so Chelsea dwellers would have you believe): elsewhere seems less fun, less heterodox, less green, less refulgent, but Chelsea shares one quality with the other districts that makes London different from almost any other city one can imagine. Chelsea's winding, narrow streets are lined with houses, small cottages and mews, Georgian crescents, Victorian terraces, and when one reflects further one realizes that London is in essence a city of houses, of single homes with small gardens with a single front door. There are a few areas of flats and apartments, but the overriding impression is of one family unit, one house. This seems to me to explain much about London, and not just the city's sprawling, generous, unstructured size but also its particular atmosphere and ambience. The house becomes the centre of the city dweller's universe, social life takes place behind the curtained windows of the dining room and sitting room, not in the streets, or squares or great public meeting places. In fact there are no real public areas in London, no great squares, no spacious boulevards. At night the vast majority of the population are back in their homes, enclosed and self-sufficient and indifferent to the life beyond their front door.

This has, it seems to me, two obvious effects that make London unusual, given its size and renown and that it is one of the great capitals of the world. First, the pace and energy of the city seem to quieten spontaneously at around eleven o'clock at night. It is as if there is a kind of tacit curfew, a feeling that to be out in the city after midnight is – if not illicit – not exactly normal. Leave a cinema or a show at the end of the evening and try to find somewhere congenial for a drink or a coffee or a meal and you are severely tested. The pubs are closed or closing, only a handful of restaurants serve meals after 11 p.m., public transport winds down, taxis disappear. The city is going to bed and those who want to stay up a little later are going to have their ingenuity and their wallets stretched to the full.

The second feature of London that extends from this home-based society is its privacy. London is a private city, intimate and reclusive. It works best for those who know its secrets, those who have learned the ropes. Even the pub – that one symbol of communal life on every street corner – represents a physical challenge to the stranger. You have to push through a heavy door to enter. You cannot see what is happening inside from the outside. It does not offer an implicit welcome to the casual passer-by, unlike the sidewalk cafe. It is a closed place, its windows are frosted, its gaze is inward-looking. Children are not admitted, its aura is masculine, gloomy, self-absorbed. Even more extraordinary, inside some pubs there are bars that operate on an overt class system: this bar, the decor says, is proletarian, for serious drinking; that bar is genteel, a place where you may bring your wife. The two rooms are often quite separate, entered by different doors.

There is no street life in London as might be recognized in Paris or Rome or Madrid, there is no community of souls in this city, there is no democratic sharing in what the city offers. To get the best out of it you have to be a member of a club. Clubs operate in many diverse ways, from the traditional gentlemen's club in St James's or Pall Mall to an avant garde theatre group, but they all point to the same conclusion. If you live in the city and if you wish to exploit it to the full you discover that again and again, to experience the best London has to offer, you have to become a *member*.

Fifty yards from my house there is a small London square, classic, pretty, with tall plane trees and rhododendrons, a lush lawn, some park benches. You come upon it, as is true of so many of London's hidden squares, quite by accident. It looks enchanting, a small green island amongst the brick and the asphalt, sheltered and tranquil. Iron railings surround it. Tired, footsore, perhaps just seeking a moment's repose, you try the gate. Locked. But people are in there, children are playing. A small sign says – 'residents only' – you walk on by, excluded. You may look but you may not touch. This little garden in Tedworth Square is yet another of London's exclusive clubs for members only. If you want to enjoy it you have to qualify for a key.

Such moments provoke attacks of spleen against London and its bourgeois smugness. You cannot live in a great city and not be alternately enraptured and repelled by it. I think of my own nine years in London, how privileged and protected they have been, and how any account of my point of view of the place does no justice at all to its dark side, London's slums and sweat shops, its poverty and meanness, its vice and brutality. Look how the glossy limousines sweep out of the Savoy Hotel on to the Strand and how there, in every shop doorway in their cardboard boxes, huddle the homeless, the drunk and the deluded. But this juxtaposition is commonplace, this is not London's problem any more than it is New York's or Delhi's or Nairobi's or Manila's. Other grudges against the city are, however, more precise and localized. Why has London neglected its river and built power stations and coal yards and warehouses along its banks? Why have so many disgusting buildings been erected everywhere else? London was never beautiful, it could never be described as stylish or splendid. Its centre – Piccadilly, Regent Street, Oxford Street, Trafalgar Square – has a solid, massy quality to it, a reflection of the prodigious success of its mercantile past and imperial dominance. But even in the 1950s London had a low, almost Venetian skyline, punctuated by its needly church spires, one that has now virtually disappeared, swallowed up by the unregulated explosion of office blocks and high-rise buildings. Why is there so much dog shit in the streets? Why are there so many cars? Why did we allow Mrs Thatcher to abolish the perfectly efficient, though inconveniently socialist, Greater London Council so that this enormous city no longer has an elected administration to run it? The litany of complaints can run and run.

But, as Dr Johnson said, 'He who is tired of London is tired of life.' And it takes only a moment for the bile and resentment to alter into invigoration and enthusiasm. In 1928 Cyril Connolly returned to London after five weeks in Spain. In his journal he recorded: 'Back in London . . . feel nothing but intense disgust. General dissatisfaction and distress.' But a few days later he writes, 'I seem to be falling in love with London . . . To feel this jungle come to life all round one in the evening, the same October mists, fires, lights, wet streets, blown leaves, to plunge into its many zones not knowing what one will discover . . .' This seems to me the authentic London voice and the authentic London experience. There is a vibrancy about the city just as there is complacency and apathy. There are maddening irritations as well as astonishing diversity. And there is also this constant prospect of discovery before you, of new places, people, experiences, views and vistas that this huge, perplexing, secret city somehow manages to keep hidden until it chooses to reveal them. A big solid hard place, pragmatic and worldly, but it still retains its powerful, irresistible allure.

1993

A New York Walk

Since 1996 I've spent between forty and fifty days a year in New York and, if I can't claim to be a local, I do feel I've come to know the place better than your average tourist: I have my habits, I have my little routines and short cuts, I am a regular in certain bars and restaurants. I may not be at home but I feel I occupy a kind of residential limbo – in prolonged and agreeable transit. I am, as they would say in France, *un familier.*

One measure of this familiarity is that there is a walk I do most Mondays to Fridays that has become as much a part of my life as similar walks are in London. It starts where I live when I'm in New York, a small hotel on 63rd Street between Park and Madison, and it forms a rough oblong shape that covers a fair bit of the Upper East Side. The Upper East Side suffers a little from its reputation – as a place where only the truly wealthy New Yorkers live, hidden away in immaculate, doorman-guarded apartment blocks. Like all clichés this one possesses a fair degree of truth. But the denizens of this bit of Manhattan do make for a fascinating passing parade, and the one place you'll see them out of their apartments and town cars is on the streets around here. People-watching doesn't come much better than on Madison Avenue.

Yet the Upper East Side is a far more heterogeneous place than its snootily upscale reputation might suggest and the first and most intriguing aspect of this walk is that, over its couple of miles or so, you will encounter as many facets of Manhattan life as you would almost anywhere else.

I leave the hotel and turn left towards Madison Avenue and, a few paces later, reaching Madison turn north, heading uptown. In the four years I've been coming regularly to New York, Madison has turned itself into one of the most remarkable shopping streets in the world, a mile-long hymn of praise to labels and logos, high prices and haute couture. This is fine if you're interested in shopping but, even if you're not, these immaculate temples of consumerism are still diverting to the eye. The Madison run actually starts a few blocks south of 63rd with Nicole Farhi, Donna Karan and Calvin Klein, but as I turn northward pretty soon I'm flanked by Armani and Valentino and up ahead loom Krizia, Ungaro and

Bulgari and so on. Also in this stretch of the Avenue are found small see-and-be-seen restaurants, such as Nello, Cafe Nosidam and La Goulou, serving international food to an international clientele, but my first break usually occurs, mundanely, at an ATM machine in Citibank and then, on 67th, I am occasionally obliged to stop for breakfast at the Gardenia Cafe. There are two potential breakfast/coffee stops on this long first stretch of the walk up Madison, but the other – another timeless classic, a Viand – is many blocks northward. The Gardenia is also a classic diner, although, fittingly for the neighbourhood, it seems slightly more genteel. A long, thin, dark room, serving American reliables – eggs, bacon, potatoes – with astonishing speed and fussless taciturnity. I drink my coffee and, if it's a Wednesday, read my *New York Observer*, a weekly, and, just possibly, the most interesting and best written newspaper in the world.

On up Madison the march of brand names continues – Dolce & Gabbana, Yves St Laurent, Sonia Rykiel. More intriguingly we encounter (on 70th) the first of five independent bookshops this walk provides. This is the Madison Avenue Bookshop, small and well stocked, famous for the contemptuous aloofness of its erudite staff.

We've been walking slightly up hill thus far, on the east side of the Avenue. At the crest of this gentle hill stands the Westbury Hotel, now converted into condominiums, and looking left down the cross streets you can see narrow, tree-crowded vistas of Central Park.

Strolling easily downhill you pass on your right the impossible fantasy that is Ralph Lauren's shop/mansion on 72nd, a two-way cross street. It's worth visiting this shop if only to see the quintessence of the Ralph Lauren vision of the good life: the dream made flesh. Across 72nd is the Madison Avenue Presbyterian Church. None of New York's churches is particularly distinguished, architecturally, but they are to be valued for their Victorian gothic contribution to the twentieth-century skyscape. Gargoyles, teetering finials and flying buttresses make the perfect decorative counterpoint to the concrete and plate glass angularities of the skyscrapers and office blocks. Diverted as you might be by the life on street level it is always worth looking up in New York every fifty yards or so. It never palls, this prospect of lofty buildings, and, particularly at night, it can be astonishingly beautiful, these soaring masses of stacked lights and the wavy ripple of mirror glass

Up ahead, on 74th Street, is the inverted grey ziggurat that is the Whitney Museum of Modern American Art. The Whitney is a great museum, not so much for what it periodically contains (though its permanent collection is superb) but for the building itself. Solidity, moneyed-heft, integrity are the quiet messages its stone, brass and mahogany seem emphatically to convey. The lifts are gigantic, the finish flawless (no expense has been spared), its scale is impressive and it is astoundingly easy to use. I don't know what it is about the Whitney that draws me so. I prefer it to the Guggenheim and MoMA (not so far away, either). I think it must be something to do with the proportion and massiveness of its construction. As I pass it every day I can go in when it's just opened. I often find myself wandering around with only the museum guards for company. In any given week I may flit in for half an hour two or three times.

On up Madison past the discreetly sumptuous wonders of the Carlyle Hotel and we are approaching my destination on 79th Street. This is the New York Society Library – where I work. This is an ancient institution by American standards, dating back to the eighteenth century. The library has moved many times in its history before ending up here in a capacious town house on 79th, between Madison and Park. The library is private – it costs $100 or so a year to join – but it provides personal access to a huge collection of books and journals (you can browse in the stacks) and, more importantly for someone like me, at its summit, rooms with desks where a transitory writer can plug in his computer and, in theory at least, work. It remains a defiantly unmodernized place, with filing cards as well as computerized catalogues, marble sculptures on the wide stairways and a politely formal way of dealing with its members. Its reading room could come out of a gentleman's club in London – tall, elegant windows, leather armchairs, periodicals displayed on circular tables, people speaking rarely and then in the quietest of whispers.

And this is where I spend my day, venturing out at lunchtime a little further up Madison to E.A.T. (80th Street) – the closest thing to a New York brasserie (as opposed to a pseudo-French one) that the city provides. It welcomes many solo diners, which seems an almost forgotten pleasure these days. Eating a proper lunch alone (rather than a bite of something on the run) is an agreeable pastime but it mustn't be rushed and needs to be accompanied by some sort of reading matter – book, newspaper or magazine. They don't chase you out, either, when you've finished. You can easily spend an hour in E.A.T. reading and eating and covertly watching the people around you at the same time.

And afterwards, if you require more diversion, just a block away on 5th Avenue is the sprawling bulk of the Metropolitan Museum, an incomparable treasure trove and again the sort of museum, in my opinion, that favours the periodic half-hour visit rather than the day-long, enervating culture-trawl. And, if the Met doesn't beguile, a couple of blocks north of E.A.T. is my favourite bookstore in the city – Crawford Doyle, another independent bookshop, which not only sells everything in print you might want to read (with great charm and friendliness) but has a thriving antiquarian business to tempt you as well.

The library shuts at the end of the working day and the second leg of my walk commences. I prefer not to walk back down Madison – it's more of a morning thing, Madison Avenue – so I stroll along 79th, heading eastwards towards Lexington Avenue. This involves crossing Park Avenue and here you are afforded one of the great American vistas: the view south down Park Avenue towards the Met-Life building at its foot. It's probably best at dusk, with some blue still left in the sky, but with enough gathering gloom to set the refulgent windows of the towering, lit buildings glowing like banked coals.

On to Lexington and a right turn southwards. Lexington is smaller (in that its buildings are lower), narrower and shabbier than its two adjacent avenues to the west and it provides a welcome contrast. From gleaming, pricey, exclusive New York, you enter a neighbourhood, a place where people actually live and shop for themselves. Gone are the designer stores, to be replaced by supermarkets, delis, Chinese laundries. Lexington has its own special bonus, however: as you walk south you are aiming for the Chrysler Building, the world's most beautiful skyscraper, its silver, art deco, hypodermic needle gleaming gold – if you're lucky – in the orange evening sun.

You start to walk up hill again, fairly soon, up the steeper rise of Lennox Hill, heading towards Hunter College (part of New York University) with its two aerial pedestrian-ways crossing the avenue. Here there is an intriguing congregation of antique shops and, within the space of a few blocks, three more independent bookstores: Lennox Hill Bookstore (on 73rd), Bookberries (on 71st) and Shakespeare & Co. on 69th. All have their own distinct character and all are worth stopping in to browse. The hegemony of Borders and Barnes & Noble hasn't – visibly – seemed to have affected independent bookselling in this part of the city, and a visit to any of the five on this walk will remind you of the advantages of plucky independence versus the chain store.

My pit-stop on the walk back is on 73rd, called the Cafe Word-of-Mouth. Downstairs is a takeaway, upstairs is almost a tea-room: Rennie

Mackintosh meets art deco, all cherrywood and taupe. The last time I did this walk I inverted it – came up Lex, went down Mad. It had snowed in the night and there were foot-high banks of frozen snow on the sidewalks. It was bitter cold, with a wind that seemed to take the skin off your face. I stopped in Cafe Word-of-Mouth for sustenance. A big caffe latte, scrambled eggs and crispy bacon. I read the newspaper and thawed out, then plodded off up Lexington to the library, full and warm.

If you want alcohol on this walk you have to go into hotels (the Mark or the Carlyle on Madison) or go further afield to the bars of Third Avenue where you're spoilt for choice. Though it's worth remembering that you can go into any New York restaurant and just have a drink at the bar without any problems. There used to be a bar on Madison called the Madison Pub – a dark semi-basement – but it closed recently. Things come and go with astonishing swiftness in New York and the Upper East Side is no exception: in the last two years I've seen an entire skyscraper rise up from Park Avenue to dominate the view from my hotel room. A favourite cafe closed (where reputedly you could get the best espresso in Manhattan); a famous landmark bookstore – Books Etc. – went, almost overnight. But this walk up Madison and down Lexington seems to me to contain, for all its regular and sudden transformations, something that remains a representative mixture of the whole city. Fashion, commerce, philanthropic art, the quaint, the banal, the unique, the down-and-dirty, high culture and nail parlours.

It's all down hill from Hunter College's crossroads. Students mill about smoking, sprawl on the steps. They seem all to be foreign, reminding you of this city's polyglot heritage, the welcome it gives (or gave) to immigrants. And indeed many of the shops on this last stretch down to 63rd and the hotel reflect that ethnic mix: pizza joints, kebab houses, Korean nail parlours, Chinese take-aways. And just at the end at the last block is A&B Stationers, home, it seems, to every foreign newspaper and magazine you could ask for. The British papers arrive twenty-four hours later and it seems bizarre, at six o'clock on a New York evening, to see the racks outside filled with the *Guardian*, *Independent* and the *Telegraph*. Bizarre but therefore somehow normal in this place, if the paradox doesn't seem too forced. Nothing, in New York, is really surprising, when you come to think about it – once you've got over your surprise.

2000

The Eleven-Year War

12 May 1986–27 March 1997

It is 1985. I am thirty-three years old and I have just hit pay-dirt (that's to say the modest seam of low-grade ore that is available to the literary novelist). My second novel, *An Ice-Cream War*, has just been published in France (under the title *Comme Neige au Soleil*) and it is a bona fide bestseller. I have been on a legendary book programme on French TV called *Apostrophes*, during which the equally legendary host, Bernard Pivot, has offered personally to reimburse any reader not captivated by *Comme Neige au Soleil*. 'Adieu, la sereine neutralité', cry the French newspapers. Pivot, whose integrity and scrupulous disinterestedness is renowned, has astonished everyone by his overt and candid enthusiasm for my novel and the whole affair has become a news event. For ten hours at the Paris Salon du Livre in the Grand Palais I sign copies to a never dwindling queue. My publishers, Editions André Balland, cannot believe what has happened. Champagne bottles are opened, euphoria reigns. It's a literary gusher – the book sells and sells. High on the bestseller lists, it racks up the sales figures: 30, 40, 50,000. On and on it goes, selling, in its first year, over 100,000 copies.

Now, foreign publishers have an easier fiscal ride than domestic ones. In Britain, your publisher presents accounts twice a year and pays the royalties owing at the same time. Abroad, the norm is different. A year after publication the figures are added up, and three months after that the cheque, if one is forthcoming, is delivered. My advance for *An Ice-Cream War* was approximately £2,000. I knew how many copies it had sold and it didn't take a mathematical genius to calculate that, fifteen months after publication, with sales of over 100,000, I was due a pretty significant royalty cheque. Authors may grumble at the delay in these payments: the book makes all this money but the publisher doesn't have to settle with you for over a year (what happens to the interest?) but that is the nature of the beast, *la règle du jeu*: just be grateful that for once your luck held up.

A year later the reckoning was made: Editions André Balland owed me a royalty payment of £57,400.

This was, in 1986, a significant sum of money (it still is, in 2001).

Susan, my wife, and I had already taken this into account – in other words we had spent it: we knew exactly what role it was to play in securing the essential underpinnings of our lives. My third novel, *Stars and Bars*, had been published in 1984 and I was already underway with my fourth, *The New Confessions*, a long book that would take me over a year to write. The French money, the French windfall, would keep the ship afloat.

But no cheque appeared on the date when it was due. I rang my agent: can we chase up the French money, please (my agents were taking a 20 per cent commission)? I remember vividly that afternoon when the return phone call came: I was in our house in Fulham, it was after lunch. I picked up the phone. 'Hello, Will? Bad news, I'm afraid . . .'

Editions André Balland would not, could not, pay.

My journal, 12 May 1986: 'Problems with Balland. They say they won't pay. A scandal. I will sue them and leave them, I will write to French newspapers and expose them.' That's all. My journal, I should say, is a resolutely pragmatic document, a simple record of my working life rather than anything more grandiose or self-conscious. Still, that note of intemperate bluster doesn't truly reflect the feelings of massive frustration and anger I felt. There were moments – twenty-minute spasms – when I wanted to kill. I simply could not believe that this had happened to me – all this effort, all this work and then the tantalizing prospect of the just reward snatched away. Moments of rage as pure as I had ever felt alternated with periods of quietistic resignation: of course, you were never going to receive this money, you fool, you dreamer, I would say to myself – the world doesn't work like that. But at base – *au fond* – it was the injustice of it all that was rammed home (and ate at my soul) that afternoon and subsequently. Over a year after the huge success of the book, with – it has to be said – everybody else taking their profits (booksellers and publisher) long before me, the reckoning day had finally arrived and the author – that hapless creature tethered forever at the end of the food chain – had to be paid his 10 per cent royalty. And it was not forthcoming.

What was to be done? I turned to my agents. Now, it can be argued (I would argue) that a literary agency has to provide two fundamental services in order to justify the 10, 15 or 20 per cent commission it charges: namely, one, sell the client's work and then, two, collect all revenues owing. The initial obligation had been discharged – now they had to tackle the second.

My agent flew to Paris – she was easily frustrated by the publishers – she sat for two hours in the lobby but no one was available to see her. She returned empty handed to London and angry letters were exchanged. The publishers claimed she was harassing them and that their Canadian distributor had gone bust, leaving them short of cash.

My journal: 15 May 1986: '[my agent] flew to Paris today to see Balland. It seems they are not the slightest bit embarrassed. To the dermatologist: my psoriasis is running riot.'

I was afflicted at the time with a bizarre form of body-wide psoriasis (dozens of circular raw scaly patches the size of fifty pence pieces all over my arms and torso, like badges – which turned out to be eczema, in the end), which was definitely stress related. The Balland affair sent it raging out of control for a few weeks.

My publishing house in France, Editions André Balland, was a small, independent one, but of some renown (they numbered a Goncourt Prize winner among their authors). They had published my first novel, *A Good Man in Africa* (*Un Anglais sous les Tropiques*), with some critical success, but no one had foreseen the huge sales of the second. In the warm afterglow of bestsellerdom, I had sold them my third novel, *Stars and Bars* (*La Croix et la Bannière*), which had been published before the storm broke. Payments were outstanding on that book also. The eponymous head of the firm, André Balland *lui-même*, was a tall, lean, much-married, droll *littérateur*, hugely experienced and widely liked. I liked him too. He had one of those badger-grey, cropped, US marine-sergeant haircuts that many elderly Frenchmen favoured long before they became the mark of the fashionable young. A month or two before the non-payment crisis, he had invited me to a grand literary lunch at the Brasserie Lipp in Paris where we had eaten and drunk well and, afterwards, we had strolled back down the Boulevard St Germain towards the firm's offices, chatting about this and that writer who had been present, talking amiably about the novel I was writing and so on. The literary life *à la française* – real, not idealized. I didn't know that would be the last time I would ever see him.

Back in London my agent could make no headway – phone calls went unanswered, letters were unreplied to. I was told that André Balland would be writing to me himself. My journal, 9 June 1986: 'Pathetic letter from Balland saying he hadn't read my contract properly and that he has a cash-flow problem. I've written to him demanding 250,000

Frs up front and the rest in monthly instalments. A good letter, it was, but a sad compromise.'

It *was* a good letter – it took me about two days to write, hunched over my French dictionary and grammar book. I have copies of our subsequent correspondence. Boyd: 'Je me trouve au bord des embarras financiers vis à vis le fisc. Souvenez-vous, c'est *mon* argent – pas le vôtre – que vous gardez à ce moment.' And so on. Balland: 'Cher William, Merci pour votre gentille lettre. Je suis extrêmement soulagé de voir que nos relations puissent reprendre leur cours normal.'

The lawyers met in Paris. Various documents that were copied to me attest to ways in which I was to be reimbursed. In August I received a cheque for 150,000 Frs – 50,000 Frs less than had been agreed. In October I received another 50,000, the money seemed finally to be on its way. Boyd to Balland: 'Cher André, Merci bien pour votre lettre. Vous savez que, moi aussi, j'ai eu les ennuis fiscaux cette année et, par conséquence, c'est crucial que les versements arrivent ponctuellement. Comme ça je peux régler ma vie, vis à vis mon banquier et le fisc. Le nouveau roman marche bien et j'espère vivement que nous pouvons oublier nos difficultés de l'année dernière et continuer notre association dans le futur. Bien à vous, William.' Balland to Boyd: 'Cher William . . . si des choses heureuses interviennent dans ma vie professionnelle, vous pouvez être assuré que j'augmenterai le montant de ces mensualités afin d'être en défaut le moins longtemps possible. A très bientôt, j'espère, André Balland.'

The monthly payments continued for a while and then stopped. I was still well short of what I was owed. My agent and I decided to sue and so we engaged a firm of English lawyers, Heald Nickinson, that had an office in Paris. There was some kind of judicial hearing (my agent and I shared the costs of the lawyers' fees) and a form of repayment was set out. I was to receive a down payment of 200,000 Frs (say £20,000) and then monthly payments of £5,000 until the amount due was settled. Matters were further complicated when we discovered on analysing Balland's accounts that other payments were also delayed, not just on *An Ice-Cream War*, but on my other two novels that Balland had published – it now appeared that I had actually been owed some £65,000.

It was by now mid 1987. By October 1987 another deal was sorted out between our lawyers and Balland's to regularize repayments. Beyond all this, life was going on: my fourth novel, *The New Confessions*, was published in Britain and was sold to a different, and very eminent French publishing house, Le Seuil (who, significantly enough, had also published the paperbacks of the first three).

And then it all goes quiet for three years, a kind of phony peace. I was now happy with my new French publisher; I'd had a fair chunk of the money owing to me, paid in dribs and drabs (I was still short by £15,000), but Balland seemed to have gone off the radar, at least as far as my journal was concerned: there is no reference between October 1987 (when the repayments scheme was formalized by the lawyers) and April 1991. More than three years of silence. The monthly payments were coming through and when they stopped, it seemed I made no fuss. I put this down to a kind of malignant unworldliness that tends to afflict novelists (there are exceptions, of course). To describe it at its most simple I think the reasoning goes like this: you, the novelist, can't believe you are actually earning your living writing novels – and to complain about being defrauded, messed about, unpaid, or ripped off under these circumstances seems somehow churlish. True, in my case, everything was going fairly well, especially in France, and I suppose I had written off the Balland affair as just one of those bad experiences that afflict writers from time to time. But looking back over my papers and journals, as I researched the background to this story, I found myself baffled and angry with myself for being so compliant and complacent. So they still owe me £15,000? – well, let's not rock the boat.

In early 1991 Editions André Balland formally declared themselves to be in financial difficulties. In French the expression is to *déposer votre bilan*. No exact equivalent exists in Britain (it's not like going bankrupt) but in the USA the expression is 'to file for Chapter 11'. What it means, in real terms, is that your bank (supervised by a court official) takes over the running of your business and you, the enterprise, admit you cannot meet your financial responsibilities. Creditors are thus warned. And I was a creditor.

In 1991 I started to receive registered letters from Paris about my status as said creditor. I had to notify the authorities exactly how much I was owed by the moribund Editions André Balland. I really didn't know what to do. And here my translator steps in. Christiane Besse (a truly remarkable woman) had (and has) translated all my novels into French and had become a close friend. As a result of the new association with Le Seuil it became clear that, over the last few intervening years (since 1989), royalties from my paperback sales (of my three Balland titles) had been properly paid to Editions André Balland but I had not received a penny. When Balland had *déposé son bilan* it had been bought by another company called Copagest. 'Copagest' is an acronym for 'Compagnie Parisienne de Gestion Automobile de la Gare de l'Est' – in short, a taxi-firm. Balland-Copagest, this unlikely coupling, had been receiving the monies due to me (from Le Seuil, from another paper-back company and from book clubs) but had neglected to pass my share along. As well as the £15,000 Balland had not paid me, and for which Balland-Copagest was liable, it seemed I was also owed other sums of money by way of unpaid royalties by the new company.

After some discussion, Christiane Besse introduced me to a lawyer in Paris called Anne Veil, who specialized in literary and publishing liti-gation. We met one afternoon in Christiane's apartment. As we took tea, Anne Veil spoke with eloquent, enormously grave, yet reassuring calm: the case was clear-cut – it was up to me. If I wanted to proceed we would institute a *procès* against Balland-Copagest. How much was involved? At that stage of accounting it appeared that, first, they should have paid me the outstanding £15,000 that Balland owed me (plus interest); second, there seemed to be some £7–8,000 of outstanding royalties that I should have received. And then there was the question of costs and damages.

A few dark nights of the soul ensued. All the old reservations about going to law came to mind (the time, the stress, the benefit accruing only to the lawyers, and so on) but it seemed to me I was in too deep now. I had already sued (via Heald Nickinson) and had achieved partial reparation. But now, by all accounts, it appeared I had been wronged yet again – all my royalties and earnings from my three books since Balland went bust had been quietly sequestered. The malignant unworld-liness that afflicts novelists for once didn't apply; this was a matter of principle – it seemed to me there was no other course of action to take. I instructed Anne Veil to sue Balland-Copagest.

French justice moves slowly, but inexorably, and French lawyers are paid half their fee up-front. It wasn't until 9 September 1993 that the 'Affaire William Boyd v Balland-Copagest (dossier no. 82231091)' was pleaded before the 3ème Chambre Civile du Tribunal de Grande Instance in Paris. Anne Veil and I were now on first-name terms and I have to say I had a confidence in her abilities that was adamantine. I felt sure we would win; she hoped for the best – she just kept warning me it would take a long time. The judgement of the tribunal was scheduled for 13 October 1993. In the meantime I had formally cancelled all the contracts of the three books I had had with Balland and had resold them to Le Seuil. I should mention that I could not have undertaken all this litigation without the tireless support and energy of Christiane Besse (all authors should be so lucky with their translators): she was busily orchestrating events behind the scenes – Anne Veil was our *force de frappe*. Looking today at the dossier we presented to the court (a formidably argued case, some thirty-five pages long) I see we were suing Balland-Copagest for 150,000 Frs (£15,000 approximately) – ('dus aux termes des relèves de comptes remis par les éditions André Balland, et non réglés depuis 1989'), 59,132 Frs (unpaid royalties for 1989 and 1990). And 103,460 Frs (unpaid royalties for 1991 and 1992). Altogether approximately £31,000. On top of that we were asking for 100,000 Frs (£10,000) 'à titre de dommages-intérêts pour le grave préjudice matériel et moral à lui causé', and another 50,000 Frs towards our legal costs. All in all, getting on for £46,000.

13 October came around. We won. Balland-Copagest were ordered to pay me the 150,000 Frs, 59,132 Frs and 162,116 Frs representing the various unpaid royalties (curiously, this last figure represented more than than we'd asked for). In the dommages-intérêts clause we received 80,000 Frs and 10,000 Frs costs. Balland-Copagest immediately appealed against the judgement. All the money that was owed to me (and which I had legally won) went into an escrow account (non-interest-bearing) to which I had no access. The fight had to go on.

We move on to May 1996 (French justice is slow but inexorable). Balland-Copagest's appeal against the 1993 judgement had been thrown out by the 4ème Chambre de la Cour d'Appel de Paris. I received a letter from Anne Veil: 'Cher William, la société Copagest et les Editions André Balland ont fait un pourvoi en cassation [lodged an appeal] contre l'arrêt [ruling] rendu en votre faveur par la Cour d'Appel. J'ai, par conséquent, été contrainte de confier vos intérêts à un avocat à la Cour de Cassation . . . Vous trouverez sous ce pli . . . la facture de ses honoraires.' Ah, another lawyer, another court, another bill. What, in the name of justice, was the 'Cour de Cassation'? It turned out that this court was, in effect, the court of last resort: it is a court designed to test the absolute propriety of a case – where the minutiae of the legal arguments and the precedents (and for all I know the punctuation of the documents) of the warring parties are scrutinized. My journal: 'The Balland case continues, into its 10th year, I would say. Balland-Copagest are challenging the appeal verdict in La Cour de Cassation which, as far as I can understand, is purely to do with legal technicalities, where they will attempt to find a point of law that is wrong and therefore overturn – *casser* – the judgement. Anne Veil said she thought we were *blindés* [armour plated] – *mais on ne sait jamais dans la vie*. There must be a ton of money in the escrow account – maybe one day I'll get my hands on it.' I was now to be represented by Maître Piwnica (whom I never met) and whose fee was £3,000.

In September 1996 the case was pleaded before the Cour de Cassation. Now we had to wait for them to pronounce their judgement. French justice is slow but inexorable.

26 March 1997. My journal: 'Fax from Anne Veil saying that we had won the final appeal against Balland–Copagest. MOMENTOUS DAY! Eleven years of litigation. I reckon I've spent £20,000 on legal fees and as far as I can tell I will receive an immediate payment of £23,000 from the escrow account. I wonder if it's over. But surely they haven't got a leg to stand on after all this?'

Well, they hadn't. And it is a measure of my exhaustion that I had to resort to upper case and an exclamation mark to register my relief that it was all done and dusted. In March 1997 I was on the final stages of my seventh novel, *Armadillo*: when the whole business had begun in 1986 ('Hello, Will? Bad news, I'm afraid . . .') I was halfway through my fourth, *The New Confessions*. Then, I was thirty-four years old; now I was forty-five. Had it all been worth it?

L'Affaire William Boyd v Balland–Copagest hadn't dominated my life over the decade of its comings and goings to the various French courts that dealt with it (Le Tribunal de Grande Instance, La Cour d'Appel de Paris, La Cour de Cassation). It had rumbled away in the background, sometimes naggingly, sometimes quite unobtrusively. Totting up the figures now, I reckon that I was paid some 75 per cent of what I was originally due after the great success of *An Ice-Cream War* – I was £15–16,000 short, in terms of unpaid royalties and I calculate that I had probably spent on the various lawyers – Heald Nickinson, Anne Veil and Maitre Piwnica – some £22,000 plus VAT. Let's say the whole adventure of fighting the case cost me close to £40,000. Editions André Balland paid me approximately £40,000 of the £57,000 they owed me (before they declared themselves in financial difficulties) and eventually, eleven years later, I retrieved £23,000 from the escrow account. So I was more or less £23,000 ahead. If I hadn't sued, if I hadn't gone to law – it's quite clear to me now – I would have received a small fraction of the money I was owed. I have absolutely no regrets about the course of action I took.

I am glad I decided to fight the *Affaire William Boyd v Balland-Copagest* as long as I did, even though my ardour, my zeal for the battle, waxed and waned (particularly when I had to sign cheques). But now that it's over I look back on the decade it lasted with some satisfaction. For me it exemplifies a strange truth about the novelist's life – indeed, a truth about any writer or artist's life: namely, that however much we love what we do, however driven or obsessed we are with our calling, our vocation, we are wise never to forget the fundamental link between art and commerce. I was thrilled to have my first book published, and my second; I was hugely pleased to have it published in French and I was exhilarated when it became a bestseller. But novels are also commodities that are designed to be bought and sold and are not just objects of delight for the author. Dickens and Balzac knew that, Joyce and Chekhov knew that – but I don't need to enlist eminent names to make the point: every author knows that. And every author knows, all too shrewdly, that if their novels sell many copies, then many people will make a great deal of money. Thus, for me, the Balland Affair is fundamentally about that commercial, money-driven, profit-motivated, commodity side of the writing life. In this particular case it went wrong, turned sour and was corrupted. But if I hadn't contested the non-payment of my royalties, if I had, instead, walked away, deciding to cut my losses, I think I would have let myself down – not just as an individual but also as a writer. In the world of commerce we, the artists, must not easily yield our ground and I see my fight (with my stalwart allies) against Editions André Balland and then against Balland-Copagest as a small symbol of that tenacity. We are not just schmucks with Underwoods, as Sam Goldwyn described us. Well, not all the time.

And what of the other participants in the story? Anne Veil still practises law with her devastating, cool expertise. Christiane Besse is still my close friend and my translator. More surprisingly, perhaps, Editions André Balland continues to exist, flourishing in its modest way, publishing fiction and non-fiction from its offices in the rue St André des Arts on the Left Bank in Paris. For my part, all my novels and short story collections are in print in France, and selling well, including the three books I published all those years ago with Balland, all the books with my current and highly estimable publishers Le Seuil. As for André Balland himself, he's abandoned the profession of publisher to become a novelist, and he's found himself – wise man – a good and reliable *maison d'édi-tion* – which happens to be the same as mine, in fact, Le Seuil. One of these days, I'm sure, I'll bump in to him in the lobby of the old house on the rue Jacob where the Le Seuil offices are and we'll shake hands, shrug our shoulders resignedly, exchange pleasantries and go our separate ways. But – I will know that I won.

2001

Anglo/Franco

A Personal A–Z

A. Avant-Propos

A few facts: I am a Scot who was born and raised in West Africa. I went to school and university in Scotland. I first visited France in 1969 when I was seventeen. I studied at the University of Nice for an academic year in 1971. I moved to live in England (in Oxford) in 1975. I moved from there to live in London in 1983. In 1991 my wife and I bought a house in south-west France. We still live in London and we still live in our house in south-west France. Everything that follows about these two alien countries that I have come to know fairly well over the past few decades is irreducibly, unapologetically, subjective and personal. It seems to me that this is the only way to encompass such a monolithic and multifaceted subject as the nature of the relationship between two nations. Generalizations about countries and their peoples are usually specious, tendentious or blandly stereotypical. The only observations of value are those that arise out of personal experience and since everyone's experience is different it strikes me as best to present such observations as randomly as they come, but marshalled under some kind of over-riding modus operandi – such as an alphabet. Out of such apparent haphazardness some sort of understanding, something meaningful – and possibly harmonious with others' experiences – may emerge.

B. Brasseries and Bistros

In a nearby village close to our house in France there used to be a perfect bistro. It was called the 'Café de France' and everything in it – the bar, the seats, the billiard table, the radio, the decor – was from the 1930s. Going in there for a drink or a meal was a form of time-travel. Then two years ago the owners retired, the cafe was sold and the dead hand of modernization took over. And so now we never go there: all the old furniture was thrown out – the old zinc bar too – and the place was smartened up and made more efficient. And in the process something valuable – a little emblem of France and Frenchness – was destroyed. I search constantly for the perfect brasserie and bistrot in France and I have to say they are becoming very hard to find. Paradoxically, such establishments are more common in British cities, where you can find fashionably retro versions of a typical *brasserie du coin*. They are lovingly recreated but they inevitably remain ersatz and inauthentic. But they are intriguing symbols, nonetheless: a British version of *une vie française* that lives on in our dreams.

C. Camus

Is Albert Camus the most famous French writer in the United Kingdom? I think it very likely – though he is run a close second by Gustave Flaubert. The reason is, I think, that almost everyone studies *L'Etranger* at school and the novel continues to haunt its readers long after the need to study it has gone. It remains enduringly modern in spirit. As does its author. Camus seems a prototypical French writer: handsome, *engagé*, moody, intellectual, sexy. And he liked football. Of course, like all those who die young his image is fixed in time, unchangingly. A friend of mine used to see him at parties at Gallimard in the 1950s – 'always surrounded by pretty girls'.

D. Dordogne

When people ask me where I live in France I always hesitate to say 'the Dordogne' because I realize it is so associated with the British. In fact I know hardly any British people in the area – almost all our friends and neighbours are French. But at the same time I am very conscious that this part of France has a powerful and curious draw for my fellow countrymen and women. I love it as much as they do, I suspect, but why do I not want to be too closely associated with these new colonialists?

E. Eurostar

There are, reputedly, some 200,000 French people living in and around London and the Eurostar link brings tens of thousands more each weekend. Sometimes when I walk up the King's Road in Chelsea, where I live, I hear nothing but French voices. My impression is that the French love London and indeed that 'London' represents 'Britain' for most of them: they do not voyage further afield. This is not true the other way round. The British range throughout France, many of them choosing to avoid Paris.

F. France

There is an idea of France that exists in the minds of the British that is a fantasy. It is impossible for any country to live up to an ideal that is so persistent and so prevalent. No doubt there is an equivalent French fantasy about the British. *Le style anglais*, for example, is a very French concept. Or let's say a very French evaluation of a form of unreflective Englishness. I have a French friend who dresses in a way he imagines is appropriate for an English gentleman – tweed jacket, striped tie, brogues, a certain type of haircut. In fact he looks very elegant and completely French – not remotely like an English gentleman.

But the British dream of France is more complex and I think more profound. It's not just a question of attitudes, values and fashion styles. It is this dream of France that sends the British there year after year, decade after decade. At its essence, I feel sure, is the conviction that, of all the countries on earth, the French have solved the problem of the quality of life, of how to live well.

G. Good Manners

I have to say that after some eleven years of living in France the welcome we have received from our neighbours, the tradesmen and the people we deal with on a day to day basis has been both warm and unaffected. I often wonder if, say, I was a Frenchman living in the English or Scottish countryside would the welcome I'd receive there measure up in the cordiality stakes. I have a strong feeling we would suffer in comparison. You see something of the difference in the small formalities of everyday behaviour that are commonplace in France but are still somewhat baffling to the English. The handshake, the kissing, the salutations on parting – 'Bonne continuation', 'Bon fin de l'après midi'

– the *Messieurs-Dames* acknowledgement as one enters a crowded shop. This quotidian politesse is very marked – but we British notice it because it is lacking in our own daily lives.

H. Hunting

Many of our French friends and neighbours in France are avid hunters. The most ardent kill migrating doves in October, luring them to feed on acorns and then shooting them from *palombières*, extravagant firing-platforms cum tree-houses in the oak woods that surround our house. Our local *palombière* is a deluxe version fitted out with a kitchen and a dining room some twenty metres above the forest floor. Hunting in France is classless, it seems to me – insofar that it's for everyone: rich and poor. Hunting in Britain is steeped in class: it's designed to be socially exclusive. Perhaps no one concept better illustrates the divide between the two countries. A book could be written on it.

I. Immensity

My English life is lived in the south-east of England, the most densely populated place in Europe. By contrast in France, even in the height of summer, I often feel isolated, a solitary presence. You forget how big France is compared to Britain – how easy it is to find yourself in an unpeopled landscape. One August, driving back from the Côte d'Azur we were caught up in a massive traffic jam on the autoroute. We decided to take the backroads home – the C and D roads – and drove across the Hérault and the Aveyron in the general direction of Cahors and then on westwards to the Dordogne. I had an impression of great tracts of empti-ness, with a few signs of cultivation and the odd ancient village. It took a full day to make our journey home but when I looked at a map of France to see the way we had come it didn't seem that great a distance – just the crossing a corner of the hexagon. You can, of course, find a similar sense of remoteness in Britain but you have to go looking for it. In our case we just turned off the motorway from the broiling hell of the Mediterranean holiday traffic and there it was – and we followed the minor, single-track roads through a virtually untouched wilderness.

J. July

23 July 1993 to be precise: this is the moment when I date the beginning of my French life. This was the first night that we spent in the old farmhouse we had bought and renovated on the Monbazillac plateau, south of Bergerac. We had bought the house two years previously, spontaneously, not really able to afford it but captivated by its perfect location. It's a solid, thick-walled farmhouse with a large stone barn, surrounded by woods, set on a hill overlooking a quiet valley, with a winding drive one kilometre long. It answered all our wishful dreams about the kind of house we imagined living in.

Having bought it and having planned to do it up piecemeal – room by room, as we could afford it – we were then visited by one of those strokes of luck that everyone needs from time to time. In 1994, the following year, a film was made based on my novel, *A Good Man in Africa*, and suddenly our cash-flow problems were eased and we were able to instruct the builders to go full steam ahead. I looked on this as a good omen, not just because it linked my old African life with my new one in France but because Sean Connery had agreed to play the role of the Scottish doctor, 'Doctor Murray', one of the two 'Good Men' in Africa that the title alludes to. 'Doctor Murray', moreover, is a portrait of my father – who died in 1978. I took all these auspicious biographical congruencies to be a form of blessing on this new French life we were embarking on – a choice that has never prompted a moment's regret ever since.

K. King's Road

Our life in France is largely rural; our nearest town of any size is Bergerac. Occasionally we will visit Périgueux. Such a tranquil life has mixed blessings for a writer: there is plenty of uninterrupted time for the imagination to work but there is an absence, nonetheless, as the weeks roll by, of the stimulation of the passing parade. You cannot be a novelist without being a compulsive observer of your fellow human beings and I find myself, for example, as the summer wears on and July gives way to August, hankering for London, for Chelsea, for the King's Road. The King's Road is not as bohemian as it used to be but I spend a good portion of each day, when I am in London, wandering up and down it. It never fails to deliver something surprising, strange, beguiling, intriguing. If I want to witness the full gamut of human types the world has to offer the King's Road has them in abundance.

L. Lunch

When we were having our house renovated in France the builders would work from eight to twelve, then they would stop for lunch. There would be an aperitif (Pernod, usually) then a full three-course lunch with a hot main course (provided by the wife of the head builder) served with wine and as much bread as you could eat. Work would start again at two and go on until six.

When our house was being renovated in London the builders would go out at odd times of the day to buy fizzy drinks, sandwiches, hamburgers and chocolate bars. They ate them fast, often not bothering to sit down.

M. Manifestations

The French are much better at political protest than the British. I was once in Marmande where a mountain of fresh tomatoes had been dumped in front of the Marie. I was denied access to Bergerac because local ambulance drivers were protesting about an insignificant pay rise. I've missed planes because lorry-drivers have blocked motorways. There is an easy formulation that claims some countries make bad citizens and good soldiers and others where the inverse applies. It seems to me that being a good citizen – caring about your rights, protesting about your rights, trying to safeguard your rights against an overpowerful govern-ment – is more valid in this day and age.

N. Nice

I first went to France when I was seventeen. I stayed in Paris for a week before hitch-hiking to the Mediterranean. I spent my last few days in a cheap hotel in Nice and came to like the town enormously. This drew me back two years later when I had the chance to study at a French university after I left school. I chose Nice unhesitatingly (I could have chosen Aix, Montpellier, Tours, Grenoble). When I lived in Nice as a student in 1971 there was a protracted postal strike in Britain which lasted many weeks, meaning that no money (my allowance) could be sent out to me. I have never been so poor and so alone. I could afford to eat one frugal meal a day at the restaurant of the *Fac de Lettres*. I lived in a small room above a cafe. The cafe owner took pity on me and every evening allowed me to eat what remained of his croissants, chocolatines and pizza – free of charge. So I survived pretty well until the strike ended. I was away from my family, friends, language, country and culture. In many ways I think Nice was the making of me.

O. Oaks

Symbol of England. But in France I live surrounded by dense oak woods, with tall ancient trees. We have a large oak wood on our property called 'Le bois de Vinaigre'. This year I am planting fifty oak saplings. And the next year. And the next.

P. Paris

I love living in London. Perhaps the only other city I could move to would be Paris. Yet Paris, beside London, seems so small. In an hour or less you can walk from Montparnasse to Montmartre, but an hour's walk in London hardly gets you anywhere.

I spent a week in Paris in 1969 when I was seventeen, sleeping on the floor of a house on the Ile St Louis, planning the great adventure of the hitch-hike to the Mediterranean coast. Even then my callow eyes were struck by the city's classy beauty. Now I go to Paris several times a year and, banal observation though it is, its claim to be the most beautiful great city of the world is effortlessly re-established.

Q. Quiet

Nowhere is as quiet as our house in France. In bed at night with the shutters closed the loudest sound you hear is the blood rushing in your ears. In the total darkness of the bedroom it is almost as if you are taking part in a sensory-deprivation experiment. The consequence of this silence in the night is that you become abnormally sensitive to noise in the day. The sound of birds – the cuckoo's call echoing through the woods – the angry sound of distant chainsaws, the creak of old beams, the battering of a stink-bug against a light shade, rain spitting on window panes, the hum of bees in the lavender, the wind in the big oaks. These are the sounds of *la France profonde*.

R. Republicanism

A few days ago, I flew from Edinburgh to London on the same plane as Prince William, the future king of Great Britain. The plane was absolutely full but this twenty-two-year-old young man sat beside his detective and around them was a protective ring of nine empty seats. Who paid for all these empty seats, I wondered? The British tax-payer? Why did he have to have *nine* seats, three full rows, empty? Why were we being kept at such a distance? I suspect the official answer would have been security but I bet the real reason is privacy. They just don't want anybody getting too close to a royal. In that case I would reply: then don't travel on commercial airlines, don't pretend you're a 'normal' passenger catching a normal plane like anyone else – why not fly in one of your royal aeroplanes, the ones that we pay for anyway.

It was not Prince William's fault – he's a nice enough lad, by all accounts – but the symbol of this young university student with his expensive and needless *cordon sanitaire* made me think. It reminded me of the undying hierarchical structure of British life: it was a sour indication of our unhealthy obsession with royalty and aristocracy and titles of all kinds.

I know that the fact I've been living on and off in France for the past ten years has made this tendency in me – this anti-royal, anti-aristo, anti-class feeling – more pronounced. It's not because France has no class-system – every society has a class-system of some kind, every society contains snobbery – but the saving grace is that because France is a republic the notion that every citizen is as good as the next seems hard-wired into the social life you lead. I feel that in my dealings with the French men and women that I meet – whether a captain of industry or a plumber, a *femme de ménage* or a novelist, a mayor or a schoolteacher, a vigneron or a *député* – there is an implicit and strong egalitarianism that functions in that encounter. We are all 'monsieur' or 'madame'; no one need defer or kow-tow; no one need assume superiority or inferiority. I find it enormously refreshing to relate and communicate with other people in France because I know that when I cross the Channel back to England I go back to the Land of Rank and Artificial Status. And, moreover, I go back to a country where so many judgements and aspirations, so many ideas of success and failure are determined by your perceived social classification. Furthermore, and even worse, this social ranking has nothing to do with ability or talent or achievement. It's all a result of an accident of birth or an expression of patronage.

I think that this is an iniquitous and degenerate situation and it breeds other noxious side effects: snobbery, pretentiousness, hypocrisy, class-hatred, social shame and so on. Almost everything I dislike about British society can be traced back to this type of aristocratic ranking and its outmoded values.

S. South

Where I live in France is, I feel, where northern Europe ends and the south – the 'South' – begins. Some people place that demarcating line further north at the Loire valley, but for me it is signified by the Dordogne river. The transition is marked: five miles north of the Dordogne feels and looks completely different from five miles south. Périgueux, the capital of the Périgord, possesses a quite different ambience from its regional rival, Bergerac, forty kilometres south, and straddling the river. A friend of mine, a Bergeracois who lives in Périgueux and works in Bergerac, tells me that the weather is different too and that those forty kilometres mean that Bergerac is usually a noticeable few degrees warmer. It's hard to determine what's different about north of the Dordogne – maybe it is something fundamentally atmospheric, a less luminous quality of the light, a preponderance of dark pine woods – but once you cross the river you notice some distinct change has taken place – the landscape is gentler, the skies seem higher, the air is sweeter. There are other more easily verifiable, more obvious signs of the south too: not just the clustered vineyards but also, in summer, the fields of sunflowers and maize and the pale mottled salmon-pink tiles on the low farm buildings and the great pitched roofs of their barns. And yet here we are not in the citrus belt, no oranges or lemons will survive the winter frosts and neither will you see any olive groves; but as you venture south to the Lot valley, down past Agen towards Toulouse, the landscape is imbued with a hint of the approaching Mediterranean, another few hundred kilometres away, but present somehow in the mineral, pure quality of the sunlight, in the flaking *crépis* of the rural churches, the shuttered fastness of the villages at noon.

T. *Tomatoes*

In our vegetable garden in France we grow, routinely, between fifteen and twenty varieties of tomatoes. In July and August I eat a flavour-rich tomato salad at least once a day – salads composed of tomatoes coloured black, purple, yellow, green and orange as well as the more normal red. I find it almost impossible to eat a tomato in England as a consequence. So if there is one fruit I particularly associate with my life in France it is the tomato.

U. *Underground*

I travel on the London Underground and (less frequently) on the Paris Métro: both are subterranean modes of transport but there all comparisons effectively end. Amongst the many things the British really, truly envy France are – in pride of place – the Lycée system and the Métro, and the TGVs.

V. *Vin*

When I occasionally begin to worry about how much wine I drink each day I console myself – or excuse myself – with the thought that I drink wine like a French person. It seems to me almost sinful to sit down to eat food without a glass of wine. And how does one signal the end of the working day without opening a bottle?

When we bought our house in France there was an old vineyard attached. Our farmer – who is also a major vigneron in his own right – suggested we tear out the old vines and replant them. Now we have our own small vineyard that produces 7,000 bottles a year: a fruity, tannic Cabernet Sauvignon, *appellation Côtes de Bergerac contrôlée*. Our first vintage was 1996; 2003 sits in its vats awaiting transfer to its oak barrels. I don't claim to be any kind of a wine expert but living beside a vineyard has given me a new understanding of this amazing drink, of how the place, the weather and the cultivation – and the luck – shape the end product. Completely impossible, now, to live without it.

W. War

The visible memory of war lives on in France more than it does in Britain. I'm talking about the First World War. You see the memorials – the rifle-toting *poilu*, the angel, the marble obelisk – in every tiny village. The few dozen names inscribed there testify to the human price France paid in the First World War. Our local village still has a population of little more than a hundred yet its small memorial records over twenty names of young men who died in 1914–18. It's impossible to imagine, as you look round at the chateau, the church, the few clustered houses, what such a death toll must have done to the community.

Memorials of the Second World War also linger more prevalently than across the Channel. On the Atlantic beaches the winter storms slowly slide Hitler's vast blockhouses out to sea. Each year these monstrous concrete gun emplacements creep further down the dunes as the coast erodes. And here and there on remote country lanes you will come across a plaque or a headstone marking some frantic ambush of the Resistance movement, a list of the names *fusillés par les Allemands* and the date of the fatal encounter.

X. Xavier Rolland

Is the name of a young farmer who lives near our house. He works his farm alone, milking his 150 goats, ploughing and harvesting his few hectares of fields with corn, sunflowers and maize. He is possibly the hardest working person I have ever encountered. The demands of the unending routine of his daily round – despite the advantages of machinery – make the quality of his life closer to a nineteenth-century counterpart than a modern farmer. The precariousness of his existence is shaped and controlled by the exigencies of the Common Agricultural Policy of the EEC. He ploughs his fields to the very edge of the roads. He obliterates hedgerows and ancient ditches and cuts down trees and woods to gain a few extra square metres to increase his subsidy. He takes two days off a year to visit the agricultural fair in Paris. He is 'close to the land' but his relationship with nature seems more like that of a tenant with a rapacious and demanding landlord. There seems no love of the countryside: the size of the field, its harvest and the compensation he receives from Brussels seem to blind him to the beauty of the place he lives and works. He's a young man – the decades stretch ahead. I wonder what will become of him.

Y. Youth

Last year I went back to Nice and revisited the places I used to frequent as a nineteen-year-old. In 1971 I rented a room in an old lady's flat in the rue Dante. In 2003 I stood at the door to the stairway and told myself that, thirty-two years ago, I had stood on this exact spot, this very spot. I had a beer in the cafe I used to visit every night. The decor was the same but the kindly *patron* had long since retired. I took a photograph of the small hotel I had stayed in on my first night. I walked around the *quartier* that I had known so well but could summon up no ghostly version of my younger self – I experienced no Proustian shiver. Yet my few months in Nice in 1971 were wholly formative for me. It was in Nice that I learned to speak French and where, for the first time, I lived alone and found myself. It comes as no surprise to me that France called me back.

Z. Zone

'Le Zone', to give it its full name, is the name of a small beach bar on the Atlantic coast near Arcachon that I frequent from time to time. I love the ocean and the beach but I don't like being in the sun: 'Le Zone' provides the perfect solution. I sit in the shade of a wide umbrella with a cold beer and a book and watch the comings and goings of the beach, the breakers creaming in, the sound of surf in my ears.

In a dark and rainy London in the middle of the Second World War, the writer and critic Cyril Connolly drew a circle on a map of south-west France and indulged in a little wishful thinking, dreaming of peace. Wish number one: a yellow manor farm inside this magic circle . . . 'A golden classical house, three storeys high with *oeil de boeuf* attic windows looking out over water . . . a terrace for winter, a great tree for summer and a lawn for games, a wooded hill behind and a river below . . .' and so on. Connolly was articulating a dream of pleasure and escape that we all indulge in from time to time. I understand its power and I have responded to its siren call. I realize how lucky I am to have this double life, this Anglo/Franco existence. And, though we live in a house with some of the components Connolly requires, I find that it's on this Atlantic beach that I feel most at one with my adopted country.

I think this has something to do with the inherent democracy of a beach in summer. Beach clothing, the essential idleness and content-ment of beach life, erase society's divisions and stresses in the same way as a tan homogenizes complexions. In this beach bar we are all anony-mous. Most of the time as I sit here and read my book (and make notes) the people around me are French adolescents. I might as well be invisible. I sit and listen to their conversations, I watch their manoeu-vrings, their games and ploys. These urgent, bright, lithe girls and boys pay no attention to me, a middle-aged man with a beer, a book and a pen in hand. In this beach bar on the edge of the Atlantic on the west coast of France I feel I have been accepted. I am in my magic circle. My magic French circle. Anglo/Franco coalesce and commingle, become one.

I have found my zone.

2004

LITERATURE

While I was at university (1971–5), studying English Literature, my taste was shaped not so much by the syllabus of the courses I was following or the academic criticism I read for my essays but by the books pages of the Sunday Times and the New Statesman. In the Sunday Times I went – unfailingly, immediately – to Cyril Connolly's weekly review, and in the back half of the New Statesman I read everything that was on offer.

The seduction of Connolly's hedonistic, unscholarly, romantic enthusiasms is easily explained. I have read, over the years, almost every word he has written and he figures frequently in these pages. The New Statesman had an altogether more acerbic, influential effect. In the early 1970s I waited each week for its arrival with a hungry expectation that has never been repeated with any other publication. The literary editors in those years were Claire Tomalin and Martin Amis and when you draw up a roster of its contributors at that time some of its allure can be explained: Julian Barnes, Craig Raine, Blake Morrison, James Fenton, Christopher Hitchens, Peter Conrad, Jeremy Treglown to name a few. The house style was mordant, knowing, witty and took no prisoners. It shaped my own reviewing practice and my early reviews, including one for the Statesman itself that I present here for sentiment's sake, were an effort to achieve a similar cool, intellectual stringency. As a result I have to admit that, while I hope I was never ruthlessly or maliciously savage, I was often very harsh as a reviewer in my early days – something I take care to recall when I receive the odd critical spanking myself.

Later, in the early 1980s I became a regular reviewer of novels in the Sunday Times. This is perhaps the most thankless form of reviewing available, but a good apprenticeship for the tyro critic. To be given four novels and, say, 800 words in which to summarize and review them – amusingly, cleverly, accurately – is a taxing and demanding subclass of critical writing whose particular merits are very hard to explain to anyone who hasn't attempted it. However, as you are at the bottom of the contributors' food chain, your copy is also the first to be cut if space is required. This happened regularly and the corresponding terseness has not made the reviews wear all that well. Consequently, only a few of my Sunday Times reviews make it into this volume.

My first novel, A Good Man in Africa, was published in 1981 and as I

*published more books myself and gave up my teaching at Oxford (I was a college
lecturer there, at St Hilda's College, from 1980–83) to move to London and
write full-time I was happy to give up the three-weekly review. It's hard work;
you burn out. I carried on reviewing but I felt I'd paid my dues in the salt-
mines of critical writing.*

*The organizing principle in this section has been to present the reviews as I
wrote them, starting in 1978 and moving on, rather than arrange them under
any thematic or geographical scheme. This is what came across my desk as the
years went by. As time has progressed the space provided in which to write has
steadily grown. It is a welcome corollary: the luxury of having a few more pages
in which to expound your opinions is all the sweeter because of that earlier discipline.*

Patrick Kavanagh

(Review of *By Night Unstarred*)

Patrick Kavanagh repudiated his early and best-known book *The Green Fool* as 'Stage-Irish autobiography', and in one sense his so-called 'auto-biographical novel' *By Night Unstarred* looks like an attempt to reclaim Irish rural life from the lush romanticism and sometimes strained folksiness that marred the earlier venture. *Tarry Flynn*, Kavanagh's only other major fictional work, also has its roots in his formative years and like *The Green Fool* concerns itself with the growth of the poet against the background of the Irish countryside. Although Kavanagh was much more pleased with *Tarry Flynn* – modestly finding it 'uproariously funny' – both it and *The Green Fool* are damaged by Kavanagh's semi-mystical love of nature and a certain platitudinous idealism that occurs whenever the subject of the poet's privileged insight and depth of feeling is raised.

By Night Unstarred on the whole avoids these pitfalls; largely, I suspect, because the main portion of it has nothing to do with poets or poetry. Although claiming to be a 'novel', the book really consists of an unfinished short novel and a short story that would have been far better left unjoined. Peter Kavanagh, the author's brother and the editor, has sought to produce a unified work of fiction by labelling the two disparate stories parts 1 and 2, and by supplying an apologetic explanatory interjection that in the end only exposes the artifice of the link.

Part 1 is far and away the most successful of the two, and, not surprisingly, the least autobiographical. Set in the parish of Ballyrush near Dundalk at the beginning of the century it charts the remorseless rise to prosperity of a weaselly Irish peasant called Peter Devine. Initially an impoverished farm labourer, he impregnates the local half-wit Rosie and has to flee the wrath of her family and the censure of the parish. He returns seven years later an obsessed and oddly motivated man. Maniacally set on becoming the richest man in the county, he courts the bulky daughter of the wealthiest farm-owner in the district and enlists the help of various colourful local characters to this end. By sly manipulation and unscrupulous use of the village gossips a myth grows up about his eligibility and fairly soon he is accepted as a suitor. Devine's sole interest is in wealth and his romantic yearnings are wholly subservient to this drive ('When he noticed her wobbling breasts beneath the loose blouse he dreamt of the field before the door with the deep hollow in the middle'). Ultimately his dedication proves highly successful, and in material terms Peter Devine triumphs in everything he does from siring children to planting potatoes. The end of part 1 sees him poised on the edge of bourgeois prosperity – a rich mill owner and county councillor – with his financial horizons beginning to broaden: 'The priest had smoked three cigarettes since coming into the room: a bit of money in a cigarette factory would be no dead loss, he thought.'

The strength and vigour of Kavanagh's portrayal of the villagers of Ballyrush are due to the constancy of his ironic gaze; a steadfastness of viewpoint that *The Green Fool* and *Tarry Flynn* sadly lacked. Kavanagh sees all too clearly that country people are as pusillanimous, bitchy and determinedly mercenary as the rest of us, if not more so: 'The misfortune of a neighbour provided nearly all the best delights of that part of the country.' And Peter Devine, who dominates part 1, is explicitly alluded to as a personification of 'the slime-stuck peasant unconscious of cities, of cultures, of everything but the power of money'. There is a sharp Flaubertian cynicism in evidence, free from any romanticism or fond simplicity, which makes Ballyrush as mordant a picture of a rural community as Yonville in *Madame Bovary*.

Part 2 jolts uneasily some decades ahead and the central figure now becomes 'Patrick Kavanagh' (in an Isherwoodian third-person return to his younger self) fruitlessly searching for a job in Dublin. The Devines have resurfaced as the De Vines, now, thanks to Peter's acumen, a large, vastly wealthy and powerful Dublin family with an interest in the arts. Patrick's attempts to advance himself – and thereby to marry the girl he loves – are continually thwarted by his refusal, or inability, to ingratiate himself with the monolithic De Vine family. The cynicism of part 2 is of a more embittered and personal sort. Kavanagh's skilful, distanced irony turns to shrill vituperation and the personal venom is all too apparent in the vignettes of literary and middle-class poseurs.

This is where the autobiography obtrudes and once again Kavanagh returns to the question of the poet's role and function in society which, with the weight of personal invective behind it, inevitably damages the fiction. By all accounts the first fifty years of Kavanagh's life were remarkably unpleasant and frustrating, and it seems he had every justification for bitterness and self-pity. And it's the self-pity in the end that emerges and weakens this section of the novel and which makes 'Patrick Kavanagh' such a hard character to sympathize with.

1978

Scottish Fiction

(Review of *The Cone-Gatherers* by Robin Jenkins
and *Beattock for Moffat* by R. B. Cunninghame-Graham)

The Cone-Gatherers starts badly. Two idealized, noble Scottish peasants
are collecting pine cones in a Scottish forest, Nature tingling vibrantly
all around:

The time came when, thrilling as a pipe lament across the water, daylight
announced it must go: there was a last blaze of light, an uncanny clarity, a
splendour and puissance: and then the abdication began.

Ah, that skirl on the pipes . . . One has an image of the author halfway
through his third Glenfiddich, Kenneth McKellar booming from the hi-
fi, biro bulging with patriotic affection. All this is rather unfair to Robin
Jenkins, who is in fact a prolific and serious novelist who's been writing
steadily for the last thirty years. But he has spent much of this time
abroad and various passages further on in *The Cone-Gatherers* do tend
to lapse into the exile's ghastly shortbread-box impression of Scotland
that gives Scottish literature – Scottish anything, come to that – a bad
name.

The Cone-Gatherers (first published in 1955) is a moody, heavy-
hearted story of two brothers, one tall and sullen, the other hunch-
backed and angelic, whose job it is to harvest pine cones – for eventual
reforestation – during the Second World War. This they do on the
massive estate of one Lady Runcie-Campbell somewhere on the west
coast of Scotland. The hunchback, Calum, a timorous, nature-loving
simpleton with, yes, a face like a Donatello cupid, pale and ringed
with soft curls, attracts the venom of the Lady Squire and of her baleful
gamekeeper Duror. Lady Runcie-Campbell's distaste is based on solid
bourgeois *snobisme*. Her frail son Roderick is fascinated by the cone-
gatherers' arboreal expertise and it just isn't right that the little chap
should be intrigued by the lower orders (Jenkins indulges in some
ponderous satire on this point). Accordingly Lady Runcie-Campbell
colludes with the grimmer motives of Duror, whose splenetic loathing
of Calum is less easy to understand, even though the hapless cripple

has made the mistake of freeing half-throttled rabbits from the game-keeper's snares.

Duror's poisonous hatred, however, provides much of the narrative impulse of the book, insofar as it compels him, again and again, to attempt to rid the estate of the cone-gatherers' presence. To this end he contrives to tip the animal-doting Calum over the edge of sanity by brutally slitting the throat of a deer before his eyes, casting slanderous aspersions about his alleged depravity to the rest of the estate staff until finally — at wits' end himself — he resorts to telling anyone who will listen (the village doctor and a shocked Lady Runcie-Campbell included) that he has witnessed Calum masturbating in the woods.

Clearly the picture of Scottish rural life is so unlikely and removed from its model that Jenkins has other interests in mind than those of documentary realism. Drawing on Scottish ballads and minstrel songs, *The Cone-Gatherers* is evidently meant to function as a fable: a moral tale of evil confronting innocence. However it largely fails in this respect because its mood and atmosphere are so tried and tested, so much a feature of hack Scots mythology.

Indeed the only character who truly comes alive is Duror, the game-keeper. Duror's wife is an obese wreck, a quivering bedridden tub of lard whispering endearments every time he returns home. Calum is the handy objective correlative upon which Duror can vent his frustration and poignant misery. The hunchback's exultation in the simple natural pleasures of life stands as an intolerable rebuke, a permanent reminder of an attitude to life that he, Duror, can never hope to attain. Eventually — inevitably — Duror has his way and Calum becomes the victim of the gamekeeper's violent expiation. The ending — blood and sap dripping from the cones — comes as no surprise.

It's a pity really, because in the figure of Duror, with his grotesque wife and his perfervid misanthropy, one senses an altogether different history striving to take shape: an altogether more unpleasant, malevo-lent, and — dare one say it? — more Scottish novel.

The Cone-Gatherers is one of a new series called 'The Scottish Fiction Reprint Library'. One book this series could happily have omitted is *Beattock for Moffat*. R. B. Cunninghame-Graham's fame as a champion of human rights, intrepid explorer and, more dubiously, founder of the Scottish National Party is reasonably secure. His advancement here as an exemplar of the 'best of nineteenth- and twentieth-century Scottish fiction' is misguided if not downright absurd. In fact only the title story

of this collection – a wry account of a chronic consumptive striving to
get to Scotland before he dies – has anything to do with the country.
The rest range between South America, Spain, Morocco and Paris, and
contain nothing that would make them stand out from the mass of
Edwardian *belles-lettres* (Cunninghame-Graham was a friend of Conrad,
Wells and other luminaries of the London literary scene).

The journey theme of 'Beattock for Moffat' is repeated in many of
the other stories here as it affords Cunninghame-Graham an opportunity to display his familiarity with foreign climes. The stories, however,
are either thinly disguised travelogues – crude narratives related round
a bubbling hookah in some souk or by a lonely campfire on the Pampas
– or else (in three stories about the Parisian demi-monde) rebarbative
examples of clubmen's innuendo:

Lesbos had sent its legions, and the women looked at one another apprecia-
tively . . . with their colour heightening when by chance their eyes met those
of another priestess of their sect.

Scottish fiction, if there is such a genre, can surely do better than this.

1978

Frank Tuohy

(Review of *Live Bait* by Frank Tuohy,
The Good Husband by Pamela Hansford Johnson
and *The Cutting Edge* by Penelope Gilliatt)

Many of the stories in Frank Tuohy's latest collection have a foreign context – and are all the better for it. This represents a partial return to the worlds of his first exceptional volume *The Admiral and the Nuns* (1962) and, I'd like to think, a move away from the less remarkable *Fingers in the Door* (1970), which dwelled a little too lengthily on the foibles of the gin-and-tonic belt. Not that Tuohy's observations aren't generally valuable; but when the scene shifts abroad the grim predictability that dulls most English short stories recedes and his own subtle talent emerges.

In fact there seems to be some ever-looming Platonic archetype of the 'well-made' short story which cramps most of our practitioners of the genre, producing endless refined and scrupulous chartings of emotional crises among distressed gentlewomen or the timorous progress of middle-class love affairs. By contrast, there is an almost palpable widening of horizons and effect in Tuohy's foreign stories. For example, the callous randiness of a retired professor groping a former student in 'A Summer Pilgrim'; or the candid lust of a rebarbative businessman searching downtown Tokyo for his Japanese mistress in 'Nocturne with Neon Lights'.

In comparison, the local offerings – 'The White Stick', 'Love to Patsy' and 'A Ghost Garden' – with their familiar middle-class intellectual background, appear whimsical and affected. It is essentially the feeling of over-worked parochialism that is responsible for the ordinariness of the long title story, a rather ponderously symbolic tale of a lonely and unpopular boy and his attempts during a summer holiday to catch a huge pike in the lake of a nearby manor house. It is not merely a question of more exotic scenery adding extra spice; Tuohy's strength lies in the way he captures the unusual mood and viewpoint of the expatriate, the exile and the temporary alien. The barriers of language and culture give rise to a slightly baffled and tentative querying of reality; perspectives shift and blur, appearances bemuse and all our certainties suddenly lack foundation.

In *Important to Me*, subtitled 'Personalia', Pamela Hansford Johnson stirringly declares that 'if you are saying something really complex you should do your best to spell it out to the reader in so far as it is possible'. On her own terms, then, it can only be concluded that complexities have no part to play in *The Good Husband*: it is a story of true slightness, an album of inconsequentiality. Miss Johnson has only her past record to blame for the disappointment: the continuing saga of merchant banker Toby Roberts quashes most expectations that *The Good Listener* (1975) might have built up. As the title suggests, *The Good Husband* is an account of Toby's marriage at the age of thirty to a woman ten years his senior and the steady but mild erosion of his at first passionate love. The decline comes about purely as a result of what we now recognize as his basic flaw – if not his sole character trait – namely his lack of commitment, his complacency. This is rather crudely spelled out in a dream, where a portrait of Toby is unveiled to reveal a blank canvas. For all the lucid prose and evident craftsmanship, it's hard to imagine such a redoubtably bland character as Toby providing material for one novel, let alone two, in spite of Miss Johnson's pointed allusion to Rastignac in both books. I'm afraid there's no chance that 'Le démon du luxe le mordit au coeur'; and the world Toby inhabits bears as much resemblance to Balzac's Paris as a wet Sunday in Arbroath.

There's a similar looseness, an almost decadent lack of direction, in Penelope Gilliatt's *The Cutting Edge*. The narrative hovers around the affection between two often-separated brothers – Benedick and Peregrine, a musician and a writer, respectively down and out in Istanbul and Positano – who are eventually reunited in the compliant arms of Benedick's ex-wife. There's an air of plundered notebooks about the desperately sparkling conversation and the redundant cast of eccentric minor characters, who look suspiciously like rejects from Miss Gilliatt's latest collection of short stories, *Splendid Lives*. At one point she says conversation is like 'the sound of souls buzzing in a glass prison of a world which they cannot escape but still try to understand'. This is all very well, but the chat has to be fairly remarkable if it's to continue to sustain our interest: 'We are the trustees of no culture but our own,' and so on. It's a shame, because Miss Gilliatt's laconic style occasionally creates moments of accurate poignancy which are worth pages of brittle dialogue and recycled *aperçus*.

1978

Edward Thomas

(Review of *The Collected Poems of Edward Thomas*)

There is a dogged vein of empiricism running through English poetry of the twentieth century – with its starting point established a hundred years earlier – and which, despite attempts to obscure or ignore it, continually breaks surface. This faith in the fixedness and certainty of the phenomenal world need not – again, despite its detractors' cries of parochialism and cramped horizons – be regarded as a weakness. It does not preclude more ideological or abstract flights and really only stipulates that they should begin from the reality of our spatio-temporal world, in the same way as Shelley's 'Ode to the West Wind' has as its unshakable substructure a precise knowledge of cloud patterns and verifiable meteorological effects.

Thomas patently belongs within this tradition, and indeed consciously allied himself with his Georgian fellow-writers in reaction to Pre-Raphaelite vagueness and pretension, and because of this – like Hardy – his verse has been slow to gain the recognition it deserves. One of the benefits of a collection such as this, with the poems in strict chronological order and the variant readings and rough drafts set out on facing pages, is that the full richness and honest toil of Thomas's development can be all the better appreciated.

Admittedly, some of the emendations seem wholly inconsequential, and the recording of a solitary spelling mistake or cancellation appears a profligate waste of expensive paper in an expensive book. However, on the whole, one would not wish the editorial practice any different, for the easy comparison of alternatives and second thoughts it affords provides fascinating examples of the poet at work and overall should make this a far more rewarding and compelling edition of the collected poems than the others available.

The briefest glance at the variations Thomas considered confirms his easy style as the product of long and artful endeavour. Acutely sensitive to the rhythms of everyday speech, he relied, in his manuscripts, on a private punctuation of different sized gaps between words. And although these have not been reproduced here, we can still witness the constant redaction that produces the distinctive conversational tone with its sophisticated

employment of conversational rhetoric – understatement, allusion and
qualification – to advance the calm argument of the poem.

Two intriguing features emerge strongly from a re-reading of all 141
of Thomas's poems. Like the best poets of the countryside the implicit
shift from the natural to the human situation occurs subtly and without
overt contrivance (famous examples being 'Tall Nettles' and 'Cherry
Trees'). But Thomas's work progressively reveals a growing dissatisfaction with that latter state which expresses itself variously in images of
displacement, brooding dark woods, ending roads and, more damagingly,
occasional death-wishing (see 'Rain', for example). There is some
evidence to suggest that his compulsion to enlist and then to get to the
front was prompted by these more morbid thoughts than the famous
fistful-of-English-earth excuse. 'I have given up groaning,' he wrote,
'since the war began'; and Thomas's war diary (usefully included in an
appendix here) is an almost jaunty document full of sharp-eyed natural
observations and wholly free from angst and despair. Thomas's darker
moods were fuelled by nostalgia and give rise to the second feature of
his verse – what Edna Longley has aptly called 'imaginative archae-
ology'. It can also be seen as a creative exploitation of history and
the past; an exploration of Time's dim perspective which, although the
present inevitably suffers in comparison, serves as a buttress to the infir-
mities of the actual moment. I suspect that this, rather than the evocation of place-names and landscapes, contributes more to that tradition
of 'Englishness' to which Thomas belongs. The past is a more reassuring
dimension – as many contemporary poets have lately discovered – and
its signs lie everywhere around us, observable, concrete and unambiguous:
key terms, these, in the essential pragmatism that so conditioned Thomas's
vision of the world and which he scrupulously related, in his short
poetic life, through his fine and careful 'language not to be betrayed'.

1978

J. G. Ballard and Kurt Vonnegut

(Review of *The Unlimited Dream Company* by
J. G. Ballard and *Jailbird* by Kurt Vonnegut)

There are two easily distinguishable strands in J. G. Ballard's work: on
the one hand his apocalyptic records of natural disasters represented by
his first four novels, and on the other his more memorable delineations
of paranoically obsessed individuals – the line which he has tended to
follow in recent years. The two modes overlap occasionally, as in *High
Rise*, but Ballard is more acclaimed – and rightly so – for his studies of
the neurotic psychopaths that people the pages of *Crash* and the brilliant *The Atrocity Exhibition*. These two are arguably Ballard's best books
to date; the brutal pornography and sustained radical vision of *Crash*,
along with the complex demented fictions of *The Atrocity Exhibition*,
make them two of the most striking and original English novels since
the Second World War.

Ballard's style, too, contributes immeasurably to the bleak tensions of
his novels. It is as distinctive and original, in its own way, as Hemingway's,
and is employed with the same single-minded purpose. Ballard's vocabulary is consciously limited and repetitive; we hear a lot about 'postures'
and 'musculature', 'contours' and 'geometry'. Landscapes are 'mimetized'
or 'modulated'; actions are 'neural', 'crazed' or 'deranged'; the characters
'exhausted' or 'enigmatic'. There is a technical abstraction about Ballard's
highly stylized use of language that owes a lot to the unemotional frank
muscularity of medical text books and the instruction manuals of sophisticated weapons. This both heightens and confines the world of his
novels but also reduces its characters to the anonymous status of case
histories; their personalities are undeveloped, their interest or value
existing only insofar as they represent a trait or abreaction.

The Unlimited Dream Company exhibits all these features but abandons Ballard's firm grip on the seedy realities of contemporary urban
life for some rather laboured mythopoetic effects. More interestingly it
represents a development of ideas formulated in his last remarkable
collection of short stories *Low Flying Aircraft*, particularly in the stories
'The Ultimate City' and 'My Dream of Flying to Wake Island'. Both
concern the general idea of flight as a symbol of escape and freedom

and involve the realization or projection of the possibility of an Utopian enclave. *The Unlimited Dream Company* takes these notions – so evocatively expressed in the stories – and expands them to novel length. Blake, an unhappy misfit with deviant tendencies, steals a light aircraft from Heathrow and crash-lands at Shepperton. His miraculous survival of the crash not only brings about his deification by the town's inhabitants but also unlocks fabulous powers within himself. Blake causes thickets of tropical flora and fauna to sprout and flourish all over Shepperton's streets and public parks and soon the town becomes the familiar Ballardian enclosed world bounded by impenetrable palisades of bamboo. Within this community Blake 'dreams' for the suburbanites. They become birds and fish, they shed their clothes and impediments – work, consumer goods, money, morality – of the twentieth-century world. With the aid of gallons of Blake's liberally ejaculated semen Shepperton returns to a state of guileless prelapsarian innocence, with the inhabitants finally, as a result of Blake's teaching, learning to fly. Flight, that unnatural occupation of an alien dimension, represents for humans a sublime transcendental impulse, and Blake is clearly a perverse Christ figure – the admixture of theology and suburban humdrum owing a lot to Stanley Spencer's Cookham paintings – and his liberation of the populace has an overt Messianic aspect combined with folk myths of regeneration and rebirth. The book ends on a note of gigantic epiphany, the Sheppertonians flying up and away to their new world, Blake left as sole guardian of the town, content in what he has achieved – a kind of One Mind totality, a pantheistic unification of 'animate and inanimate, of the living and the dead'.

The Unlimited Dream Company represents a new direction for Ballard, but one which his various talents in the end don't quite manage to bring off. The fervent lyricism of much of the book is sometimes embarrassingly over-intense, and the symbolic machinery creaks rather in the working out of its mythic programmes and objectives. Ballard's charting of an elemental human aspiration has its moments – usually in the form of powerfully written evocations of Blake's dream-fantasies – but the overall structure seems an amalgam of styles and moods – myth, fable, surrealism, robust Ballardian crudeness – that never really coheres. A similar thematic concern informs 'My Dream of Flying to Wake Island', but the subtle ramifications of the hero's obsessive unearthing of a crashed Second World War bomber in some nameless dunes and his hopeless desire to fly it to an abandoned American airbase in the Pacific achieves everything *Dream Company* sets out to do but with more economic and, ultimately, more potent methods.

Kurt Vonnegut is another writer with a distinctive tone of voice, though as is the case with most conscious stylists Vonnegut wears his as a badge rather than using it as a technical device. Vonnegut's ironic resigned parentheses ('So it goes', 'ho hum') are so well known that it will come as no surprise to aficionados to learn that in this novel he opts for at least three: 'Peace', 'and on and on' and 'Strong Stuff'. *Jailbird* is the story of a put-upon failure, one Walter Starbuck, Nixon's former adviser on youth affairs, arrested and imprisoned for his part in the Watergate fiasco. Starbuck is the classic innocent figure, hapless and helpless, whose very insignificance and impotence lends his observations on contemporary American life the indirect veracity and impact of a Candide. Vonnegut covers here similar ground to Joseph Heller's *Good as Gold* (attacks on Washington wheeling and dealing, McCarthyism, the multinationals) and while one acknowledges the urgent necessities lurking behind the writing of them both are less than successful. Heller's hatred for Kissinger and tiresome reworking of the same three jokes overbalance the genuinely funny moments, while Vonnegut on this occasion falls prey to his usual affliction of winsomeness. Far the most effective section of the book is Vonnegut's prologue, a discursive rambling introduction that has little to do with the subsequent tale but skilfully utilizes all the ploys and devices available to modernist fiction with an assurance and aplomb that makes the *nouveau roman* look like the product of a first year creative writing class.

1980

Katherine Mansfield

(Review of *Katherine Mansfield: A Biography* by Jeffrey Meyers)

Katherine Mansfield died of tuberculosis on 9 January 1922 at Gurdjieff's Institute, the Prieuré, near Fontainebleau. D. H. Lawrence commented that it was 'a rotten, false, self-conscious place of people playing a sickly stunt' and, having earlier accused her of 'stewing' in her illness, he must have seen a singular aptness in her dying there. For in one sense, as this biography makes clear, most of Katherine Mansfield's life had been composed of sickly stunts of one sort or another.

Born into a prosperous New Zealand family in 1888, she spent her childhood and early adolescence hankering for release, already thinking of herself, according to Meyers, as 'an artist who lived in a world of her own'. She felt stifled by the bourgeois philistinism of life in the colonies and left to go to school in London at the age of fourteen. The abandoned country soon became transformed in her imagination – as is common with most exiles – into a land of beauty and innocent childhood pleasure. She returned there briefly in 1907 but from 1908 onward lived in England and Europe. It was a notably unhappy existence too, spent in a succession of drab rented properties and hotels and featuring, among other mishaps, a temporary addiction to Veronal, an abortion, a one-day marriage, lesbian relationships, continual ill-health and, most unfortunately perhaps, marriage to Middleton Murry.

At the centre of any biography of Katherine Mansfield lies her relationship with Middleton Murry, who was at one point, according to the *Dictionary of National Biography*, 'the most hated man of English Letters in the country', and who described himself as 'part snob, part coward, part sentimentalist'. It was a highly unsatisfactory liaison from the start, with Katherine Mansfield having to coax a reluctant Murry into her bed, and its unpropitious beginnings heralded a succession of bitter rows, partings and brief reconciliations. Murry's subsequent idolization of his dead wife has tended to obscure the picture but Meyers's careful delineation of the facts makes the nature of the relationship clear. Where Murry is most condemned is not so much in the see-sawing marital strife but in his lukewarm and even callous response to her progressively worsening illness. He was often absent from her during her long periods of attempted convalescence on the Continent and provided skimpy financial support. However, it has to be said that she was not averse to employing her fragile condition to its full dramatic effect. One visitor to the Murry household had this to say:

Katherine was 'draped' on a couch (it was one of her not-so-good days) . . . People stood around, adoring her, talking quietly to her. I was not prepared for this adoration and the whole picture, to my provincial, down-to-earth view, was utterly artificial, all affectation.

One can imagine that after a while the impact and concern the disease aroused in Murry began inevitably to lessen. A similar suspicion of histrionics and melodrama is also evident in her edgy friendships with Virginia Woolf (who once described her, with characteristic acerbity, as 'a civet cat got up for street-walking') and D. H. Lawrence. There were few interludes of contentment in the Murry/Mansfield relationship, which is scarcely surprising considering it was made up of two people with more than their fair share of intense self-absorption and weakness. Lawrence referred to them in a letter as 'Two mud worms . . . playing into each others long mud bellies.'

Meyers places most of the blame on Murry, and it is true that his appalling behaviour after his wife's death cannot be excused, but they both share an equal guilt for their unhappiness while she was alive. There is an inescapable air of acute self-consciousness about their lives, an artistic pomposity and pretentiousness that allowed Katherine Mansfield quite openly to compare herself with Keats and Chekhov as fellow tuberculosis sufferers, but also, one suspects, thereby elevating herself by association into this select company. This might just be acceptable if the literary output justified it, but the slightness and ephemerality of her talent cannot live up to the role-playing. The narrow restricted worlds of her stories, the absence of plot, the factitious reliance on mood and atmosphere to give brief inconsequential episodes more weight and timelessness, are only partially compensated for by a certain directness of language and sharpness of observation. The mystique surrounding her life and the adulation she has received in countries like France have boosted the reputation of her stories and given them a literary importance far beyond their real merit. The effect has been remarkable. The English short story today still labours under her vapourish influence.

Meyers's biography goes some way to correct this. It is balanced and thorough and, despite his annoying tendency to ascribe rather glib psychological motives, his assessment is on the whole careful and unemotional. One senses little affection but some pity for his subject, which, overall, seems to have been the reaction of most of the people she encountered in her short and frustrated life.

1979

Toni Morrison

(Review of *Song of Solomon*)

Normally the pretensions of an American novel bear a direct proportion to the number of pages printed. The simple formula being: the thicker the volume the more serious the message contained. What is both striking and gratifying about *Song of Solomon* is the absence of transatlantic largesse and hyperbole in a novel that clearly sets out to be significant.

Toni Morrison's well-structured story concerns itself with two generations of a black American family from the 1930s to the 1960s. Macon Dead is a wealthy Chicago landlord eager for bourgeois respectability. But like most façades of middle-class content this one hides the usual catalogue of fear and frustration. Macon's unorthodox sister Pilate and her own Bohemian household of illegitimate daughter and grandchild stand as a permanent rebuke to Macon's ambitions. Macon's son Milkman hovers uncertainly between the two families, attracted by the life in one and the comforts of the other. Milkman's dilemma is essentially that of the modern black American confronted by the brutal historical circumstances of his presence in the USA and at the same time drawn to the powerful consumer allure of contemporary society. As some kind of a way out he decides to attempt to trace his lineage and the search for his roots becomes – as in Alex Hailey's book – a quest for his own identity and self-respect.

In a Southern town called Shalimar he discovers the clues to his ancestry in a song the children sing about his great-grandfather Solomon, a near-mythical figure who is reputed to have flown back to Africa. The fulfilment of his search, the new knowledge of the unity and special nature of his heritage coincides with the development of Milkman's hitherto complacent character and a conformation of values – embodied in his aunt Pilate – he had thought dated and whimsical.

In *Song of Solomon* Toni Morrison consciously invokes a comparison with *The Great Gatsby* when she adapts the famous guest-list episode from Jay Gatsby's party. In the names of the guests Fitzgerald encapsulates an entire society and Toni Morrison uses the device for the same purpose here. At the climax of the novel Milkman sees that the bizarre and colourful names of the black people he knows have real meaning too and bear witness to the past. In fact the lesson of *The Great Gatsby* can be seen everywhere in this novel. There is the same economy, the same discipline and the same potent manipulation of symbol where Solomon's magical flight becomes – like the green light at the end of Daisy's pier – an abiding and passionate metaphor for all kinds of human aspiration.

1979

Penelope Shuttle and Peter Redgrove

(Review of *The Wise Wound*)

On 4 April 1852 Flaubert wrote to his mistress Louise Colet: 'I'm very anxious about your English troops, though I've nothing to reproach myself on that score.' A few months later he complains that:

If I haven't written to you for the last few days, it is because I was expecting every morning a letter from you, informing me of the event, the delay of which was causing me such hideous anxiety. You don't realise in what a state you put me. I can't understand how I can work in the midst of this worry.

Then, a few days after, the relief is enormous: 'At last, God be praised, there is nothing further to fear, and blessed be the redcoats.' It sounds very much as though Flaubert is celebrating the British Army's liberation of some besieged town in which his mistress has been imprisoned, but in fact he is talking about Louise Colet's period, the monthly appearance of which was agonizingly attended upon by the writer. Flaubert was paranoically afraid of becoming a father – hence the stressful concern – but it is his attitude to Louise Colet's menstruation that is particularly interesting, especially after Penelope Shuttle and Peter Redgrove's important book. Flaubert's sulks, petulance and selfish joy usefully illustrate the three major arguments of *The Wise Wound*.

First (and in this case most amusingly), there is the coyness exhibited by the creator of Madame Bovary, champion of free expression and paradigmatic exponent of the *mot juste*, which is typical of the forest of taboos surrounding the subject, the shifty evasiveness associated with any rare discussion of menstruation. 'English troops' and 'redcoats' aren't included in the list of synonyms on page 54 but they vie with the most absurd ('reggie', 'reading a book') in their referential distance from the thing they purport to describe. Secondly there is the animosity directed at Louise Colet herself. She is causing Flaubert 'hideous anxiety' by not menstruating on time; she is putting *him* in a state. This animosity is part of a larger classic male reaction to an exclusively female process: men can't partake and are therefore hostile. Thirdly, there is the wider effect of the female's menstruation on the male – Flaubert manages to work but only just, he's under pressure. If one could track down the passage of *Madame Bovary* Flaubert was writing at the time would it show any imprint of this transmitted menstrual tension? The notion may sound whimsical but it's an idea Shuttle and Redgrove invite us to take very seriously indeed and is one which, for the male reader, is intensely interesting and controversial.

All three arguments are lengthily considered by Shuttle and Redgrove but, although backed up by extensive research, their plausibility diminishes as the exposition proceeds. The opening chapters, by and large, straightforwardly examine the physiological nature and effects of menstruation and strip away centuries of male deceit and hypocritical *pudeur*. This is immensely valuable and done with lucid expertise. So too is the historical, anthropological and psychological discussion of male attitudes.

The period (another metaphor-word, but among the least objectionable) is no longer something to hide, ignore or be ashamed of, but is – contrastingly – a time of fruitful self-awareness, a unique opportunity for self-knowledge, increased creative powers and heightened sexual pleasure. There is some truth here no doubt, and the motives are entirely praiseworthy, but one questions the general applicability of their conclusions. Clearly it's an area of experience denied to the male – though there are benefits accruing to him also – but a little research soon establishes that, despite widespread support for the Shuttle/Redgrove mission, for many people pain stays painful and cramps remorselessly cramp.

The Wise Wound is a valuable and long overdue book but Shuttle and Redgrove's evident heartfelt proselytizing zeal and fervour incline them on occasions to carry their polemic just a little too far. This is especially prevalent when they come to look at the wider socio-cultural effects of menstruation: they advance the proposition that in some way or another almost everything in life is ultimately connected to the monthly evacuation of the womb lining. For example, they say that 'anxiety and aggression are tied cross-culturally to strong menstrual taboos'. This conclusion is derived from experimental work that has been carried out in the past and as such is unexceptionable. But in the next sentence Shuttle and Redgrove go on to assert that 'we cannot forget that our own society practises systematic menstrual ignorance and is one of the most bellicose in human history'. So menstrual ignorance leads to war?

This sort of wild reductionism is understandable but is patently absurd, and it's a shame that they yield to temptation because the Erich von Däniken aspects of the book tend to cloud its essential value and encourage those who have a vested interest in dismissing its worthier conclusions. The problem lies in the book's scope and ambitions. The final chapters, for example, on the menstrual connections with witch-hunts and the horror film genre are interesting but belong to another book altogether and only serve to distract our attention from its main import. Similarly, the embattled, insistent style, with its exclamation marks and stressed passages, has a hint of the soap-box about it: the reader is bludgeoned unnecessarily into accepting the validity of the arguments, whose case doesn't require such shock tactics. The evidence speaks more forcefully when allowed to do so for itself.

The God of Glass is a 'novelization' of Peter Redgrove's award-winning radio play of the same name. It has close links with the concerns of *The Wise Wound*, its theme being, so the author informs us, the 'dire consequences of masculine non-participation in feminine blood-mysteries'. Geoffrey Glass, a black African living in England, employs his shamanistic powers to exorcize the demons from certain possessed young girls in an English village. Glass subsequently becomes the founder of a new religion that 'triggers-off a movement towards self-discovery that permanently alters mankind', allowing men to participate so fully in feminine blood-mysteries that ultimately they can conceive and give birth themselves.

The book is subtitled 'A Morality' and its didactic intentions over-whelm its rather unconvincingly imposed supernatural narrative. As a companion piece to *The Wise Wound* and as a dramatization of some of its themes *The God of Glass* has its interest but as a novel it is unsuc-cessful, largely because its hybrid elements – prose tract, clumsy polemic and radio drama – coexist uneasily, though there are two passages of remarkable intensity (an attempted exorcism and the flaying of a body) that testify to Redgrove's descriptive powers.

His latest novel, *The Sleep of the Great Hypnotist*, has its origins in a poem of the same name in *From Every Chink of the Ark*, and which, like *The God of Glass*, translates unhappily into prose fiction. In this case Redgrove's purpose is to stimulate a revival of interest in the therapeutic possibilities of hypnotism. He appears to have an almost Lawrentian faith in the novel as a vehicle for social change but ignores the subtlety required to bring about the reader's assent. He seems to be alluding to this failure when in another author's note he states that 'those who doubt that hypnotism is capable of the kind of effects described in this novel should consult *Hypnosis and Behaviour Modification: Imagery Conditioning* by William S. Kroger and William D. Felzer.' It's as if he senses that the novel is not the ideal medium and that if in the end we have to go to Kroger and Felzer for verification and the facts we might as well miss out the fiction altogether.

Penelope Shuttle's novels are, I suspect, an acquired taste. Although she appends no suggestions for further reading, *The Mirror of the Giant* also dramatizes certain ideas from *The Wise Wound* beneath its super-natural, ghost-story surface. Set in a contemporary English village popu-lated with such pretentiously named characters as Theron, Vellet and Ash, the book does achieve on occasions a certain mythic resonance through the use of the present tense and brooding evocations of atmos-phere. However, the affectations of style ultimately become gratingly over-insistent and self-consciously 'poetical':

The moon is running backwards for Beth. She catches words in the folds of her skirt. Dark-odoured, she moves back to her chair, and tells Tabitha her story. The whispering of Centaurs, that rain outside and the thread of Beth's story running through it.

This passage is poetic only in its obvious attempts to render that kind of effect. The hallucinatory quality of the images is dauntingly impre-cise and the book is full of phrases like 'our rage burning us like the edge of the moon', 'drenched in an elvish sweat', and 'the woodland of the scissors' which are quite opaque and literally incomprehensible. What precisely is the nature of an *elvish* sweat? In what way does the edge of the moon burn? The words function in an entirely limited manner that is in reality fundamentally *un*poetic. It was Pound who said poetry should be at least as well written as prose: novelists should return the compliment.

1980

War in Fiction

(Review of *The Wars* by Timothy Findley, *War and Remembrance* by Herman Wouk and *Going After Cacciato* by Tim O'Brien)

These three novels deal respectively with the three greatest wars of this century and they each represent different – and ultimately unsuccessful – methods of tackling the awkward problem of war in fiction. War, thanks to television, is now familiar to us all. Not only have there been long and immensely popular documentary serials about the First and Second World Wars, but the slightest border raid or counter-insurgency operation is filmed and recorded by dozens of camera crews and reporters. The magazine shelves of any W. H. Smith testify to the popularity of war and its paraphernalia of equipment and hardware. It seems to be one of those subjects that we just can't know enough about.

But curiously enough this plethora of documentary material, this mountain of close detail, seems scarcely to have affected the fictional presentation of war whether in novels, film or TV. There exists a wide gulf between what we can see for ourselves as the brute facts and the imaginative presentation of them. Admittedly the gap has narrowed in recent years as can be seen from the contrast between R. C. Sherriff's *Journey's End* and Mailer's *The Naked and the Dead*, but it remains, nevertheless, resolutely there.

The first point of contention, and one that raises significant doubts about serious war novels, is this. Any one man's experience of war or battle – unlike, for example, tennis or bridge – *has* to be an exclusively subjective, quirky and highly personal affair. It will be a compound of his own intricate personality and the infinite variety of occurrences a war or battle provides. And yet one's reading of any account suggests that the experience is instead fundamentally a common one; a moderately varied but essentially repetitive parade of stock attitudes and conclusions. Furthermore, the basic judgement of nearly all war novels runs along these sort of lines: 'War is hell/shocking/depraved/inhuman *but* it provides intense and compensatory moments of comradeship/joy/ vivacity/emotion or excitement.' What appears most damaging is not so much the fatuity of the idea but that this formula represents an orthodoxy in the fictional treatment of war that – with a few exceptions –

is only paralleled in the pulpier forms of modern romance writing. This may be taken as unduly harsh, but it seems that writers of serious war fiction still consciously or unconsciously echo this position to such an extent that it is not only an inaccurate picture but can give rise to questions of irresponsibility.

The two basic errors behind this attitude are (1) a failure to come to terms with or to understand the true nature of battle (a fault shared with military historians) and (2) a tendency to qualify and to some extent condone warfare through the ennobling effects its 'heightened awareness' imposes on the combatants. The first can possibly be explained by lack of experience or information but the second is an evaluative judgement that is so widespread that it has moved from the world of fiction to infect the more factual documentary or historical account and which has, not unnaturally, almost entirely influenced film or TV dramatizations.

Timothy Findley's *The Wars* is a good example of the first problem. It tells the story of a young Canadian officer's experiences of the First World War and his ultimate nervous collapse. The narrative moves forward and backward in time; we share the reflections of the archivist/author as he sifts through the family papers, we hear reminiscences of the long dead hero, extracts from a child's diary and so on, gradually building up a composite picture of the young soldier. It's sensitively and carefully done, but the setting of the war appears almost as a gratuitous extra, a vaguely glamorous and emotive background to the torments of the young man. World War I seems especially prone to this sort of treatment – for example, Susan Hill's *Strange Meeting* and Jennifer Johnson's *How Many Miles from Babylon* – where the residual nostalgia of the period is all important rather than the war itself. Often the setting appears as a hindrance, something to be got out of the way as quickly as possible. For example, here Findley talks about a German-held ridge at Passchendaele:

The casualties were terrible, rising in numbers by the hundreds by the day. It seemed to be an impossible objective and it was here that many of the troops surrendered to the Germans rather than press on with the hopeless attack.

This reads like a second-rate official history: the words are so overworked and familiar that they have become virtually devoid of meaning. This is not entirely Findley's fault; he has merely aligned himself with the conformity of style that continues to surround most descriptions of violent action. For, despite Hemingway's revolution, the description of action by otherwise creditable writers remains in a lamentable state. And although Hemingway must be held responsible for much of the wrong-headedness that surrounds war fiction he was the first to sense the real inadequacy of writing about action and sought to change it. He succeeded nowhere more brilliantly than in the short linking sections between the stories in *In Our Time*. They still stand as a model of what can be achieved and Hemingway never quite recaptured their refined and precise tone. It was certainly absent from *For Whom the Bell Tolls* where Hemingway's interests revolved more around notions of heroism, bravery and duty, and the exact and scrupulous recording of experience had given way to the perverse idea of 'grace under pressure'.

This pervasive myth, and related versions of it, has probably replaced patriotism as the best reason for going to war, as can clearly be seen from any modern army recruiting campaign. It is possibly more preva-lent in American fiction (where war is a favourite subject), prompted initially by Hemingway's virility cult and reaching its flamboyant peak in Norman Mailer's *Why Are We In Vietnam?* The existence of this atti-tude helps explain both the tragedy of My-Lai (and its innumerable unremarked siblings) and the farce of Lt. Calley's trial. For Calley and his men the war was totally unlike anything they had been prepared for; and for the USA their soldiers just didn't commit that sort of crime. Both sides had been deluded as to the reality of warfare. Significantly, only in Vietnam has this sensation of utter bafflement and disillusion on the part of the fighting soldier been adequately recorded though it is a common, if not *the* common experience of every conflict, shared by the French knights at Agincourt, the British at the Somme and the Marines at Da Nang. Confusion and mental disintegration are inevitable when one's expectations of warfare have been conditioned – at the simplest level – by such things as Marvel Comic's 'Our Army at War' series, where the legendary Sgt. Rock of Easy company fights the good fight with an ascetic and almost saintly purpose. But the mood and tone are equally evident in more sophisticated writings from *The Red Badge of Courage* to the recent and wildly over-acclaimed *Dispatches*.

Nobody could be more sincere about war than Herman Wouk as his mighty 1,000-page opus *War and Remembrance* makes clear. It is part of a subgenre of war novels that begins with *The Naked and the Dead* and includes Jones's *From Here to Eternity* and Shaw's *The Young*

Lions. The huge all-encompassing canvas, the cast of thousands, the flitting from continent to continent, the way lives interlock and events conspire together ultimately fail in the presentation of truth precisely because the novelist's necessarily considerable organizational role looms above the fiction like a player at a chess board. And curiously it is also in the nature of these books to have very little action in them; we become more interested in the characters – will John marry Jane next leave, will Fred get promoted, etc. – than in their circumstances. Wouk goes one step beyond this too, acting as military historian, strategist and providing a layman's guide to the Final Solution and the making of the Atomic Bomb, until the book sags under the weight of its good intentions.

Going After Cacciato, set in Vietnam, recounts the desertion of Cacciato, a 'dumb as a dink' infantryman who decides to go AWOL and head for Paris. The other members of his patrol follow in hot pursuit across Burma, Iran, Turkey and Europe until Cacciato is finally cornered in a seedy hotel in Les Halles. The fantasy (the epigraph from Sassoon, 'Soldiers are dreamers', rather gives the game away), the whimsical jokes, the conscious presentation of absurdity, all point inescapably to the weighty influence of *Catch-22*. If there has ever been a book begging not to be imitated it is Joseph Heller's seminal and unique condemnation of warfare. All imitators suffer in comparison and *Going After Cacciato* is no exception. O'Brien's book is an expansion of one episode in *Catch-22* where, at the end of the novel, Orr ditches his plane in the Mediterranean and paddles his rubber dinghy to Sweden. In *Catch-22* Orr's escape is the final inspiration for Yossarian: Orr, who everyone thought was quite mad, eventually triumphs. *Going After Cacciato* is a Vietnamese reworking of this theme but Cacciato's toiling journey cannot sustain interest; the initially amusing notion just can't be stretched out into a novel. The best sections of the book are the descriptions of operations in the paddy fields and jungles of Vietnam where the author fought himself, but which he portrayed far more efficiently in his autobiographical account *If I Should Die in a Combat Zone*.

It is the Vietnam war – the most scrutinized and observed conflict ever – that has forced us to re-examine most serious war fiction and which exposes its inadequacies. All the newspaper accounts and newsreel pictures – of heavily armed men firing endlessly at jungle, napalm blooming in straw villages, the almost complete absence of enemy dead and wounded – spoke of experiences wholly unlike those encountered in novels. As the vast majority of us are non-combatants we are wholly dependent on the accounts of others when it comes to learning about war. It is an aspect of experience – unlike, say, childhood, love, loneliness – where verifiability is hard to come by. Vietnam, more than anywhere, showed the almost divine illogicality of warfare, when a peasant army defeated the most powerful nation in the world. Beside it *Catch-22* reads like a model of propriety and good sense – reality confounding art once again. The reaction to this has yet to be felt. Very few accounts of the war have yet appeared and most of these are documentary. There has been no true Vietnam war novel up to now; those that have been published – such as *Going After Cacciato*, Robert Stone's *Dog Soldiers* or even Dinah Brooke's *Games of Love and Death* – are really written around the subject. One reason for this is that Vietnam, having exposed the redundancy of war fiction, has literally left writers wordless. The same fictional silence surrounds the Biafran war – one of the most tragic, haphazard and amateur conflicts of all time – which is all the more surprising considering Nigeria's lively and impressive literary talents. It seems that there just do not exist the modes and structures within the genre of war fiction to come to terms with experiences utterly different from those we have been led over many years to expect.

However, there are signs of change. The first indications of this shift of opinion, the beginnings of a reassessment, do not lie in fiction or the cinema (unless Francis Ford Coppola's much heralded *Apocalypse Now* proves me wrong) but, strangely enough, in military history. Three books have appeared in the last few years that mark an entirely new if not revolutionary approach to their subject and which can be simply classified as looking at the realities of war from the ground up. They are Martin Middlebrook's *The First Day on the Somme*, Len Deighton's *Fighter* and John Keegan's exceptional study *The Face of Battle*.

One reading of *The Face of Battle* will show how wide of the mark most war novelists are and should convince anyone of the falseness of the so-called realities of warfare that have hitherto been accepted as accurate. Len Deighton's *Fighter* is the best means of getting behind the thick cloud of myths surrounding the Battle of Britain. This is not to say that effective novels of war have not been written. Examples of convincing accounts of war – in line with the conclusions of the three books mentioned above – can be found in, for example, the Caporetto chapter in *A Farewell to Arms, Catch-22*, and Christopher Wood's fine novel about Cyprus and EOKA, *Terrible Hard, Says Alice*, but they form a small minority and on the evidence of these three new novels it seems they are more than likely to remain in that state.

1979

William Golding

(Review of *Rites of Passage*)

Towards the end of William Golding's novel – *Rites of Passage* – its protagonist Edmund Talbot remarks to a naval lieutenant that 'life is a formless business, Summers, Literature is much amiss in forcing a form on it!' The notion is a central one in Golding's work and also in any appreciation of it, for literature, we are now fully aware, cannot do other than impose a form, even when aping life at its most random and contingent. From one point of view Dean Jocelin's vision and construction of his cathedral spire is a prolonged debate on the futility of the entire purpose of trying to shape and create something out of redoubtably intractable material – the writer's problem no less than the medieval architect's. Golding goes further than this. Not content with the struggle to shape and form he also seeks answers to grave and essential questions about the human condition: 'the unnamable, unfathomable and invisible darkness that sits at the centre' (*Free Fall*). This overall seriousness of intent on Golding's part – the sense that his novels are meditations on or dramatizations of life's most seminal concerns – is at once his great strength and his weakness, an advantage and a constraint; some of his novels are immeasurably enhanced by it, others find the freight of significance too much to bear.

Perhaps the problem can be conveyed more precisely by recording a remark Graham Greene made. Greene complains that 'I would like to ascend into myth but find my books so often muddy with plot.' This, I suspect, is not only a piece of self-criticism (misguided, in my opinion) but also a wishful indication of the way Greene would like his books to be read. It's a plea for less popular assessment, a desire to be rated – or to write – on a deeper more elemental level. Golding, on the other hand, suffers from the opposite reaction. Not only in the reverential, solemn way people approach his work but also, from his fourth novel onwards, in some impulse governing the way he writes.

Most novels tend inevitably towards what we can call the world of history – the rich infinitely varied world of phenomena, of appearances and details. Indeed, it can be argued that there is something in the novel form itself that fosters and encourages this inclination. This is what

Greene is bemoaning – the pull is too hard for him to resist. Golding, alternatively, has determinedly steered his fiction towards the other pole: that of myth, and all the more single-mindedly since *Free Fall*. Of course, in most serious fiction both elements coexist, but in varying degrees and, by and large, the mythic features are subordinate, the *referential* aspects of the form claiming most of our attention. This duality also applies to Golding. *Lord of the Flies*, he has related, started out primarily as an attempt to portray what children are really like, in opposition to the anodyne Victorian image in *Coral Island*. However, the novel is more than that, clearly – or at least became more than that – developing into the first exploration of now familiar Golding themes: an examination of innocence, the dark truth about human nature and a delineation of his particular Manichean vision of the world.

But what made Golding's first three novels so remarkable (and I would rate *Pincher Martin* as high as any) was the extent to which he managed to introduce the mythic element without threatening the tenuous equilibrium that has to exist between the specifics of history and the generalities of myth. *The Inheritors* captures with marvellous ability a wholly realistic sense of the Neanderthal world as well as re-enacting on the wider level the confrontation between Innocence and Experience. So too *Pincher Martin* is at once the story of a real man marooned on a rock in the middle of the Atlantic as well as an elaborate parody of the Creation, an illustration of man's immense ego and his futile heroism.

Many commentators see Golding's first five novels as forming a homogeneous unit, but I would be inclined to mark the division after *Pincher Martin*. Both *Free Fall* and *The Spire* significantly tip the balance towards myth and concentrate attention rather more on the solution of what might be termed spiritual or aesthetic dilemmas. Significance is no longer tethered to fact. One is too conscious of the huge abstractions bulking beneath the narrative and its surface details. There is, at the back of the reader's mind, an overpowering, and at times enervating, awareness of correspondence: the fact that nothing in these novels is offered for its own sake, but is there to serve the rhetoric of the mythopoeic impulse. In *Free Fall* and *The Spire* the mythical *sous-texte* of the novels dominates to the detriment of the fiction. There is on occasion a certain inflated, striven-for trenchancy in the prose (a failing Conrad was also prone to), as well as passages of great power. There simply isn't enough 'muddy plot' obscuring the vision. Not that the vision is ever crystal clear – Golding's answers are never unambiguous and succinct – it is instead that one knows one should always be seeking the analogical matrix that lies beneath the prose, striving all the time to 'see into the life of things'.

The two books that followed *The Spire* – *The Pyramid* and *The Scorpion God* – represented a hiatus in the Golding oeuvre. *The Scorpion God* consisted of three novellas and *The Pyramid* was an untypical, Trollopian novel recrafted from some early short stories. It wasn't until the publication of *Darkness Visible* last year – after a self-confessed eight-year block – that the sequence of Golding novels proper continued. To put it at its most simple, *Darkness Visible* is an uneven, strained attempt to reconnect the twin worlds of muddy plot and myth that had diverged since *Pincher Martin*. To some extent it succeeds brilliantly, as in the opening chapter dealing with the blitz and the simple hero Matty's exposure to the pentecostal firestorm, and the later chapters treating his life and education. However there is something disconcerting about the book's self-conscious modishness – terrorism, paedophilia – and for once Golding's superb organizational grasp of his material seems to have deserted him almost completely. There is no doubt that the writing of the novel was something of a purgative experience – Golding has stated that he has refused to read a single review of the book – and it will come to be seen, I suspect, as something of a curiosity – an aberration in what is otherwise a career of masterly technical control and authorial self-assurance. Its, so to speak, emetic properties have clearly proved efficient, and we now have, a year later, a novel which has not only won the Booker prize but, more importantly, reaffirms a memorable return to form and the literary stature of its author.

Many reviewers of *Rites of Passage* have qualified their praise, ranking it with *The Pyramid*, seeing it as something of a perfect minor work. It is far more than this: rather it's a return to tried and tested techniques; in many ways a look back at what has come before and a summary of the preceding novels' achievements. Golding's best novels take place in a confined world: the island in *Lord of the Flies*, the rock in *Pincher Martin*, language in *The Inheritors* – further confined by the characters' vastly limited conceptual boundaries. Similarly, *Rites of Passage* takes place on an ageing man-of-war, en route with a party of emigrants for Australia, at some point towards the end of the Napoleonic wars. The main burden of the narrative is taken up by a privileged young passenger called Edmund Talbot, who is recording the events of the passage in a journal for the benefit and amusement of his aristocratic patron. This journal in itself is a superb example of literary mimicry on Golding's part, a feat of imaginative sympathy with the early nineteenth century that comes close to the intellectual efforts required to render Neanderthalers' world-view in *The Inheritors*. Talbot is contemptuous and sneering about his fellow passengers, particularly an impoverished clergyman named Colley, who somehow manages to attract the disdain of just about everyone else on board. Talbot's voyage and journal proceed with their unremarkable catalogue of seasickness, minor tiffs, a brief flirtation and sex-bout with a meretricious female passenger, and a tour of the bowels of the ship. Talbot has little out-of-the-ordinary to report until the Reverend Colley, in the course of delivering a sermon to the huddled masses in steerage, gets drunk on navy rum and makes an exhibition of himself capering about the deck semi-nude and finally pissing up against a mast in full view of the other passengers. Colley's reaction to this inebriated display is, however, extreme. He lies face down on his bed in a kind of catatonic trance for four days before finally dying of shame. On going through Colley's room, Talbot discovers a long letter that Colley had been writing to his sister and he duly transcribes it into his journal. The narrative point of view shifts and the events of the voyage are retold by Colley. This change in perspective completely alters our conception of events as Talbot has thus far related to us. Colley has been the victim of callous persecution at the hands of the officers of the ship and the captain himself. He has been humiliated in front of the ship's company during the traditional crossing-of-the-equator cere-mony. Colley's idea of his own nature and his standing in the eyes of his fellow passengers is revealed as hopelessly and tragically inaccurate. Talbot's journal and narrative have also to be reassessed and he sees himself as being unwittingly responsible for Colley's bizarre demise. This sudden, final change of viewpoint causing a reanalysis of all that has passed before is a feature that occurs in all of Golding's first three novels. Here it is handled with great skill and deftness, used not only as an instrument of humorous irony and a subversive literary technique (as remarkable as Conrad's similar exercise in *Under Western Eyes* – a writer to whom Golding comes to bear more and more resemblance) but also as a means of focusing on the themes of guilt, persecution and delusion which were only intermittently apparent in Talbot's self-opinionated journal. Now Talbot is able, with the aid of Colley's letter and the impromptu inquest held after his death, to fill in the gaps in his own defective and subjective account of what has been going on in the ship. The hidden and unknown act which brought about Colley's insupportable shame and eventual death is suddenly made clear.

Rites of Passage and *Pincher Martin* are the only two Golding novels where a revelation of what takes place at the end will completely ruin the reader's enjoyment of the book – a sufficient testimony to the renewed status of muddy plot. However, *Rites of Passage* contains greater riches than pure narrative entertainment. Riches which, on the basis of only two readings so far, I can only hint at. Like *Lord of the Flies*, *The Inheritors* and *Pincher Martin*, *Rites of Passage* has 'at its back' another text. (For the preceding three, they are, respectively, *The Coral Island*, Wells's *Outline of History* and *Robinson Crusoe*). In this case it is Coleridge's 'The Rime of the Ancient Mariner'. One comparison will have to suffice. Just before the Mariner is freed of his albatross he looks over the side of the ship:

> Beyond the shadow of the ship
> I watched the water snakes . . .
> Within the shadow of attire: Blue, glossy green, and velvet black
> They coiled and swam; and every track
> Was a flash of golden fire.
>
> O happy living things! no tongue
> Their beauty might declare:
> A spring of love gusht from my heart,
> And I blest them unaware! . . .
>
> The self-same moment I could pray;
> And from my neck so free
> The Albatross fell off, and sank
> Like lead into the sea

Colley, just before his final ordeal, looks over the side of the ship:

I gazed down into the water, the blue, the green, the purple, the snowy, sliding foam! I saw with a new feeling of security the long green weed that wavers under the water from our wooden sides . . . It seemed to me then – it still seems so – that I was and am consumed by a great love of all things . . .

There are many other obvious echoes. Just as Golding challenges the dogmas of his literary starting points in his first three novels so he 'deconstructs' Coleridge in *Rites of Passage*. To put it at its most brief, Colley is at once Mariner and Albatross, and the purgatorial sufferings which lead to redemption in the poem are pointedly, and with wicked irony, eschewed here. In the poem the Mariner confers his blessing on the water snakes and is freed from the albatross by his unselfish act. Colley, re-enacting the Mariner's part with a more literal accuracy, goes on from this point to assume an albatross which leads to his squalid end. His geographical passage across the equator, his physical move over the white line painted on the deck to separate 'gentlemen' from 'people', symbolizes his own transit from the factitious world of civilized appearance to the darker realms of the unconscious, which ultimately brings about his doom. This is a multi-layered and marvellously intelligent novel with endless subtle allusions and reverberations and effortlessly marshalled cross-references. It is also a witty and solidly realistic account of life on a sailing ship at the beginning of the last century. There is an exuberance and confidence about the book that signals the author's own awareness of his return to former strengths. The balance is triumphantly right.

1981

Philip Roth

(Review of *Zuckerman Unbound*)

Philip Roth's last book, *The Ghost Writer*, featured an unknown novelist called Nathan Zuckerman and dealt with the visit he paid to the home of a literary giant. In *Zuckerman Unbound* Zuckerman is now a celebrated and notorious author, whose novel, *Carnovsky*, has brought him overnight fame. *Zuckerman Unbound* details his inept attempts at coping with being a celebrity and, more seriously, considers the connections that exist between a writer's life and his art.

The Zuckerman/*Carnovsky* link seems parallel to that between Roth and *Portnoy's Complaint*. *Carnovsky* is a graphic account of the sex life of its eponymous hero and the simple equation that exists in the minds of its readers is that Zuckerman and the fictional Carnovsky are, in actual fact, interchangeable. There's a lot of amusing detail about the pressures of living with fame, reminiscent in parts of Woody Allen's film *Stardust Memories*. Allen's paranoia is also echoed in Zuckerman's fears that he will end up the victim of some deranged fan. Zuckerman finds himself pestered by the usual collection of cranks and weirdos, but is dogged more persistently by one Alvin Pepler, a contemporary who hails from the same town – Newark, New Jersey. Pepler had achieved a short span of fame as winner on a nationwide quiz show, a success brought to him by virtue of his photographic memory. But the quiz show was rigged (a genuine scandal in the fifties) and Pepler was 'defeated' by another contestant and condemned to return to the obscurity from which he'd briefly emerged.

Pepler's obsessions and his grandiose ambitions (he wants Zuckerman to help promote his book) are irritating, but later Zuckerman becomes more intrigued with this extraordinary character. For a while he contemplates writing Pepler and his life into a novel and begins to make transcriptions of everything he says. This illustration of a writer engaged in the process of turning life's raw materials into art bears on the book's wider theme, namely the persistent identification the public makes of the artist with his creation. Or, as Zuckerman cogently puts it, confusing the 'dictating ventriloquist with the demonic dummy'.

The most serious consequences of this sort of identification are experienced by members of the artist's family, especially if – as in the Roth/Zuckerman case – characters, such as parents, play a large part in the fiction. It's in his relationships with members of his family that Zuckerman sees the genuine damage that his fame has caused. The incomprehension of his parents and brother, the sense of betrayal that they feel, have opened up an unbridgeable gap between them. The novel ends with Zuckerman returning to his native Newark, the setting for *Carnovsky*. It has all changed, to such an extent that it is almost unrecognizable. Roth seems to be leaving us with a symbolic reminder of the difference between life and art, a warning not to mistake the illusion for the illusionist.

It was T. S. Eliot who emphasized the gulf between the 'man who suffers and the mind which creates'. It's a separation that Zuckerman insists on throughout the novel too. There's no connection, he repeats, between what happens in his novels and what's happened in his life. *Zuckerman Unbound* is a very funny account of the consequences of not observing the distinction. Some consequences are easy to live with – Zuckerman's sexual renown allows him to bed film stars – others are very sad: Zuckerman senior's dying word to his son is 'bastard'. But essentially Roth, I think, is playing an elaborate joke on the reader. In *Zuckerman Unbound* we constantly hear of other readers' stupidity in taking Zuckerman for his fictional hero Carnovsky, and we sympathize with Zuckerman's frustration. But at the same time – I've been doing it throughout this review myself and, I guarantee, it will occur in every notice the book receives – we identify Zuckerman with Roth and talk about *Zuckerman Unbound* in terms of Roth and the reception of *Portnoy*. Perhaps all that Roth is pointing out in laying this trap for us is simply to show how instinctive such a response is; that it'll be made anyway, no matter what the writer tries to do. Is it an error on the reader's part, though? Is the reader hopelessly unsophisticated? Roth doesn't actually come out and say so, but I think that throughout the novel – especially in the way he reacts to Pepler – he drops hints that the notion of the separation of the artist from his art is, in a significant sense, something of a convenient piece of camouflage for the artist. Certainly Eliot for one – who energetically pursued this line throughout his life – was not doing it disinterestedly. *Zuckerman Unbound* is an elegant and amusing contribution to the debate.

1981

Kurt Vonnegut (1)

(Review of *Palm Sunday*)

In 1975 Kurt Vonnegut published a collection of reviews, articles and speeches under the annoying title of *Wampeters, Foma & Granfalloons*. Now, six years later, he has done much the same in *Palm Sunday*. He calls the book a collage but adds that

As I arranged those fragments in this order and then that one I saw that they formed a sort of autobiography, especially if I felt free to include some pieces not written by me. To give life to such a golem, however, I would have to write much new connective tissue. This I have done.

The other contributions are a history of the Vonnegut family written by a cousin, a letter from his daughter and miscellaneous extracts from work by other relatives. The result is far more effective than the earlier book. Indeed were it not for the 'connective tissue' *Palm Sunday* would be dangerously inconclusive and slight. For the plain fact of the matter is that Vonnegut hasn't done that much reviewing or public speaking in the intervening six years. Even without the extra help provided by his family some of the pieces included here are clearly no more than padding. There can be no other reason for reprinting his short story 'The Big Space Fuck' or subjecting us to a truly appalling libretto for a musical version of *Dr Jekyll and Mr Hyde* – which the producers quite rightly turned down. It is Vonnegut's musings and speculations on and around the circumstances that prompted this or that address or introduction to a book that prove in the end to be far and away the most rewarding elements of *Palm Sunday*. They do, as he intended, form a partial auto-biography – a 'sort of life' – which reveals the author to us in a genial and unselfconscious way and raises hopes that this will prove to be a trial run for a fuller, longer account of his life.

I have often suspected that a reader's reaction to Vonnegut's style depends largely on the mood he or she happens to be in at the time. It's quite possible one day to be entertained, and the next to be irked and infuriated. This is not a result of inconsistencies in Vonnegut: his tone of voice has remained remarkably consistent through his writing career – a curious blend of *faux naïveté* and profanity, of innocence and deep irony. It produces, in *Palm Sunday*, such effects as these:

As for literary criticism in general, I have long felt that any reviewer who expresses rage and loathing for a novel or a play or a poem is preposterous. He or she is like a person that has put on full armour and attacked a hot fudge sundae or banana split.

and

Dog poisoning is still the most contemptible crime I can think of.

and

He was an abstract impressionist you see. His paintings just looked like bright weather . . .

and

The apathy of the University of Chicago is repulsive to me. They can take a flying fuck at the moooooooooooooooon.

To me this appears, respectively, to be: largely correct; fake, coy and stupid; nicely put; and childish but forceful.

However, it's unfair to quote Vonnegut out of context, because, such is the nature of his style, you can find examples to suit any accusation you choose. Moreover, beneath the mannerisms lies an amenable personality whose opinions are not without merit and relevance. Vonnegut's *bêtes noires* are worthy and well known and include such targets as multinationals, pollution, organized religion, war and inhumanity. If a new note appears in *Palm Sunday* then it's a plea to abandon the nuclear family and to return to the extended one. Vonnegut talks wistfully of Ibo tribesmen who know or are related to upward of a thousand people. Speculating on the fact that one in three Americans is or will become divorced, he offers this explanation:

The nuclear family doesn't provide nearly enough companionship . . . In a nuclear family children and parents can be locked in hellish close combat for twenty-one years or more. In an extended family, a child has scores of other homes to go to in search of love and understanding. He need not stay at home and torture his parents, and he need not starve for love.

This particular direction of Vonnegut's thought seems to have been caused by the breakdown of his twenty-year-old marriage and the dispersal of his six children. Without rancour or sentiment he chronicles their lives and assesses their characters and future. He regards his family in the same way as he contemplates other people: alien but generally nice beings who are difficult to understand or fathom, whether they are leading aimless or purposeful lives. This is particularly evident when he savours the irony of the fact that – a professed and radical atheist all his life – not only his wife but also both his daughters should have recently become fervent born-again Christians.

Unlike the hostage-diplomat, the explorer or the film star, the novelist's life is on the whole a dull unremarkable affair. Auden's poem sums it up perfectly. The novelist

> Must struggle out of his boyish gift and learn
> How to be plain and awkward, how to be
> One after whom none think it worth to turn.

Vonnegut is no exception. He lives in New York with his second wife, smokes fifty cigarettes a day, and writes. So when it comes to autobiography something other than the facts must be present if the account is to grip and intrigue. The answer is to cultivate a tone of voice – a literary personality who may bear no relation to the real one but whose idiosyncrasies and manner provide a point of view, an angle of vision, that redeems the otherwise banal details and unexceptional events. In fact this dictum may well apply to any published writing where the first person pronoun is frequently in use.

Nabokov in *Strong Opinions* achieves this superbly. The spry, dandified inconoclast is highly engaging and teasingly outrageous. So too with Graham Greene in *A Sort of Life* and the recent *Ways of Escape*. The measured self-deprecating ironic gaze suits the recollections admirably. It doesn't matter if the real Nabokov and Greene bear scant resemblance to their literary siblings – indeed there is something to be said for maximizing the distance between the two – the pleasure resides in the pose, the imposture. Vonnegut may or may not be like the portrait he presents of himself here. The point is that he has found his voice and it informs and colours the moderately interesting facts and tendentious opinions in a beguiling and sympathetic way. When talking about Thoreau, Vonnegut observes that 'Thoreau, I now feel, wrote in the voice of a child, as I do.' That is Vonnegut's voice, his particular imposture, and, like any child, its pronouncements can be maddening or inspiringly perceptive. There are enough of the latter to make us hope for more in the future.

1981

John Fowles

(Review of *Mantissa*)

John Fowles's curious new novel starts off with epigraphs from Descartes, Marivaux and Lemprière and then launches us into a steamy soft porn sex fantasy which wouldn't shame Harold Robbins, Sydney Sheldon and other masters of the genre. It features one Miles Green, a novelist, who is suffering from amnesia and is convalescing in a bizarre experimental hospital. Treatment is administered by the stern and emotionless Dr Delphie – 'Her dark hair was bound severely back at the nape, she wore no make up, yet there was something elegantly classical about her face' – and pneumatic West Indian, Nurse Cory, altogether warmer and more fun. Their cure consists in attempting to excite sexually the drugged and dozy Green, to which end he's ordered – forced – to fondle their naked bodies. Lack of response on Green's part compels them to clamber into bed with their meekly protesting patient. There more thoroughgoing stimuli are applied, the therapy gets more intimate, and so on and so forth for the next forty pages or so.

It turns out – and it doesn't come as that much of a surprise – that in fact all this has been *written* by Green, but just as the reader stifles a yawn, thinking that this is just another exercise in the fiction/fabulation game, a further dimension is added when the hospital room door bursts open and in stalks Erato, muse of lyric and amorous poetry – and by extension anything to do with love and sex as they make an appearance in fiction. It is on this relationship – between Green and Erato – that the rest of the book centres. It transpires that Erato was both Dr Delphie *and* Nurse Cory; indeed Erato is the archetype behind all the female love objects in world literature – Lesbia, the Dark Lady, T. S. Eliot's typist – and not just those thronging Green's fevered imagination.

What follows over the subsequent three parts of the novel is a sustained debate – alternating with a fair amount of flirtation and sexual banter – between Green and Erato, in which literature and life, art and reality and the difference between male and female sexual natures are given a fairly thorough airing. It's reminiscent of a facetious and camped-up version of those dialogues eighteenth-century philosophers employed to dramatize their views on epistemology, theories of causation or proofs for the existence of God. Green and Erato – as befits the relationship between a writer and his muse – wrangle and row, moon and caress and steadily talk themselves into bed. (We never really establish the extent to which we're still inhabiting Green's torrid imagination, but then that ambiguity is entirely deliberate.) Some of the chat is intelligent and perceptive, some of it appallingly winsome, but overall the main response it provokes is irritation and tedium.

The source of this reaction is a feeling – profound in my case – that the last word on the fictionality of fiction was uttered a long time ago, and that this sort of literary games-playing – knowing, self-referential, tongue in cheek – is very old hat. Some of the topics raised in the novel are interesting, notably on the odd relationship that can spring up between a male writer and the female characters he creates, but it's small compensation for what turns out to be an over-attenuated *jeu d'esprit*.

One of the advantages of writing a novel about a novelist writing a novel is that you can pre-empt any critical reservations that might arise over your own text. It's part and parcel of the 'knowing' aspect of the enterprise, and sure enough nothing I've objected to here hasn't been anticipated in one form or another by Fowles/Green.

'Serious modern fiction,' says Green, 'has only one subject: the difficulty of writing serious modern fiction. First it has fully to be accepted that it's only fiction, can only be fiction, must never be anything but fiction, and therefore has no business at all tampering with real life or reality. Right?'

To be fair to Fowles, a lot of the post-structural, deconstructivist jargon is sent up (albeit heavy-handedly) and there is a muted note in the book which would seem to set Fowles down on the old-style 'reflective' side of the fence rather than the modish 'reflexive'. The key to this solution resides in the Cartesian epigraphs, in that there's a Fowlesian doubt that won't go all the way with the total absence of the author and the absolute autonomy of the text. There's also a powerful hint to this effect in the final paragraph, but its Jamesian accumulation of subordinate clauses plus some dodgy grammar (I think there's a main verb missing) means that this conclusion can't be stated with any certainty.

So *Mantissa* isn't simply a more radical reworking of the dallying with metafiction we witnessed in *The French Lieutenant's Woman*. Its speculations arise out of various tensions generated by the writing process (namely writing about sex, women, the nagging demands made on a novelist by post-modernist criticism and – if I surmise correctly – bad faith *vis-à-vis* the same) and to that extent anyone interested in Fowles – *pace* the author/text dissociation – may find this novel intriguing. But on the whole it's heavy going and with scant returns. Interestingly enough a related exercise was expertly achieved by Martin Amis in *Other People* (both open with an amnesiac/aphasic in hospital). And as for the delights and frustrations of the relationship between a writer and his muse one should go no further than Anthony Burgess's version in the marvellous *Enderby Outside*. A 'mantissa', so Fowles informs us in a foot-note towards the end, is 'An addition of comparatively small importance, especially to a literary effort or discourse,' *OED*. Another pre-emptive critical strike, but one that just about sums it up.

1982

Kurt Vonnegut (2)

(Review of *Deadeye Dick*)

Every time I open a novel by Kurt Vonnegut the same words spring to mind: 'Coy', 'Arch', 'Winsome' and 'Cute'. But they are equally quickly dispelled. I suspect that Vonnegut's tone of voice — and a remarkably consistent one it is — either wins the reader over fairly promptly or not at all. In my own case it's the former effect that occurs, certainly with the category of novel which we can safely demarcate 'late' Vonnegut: the sequence of books beginning with *Breakfast of Champions* and including *Slapstick*, *Jailbird*, *Palm Sunday* (autobiography) and this, the latest.

In these novels — and in *Slaughterhouse 5* — the connection between life and art is straightforwardly causal. It seems to me that all the books mentioned emerge directly from the author's baffled observation of human life and nature and effectively dramatize certain questions (and attempt to come up with some answers) that the observation engenders. Vonnegut considers our swarming damaged planet and contemplates our bizarre behaviour-patterns. He looks at the way we exploit and corrupt each other; he marvels at the multitude of toxic chemicals we happily ingest; he ponders why we spend so much time inventing devices that can so easily bring about our annihilation as a species — and so on, as he would say. But he also focuses his gaze more precisely: on the sex-game, as he terms it; on the connection between love and common decency; on how to cope with the random fatalities of life, with sudden and incomprehensible bereavement. In this sense Vonnegut is the most overtly humane of that remarkable generation of American novelists to which he belongs, and it's to his undying credit that no sentiment, pap or any kind of emotional sop ever clouds or diminishes the cool, ironic, unapologetic quality of his vision.

In many ways Vonnegut exhibits — in his candour and disarming openness, the way he squares up these Big Issues — an archetypal Americanness. But he avoids the typical American response: an appeal to the heart, whether in the form of God, the flag, Mom or apple-pie. He seems to lack the sophistication of a Roth or Heller; he has, in the best sense of the word, the most popular approach. But that type of naivety and simplicity is illusory. Vonnegut's verdict on the world and its denizens is as hard-nosed and unconsoling as any his peers can offer up. And it's this seeming paradox – the gum-chewing hick from middle America combined with a brand of cynicism almost classical in its consistency – that makes his work so intriguing.

Deadeye Dick exhibits all these qualities in the most satisfactory ways. The story relates the life of Rudolf Waltz from Midland City, Ohio. Rudy is, in his own terms, a 'neuter' – he takes no part in the sex-game. He works as an all-night salesman in Schramm's drugstore. His main aim in life is to be inconspicuous. This is partly owing to his crippling shyness but is also as a result of an accident he was responsible for when he was twelve. In a moment of elation young Rudy fired a gun over the roof-tops of Midland City. The bullet, falling many miles away, drilled a hole between the eyes of a pregnant woman. Thus Rudy became a double murderer, and thus he earned his nickname, Deadeye Dick.

This sort of picaresque autobiography (Rudy is the narrator) allows Vonnegut's distinctive style and approach to function at their most effective. Various characters in Midland City are introduced to us and the mundane course of Rudy's life steadily progresses. People die, people are unkind to and misunderstand each other. In the end a neutron bomb accidentally explodes in Midland City, wiping out the population but leaving the buildings intact. Fortunately, by this time, Rudy and his brother Felix have left and have set up in a hotel they've bought in Haiti. Rudy's final comment is 'we are still in the Dark Ages', but there is no sense of Vonnegut passionately indicting man's inhumanity to man. His stance is, if anything, more disinterested than ever. The book opens with a warning: 'Watch out for life.' Rudy survives – to the extent that anyone survives – through a policy of mental non-engagement. In his attitude to others he is selfless and caring, but intellectually he is entirely uncommitted. Behind the wit and the humour this is the bleakest Vonnegut since *Slaughterhouse 5*.

1983

W. H. Auden

(Review of *The Orators*)

The Orators by W. H. Auden was published in 1932 when Auden was twenty-five. It is an immensely precocious, rambling, difficult and eccentric work, mainly in prose and almost entirely forgotten. Today, outside libraries, it is only available in *The English Auden*, a collection of his poems, essays and dramatic writings from 1927 to 1939. *The Orators*, I suppose, is subsumed under 'dramatic writings', but it's not in any sense a play, or even a piece for several voices. It is in actual fact an unclassifiable oddity, a maverick work in Auden's output, impossible to label or pigeonhole. It is fiction, but it's neither a novel or a short story. It contains parodies, lists, geometric drawings, diagrams, odes, doggerel and straightforward poems too. And, to be honest, it is long-winded occasionally, and, at times, maddeningly opaque with a rich seam of cock-eyed, socio-cultural analysis. Auden himself, in later life, said of it, 'My name on the title page seems a pseudonym for someone else, someone talented, but near the border of sanity.' So why do I keep on reading it all the time?

Two main answers and lots of minor ones. I re-read it chiefly because it's very funny and also for the access I gain into an astonishingly vivid, entrancing and daft imagination. Auden is my favourite poet, but in the prose of *The Orators* the control and discipline of poetry are abandoned. If you like the Audenesque tone of voice, its particular tropes and obsessions, then here you will find it writ large, lavishly piled on. It is, I think, something to be dipped into or picked over and, although it was vaguely designed as a coherent statement, its parts are infinitely richer than its whole.

The Orators is subtitled 'An English Study' and is, rather as *The Waste Land* intended, meant to be a survey of the state of England, and the moral and spiritual health of the populace. This all sounds eminently serious and dull but, being Auden, it is Englishness that comes through rather than *gravitas*, and the ills of society are very idiosyncratically diagnosed. There is none of the monumental distanced *angst* striven for in Eliot's poem. The needs and desires voiced – though genuine – are much more the needs and desires of W. H. Auden Esq., one suspects, rather than the unspoken pleas of a generation.

The book is divided into three sections, sandwiched between a prologue and an epilogue. Part One is called 'The Initiates' and is itself subdivided. It opens with an 'Address for a Prizeday', a hectoring speech analysing the current problems of the population. The English, it transpires, can be classed as four different types of lover. Excessive Lovers of Self, Excessive Lovers of Neighbours, Defective Lovers and Perverted Lovers. All this has at root some ostensibly serious purpose, to do largely with Auden's preoccupation with psychosomatic illness as inspired by people like Groddeck and Layard. But this can be safely set aside, for the 'seriousness' of *The Orators*, it seems to me, is only a starting point – a sort of skeleton of the book which gives it a rough structure and shape but which is really only there to provide support for the fleshing out of the text. It provides Auden's talent with the excuse it has been waiting for. Having classified the population in this way he can now get on with describing them. The Excessive Lovers of Self: 'Habitués of the mirror, famous readers, they fall in love with the voice of the announcer, maybe, from some foreign broadcasting station they can never identify.' The Defective Lovers: 'They sit by fires they can't make up their minds to light, while dust settles on their unopened correspondence . . . Wearers of soiled linen, the cotton wool in their ears unchanged for months. Anaemic, muscularly undeveloped and rather mean. Hit them in the face if necessary.' And so on for two delightful pages.

The following sections, 'Argument' and 'Statement', introduce the atmosphere of war, insurrection, civil unrest and the emergence of a Leader who will guide the true of heart to victory and a new life. Once again the rather 'loony' message is the excuse for more virtuoso comic description. A bizarre and fantastic atmosphere of risk, threat and paranoia is conjured up. And here too are all the familiar ingredients of the Audenesque landscape: public schools, the OTC, mines, mills, crags, borders and spies. 'The fatty smell of drying clothes, the smell of cordite in a wood, and the new moon seen along the barrel of a gun . . . Rook shadows cross to the right. A schoolmaster cleanses himself at half term with a vegetable offering; on the north side of a hill, one writes with his penis in the snow "*resurgam*".'

You will be beginning to gain some idea of the tone of *The Orators* – the sinister-comic-eccentric voice at its most developed. The mood is sustained in the final section 'Letter to a Wound'. This is based on

Auden's own experience after an operation he underwent on an anal fissure which took many months to heal. The letter forms a curious coda: a love letter, it shows the extent to which illness and sufferer become one.

Part Two is 'Journal of an Airman' and the triumph of *The Orators*. It should be included in every anthology of the English short story. In it the vague impulses and solutions, needs and prognoses that preoccupied Part One are splendidly focused and dramatized in the diary of a neurotic aviator. The battle lines are drawn. The airman and his comrades face the Enemy. Although meant to function as a metaphor, the Enemy turn out to be suspiciously like the English middle classes at their smug, bourgeois worst. A strange civil war or revolution seems to be in progress in a landscape which is half Icelandic, half Cotswolds, with moors and ice floes, golf links and country pubs. The airman's tortured and paranoid voice leads us through the mounting conflict with notes and jottings, attempts at aphorisms and pensées. The need for a true Leader re-emerges, while the airman frets about his fear of his mother and his love for his homosexual uncle Harry. The voice is uniquely Auden's – D. H. Lawrence meets P. G. Wodehouse by way of Freud and Ealing comedies, if you see what I mean.

   Throughout, the airman keeps trying to define and fix the Enemy in his mind and encourage in himself the right elements of daring and fearlessness. 'Three kinds of enemy walk – the grandiose stunt – the melancholic stagger – the paranoic sidle. Three kinds of enemy face – the fucked hen – the favourite puss – the stone in the rain. Three enemy traits – refusal to undress in public – proficiency in modern languages – inability to travel back to the engine. Three kinds of enemy hand – the marsh – the claw – the dead yam.' And manically on and on. The journal has all the elisions, fractures, non sequiturs and private references one would expect. But what is most striking and admirable is the way Auden has seized on the potentiality of this literary form and exploited it to the full. Hint, allusion and half-meaning suddenly become potent assets: the briefest references can conjure up the density and detail of a long novel.

Here are some examples.

Tea today at Cardross Golf Club. A hot bed. Far too many monks in Sinclair Street.

Thursday

The Hollies. Some blazers lounge beneath a calming tree; they talk in birds' hearing; girls come with roses, servants with a tray, skirting the sprinkler preaching madly to the grass, where mower worries in the afternoons.

Fourteenth anniversary of my uncle's death. Fine. Cleaned the airgun as usual. But what have I done to avenge, to disprove the boy's faked evidence at the inquest? NOTHING.

Monday – Interviewed A about his report.

Tuesday – Pamphlet dropping in the Bridgenorth area.

Wednesday – Address at Waterworm College.

Thursday – The Hollies. 7.30.

Friday – See M about the gin to be introduced into the lemonade at the missionary whist drive.

Saturday – Committee meeting.

Sunday – Break up the Mimosa's lecture on blind flying.

We are drawn into the batty, surreal world of the airman. We are his confidant, his confessor. We share his worries (his errant love of Uncle Harry, his betrayal of Derek), his grief (Derek's death, a crash: 'His collar bone was sticking through his navel'); his love for E; the dangers of war ('A feint landing by pleasure paddle steamers near the bathing machines'); his own perpetual struggle to be heroic (28th. 3.40 am. Pulses and reflexes normal . . . Some cumulus cloud at 10,000 feet. Hands in perfect order').

The final section of *The Orators* is all poetry – six odes – with examples of Auden at his most silly ('Christopher stood, his face grown lined with wincing/In front of ignorance – "Tell the English," he shivered,/ "Man is a spirit"'); evocative ('After a night of storm was a lawn in sunlight'); and typical ('Go south, lovey, south by Royal Scot/Or hike if you like it, or hire a Ford'). But the odes are a mixed bunch, and the best have been reprinted elsewhere, as have the other poems in the body of the book. As a result the work itself has fallen into obscurity, remembered if at all as the original context for a few more famous poems ('By landscape reminded of his mother's figure' and the superb sestina 'We have brought you, they said, a map of the country'). This is a real shame, for in *The Orators* one encounters the Audenesque at its most vivid and ill-disciplined and, accordingly, most fecund and distinctive. But more than that it reveals the vast range and scope of Auden's astonishing eye for detail, Dickensian in its precision and accuracy, and provides us with that rare opportunity: to find in prose the word by word, line by line delights of poetry.

1984

Djuna Barnes

(Review of *Selected Works of Djuna Barnes*)

'Djuna was tall, quite handsome, bold voiced and a remarkable talker, full of reminiscences of her Washington Square New York life and her eccentric childhood somewhere up the Hudson.' So Janet Flanner – Paris correspondent of the *New Yorker* between the wars – recalls Djuna Barnes in *Paris Was Yesterday*. It's not much, but it's about the most we ever get on the shadowy figure of the author of *Nightwood*, that acclaimed 'black' innovatory work of the 1930s. It is true that many of the auto-biographies and memoirs of the Lost Generation make reference to her (largely of the '. . . saw Djuna last night . . .', 'Djuna Barnes was there' variety), but there is very little more and the air of mystery is main-tained. It's not dispelled, either, by this latest edition of her best-known work; there is no biographical sketch or critical introduction to *Nightwood*.

Monroe Wheeler, George Davis, Kay Boyle, Stephen Vincent Benet . . . ? Not exactly names to conjure with, but they, along with Djuna Barnes, were all members of that extraordinary gathering of talent in Paris in the 1920s and 1930s. And it is not unreasonable to speculate that Djuna Barnes's name would have about as much *éclat* as that of, say, Glenway Wescott – another critically esteemed young writer of the time – had it not been for the fact that T. S. Eliot wrote an introduc-tion to *Nightwood*, thereby assuring her of the attention of Eliot scholars and at least a footnote in the annals of that astonishingly fecund literary period.

That was in 1936, however, and Djuna Barnes had established some-thing of a reputation for herself before that as a playwright, author of short stories and wit. Born in 1892 she came to New York City at the age of twenty to study art. She supported herself through popular jour-nalism and achieved some success there with one-act plays and an illus-trated book of poems. She was a member of the New York artistic set that frequented Greenwich Village in the heyday of its rather strained post-*fin-de-siècle* bohemianism in the pre-war years.

She moved to Paris in the early 1920s, and her next two literary endeavours were novels: *Ryder* and *A Ladies' Almanack*. Both are mannered parodies of literary styles, *Ryder* retaining a slight interest through its putative autobiographical links with the author's life, and *A Ladies' Almanack* through its *roman à clef* satire of lesbian bluestocking cliques in Paris. *A Ladies' Almanack* is a heavy-going parody of an Elizabethan chap-book. There is a certain facile brilliance in the book's baroque wordiness, and Barnes enjoyed considerable notoriety as a result of having written it.

None of these early works is reproduced in this selection, which is something of a pity for they are of more intrinsic interest than *The Antiphon* (1958), a ponderously overwritten and overblown attempt to recreate a Jacobean play, full of ghastly mock-Elizabethan English lines like 'The flank-plume of the greater bird of paradise/Racked not more pride, than did the dancing lappet.'

The early works that are offered instead are a selection of her short stories first published in magazines and journals such as *Dial* and the *Little Review*. Here much of the flamboyance of *Ryder* and *A Ladies' Almanack* is abandoned for an elliptical terseness and an overdeliberate attempt to render physical sensations. These brief, shapeless tales reflect something of Djuna Barnes's skill as a stylist but the effort is marred by the glum aristocrats and neurotic pampered children she seems to prefer as characters. These improbably named figures – Dr Katerina Silverstaff, Princess Frederica Rholinghausen, Moydia – together with a perpetual air of *cafard* and decadent morbidity, give the stories an arch, affectedly gnomic quality which finally overcomes the sporadic excellence of the prose.

Djuna Barnes's reputation rests finally on *Nightwood*, which belongs to that small class of books that somehow reflect a time or an epoch, are repeatedly mentioned and infrequently read. In this context one thinks of Connolly's *The Rock Pool*, Paul Bowles's *The Sheltering Sky* or Delmore Schwartz's *In Dreams Begin Responsibilities*, all heralded in their time as signs of a promise which we can now see as never having been likely to materialize.

The book is divided into eight parts with no real development, and features a set of distraught tormented characters whose lives haphazardly interlock. The book opens with Felix, a Wandering Jew figure, coming to the aid of a young girl called Robin Vote. He falls in love with her and they marry and produce a retarded child called Guido. Robin, however, is a confused and errant wife who spends long periods away from home, eventually eloping with Nora Flood. Later, another lesbian, Jenny Petheridge, appropriates her and Nora is abandoned. She, in turn, seeks advice from the mysterious Dr O'Connor who, apropos of nothing, delivers a peroration on Night, Sleep, Dreams and the Human Condition.

This outburst forms the rhetorical centre of the book and provides us with some grounds for seeing the doctor as some kind of controlling presence. Eventually the demented Robin manages to escape from Jenny Petheridge and finds her way back to Nora. The final scene is a freakish encounter between Robin and Nora's dog. Robin gets down on her hands and knees and advances on the puzzled animal, which naturally begins to bark:

He let loose one howl of misery and bit at her, dashing about her, barking . . . Then she began to bark also crawling after him – barking in a fit of laughter, obscene and touching.

At this point the baffled hound – 'his eyes bloodshot' – gives up and lies down beside the now weeping Robin, prepared, it seems, to accept her dogginess after all. This self-imposed degradation on Robin's part clearly contains the book's symbolic import, and is no doubt what prompted T. S. Eliot's remark that it possessed 'a quality of horror and doom very nearly related to that of Elizabethan tragedy'. Today the nihilism and the loaded 'relevance' seem instead unintentionally hilarious.

1984

Nadine Gordimer and Dirk Bogarde

(Review of *July's People* by Nadine Gordimer
and *Voices in the Garden* by Dirk Bogarde)

The slimness of Nadine Gordimer's new novel gives little indication of the scope and momentous nature of its setting – namely the fall of South Africa. The date is an unspecified near future, the country is in the grip of a savage civil war. There is widespread rioting and looting. Jumbo jets packed with fleeing whites are downed by Sam missiles as they take off from Johannesburg airport.

Maureen and Bamford Smales, with their three children, escape from their ravaged suburb with the aid and assistance of their faithful black servant July. He leads them through the bush to his isolated village in some tribal trustland. There the Smales uneasily settle in, living in a native hut, trying to cope with their radically altered circumstances as the news bulletins chart the course of the Republic's last days.

This change in their fortunes inevitably transforms the relationship that existed hitherto between the Smales and July, and Nadine Gordimer uses this ironic reversal of roles to great effect. The family's survival is now fully dependent on July's goodwill and determination and, also, on that of the other villagers. July remains kind and dependable but a subtle shift in his attitude towards his charges – especially Maureen – steadily becomes evident. No longer a compliant servant, July gladly takes up the responsibilities of provider and protector and Maureen witnesses, with some misgivings, the real man emerging from the stereotypical personality his race and the master-servant relationship had conferred on him.

July's People is a fine and thoughtful exploration and critique of certain South African and colonial values, made all the more convincing through an absence of overt polemics or stridency. It's also an extremely gritty portrayal of the details of deprivation, as the Smales attempt to adapt to the lifestyle of rural Africans. Again and again Maureen has her assumptions and preconceptions challenged and undermined through the pressures, tensions and irritations of their enforced seclusion. Unaccommodated woman, she finds, is a state she's not well suited for. The novel ends with the arrival of a helicopter – we don't know whether it's friend or foe – and Maureen impulsively runs off through the bush to the spot where it has touched down, abandoning the village, her husband and children in a desperate attempt to flee her responsibilities.

We never learn her fate. This fashionably 'open' and ambiguous ending gives rise to one dissatisfaction in an otherwise very accomplished and beautifully written novel. Put simply, *July People* is an investigation of certain types of human relationships – black and white, servant and boss, husband and wife – under extreme stress. But its background of inter-national disaster and war consorts less easily with the nuances of psycho-logical insight with which it is really concerned.

It's not just a question of the sketchiness of Gordimer's political predictions but also that the 'escape and survival' literary tradition with which the novel aligns itself – and which is handled most effectively – demands a less ethereal narrative conclusion. Having got us so inter-ested in what is going to happen to the Smaleses there's a genuine sense of disappointment when we find that it's left to us to supply a conclusion.

There's no such problem in the case of Dirk Bogarde's second novel as, from the outset, it fails to arouse even a suspicion of curiosity about the destinies of the empty characters that populate its pages. The rambling storyline concerns an aged English couple who live in a sumptuous villa on the Côte d'Azur, and the various guests they receive there over the course of the summer. They include an English youth and his German girlfriend and a tyrannical Italian film director and his acolytes. The characters swim, drink, eat, make love and indulge in very long dialogues about their various pretty inconsequential problems. They appear to be assembled there not to satisfy any demands of plot but rather to provide excuses for elegant descriptive set-pieces:

The terrace was deserted, shaded, the fountain bubbling softly, a bowl of full blown roses, deep cane chairs, in a bucket a bottle of Laurent Perrier, a neat white cloth about its shoulders, two glasses; moisture beading.

Bogarde actually does this sort of thing very well, albeit with a heavy emphasis on up-market consumerism, and makes this life of sybaritic languor almost palpably appealing. We have a close and precise acquaintanceship with the objects and accoutrements of this world – the drinks, the decor and the clothes – but Bogarde's descriptive abilities fail to enlighten us about the individuals who inhabit it.

1981

Michel Tournier

(Review of *Gemini*)

Gemini, first published in France in 1975 under the title *Les Météores*, is Michel Tournier's third novel. His first was *Friday* and his second, winner of the Prix Goncourt, was *The Erl King*. We are fortunate to have them now all excellently translated into English, for they represent a sequence of remarkable and extraordinary books, each characterized by Tournier's highly distinctive way of looking at the world and by a speculative, imaginative philosophy that seems quite alien to British traditions of thought.

Tournier was trained as a philosopher, but his intellectual allegiance is not to the analytical, empirical methods we are most familiar with in this country but rather to the great metaphysical systems which we recognize, in our insular way, as being particularly European. Tournier's approach, to simplify considerably, is to seek for significance in things, to see always in the random occurrence or the individual object some intimation of the universal, some hint of the divine or cosmological plan. In *Friday* he retold Defoe's *Robinson Crusoe*, reconstituting the well-known aspects of the classic adventure in terms of a potent and evocative mythology of human nature. In *The Erl King* the life of a bizarre paedophilic giant and the Second World War are so combined and inter-woven as to explore the mysterious workings and consequences of personal and global destiny.

Gemini is a similar exercise. In it the compelling notion of twinship – the enclosed self-sufficient world of twins, and its disruption – becomes an elaborate model for the way we encounter and deal with the phys-ical universe, the world of phenomena. Jean and Paul Surin are iden-tical twins. Their childhood and youth is one of idyllic and almost unreal harmony. They speak a private language, and their communion with each other is intense and profoundly satisfying. When the pairing is broken – Jean meets a girl, then runs away – Paul strives vainly to find him, touring the world in a frantic search for, literally, his other half.

The breaking of the bond forces Paul to enter the unfamiliar milieu of what Tournier calls dispaired twinship and its fractured perceptual world, conditioned by defective dispaired vision. Essentially, the final third of the novel is to do with Paul's coming to terms with his 'disability', with attempting to regain something of the wholeness and 'ubiquity' he experienced when paired with his twin. Burrowing under the Berlin wall (another loaded symbol of disjunction) in pursuit of Jean he is hideously injured. His left arm and leg are amputated, his emotional deprivation now loathsomely figured in his missing limbs. But this appalling setback forces him into self-reliance; the pursuit of the other twin is now necessarily over.

The novel's end sees Paul coming to terms with his solitariness. He achieves a new integration and fusion with the world around him which – though different – is as immediate and satisfying as that he'd reached with his twin:

A cloud forms in the sky, like an image in my brain, the wind blows as I breathe, a rainbow spans the heavens in the time it takes my life to become reconciled to life . . . just as twinship has its own language . . . so has dispaired twinship. The dispaired (twin) hears the voices of all things as the voice of his own moods.

The grand theme of *Gemini* is, in essence, to bring about a restoration of the abstract with the particular, to recombine the numinous with the everyday. Paul's triumph at the end of the book makes it clear that such achievements aren't confined to twins.

1981

Milan Kundera

(Review of *The Unbearable Lightness of Being*)

This novel begins with a myth. Suppose that every act we committed in our life on earth was destined to be repeated, not just once, but in an endless series of cycles. In that case everything we did, trivial and grand, from minor sin to major goodness, would be invested with a momentous importance simply because of its permanence in the scheme of things. Every act of kindness, selfishness, deceit, self-regard would be etched on existence for ever. And, consequently, we would think twice, thrice, many times, before acting – our lives would be weighted down with import and significance, with unbearable responsibility.

But if, on the other hand, life is instead merely an endless linear flow of time, then every act, every moment, is at once unique and lost for ever – gone in an instant, never to return. The upshot of this theory is that life becomes an affair of utter insignificance, a droll succession of inconsequences – living (Being) is frivolous, transitory, light.

Kundera introduces these two opposing notions at the outset of this – his fifth and best – novel and throughout further opposes their two related qualities of lightness and weight. Which is better (I paraphrase drastically) – a life lived burdened by the weight of responsibility? Or a life lived unfettered by duty and moral injunction: a life of perfect, airy freedom?

This dilemma summarizes what I take to be the essence of this complicated and thoughtful novel. In a typically Kunderan manner, these questions emerge from a disjointed and rambling blend of wry philosophical speculation and fiction. Kundera himself discourses on and redefines a variety of subjects and categories (including vertigo, dreaming, nudity, betrayal, noses, abroad and WCs, among others) while, fictionally, the choices are dramatized in the lives of a pair of couples – Tomas and Tereza and Franz and Sabina – each of whom represents, in varying degrees, one or other aspect of the polarity of lightness and weight. Franz and Sabina have their roles to play in the enacting of ideas, but the central couple is Tomas and Tereza.

Tomas is a successful surgeon and philanderer who, by a series of chances, ends up one day in a provincial hotel where he attracts, inadvertently, the love of a waitress – Tereza. On impulse Tereza follows him to Prague where they become lovers and soon fall in love. Even after they are married, however, Tomas continues to sleep around, but his life has changed more than domestically with the arrival of Tereza, for Tereza is afflicted with 'weight' – a sense of the unbearable responsibility of being. And Tomas, one might expect, is lightness personified. But soon he finds – like it or not – that his soaring irresponsibility begins to be tethered: he gains – metaphysically speaking – weight.

He renounces a prosperous career as a surgeon in Zurich to follow Tereza back to Prague after the Russian invasion of Czechoslovakia. There, his career charts a steep decline owing to an ill-timed political article he has written. From top surgeon he descends to local GP, and from there to window cleaner. Ultimately, Tereza persuades him to leave the city and they go to work on a farm in the country where, before they die in a car smash, they find their own brand of happiness and Tomas – or so I take it – shoulders the burdens of responsibility and contentedly renounces 'lightness'.

'Weight', as Kundera defines it, is to do with love, compassion and a true sense of the absurd dictates of chance and contingency. 'Lightness' is to do with sex, frivolity and irresponsibility. In the novel Kundera debates and counterposes the reasons for and the consequences of choosing one or the other. The dialectic is urbanely, wittily and cleverly orchestrated. One senses too – and Kundera encourages us to think so – that the conflict is a highly individual one ('The characters in my novels are my own unrealised possibilities') born out of his own personality and his experience at the hands of the malign and bizarre forces of recent European history.

In a significant sense, then, *The Unbearable Lightness of Being* can be described as an intensely moral book which, for all its superficial postmodernist totems (paraded fictiveness, blatant authorial intervention, disdain of basic narrative convention), would satisfy the most stringent and traditional imperatives of Leavisite 'relevance' and 'value'. For, in the novel, Kundera is really attempting to answer the key questions of how we should live our lives, given the sordid, perplexed and fraught nature of the human condition, and of the place of Love in a world seemingly compromised by corruption, self-delusion and evil.

His answer is dramatized – most movingly – in the death from cancer of Tomas and Tereza's dog Karenin (the name is no accident). The animal's slow, puzzled, wracked demise becomes a focus for all those traditional verities – compassion, understanding, disinterested love – so opposed to 'lightness' and all it stands for. On the penultimate page of the novel Tereza apologizes for the way she has literally and metaphorically brought him down. 'Haven't you noticed I've been happy here?' Tomas says.

The Unbearable Heaviness of Being is of course a far more complex notion than this review can convey. It's not, for example, to be confused with earnestness or commitment, and has *nothing* to do with political ideology (an elaborate disquisition on the phenomenon of 'kitsch' denies weight to the passionate idealists of both East and West, Left and Right). It seems to be, to simplify once again, a steadfastly ironic facing up to all the sadness of the human condition, coupled with an awareness of the value of the modest and fleeting moments of happiness it can also provide (Tomas's declaration occurs on the last night of his and Tereza's life). The modish *succès fou* of this book does it a huge disservice: this is a clever, thoughtful, intellectually stimulating, occasionally flawed novel, but its central concerns are perennially valuable and humane.

1984

Evelyn Waugh (1)

(Introduction to *Labels*)

Evelyn Waugh was not fond of *Labels*, his fourth published book. In an interview given later in his life he referred to it dismissively as 'a collection of essays bundled together'. In 1946, when he edited all his travel writing for the compilation *When the Going Was Good* only fifty of *Labels*' 200 pages were included. Indeed, superficially, there does not appear much to recommend the book. An account of a cruise in the Mediterranean is hardly exotic. A few weeks on a luxury liner would not qualify one as an intrepid traveller. Also, the assignment was undertaken solely for money (although I realize that this does not imply, a priori, that the work will be bad) and was written up at speed over a period of two months in early 1930. And yet, in my opinion, this, the first of Waugh's many travel books, is his best and most fascinating, and, for reasons which we will discover, it is a highly significant document with an important bearing on the development of Waugh's oeuvre and is a vital clue as to why Waugh's personality took the abrasive, complex and troubled course it did.

In 1929, when the trip that was to provide the raw material for *Labels* was undertaken, Waugh was twenty-six years old. He had just published his first novel, *Decline and Fall*, to tremendous critical and popular acclaim. He was a 'fashionable' young writer, a self-appointed spokesman for Modern Youth and made regular appearances in the gossip columns. Life had finally taken a dramatic turn for the better. For, after the pleasant distractions and rowdy hedonism of Oxford, Waugh's fortunes had reached a low ebb. He attempted vainly to become an artist and illustrator but lack of money drove him to badly paid jobs in remote preparatory schools. While his Oxford contemporaries were establishing reputations for themselves Waugh was miserably unhappy. He wanted to be an artist, he wanted to move easily in English high society, he wanted to be wealthy and he wanted to be in love. In the disappointing years following his university career it looked very unlikely that he would ever achieve any of these ambitions. But then the publication of *Decline and Fall* (1928) changed everything. He was now a novelist (albeit a reluctant one), celebrated, wined and dined, had made some money and there was now the prospect of making more, and he was married. Waugh had married (just prior to the publication of *Decline and Fall*) a pretty girl called Evelyn Gardner. They were known to their friends as 'he-Evelyn' and 'she-Evelyn'. Evelyn Gardner was 'modern' (her blonde hair was cut in a short bob), wanted to write herself, and was well bred – she was the daughter of Lord Burghclere. Everything seemed to be perfect. They were both very happy and they lived in a small flat in London in Canonbury Square.

In the winter of 1928 'she-Evelyn' fell ill with a bad attack of German measles. To help her convalesce and to allow Waugh to write a travel book (while he gathered material for his next novel) a Mediterranean cruise was planned. Waugh's agent managed to negotiate the Waughs' free passage on the MY *Stella Polaris* in return for favourable mentions of the ship in *Labels*. In the gossip column of the *Daily Sketch* their departure was reported thus: the Waughs

were about to spend the proceeds of *Decline and Fall* in a tour of Southeastern Europe and the Levant . . . in the most luxurious boat in the whole Mediterranean . . . Mr Waugh is going to write a travel diary about the trip . . . But there is more to come: 'I am really going to concentrate on drawing during the voyage . . . I hope I can bring back enough sketches to hold an exhibition in June, and, if it is successful, abandon writing for painting.'

We can see how the idea of earning his living from the pen was still essentially uncongenial to Waugh.

But the voyage was not a success. The couple caught a train to Monte Carlo, where they were to board the *Stella Polaris*, but on the journey south she-Evelyn fell ill once more with a high fever. She was ill throughout the first portion of the cruise – Naples, Haifa, Port Said – with what was later diagnosed as pneumonia. She-Evelyn was moved to hospital in Port Said and the *Stella Polaris* sailed on without the Waughs. When she-Evelyn was feeling better they moved to a large hotel near Cairo. For the first time the two of them actually began to feel they were on holiday.

From Egypt they sailed to Malta where they managed to rejoin the *Stella Polaris* for the rest of her voyage – Crete, Constantinople, Venice, Ragusa and Barcelona were among the places they visited. The enforced delay in Port Said and Cairo and the medical bills that ensued there meant that Waugh had spent far more than he had planned on the cruise. On the way home to England he wrote as many newspaper articles as he reasonably could in an attempt to defray his expenses.

The trip had been something of a disaster, but none of this appears in *Labels*. The itinerary is the same but the circumstances of the voyage are altered beyond recognition – to the extent that a pronounced fictional element enters the narrative. The single, simple reason for this is that shortly after their return to London the Waughs' marriage collapsed irretrievably.

This process had been accelerated by the now pressing financial reasons for Waugh to write his second novel (which was to be *Vile Bodies*). In order for him to do this quickly he had to be alone and away from the social distractions of London. Waugh went to stay in a pub near Oxford – the Abingdon Arms in the village of Beckley – and immediately set to work on his novel. She-Evelyn remained in London, now fully recovered and determined to enjoy the social round after the enervating problems of her two-month cruise.

This is not the place to analyse the reasons for the breakdown of Evelyn Waugh's marriage. To put it simply, she-Evelyn met another man with whom she fell in love. She told Waugh this and he abandoned his novel and returned home in an attempt to win her back. She-Evelyn promised never to see her lover again but their reunion proved to be an unhappy time together. After two miserable weeks they decided to get divorced.

Waugh was devastated by the failure of his marriage and by what he saw as his public humiliation. I do not believe that it is an overstatement to say that his divorce and his wife's betrayal affected him for the rest of his life. It brought about a profound change in the way he saw the world and in the way he presented himself to others. It was a major reason for him embracing the Catholic faith a few years later and its reverberations can be detected in almost all his subsequent fiction.

In the months following the separation Waugh wrote *Vile Bodies*. Much of that novel's remorseless clear-eyed cynicism is a product of Waugh's bitter and misanthropic mental state at the time.

Labels, which he had to begin almost immediately after, must have seemed like the most thankless of tasks: to relive in prose the two difficult months preceding his wife's betrayal. Waugh set about it with professional purpose. The book is based on detailed diaries (which he later destroyed) which he had kept throughout the trip, but she-Evelyn is expunged from the record. Waugh presents himself as a bachelor, travelling alone, a reserved and supercilious presence observing his fellow voyagers with a neutral, objective gaze. Amongst his travelling companions is a young couple, Geoffrey and Juliet, who are on their honeymoon:

a rather sweet-looking young English couple – presumably, from the endearments of their conversation and marked solicitude for each other's comfort, on their honeymoon, or at any rate recently married. The young man was small and pleasantly dressed and wore a slight curly moustache; he was reading a particularly good detective story with apparent intelligence. His wife was huddled in a fur coat in the corner, clearly far from well.

Geoffrey and Juliet: he-Evelyn and she-Evelyn.

In this curious, schizoid way Waugh contemplates himself and his ex-wife. Indirectly, from time to time we learn of Geoffrey and Juliet's difficult voyage, of Juliet's illness and hospitalization, of Geoffrey's deep concern and worry. From time to time, too, Geoffrey and Waugh go out together and visit the sights of Port Said. It is not putting too fine a point on it, I think, to see in *Labels* Waugh bidding farewell to his former self. An altogether tougher, more self-sufficient and, it has to be said, unpleasant persona emerged.

'The young man was small and pleasantly dressed and wore a slight curly moustache.' Waugh was blond and only five foot five inches tall. He was a small, fair, boisterous young man. 'Faunlike' and 'childlike' are adjectives contemporaries used to describe him in the Twenties. It is worth recalling this – and his diminutive size – especially in the face of the image of Waugh that has survived (in Britain at least) after his death. Waugh is remembered as an aggressive man, a snob and of reactionary tastes and political opinions. Fat and choleric, playing out a role – very deliberately – of a testy colonel or outraged Tory squire; dressed in loud-check tweeds and brandishing an ear-trumpet, the image of the elder Waugh is calculated to give offence. It was an ideal mask to hide behind. The great value of *Labels*, once one knows its history, is that we can see the first steps in the construction of that mask which, with various adornments, was to serve him well throughout the rest of his life. Only in his fiction was it allowed to drop; only there can we see, to employ T. S. Eliot's dichotomy, the 'man who suffers' behind the 'mind which creates'. And this honesty is what redeems Waugh the artist in the end, no matter how repugnant we find the man he forced himself to be.

This too explains much about *Labels*. The book is by a man at his most vulnerable, writing about a period in his recent history which must have been, thanks to the cruel ironies of hindsight, almost unbearably painful. This must go a long way to explain the hauteur in the tone of voice, the mandarin pomposities that surface occasionally in the style and the disdain and xenophobia that are apparent in the content.

These were not new attitudes. Even as a schoolboy Waugh understood how to be superior. But in *Labels* we see the fashioning of a creed, and aesthetic, that was to see Waugh through until his death. I do not think that anybody reading the book 'blind', as it were, would guess its author's age to be twenty-seven. The voice has the confidence of a man almost twice that age; of a man unlikely to be persuaded that there are other points of view with equal validity.

In this sense it is also a very English book, and manifests a very English sense of its own essential superiority and worth in comparison to all the other races of the world. It is an Englishman who contemplates other cultures and civilizations armed with

a vague knowledge of History, Literature and Art, an amateurish interest in architecture and costume, of social, religious, and political institutions, of drama, of the biographies of the chief characters of each century, of a few anecdotes and jokes, scraps of diaries and correspondence and family history . . . fused together . . . so that the cultured Englishman has a sense of the past, in a continuous series of clear and pretty *tableaux vivants*.

As it happens this is still a pretty good definition of the 'cultured Englishman', and it represents the point of view of the sort of man Waugh aspired to be. But such a man would be unlikely to admire Gaudi's *Sagrada Familia*. And here again we come to the complexity and contradiction that underlie all of Waugh's work. He was a deeply sensitive man who behaved like a boor; an aesthete with precise refined tastes who dressed like a bookmaker . . . a long list of such antitheses can be compiled. And it is in these conflicting impulses that we find, I believe, the key to the many and varied pleasures his books provide, and *Labels* is no exception. We experience a frisson of outrage at some racial slight, recoil at opinions of absurdly dogmatic cast and yet at the same time are challenged and intrigued by observations and judgements of genuine originality and acuity. In the end Waugh's brilliance – one might say his particular genius – is to defeat all easy categorizations. For, whatever

Labels' fascinating autobiographical pertinence, it is also a tremendously fresh, funny and stimulating book. But there is no denying that a knowledge of the circumstances in which it was written adds considerably to its overall impact. It is ultimately a sad book; it is the fruit of sad and chastening experience, and no one acquainted with Waugh's own personal grief, and understanding the poignancy of his hurt and disillusion, can dismiss the book's final lines as merely the product of a precocious or affected sagacity:

Fortune is the least capricious of deities, and arranges things on the just and rigid system that no one shall be very happy for very long.

1988

Raymond Carver

(Review of 'Where I'm Calling From',
The Selected Stories)

'The style is the man,' Buffon said, and one wonders what he would make of a man who wrote like this:

This friend of mine from work, Bud, he asked Fran and me to supper. I didn't know his wife and he didn't know Fran. That made us even. But Bud and I were friends. And I knew there was a little baby at Bud's house. That baby must have been eight months old when Bud asked us to supper. Where'd those eight months go?

These are the opening lines of a short story called 'Feathers' and in them we are presented with what one might call stereotypical Raymond Carver: the demotic first person voice, the short sentences, the reduced vocabulary, the pointed unliterariness (the ugly repetitions of 'know' and 'Bud'). A few more sentences and the picture is complete: Bud and the narrator are blue-collar workers, the context is parochial – white, working class, middle America – and the events of the story, its narrative, minimal in the extreme.

This selection of thirty-seven stories was made by Carver himself before his premature death in 1988 at the age of fifty. The consistency of tone, style, setting and mood of the stories is remarkable, and, with a few variations, they roughly conform to the stereotype outlined above. Occasionally the protagonists become more affluent (or less) and occasionally the pronoun shifts to the third person, but it is clear that Carver had found his two inches of ivory and was prepared to work it as doggedly as he could.

And there is nothing wrong with this. The only danger is that by confining your focus and by making your voice so insistently individual and unchanging an element of self-parody unwittingly creeps in, and the writer becomes a victim of his own success. There may be a rough rule of thumb here that needn't only apply to writers, namely: the easier it is to parody an artist's style, the sooner the artist ought to change it. Something similar happened to Hemingway, a writer with whom Carver can stand some comparison. The style of Hemingway's early stories was as terse, uncompromising and idiosyncratic as Carver's and it made a similar impact. Each man, it seemed, had found a fully formed and distinct voice that was perfectly attuned to their particular vision of the world and that harmoniousness lent the prose an unmistakable authority and literary heft. But it was not sustainable; or rather it *was*, but a price had to be paid when every Eng. Lit. undergraduate could soon turn in a passable Hemingway parody with no trouble at all. And something of the same law of diminishing returns applies to Carver's stories, even though, as he himself claimed, he made efforts in his last collection to broaden his canvas and enrich his palette. In a late story such as 'Blackbird Pie' where the narrator appears to be an academic, the voice is educated and peppered with literary allusions but it seems epicene, uncarveresque. We want a misanthropic redneck in a trailer park musing on how awful life is.

This phenomenon, this double bind, occurs in various art forms but bears particularly on short story writers and painters. Throughout the ups and many downs of his career Scott Fitzgerald was constantly asked to reprise his tales of ditsy flappers in the Twenties, and Picasso's reputation is still haunted by the enormous popularity of his 'Blue period' paintings. Any number of other examples come to mind but the 'problem' remains the same: what is first acclaimed as powerful and original soon becomes confining and restricting. The artist wants to develop and advance but does so at the risk of losing what has drawn the public to the artist in the first place.

Thirty-seven short stories may seem a smallish oeuvre upon which to build a significant reputation yet there is no doubt that Carver's achievement is considerable and that he deserves his place in the pantheon of American letters. The down-and-out, the hobo, the underachievers of American life have all had their chroniclers (from Damon Runyon to John Fante to Charles Bukowski) but Carver's bleak but fundamentally humane point of view has a distinct late twentieth-century feel to it, if only because it is so resolutely low-key, the prose studiedly refusing to indulge in sentimentality, sensationalism or bathos. In spite of all the despair and waste, the hardship and relentless grind, Carver's stories do somehow seem to celebrate some lasting aspects of the human condition, however minimal, conjuring up something marginally positive, a quality of fellow feeling that may amount to nothing more than a recognition that – at the end of the day – we are all in this mess together, but which gives the stories a compelling dry-eyed poignancy, a bitter but intensely moving authenticity.

1993

Michael Ondaatje

(Review of *The English Patient*)

In a semi-ruined villa somewhere in the north of Italy in the final year of World War Two a young Canadian nurse called Hana – numbed by the horrors of war – cares for a hideously burned aviator who has no name. He is the English patient, his brittle, cauterized skin the colour of aubergine. He is alone in the villa, the nurse his sole company, left behind to die, one assumes, by the field hospital that once occupied the building. The nurse bathes him, reads to him, listens to him and injects him with morphine to mask the agony of his terrifying burns.

This is the opening of Michael Ondaatje's new novel, and it is hard to imagine a better and more disturbing *mise en scène*, combining as it does all manner of romantic, gothic and mysterious elements: a young and beautiful woman tending to a terminally disfigured man in an antique and classical landscape ravaged by war. What secrets lie here, what explanations, what undercurrents of feeling, of emotion? Guilt and loss, pain and redemption, endurance and love . . . The book is gravid with the potential to move and beguile.

And Ondaatje does not disappoint. A poet turned novelist, his interest in his characters and their situation leans heavily towards their symbolic and elegiac aspects. And indeed, this curious conjunction of nurse and patient could have occurred in any war in any place in almost any time. A reader expecting the conventions of a realistic novel such as Hemingway's *A Farewell to Arms* (another juxtaposition of nurse and patient in an Italian war) will be frustrated. Ondaatje eschews the nuts and bolts of period detail, the roughage of authentic fact, for the trenchant reverberation of metaphor and image. And in so doing the book sets entirely its own tone and its own conventions. To ask a question of it along the lines of: would the senior staff of a World War Two army field hospital *really* abandon a traumatized young nurse and one of its badly burned patients in a bomb-damaged villa while it moved on to safer and more secure quarters? is redundant, not to say pedantic. Ondaatje's novel is hermetic and self-sufficient, its conventions and its final reality – and its strange power – belong to it alone.

In the event the nurse, Hana, and her patient are not left to each other's company for long. They are joined by a man named David Caravaggio, a friend of Hana's late father. Caravaggio, a former cat-burglar from Toronto, has spent the war in intelligence and is himself recovering from wounds, only this time wounds inflicted by torture – his thumbs have been amputated. He claims to be concerned for Hana's health and safety but it soon becomes clear that his real interest is in the English patient. Soon the trio is augmented by a fourth figure – a young Sikh bomb disposal expert, called Kip, who billets himself in the villa grounds while he tries to defuse the multiplicity of booby traps that the retreating Germans have set in the Tuscan countryside.

Slowly, steadily, the histories of these four emerge as they converse. We learn of Caravaggio's capture and torture, of Kip's training in England and his mastering of the precise and delicate art of bomb disposal, of Hana's experience of the suffering and agonies of the dressing stations – the endless stream of broken and dying young men she tried to tend and comfort. And slowly too we begin to learn more about the English patient. A history begins to take shape, piecemeal, of his life before the war. We discover he was an Arabist and explorer in the Sahara, a scholar-soldier on the T. E. Lawrence model. We are told also of a doomed love affair with an Englishwoman, Katherine Clifton, the wife of a colleague, and its ultimate tragedy, and of his own final crash and rescue from his burning aeroplane by the Bedouin.

Ondaatje's method and approach in the relating of these contrasting histories are both unusual and admirable. The narrative point of view is omniscient – we enter and quit the minds and experience of the other characters at will. Stylistically too the tone is fluid and changing. Tenses move from the present to the past and back again. Dialogue is presented with and without quotation marks. We transfer easily from meditation to monologue, from reverie to orthodox description. Anecdotes and digressions blend and recur: there is a disquisition on winds, on the fusing of bombs; key texts are referred to repeatedly – Kipling's *Kim* and Herodotus' great *History*. The language is lucid and vivid, certain moments, certain images, held and rendered with a clarity that gives them the lyric force of an epiphany:

They found my body and made me a boat of sticks and dragged me across the desert. We were in the Sand Sea, now and then crossing dry riverbeds. Nomads, you see. Bedouin. I flew down and the sand itself caught fire. They saw me stand up naked out of it. The leather helmet on my head in flames. They strapped me onto a cradle, a carcass boat, and feet thudded along as they ran with me. I had broken the spareness of the desert.

Back at the villa, Hana and Kip enter into an intense but platonic affair and Caravaggio's inquisition of the English patient becomes more suspect and thorough. Dosing the patient with morphine to make him more garrulous, Caravaggio begins to dig for the truth. We learn more about events in the Sahara just preceding the war. Caravaggio suspects that the patient is in fact a man called Ladislau Almasy, a Hungarian explorer who, when the war came, flew with the Afrika Corps and guided German spies across the desert behind British lines. Bit by bit, under Caravaggio's prompting, the identification of Almasy and the English patient becomes more plausible and the events that led to his blazing fall from the air and hellish disfiguration are revealed as a bizarre and tragic confluence of his love affair with Katherine Clifton and an episode of espionage skulduggery and double bluff that went disastrously wrong.

It would be unjust to spell this out in any more detail. The truth about the English patient is revealed by degrees, teased out from the warp and woof of the narrative in a manner that is both bold and confident. Ondaatje diverts and muddles the linear flow of the novel most skilfully here: the structure of the story circles, recoils, coagulates, pauses and digresses while moving us inexorably forward (as it must – one can only tamper and meddle with linearity: the novel will have its way in the end). From time to time – for my taste, at least – the romantic elements grow a little too heady and the moody atmospherics of the cast and their situation veer dangerously towards cliché and self-parody. This is particularly true of the English patient's love for Katherine Clifton, who emerges as an improbable cross between Virginia Woolf and Mary Astor. One night in the desert she recites some poetry: 'I am a man who did not enjoy poetry until I heard a woman recite it to us. And in that desert she dragged her university days into our midst to describe the stars – the way Adam tenderly taught a woman with gracious metaphors . . . That night I fell in love with a voice. Only a voice. I got up and walked away.'

But these are rare lapses. Normally the rigour of the language effectively counterposes the pitfalls of sentiment and bathos with commendable skill and *The English Patient* – through the intelligence and originality of its structure and the passion and potency of its telling – marks a significant advance in Michael Ondaatje's growing reputation.

1998

Albert Camus

(Review of *Albert Camus: A Life* by Olivier Todd)

I would wager that, of all post-war French writers, the best known in Britain, the most widely read and the most cherished is Albert Camus. I use the word 'cherished' advisedly because Camus is one of those writers who, as our reading matures, introduces us to the world of literature. Or, to put it another way, Camus is one of those writers who produced one of those books that marks a reader's life indelibly. I refer of course to *L'Etranger*. It is like *Catcher in the Rye* or *Catch-22*, like *Lucky Jim* or *Brideshead Revisited* (and a handful of others) – one remembers vividly the actual reading of the book itself, the sense of unfolding revelation afforded, however modest, of doors being opened, the power of one writer's imagination impinging irrevocably on your own.

In Camus's case a reading of *L'Etranger* was invariably followed by *The Myth of Sisyphus*, then *The Plague*, *The Fall* and so on – the urge to consume the entire oeuvre was a vital part of this writer's allure. And yet one knew very little about Camus himself, other than he was Algerian, liked soccer, had won the Nobel Prize and died young (he was forty-six) in a car crash.

Which was why the publication of Olivier Todd's superb biography of the man was so welcome: clear-eyed, compendious, with full access to the Camus's archive, it fulfilled every expectation and its publication in France last year was a cultural event. It is rare and gratifying to have an English 'version' (more of that later) so swiftly.

Camus was born in 1913. Ten months after his birth his father was dead, a conscripted soldier, an early victim of the Battle of the Marne, a tragedy that condemned the surviving members of his family – a wife and two sons – to a life of near abject poverty. Camus, like James Joyce, never forgot the genuine privations of his early life and, also like Joyce, he saw his intellect as a source of escape. He was bright, ambitious and, one senses, remarkably sure of his destiny. As a young man in 1930s Algeria he joined the Communist party (and was expelled), plunged himself into the world of theatre – acting, producing, directing – married and divorced (his first wife was a morphine addict) but all the while nurtured dreams of becoming a writer.

Camus was also tubercular, gravely so, and his life from the age of seventeen was dogged with bouts of ill-health and the enervating pre-antibiotics treatments of his lesioned lungs. In Algeria, in the years before the start of the Second World War, the young Camus established a formidable reputation as a campaigning journalist, a left-wing intellectual with a fully developed social conscience and, it has to be noted, a compulsive womanizer. It was only the outbreak of war that took him to Paris (he was too unwell to be called up) where he began writing *L'Etranger* in 1940.

The novel was published in 1942, followed shortly after by the philosophical essay *The Myth of Sisyphus*. Camus, remarkably, was only twenty-eight years old. By the time of the liberation of France he was already acclaimed in intellectual circles and his trenchant journalism in the resistance newspaper *Combat* added to his renown.

Indeed, Camus often thought that fame came too early to him: in the late 1940s he was an internationally bestselling author, his name (to his constant irritation) was for ever linked with Sartre as a founder of Existentialism and his life subsequently became that of the classic Left-Bank *intello* moving in all the right socio-cultural circles. He worked for his publishers, Gallimard, he travelled, he had many love affairs, he hobnobbed in the fashionable cafes and brasseries but he always remained, it is clear from Todd's account, something of an outsider. This may simply have been a matter of temperament, or it may have been the ever-present proximity of death (the severity of Camus's tuberculosis is one of the book's key illuminations), or it may have been the fact that he was a *pied-noir*, an Algerian, never feeling truly at home in France.

In the event, he quarrelled bitterly with Sartre and after the start of the Algerian war in 1955 found himself even more isolated by his refusal both to support the FLN freedom fighters and to condemn France's colonial oppression. Ironically, it was at this stage, in 1957 aged forty-four, that he was awarded the Nobel Prize for Literature and his elevation to the Pantheon was assured.

And then he was killed, on 4 January 1960, in a car crash, being driven back to Paris from his new home in Provence and the legend, and the disputes about his greatness, or lack of it, began.

Todd's biography is both remarkably thorough and candid, and will prove indispensable to all those interested in Camus's life. However this English translation falls short on several counts. First it has been severely abridged: 'some material not of sufficient interest to the British and

American general reader has been omitted', so runs the translator Benjamin Ivry's introduction. This is disingenuous – only the economics of publishing could explain such significant cutting. Much has gone: notwithstanding the natural brevity of English, Todd's 767 pages of French text somehow become 420 English ones. Furthermore, in Todd's concluding chapter in the French edition he makes a profound and highly important comparison between Camus and George Orwell as exemplary figures of the heterodox left. This is mysteriously omitted in the English edition – but surely this would be 'of sufficient interest' to the anglophone general reader? Further comparisons between the two texts throw up other anomalies. For example: a chapter entitled 'Un regard myope' becomes in English 'Algerian Grief'. The harmless adjective *'foutu'* ('done for' in my dictionary) is a coarse 'fucked-up' in the English text (Ivry tends to inflame the mildest profanities). 'Je n'ai plus un sou' is rendered as 'I don't have a dime' (what could be wrong with 'I don't have a sou'?). Certain infelicities of style draw attention to themselves: 'His palling around deepened into friendships, as Albert became more choosy.' The French is: 'Des copains deviennent des amis. Albert cloisonne.' Todd's own style is punchy and terse and written in the present tense – which one would have thought would have favoured the English version, but here all present tenses have routinely been made past.

Still, despite these nagging worries and a sense of disquiet at being served up something indubitably boiled down, this biography remains completely fascinating for the portrait of Camus that emerges and, incidentally, for its depiction of the snake-pit of post-war French intellectual and political life. The debate over Camus's status still rages across the Channel (interestingly, it is far more secure here) but Todd, I think, establishes the nature of Camus's appeal and importance with great insight and skill. Its essence is contained in Camus's own modestly couched ambition: 'What interests me is knowing how we should behave, and more precisely, knowing how to behave when one does not believe in God or reason.' These are, in the end, interests we all possess, and answers we all seek. This is what provides the universal element in Camus's work and this is what will make it endure.

1997

Jean-Jacques Rousseau

(Review of *The Solitary Self: Jean-Jacques Rousseau in Exile and Adversity* by Maurice Cranston)

This is volume three of the late Maurice Cranston's magisterial and definitive biography of Jean-Jacques Rousseau. Volume one appeared in 1983, volume two in 1991 and now the grand project is completed. Alas, Maurice Cranston did not live to see the final volume published but those of us who have been impatiently reading and waiting over the last fourteen years will not be disappointed. All of Cranston's scholarly and writerly credentials are on full display: the vast learning, quietly incorporated, the feel for the eighteenth century in all its social, cultural and intellectual aspects and, most importantly for the non-academic reader, a prose of limpid readability, a dry and worldly sense of humour and the ability to fix a character or a place or a moment with apparently effortless skill.

Volume three begins in 1762 in Switzerland with Rousseau at the height of his fame and notoriety. *The Social Contract* had been written, his novel *La Nouvelle Héloïse* has enjoyed wild success throughout Europe, turning him into a cult figure, and his treatise on the education of children, *Emile*, has fomented acclaim and hysterical derogation in equal measure. In fact it was the spiralling controversy over *Emile* that led the French *parlement* to order the burning of the book and the arrest of the author.

So Rousseau fled to the land of his birth seeking exile and asylum, but this last phase of his life was to prove as unsettled and disturbing as anything that his earlier career had witnessed. The fifty-year-old Jean-Jacques cut an eccentric figure: still living with his slatternly common-law wife Thérèse Levasseur, he was plagued by urinary problems that necessitated use of a catheter and the wearing of an Armenian kaftan to make him more comfortable (he had need of a chamber pot every few minutes, he claimed). He settled in Môtiers in the canton of Berne trying to write his biography and going for long botanizing walks in the mountains. But a quiet life was always to be denied Rousseau, however arduously he tried to create one: he had powerful friends to protect him but also many enemies determined to make his life difficult. Also his renown was such that however reclusive and anonymous he sought to be admirers would beat a path to his door for audiences. One of the most amusing and best detailed of these was with the young James Boswell (who introduced himself as 'I am a Scottish laird of ancient lineage').

Rousseau was never wholly secure or at ease in Switzerland – the cantonal governments saw him as a dangerous dissident – and his few years there were fraught with vain lobbying to confirm his residential status. Rousseau's paranoia grew, not unjustifiably, and he saw himself as dogged by malevolent enemies and persecutors. Voltaire, malignity personified, the arch rival, published an anonymous pamphlet recounting the scandal of Rousseau's children by Thérèse, all of whom he had left at the gates of an orphanage. Thus stimulated, local clerics stirred up their congregations with claims of heresy and depravity and Rousseau's house was stoned by a mob on one memorable and terrifying night. He came to loathe the village and the *canaille* who inhabited it, longing to find a country where he could be left in peace.

The philosopher David Hume, then living in Paris, invited him to England and Rousseau reluctantly accepted his offer. Hume, another well-disposed Scot, was a genuine admirer of Rousseau but the history of their relationship ended badly – in typical Rousseau-esque fashion. Rousseau was a man of spontaneous impassioned emotion and illogical mood swings. Hume records a moment when Rousseau, in a bad temper, suddenly 'rose up and took a turn about the room: but judge of my surprise, when he sat down suddenly on my knee, threw his hands about my neck [and] kissed me with the greatest warmth'. It was not to last. In 1766 Hume accompanied Rousseau to London and a wealthy patron installed him in his house in Derbyshire. Boswell escorted Thérèse thither separately from Switzerland, during which journey they had a brief, energetic affair (Boswell noting in his journal 'gone to bed very early and had done it once. Thirteen in all'). And all for a while was well until Rousseau got it into his head that Hume was the author of a satirical letter published in the English press (in fact it was by Horace Walpole) and he accused Hume of betrayal and of covertly opening his mail. Rousseau's affection and gratitude had turned immediately to passionate vilification and disdain. Hume was hurt and baffled and eventually equally outraged at the accusations. So the English period of Rousseau's life ended on this tone of mutual defamation and aggrieved self-justification. He and Thérèse returned to France where, finally, at Ermenonville near Paris, another wealthy patron provided the philosopher with a rural retreat and he passed his last years in some form of comfort and peace, dying of a stroke on 2 July 1778.

His greatest work, and his lasting monument, was published posthumously. *The Confessions* is a truly astonishing autobiography, a beguiling mix of total candour, self-abasement, vainglory and special-pleading. Hume had encouraged Rousseau to write his memoirs and Rousseau told him the work was already underway. Rousseau said, 'I shall describe myself in such plain colours that henceforth everyone may boast that he knows . . . Jean-Jacques Rousseau.' Hume commented sagely, 'I believe he intends seriously to draw his own picture in its true colours; but I believe at the same time that nobody knows himself less.' This is the key to Rousseau's abiding fascination in the modern age – he is one of the great characters of history, an absorbing psychological case study, of which we have, mercifully, copious documentation. Rousseau may not have known himself well but, thanks to Maurice Cranston's exemplary labours, we have in these three volumes of biography (to be read alongside *The Confessions*, ideally) a chance to make the acquaintance of Jean-Jacques, in all his maddening and endearing complexities, ourselves.

1997

Ronald Frame

(Review of *A Long Weekend with Marcel Proust*)

Scottish literature is very fashionable at the moment – particularly in England – its 'coolness' exemplified by the huge international success of Irvine Welsh's novel about heroin addicts in Edinburgh – *Trainspotting*. This novel has sold in its hundreds of thousands, has spawned a play, a cult film and two successful CD compilations of music from the film. This is all well and good, and a credit to Irvine Welsh's feel for the zeitgeist, but one of the less welcome consequences of *Trainspotting*'s prominence is that it has unwittingly defined what it is to be a Scottish writer, or, to put it another way, what it is to be a 'real' Scottish writer, a 'true' Scottish writer as opposed to a writer who just happens to be Scottish.

This kind of debate is one that resurfaces frequently in the cultural histories of small countries with a large diaspora. The old joke has it that the second biggest export from Scotland – after whisky – is people. Those that leave do so for all sorts of reasons; but those that stay regard the leavers differently, almost suspiciously. It has given rise to the twin categories of 'Red' Scots and 'Black' Scots. Red Scots are the ones who have left: the Black Scots have stayed behind – and the assumption is implicit that they have a closer bond with the country, with its heritage, its art and its very quintessence.

All this is by way of a preamble to try and place the writer Ronald Frame in a context. Frame is a Scot, a 'Black' Scot too, but a very cosmopolitan one, educated in Scotland and at the University of Oxford, and who, after some time abroad, returned to his homeland to live and work. And yet Frame, I feel, has never been fully welcomed or celebrated as a Scottish writer – and not just because of the cultured and sophisticated nature of his work. There is another factor that enters the complicated equation of what it takes to be a Scottish writer today and that is to do with that old British bugbear – class. The strata of Scottish society mirror those of English society almost exactly and part of what one might term the 'Trainspotting' effect on Scottish literature is that it has located the Scottish literary renaissance in a culture that is, for want of a better phrase, 'working class'. So that, to simplify somewhat crudely, the Scottish writer, if he or she is to gain full critical acceptance, not only has to live in

Scotland but also has to represent – and write about – working class life, whether it be the unemployed of Glasgow or the junkies of Edinburgh. This is not Irvine Welsh's fault but he is highly symptomatic of this dominant trend in Scottish literature that has emerged over the last ten years or so. It is a bizarre kind of self-denying ordinance: the country is richly diverse and pluralistic; its ancient institutions (law, finance, education, learning etc.) as venerable as any in Europe but, in its contemporary literature at least, its focus is proudly narrow: to be taken seriously, it now seems – to be regarded as an *echt* Scottish writer – you must write about urban life at the lower levels of society and deal with its deprived or alienated members.

Ronald Frame does not write this kind of fiction yet he is without any doubt one of the most significant writers to have emerged from Scotland in the last few decades. Frame is a prolific writer, but one of great invention and variety. His settings are European in the broad sense. He will place a story or a novel in Austria or France as readily as in Wiltshire or Perth. His style is classically lucid but he will boldly experiment with structure, producing fictions that, sometimes even in the manner they are arranged on the page, illustrate or replicate their fractured or contrapuntal nature.

Yet for all their range and scope beneath them run themes that we can now see represent Frame's essential preoccupations. He is a Proustian, insofar as memory and the past dominate so many of his novels and short stories. Time and again, in different guises and narratives, he will return to certain key ideas – that the child is father to the man, that the past permanently haunts the present moment, that a person can have a whole wardrobe of former selves, that secrecy and duplicity shape society and human behaviour as much as honesty and straightforwardness. Frame's portraits of his central characters and the social spheres they inhabit are minutely observed and wonderfully drawn. In Frame's world a choice of perfume can tell you as much about a woman as her choice of husband – perhaps even more. The superficial details of fashion, of consumerism, of manners and comportment (Frame loves to inhabit the earlier decades of this century) are clues to darker secrets, indications of deeper, more sinister waters flowing beneath the tranquil surface.

There is something akin to music in this persistent reworking of themes and leitmotifs (Frame is an accomplished musician) and he has evolved a type of book that perfectly reflects his art and its obsessions. Often he will present one substantial work of fiction – a short novel or a novella – accompanied by a sequence of shorter stories. These stories are discrete fictions in themselves but because they inevitably reflect these essential Frame concerns they often pick up and elaborate on aspects of the longer piece – as miniature variations on the larger theme, to continue the musical analogy. *A Long Weekend with Marcel Proust*, highly acclaimed when it appeared in Britain, is precisely this type of book – its central novella is even called 'Prelude and Fugue' – and is a superb introduction to the fascinating and cleverly beguiling world of Ronald Frame.

1998

Muriel Spark

(Review of *Reality and Dreams*)

'He often wondered if we were all characters in one of God's dreams.'
Thus begins Muriel Spark's shortish, beguiling, twentieth novel. The 'he'
doing the wondering is Tom Richards, a sixty-something film director
of some renown, who is recovering from a serious accident – a fall from
a crane during the shooting of his latest film, *The Hamburger Girl*. This
is about as profound as Tom gets (he is no great intellectual) and most
of his waking moments are given over to thinking about himself – his
future projects, his cares and woes, his love affairs and his wife and
family.

The mazy and improbable plot largely centres on Tom's relationship
with his daughter from his second marriage, Marigold. Marigold is plain,
difficult and demanding and an air of mutual dislike colours their respective attitudes to each other. Cora, Tom's daughter from his first marriage,
however, is beautiful and can do no wrong. Claire, Marigold's mother,
airily tolerates Tom's egotism and his regular adultery. The family congregate around Tom after the fall (many broken ribs, a shattered hip),
commiserate somewhat and go on their merry ways. Tom's film is put
on hold, retitled, then, after he has recuperated, starts up once more
with Tom restored at the helm. Tom has an affair with his leading lady,
Rose Woodstock, alienates another dysfunctional actress called Jeanne
and presides over the several misfortunes of his daughters and sons-in-
law.

It is all slightly ditsy and eccentric with a *La Ronde* style of serial
infidelities adding a certain spice. Things get serious however when
Marigold disappears: rather, things *eventually* get serious because no one
seems to notice she has gone, at first. Finally the alarm is raised, the
media are alerted, a search is initiated world wide and eventually Marigold
is found disguised as a man living with some New Age travellers. It was
all, it turns out, a way of tormenting her horrible father. Except that,
mysteriously, a taxi driver companion of Tom (a compliant ear to Tom's
convalescent witterings) has been shot at and nearly killed. Was this
Marigold's doing?

By way of compensation for his paternal neglect Tom casts manly

Marigold as a prescient Celt called Cedric in his latest absurd movie, set in Roman Britain, called *Watling Street*. Curiously, but then perhaps not, this is the movie business after all, Tom persists in recasting Rose Woodstock and Jeanne in this new film. Jeanne, now druggy and seriously unhinged, becomes a compliant agent for Marigold's wiles. Marigold, still nurturing murderous thoughts, decides to kill her father by re-enacting the original crane accident, only this time with more fatal efficiency. Jeanne is engaged as saboteur but the plans go tragically awry.

Such summaries of Muriel Spark's novels do them a misservice. What delights principally is the tone of voice, so enviably assured, such a distinct signature. In this novel the point of view is omniscient, we visit whichever character's thoughts suit the Sparkian design. The voice is cool and spare, and in complete disinterested control: 'The youth recounted his experience with Marigold but said they had parted shortly afterwards. He did not discount that Marigold was perfectly capable of hiring a hit-man if the plan suited her. The police eventually believed the boy, whose name for the present purpose is irrelevant, and let him go. Where was Marigold? Nobody knew for sure.'

The disinterest can also shade into ruthlessness. There has always been a nail-paring objectivity about Muriel Spark's authorial style (this is what drew Evelyn Waugh to praise her first novel) and it provides delectable pleasures throughout her work, *Reality and Dreams* included. This aloofness can breed a certain air of cynicism or fatalism and gives rise to the darkness that seems to haunt the story. Tom and his brood are lightweights, people we care little for, whose lives and concerns, from one point of view, seem almost nugatory.

A conclusion that is perhaps borne out by the novel's opening sentence, Tom's ingenuous aperçu. What, indeed, if we *are* mere figments in one of God's dreams? Where does that leave us? 'As flies to wanton boys are we to the Gods' – so Gloucester famously observed in *King Lear* and Spark's wise and disturbing fiction often exploits a similar sense of human insubstantiality and unimportance with great subtlety and skill. Of course there is another layer here, apart from the nihilistic, that is readily developed. We can detect a God-like presence hovering over the action of the novel – that of the author: these characters are characters in one of Muriel Spark's dreams. The dream/reality, art/life theme is further enhanced by the fact that Tom's films all start from dreams he has had. He then makes these films 'real' through the wholly unreal medium of film. Just as the plot slips and slides, and the characters' various fates chop and change almost at whim so too does our sense of the reality of what we are reading shift and blur. There is, in the end, only one person who can make sense of the whole can of worms – the artist.

However, in *Reality and Dreams* the controlling role of Muriel Spark is a little too overt, I feel. Her unique sensibility functions best when the voice is subjective, the point of view confined or in first person, as in her two wonderful late novels *A Far Cry from Kensington* and *Loitering with Intent*. This method localizes, and validates, that clear-eyed, unabashedly, brutally honest gaze on the world and its denizens. Omniscient narration has the opposite effect: the mode has its attractions but, in this day and age, it can seem a little too manipulative and knowing. Perhaps in this elderly century (and Spark makes some play with this notion) the predetermined, the ordered, the sense of everything-in-its-place is fundamentally inimical. In our novels, that most controlled of artefacts, we need at least the illusion of uncertainty, of ignorance, of the random.

Reflecting on his dream notion Tom concedes that, '"Our dreams, yes, are insubstantial; the dreams of God, no. They are real, frighteningly real. They bulge with flesh, they drip with blood." My own dreams, said Tom to himself, are shadows, my arguments – all shadows.' The dreams of Muriel Spark, as we have seen in her exemplary oeuvre, are frighteningly real, also, and bulge and drip to great effect. *Reality and Dreams*, however, is a little muted, and a certain shadowiness detracts from the real frisson. We may not have, in this latest novel, Muriel Spark in her full symphonic majesty but we can still relish the real pleasures of this work on a smaller scale – a nocturne, say, a suite, a variation on certain themes – as we wait impatiently for the major work to resume.

1999

Frederic Manning

(Introduction to *Her Privates We*)

Two brief quotations will serve as the best introduction to this unique and extraordinary novel, the finest novel, in my opinion, to have come out of the First World War. The scene takes place in the reserve lines in the Somme valley in northern France during the late summer of 1916. A corporal is dressing-down the men in his section.

'You shut your blasted mouth, see!' said the exasperated Corporal Hamley, stooping as he entered the tent, the lift of his head, with chin thrust forward as he stooped, giving him a more desperately aggressive appearance. 'An' you let me 'ear you talkin' on parade again with an officer present and you'll be on the bloody mat quick. See? You miserable beggar, you! A bloody cow like you's sufficient to demoralize a whole muckin' Army Corps. Got it? Get those buzzers out, and do some bloody work for a change.'

Nothing too unusual here: standard NCO aggression, an attempt to render the colloquial nature of the speech by dropping the odd consonant, perhaps a hint of a more refined sensibility present in the way Corporal Hamley's entry into the tent is so precisely described. But now here is the same passage as it was originally written and as it was originally meant to be read.

'You shut your blasted mouth, see!' said the exasperated Corporal Hamley, stooping as he entered the tent, the lift of his head, with chin thrust forward as he stooped, giving him a more desperately aggressive appearance. 'An' you let me 'ear you talkin' on parade again with an officer present and you'll be on the bloody mat, quick. See? You miserable bugger you! A bloody cunt like you's sufficient to demoralise a whole fuckin' Army Corps. Got it? Get those buzzers out, and do some bloody work, for a change.'

It is remarkable the change wrought by the good old Anglo-Saxon demotic of 'bugger', 'cunt' and 'fuckin''. What was familiar, stereotypical, almost parodic, becomes suddenly real – the whole situation charged and violent. And in its wider context – the First World War – a whole

new resonance emerges. Those monochrome images we know so well
– Tommies puffing on their fags, troops marching through French villages,
the lunar landscape of no man's land – suddenly have a different import.
Suddenly, a veil is stripped away. These are real men, real soldiers – and
all soldiers swear, vilely, constantly. This is a world where corporals call
their men 'cunts'.

Her Privates We was not the title chosen for the first, unexpurgated
edition of this novel which was privately printed and issued in an impression of some 600 copies, and is what you will read here. Frederic
Manning called this version of his book *The Middle Parts of Fortune*,
changing the title for the later, bowdlerized, public version. And, even
though we have had the uncensored novel for some three decades now,
the book's fame and reputation have always been associated with the
second title. Both titles, in fact, come from *Hamlet* (Act II, scene 2)
when Hamlet indulges in a bit of saucy badinage with Rosencrantz and
Guildenstern. When Hamlet asks how the 'good lads' are, Guildenstern
replies: 'Happy in that we are not over-happy / On Fortune's cap we are
not the very button.'

HAMLET: Nor the soles of her shoe?
ROSENCRANTZ: Neither, my lord.
HAMLET: Then you live about her waist, or in the middle of her favours.
GUILDENSTERN: Faith, her privates we.
HAMLET: In the secret parts of Fortune? O, most true, she is a strumpet.
 What's the news?

I take the allusion in several ways. First, I think Manning acknowledges
that the very coarseness of the book is its strongest and most shocking
asset. Especially in 1930, when it was published, even the cleaned-up
version would have seemed relentlessly profane. Second, it draws attention to the role of luck and blind chance in men's lives, particularly in
a war. And third, it advertises the book's intellectual seriousness. For
although this is a novel about private soldiers, those at the bottom end
of the army's food chain, the authorial brain informing it is rigorously
intelligent and clear-eyed. And, as if to ram that point home, every
chapter has a Shakespearean epigraph.

 Even when the book was first published, credited pseudonymously
to one 'Private 19022', it would be apparent to any reader that the

central character, Bourne, is different from the ordinary soldiers around him. The tone of voice, the intellectual nature of the book's reflection and analysis, the sardonic sensibility, all spoke of a different category of author than a mere private soldier. And when the identity of the author was eventually revealed there was even more of a surprise – but more of that later.

Her Privates We has little to do with actual combat – most of its action takes place behind the lines, in reserve or in billets as the battalion trains, does fatigues and waits for its turn in the front-line trenches. Bourne is a thoughtful and ruminative man, taciturn, an almost lugubrious presence – an older man, too, educated, but with no desire to exploit the privileges that this education, and what was then called 'breeding', would have provided for him in the army. He is friendly with the NCOs – happy to go drinking with the sergeants, and, because he can speak French, is used by the men as an interpreter, and provider of services, with the local population.

Here again, despite the classically turned prose of the novel, its modernity emerges. While they wait to go into battle, the men's interests are focused on food, drink, sex and idleness – probably in that order. Bourne observes all this and bears calm and cool witness. The men tolerate rather than respect their officers, they show no military zeal or patriotic fervour, they have no faith in their leaders and no real interest in the war: '. . . they were now mere derelicts in a wrecked and dilapidated world, with sore and angry nerves sharpening their tempers, or shutting them up in a morose or sullen humour from which it was difficult to move them.' Time and again Bourne's observations undermine the stereotype of the First World War and in so doing paint a picture of men at war that is – after decades of mythmaking and romance – both bitterly fresh and timeless.

When *Her Privates We* was published in 1930 it became an almost immediate success, some 15,000 copies selling in the first three months as newspaper columnists vied with each other trying to guess the identity of 'Private 19022'. Manning's cover was blown relatively quickly. One of the first to guess the true identity of the author was T. E. Lawrence who claimed that within six weeks of the book's publication he had read it three times.

Lawrence recognized Manning as the author because he was a great admirer of Manning's book *Scenes and Portraits* (published in 1909). When

Manning's identity was revealed to the world at large it came as something of a shock. Frederic Manning was a minor figure in Edwardian
literary circles, a Greek scholar, a poet, a belle-lettrist, friend of Ezra
Pound and T. S. Eliot – he seemed a million miles away from the foul-
mouthed soldiers in his novel, scrounging for booze and bitching about
the war.

Manning was in fact an Australian, born in 1882 to a prosperous
family in Sydney. His father was mayor of Sydney, later knighted, and
his brother became Attorney General. Manning, a neurasthenic young
man of perpetually failing health, came to England in 1903 determined to make a career in literature. And his efforts followed the
predictable path of those blessed with a modest talent, a private income
and low ambition: reviews and poems printed in periodicals, a turgid
epic poem called *The Vigil of Brunhilde*, and then finally the critical
success of *Scenes and Portraits*, a series of imaginative dialogues between
historical figures which display a refined and ironic intellectual
preciosity but which now read as hopelessly dated. However, in 1909,
the *réclame* of the book finally permitted Manning full access into
Edwardian literary circles and it was at this time that he and Ezra
Pound became friends.

What little information there is on the early life of Frederic Manning
makes it hard to believe that one day he would write *Her Privates We*.
Before the war Manning published regular reviews for the *Spectator* and
other periodicals, and the occasional poem appeared in little magazines.
He lived in a vicarage in the countryside and, when he could afford it,
travelled in Europe. Nothing about his life distinguishes him from many
other somewhat effete and vaguely talented littérateurs that then
abounded. There seems also to have been no grand romantic passion in
his life – with either sex – and even his friendships, with the painter
William Rothenstein, with Pound, appear oddly formal and distanced.

When war broke out in 1914 Manning did not volunteer immediately because he thought he would fail the army medical. He continued
to scratch a living from his pen but eventually in October 1915 he
enlisted in the Shropshire Light Infantry and reported for training at
Pembroke Dock in South Wales.

Manning was now 'Private 19022'. Quite why he had not attempted
to apply for a commission is not clear – it is possible he had, but had
been rejected (I am indebted for much of this information to Jonathan
Marwil's *Frederic Manning: An Unfinished Life*). However after some weeks

of basic training he was selected and sent to Oxford to train as an Officer Cadet. Manning's role as a tyro officer did not last long – he was returned to his unit in June 1916 for drunkenness.

So Manning went to France in August 1916 as a private, an elderly private too, at the age of thirty-four – there were boys of sixteen at the Battle of the Somme. He was joining the secondary stages of the Somme battle that had begun with the catastrophic slaughter of 60,000 killed and wounded on the first day – 1 July – and that would fizzle out in the freezing mud and snow as winter closed in at the year's end. In August the Shropshires soon saw heavy fighting around Guillemont, in the southern section of the Somme battle front, and later, towards the end of the year, on the Ancre front at Serre. Manning's war as a private soldier lasted just over four months. He returned to London at Christmas 1916, again to attempt officer training.

Those four months on the Somme front provide the background for *Her Privates We*. Bourne's war, in the novel, is very close to Manning's both geographically and in terms of the experience undergone. Just as Bourne was transferred to signals, and thus to comparative safety, so too was Manning. And just as Bourne was constantly urged to apply for a commission so too, one must suppose, was Manning. In any event, when complied with, the new experience was not a happy one. Manning duly became a lieutenant in the Royal Irish Regiment but his drinking problems became more serious (in the novel, Bourne is an intermittent but redoubtably heavy drinker). In August 1917, in Dublin, Manning was summoned before a court martial and severely reprimanded. In October 1917 he was in hospital, suffering from *delirium tremens*. Shortly after, he offered to resign his commission and was accepted. But Manning carried on drinking and was described by his battalion medical officer after one binge as being in 'a stupor, quite unfit for any duty, evidently the result of a drinking bout'. Manning's own account was blunt and factual: 'From some time . . . I had been suffering from continual insomnia and nervous exhaustion. I was in an extremely weak condition of health generally, and in those circumstances had recourse to stimulants.' Manning's self-diagnosis is more easy to understand in this the day and age of post-traumatic stress disorder but in 1918 he met with little sympathy: his military career was over.

After the war Manning took up his old life as a jobbing man-of-letters again – literary journalism and hack work in the shape of a biography of a famous naval architect. He moved in the same obscure literary and intellectual circles as before, returning to Australia in 1925 for a visit. But there is a sense of the decade of the 1920s being one long slow slide of apathy and disillusion. He published a small book on Epicurus and wrote reviews for T. S. Eliot at the *Criterion*. Manning, a lifelong chain-smoker, was still drinking heavily and, inevitably, health problems returned. He had thirteen teeth extracted. Photographs at the time show a gaunt, seamed face, prematurely aged. It was only when the publisher Peter Davies urged him to write his war memoirs that some form of energy returned and *Her Privates We* was composed in a few galvanized weeks. Manning had never written so easily, before or since.

But the success and fame of the novel, as well as temporary prosperity, brought little contentment. Manning's health was failing and it seems he was by now suffering from emphysema. He travelled to Australia again in 1932 and passed sixteen isolated months there. Manning returned to England but spent most of his time in and out of rest homes and hospitals. He now needed oxygen to help him breathe. Any cold or attack of flu brought with it deadly risks. Early in 1935 Manning contracted pneumonia which, coupled with his chronic emphysema, proved swiftly fatal: he died on 22 February. He was fifty-two years old.

At the centre of Frederic Manning's short and disappointed life stands the monument of *Her Privates We*. It was a book that Ernest Hemingway read each year, 'to remember how things really were so that I will never lie to myself nor to anyone else about them'. Hemingway has got to the heart of the book's dogged and lasting appeal. There are many superb memoirs and testimonials about the First World War that have stood the test of time and become classics. Owen, Sassoon, Blunden and Graves are permanent members of the poetry canon. It is perhaps somewhat strange that, apart from *Her Privates We*, there are no English novels that came out of the Great War with a similar status. Yet it is precisely because *Her Privates We* is a novel that its reputation and its import are so remarkable and so affecting. Fiction adds a different dimension that the purely documentary and historical cannot aspire to. As Hemingway said on another occasion: 'I make the truth as I invent it truer than it would be.' This is what the novel does and this explains the enduring power behind *Her Privates We*. Something in Manning's persona made him wish to write a novel rather than a memoir. Perhaps fiction gave him that freedom to reinvent himself as Bourne, made him truer than he would be, and perhaps fiction gave him that freedom to be honest in a way that more decorous autobiography would not permit. For, finally, it is the unremitting honesty of *Her Privates We* that stays in the mind; its refusal to idealize the serving soldier and military life; the absolute determination to present the war in all its boredom, misery and uncertainty; its refusal to glorify or romanticize; the candour that makes a soldier say about the civilians back home, 'They don't give a fuck what 'appens to us 'ns.' We know now that all this was true – but we needed Frederic Manning to bear fictional witness for us, to make it truer.

If we only had the expurgated edition of *Her Privates We* it would still remain a great and original novel. It may seem a somewhat large claim to make but the restoration of these stark curses, oaths and swear words in the unexpurgated version has the curious effect of making the First World War seem somehow modern and more contemporary – of making it closer to us, removing the decades that lie between our time and the summer of 1916. After all, it was not that long ago. My grandfather and my great-uncle both survived the First World War: one was wounded at Passchendaele, the other at the Somme, in August, at about the time Manning arrived there. These famous names still resound awfully, even now – Passchendaele, the Somme – names with their great freight of history and of potent abstract nouns – courage, duty, sacrifice, heroism. But, funnily enough, it is the thought of my grandfather and my great-uncle swearing – 'fucking' and 'cunting' with the rest of the poor benighted infantry – that makes them real to me. I understand their ordinariness and humanity. Therefore I understand all the better what they endured.

1999

Alan Ross

(Review of *Winter Sea: War, Journeys, Writers*)

The winter sea is the 'white sea of memory', as Alan Ross describes it, 'of fear and adventure, of camaraderie and consolation . . . on which nothing and everything is written.' In this beguiling and atmospheric book Ross revisits a portion of his past life when, during and just after the war, on active service as a young naval officer in his early twenties, he came to know the northern towns and cities of the Baltic and North Sea littoral – cities such as Tallinn and Bremen, Oslo, Hamburg and Wilhelmshaven.

Fifty years on from those grim days, Ross retraces his steps or follows up leads from his past. A German naval officer whom he befriended in 1945 just after the war had ended – Schlemmer – who went to live in Estonia, and who wrote occasionally from Tallinn, prompts a visit to the city in the vague hope of finding Schlemmer's grave or, failing that, checking out the habitat of his old companion, trying to imagine how he must have lived out his life in this curious town – once German occupied, then Soviet occupied and, today, uneasily, freely Estonian once again.

Ross, now in his mid seventies, has the wonderful advantage of the long view and his ruminations – precise and beautifully observed – brim with a gentle, worldly sagacity. He has created here a form of travel-memoir which he has made very much his own. The journey acts as a kind of Proustian trigger, prompting reflections on the history of the places he visits, on his own life, and also on other travellers and writers who have preceded him. In Tallinn, for example, he comes across the ghostly traces of Arthur Ransome, who lived in the city in the early 1920s. In Oslo, Ross recalls his first reading of Knut Hamsun's great novel about the place, *Hunger*, a book given to him by a fellow officer whilst on convoy duty on the Murmansk run. In 1996 Oslo, Ross, map in hand, retraces the steps of Hamsun's starving protagonist as he meanders the streets looking for a square meal and trying to scrape a living as a writer. Wilhelmshaven prompts memories of Ernst Jünger, Hamburg of B. Traven, Bergen of Nordahl Grieg and so on.

The tone of voice is discursive and conversational, the observations and reflections setting off other memories, drawing in other facts and coincidences, such as the fact that Graham Greene had visited Estonia in the thirties, 'For no other reason,' Greene explained, 'except escape to somewhere new.' Greene – almost parodically – had spent his time in Tallinn vainly searching for a brothel 'which had been run by the same family in the same house for three hundred years.' The person who had given him the (wrong) address was Moura Budberg, mistress of Gorky and H. G. Wells, whom, by coincidence, Ross had come to know at the end of her life when she lived on the Cromwell Road and still attempted to run a kind of salon. 'Her invitations were peremptory,' Ross writes. 'Any excuses . . . were brushed aside as if of no account. "Just come in for a little moment," she would wheedle in her husky voice, which remained distinctive and seductive long after all other physical charms had fled.' In a seamless series of segues Ross visits Tallinn on the trail of a wartime encounter, reads a biography of Ransome, recalls Greene's frustrating sojourn in the place which in turn prompts a brief reminiscence about a strange and exotic literary *grande dame* living out her final years in London.

And so the book effortlessly progresses, as Ross leads you to these half-forgotten, chilly, northern, moodily scenic cities. The art, of course, resides in it seeming effortless, and one remembers that Ross has written two classic volumes of autobiography – *Blindfold Games* and *Coastwise Lights* – to which this volume, and its predecessor, *After Pusan*, are, as it were, generous appendices and afterthoughts. One remembers also that Ross is a fine and accomplished poet, and the book is interleaved with the poems that the visits and the recollections have inspired. Ross's prose too recalls his poetic vocation. He is a sensualist, responding to the physical sensations of place and weather conditions, of psychological mood and unfolding panorama. Unlike Greene, who travelled in a frantic flight from boredom, Ross, one senses, travels in search of beauty and difference, seeking varieties of experience, the more palpable and impressionistic the better. Ross has been and still is an inveterate, nomadic traveller but he can savour the bleak north with as much evocative resonance as the warm south: 'Clear light, the trees just starting to turn. Out at sea ships tow filigree wakes over water suggestive of glycerine. The wooded curve of Tallinn Bay protects its islets like an outflung arm.' The book is generously studded with such passages of transfiguring beauty but is made memorable not simply by the clear and candid eye with which the world is observed – and made visible to us – but, more importantly,

by the implicit sense of experience that resides in this sequence of journeys; experience of a life lived fully, of cruelties and hardships witnessed
and undergone, of moments of happiness and pleasures tasted with gratitude – but with never a shred of complacency.

Recalling his days on the Murmansk convoys, and the solace which
reading provided then, Ross remarks that, 'When for so long the war
seemed shapeless and infinite, it was from writers who had made something of tough and exacting conditions that we learned to value the
experience for its own sake, without questioning its purpose.' In lazier,
softer times than those that same need remains. Perhaps more than ever
we ought to strive to 'value the experience for its own sake' and thereby
derive something of lasting worth from the exercise. A book such as
Winter Sea provides superb and exemplary instruction.

1998

Charles Dickens

(Introduction to *Martin Chuzzlewit*)

The first problem about *Martin Chuzzlewit* is its title. 'What's in a name? that which we call a rose/By any other name would smell as sweet,' opines Juliet, and normally I would agree, but I feel that in the case of *Martin Chuzzlewit* the axiom does not neatly apply. *Martin Chuzzlewit* is one of those novels that would benefit from a title change. It is a problem that emerges only once the book has been well begun, as a vague niggle at first, then a growing worry, and then, by the time one has reached the end, it is a full-blown puzzler. Why on earth is the book called *Martin Chuzzlewit*? More precisely: *The Life and Adventures of Martin Chuzzlewit*? Who, in all honesty, gives a fig about young Martin – whose story, I roughly calculate, probably occupies barely a fifth of the text – so why should the book be named after him? When one thinks of the great eponymous Dickens novels – *Oliver Twist, David Copperfield, Nicholas Nickleby* – it is apparent that *Martin Chuzzlewit*, though it would seem to be in the same family, is manifestly not. And this misnomer goes some way to account, I think, for the novel's surprising though significant neglect. For one of Dickens's greatest novels it is, without doubt, under-read and undervalued. It is as if it has been placed, as it were, in the wrong pigeon-hole: it shouldn't be with *Oliver Twist* and *David Copperfield* but with, say, *Great Expectations* or *Our Mutual Friend*. Readers are expecting Dickens to offer them something they are familiar with, and something that he does unsurpassably well, and in the event the central character is almost insignificant, and was there ever such a bland pair of lovers as young Martin and Mary? It is not conclusive evidence, though telling enough all the same, but in a recent biography of Dickens the index cites only nine fleeting references to the novel, the longest being a couple of paragraphs dealing with the American episodes and their sources. Clearly, *Martin Chuzzlewit* is something of a square peg in a round hole; *Martin Chuzzlewit* is an odd fish.

And yet at the same time *Martin Chuzzlewit* is, I think, the most sheerly *funny* of all Dickens's novels, with a teeming energetic humour that continues to delight some hundred and fifty years after its first publication. It contains enduringly celebrated Dickens creations, notably

Seth Pecksniff and Mrs Gamp, a whole gallery of brilliantly rendered minor characters and writing of a verve and vigour, and imaginative audacity, that is the equal of anything else in the oeuvre. Dickens himself was highly pleased with the book as he was writing it. 'You know, as well as I,' he confided to his friend and future biographer John Forster, 'that I think *Chuzzlewit* in a hundred points immeasurably the best of my stories. That I feel my power now, more than I ever did. That I have a greater confidence in myself than I ever had. That I *know*, if I had health, I could sustain my place in the minds of thinking men, though fifty writers started up tomorrow. But how many readers do *not* think!' The somewhat plaintive self-justification is highly revealing, as is his evident ambition and confidence. It was prompted by the comparative failure of the novel, which was appearing in monthly parts throughout 1843 and the first half of 1844. By Dickens's standards it was not doing well. *Pickwick* and *Nickleby* sold 40–50,000 copies a month: *Chuzzlewit* never rose much over 20,000.

It must have been hard for Dickens to comprehend this baffling shortfall. He was thirty-two years old and at the very apex of his fame. *Chuzzlewit* was his sixth novel, destined to follow the unequivocal triumphs of *Pickwick*, *Oliver Twist*, *Nickleby*, *The Old Curiosity Shop* and *Barnaby Rudge*. He was in a real sense a mature novelist with a massive readership and in full and confident apprehension of his particular genius. He had special hopes for *Chuzzlewit* also: it was to be more deliberately structured than the picaresque form of its predecessors; moreover it was to have a clear moral agenda – it was designed to illustrate, according to Forster, 'more or less by every person introduced, the number and variety of humours and vices that have their root in selfishness'. And throughout the novel Dickens dutifully reminds us of this great theme of 'Self', addressing little homilies to the reader, explaining motives and consequences, just in case the outlines of the grand plan are becoming a little blurred. But it does not work, or rather it works, but only in the most general sense. Yes, one can see what he is driving at, but this sententious overview is an afterthought; it has nothing to do with the success, nor of the greatness, of the novel.

And here we enter the realm of speculation, somewhat. *Chuzzlewit* is a huge novel, more than half a million words I calculate, which was written more or less continually over a period of eighteen months. Your average late twentieth-century novelist, producing a lean, well-tooled 200 pager every three or four years, must stand in shamefaced awe at this superabundant energy. Dickens's letters are full of it – 'writing like a Dragon', 'powdering away at *Chuzzlewit*', 'writing merrily'. Again he declares to Forster: 'I have been all day in *Chuzzlewit* agonies – *conceiving only*. I hope to bring forth tomorrow' (my italics). The demands of monthly serial publication must have made this form of writing rhythm inevitable. A day of feverish thought and plotting followed by days of feverish writing. Even if we did not have Dickens's own words for it the internal evidence of the text would suffice to establish that the novel was composed in this manner. You can chart the rise and fall of his energies and enthusiasms, easily spot the longueurs and the padding. That the novel is generally so unflaggingly zestful is what is astonishing: the fact that it is not wholly sustained, that it occasionally goes off the boil, meanders and loses its way, is not only inevitable, it is also – thank God – only human.

In every artist's head, certainly in every novelist's, there is an ur-version – a perfect Platonic vision – of the art form he or she intends to produce. For various reasons – usually a blend of impossible ambition and pragmatic constraints – something different, and, rarely, something better, emerges. And this, I think, is what occurred with *Martin Chuzzlewit*. We know in fair detail what Dickens hoped the *Chuzzlewit* he was writing would be: we can only be grateful that it didn't come off.

Because it has to be said that, for all his hopes about producing a more sophisticated and better-structured novel than its predecessors, *Chuzzlewit* – judged by Dickens's criteria – fails. It is uneven, it is ungainly, it sags and from time to time bores and baffles. The most signal example of this, as I have already suggested, is the superficiality of the eponymous hero. But the American episodes are another instance of bad planning (apparently an attempt, in response to the disappointing sales, to win new readers). When Martin and Mark Tapley go to seek their fortune in the New World the whole tone of the novel changes. It reads today as laboriously heavy-handed satire, but I suspect that, even in 1843, when the narrative switched back to England and the Pecksniffs, a sense of relief would be inevitable. This is not to say that the novel is badly plotted: on the contrary, Dickens keeps the strands of various storylines taut and neatly interconnected. As the novel progresses, the geographical displacements of minor characters – Mark Tapley, Bailey, Mrs Gamp – function very effectively as *points de repère* for the multi-levelled plot. Young Bailey, for example, neatly takes us from Mrs Todgers's boarding house, to the Anglo-Bengalee Assurance Company, which links us again with Jonas Chuzzlewit and the unfortunate Merry Pecksniff. Another device Dickens employs is deliberately to withhold information from us, while at the same time letting us know that the information is highly significant. This is a form of teasing on the part of the omniscient novelist that can occasionally verge on the arch. An obvious instance is the 'dirt' that Nadgett digs up on Jonas Chuzzlewit. He hands the details to Tigg Montague who reads them with mounting glee. Dickens knows, Nadgett knows and Montague knows . . . but we don't. The reader's curiosity is distinctly piqued. Also the invalid Lewsome confides to John Westlock that he has a dread and vital secret to impart and will do so as soon as he recovers his health. This knowledge ticks away like a buried time bomb as the story continues elsewhere. Another tribute to Dickens's skill in the mechanics of novel writing is that nothing is wasted. I am sure every reader would have forgotten that young Martin designed a grammar school while he was briefly Pecksniff's pupil. But it delivers a pleasant frisson of surprised recognition when, hundreds of pages later, Martin and Mark return to England and discover Pecksniff humbly receiving the plaudits of an admiring crowd as the foundation stone of Martin's grammar school is laid.

All these techniques are narrative skills that Dickens possesses in abundance, that contrive to keep the story moving, that deliver a sense of something shapely and well constructed (though he doesn't hesitate to resort to absurd coincidence when he is in a tight spot). But they are the sort of manipulations that, I would suggest, manifest themselves in the day to day business of writing and plotting the monthly numbers. The component parts – the whirring cogs, the levers and the pulleys – are all functioning well: it is only the grand design of the machine that is flawed.

Not that this unduly matters, I repeat. The poet and critic Craig Raine suggests, quite rightly I believe, that '*finally*, we read Dickens for his brilliant detail'. Detail like this, for example: 'his fingers, clogged with brilliant rings, were as unwieldy as summer flies but newly rescued from a honey pot'. This is masterfully done, not simply in terms of the visual analogue provided – one knows exactly the degree of vulgar flashiness we are dealing with – but also for its undertones, of 'flies round a honey pot', of the element of corruption – there is something candidly disgusting about this image. The fact that the simile is applied to Tigg Montague in his newfound glory makes it all the more apt.

And the fact too that this is but one image in a marvellously burnished paragraph devoted to a description of Montague Tigg turned Tigg Montague is further evidence of Dickens's prodigality.

A little later, in the extraordinary pages that make up our introduction to the Anglo-Bengalee Disinterested Loan and Life Assurance Company, we find this: 'Look at the green ledgers with red backs, like strong cricket-balls beaten flat . . .' The strength and sheer originality of this simile almost draw you up short. A cricket-ball beaten flat? Something I doubt anyone has ever seen, but in the forcing jar of Dickens's imagination it not only is readily visualized but it also provides a vision of these mighty ledgers that is perfectly precise.

These 'brilliant details', the quality of writing, the very palpability of Dickens's descriptive prose, are the nuggets we quarry from the great bulk of the novels and *Martin Chuzzlewit* is richly provisioned with them. But there are moments when Dickens, in full flow, is able to extend this feeling of physicality through entire paragraphs. Here, for example, is part of a description of Mrs Todgers's boarding house:

In particular, there was a sensation of cabbage; as if all the greens that had ever been boiled there, were evergreens, and flourished in immortal strength. The parlour was wainscoted, and communicated to strangers a magnetic and instinctive consciousness of rats and mice. The staircase was very gloomy and very broad, with balustrades so thick and heavy that they would have served for a bridge. In a sombre corner of the first landing, stood a gruff old giant of a clock, with a preposterous coronet of three brass balls on his head; whom few had ever seen – none ever looked in the face – and who seemed to continue his heavy tick for no other reason than to warn heedless people from running into him accidentally. It had not been papered or painted, hadn't Todgers's, within the memory of man. It was very black, begrimed, and mouldy. And, at the top of the staircase, was an old, disjointed, rickety, ill-favoured skylight, patched and mended in all kinds of ways, which looked distrustfully down at everything that passed below, and covered Todgers's up as if it were a sort of human cucumber-frame, and only people of a peculiar growth were reared there.

All the familiar Dickensian tropes are pressed into service here. Comic exaggeration, the swaggering simile ('balustrades . . . [that] would have served for a bridge'), personification, the conversational aside ('It had not been papered or painted, hadn't Todgers's'), the piling on of adjectives and then, finally, the startling transmogrifying image – of Todgers's as a human cucumber-frame – that leaps from the page and delivers us Todgers's in a manner so fresh, so audacious, that any sense that this was merely another run-of-the-mill tumbledown dwelling, of the sort that has been described in literature countless times before, is entirely banished from our minds.

There are also other, more covert, talents at work in passages like this: to do with punctuation and rhythm and sentence cadence. This is hard to analyse, and it may even be an instinctive gift, but Dickens, it seems to me, has a superb sense of timing, of when to throw in a short sentence – 'It was very black, begrimed, and mouldy' – amongst longer ones; of when to allow the parenthetical clauses to build and mount; of when to introduce repetition ('The staircase was very gloomy and very broad'); and so on. This ability to orchestrate the pace of these bravura passages in no small manner contributes to their success. The way a paragraph like this is structured acts as a kind of invisible matrix upon which the ideas and images may confidently rest; and Dickens shows himself as deftly accomplished with these more recherché technical gifts, as with the principal ones of story, character and language, allowing them discreetly to distribute and enhance the various forces of the words he employs. One may admire the splendid ambition of the architect but one should never forget the less ostentatious labours of the engineer. Dickens, as we have seen, was a formidable exponent of both professions.

There are many passages of similar brilliance in *Martin Chuzzlewit*, as there are in all of Dickens's novels, but *Chuzzlewit*, to my mind, is amongst the most amply provided. Furthermore, it is not simply a matter of sparkling and pyrotechnical description. *Chuzzlewit*, it is worth reiterating, is Dickens's funniest novel, and it is the ever present, and effervescent, sense of comedy, alongside the virtuoso wordplay and image-mongering, that makes paragraphs like the one quoted above so memorably effective.

If, in some notional parlour game, I were asked to select the most sustained passage of comic writing in English literature, to choose a *tour de force* that one could confidently present as an exemplar of the comic form, then I think I would offer up as my choice the penultimate chapter of Evelyn Waugh's *Scoop*, where Salter, the hapless news editor, follows William Boot to Boot Magna, the family home, and tries to persuade him to rejoin the staff of the *Daily Beast*. Every time I read these pages

I laugh again and exult at Waugh's impeccable comic sense. Comparisons are invidious, and the comic styles are so different in any case, but I now believe that the pre-eminence of the penultimate chapter of *Scoop* is seriously challenged, if not overthrown, by chapters eight and nine of *Martin Chuzzlewit*, pages which deal with the Pecksniff family's trip to London, their arrival at Todgers's, their visit to Miss Pinch and concluding with the Sunday dinner given in the Pecksniffs' honour by the gentlemen lodgers. Waugh's style is all to do with restraint, the humour is implicit, everything is merely presented – shown – and it is the reader who, automatically, fleshes out the context and significance, and supplies the humour and absurdity. Waugh sets the charges, if you like, and the reader detonates them. In Dickens the reverse is true – Dickens *tells* as well as shows – and it is a remarkable tribute to the potent verve and dynamism of his style (and perhaps to the fact that, at root, senses of humour barely change) that, a century and a half on, these forty pages or so of *Martin Chuzzlewit* provide such fecund and inventive writing as well as such rich and apparently timeless comedy. They are, in my opinion, unmatched in all his other novels.

But Dickens, as has been frequently observed, can all too easily make his critics appear clever. This may be a weakness apparent in a certain type of talent or genius – not so long ago Mozart was mocked for his 'horrible little tunes' – a type that is generous and lavish, open and unguarded, the very opposite of the costive or over-intellectual artist. Dickens takes great risks (he was, it should always be remembered, writing for a huge popular audience) and he leaves hostages to fortune in every chapter. It is not difficult to deplore a ghastly passage like this, apostrophizing on the attraction between John Westlock and Ruth Pinch:

Merrily the tiny fountain played, and merrily the dimples sparkled on its sunny face. John Westlock hurried after her. Softly the whispering water broke and fell; and roguishly the dimples twinkled as he stole upon her footsteps.

Oh, foolish, panting timid little heart, why did she feign to be unconscious of his coming! Why wish herself so far away, yet be so flutteringly happy there!

Can this be the same man who can write, with the laconic quietism of a Kurt Vonnegut, of a child's death: 'Smart citizens grow rich, and friend-less victims smart and die, and are forgotten. That is all'? The answer is 'yes' and there is a complexity of reasons required to explain why this can be. Briefly, it is a combination, I would suggest, of *autre temps, autres moeurs*, and various impulses existing in the Dickens psyche. And there is no doubt that raw sentiment, in serious literature, is today almost wholly discredited and *démodé* to such an extent that we are embarrassed when we come across it in an artist we admire and revere. It is instructive to compare the contemporary responses to another comic genius – Charlie Chaplin (with whom, in the life and the work, there are many parallels) – who, forty years after Dickens's death, also won enormous popular acclaim with a similar blend of comedy and unadulterated sentiment. In Chaplin's case modern audiences feel happier analysing the complex architectonics of a pratfall or elaborate gag than responding to the two-fisted hauling on their heartstrings that many a Chaplin film indulges in. But Dickens is the greater artist (and, of course, his art form infinitely more rich and complex) and his genius, unlike Chaplin's, more easily survives the excesses of an overloaded heart.

There are two broad reasons for this: one to do with content and one to do with form. Dickens proclaimed that *Martin Chuzzlewit* was to do with 'Self'. But, as with many of the ostensible subjects of his great novels, this formulation is just another way of saying that it is to do with 'Money'. Money and the getting of it are the key factors underpinning the narrative and moral strands of *Martin Chuzzlewit*. Martin wants money, as do Pecksniff and Jonas Chuzzlewit and Montague Tigg. *Chuzzlewit*, like many a Victorian novel, has as its starting point a potential inheritance, and the material changes that inheritance will bestow: who will get what and how will their lives alter thereby? It was a theme, to put it bluntly, very close to Dickens's heart. But against this need, against this motive force, Dickens sets characters for whom these pecuniary desires hold no attraction. Tom Pinch, Mark Tapley and Ruth Pinch, for example, lead lives in which the getting of money has no part to play beyond essential pragmatic concerns. (Symbolically, Tom sends back Mrs Lupin's fiver without breaking it.) Their lives are driven instead by principles of simple human decency, and the moral tensions of the novel revolve around these counterposing tendencies. Money versus decency, and the eventual triumph of decency, is a sloganizing redaction of what *Martin Chuzzlewit* is 'about'. It is not resolved in a satisfactory way because the comic form, the serious comic form, fights against this type of cosy sententiousness. This sort of conclusion is one where art is designed to console, but if it is to console in this way then it has to be handled, and the reader manipulated, with cool and masterly skill. A glance at the final paragraphs of *Martin Chuzzlewit* will illustrate just to what extent Dickens has lost this fingerparing, objective poise.

But it does not matter: the cute verities that Dickens endorses in the novel's conclusion do not undermine its greatness (and in fact I defy anyone not to be delighted that young Bailey turns out to be alive after all. There is a small place for sentiment, one must grudgingly concede, however hardnosed we like our comedy to be in this day and age) because the triumph of decency, if we may so term it, is not why one values the novel. Because, to contemporary readers, its value must be to do with, in the end, questions of contemporary response. It is right that we should not bend Dickens's work into some grotesque modern distortion – 'The Existential Dickens', or 'Dickens as Marxist' or some such parody. He was an early Victorian, inescapably, with all the emotional and intellectual baggage that is implied in that classification. But at the same time it is vital for each new generation of readers to reassess and re-evaluate the great works of the past, and if we are to read *Martin Chuzzlewit* today, and derive pleasure from it – and not just as an anthropological curiosity – we must ask ourselves what there is in the novel that defies history, as it were, that makes it always valid.

My own response to this question would be that it lies in the comedy. The unequivocal fun and exuberance are crucial, as I have suggested, but there is a note in *Chuzzlewit* that is new in Dickens and marks *Chuzzlewit* as a precursor of the darker, later novels. The high-spirited comedy is mixed here and there with a brand of humour that one might designate 'brutal' or 'cruel'; moments where Dickens, like all great comic novelists, recognizes the indifference of the universe to mankind's fate, recognizes that, to quote Evelyn Waugh, 'Fortune is the least capricious of deities, and arranges things on the just and rigid system that no one shall be very happy for very long.' One thinks in this context of the tenacious, indestructible fraudulence of Pecksniff, of Merry and Cherry and their respective fates, of Jonas Chuzzlewit's bleak lechery and near-demonic possession, of the ruthless mockery of Chuffey and Moddle, of Mrs Gamp and her gallows humour, of Montague Tigg and his ebullient conning of trusting investors. Dickens's comic vision of the world, despite his neat pairing off of happy young lovers, despite, one might say, his best intentions, is too sagacious, too clear-eyed and realistic, to pretend that all's well that ends well. There is a moment, early in the novel, where Dickens is guying the rebarbative smugness of the Pecksniff family. 'What words can paint the Pecksniffs in that trying hour? Oh, none: for words *have naughty company among them*, and the Pecksniffs were all goodness' (my italics). At the end of the novel 'all goodness' seems to have triumphed but the jollity and benignity appear forced and self-deceiving. Tom Pinch may be bedecked with flowers and mellow harmonies may enfold him but we know what the world is really like because Dickens has just shown us, with fierce accuracy and intoxicating humour. It is the naughty company of words that we celebrate and recall: this is what gives *Martin Chuzzlewit* its edge, its wild glee, its cautious disquiet, and its greatness.

1994

Gustave Flaubert

(Review of *Madame Bovary*)

'Madame Bovary c'est moi', Flaubert famously observed, but was he talking about the book as a whole or its heroine? Titles are important clues as to how a book should be read: *Madame Raquin*, *Miss Emma Woodhouse*, or even *Emma Bovary* carry a different freight than the originals do. And if titles are significant then subtitles represent another covert shove in the right direction. *Madame Bovary* was originally subtitled *Moeurs de Campagne*. 'Moeurs' – in my *Petit Robert* – is defined thus: 'habitudes (d'une société, d'un individu) relatives à la pratique du bien ou du mal' – a far more nuanced term than the usual English translation of 'customs'. 'Customs of the countryside' will not do.

Both the title 'Madame' and the subtitle speak of decorum, or, more precisely, bourgeois decorum. *Madame Bovary* is a book about the 'bourgeois' of provincial France and their 'habitudes relatives à la pratique du bien ou du mal'. And the *mal* in question here is the adultery of Emma Bovary, the causes and the consequences thereof. Emma Bovary dreams of a different life and her dreams are driven by romantic literature, good and bad. Every choice she makes in her life is vitiated by this corrupting influence: she sees the world through a glass, rosily. Her marriage to the widower Charles Bovary, country doctor, her affairs with Rodolphe, the libertine, and Léon, the clerk, are a series of straw-clutching efforts to escape.

Flaubert, a bourgeois who lived in the provinces, loathed the bourgeois and the book is a sustained dissection and condemnation of this sensibility and class. When he quoted Voltaire's dictum that 'the history of the human mind is the history of stupidity', he meant it from the bottom of his heart.

Everybody in the novel is stupid: Charles Bovary is stupid for loving Emma; Homais, the insufferable chemist, is a smug monster of stupid homilies. Emma's two lovers are stupid and selfish in equal measure. Nothing escapes Flaubert's gimlet eye and the precision of his detailing. And God is in the details of this novel, so lovingly reproduced in a perfectly fashioned prose that we forget we are dealing with a dull tale of provincial adultery. If Flaubert's pen is dipped in bile it is so that he may write all the more clearly – phrases even italicized so they will not escape notice, relish and censure. The effort and art in this procedure were both phenomenal and revolutionary. One detail will have to stand for the mass. Emma's daughter Berthe is brought into a room to say goodbye: '. . . la servante amena Berthe, qui secoua au bout d'une ficelle un moulin à vent la tête en bas'. Most novelists might have mentioned a toy, a few might have chosen a windmill, but only Flaubert would have had it dangling upside down on a string.

Emma, ruined, poisons herself; Charles dies – of grief – and the impossible Homais triumphs and is awarded the Légion d'Honneur. Flaubert is unremittingly and uncompromisingly bleak in his final vision – no consolation is offered. 'I remain glued to the earth,' he wrote to George Sand, '. . . everything disturbs me, everything lacerates and ravages me, though I make every effort to soar.' It is his rage against the bourgeois spirit that informs his novel and his furiously precise prose but that alone cannot explain the book's endurance as a classic. We are all, in our own way, bourgeois – like Emma Bovary – and even Flaubert admits he made every effort to soar. For to think that life might be better is no shame – it is, indeed, to be human. In the end, *Madame Bovary, c'est nous.*

1999

Cyril Connolly

In early 1945 Evelyn Waugh was languishing in Yugoslavia, bored and
dispirited, waiting for the war to end. He had recently completed
Brideshead Revisited, the most important novel of his career, when
Nancy Mitford sent him a copy of *The Unquiet Grave* by Cyril
Connolly. Waugh read and reread Connolly's book and scribbled his
reactions on the margins. The marginalia are extensive, full of insight
and full of self-delusion. Waugh used the opportunity both to excoriate
and analyse his old acquaintance ('friend' is too loaded a word for their
complex relationship) and the comments he made on the book are fascinating, not just for what they say about Connolly but also for the light
they throw on Waugh himself.

For Waugh was obsessed with Connolly: fascinated and irritated by
him; alternately admiring and contemptuous; secretly envious and
publicly derisive. These are a set of contrasting reactions easily understood by Connolly fans (amongst whom I count myself among the
most ardent) because you cannot read Cyril Connolly for very long
without wanting to acquire – and then develop – a relationship with
the personality of the man himself. This is rarely the case with readers
and writers. Everyone is curious (I'm deeply curious about the character of Evelyn Waugh, for example) but the dislocation between the
mind that creates and the man who suffers (in T. S. Eliot's phrase) is
usually happily observed. My admiration of Waugh's novels is not
diluted by his rebarbative personality. But with Connolly there is a
marked difference and the difference is that the artist and the man are
so conjoined and intermingled that you cannot savour the one without
the other and vice versa. Connolly famously declared that it was the
'true function' of a writer to try and produce a masterpiece 'and that
no other task is of any consequence'. Whatever the veracity of this
claim (dubious), there's no doubt that one of the great frustrations of
his life was that he himself so conspicuously failed to live up to his
own stern injunction. Yet the more one reads and the more one learns
about him perhaps the fairest conclusion to arrive at is that Cyril
Connolly's greatest memorial – his particular masterpiece – is precisely

that conjunction of life and work: that both how he lived (1903–74) and what work he produced form a unique and lasting whole. To invert the old saying: in Connolly's case we cannot see the trees for the wood. It's the wood – whole and entire – that interests us and not so much the individual oaks and elms.

This may seem harsh but, while almost everything Connolly wrote was stylish and intelligent, informed and passionate, there is no one book, or sequence of writings, that one can hold up as unequivocally excellent or fully achieved. The famous parodies are clever but finally lightweight and ephemeral; the millions of words of literary criticism and journalism suffer from the built-in obsolescence that undermines all journalism, however fine. *Enemies of Promise*, that precocious memoir, is good – but patchy. *The Unquiet Grave* is maddeningly flawed – pretentious, self-serving, arch – as well as achingly honest and true. *The Rock Pool* (Connolly's one novel) is an interesting failure – and so on. Yet the sum of his uneven parts adds up to something formidable. He's a writer for all seasons, for all readers. Waugh sneered at his amateur psychoanalysing. 'We love only once,' Connolly wrote, 'and on how that first great love affair shapes itself depends the pattern of our lives.' 'Nonsense,' Waugh mocked in the margin. But there was never a truer comment made about his own life and situation and perhaps it pained him to see Connolly hitting a personal nail so squarely on the head.

Thus one's reading and relish of Connolly's work is shaped and conditioned by what one knows of the man himself to a degree not shared by any other writers. More will be derived, for example, from reading the prefaces to the monthly issues of *Horizon* (which magazine he edited from 1940–49) if you know about the history of *Horizon*, Connolly's editorial lifestyle, his love affairs, the animosities and gossip that surrounded that period of London cultural life. *The Rock Pool* – selfconscious, straining for effect – becomes far less unwieldy once you know the background to its composition and who the thinly disguised characters are based on, and so forth.

This is not to denigrate or diminish Connolly's skill as a writer and literary journalist. I first came across his work during the late sixties and early seventies when he was writing a weekly book review for the *Sunday Times*. At school and university I read Connolly's weekly review religiously, whatever the subject, with – at that time – no insider knowledge about the man. What stimulated me was, I think, his enthusiasm. This was no dry, jaded don routinely turning out his 800 words, no embittered hack assailing grander reputations for the sake of a weekend's frisson. Though I now know the drudgery of the weekly review caused him intense pain it never seemed to come through in the writing. He could pick and choose, of course, and the books he wrote about reflected his passions – French literature, the classics, the Augustans, the great Modernists – and his passion was contagious. From the reviews I moved on to *The Unquiet Grave* and was completely captivated by it. This 'word cycle', a loosely yoked collection of *pensées*, lengthy quotations, reflections on literature and autobiography, in many ways earns all of Waugh's strictures – snobbish, fey, posturing, self-pitying – yet I can think of few better evocations of intellectual melancholy, if I can put it that way, of the dissatisfactions inherent in a life nurtured by and charged with European culture: of individual human insufficiency confronted by the great artistic ideals and achievements. Connolly is no Montaigne, he has none of his calm, resigned sagacity (though Montaigne is one of the presiding spirits of the book), but Connolly captures something ineffably present in the human spirit. And as he roves through world literature trying to pin down these emotions he does so with a candour and a kind of gloomy relish that are very easy to identify with (particularly when you are young: it is a perfect book for the young, would-be littérateur). We have all felt like this, have reached to art for solace and found only more despair, but only Connolly could be so unashamedly candid about it and make a virtue of his inadequacy.

This honesty, try as he might to disguise it, surfaces again and again in his writings and I think is what makes him perennially modern. Connolly is always confessing his failures one way or another and like all great confessors (Rousseau and Boswell spring to mind as real Connolly precursors and fellow-spirits) we are both appalled by what they tell us and at the same time drawn to them. We're all human – all too human – but not all of us will admit to it in print. The vicarious thrill and recognition we take in confessional writings is one of the great literary pleasures and is nowhere more evident than in Connolly's *London Journal*. Here we have the essence of the young Cyril, just up from Oxford, out of pocket, out of love, fretting and dissatisfied. I think the *London Journal* deserves its place alongside *The Unquiet Grave* and *Enemies of Promise* as representing the best of Connolly. One regrets that this fragment is all we have (it seems Connolly was more of a notebook-jotter than a journal keeper). On the evidence of these few pages he could have been our modern Boswell – and how wonderful it would have been to have Connolly's *journal intime* to set alongside Virginia Woolf's diaries – fascinating, yet highly contrived and self-conscious, written, unlike Connolly's, with both eyes firmly fixed on posterity.

Connolly earns my further affection by being the great self-appointed anti-Bloomsbury figure. He drew up the battle lines himself early in life, placing himself in Chelsea ('that leafy tranquil cultivated *spielraum* . . . where I worked and wandered') precisely to counter what he saw as the desiccated fastidiousness, the preciosity, the snobism and the cliquishness of Bloomsbury. Chelsea, by contrast, was more open to Europe, more grubby, sexier, more rackety, more worldly and hedonistic. It was not simply a question of the new generation rejecting the values of the older, he saw instead a real opposition: of contrasting lifestyles, of political and cultural values, of attitudes to art. And it was an opposition that he maintained all his life: there was always in his life not just a love of European culture (especially that of France and Spain) but also a love of beauty, of women, of alcohol and food, of sea and sunbathing, of idleness and travel. Connolly is one of the great evokers of place and of pleasure: whether he is talking about a meal of a rough red wine and *steak-frites*, or wandering through Lisbon or Rome looking at architecture, one feels through his words the physical relish he takes in the experience. He makes you want to do the same things and derive the same intense enjoyment as he does. When he writes that he wants to live in France, somewhere in a magic circle embracing the Dordogne, Quercy, the Aveyron and the Gers, in a 'golden classical house, three storeys high with *oeil de boeuf* windows looking out over water . . . [with] a terrace for winter, a great tree for summer and a lawn for games; a wooded hill behind and a river below, then a sheltered garden indulgent to fig and nectarine . . .' you respond, instinctively, 'How true, that's exactly where I want to live and how I want to live as well.' In a curious way he is both a great and dangerous role model: most of us share, to one degree or another, Connolly's prodigious appetites, both venal and exalted, and most of us share, to one degree or another, Connolly's failings, both petty and debilitating. This small, podgy, balding, pug-faced, funny, gossipy, lazy, clever, cowardly, hedonistic, fractious, difficult man somehow manages to enshrine in his work and life everything that we aspire to, and that intellectually ennobles us, and all that is weak and worst in us as well.

I think this explains both the fascination and repulsion that Waugh felt. Physically and temperamentally they were not far apart: both small, egotistical, selfish, stout and unhandsome. Waugh took the opposite route to Connolly and studiously and desperately reinvented himself as a parodic Tory squire cum reactionary man of letters. It is a facile over-simplification, but Waugh decided to live a lie while Connolly remained true to himself – however flawed or inadequate that self happened to be. Both men were consumed with self-loathing: both of them, Waugh said, were 'always tired, always bored, always hurt, always hating'. Waugh became the rich and acclaimed novelist, with a large family, living in a country house; Connolly was always indigent, the hard-up journalist scraping a living but, somehow, seeming to attract a succession of beautiful women prepared to put up with him. Waugh's life appears superficially the more successful and achieved and yet, for all his endless moaning, Connolly seems far and away the happier man. The secret, I think, was in his resolute secularity and worldliness: he did not seek solace in spirituality (as Waugh did), instead he took both simple and intelligent pleasure in what the world offered, whether it came in the shape of a building, a marsupial, the company of friends, a fine claret, a train journey, a cigar, a sunny terrace, a beautiful woman, a good book, a Georgian teapot or a painting. That relish of life and its potential joys (and the sense of their fragility and transience) permeates his work and gives it its enduring value – and, I suspect, for I never met him, permeated the man as well. There is a wonderful passage in the *London Journal* that, I believe, sums up the essence of the Cyril Connolly appeal. It was written in 1929. Unhappy in love, paranoid, fed up with London and duplicitous friends, the young Cyril Connolly flees to Paris for consolation and takes a room at the Hôtel de la Louisiane on the Left Bank:

Hôtel de la Louisiane

. . . I have a room for 400 francs a month and at last I will be living within my own and other people's income. I am tired of acquaintances and tired of friends unless they're intelligent, tired also of extrovert unbookish life. Me for good talk, wet evenings, intimacy, *vins rouges en carafe*, reading, relative solitude, street worship, exploration of the least known *arrondissements*, shopgazing, alley sloping, café crawling, Seine loafing, and plenty of writing from the table by this my window where I can watch the streets light up . . . I am for the intricacy of Europe, the discreet and many folded strata of the old world, the past, the North, the world of ideas. I am for the Hôtel de la Louisiane.

Yes, yes! you cry spontaneously, when you read this. So am I. I'm for all this too. I'm for the life of the Hôtel de la Louisiane. And this, in the end, also explains why we are for Cyril Connolly.

2000

Keeping a Journal

4 November 1977. 9.30 a.m. The painter Keith Vaughan, dying of cancer, opens his journal and prepares to record the moment of his death: 'The capsules have been taken with some whisky,' Vaughan writes and keeps on writing, quietly waiting for oblivion to arrive. 'I don't quite believe anything has happened though the bottle is empty. At the moment I feel very much alive . . . I cannot believe I have committed suicide since nothing has happened.' Vaughan writes on for a few more lines and then the editor adds, 'At this point the words lapse into illegibility and stop.'

In December 1945, Edmund Wilson opens his journal to log the beginning of a love affair: 'I loved her body which I had first seen in a bathing suit – taller than my usual physical type – there was nothing about it that displeased me – her breasts were low, firm and white, perfect in their kind, very pink outstanding nipples, no hair, no halo round them, slim pretty tapering legs, feet with high insteps and toes that curled down and out.'

On 1 May 1792, Gilbert White, a country curate, opens his journal to observe that, 'Grass grows very fast. Honeysuckles very fragrant and most beautiful objects! Columbines make a figure. My white thorn, which hangs over the earth house, is now one sheet of bloom, and has pendulous boughs down to the ground.'

On 21 June 1918 Katherine Mansfield opens her journal to ask, 'What is the matter with today? It is thin, white, as lace curtains are white, full of ugly noises (e.g. people opening the drawers of a cheap chest and trying to shut them again). All food seems stodgy and indigestible – no drink is hot enough. One looks hideous, hideous in the glass – bald as an egg – one feels swollen – and all one's clothes are tight. And everything is dusty, gritty – the cigarette ash crumbles and falls – the marigolds spill their petals over the dressing table. In a house nearby someone is trying to tune a cheap cheap piano.'

Four journal entries by four compulsive journal-keepers, each journal functioning for its author in a different way, satisfying different needs. Why did these people feel the urge to write these observations down?

What is the strange allure of the journal? What does it do to your life?

It's hard to come to any conclusive answer, to explain why a journal is something you have to keep. The simple reason is that the journal is all things to all men and women, a kind of literary text that is famously hard to define, and whose *raison d'être* has rarely anything to do with fame or notoriety, narrative excitement or exoticism. There are many sorts of journals: journals written with both eyes fixed firmly on posterity and others that were never designed to be read by anyone else but the writer. There are journals content to tabulate the banal and humdrum details of ordinary lives and journals meant expressly to function as a witness to momentous events of history. There are journals that act as erotic stimulants or a psychoanalytic crutch and there are journals designed simply to function as an *aide-memoire*, perhaps as a rough draft for a later, more polished account of a life, and so on. But buried within these varying ambitions and motivations is a common factor which unites all these endeavours – the aspiration to be honest, to tell the truth. The implication being that in the privacy of this personal record things will be uncensored, things will be said and observations made that couldn't or wouldn't be uttered in a more public forum. Hence the adjective 'intimate' so often appended to the noun 'journal'. The idea of secret diaries, of intimate journals somehow goes to the core of this literary form: there is a default-setting of intimacy – of confession – in the private record of a life that not only encourages the writing of journals but also explains their fascination to the reader.

In the case of Keith Vaughan this intimacy reaches unparalleled levels of candour. I can't think of any other writer who has ever been writing deliberately at the very moment of his death, trying to record the last moments of conscious life. This in itself is enough to make Vaughan's journal unique but it is typical of his tone of adamantine honesty throughout: his is the most unsparingly, harrowingly honest of the dozens of journals I have read over the years. I had the opportunity once to see the manuscript and the sight of that final page with the words tailing off into weakening squiggles freezes the soul. It is as if the terminal downward slash of the pen scarring the page (as his hand went limp and slid away) symbolizes the fall into the void that Vaughan longed for and had at that moment entered. And I wonder if there is something even more symbolic in that image that brings us closer to the root of the compulsion, the potent need that some of us feel to keep a journal.

Vaughan's marks on the page and their sudden cessation seem to me to sum up what is taking place in journal-keeping in a fundamental way: we keep a journal because we want to leave a trace of some kind. Like the prisoner who scratches the passing days on his cell wall, or the adolescent who carves initials into the trunk of a tree, or even an animal depositing his spoor, the act of writing a journal seems to say: I was here – here is some record of my journey.

My own serious journal-keeping has two distinct phases. The first began when I was nineteen, in 1971. I kept an almost daily journal for two years and then suddenly stopped, for reasons I now can't recall – the journal gives no clue. I took it up again ten years later in 1981, and have kept it going steadily (though not daily) ever since. So, approximately half my life has now been set down in journal-form, but what's interesting to me is that the two journals have quite different intentions. The first was motivated by a drive for total candour: it's an urge common to many journal-keepers, that impulsion to set down on paper exactly what was going on in your life with no shame, prudery or cover-up. The second journal is of the *aide-memoire* variety: in 1981 my first novel had just been published and I thought it would be intriguing simply to record the everyday details, the ups and downs, the checks and frustrations, successes and failures of my writing life as time went by – and the second novel was published and then the third and then the fourth, the fifth and the sixth, should I ever reach those numbers. And so it has gone on over the last twenty-two years: it's now a document of close to 2,000 pages and of abiding interest to its author. I refer back to it constantly.

But a couple of years ago I decided to reread the journal I had kept between the ages of nineteen and twenty-one. It was a disturbing experience, like encountering a total stranger, a doppelgänger who had lived my life, but whom I barely recognized. The account I would give now of the factual events of those years would be essentially the same but the psychological and intellectual content seem to belong to somebody else. The journal is full of the usual undergraduate pretensions and musings and faithfully recalls the torrid roller-coaster that was my emotional life at the time. But there was also a kind of pitiless self-examination of almost everything I did that I could not remember ever undertaking. And I was very hard on myself – often insulting myself crudely and ruthlessly in the second person (and not very imaginatively:

'you bloody fool', 'you stupid cretin', sort of thing). Clearly, I had been much unhappier then than I thought, much more troubled and inse-cure. Yet if I had been asked before I reread the journal what I had been like in my late teens I would have said carefree, easy-going, rela-tively content.

But the hard evidence of my journal is irrefutably there and I value its honesty and have to acknowledge its truth. However, this schism between my memory of my earlier self and the historical facts made me wonder if the journal served another, more covert purpose for its keeper, namely to chart that progression of selves that we are at various stages of our life. We do change as people – even though our funda-mental natures may remain the same. Whether we are in love or out of love, rich or poor, happy or sad, healthy or beset by illness will affect the self that we are at any given moment. Ageing and the getting of wisdom contribute to this constant metamorphosis as well but, as we move through time, it's as if we shed these selves in the way a snake will slough off its skin: the glossy new scales bearing no imprint of the weathered, dull integument that was once there. And it seems too that we can be certain that our memories will play us false about our past: only the journal remains as witness to the series of individuals we were in our lives.

This thesis that we are an anthology, a composite of many selves, was put into practice when I decided to write my last novel, *Any Human Heart*, as the fictional intimate journal of a fictional writer. Over 500 pages, from 1923 to 1991, the protagonist ages from a seventeen-year-old schoolboy to an eighty-five-year-old man. The various journals he keeps during his life, among other things, record these transformations in himself. It was a paradoxical exercise because in writing the fictional journal I had to remain true to another constant that is a defining feature of the journal-form. For the journal – relating as it does a life-story, or part of a life-story – does so in a manifestly different manner than the other forms available, whether biography, memoir, or autobiography. All these last three are fashioned by the view backward, informed by the 20/20 vision of hindsight. Only the journal truly reflects, in its dogged chronology, the day-by-day, week-by-week progress of a life. Events have not yet acquired their retrospective gloss and significance; meetings and people, projects and schemes have not matured or devel-oped. The impenetrable judgements of the future more often than not undermine the honest analysis of the present. That job you were so excited about has not yet turned tedious; that thriving dot-com company you sunk your savings into has still to go belly-up; that pretty woman/good-looking man you met at the party last night has not become your wife/husband – and so on. The journal has to have the same random shape as a human life: governed by chance and the haphazard, by that aggregate of good luck and bad luck that everybody receives. Biography and autobiography dilute this inexorable fact, shaped as they are by the wisdom of hindsight and the manipulations of ego, and are literary forms that are, in many ways, as artificial and contrived as fiction. But, by definition, a journal cannot do this: it's written as the future unspools into the present. There are glances backward, true, but in its essence it mimics and reflects our own wayward passage through time like no other form of writing.

There is one further fundamental stipulation I would make: no true journal worthy of the name can be published while its author is alive. Only a posthumous appearance guarantees the prime condition of honesty. However interesting, journals and diaries published while their author is alive seem to me (with very few exceptions) to be bogus in some crucial way. This is particularly true of politicians' journals – Clark, Benn, Castle et al. They have a different agenda (their very publication makes that point) and thus they can't be totally honest, certainly not about their author, and thus they lose their legitimacy as true journals – they've sacrificed that potent alchemy of confession and confidentiality that all great journals require – for the quick fix of controversy and renown. If you're going to publish your intimate journal while you are still alive you reduce it to another category of writing – your journal becomes a form of bastard-journalism or bastard-autobiography. There's something inherently contradictory about being a living writer acclaimed for your published journals: you have to be dead to escape the various charges of vanity, of special-pleading, of creeping *amour-propre*. More to the point, because of these suspicions, we can't read such journals in the same way: only the posthumous journal can be read purely.

However parochial they are, however apparently insignificant the entries, the pages of a journal offer us, as readers, a chance to live the writer's life as he or she lived it, after he or she has lived it. On occasion, we are provided with the curious godlike knowledge of their destiny. Reading Virginia Woolf on 26 February 1941, a month before she commits suicide, provokes a bizarre conjunction of subjectivity and objectivity. She comments: 'Food becomes an obsession. I grudge giving away a spice bun. Curious – age or the war? Never mind. Adventure. Make solid. But shall I ever write again one of those sentences that gives me intense pleasure?' We actually know the negative answer to that question: we share the quiddity of her day and at the same time note that her vital clock is nearly wound down. Similarly, on 16 May 1763 James Boswell writes: 'I drank tea at Mr Davies's in Russell Street, and about seven came in the great Mr Samuel Johnson, whom I have so long wished to see. Mr Davies introduced me to him. As I knew his mortal antipathy to the Scotch, I cried to Davies, "Don't tell where I come from."' As he describes his first sight of Dr Johnson we participate in the thrill of the young man's meeting with the literary lion but there's an extra frisson delivered by the foreknowledge that the mortal antipathy won't frustrate the riches that ensued from that encounter.

But often we read with the same ignorance as that of the journal-keeper as he writes. The mundane flow of the day engulfs us similarly. Francis Kilvert notes on 21 September 1870: 'Went to the Bronith. People at work in the orchard gathering up the windfall apples for early cider. The smell of the apples very strong. Beyond the orchards the lone aspen was rustling loud and mournfully a lament for the departure of summer.' We are with Kilvert that day. 'The smell of the apples very strong' bears a kind of witness to 21 September 1870 that has as cogent and undeniable a validity as any other. Which brings me to the final characteristic of journal-keeping: it is the most democratic form of writing available, perhaps even more so than a letter. The letter presupposes another person in order to function; the intimate journal is designed to be read by only one pair of eyes, the author's (even though others may be hoped for one distant day). Therefore it is judged by standards of truth, integrity, honesty and immediacy that require no special education, talent or gift. Poetry, the novel, biography, the essay and journalism are weighed up by different criteria, different forms of evaluation – and therefore different categories of success and failure too. D. H. Lawrence defined the novel as 'the bright book of life'. Not everyone can write a novel but everyone is, in theory, capable of keeping a journal. And if you keep a journal – a true intimate journal – then it becomes, in a real sense, the book of *your* life and is therefore a unique document. But there is more to it than simply that, I feel, for we all share the same fate and – as we live, as long as we live – we all submit to the same condition: the human condition. In that case, then, the book of a life, an intimate journal – if it is true, if it is honest – will speak to everyone who has a chance to read it: it will be, in a curious way, both completely individual and universal. This is what happens when we read a journal: 'The smell of the apples very strong' is, in its own way, perfect and unimprovable – 21 September 1870 is fixed for us, for ever.

2003

Three French Novels

I write these words in France on the eve of war [the invasion and occupation of Iraq]. A few days ago I travelled from London to my house, not far from Bordeaux in the south-west, by train, stopping off, en route, for a few hours in Paris. Fortuitously, I have covered a great swathe of this country and the weather, for March, is sublime: cool, dry and sunny – the hedgerows and the plum trees are dense with blossom. And to sit on a wicker chair in a Parisian sidewalk cafe with a cold beer on the table and the sun slanting warmly on the façade of the Louvre is to reinforce the abiding impression that there is no city in the world as beautiful as Paris and that – surely, also – France is the best country in the world when it comes to the quality of life. The things that give us pleasure, the buildings we see, the landscapes we traverse, what we drink, what we eat, what stimulates us aesthetically, and so on, seem to have been sorted out better here, if I can put it that way. Centuries of refinement have created a country where even the simplest, most democratic pleasures – a loaf of bread, a *café au lait*, a glass of wine – have a depth of meaning, a quality of enrichment that is somehow lacking elsewhere.

But there is another side to France, a more complex, darker one that coexists with its sophisticated hedonism, and the three books I've chosen all in their own way exemplify this admixture. Rather than range through French literature and select a Molière with a Proust and a Sainte-Beuve, or a Rimbaud with a Racine and a Montaigne, I have deliberately limited myself to the twentieth-century novel. On no other country in Europe (with the possible exception of Germany) does the last century cast such a sombre shadow and each of these novels hints at or explores the three great traumas France has endured during those hundred years and still endures today.

The first, moving chronologically by publication, is *Le Grand Meaulnes* by Alain-Fournier. I read this novel in my teens and I can still recall the impression it made on me then. It is a great novel of adolescence – you might say *The Catcher in the Rye* of contemporary French literature. It deals with the relationships between three school friends in provincial France at the end of the nineteenth century and the adventures that befall its eponymous hero, Meaulnes. The boys discover, in the depths of the French countryside, a lost domain, an old manor house, and at the same time are captivated by the girl who lives there, Yvonne. It's hard to analyse the magic that this book works. It's to do with secrecy, with the stirrings of adolescent sexuality but, more movingly, with the transience of our childhood pleasures and pains. Lurking behind the sunlit felicities of the simple story is the idea of death and its inevitability. All the more poignantly, the novel was written and published in 1913, a year before the outbreak of the First World War. Alain-Fournier, twenty-eight years old, was killed in the first month of the conflict and his body never recovered. The *memento mori* prescience of the novel's atmosphere found an eerie parallel in the author's own fate. And the undertone of melancholia that sits beside the precise and beautiful descriptions of a provincial adolescence is very French.

There's a similar but more brazen confrontation with the human condition in my second choice: Albert Camus's celebrated *L'Etranger* (*The Outsider*). Its status as a modern classic makes it difficult to imagine what it must have been like to read this short, laconic novel at the time of its publication in 1942 in the middle of the war, with France occupied by the invading Germans.

Camus's hero, Mersault, is a truly modern man in his godlessness and his uncompromising, ironic understanding of the absurd nature of human existence. He is chillingly and brutally honest in his refusal to ameliorate his relentless non-conformity. Again the extra-literary resonances of the novel contribute to its exemplary nature. Camus was an Algerian, a citizen of France domiciled in North Africa. There is, in Mersault's blunt diffidence, his absolute disinterestedness, a challenge to the culture of France and Europe. Here is a Frenchman with a different and very uncomfortable attitude – but who is as French as any Parisian waiter, for all that. These tensions foreshadow the Algerian war of the 1950s – effectively a French civil war – whose ramifications are still powerfully felt in the country half a century on.

My third novel was published in 1970 and won the Goncourt Prize of that year. Michel Tournier's *Le Roi des Aulnes* (*The Erl King*) is an extraordinary account of the life of one Abel Tiffauges, whom we follow from ungainly schoolboy to humble *garagiste* to a prisoner of war of the Germans in East Prussia. There he is transformed into, literally, a form of ogre – a child stealer (the erl-king of legend). The novel is a haunting mixture of beautifully observed reality (Tiffauges's boarding school is enduringly horrible) and an expert reinvention of familiar myth. While it deals with the Second World War and the Nazi terror it is also an example of the kind of novel that only a French writer can achieve. Tournier is an immensely learned author with powerful opinions of true and controversial intellectual heft. And although he uses these ideas to buttress the cultural and literary leitmotifs of the novel they never overwhelm it. There is a tendency to denigrate French abstract thinking by contrasting it with Anglo-Saxon plain speaking. Each cultural predisposition has its extremes: impenetrable pretentious waffle on the one hand and pipe-and-slippers philistinism on the other. Tournier's novel manages, however, to walk a line between intellectual profundity and narrative excitement with unusual poise and fascinating, stimulating flair. It is a very French novel.

Which is why I admire it so. I love France, I love its culture and its people. I was educated in one of its universities and I have lived in the country for ten years now. But like all countries and all peoples there are complexities of attitude, problems of understanding and comportment. All three of these novels explore aspects of the French 'character' and in so doing elaborate, sometimes inadvertently, on themes peculiar to it. Generalizations about a country or its population are facile and effortlessly disproved (I'm speaking as a spendthrift Scotsman), but Camus said once, 'si tu veux être philosophe, écris un roman.' Novels, then, with their complexity, their scope, their built-in engagement with our common humanity, may be an ideal way of getting under a nation's skin. So what do these three tell us about France? My feeling is that all three of them are darker than they may first appear and I think one can point to a strain of pessimism in French life and behaviour that these works echo. When Camus says, 'everything that exalts life adds at the same time to its absurdity' he is not airing some convoluted intellectual trope but facing up to a pitiless fact about our existence that we would be better off acknowledging. Does this darkness contribute to that wilful stubbornness, that contrariness we non-French so often find in the French? Perhaps so – and *tant mieux*, I would add. The world seems palpably, rebarbatively absurd this week, hellbent on war. A dose of French contrariness is both provocative and salutary in the face of the new hegemony to whose tune we seem obliged to march, these days. A discordant note in a military band has never been so welcome.

2003

Evelyn Waugh (2)

(Introduction to *A Handful of Dust*)

Madame Bovary rewritten by Noël Coward. Is this too harsh – or too glib – a redaction of *A Handful of Dust*, considered by many readers to be Evelyn Waugh's finest novel? My one-sentence summary is not intended to be facetious but arose from a thought-experiment I imposed on myself. I tried to imagine what it must have been like to read the novel when it was first published (in 1934), to imagine what the experience must have been to read Waugh without the mighty baggage of the posthumous reputation. The problem is that we know too much about Evelyn Waugh – the biographies, the journals, the letters and the memoirs flesh him out in a manner rare amongst twentieth-century British writers. Virginia Woolf runs him close, Philip Larkin is coming up on the rails, but it is unusual to have so much information so comparatively soon on a writer who died only a generation ago. This weight of public judgement and analysis (and self-analysis) makes it hard to return to the novels as an innocent and unknowing reader: the bloated Catholic apologist, the misanthropic, check-suited Tory squire, stands at your shoulder and hindsight's 20/20 vision provides answers that are both too swift and too pat. Hence the attempt at a thought-experiment and hence the reference to Noël Coward and *Madame Bovary*. And in this spirit it seems to me that above all else *A Handful of Dust* – this complex, fraught, tension-riven novel – is essentially, pre-eminently, two things: namely, it is a society novel (which is not the same as a novel about society) and a novel about adultery. I had forgotten how *Tatlery* the book is: how it was so plainly written for a small elite of London and County readers who would pick up the many smart references and the in-jokes. It is bright and brittle and knowing in its depiction of that milieu and written with an insider's ease and familiarity. This tone of voice seems a little mannered and tiresome today (as indeed does Noël Coward's) but it was designed at the time to play to a well-heeled and well-connected gallery.

It is also a brutally cold and clear-eyed look at a wife's betrayal of a loving husband. Brenda Last, like Emma Bovary, is a provincial lady married to a stuffy and somewhat dull, prematurely aged man ('a bore', as Cyril Connolly dubbed Tony Last). John Beaver is a metropolitan version of the clerk who takes his pleasure selfishly and lovelessly. From here the comparisons begin to grow a little strained. Flaubert may have said 'Madame Bovary c'est moi' but Waugh would never have made that claim about Brenda. *A Handful of Dust* is a portrait of adultery seen from the side of the blameless cuckold – there can be few more ruthless and unredeeming literary portrayals of a woman than Waugh's of Brenda Last. As the affair between Brenda and Beaver continues and the lies become more and more brazen (and therefore condemnable) one begins to question the veracity of the earlier portrayal of the Lasts' marriage: how could Tony Last (a good man, though set in his ways) have ever married anyone as vapid, heartless and lacking in human warmth as the Brenda who takes up with Beaver? I would argue that the portrait of Brenda is inconsistent and dislocated (wife and adulteress seem different people) because it is not her character that particularly interests the author but the nature of what she has done to her marriage. The betrayal is everything and Waugh is unsparing in the way he wrings every final humiliation from it.

This is not all that surprising given the circumstances in which *A Handful of Dust* was begun. Waugh travelled to Fez, in Morocco, to write the book in January 1934. The preceding months had seen him much preoccupied with an unhappy love affair with Teresa Jungman (Waugh had proposed marriage, she had turned him down – Waugh was distraught and miserable) and with the continuing consequences of his own divorce from his first wife Evelyn Gardner, a complicated process which involved appearing at an Ecclesiastical Court to testify to the flawed and insincere nature of his marriage in an effort to have the religious authorities declare the union null and void, Evelyn Gardner (she-Evelyn) had had an affair with John Heygate in the first year of her marriage to Waugh. The publicity and grim procedures surrounding the eventual divorce (announcements in *The Times*, for example; meeting the lover in a lawyer's office so he could be formally identified as co-respondent) and the acute embarrassment (and his own perceived shame and ridicule) that Waugh suffered within his circle of friends had a monumental and lasting effect on his life and personality. It is no wonder that adultery, betrayal and heartlessness so dominate the pages of the novel he began to write.

Waugh wrote fast: he finished *A Handful of Dust* in four months, dispatching sections to the typist as he completed them. But he was having trouble with the ending (there is a very useful account of the composition of the novel in volume 1 of Martin Stannard's fine biography). Before starting *A Handful of Dust*, Waugh had just written a travel book (in a month), an account of his recent travels in the hinterland of British Guiana, published under the title *Ninety-Two Days*. It was a job of work and was not a book he held in much esteem. However, the trip had given him the material for a short story, 'The Man Who Liked Dickens'. In the novel, Tony Last, having discovered Brenda's adultery, also leaves Britain to travel into the jungles of British Guiana and his famous fate − compelled to read Dickens for the rest of his life to the baleful settler-cum-gaoler Mr Todd − is essentially Waugh's short story 'The Man Who Liked Dickens' stapled on to the end of his unfinished novel about adultery. Henry Green wrote to Waugh when the book came out and said, 'I feel the end is so fantastic that it throws the rest out of proportion. Aren't you mixing two things together? It seemed manufactured and not real.' This is one novelist's intuition analysing a fellow novelist's work with great and embarrassing acuity. Waugh defended himself stoutly: 'wishing to bring Tony to a sad end I made it an elaborate and improbable one'. Adding that it was a 'conceit in the Webster manner'. This is disingenuous: I would argue that Waugh needed an ending and realized that he had already written something that would do. He was an assiduous recycler and re-user of his own experiences and other writings and *A Handful of Dust* is evidence of his economy − both *Ninety-Two Days* and 'The Man Who Liked Dickens' were press-ganged into solving the problem of his novel's conclusion.

There is nothing wrong with this − most novelists have occasion to do something similar from time to time, though perhaps they do it more covertly than Waugh. But I think the history of the novel's composition and the evidence of its frankly cobbled-together ending undermine claims for the book's thematic consistency and its structural cohesion. *A Handful of Dust* is characterized by several such tensions: not merely in its structure, but also in its tone of voice, its characterization, comedy − the novel is full of uneasiness. The key to Waugh's objective in finding the right ending to the story lies in his phrase 'wishing to bring Tony to a sad end' rather than any huffing and puffing about Websterian conceits. Waugh wanted to bring Tony to a sad end because this was the nature of his comic genius − it is pitiless and ruthless, and this is what makes it both modern and enduring. Tony, that most wronged of decent men, is served up with his own particular circle of hell through no fault of his own. Brenda, in contrast, one of the most empty and unpleasant women one can imagine, is rewarded with marriage to Jock Grant-Menzies, MP, one of Tony's rich friends. This was the way the world worked for Waugh (and it certainly must have seemed so as he wrote the novel in 1934) – in his best work he always refused to allow his art to provide any form of easy consolation. At the end of *Labels*, the travel book he wrote in the immediate fallout of his own broken marriage, and in the full knowledge of the nature of his wife's betrayal, he wrote: 'Fortune is the least capricious of deities, and arranges things on the just and rigid system that no one shall be very happy for very long.' This is very bitter, but it also happens to be very true, in the main. It was a world-view that underpinned Waugh's work and, I believe, was one that continually fought against his newly acquired Catholic faith. It provokes an unhappy tension in his work that begins to emerge in the novels after *A Handful of Dust* (with the notable exception of *Scoop*, his real masterpiece, in my opinion). The new seriousness that critics began to see in his work – in *Brideshead Revisited* and in *The Sword of Honour* trilogy, for example – is Waugh's attempt to use his religious faith to combat or obscure this instinctive view he possessed of the human condition. He saw life as anarchic, indifferent and absurd. Waugh, to put it crudely, could not, or did not, want to write in this spirit any longer (which is fundamentally Godless) but it was one that came all too naturally to him. In *A Handful of Dust* we see its apotheosis.

Waugh wrote very fast and he always had financial reimbursement for his writing very close to the forefront of his mind. This is not to say he wasn't an artist – he definitely was, as were Balzac and Dickens, two other speed-merchants – but he was not an artist in the sense that, say, Flaubert, Joyce and Nabokov were. One fact about *A Handful of Dust* makes this very clear: before the book was published in Britain it had been serialized in five parts in the American magazine *Harper's Bazaar*. Because 'The Man Who Liked Dickens' had been published separately as a short story in America, Waugh found himself in copyright difficulties (this conflict also testifies tellingly to the virtually unchanged, bolted-on aspect of the Mr Todd conclusion). Consequently, he wrote a new ending for the serialized version of the novel. In the light of this evidence I find it very hard to accept that there is some schematic master-plan for *A Handful of Dust* and that its various components were always designed to harmonize and complement each other. This is what Henry Green sensed – one craftsman looking at another craftsman's work – and his complaint is wholly justified. Waugh's response is a little desperate: if the book is so intricately stitched together, then just how easy can it be to write an entirely new ending for it? However, the serialization ending is very interesting in itself and it inadvertently says as much about the novel's underlying intentions, I would claim, as the published book version does. We will return to it later.

Waugh was one of the most confessedly autobiographical of writers. All his novels – with the exception of *Helena*, perhaps – are rooted in his own experiences, even the most exuberant and grotesque comedies. *The Ordeal of Gilbert Pinfold* and *The Sword of Honour* trilogy are particularly good examples of this tendency, but the life/art nexus is strongly present in all his novels. Novelists of this sort do not necessarily possess the fingernail-paring artistic objectivity of a Joyce or Nabokov. Themes and leitmotifs, images and metaphors tend to emerge more unconsciously with this category of writer. That Waugh wrote so quickly also testifies to something subconscious and instinctive in his art rather than highly planned and artistically organized. True, there are repeated themes in *A Handful of Dust* that appear to run coherently through it – lists of objects that define a character, images of beasts and animals, for example; the idea of the celestial city, of Gothic fantasy and romance – but such synthesis is not the overriding impression the novel conveys, I would claim. On the contrary, *A Handful of Dust*, structurally speaking, is highly variable, not to say disorganized, and the machinery of the novel – its nuts and bolts, its pulleys and levers – suggests, when analysed, something altogether more inchoate and thrown together.

Take the question of point of view, for example. The narrative voice is omniscient: namely, the author is at liberty to enter any character's mind and tell us, the readers, what he or she is thinking. Godlike, the author can flit here and there, and present the novel's world in all its objectivity or subjectivity as he pleases. As the twentieth century moved on, omniscient narration became less and less favoured, or else was used with deliberate knowingness. It was the most popular narrative method of the great Victorian novelists and, surprisingly, *A Handful of Dust* sounds at times very Victorian in its use of omniscience. Waugh does not hesitate to employ what we might call the Dickensian apostrophe: a moment in the text when all suspension of disbelief is cast aside and the novelist addresses the reader in his own voice. For a book regarded as bleakly modern it is in places creakingly antique. Waugh favours the use of the bracketed aside quite frequently. For example, early in the novel after Tony and Brenda have breakfast there is a two-line parenthesis: '(These scenes of domestic playfulness had been more or less continuous in Tony and Brenda's life for seven years.)' Whose voice is this, thus distinguished from the surrounding expository prose? It is Waugh, himself, filling in a bit of background, ignoring the modernist injunction, 'show not tell'. And Waugh does a lot of 'telling' in this novel, often clumsily, which is surprising given that the novel's strongest technical virtuosity is otherwise its economy and spareness. *A Handful of Dust* is at its most accomplished and convincing when Waugh does the opposite of apostrophize and tells us virtually nothing: when what is implicit in the few words used detonates so much more effectively than any amount of elaborate explanation. I find Waugh's manifest awkwardness with the omniscient voice perplexing – seeing it as evidence (with the aid of hindsight operating, I admit) of something hurried rather than fully or carefully considered. The opening of chapter three, 'Hard Cheese on Tony', almost reads like a parody of Dickens: 'It is not uncommon at Brat's Club, between nine and ten in the evening, to find men in white ties and tail coats sitting by themselves and eating, in evident low spirits, large and extravagant dinners.' The tone is avuncular, the overview authorial, the tense is present – and then it shifts back to the past tense for the arrival of Jock Grant-Menzies: 'It was in this mood and for this reason that, one evening towards the middle of February, Jock Grant-Menzies arrived at the club.' This would not seem out of place in Trollope.

By dramatic contrast you then find passages as elliptical as this conversation between Tony and Brenda after Brenda has seen Beaver in London:

'Barnardo case?'

Brenda nodded. 'Down and out,' she said, 'sunk right under.' She sat nursing her bread and milk, stirring it listlessly. Every bit of her felt good for nothing.

'Good day?'

She nodded. 'Saw Marjorie and her filthy dog. Bought some things. Lunched at Daisy's new joint. Bone-setter. That's all.'

'You know I wish you'd give up these day trips to London. They're far too much for you.'

'Me? Oh, I'm all right. Wish I was dead, that's all . . . and please, please, darling Tony, don't say anything about bed, because I can't move.'

Underneath these commonplace exchanges lurks the ticking time bomb: *Brenda hasn't mentioned Beaver.* She hasn't exactly lied, true, but we, the readers, will be hugely aware of the omission. It's at this moment that we know for the first time she will have an affair with Beaver and will betray Tony. It is what is *not* said, what is left out, that makes these few lines function so effectively. But such skilful reticence isn't consistent in the novel: implicitness and explicitness coexist, often uneasily. This is not a sign of a writer exercising total mastery over his material.

Such signs are legion, however, in the passages leading up to the death of Tony and Brenda's child John Andrew in a hunting accident. Before the fateful hunt Waugh uses a device that can only be called cinematic: a series of short scenes juxtaposed, sometimes no more than a few lines of dialogue, a method that, in a film, would be known as cross-cutting, or even, at its most rapid, montage. Again, it is the absence of interlinking passages that is conspicuous. Often the speakers of lines aren't identified, neither is their location. Waugh was an avid cinema-goer and he doubtless realized that here was a method of moving narration along without the need for pages of expository prose. And such descriptive passages as there are demonstrate the old adage of 'less is more' to near perfection:

She hit him and the horse collected himself and bolted up the road into the village, but before he went one of his heels struck out and sent John into the ditch, where he lay bent double, perfectly still.

Everyone agreed that it was nobody's fault.

Terse, heavily monosyllabic, the words do their job with perfect thriftiness – and then the overused phrase 'bent double' seems, at first, slack or lazy, until you realize, as you visualize exactly what the words describe, that there is no more expressive way of conveying the fact that John Andrew is actually dead. A little boy bent double in a ditch.

Sustained passages of brilliance like this can function as an ideal model of how to maintain narrative power. The pages that lead up to the death of John Andrew are a tour de force. But then you come across a section, such as the following, when Tony learns that Brenda is going to sue for heavy alimony.

He hung up the receiver and went back to the smoking room. His mind had suddenly become clearer on many points that had puzzled him. A whole Gothic world had come to grief . . . there was now no armour glittering through the forest glades, no embroidered feet on the green sward; the cream and dappled unicorns had fled . . .

Just in case we hadn't got it, Waugh resorts to telling not showing, in a manner that is over-obvious and over-larded. Time and again in the novel, these inconsistencies and dissonances are revealing. And what they reveal, I would argue, is that *A Handful of Dust* is not the harmonious whole, the masterwork, that critics have claimed it to be. Inside the structure of omniscience and Victorian apostrophe, a leaner, more oblique, more modern novel is struggling to coexist. Pages of rapid cross-cutting and terse dialogue consort unhappily with ponderous explication, authorial asides and forced humour (*A Handful of Dust* is the least funny of all Waugh's novels: look at the interminable ten pages of Tony and Jock's drunken spree). What is in fact a dark and acerbic exposé of contemporary decadence and ennui is overweighted at the end by the battened-on symbolism of a previously written short story.

I see other inconsistencies that point to further warring intentions. Take the portrait of Brenda, for example. At the beginning of the novel she seems sweet: loving and tolerant of Tony – yet she takes to adultery effortlessly and without a qualm: indeed she's rather good at it. Scenes are then presented to show Brenda in the worst possible light as someone utterly without feeling and casually cruel. The famous exchange when she learns that 'John' has died and instantly thinks it is John Beaver, rather than John Andrew her son, is perhaps the best example (though I've always felt the scene sells itself short – no one really refers to Beaver as 'John', so when she says 'John' the reader will automatically think of the boy. The joke requires a double take (you have to remind yourself of Beaver's Christian name) and in that split second the shock effect rather loses its potency). More to the point are her lying telephone calls to Tony when Beaver is in bed with her: there is nothing in Brenda as she is first presented to us to hint that she is capable of such icily calm duplicity – this is the behaviour of a serial adulteress. Some other process is going on here, I would argue, in her changing portrayal. Similarly, critics who contend that Tony is meant to be seen as a buffoon and that his love of his big, ugly, Victorian Gothic house is risible are not reading the book closely. Waugh – whose own tastes were maverick and the opposite of à la mode – lovingly celebrates Hetton and Tony's love for the house. The precision of the writing about the architecture does not remotely hint at mockery – on the contrary, every word speaks of relish and approval. If Tony's taste is meant to be absurd then what of Mrs Beaver's ghastly interiors? Surely Hetton is meant to represent values, however out of fashion, that are fundamentally sound and worthwhile and deliberately set in opposition to the shoddy trendiness of Mrs Beaver. What these discordancies illustrate is the effects of attempting to shape *A Handful of Dust* into something it isn't. My contention is that, at root, *A Handful of Dust* was written to be Waugh's own exploration of betrayal and marital humiliation and that it is, in its special way, a form of revenge against the damage inflicted on his psyche by Evelyn Gardner. Brenda's casual adultery and the disasters it sets in train are meant to be condemned in the most stern and merciless terms. Waugh gives her no escape route: her lover is a waster and a sponger, a hopeless remittance man. Her betrayed husband, by contrast, is sincere, decent and loving. Furthermore – and this is the killer blow – Brenda has so lost her sense of value that she cares more about her boyfriend than she does about her son. It is an unyieldingly cruel and vicious portrait of a worthless woman.

One more piece of evidence: towards the end of the novel when Tony is sailing to South America he has a shipboard romance with a young girl called Thérèse. In the previously quoted letter to Henry Green, Waugh admits, 'I think the sentimental episode with Thérèse is probably a mistake.' He was right: it's a mistake because we think that it is positioned there so that Tony will find some romantic reward for his sufferings – and the romance is painted with real tenderness – but it turns out that, as soon as Thérèse finds out Tony is married (i.e. not divorced) she loses all interest in him. Yet another insincere woman dissembling to try and catch a husband. Martin Stannard, in his biography, points out that Thérèse was originally named Bernadette but the name was changed in the manuscript. Prior to writing the novel Waugh had proposed to Teresa Jungman, had been rejected and was severely heartsore (he dedicated the Dutch edition of *A Handful of Dust* to her). Circumstantial evidence? Yes, perhaps, but the more it mounts the harder it becomes not to read *A Handful of Dust* as Waugh's individual cry of pain.

The novel is full of hate and scorn, not just for Brenda, but also for the society in which she moves. The smart world of metropolitan London is portrayed by Waugh as utterly dissolute, genuine venom lurking beneath the ostensible social satire. The only woman in that world who escapes total censure, interestingly enough, is the morphine addict Mrs Rattery – who is of real and coolly efficient support to Tony in the hours after John Andrew's death. Mrs Rattery, morphineuse and aviatrix, can retreat from the social whirl through her drugs, her self-absorption (her endless games of patience) or – physically – by taking to the air in her flying machine. There is something enviably godlike about her impassivity and emotional distance from the rest of the characters in the novel.

The social world of the novel – of night clubs and house parties, soirées and silly fads – is the world that Waugh himself occupied and was intimate with. It is depicted with a cold and unsparing eye and I would suggest that this explains the title Waugh eventually chose (he was going to call the book *A Handful of Ashes*). 'I will show you fear in a handful of dust' is about the emptiness at the heart of this section of society. Eliot's poem, to put it very simply, seems notionally about seeking some form of restoration (rain, rebirth, regrowth), redemption (some Grail substitute) or salvation (some spiritual peace) in a world turned waste land. But looked at from a slightly different angle (again trying to ignore the poem's reputation and critical baggage acquired over the years) it can be argued that in fact *The Waste Land* is all about sex – seedy, unsatisfactory, loveless, dangerous, destructive sex. It abounds in references to sex, is steeped in it, almost obsessively so. The context of the four lines Waugh cites as his epigraph (and usually authors do not choose epigraphs lightly) comes just before the introduction of the 'hyacinth girl'. Would one think of Brenda Last? '. . . your hair wet . . . /I was neither/living nor dead, and I knew nothing/looking into the heart of light, the silence.' Brenda, with her 'fair underwater look' (not a bad description of Evelyn Gardner, either) . . . Circumstantial evidence, admittedly, but the file is growing.

Waugh wrote the first two-thirds of this novel at great speed, fresh from his rejection by Teresa Jungman (his one great love after Evelyn Gardner) and his regular testimony to the Roman Catholic authorities about the sham and frivolity of his first marriage. That bitterness and resentment found its place in the bleak story of Brenda Last's betrayal of her husband and the curse they suffered of their child's awful death. And then Waugh stopped, unable to think how to conclude the book, knowing only that he wanted Tony to come to 'a sad end'. In the event he took over, almost wholesale, an earlier short story and hitched it on to his incomplete novel. Fiddling around here and there with themes and images, chapter headings and symbols, he endeavoured to give the book some coherence. But in fact the most integral conclusion to the book was the one he had already written to complete the American serialization. It is a very short final section, some seven or eight pages, and is meant to come after Tony and Brenda have agreed to a divorce.

It picks up the story after Tony has returned from an uneventful tourist trip in the Caribbean and is met at Southampton docks by Brenda. The couple are reconciled, after a fashion (Beaver, tiring of Brenda, has tried and failed to seduce Mrs Rattery, and has gone abroad), and Tony, it appears, has forgiven her – or decided to ignore – her aberration. Months later they go up to town (Brenda is now pregnant). Tony goes to see Mrs Beaver about Brenda's flat and makes a deal to keep it on (Brenda knows nothing). The implication is that Tony will be coming up to town more frequently himself and will need the flat to entertain girl-friends. In the final lines of the chapter Tony lies to Brenda:

'Did you get rid of the flat?' she asked.

 'Yes, that's all settled.'

It's not exactly a lie but the reader knows (as the reader knew earlier when Brenda committed her sin of omission) that Tony is going to find the flat very useful indeed. The last line reads: 'And the train sped through the darkness towards Hetton.'

The changes of emphasis are hugely significant: in the novel Tony's fate is as a helpless victim; Mr Todd's torture a symbol of the malign indifference of the universe. In the magazine version he is instead actively responsible for his own unpleasant transformation. Given the bitterness and contempt that inform the novel this alternative ending seems to me to be truer to the novel's potent undercurrents than the short story Waugh recycled to finish off his sombre, disturbing tale of adultery, betrayal and the death of hope. Waugh republished the ending in 1963 as an appendix to the uniform edition of *A Handful of Dust*, describing it as a 'curiosity'. We have to take it that he wanted it preserved. So why didn't he use the ending that was specifically written for his novel? Perhaps because it would have seemed too brutally, too unsparingly cynical. Tony Last has become like everyone else in *A Handful of Dust* – corrupt, selfish, venal and heartless. He still has Hetton – he still has Brenda (with another child on the way) – but he now speeds through darkness to reach his home.

2003

Ernest Hemingway

(Review of *True at First Light*)

'Honey are you bored? I'm perfectly happy reading and not being wet in the rain. You have to write letters too.'

'No. I love for us to talk together. It's the thing I miss when there's so much excitement and work and we're never alone except in bed. We have a wonderful time in bed and you say lovely things to me. I remember them and the fun. But this is a different kind of talking.'

It certainly is: it is mawkish, badly composed, embarrassing and toe-curlingly cute and is written, not by Danielle Steele, but by Ernest Hemingway. This passage is lifted, almost at random, from one of the interminable dialogues in what purports to be the latest and final posthumous Hemingway novel, edited – if that is the correct word – by Hemingway's son, Patrick. The work was done, so Patrick Hemingway tells us in an introduction, along the following principles: '[the] untitled manuscript is about two hundred thousand words long and is certainly not a journal. What you will read here is a fiction half that length . . . which I have licked here into what I hope is not the worst of all possible shapes.' And that is all, apparently, that we need to know.

The existence of this African journal is well known. It was written in the mid 1950s and extracts were published after Hemingway's death by his widow in *Sports Illustrated* in 1971 and 72. The text emerged from the disastrous hunting trip Hemingway made to Africa in 1953–4 with his fourth wife, Mary. During the trip Hemingway was involved in two light-aeroplane crashes, one of which injured him severely. In the second crash Hemingway fractured his skull, dislocated his shoulder, ruptured his liver, right kidney and spleen and his face and head were badly burned. It could be argued that the health problems he suffered thereafter precipitated his notorious decline into terminal alcoholism and depression.

But not a word of this appears in *True at First Light*. Instead the book concentrates on the few weeks of the hunting trip that took place before Xmas 1953. Most of the action in the book – narrated by Ernest Hemingway – revolves around two significant events: first, the need to protect the camp against a possible raid by escaped Mau-Mau insurgents (this threat suddenly disappears) and second, the efforts made to help Hemingway's wife, Mary, shoot a large lion which prowls around the vicinity. Added to these concerns are various hunting and camp-related activities – shooting game for the bearers, going into town for supplies, nattering round the campfire, relations with the African staff and so on. Most curious, though, is a kind of semi-covert 'affair' going on between Hemingway and an African girl called Debba – whom Mary refers to as 'your fiancée' – who lives in a nearby village. There are many visits to Debba and a certain amount of harmless physical contact ensues: 'Debba said nothing. She had lost her lovely Kamba impudence and I stroked her bowed head, which felt lovely, and touched the secret places behind her ears and she put her hand up, stealthily, and touched my worst scars.'

Mary finally shoots her lion, Ernest shoots a leopard, there are long conversations around the campfire, Mary goes to Nairobi, Ernest visits Debba, the African landscape is regularly described, more animals are shot and, fundamentally, that is about it. One is left at the end with a feeling of saddened bafflement, rather than gratitude, wondering why this book would ever have been thought worth publishing.

The answer, of course, is that these are the final sweepings from the great *vide grenier* that has been the story of Hemingway's posthumous publication. It began with *A Moveable Feast* and continued with the novels entitled *Islands in the Stream* and *The Garden of Eden*, a collection of bullfighting articles which became *The Dangerous Summer*, various short stories and the African safari excerpts published in *Sports Illustrated*. *A Moveable Feast* apart, which Hemingway had, at least, actually submitted to his publishers before he died (and then withdrawn), all this work was deemed by the author to be unpublishable: his family has thought and chosen to do otherwise.

The ethics of this enterprise may be dubious but critically and artistically they have been close to ruinous as far as Hemingway's reputation is concerned. *True at First Light*, the case in point, is a particularly lethal blow. The book is, frankly, often hilariously bad and embarrassing. Apart from the desperate archness and tedium of much of the dialogue, it has no organization, it rambles and repeats itself and it contributes nothing to the Hemingway oeuvre that was not already, more resplendently, there. There are, to be fair, some better moments. The account of Mary shooting her lion is tensely and effectively done; there are some

lyrical passages of description of landscape (one of which gives the book
its title) and, for biographers, the odd insight may be afforded – into
Hemingway's prodigious drinking, for example, and also some light may
be thrown on his brag to have been married to a Wakamba girl and
her sister.

A further miscalculation – on Patrick Hemingway's part, I suppose
– was pointedly to call this book a 'novel'. Biographers have always
referred to the manuscript as a 'journal' and even Mary Hemingway
classified it as a 'semi-fictional account of our African safari'. Some sort
of fudge of this order might have been advisable, especially in this day
and age, when we readily accept that memoirs, travel writing and
reportage will have a hefty dose of the fictive in the mix, but for Patrick
Hemingway to carve out 50 per cent of the text, 'lick it into shape' and
categorize it as a novel seems not only misguided but absurd as well.

Hemingway himself animadverts on this very topic in *True at First
Light*. 'My excuse is that I make the truth as I invent it truer than it
would be. That is what makes good writers or bad. If I write in the
first person, stating it as fiction, critics now will still try to prove these
things never happened to me.' This sounds like an attempt to form the
artistic credo behind the African manuscript. It is so palpably Hemingway
himself at the centre of the stage – he reminisces about his past, he
quotes a hostile letter to him from a woman reader in Iowa, for instance
– and the touchstones with his life are so vividly present that it is as if
he is deliberately trying to pre-empt this tendency, as he perceives it,
of critics' efforts to fit the fiction to the creator. So, quite blatantly, he
calls the narrator Ernest Hemingway; he calls his wife Mary; he fills the
book with verifiable facts and persons and attempts no artful disguise.
Everything about this endeavour stresses the documentary and the real.

Paul Fussell has written (in *The Great War and Modern Memory*) of
'the necessity of fiction in any memorable testimony about fact'. *True
at First Light* is in no way memorable testimony but one can see how
this modus operandi would appeal to Hemingway as it makes it all the
easier subtly to embellish, to foster the mythic tendancy: Papa
Hemingway out on the veldt at dawn, gun in hand, hunting his prey –
wife, booze and Kamba bride waiting for him back at home. And for
the reader too, this notional autobiographical candour has the effect of
making the aggregate of meandering anecdotage relatively more interesting in that, as is usual in this sort of writing, it is easier to fillet out
the fictive decoration from the facts than the other way round – the

whole sorry business of the 'affair' with Debba being a fine example. However, Patrick Hemingway – for sound marketing reasons, doubtless – would have us read this book as a novel, which proves a frustrating and impossible task in the end: the book remains studiedly grounded in the biography and in its particular place and time. *True at First Light* has to be read in this spirit, as non-fiction, with all the usual caveats that apply.

And what it tells us is old news indeed: namely that by the mid 1950s, the Nobel Prize in his pocket, Hemingway was subsisting on 'Hemingway', that the writer had become more important than the work itself. Chronologically, the African manuscript follows the critical disaster of *Across the River and into the Trees* (which Delmore Schwartz described as 'extremely bad in an ominous way') and the huge commercial success of the novella *The Old Man and the Sea*. This last had won the Pulitzer for Hemingway in 1952 and in 1954 he had won the Nobel. *Across the River* had been Hemingway's first published novel for ten years. Now, in the mid 1950s, he was, in terms of public recognition, at the very apogee of his career as a writer. Yet by the time Hemingway sat down to write up the account of his African safari the ominous decline that Schwartz had spotted was clearly in freefall. And, indeed, it must be admitted, everything that is bad in *True at First Light* is also present in *Across the River*. What the publication of *True at First Light* actually achieves – this 'novel' hacked out of a disorganized work in progress – is to confirm beyond all reasonable doubt that the death of Hemingway the novelist had occurred some time at the end of the 1940s. All efforts to revive the corpse proved to be vain.

And nobody tried harder than Hemingway himself, as the publication of the posthumous novels reveals. Two hundred thousand words of unusable manuscript is no small price to pay. It is, in a backhanded way, a tribute to Hemingway's own vanishing instinct as a writer that, even as he created them, he recognized that his fictional efforts were truly moribund and he kept them locked away from public view until his death and the family intervened. And yet, despite all the damaging evidence of the late work and the posthumous novels, Hemingway remains, in my opinion, one of the most important writers of the twentieth century, but his greatness resides almost entirely in his short fiction. His revolutionary short stories, written in the 1920s and 30s, blending tremendous complexity with radically new expression, rank him along with Chekhov, Joyce and Kipling as one of the great masters of the form.

Paradoxically, the one service that publication of *True at First Light* might render is to furnish a metaphor or lasting image for the awful spectre of Hemingway's decline as a writer. He writes that, 'In Africa a thing is true at first light and a lie by noon, and you have no more respect for it than for the lovely perfect weed fringed lake you see across the sun-baked salt plain. You have walked across that plain in the morning and you know that no such lake is there.' Hemingway's real gift – his genius – was true at the first light of his writing career but by noon he was living a lie.

1999

Evelyn Waugh (3)

(Review of *Collected Travel Writing*)

It is 1959, you are a retired brigadier living in Dar es Salaam, Tanganyika. A friend of yours, a colonial officer, has offered to drive you up country to Morogoro. But when your friend arrives he is already accompanied by a stranger: a stout, elderly man named Evelyn Waugh. You have a long day's journey ahead of you. In his book, published a year later, *A Tourist in Africa*, Waugh describes you as a man of 'imperturbable geniality' and adds of his two travelling companions, 'I don't know if they enjoyed my company. I certainly enjoyed theirs.' I wonder . . . How one would love to know what the retired brigadier really thought.

I mention this tiny incident because one of the experiences of reading Waugh's travel writing is that I constantly speculate what it must have been like actually to meet him while he was on the road, as it were. It strikes me that a day in a hot car driving through the African bush with Evelyn Waugh could well qualify as a minor circle of hell. He was not a tolerant or easy man, that much is clear, but he also had a weak grasp of how he himself was perceived. He was genuinely traumatized after a visit to the Caribbean to discover that his hosts thought him 'a bore'. I remember once meeting Fitzroy Maclean — and there was little love lost between him and Waugh — and asking him what Waugh had been like when they knew each other during the war. Maclean said, with candour — and no axe to grind, as far as I could tell — that he had never, in his entire military career, met an officer so loathed by the men who served under him.

One of the reasons why one tries to imagine an encounter with Waugh on his trips abroad is that he seemed always to be travelling under duress of one sort or another. And such duress is not conducive to congeniality: there never appears to be any real enthusiasm for the journey or curiosity about the places and people he will discover. You are left with the impression that he was more or less permanently disgruntled, quick to complain, a moan always on his lips, the spectre of terrible boredom forever hovering at his shoulder.

As Nicholas Shakespeare makes clear in his excellent introduction to this omnibus, Waugh's travel writing was, in the pure sense, hack work.

Waugh wrote travel books for the money and, later in life, also undertook assignments to escape the severities of the English winter. Waugh was completely open about this: even in his first volume, *Labels*, he advertised the ulterior motives of the enterprise, and it is not surprising that his travel writing is redolent of the dutiful task and the looming deadline. It rarely shines.

Mind you, if one was to be honest, one would have to confess that as a genre travel writing – at book length – with a few notable exceptions, makes tedious reading. Shakespeare is all too well aware of Waugh's shortcomings but makes the valid point that the seven travel books in this collection form a kind of covert autobiography. We receive opinions, discover attitudes and prejudices that are unadulterated by fiction: we are permitted a direct glimpse of the man. And it's a good point to make, but Waugh, it seems to me, always adopted a mask when he wrote a travel book and the comments and reflections often appear on closer examination to be disingenuous or assumed. I'm not so sure we uncover the truth or learn much more about this difficult and hugely complex man.

I had read all these books before but thought it might be a useful exercise to reread the first and last of his travel writings – *Labels* (published 1930) and *A Tourist in Africa* (1960) – to see what differences there were between the young man, recently published and recently married, and the prematurely old, eminent writer, full of cafard and *taedium vitae*, looking at the world with a carefully cultivated jaundiced eye. *Labels* has always been the most interesting of Waugh's travel books because it witnessed and was written as his first marriage collapsed. When you know the facts behind the book it appears almost as a fiction: Waugh, the narrator, looks on at himself and his wife Evelyn, thinly disguised as travelling companions, posing as a detached and disinterested observer. Little of the acute misery he was suffering as he wrote it is obviously present, except for the final paragraph, and it has, like all his travel books, an air of hoops being doggedly jumped through. The pages on Gaudi's Sagrada Familia in Barcelona would challenge the most soporific guidebook.

In *A Tourist in Africa* Waugh, in his mid fifties, is now playing the part of the choleric, aged author. He can barely bestir himself to make any effort to engage our interest, spending pages, for example, summarizing books he has read on the voyage out to Mombasa. Occasionally you sense his spirits rise such as when, in Dar es Salaam, he comes across a man calling himself Bishop Homer A. Tomlinson, an American madman who was travelling the world crowning himself king of every country he found himself in. For a couple of pages the book turns into pure Waugh: the wholly relished black humour, the refusal to judge or comment, the clinical description of total absurdity. But such occasions are rare.

Even the fabled style slips. *Labels* is far more garrulous than mature Waugh, almost chatty, which is not surprising given the author's age. *A Tourist in Africa* is interesting insofar as it shows the Augustan verities of his writing turning decadent: the matchless prose becoming slack and pompous: 'For me a voyage is the time to read about the places for which I am bound and to study the bestsellers of the past year. I got through two books a day and never found myself without something readable.' Clichés ('breakneck speed') and the use of the same adjective in the same line are sure signs of his lack of energy and interest, not even picked up at proof stage: 'Over great areas the tsetse fly keeps man away. The great European settlement,' etc.

Waugh had little respect for his travel writing but Nicholas Shakespeare is right to claim that there are flashes of insight. Talking about Cecil Rhodes, Waugh contrasts the lives of the politician and the artist: the politician 'fading into a mist of disappointment and controversy', the artist 'leaving a few objects of permanent value that were not there before him and would not have been there but for him.' This is very close to a personal credo, in fact: this was how Waugh saw himself and is both an exalted and humble definition of what a genuine artist hopes to achieve. Spontaneously addressing a school in Rhodesia he says he has been studying the wonders of the English language for over fifty years and every day still has recourse to a dictionary. There are nuggets of gold in these overworked seams but they are hard to find.

However there is one link between the first and last of these travel books that does resonate. When Waugh wrote *Labels* he had been cuck-olded and was contemplating the impending and very public shame of his divorce. That personal hurt comes to the surface at the end of the book as his boat moves slowly up the Thames to its berth: 'I woke up several times in the night to hear the horn again . . . It was a very dismal sound, premonitory, perhaps of coming trouble, for Fortune is the least capricious of deities, and arranges things on the just and rigid system that no one shall be happy for very long.' Bleak words from a twenty-six-year -old who has just seen his world collapse. But the end of *A Tourist in*

Africa sees a similar bitter envoi as he leaves the continent: 'Cruelty and injustice are endemic everywhere.' It was while Waugh was away from home writing *Labels* that his wife betrayed him. And I have always thought, myself, that the collapse of Waugh's first marriage was the determining event in his life, that this cataclysm shaped him in one way or another for the rest of his days. The saddened, humiliated young man of *Labels* is maybe not so far removed from the posturing clubman roving round Africa. Perhaps that helps explain why there is always something joyless in Waugh's travels.

2003

The Short Story

'Aristocrats? The same ugly bodies and physical uncleanliness, the same toothless old age and disgusting death, as with market women.' This observation comes from a notebook that Anton Chekhov kept during the last six years of his life between 1898 and 1904. In it he jotted down snatches of conversation he had overheard, anecdotes, aphorisms, interesting names and embryonic ideas for short stories. This entry about aristocrats and market women belongs to the last category. The more one has read of Chekhov the more one can envisage the short story that might have grown from this bleak comparison. The point is well made and as true today as it was in nineteenth-century Russia – death is the great leveller – but more interestingly these twenty words can lead us towards an initial way of understanding the short story as opposed to its larger sibling, the novel. I would argue that you could write a short story inspired by Chekhov's words but they wouldn't be sufficient for a novel.

What draws a writer to the short story? Some writers rarely tackle it, or else, in a full career, only write half a dozen stories. Others seem perfectly at home with the form and then let it drop. And then there are those for whom the novel appears the threat. Yet William Faulkner regarded the short story as harder to write than a novel. Many of the greatest short story writers have steered clear of the long form, by and large: Chekhov, J. L. Borges, Katherine Mansfield, V. S. Pritchett, Frank O'Connor. My own case is perhaps typical: I have written eight novels but I cannot stop writing short stories – something about the short form draws me back again and again. The aesthetic pleasures on offer are fresh and beguiling.

It's important to remember that the short story as we know it is a comparatively recent phenomenon. The arrival of mass-market magazine publication and a new generation of literate middle-class readers in the mid to late nineteenth century saw a boom in the short story that lasted maybe a hundred years or so (things are different today). Many writers were initially drawn to the form simply as a way of making money. Particularly in America: Nathaniel Hawthorne, Herman Melville and Edgar Allan Poe all subsidized their less well-remunerated novel-writing careers by writing stories. In the 1920s Scott Fitzgerald was paid $4,000 for a story by the *Saturday Evening Post* (a vast sum today – multiply by ten to get some idea of a comparison). Even John Updike, in the 1950s, reckoned he could support his wife and young family by the sale of five or six stories a year to the *New Yorker*. Times have changed.

The popularity of the short story – indeed its very availability – has, unlike the novel, always been driven by and has always been somewhat at the mercy of commercial considerations. When I published my first collection of stories, *On the Yankee Station*, in 1981, many British publishers routinely brought out short story collections. Not any more. Moreover, there was a small but stable marketplace where a story could be sold. A short story writer could place his or her work in all manner of outlets. The stories in my first collection, for example, had been published in *Punch*, *Company*, *London Magazine*, the *Literary Review*, *Mayfair* and broadcast on the BBC. As a young writer I started writing short stories because at the time it seemed logical: this was my best chance of getting published.

All this talk of money and strategy masks the tenacious appeal of the form. In the end writers write short stories because a different set of mental gears are engaged. Melville wrote short stories as he laboured with *Moby-Dick* saying, 'My only desire for their "success" (as it is called) springs from my pocket and not my heart.' And yet, in the process, he wrote works of short fiction ('Bartleby' and 'Benito Cereno' amongst others) that are timeless classics. The point being that something else occurs in the writing – and reading – of a short story that is on another level from the writing and reading of a novel.

The basic issue here, it seems to me, is one of expansion versus compression. To go back to the remark I made apropos Chekhov's little *memento mori* about aristocrats and market women: we see that the ideas, the inspiration, that will drive a novel, however succinctly expressed, have to be capable of endless augmentation and elaboration. The essence of almost every short story, by contrast, is one of distillation, of reduction. It's not a simple question of length, either: there are twenty-page short stories that are far more charged and gravid with meaning than 400-page novels. We are talking about a different category of prose fiction altogether.

A common analogy is to see the novel as an orchestra and the short story as a string quartet. Beautiful and rich music will be produced by them both but the imbalance of scale will always favour the novel when it comes to variety, nuance, texture, power and so forth. But the analogy strikes me as false because once again it is all about size, and this leads us in the wrong direction. The music produced by two violins, a viola and a cello cannot ever sound anything like the music produced by dozens of instruments, but a paragraph or a page from a short story is indistinguishable from a paragraph or a page from a novel. The short story draws on exactly the same resources as does the novel – language, plot, character and style. Nothing – none of the literary tools that novelists require to write their novels – is denied the short story writer, which is not true for a composer of chamber music as opposed to orchestral. A more pertinent comparison – to try and pin down the essence of the two forms – is poetry: to compare the epic with the lyric. Let us say that the short story is prose fiction's lyric poem, contrasted with the novel as its epic.

There are many definitions of the short story. V. S. Pritchett defined it as, 'something glimpsed from the corner of an eye, in passing.' John Updike has said, 'More closely than my novels . . . these efforts of a few thousand words each hold my life's incidents, predicaments, crises, joys.' Angus Wilson observed that, 'Short stories and plays go together in my mind. You take a point in time and develop it from there; there is no room for development backwards.' All things to all writers, then: the quotidian epiphanic moment, the submerged autobiography, a question of structure and direction. I could cite other definitions – some contradictory, some far-fetched – but all, in their own way, possessing some cogency. If the house of fiction has many windows so too, it seems, does the house of short fiction.

Therefore it might be worth trying to categorize the short story in a bit more detail, to try and classify its multifarious forms. I have published three collections of short stories over two decades, a total of thirty-eight stories, in all. Perhaps there are another four or five uncollected ones out there – juvenilia in university magazines, the odd one-off commission for an anniversary (I seem to remember I wrote something about *1984* and Orwell) or a themed number of a magazine or anthology. In any event what repeatedly draws me to the short story is its variety – the enticing possibility of adopting different voices, structures, styles and effects. Looking at other collections by other writers, I gradually came to the conclusion that there are in fact basically seven types of short story and that within these seven categories almost every kind of short story can be accounted for. Some of them will overlap, one category will borrow from a seemingly unrelated type, but these denominations seem, by and large, to subsume all the species of the genus. In this diversity we may begin to see what short stories have in common.

The Event-Plot Story

This term was coined by the English writer William Gerhardie in 1923 in a short, fascinating book he wrote on Chekhov. Gerhardie uses this appellation to distinguish Chekhov's stories from everything that had preceded him. Up until Chekhov, all short stories, virtually without exception, were event-plot ones. In these stories the skeleton of plot is all important, the narrative is shaped, classically, to have a beginning, middle and end. The revolution that Chekhov set in train – and which reverberates still today – was not to abandon plot, but to make the plot of his stories like the plot of our lives: random, mysterious, run-of-the-mill, abrupt, chaotic, fiercely cruel, meaningless. The stereotype of the event-plot story is the 'twist-in-the-tail' famously developed by O. Henry but also used widely in genre stories – ghost stories (W. W. Jacobs, for example) and the detective story (Conan Doyle). I would say that today its contrivances make it look very dated, though Roald Dahl made something of a mark with a macabre variation on the theme and it is also a staple of self-appointed yarn-spinners (Jeffrey Archer, for example).

The Chekhovian Story

Chekhov is the father of the modern short story and his influence is still massive and everywhere. James Joyce pointedly claimed not to have read Chekhov when he published *Dubliners* in 1914 (most of Chekhov's work had been translated into English since 1903) but the pointedness of the disclaimer is highly disingenuous. *Dubliners*, one of the greatest short story collections ever, owes a great deal to Chekhov: or to put it another way, Chekhov liberated Joyce's imagination in the same way Joyce's example later liberated others.

What is the essence of the Chekhovian short story? Chekhov wrote to a friend that, 'It was time writers, especially those who are artists, recognised that there is no making out anything in this world.' I would say that the Chekhovian point of view is to look at life in all its banality and all its tragicomedy and refuse to make a judgement. To refuse to condemn and refuse to celebrate. To record the actions of human beings as they are and to leave them to speak for themselves (insofar as they can) without manipulation, censure or praise. Hence his famous retort when he was asked to define life. 'You ask me what is life? That is like asking: what is a carrot? A carrot is a carrot and that's all there is to it.' But the effect of this world view as expressed in his stories has had an astonishing influence. Katherine Mansfield and Joyce were among the first to write in the Chekhovian spirit but his cool, dispassionate, unflinching attitude to the human condition resounds in writers as diverse as William Trevor and Raymond Carver, Elizabeth Bowen, John Cheever and Muriel Spark.

The 'Modernist' Story

I choose this title to introduce the other giant presence in the modern short story – Ernest Hemingway. I use the term to convey the idea of obscurity and deliberate difficulty. Hemingway's most obvious revolutionary contribution to the short story was his style: pared down, laconic, unafraid to repeat the most common adjectives rather than reach for a synonym. But his other great donation was a purposeful opacity. When you read Hemingway's early stories (far and away his best work, as it happens) you understand the situation at once. A young man is going fishing, he camps out for the night. Some waiters gather in a cafe. In 'Hills Like White Elephants' a couple at a railway station wait for a train. The mood is tense between them. Has she had an abortion? And that's about it. Yet somehow Hemingway invests this story and the others with all the covert complexities of an obscure modernist poem. You know there are hidden meanings here and it is the inaccessibility of the subtext that makes the story so memorable. Wilful obscurity in the short story works: over the length of a novel it can be very tiresome. This idea of modernist obscurity overlaps with the next category.

The Cryptic/Ludic Story

Here the story presents its baffling surface more overtly as a kind of challenge to the reader – Borges and Vladimir Nabokov spring immediately to mind. In these stories there is a meaning to be discovered and deciphered whereas in Hemingway it's the tantalizing out-of-reachness that entrances. A Nabokov story such as 'Spring at Fialta' is meant to be unravelled by the attentive reader – and it may take several goes – but the spirit behind its teasing is fundamentally generous: dig deep and you will discover more, is the implied message. Try harder and you'll be rewarded: the reader is on his mettle. One of the great cryptic short story writers is Rudyard Kipling, something of an unacknowledged genius of 'suppressed narration' as it is sometimes known: stories like 'Mary Postgate' or 'Mrs Bathurst' are wonderfully complex and multi-layered. Critics still argue passionately about the correct readings.

The Mini-Novel Story

It establishes its remit in its title. Like the event-plot story this is one of the first forms the short story took. In a way it is something of a hybrid: half novel, half short story – trying to achieve in a few dozen pages what the novel achieves in a few hundred: a large cast of characters, lots of realistic detail. Chekhov's great story 'My Life', for example, belongs to this category. It has a span of many years, characters fall in love, marry, separate, children are born, people die. All the matter of a Victorian three-decker is somehow compressed into its fifty or so pages. These stories tend to be very long, almost becoming novellas, but their ambition is clear. They eschew ellipsis and allusion for an aggregation of solid fact, as if the story wants to say, 'See: you don't need 400 pages to paint a portrait of society.'

The Poetic/Mythic Story

In strong contrast, the poetic/mythic story seems to wish to get as far away from the realistic novel as possible. This category is wide and includes writers as varied as Hemingway (his terse and brutal one-page vignettes that interleave his *In Our Time* story collection), the stories of

Dylan Thomas and D. H. Lawrence, J. G. Ballard's moody riffs on inner space to the long prose poems of writers like Ted Hughes and Frank O'Hara. This is the short story-quasi-poem and it can range from stream-of-consciousness to the impenetrably gnomic.

The Biographical Story

This is the one category that seems harder to define. One way of putting it would be to describe it as the short story deliberately borrowing and replicating the properties of non-fiction: of history, of reportage, of the memoir. Borges's stories play with this technique regularly. The over-weening love of footnotes and bibliographical annotation in younger contemporary American writers is a similar example of the genre (or to be more precise they represent a hybrid of the Modernist Story and the biographical — if my taxonomy is correct). Another variation is to introduce the fictive into the lives of real people. I've written short stories about Brahms, Wittgenstein, Braque and Cyril Connolly, for example — imagined fictive episodes in their real lives, yet have drawn on all the research that would be required as if the piece were an essay. A very valid definition of biography is that it is 'a fiction conceived within the bounds of the observable facts'. The biographical story plays with this paradox and in so doing attempts to have its cake and eat it, to capture the strengths of fiction and the non-fictional account simultaneously.

Today, in the UK especially, it has never been harder to get a short story published. The outlets available to a young writer that I benefited from in the 1980s have virtually dried up. Yet, despite the state of publishing, the short story seems to me to be undergoing something of a revival, both here and in the USA. The socio-cultural explanation for this would perhaps be the massive increase in creative writing degree courses. The short story is the perfect pedagogical tool for this kind of education and conceivably the tens of thousands of stories being written (and read) in these institutions are cultivating a taste for the form in the way that the mass-circulation magazines did in the late nineteenth and early twentieth centuries. However, I feel that there may be a different reason why readers of the short story have never really gone away. And once again, this has nothing to do with length. The well-written short story is not suited to the sound-bite culture: it's too dense, its effects are too complex for easy digestion. If the zeitgeist is influencing this taste then it may be a sign that we are coming to prefer our art in highly concentrated form. Like a multi-vitamin pill, a good short story can provide a compressed blast of discerning, intellectual pleasure, one no less intense despite the shorter duration of its consumption. To read a short story like Joyce's 'The Dead', Chekhov's 'In the Ravine' or Hemingway's 'A Clean Well-Lighted Place' is to be confronted by a fully achieved, complex work of art, either profound or disturbing or darkly comic or moving. The fact that it takes fifteen minutes to read it is neither here nor there: the potency is manifest and emphatic.

Perhaps that's what we are looking for, as readers, more and more these days – some sort of aesthetic daisy-cutter bomb of a reading experience that does its work with ruthless brevity and concentrated dispatch. But, as writers, we turn to the short story for other reasons. I think, finally, it comes down to this ability that the short story offers to vary form, tone, narrative and style so quickly and so dramatically. Angus Wilson said he began writing short stories because he could start and finish one in a weekend before he had to return to his job at the British Museum. There is a real investment of effort, to be sure, but it's not the long haul of the novel with its years of generation and execution. You can write a plot-event story one week and a ludic/biographical one the next. Chekhov, the quintessential short story writer, referred to this same pleasure in the notebook I quoted from above. He had copied down something Alphonse Daudet had written and it obviously resonated strongly with him too. All short story writers will know what he means. Daudet's words were these:

'Why are thy songs so short?' a bird was once asked. 'Is it because thou art so short of breath?'

The bird replied: 'I have very many songs and I should like to sing them all.'

2004

Anton Chekhov (1)

An A–Z

A. Anton

Anton Chekhov died a hundred years ago, on 15 July 1904. He was forty-four years old. His lungs were ravaged by tuberculosis. In Russia Chekhov is revered as a short story writer of genius; his plays are considered as extremely interesting but somehow ancillary and complementary to his main achievement. And this Russian conception of his work has some validity: Chekhov, whatever his standing as a playwright, is quite probably the best short story writer ever. Like certain great pieces of music, his stories repay constant revisitings. The two dozen or so mature stories he wrote in the last decade of the nineteenth century have not dated: what resonated in them for his contemporaries resonates now, a hundred or more years on. Chekhov, it can be argued, was the first truly modern writer of fiction: secular, refusing to pass judgement, cognizant of the absurdities of our muddled, bizarre lives and the complex tragicomedy that is the human condition.

B. Biarritz

Chekhov visited Biarritz in south-west France in 1897. His health was failing and he had to seek a warmer climate in the winter months. For an effectively monoglot Russian writer (scant French and a little German) and a semi-invalid he had travelled fairly far and wide in his life. In Europe he knew Germany, France and Italy (how one wishes he had visited England). In 1890 he made an epic eighty-day trans-Russian journey to Sakhalin, a prison island in furthest Siberia. The book he wrote about the conditions of the prisoners there is earnest but dull; it does not live up to the near-intolerable struggle it took to reach the place. He came home by steamer via the orient: Hong Kong, Singapore, Ceylon and then through the Suez Canal to Odessa.

C. Critics

'Critics,' Chekhov said once to Maxim Gorky, 'are like horse-flies which prevent the horse from ploughing. The horse works, all its muscles drawn tight like the strings on a double bass and a fly settles on its flanks and tickles and buzzes . . . he has to twitch his skin and swish his tail. And what does the fly buzz about? It scarcely knows itself; simply because it is restless and wants to proclaim: "Look I am living on the earth. See, I can buzz too, buzz about anything".' Chekhov went on: 'For twenty-five years I have read criticisms of my stories and I don't remember a single remark of any value or one word of valuable advice. Only once [a critic] said something which made an impression on me – he said I would die in a ditch, drunk.'

D. Drink

Untypically for a Russian of his era, Chekhov was not a heavy drinker. His elder brothers Kolia and Aleksandr were chronic alcoholics and perhaps the memory of the squalor of Kolia's wasted life (he was a hugely talented painter who died aged thirty-one) put Chekhov off. Yet Chekhov's last act in life was to drink a glass of champagne. Fatally ill, he had travelled to the German spa town of Badenweiler in the vain hope that German doctors might save him. German medical etiquette demanded that, when the patient was near death and there was nothing more that a doctor could do, a glass of champagne would be offered. Chekhov knew what this meant. He accepted the glass, muttered '*Ich sterbe*' ('I'm dying') and drank it down. His last words were: 'I haven't had champagne for a long time.' Then he died.

E. Event-Plot

This is William Gerhardie's phrase – one he uses to describe the kind of fiction written before Chekhov. Gerhardie, who is tremendously acute about Chekhov (he published a passionately enthusiastic short book about him in 1923), spoke with real authority. An Englishman, born in Moscow in 1895, wholly bilingual, Gerhardie idolized Chekhov (whom he read in Russian long before he was translated). Gerhardie himself was described in his 1920s heyday as 'the English Chekhov' and they do share a similar philosophy of life – though Gerhardie's talent had a briefer flowering. Gerhardie's analysis of Chekhov's genius maintains that for the first time in literature the fluidity and randomness of life were made the *form* of the fiction. Previous to Chekhov, the event-plot drove all fictions: the narrative was manipulated, tailored, calculatedly designed, rounded-off. Tolstoy, Flaubert, Dickens and Turgenev could not resist the event-plot powering and shaping their novels. Chekhov abandoned this type of self-conscious 'story' for something more casual and realistic. As Gerhardie says, Chekhov's stories are 'blurred, interrupted, mauled or otherwise tampered with by life'. This is why Chekhov's stories still speak to us a hundred years on. His stories are anti-novelistic, in the traditional sense. They are like life as we all live it.

F. Faith

Chekhov's personal world was a Godless one: despite his orthodox religious upbringing, he asserted, in 1892, that 'I have no religion now.' He wrote about religious folk, indeed one of his greatest stories is entitled 'The Bishop'. But intelligent people who believed in God seemed baffling to him. 'I squandered away my faith long ago and never fail to be puzzled by an intellectual who is also a believer.'

G. Grigorovitch

In 1886 Dmitri Grigorovitch, a distinguished Russian writer, wrote Chekhov a letter which changed his artistic life. Up until that date Chekhov had earned his living as a composer of humorous short stories, almost like variety sketches (he was a qualified doctor but it was his writing that sustained him financially). He published these *jeux d'esprit* under a pseudonym, 'Antosha Chekhonte'. The vast majority of them have not aged well: arch, knowing, manifestly trying to be funny, these stories were hack work. Then in 1886 he published a story, 'Requiem', under his own name. Grigorovitch was hugely impressed, and wrote to Chekhov acclaiming his talent and urging him to abandon his comic squibs. 'Stop doing hack work . . . better go hungry . . . save up your impressions for work that has been pondered, polished, written at several sittings.' Chekhov was overwhelmed by this letter and his reply is valuable if only because it is perhaps the only time that Chekhov drops his guard and gushes. 'Your letter struck me like lightning. I almost burst into tears, I was profoundly moved and I now feel it has left a deep trace in my soul.' Grigorovitch's passionate urging worked. For Chekhov it was a Damascene moment. The eighteen years remaining to him bear witness to his new zeal as a serious artist.

H. Home

Chekhov was born in 1860 in the Crimea, in a town called Taganrog, far to the south of Moscow on the Sea of Azov. More Levantine than European (Turkey was 300 miles away), Taganrog was a hot, fly-infested port with a varied population – Russians, Greeks, Armenians, Italians. Chekhov's father was an indigent grocer whose debts eventually caused the family to flee to Moscow. Chekhov had four brothers and one sister – Aleksandr, Kolia, Vania, Misha and Masha. Very early in his life Chekhov became the family breadwinner. He supported them all – doggedly and in the main ungrudgingly – until his death.

I. Intimacy

In his short life Chekhov had many lovers but he had, as we would now term it, a real problem with commitment. Most of the women he had affairs with would have been happy to marry him but Chekhov was always careful to keep them at a distance, to break the relationship off if it seemed likely to become too heated.

J. The Japanese Girl

On his voyage back through the orient from his travels to Siberia Chekhov went to a brothel in Hong Kong. He wrote to a friend, 'The Japanese girl . . . doesn't put on airs, or go coy, like a Russian woman. And all the time she is laughing and making lots of *tsu* noises . . . When you come, the Japanese girl pulls with her teeth a sheet of cotton wool from her sleeve, catches you by the "boy", gives you a massage and the cotton wool tickles your belly. All this is done with coquetry, laughing, singing and saying *tsu.*'

K. Koumiss

A fermented mare's milk that was believed, in the 1890s, to be a defence against tuberculosis, as a source of 'good' bacilli. In 1901 Chekhov undertook a koumiss cure, drinking four bottles of the milk daily. He gained twelve pounds in weight in a fortnight. A month later he was still coughing blood.

L. Lika Mizinova

The one true love of Chekhov's life? Chekhov married the actress Olga Knipper in 1901 when he had three years left to live. It was a union that dumbfounded and outraged most of his family – it seemed incomprehensible. It has subsequently been presented as one of the great romances of the twentieth century. My own theory is that his long affair with Lika Mizinova was the real love story. He met Lika in 1889, she was a teacher, an aspiring opera singer, blonde and buxom and nineteen years old. Chekhov was ten years older. For almost a decade they conducted a bantering, passionate on-off love affair. No other woman in Chekhov's life held his affections so long but he always refrained from proposing marriage. Frustrated, Lika had an affair with Chekhov's close friend and business manager Ignati Potapenko (a married man). They had a child together. Betrayal enough to break up any relationship, one would have thought – but Chekhov kept seeing Lika. Her career failed, she grew plump but something kept drawing him back to her. They last met in 1897 but Lika remained very friendly with Chekhov's brothers and sister. She is often considered to be the model for Nina in *The Seagull*.

M. 'My Life'

This is the longest story Chekhov wrote, it's almost a novella and is, in my opinion, his greatest. In it you will find all the key Chekhovian tropes: the black humour, the candid depiction of the absurdity of life, its fleeting happiness, its 'weirdness and vulgarity' (as Stanislavsky put it), its brutal randomness. This dark Chekhovian comic ruthlessness found its way into English literature via William Gerhardie. Katherine Mansfield plagiarized Chekhov but she responded to his more elegiac tone. Gerhardie sensed Chekhov's tough realism, his acknowledgement of life's bland cruelty. Gerhardie in turn was a huge influence on Evelyn Waugh (Waugh's early comedies are extremely Gerhardian, a fact that Waugh himself acknowledged later in life). This tone of voice has subsequently come to seem very English, but it was there in Chekhov first. My other favourite Chekhov stories in no particular order are: 'The Lady with the Dog', 'In the Ravine', 'A Visit to Friends', 'Ionych', 'The Bishop', 'The House with the Mezzanine', 'Three Years'.

N. Nice

Chekhov went to Nice in 1898 to protect his damaged lungs from the ravages of the Russian winter. It's a city I know well, I spent most of a year there in 1971. Like Biarritz, Nice is a place where, here and there, the ghost of Chekhov haunts its streets. At the turn of the century it was popular with Russians and Chekhov stayed in a Russian pension in the rue Gounod. The room I rented was on the rue Dante, a few blocks away. Chekhov liked Nice (the weather was good) and tolerated the routine and circumscribed life he lived there. Nice was a good place to read, he said, but not to write.

O. Olga Knipper

A leading actress at the Moscow Art Theatre. She acted in the earliest productions of Chekhov's four finished plays – *The Seagull*, *Uncle Vanya*, *Three Sisters* and *The Cherry Orchard*. Chekhov married her in 1901, three years before he died. Olga survived him by fifty-five years, dying in 1959 (she also survived Hitler and Stalin). She was an ardent keeper of the flame but, despite her efforts to portray it otherwise, there is no disguising that the marriage was a strange one. They spent much more time apart than together (hence their copious and affecting correspondence): she acting in Moscow, Chekhov convalescing in Yalta on the

Black Sea. Sometimes she even kept her Moscow address from her husband. She and Chekhov tried to conceive a child but failed. There is strong evidence, however, that she was unfaithful to him and miscarried another lover's child in 1902.

P. *Pavel Egerovitch Chekhov*

Chekhov's father. The son of a serf, he was both absurdly devout and a ruthless disciplinarian. He beat his sons remorselessly. Chekhov saw it as the watershed in his life the day he woke knowing that he would not be beaten by his father. Yet this sentimental, sadistic boor was financially supported loyally and tirelessly by his third son throughout his life, living with him in his various establishments and particularly at Melikhovo, the small estate Chekhov bought to the south of Moscow and which, of all the places he lived in (from 1892 to 1899), he most loved. Pavel Chekhov effectively ran the estate with shrewd serf-like application. He died in 1898, aged seventy-three, on an operating table when the surgeon was attempting to rectify a gangrenous hernia. Pavel had forgotten to put on his truss and developed the fatal hernia by picking up a 20-pound bag of sugar. Chekhov declared it the end of an era, that 'the main cog had jumped out of the Melikhovo machine'. He never loved his father but he had never let him down. He abandoned Melikhovo shortly after his father died.

Q. *Quinine*

At Melikhovo Chekhov had two dachshunds which he called Quinine and Bromine. Quinine was his favourite. The most natural and unposed photographs of Chekhov show him sitting on the steps of his veranda with Quinine tucked under his arm.

R. *Real Lives*

Chekhov said: 'Every person lives his real, most interesting life under the cover of secrecy.' By this I take him to mean that other people are fundamentally opaque, mysterious – even people you know very well, your wife or husband, your family. Janet Malcolm, who has written a profound and insightful book on Chekhov (called *Reading Chekhov*), says that 'We never see people in life as clearly as we see the people in novels, stories and plays; there is a veil between ourselves and even our closest intimates, blurring us to each other.' This, it seems to me, is the great and lasting allure of all fiction: if we want to know what other people are like we turn to the novel or the short story. In no other art form can we take up residence in other people's minds so effortlessly. Chekhov tells us a great deal about his characters but, however, resists full exposure: there always remains something 'blurry', something secret about them. This is part of his genius: this is what makes his stories seem so real.

S. Aleksei Suvorin

A vastly wealthy, right-wing publisher and newspaper magnate and prob- ably Chekhov's closest male friend. Chekhov achieved a bond with Suvorin which is hard to explain, given the latter's rebarbative politics. It's rather as if George Orwell's best friend had been, say, Julius Streicher. I suspect Suvorin functioned as something of a surrogate father for Chekhov (he was twenty years older) – also he paid him well and Chekhov's fame largely came about through his stories appearing in Suvorin's publications. Suvorin had no illusions about Chekhov: '. . . a man of flint and a cruel talent with his harsh objectivity. He's spoilt, his *amour propre* is enormous.' They fell out, finally, irrevocably, over the Dreyfus affair. Chekhov was an ardent Dreyfusard; Suvorin unashamedly anti-Semitic. There was no rapprochement and Suvorin bitterly regretted the rift. Asked about his politics once, Chekhov declared that he wanted only to be a 'free artist'. Like Vladimir Nabokov, he was deeply distrustful of fiction that openly proselytized for any political ideology. Chekhov's view of the human condition, given his own terminal illness, was bleakly clear-eyed. 'After youth comes old age; after happiness, unhappiness, and vice versa; nobody can be healthy and cheerful all their lives . . . you have to be ready for anything. You just have to do your duty as best as you can.'

T. *Theatre*

Chekhov was both drawn to and exasperated by the theatre. He wrote his first plays purely as a way of making quick money. One always feels that he was somewhat amazed at the acclaim his later plays achieved. Seen in the light of the mature stories, the plays are clearly heavily indebted to the fiction in their mood, themes and settings – which is what made them so revolutionary and, later on, so influential. But the plays lack the seamless authority of the fiction: there are great characters, wonderful scenes, tremendous passages, moments of acute melancholy and sagacity but the parts appear greater than the whole. Perhaps only in *The Cherry Orchard* does everything fuse and the drama takes on an autonomy of its own. Days before his death he conceived the idea for a play about passengers stranded on an ice-bound ship. Perhaps his premature death makes the plays that Chekhov never wrote the real loss. The stories are fully achieved: a genuine apotheosis.

U. Uncle Vanya

Tolstoy went to see *Uncle Vanya* and loathed it. Chekhov was backstage and asked what Tolstoy's opinion was. A kindly interlocutor said that the great man hadn't 'really understood' the play. Chekhov saw through that one. But then he was told that even though Tolstoy hadn't enjoyed *Uncle Vanya*, that he thought Chekhov was an appalling playwright, he was not as bad as Shakespeare. Chekhov found this delightfully, hilariously amusing.

V. *Vanity*

Chekhov was six foot one inch tall – a very tall man for the end of the nineteenth century. He was handsome: in early photos he looks burly and strangely Asiatic. The familiar images of his last decade, goateed, with pince-nez, slimmed by his illness, carefully dressed, testify to a man who was proud of his appearance and knew he was attractive to women. He had a terror of going bald.

W. Writers

Chekhov wrote in a letter to Suvorin, 'Remember, that writers whom we call great or just good and who make us drunk have one common, very important feature: they are going somewhere and calling you with them, and you feel not with your mind, but your whole being, that they have a goal, like the ghost of Hamlet's father.' He also said: 'Writers must be as objective as a chemist.'

X. X-rays

An X-ray of Chekhov's lungs early in his life (had such a thing been available) would have shown the shadowy traces of the 'tubercules': latent walled-in lesions of the bacillus *Mycobacterium tuberculosis*. Chekhov probably caught the disease in childhood. And he saw his brother Kolia die of it in 1889. Moreover, Chekhov was a doctor: he knew exactly what was in store for him. The bacilli lie dormant in the body, kept at bay by the immune system. At moments when the immune system is under stress or weakened the bacilli break out of the tubercules and begin to spread extensively in the lungs. The lung tissue is then effectively eaten by the bacilli – *consumed* – hence the nineteenth-century name for the disease: 'consumption'. In Chekhov's time – the pre-antibiotic era – the only cure was isolation, rest and good nutrition. In the last years of his life Chekhov's lungs became increasingly devastated. The amount of lung tissue available for the exchange of gases in the breathing process radically decreased. Chekhov died of breathing failure, exhaustion and general toxaemia (the tuberculosis had also spread to the spine).

Y. Yalta

A popular resort much favoured by tubercular patients. Positioned in the Crimea on the Black Sea it had a congenial climate. Chekhov moved there in 1899 and built a house, only returning to Moscow in the summer. The fact that he had taken up residence made the resort instantly chic – other invalids suddenly wanted to convalesce there rather than anywhere else – something that he doubtless found wryly amusing. His famous story 'The Lady with the Dog' is set in the town. Many of

Yalta's transient lady visitors fancied themselves as the model for Anna, the eponymous heroine. Chekhov's Yalta house is now a museum, its furnishings and decor theoretically unchanged since Chekhov lived there.

Z. Zoo

About a month before he died, the desperately ill Chekhov visited Moscow zoo. Chekhov loved animals. Apart from his dachshunds and the livestock on his estate he also had as pets two mongooses and, in Yalta, a tame crane. Conceivably, during that visit to Moscow zoo, Chekhov might have seen a cheetah in its cage. Donald Rayfield, Chekhov's best and definitive biographer, speculates that Chekhov's sexuality was like that of the cheetah. The male cheetah can only mate with a stranger. When the male cheetah mates with a female cheetah familiar to him he is – bizarrely – impotent. It's a fanciful image but one worth contemplating: the dying Chekhov staring at a cheetah in its cage. Perhaps this explains this rare man's extraordinary life and the view of the human condition that he refined in his incomparable stories. Perhaps it explains his enigmatic, beguiling personality: his convivial aloofness; his love of idleness; his immense generosity; his hard heart. For this artist to avoid impotence only strangers would do; it only worked with strangers. Anton Chekhov was a cheetah.

2004

Anton Chekhov (2)

Anton Chekhov and Lika Mizinova

Consider this situation. You are a handsome, celebrated writer in your thirties – male and unmarried. You have been having a passionate affair for some years with a beautiful young woman (a decade younger than you) that has reached such a pitch that the next logical step is marriage. She wants desperately to marry you, but, however much you are attracted to this young woman, you inevitably draw back: you cannot commit and so the affair effectively ends. But the young woman, spurned in this way, hugely frustrated, embarks on a fresh affair – but this time with one of your close friends (who also happens to be married) and who is also your business partner. These new lovers decamp to Paris where the young woman becomes pregnant and duly has a child. Whereupon her faithless lover abandons her and returns to his long-suffering wife.

What does one do, embroiled in such a soap opera? Cuckolded in this way by a real friend, how does one feel or respond? Do you laugh it off, chalk it up to experience, move on? Or are there deeper wounds, more profound regrets, moments of poignant self-analysis, of possible self-loathing? Or do you write it all up and put it in a play?

Exactly this situation happened to Anton Chekhov in 1894. Chekhov had a prolonged affair with a young teacher and apprentice opera singer called Lydia ('Lika') Mizinova. When marriage was ruled out by Chekhov she began an affair with his friend Ignati Potapenko. This ménage moved to Paris, Lika had a child, Potapenko returned to his wife and Lika returned to Russia. Chekhov affected to be unconcerned.

I have been reading a great deal and writing a fair amount about Chekhov recently (this year sees the centenary of his death) and have become very familiar with his various biographies. Chekhov had a rare and complex personality. He was much loved, but remained a closed and sometimes cool acquaintance. He was incredibly generous but was often ruthlessly hard-hearted. He loved the company of women but he was terrified of marriage. When he did marry towards the end of his short life it was only because ill health (he was dying of tuberculosis) would ensure that husband and wife were more apart than together. Reading Russian, French, American and British commentaries and accounts of his life, I have found that there is one consensus that emerges in the face of these conundrums. Namely that Chekhov was constitutionally incapable of falling in love and giving himself fully to a woman; that something in his nature always drew him up short; that he was always destined to be a loner.

And yet, and yet . . . The nature of his relationship with Lika Mizinova struck me as something of an exception to his usual amours (Chekhov was promiscuous with his affections). As I read about Chekhov, the story of his affair with Lika nagged at me: it seemed different from his other romantic entanglements. I began to wonder if Lika was the one that got away.

The facts are relatively straightforward. Anton Chekhov met Lika Mizinova in 1889, she was nineteen and a friend of his sister, Masha, who taught at the same school. Chekhov was twenty-nine and on the verge of his great literary fame. Lika was very pretty: grey-eyed with dark eyebrows, buxom, with a mass of curly ash-blonde hair and a chain-smoker (somewhat daring for the 1880s). Chekhov fell for her and an affair began. It's worth bearing in mind that, amongst artistic circles in pre-Revolutionary Russia, social and sexual behaviour seem remarkably 'modern' – not far removed from the norms of today. The Moscow and St Petersburg intelligentsia led similar lives to fin de siècle Parisian artists and writers. Fun was had. Life was good.

The precise nature of Chekhov's affair with Lika is best derived from their letters. Apart from his wife, Olga Knipper (whom he married towards the end of his life), and his sister, Masha, Lika is his most regular female correspondent. Ninety-eight letters survive from her to him, sixty-seven in the other direction, though it seems there were many more, now lost. The tone of these letters is fascinating: it is almost consistently one of bantering flirtation, of feigned identities (idiot lover, childish sweetheart and so on), of joking, of sexual innuendo. Chekhov is always speculating that Lika has other admirers, direly warning her off other men. There is, clearly, an erotic undercurrent to these letters and this persistent role playing, as if they were designed to stimulate. For example: 'Ah, Lika, Lika, diabolically beautiful Lika! . . . Do not despair but come to us, and we will hurl ourselves upon you with might and main.'

A year later Chekhov alluded to a friend that he might marry Lika, then added, 'I doubt if I'll be happy with her – she's too beautiful.' Maybe this was the problem: Lika's beauty attracted constant admirers, she was the cynosure of all male eyes. A friend would walk down a

Moscow street with her and count the number of male heads turning. She was evidently strikingly attractive. Chekhov tried not to be jealous as other men fell for her, but he still would not commit to matrimony. Then Lika had an affair with the painter Levitan, another of Chekhov's friends. It was as if Lika was challenging him, but Chekhov responded only with more jokes and ironies. However, Chekhov was obviously wounded: he parodied Levitan and Lika with some cruelty in a story he wrote in 1891 called 'The Grasshopper'. Levitan refused to speak to Chekhov for three years. Lika persisted. Like no other woman he knew – and he knew a lot – Lika got under his skin.

A year later, 1892, the affair was back on. Lika, wiser now, was aware that it was best for her to bide her time. Chekhov dallied with other admirers but he was always drawn back to Lika. The on-off affair continued: she visited him at his country estate, he came to her flat in Moscow – but Chekhov still kept her at bay. As long as Lika wanted him, Chekhov could maintain his ironic distance. The affair with Levitan had touched him to a degree, but he could not have imagined what she would do next to stimulate his jealousy.

Lika's affair with Ignati Potapenko began at the end of 1893, four years after she and Chekhov first met. It was undisguised and Chekhov appeared to give the union his blessing, even allowing the lovers to stay together at Melikhovo, instituting an odd ménage à trois. Lika conceived her child here at this time. Chekhov's sister, Masha, was disgusted by her brother's supine behaviour. Yet, even now, Chekhov could still write to Lika: 'Darling Lika, today at 6.30 pm I shall leave for Melikhovo, would you like to come with me?' He was playing a curious and dangerous game, both desiring her and letting her betray him – the immediate consequence of which was that Lika left Moscow for Paris to be with Potapenko.

But even in Paris Lika and Chekhov wrote regularly, tormenting each other with coy invitations and hard irony. Chekhov was beginning to block out the ideas for *The Seagull*, in which the central character of Nina was to be very close to Lika. Potapenko kept the fact of Lika's pregnancy from Chekhov and the two men were still sufficiently firm friends to travel together on holiday in the summer of 1894. Lika, meanwhile, went to Switzerland to have her child. Chekhov couldn't stop writing to her: 'You refuse to answer my letters, dear Lika . . . I'm not very well. I have an almost continuous cough. I seem to have lost my health as I lost you.'

In fact more had changed. The tone of their letters seems to signal that some sort of watershed had been reached. Chekhov by now could not ignore the fact that Lika was pregnant and expecting Potapenko's child: nothing could ever be the same. Lika gave birth to a girl, Christina. Potapenko, under enormous pressure from his wife (she threatened to kill herself and her children), told Lika he could never see her again.

Lika's life was in disarray: abandoned and impoverished (and noticeably plumper) she returned to Moscow. The birth of Christina seemed to have made Chekhov resolve to see her no more. Yet in early 1896 Lika was once again at Melikhovo, as Masha's guest. Old feelings stirred in Chekhov. Despite everything, the love affair resumed. The next few months seem to have been the happiest the two of them shared. But as the year moved on the old pattern re-established itself. Mutual happiness provoked Chekhovian insecurity. Chekhov seems to have promised marriage and then reneged. Meetings were arranged and cancelled – Lika began to grow angry again. She was unaware that her character was about to be exposed on the Moscow stage in *The Seagull*.

Chekhov was understandably worried about the opening of the play (in October 1896). Both Potapenko and his wife – and Lika – were all naturally most eager to see the first performances and Chekhov had genuine reason to think that Potapenko's wife might attack Lika. In the event he contrived to keep the parties separate. The first night was one of the most epic flops in the history of Moscow theatre, but, despite the huge controversy, Lika did not take against the portrayal of her character. A few days later she was back at Melikhovo and once again there was talk of marriage. And once again, Chekhov balked – he asked her to wait 'two or three years'. Lika had had enough – and she still had other suitors of her own. She ruefully conceded that marriage – or 'bliss' as they termed it – was unlikely to come about. She signed herself, 'Goodbye. Your twice rejected L. Mizinova.'

And that really should have been the end of the affair. It had lasted seven years, but life was about to calamitously imitate art. Just as in *The Seagull* Chekhov had Nina's child die, so too, now, Lika's child sickened and died. Lika came to Melikhovo for comfort and to grieve, playing patience at a desk in Chekhov's study as he worked. There seemed a kind of inevitability that she should seek him out in her darkest hour.

But Lika wound up the affair herself shortly after a final meeting: Chekhov's prevarications eventually convincing her that nothing would come of it. Lika went back to Paris to pursue her career as an opera singer. She wrote to Chekhov: 'To dear Anton Pavlovich, in kindly memory of eight years' good relations.' Then she quoted some lines of poetry:

> Whether my days are clear or mournful,
> Whether I perish, destroying my life,
> I only know this: to the grave
> Thoughts, feelings, songs, strength
> All for you!

'I could have written this eight years ago,' she added, 'and I write it now and I shall write it in ten years' time.'

They still corresponded with each other but Chekhov, now terminally ill, had met the actress Olga Knipper who was ultimately to become his wife (in 1901, much to the shock and initial outrage of his family). Lika remained close to Masha and to Chekhov's younger brother and found some sort of domestic happiness with the theatre director Aleksandr Sanin-Schoenberg. Chekhov died in 1904. Lika outlived him by thirty-three years, dying in Paris in 1937.

What is one to make of such a relationship, as passionate and as stormy as they come, it would seem? Donald Rayfield, Chekhov's best biographer (and to whom this chronology is much indebted) speculates that Chekhov's sexuality was stimulated by newness, by strangeness – lovers who became familiars lost their appeal. My own feeling is that Chekhov genuinely loved Lika – his sister Masha felt the same – but that something to do with his own impending mortality (he knew he had tuberculosis from an early age) and the need – like the writer Trigorin in *The Seagull* – not to be distracted from his work in the years he had left to live made him pull away from any romantic commitment that would be all-encompassing. His eventual marriage was full of love and affection but it was one of long separations and it misses the *sturm und drang* of the Lika years.

And Lika? Clearly, when she met Chekhov she was a young woman of tremendous beauty and incandescent sex-appeal, coupled with an unaffected, bohemian nature. She started as a teacher, failed as an opera singer and a milliner, worked as a secretary, tried to be an actress, had too many love affairs, smoked too much, put on weight and lost it again. Masha speculated that the fastidious Chekhov might not have been able to cope with such a rackety personality. And maybe Chekhov sensed that. He wrote to her once explaining his persistent reticence: 'A huge crocodile lives in you, Lika, and as a matter of fact I'm doing the wise thing in obeying common sense and not my heart, which you've bitten into.' The crocodile bit Chekhov's heart and he recoiled, reluctant to go there again. What would life have been like with the lovely, dangerous crocodile Lika? Chekhov decided to play safe. One wonders what regrets he lived with.

2004

Richard Yates

(Review of *A Tragic Honesty* by Blake Bailey)

'Mostly we authors repeat ourselves,' Scott Fitzgerald observed late in his life. 'We learn our trade, well or less well, and we tell our two or three stories . . . as long as people will listen.' There's a lot of truth in this remark (though some authors have more than two or three stories to tell), but in the case of the American writer Richard Yates, subject of this fascinating biography, there was only one story that obsessed him and Yates, essentially, told it again and again in both his long and short fiction whether people were listening or not.

Richard Yates was born in Yonkers, NY, in 1926 into a thoroughly dysfunctional family and his own tortured psyche and that of his mother and relatives provided him with the raw material of his fiction for his working life. Yates was mentally unstable and an alcoholic (as was his only sister). Their mother was a self-appointed 'Bohemian' sculptress who divorced her dull, middle-management husband as soon as was feasible and took her children off on a series of flits through pre-Second World War New England and Greenwich Village, somehow managing to keep one step ahead of the bailiffs and the creditors but royally messing up her children in the process (in her cups, she was in the habit of slipping into bed with her pubescent son).

A scholarship pupil at private school, Yates was the talented poor boy who wanted to be a writer and he achieved relatively early success with his short stories. After graduating he served briefly with the US Army at the tail end of the war, married early and spent some time learning his trade, as Scott Fitzgerald put it, in France and London. The trouble with Yates was that he wanted to be a writer – and a 'writer'. The ghost of Scott Fitzgerald haunts his life both as an artistic exemplar and as a ruinous role-model. Yates's writing career was lived out against a background of eighty cigarettes a day, prodigious boozing and manic depression. The handfuls of pharmaceuticals he took to keep himself relatively sane were never designed to be washed down with Jack Daniels and it has to be said that, very early on, Yates placed his finger squarely on the self-destruct button and held it there. Marriages and relationships collapsed with regularity and the literary career that he embarked on so promisingly with his first novel *Revolutionary Road* (1960) soon evolved itself into a long, slow slide of falling sales, missed deadlines, alienated publishers and the law of diminishing returns.

Yet throughout his life Yates was sustained by grants, prizes, spells in Hollywood writing scripts, temporary creative-writing teaching posts (with a brief, unlikely period as a speech writer for Bobby Kennedy) and the affection and support of steadfast friends and colleagues. As a young man he was tall and moodily good-looking. Yet for all his charisma he was, I suppose, that sad literary figure the 'one book wonder'. His first novel, *Revolutionary Road*, turned out to be his *chef d'oeuvre*. It was written to be the *Great Gatsby* of the 1960s and it still has its fervent adherents. Reading Yates's fiction today one has to say that, looking at the work as a whole (six novels and two collections of short stories), there don't really seem to be grounds for resurrecting him as a forgotten master. His style is classically realistic and elegantly turned but the one-note tango of his inspiration finally enervates. John Updike – who one might argue overtook and outshone Yates as the pre-eminent chronicler of middle-class American angst and adultery – is in a different league. Yates is like many figures in twentieth-century American literature: an early flowering of an intriguing talent rendered nugatory by crowding, tormenting demons – drink, drugs, self-doubt, self-loathing, burn-out and so on. Fitzgerald is the obvious precursor but Hemingway was equally undone, as were writers like Berryman, Capote, Kerouac, Cheever and many more.

Yates in his middle age wound up in Boston, living in a bleak, roach-infested apartment with just enough money to feed himself in an Irish pub up the block. He looked like a derelict with a crusted beard, greasy clothes, muttering to himself as he trudged between his apartment and the bar. What sustained Yates – what kept him alive, I suppose – was his romantic vision of himself as an artist. He wrote all the time, even if what he wrote was inferior stuff, and pursued his vocation with a dedication that is in the end amazingly impressive, even if it was self-delusory. A friend described him as 'fun to be around but a pain in the ass'.

Unfortunately, as his life spiralled downwards the 'pain in the ass' aspects seemed to dominate. Yates was both bitter and aggressive, his moods swung violently because of his bipolar disorder and the vast amounts of alcohol he consumed. He fought with friends and his family; through his drink-driven dementia he made a regular public spectacle of himself and was in and out of mental institutions. But it was, so his doctors claimed and pleaded with him, his refusal to give up alcohol that was destroying his life. Eventually, however, it was his manic smoking that killed him. In the early 1990s Yates wound up teaching creative writing at a university in Alabama. Virtually immobile owing to his chronic emphysema, he became a familiar figure driving around campus in a clapped-out Mazda alternately puffing on a cigarette and clamping an oxygen mask to his face. He quit smoking a few months before he died and was astonished at how easy it was to give up. By then it was too late: he was rushed into hospital for a routine operation on an inguinal hernia (caused by his fits of coughing) and died alone in the night, asphyxiated by his own vomit. It was 1992: he was sixty-six years old.

'To write so well and be forgotten is a terrifying legacy,' a critic commented posthumously. Yates was a fine writer, but the very uneven quality of his work will always have him categorized as a minor twentieth-century American novelist despite the tremendous debut he made with *Revolutionary Road*. However, in a curious way, his hellish life itself may be what he will be remembered for. Blake Bailey has written a fully documented, wonderfully clear-eyed, shrewd and sympathetic account of what must be one of the most nightmarish journeys across this vale of tears that any novelist has undertaken. Yates's battered, wheezing, ascetic indefatigability is almost heroic but, as with many artists who embark on this kind of slow suicide, one is left with the feeling that at root it is caused by an innate sense of the limits of their talent – by their awareness of just how far they fall short of the genuinely great – that sends them down the slippery slope to their own self-destruction.

2004

ART

In my late teens I decided that I wanted to go to art school and become a painter. I was good at art, I took my A-level a year early and, to be honest, at that stage of my education I was more enthused about art than I was by literature. This was not to be: my father's implacable objection to this plan provoked no rebellion in me and so I decided to follow the path of literature instead, a calling about which he was marginally less disparaging. Decades on, I have to concede that perhaps he was right to dissuade me. But, all the same, my old ambition still nags at me from time to time. It was Karen Wright, editor of Modern Painters magazine, who in 1998 unwittingly re-opened this small Pandora's box when she asked me to write for her journal and then, a little while later, invited me to join its editorial board.

Suddenly, I had a toe in the world I had hankered to belong to as a schoolboy and I found that, even if I couldn't be a painter, at least I was happy to write about art. It was not a difficult compromise.

Most of the pieces I have written for Modern Painters and other magazines and newspapers have been largely about British painting, post World War Two. I am no expert in the fine art, scholarly sense, but I feel British painters of that era are both underestimated and undervalued. I was more than prepared to try and boost reputations unjustly in decline.

The other feature of my connection to Modern Painters was that it provided me with the opportunity to invent my fictitious American painter Nat Tate (see pages 373–5) who, for about a week or ten days in 1998, enjoyed a certain notoriety on both sides of the Atlantic, as indeed did I, as the perceived perpetrator of a hoax on the New York art world. Nat Tate seemed to have a strange half-life for a while (I was interviewed on Newsnight about his work and there was a Channel 4 documentary made about him) and his réclame still rumbles on. Most interestingly for me, however, is that Nat's curious existence has returned me, if not to painting, then to drawing again: from time to time I discover a 'lost' Nat Tate and give it to a friend as a present. I am Nat's only begetter, after all, and also the source of all his surviving art: perhaps the old ambition has been lying dormant all these years and may be beginning to stir again.

Georg Grosz

(Review of *World War One and the*
Weimar Artists by Matthias Eberle)

It is hard to gauge now – in this era of outrage and daily disaster –
what the effects of the sinking of the *Titanic* were on the popular imagination in 1912. Was it simply one of shock and blank astonishment?
Or did it give rise to darker premonitions? Matthias Eberle suggests, in
this very intriguing if somewhat earnest book, that – certainly as far as
German artists were concerned – it was a seminal date, the beginning
of a process of profound suspicion and disenchantment with the mech-
anized forces of industry that reached its apotheosis in the 1914–18 war.
That fervid exultation in dynamism and the heroic potential of mechanics
so eagerly celebrated by the Futurists and, one suspects, by the world
at large as well as the German artists, received its gory comeuppance
on the Western Front. The fragility of the human body and the transience and futility of human aspirations were all too cruelly exposed
when the machines they were pitted against took the form of trench
mortars and howitzers.

No one was better placed to observe this than Otto Dix, a machine-
gunner on the Western Front who no doubt on many occasions had
the opportunity to observe at first hand the effect of high technology
on the lumbering Tommies slogging across the mud. Dix had joined
the war full of sub-Nietzschean enthusiasm for the fight. He was swiftly
disillusioned and that disillusion manifested itself in his art. The same
bitterness occurred in other German artists in a curious unity of vision
which was called – in opposition to Expressionist and Futurist excesses
– the *Neue Sachlichkeit*, the 'New Objectivity'. Dix, Grosz and
Beckmann are the most famous exemplars of the grouping and each
is the subject of an essay in this book. Dix and Grosz are the most
commonly linked and I suppose the most well known, but one of the
bonuses of this book was to discover that the same strains in Dix and
Grosz appear in Max Beckmann's work. Indeed there are stronger
parallels between Dix and Beckmann than one might have surmised.
Each was influenced by Nietzsche, each saw active service and their
war experiences produced in them tortured, morbid obsessions with

sex, human cruelty and vague religious impulses. Grosz's work exhibited similar tendencies but, interestingly, it was not produced by a spell
at the front. Grosz was first declared unfit for military service. Later
he was conscripted, but after a nervous breakdown of sorts he was
sent to a sanatorium. A medical student, who thought he was perfectly
fit, ordered him out of bed. In a fury, Grosz attacked him and was
promptly beaten up by the other patients with, by all accounts, considerable glee. It was this trauma which accelerated his acerbic cynicism,
not any spectacle of mass destruction.

For all their power, there is something unpleasantly pathological in
the work of all three artists. There is a kind of righteous nihilism which
one can applaud: their portrayals of the horrors of war (no British artist
has painted anything so scarifying); their excoriation of the sleek industrialists and corrupt businessmen and so on. It is a little harder to
explain away, however, their morbid obsession with sex. One could say
that after the war, once the fighting was over, the crude commerce of
prostitution served as a useful symbol of the degeneracy of the human
spirit, but it rings somewhat of special pleading, especially when one
is faced with its lurid prominence in the work of all three men. Both
Dix and Grosz, for example, independently produced a series of etchings on sex murders. The answer lies, rather, in the complex individual
personalities of the artists than in any *Neue Sachlichkeit* programme.
Their respective traumatization – coincidentally – engendered the same
symptoms.

It may be, of course, a national psychosis: it is tempting to see Weimar
Germany (or rather one's received image of Weimar Germany) suffering
– so to speak – in the same way as its artists, especially when one
takes into account the German race's propensity for doing things en
masse. It is a theory that gains some further credence when we look
at Britain between the wars. If we accept that the *Neue Sachlichkeit*
artists represent the most significant cultural response to the Great War
in Germany then its corollary in Britain is the war poets – Owen,
Sassoon, Rosenberg, Gurney et al. What a fascinating contrast they
make. The same shock and condemnation of the horrors of war
provides a powerful stimulus for their respective arts, but nowhere in
the British response do we encounter this purulent nihilism reflected
through overt sexual loathing and revulsion. Is this simply a sign of the
dissimilarity between the British and German psyche? Or is it merely
the difference between victor and vanquished? Searching for an answer,

it is perhaps significant that Grosz himself later (in 1933) disowned and repudiated his post-war etchings because he considered that the relentless cynicism of the Weimar artists and writers had contributed to the rise of the Nazis.

1988

Keith Vaughan

(Review of *Keith Vaughan: His Life and Work* by Malcolm Yorke)

Keith Vaughan was born in 1912. Later in his life he was to reflect on what he regarded as one of the more auspicious omens of his birth. He was a healthy baby, 'but it was also observed that my penis possessed a loose and easily retractable foreskin which was not considered necessary to circumcise. For this piece of good fortune I have had many occasions to be grateful.' We shall see why in due course. In this nugget of autobiographical information are preserved many of the qualities that make Vaughan such a distinctive artist and personality: his unflinching candour, his formal exactitude, his dry wit, his lifelong obsession with his cock. All key aspects of his life as a man and, though perhaps not in every respect, his work as an artist.

Although he expressed satisfaction with his foreskin other features of Vaughan's childhood were less happy. His father died when he was very young, and he grew up in a close, neurotic household composed of his mother – an omnipresent source of irritation for most of his life – and his younger brother Dick, a weak, insecure boy who totally depended on Vaughan for amusement and regular consolation.

Vaughan's father's death reduced the family to a level of bourgeois penury. Mrs Vaughan had to work hard to 'maintain standards', and constant economy was the order of the day. But in compensation the cultural atmosphere of the life they led was rich. At a young age Vaughan was an accomplished pianist and would accompany his mother on the violin. He also won a Royal Drawing Society award when he was seven years old. The intimacy of the family was broken, however, when he was sent away to boarding school two years later, to Christ's Hospital in Sussex. Here he suffered the usual humiliations visited on sensitive boys at single-sex boarding schools – corporal punishment, bullying, smut, filth etc. – and Vaughan begged his mother to take him away, in vain. By his account his adolescence seems to have borne more than the usual burden of guilt, misery and isolation.

It was at school that Vaughan's particular sexual nature began to assert itself in a manner that was unequivocally homoerotic and masochistic. And it was at Christ's Hospital that he commenced a programme of regular and ingenious masturbation that was to prove lifelong. He retained nothing but unhappy memories of his schooldays but, whatever tribulations his psyche was undergoing, the seeds of his education as an artist were also sown. In the fields of music, literature and painting his years at school had not been unproductive.

It was his skill at drawing that led him, almost directly on leaving school, into the advertising world. He became a layout artist in the advertising services branch of Unilever – Lintas – where he spent most of the 1930s. The Lintas years functioned for Vaughan as a surrogate university and art school. Here he found a set of like-minded colleagues and friends who were also artists, intellectuals and eccentrics, happy to accept Vaughan on his own terms. Vaughan still lived at home with his mother but he began to experience a measure of independence too. He would spend weekends in a converted railway carriage on the Sussex coast at Pagham with a group of friends, where they would sunbathe and swim in the nude. In his memories, Pagham became one of the magic places of his life.

In other respects the broad character of Vaughan's life in the thirties seems to be one of naively earnest and dogged cultural self-improvement: endless courses of reading, playing and listening to music, visits to the ballet (an obsession) and theatre. And in many ways the pattern of life he established for himself at that time was to remain constant. On one side single-minded artistic endeavour, and on the other an equal dedication to enriching his erotic experience.

Like many middle-class homosexuals of that era most of Vaughan's sexual partners were working class, but in Vaughan's case this arose out of expediency rather than from some Forsterian fantasy. Throughout his life Vaughan yearned – vainly as it turned out – for a romantic lover who would be his social and intellectual equal. Less orthodox, however, were the refinements of his masochistic auto-eroticism. He tried to construct a primitive machine that would deliver electric shocks to his genitalia; he pushed a needle through his foreskin, and when his mother left the family home at weekends he would endeavour to bind himself to the upturned legs of the kitchen table.

It was the war which changed everything. It removed him from the cosy world of Lintas and his family, and thrust him into an entirely new set of social encounters and environments. A committed pacifist, he registered as a non-combatant and was drafted into the pioneer corps. The manual work the corps carried out was routine and mindlessly laborious. It took him to parts of England he had never visited; it reintroduced him to communal life, but without the terrors of boarding school. Moreover, it initiated his development as a serious artist, forcing him out of the 'years of dilettantism' of the Lintas period, and gaining him access to literary and artistic circles in London, that hitherto had been unapproachable, where he began to meet and be influenced by other contemporary artists – most notably Graham Sutherland.

The year 1939 also saw the start of his celebrated sequence of journals which he was to continue, almost without interruption, until the end of his life. The journals form an astonishing document. With complete candour Vaughan describes every aspect of his personality on the page. It is no exaggeration to say that they represent one of the most extraordinary, and greatest, pieces of confessional writing of the century.

From the outside, friends and colleagues variously described Vaughan as intelligent, charming, diffident, somewhat aloof, critically acute and astringently witty and generally good company. The self-portrait that emerges from the journals is considerably at odds with this, at once fierce, cold and anguished. They are excellently and lucidly written but what is so striking is the unsparing honesty, the brutal objectivity. The self-analysis is relentless. Full of self-doubt, seeded with contempt and rare exhilaration, Vaughan probes and reiterates his dilemmas and anxieties – both artistic and personal – with a determination and dedication that are prodigious. So far as his development as an artist is concerned it is as if Vaughan had realized that for him the route to success was through sheer persistence and hard work rather than inspiration and imagination. True, Vaughan had Sutherland's own huge discipline and effort as an early model, but this tenacious and unceasing toil in the older artist must have chimed with elements that already existed in his own personality. A working practice was established that he was not to deviate from. Vaughan was not, it seems to me, a naturally gifted draughtsman in the way that, say, Augustus John was. The line in a Vaughan drawing is not fluid and suggestive but firm and heavily scored. Sketchbooks are filled with dense dark pencil drawings, fretted with cross-hatching, which are worked up in the studio into sombre, muted gouaches or oils in which form and composition dominate. The whole artistic achievement of Keith Vaughan from World War Two onwards is a strenuous, laborious one; its nature is obstinate, striven-for, built up slowly and steadily, relying on constant effort and patience to see the work through to a successful culmination, rather than afflatus or spontaneous invention.

After the war, during the forties and fifties this dedication began to pay off. Vaughan's reputation grew and he began to move in established metropolitan artistic and literary circles. He taught at Camberwell, Central and the Slade. He was friend and associate with many of the artists that make up the neo-romantic movement, notably Robert Colquhoun, Robert MacBryde and John Minton. By 1950 his career was firmly established. On a personal level it seemed that he had found some measure of happiness too. He set up house with one of his painting students, Ramsay McLure, but although they remained together for the rest of Vaughan's life the passion swiftly dimmed and Vaughan returned to his old methods of obtaining sexual satisfaction. At some time in the fifties he bought a machine from Gamages department store which he adapted to pass electric current through his genitals. For the rest of his life it was to the machine he turned when he was in need of sensual excitement or consolation.

Biographically, the last thirty years of Vaughan's life were uneventful. His subject matter remained remarkably constant – more often than not the male nude in a landscape – as his style became more abstract. He showed regularly and the prices he commanded rose steadily. He and McLure moved to a flat in Belsize Park, and increasing prosperity soon allowed him to buy a cottage in Essex. McLure lived there while Vaughan led a solitary life in London during the week, returning to the country at weekends. Vaughan's working routine was quickly established and rarely varied. He would paint in the mornings and break for lunch at 12.30. After lunch there would be a siesta followed by a shorter period of work until seven when he had his first whisky. He took great care over his solitary dinner and made sure to drink a bottle of good wine. After dinner he might watch TV, listen to music, or write in his journal.

Sexually he resorted more and more to the machine. He went on occasional 'lust sleuthing' forays in Soho looking for rough trade but he came to rely on masturbation for sexual release, perfecting the operating procedures of his machine and employing other flagellatory or masochistic props – metal-tipped canes, needle and thread, mustard and red pepper.

The last ten years of Vaughan's life as evidenced by the journals represent, as their editor Alan Ross describes, 'a descent into hell . . . redeemed by . . . frankness, spleen and dry humour'. Self-analysis, nostalgia and misanthropy are mingled with despair and meticulous chronicling of his experiments with the machine (which, in a display of typical Vaughan candour, he kept on open show in his studio). Yet to the outside world, until the onset of his final illness, he appeared little changed; still teaching, still painting successfully, still reluctant for company, yet, when he was persuaded to go out, apparently enjoying himself. In 1975 he developed a malignant cancer of the bowel and underwent a colostomy. Radiation treatment followed and Vaughan became a semi-invalid, becoming progressively iller as the cancer advanced and complications set in. On the morning of 4 November 1977 he decided to commit suicide. He swallowed the pills with some whisky and sat down to record his final thoughts in his diary before he died. 'Oblivion holds no terrors for me,' he wrote. These last pages of this extraordinary document are very moving, full of stoic resignation and dignity. The final lines read: '65 was long enough for me. It wasn't a complete failure, I did some . . .' And then nothing.

He did some good work. Vaughan's posthumous artistic reputation continues to grow as indeed does his personal fame, owing to the publication of the journals last year. Malcolm Yorke's fine biography is a valuable and diligent adjunct to them, filling in many of the gaps and also setting Vaughan's work firmly in its artistic and historical context. Inevitably, though, the journals form the best and unique access to Vaughan's strange and complex personality. Any biography would suffer by comparison in this regard but one senses here and there that, however well-equipped Yorke is to talk about the work, the life of Keith Vaughan – or rather the life *in* Keith Vaughan – remains something of a mystery to him.

1990

Stanley Spencer

Stanley Spencer is an odd fish. The responses to his work are both complex and contradictory – they always have been, and the new exhibition at the Barbican, 'Stanley Spencer: The Apotheosis of Love', will prolong the debate. In my own case, one of the most nagging of the many dilemmas his art provokes is this: for someone who could clearly paint so well, why did Spencer often paint so badly? It is not simply a matter of indolence or easy nonchalance on his part: there is nothing slipshod about his bad paintings, indeed in places they are rendered with fanatical, pedantic diligence, but for me the great problem at the centre of his achievement remains this schism, this schizophrenia of technique. It is rather as if a chess grandmaster voluntarily switched to draughts, or Chopin confined himself to ragtime.

When you look closely at, for example, the extraordinary deftness and skill with which Spencer has painted the shadow of Patricia Preece's lace negligée as it falls on her thigh (in the remarkable *Patricia Preece, 1936*), or the way, in the great self-portrait of 1959, the cropped grey fringe falls over the seamed brow, you wonder how the same man could have produced the simplicities and inept distortions of *Villagers and Saints* or *The Lovers*. It is like setting a Lucian Freud beside a Beryl Cook. In the end such a wilful abdication of talent – if there is no obvious reason: sloth, drink, drugs, penury or mental collapse – remains baffling.

Perhaps this sort of deliberate shift – from the refined to the unrefined, from the subtle to the crude – occurs when innocence is overvenerated, and in Spencer's case this notion may be particularly apt. Broadly speaking, what we value in the native or the primitive – the pleasure prompted, say, by a Grandma Moses or an African carving – is the delight we take in seeing aspects of our world depicted in a manner unmediated by sophistication, by familiar cultural reference, by centuries of tradition and so on: all the rules and regulations, expectations and assumptions of a mature art form. I suppose that motives of this sort may inspire the highly accomplished artist to attempt to reproduce these effects, to scour away the gunge and clutter of too much skill and civilization, too much thought and reflection. By fashioning a false innocence we may borrow some of the properties of the real thing: fool's gold has duped many a gnarled prospector.

Certainly Spencer in his early work followed the example of the quattrocento with genuine success, but no pictures in this exhibition date from before 1933, and their naivety, their distortions and simplifications have moved on from emulation or the influence of classical traditions. Spencer's *faux-naïf* style is from this time onwards *sui generis* – it stands or falls on its own.

And its putative success would have been far easier to establish or defend if it were not counterposed – and undermined – by examples of a technical skill and artistry unshakeable in its self-assurance and triumphant in its exceptional ability. For example, *Nude Portrait of Patricia Preece* is one of the great disturbing portraits of the twentieth century. Initially, it is the arrant candour of the image that unsettles and disquiets. The almost palpable weight of the large, pendulous, blue-veined breasts, the folds and creases of slack flesh, all the flaws and discrepancies of a particular body that give an individual her, or his, physical quiddity. Then almost unconsciously you grow aware of the variety of skin tone – the chicken-fat yellows, the tarnished greens and licheny blues, the raw pinks and dirty browns, the blurry roses and clotted creams. Patricia Preece's body seems extraordinarily *lit*, as if by some sublime cinematographer, until you realize that this is in fact what we are actually like, that human skin, closely observed, looks like this, that this improbable assemblage of pigments on a canvas is the product of an artist's eye scrutinizing what he sees in front of him. Steadily, other aspects of the portrait emerge: the unusual intensity of Patricia Preece's big-eyed stare, the troubling ambiguity of her expression – a tension? or a superb confidence? Then, inevitably, ideas of artist and model intrude on the reverie of portrait and spectator. This model is the artist's wife. Even if you knew nothing of Spencer's fraught relationship with Preece you would concede the astonishing intimacy of the portrait, acknowledge what it offers up and exposes to the viewer's gaze, what emotions and potential history are implicit in it. The unequivocal power of this and other portraits set the standards by which the rest of Spencer's work is to be judged, and, as with all great artists, the criteria are established by the artist himself.

The physical layout of the exhibition is constructed roughly along lines that Spencer envisaged. It was an idea that originated in the early 1930s after the completion of the Burghclere chapel (and was probably inspired by it). Spencer conceived of a notion of displaying his work which he referred to as the Church-House project, or a 'church of me' as he sometimes described it, a collection of pictures that would represent a conspectus of his unique imagination, in both its sacred and secular dimensions. The architecture of this building was vague but was approximately churchy in configuration – a long nave, with side chapels, a transept, an altar and altarpiece. He made rough sketches of this scheme over the years and it is fair to say that almost anything he painted after its conception had its place somewhere in the rambling aggregate of buildings, small rooms, alcoves and corridors that the Church-House design had now become. He was, to put it another way, painting to equip and fit out his own private gallery which, when completed, would be a summation of his life's vision. Clearly, it was always going to be impossible to reproduce this ambitious plan in its entirety, but the Barbican has made a good stab at it, first by assembling a large and significant proportion of those pictures, and second by physically recreating something of the church effect. In the 'nave' of the gallery pictures are grouped under generic titles, set in alcoves, and on either side are a couple of 'rooms', or 'chapels', one containing the magnificent portraits of his formidable second wife Patricia Preece, the other for the 'Christ in the Wilderness' series, the small square paintings set high up on the wall, like a frieze. A large and bizarre crucifixion (of 1959), a kind of horrific cartoon, acts as the altarpiece, and to the left the gallery continues, as one arm of an extended transept into rooms containing the *Port Glasgow Resurrection*, and the Hilda Chapel, a homage to Spencer's long-suffering first wife, containing the enormous, unfinished *Apotheosis of Hilda*.

It was worth the effort: the arrangement conveys a vivid sense of Spencer's idiosyncratic personality and obsessions, and you gain some sense – however stylistically distinct the work is – of its unifying factor, that joyous celebration of life's diversity. The Patricia Chapel is the most effective. There is an almost visceral shock experienced as you walk in, with four of the big pictures hung virtually frame to frame: the two double portraits and two nudes, and, to each side, two portraits. The viewer stands there, faced with this vision of flesh, pinned in a crossfire of Patricia Preece's unflinching stares, nervously privy to Spencer's candid exultation in his wife's – and his own – nakedness.

But here lies the problem. To move from the profound and disturbing power of the Patricia Chapel back to the 'nave' of the gallery is to experience a marked diminution of effect, a diminution brought about by a number of factors that we will come to see are typically Spencerian. To put the contrast very simply, you move from refulgent, life-sized, superbly painted portraits to large long rectangles of canvas crowded with small figures. The juxtaposition is disquieting. But this shape of canvas crowded with its clustering figures was highly popular with Spencer. It embodies what might be termed the predella effect. A predella is part of an altarpiece, a horizontal strip, or separate painting below the main painting, often used, so my Pevsner informs me, 'for a number of representations in a row'. Its effect was deliberately designed to be subsidiary. The votary would approach the altar, overwhelmed and awestruck by the vast crucifixion, or transfiguration, or whatever, above it, then kneel, and then his eye would be caught by the predella. The same emotions are experienced in this exhibition on emerging from the Patricia Chapel – nothing matches the power or impact of its pictures. And many of Spencer's most famous paintings are predella-like, not just in format but in design, containing large 'numbers of representations in a row'. The *Port Glasgow Resurrection*, the 'Last Day' sequence, the 'Christ's Passion' sequence, and so on, all reflect this strong linear component. The eye need not necessarily travel from left to right as if reading a text, but it does (in pictures of this sort and shape this is the eye's natural tendency – it has to be cajoled into roving). Furthermore, if you look closely at, for example, a panel of the *Port Glasgow Resurrection*, *The Reunion of Families*, 1945, in purely painterly terms, ignoring its religious import and not attempting to assess its particular meaning, then the first quality that strikes you is the mutedness of the palette. The colours are uniformly sombre and subdued: beige, stone, moss green, grey, dull cinnamons and umbers. There is nothing rich here, nothing vibrant or glowing. At first I thought this might be a side effect of the very unsatisfactory lighting in the gallery or of the curious colouring of the walls the pictures are mounted on – a pale puce – but in fact this dullness is a feature of many of the large paintings on display. Unusually, reproductions of Spencer's pictures tend to flatter the originals. His colours are predominantly dusty, flat, depthless – even the famous *Desire* from the 'Beatitudes of Love' series shines on the page in a way it does not on the canvas. It is not hard to see why this should be so. In *The Reunion of Families* (or any number of other examples) the paint is applied very thinly, so thinly that the warp and woof of the canvas is rarely obscured by the pigment. There is absolutely no sense of any joy or satisfaction in the plastic tactile sensation that comes from the application of paint to canvas from loaded brush, no exploration of the fundamental possibilities of oil. Oil paint is used in these cases simply for its basic colour properties, and even then within this oddly reduced, dull range. The paint seems heavily thinned with turpentine, often leaving the squaring-up, pencilled grid clearly visible behind the near-transparent smear of colour. Of course, in these large pictures Spencer reproduces an overwhelming *effect* of texture, but this is more a result of his love of pattern and minute detail, which is depicted with assiduous and mind-boggling patience. In the great olive drab swathe that is *Love on the Moor* every brick in the wall which runs along the top of the picture is dutifully painted in, as is every dogtooth and stripe, herringbone and polka dot, dart and flick on the clothes of the picture's swarming population.

Staring at square yards of these paintings two comparisons came to mind as I tried to register and evaluate their effect. First of all they seemed to possess the properties of tapestries, rather than paintings. The absence of depth of field is the clearest similarity, and the flatness of the visual plane and the diminished or non-existent perspective are very tapestry-like. So too is what might be termed the picture's dogged egal-itarianism. The very top right hand corner of *Christ Delivered to the People* – a branch of a tree, a wall, a neutral section of street – is rendered with precisely the same care and attention, sharpness of focus and concentration on detail as is Christ's face! This is the democratic deadening effect of tapestry, one stitch enjoying exactly the same status as another, but is not normally a consequence of painting, except in one genre of it – which brings me to the second comparison – namely hyperrealism. One is hugely impressed, full of admiration, before these large Spencer pictures, almost stunned by these vast testimonials to his prodigious diligence and tirelessness, in much the same way as one is amazed how this or that airbrush-wielding hyperrealist has captured every gleam and warped reflection, every twinkle and dent, in the chrome innards of a Harley Davidson. Look at the *Waking Up* panel of the *Port Glasgow Resurrection*. Each leaf is there, every blade of grass, every petal on the primroses (yet the babies have the individuality of lumps of dough, strangely). But this sedulous industry – like hyperrealism – is in the end a facile talent, indicative more of a certain hyper-patient cast of mind than of genuine artistry or genius. And nowhere is this better illustrated than in the huge unfinished canvas (twenty feet by six feet) *The Apotheosis of Hilda*.

Perhaps 'barely started' would be a more apt description than 'unfinished', as only the top left hand corner is actually painted, approximately
one twelfth of the canvas. The rest is ready for painting, and in a way
that is highly revealing of Spencer's methods. In fact the expanse of
white canvas is more like a sheet from a giant sketch pad: most of the
rest of the composition has been drawn on the surface in pencil, but
drawn in the most elaborate detail – even the fishnet mesh of Hilda's
gloves has been cross-hatched in. And what has actually been completed
– and this is not meant to sound flippant – forcibly reminds one of an
abandoned 'paint-by-numbers' exercise. Looking at the painted twelfth
of the picture, it is immediately obvious that the completed work would
have been the *Apotheosis of Detail* also. Spencer has painted virtually
every pebble on the ground, every brick in a wall. Here and there the
white circle of an untreated face waits for later attention. The effect of
so much effort is disorientating: clearly on paintings of this scale this
kind of method, or something similar, has to be employed simply to get
proportions right and composition exact, but it has to be said that there
is something soullessly mechanical about this laboured depiction of
minutiae: leaf by leaf, pattern by pattern, stitch by stitch it goes, a
monstrous pseudo-Gobelin, the triumph of pertinacity over afflatus.

What is in the end so exasperating (and I think that one word sums
up the complexity of response this exhibition stimulates in me) is that
counter-examples abound, and not just in the rapt carnality of the Patricia
Chapel. There is a portrait of Hilda Spencer – *Seated Nude* – which is
equally fine. As with the Patrica Preece portraits, it exhibits a sensitivity
to the potential and resources of oil paint far superior to anything in the
large allegories or religious paintings, not just in the freedom with which
the paint is applied, or reproduction of subtle skin tones, but also an awareness of how impasto and wash, highlight and shadow, of overt brushmark
set beside absolute smoothness can simulate the contours of the body and
properties of skin with spectacular success. The effect of the bulge of
muscle over bone on Hilda's right shoulder is achieved by thick strokes
of pale coral set just below the smooth cream highlights where the skin
is stretched over the deltoid. The axillary folds above her breast are painted
slate grey, almost scumbled, with the white weave of the canvas allowed
to show through as highlights. Over and above this technical mastery
the wholly uncompromising honesty of the painter's eye is again very
powerful. It is the antithesis of idealization, but derives its power precisely
from that ruthlessness. The flesh tones of the face are markedly darker

than the hues of the torso, suiting the slight frown on Hilda's brow and the odd, troubled, askance nature of her gaze. One needs no specialized biographical information to recognize this as a great picture; all its ingredients fuse superbly. As they do in the portraits of the Patricia Chapel and as they do, for example, in the three marvellous self-portraits of 1914, 1936 and 1959.

By emphasizing the achievements of these portraits over the religious and allegorical paintings I do not wish to denigrate work that we might normally and unreflectingly regard as quintessential Stanley Spencer. But the division exists, and the artistry and spirit that infuse the former seem only marginally present in the latter. Furthermore the allegories and religious paintings are heavily encoded, replete with possible interpretations. Some of them have a more public dimension – great religious themes – others remain irreducibly private. From this stem further ambiguities and problems of response. Standing before a picture that is manifestly the product of a personality at once so eccentric and idiosyncratic can be unsatisfying: one's own emotional and intellectual comprehension seems inadequate or nugatory. What is one to make of *The Chest of Drawers*, for example? A large woman looms over a small man rummaging in the bottom drawer of a chest. Superficially it seems to me badly painted – textureless, hurried, *faux naïf* – and as for its content I suppose it might pass muster as a private joke or whimsical *jeu d'esprit*. However, set in the full context of Spencer's life, buttressed and explicated by what we know of his personal history and his private needs and desires, from information gleaned from his letters and journals, the painting takes on a different significance and is judged by altogether different standards. But this is to make the picture an adjunct to autobiography – as a work of art it still seems to me deficient. By this I don't want to imply that great or good art must necessarily have an accessible public dimension – I am not insisting that the cryptic and the obscure exclude themselves from evaluation by their very nature. On the contrary, the truly private import of, say, the *Leg of Mutton Nude* will probably remain for ever buried. But the picture exists for us in a way that, for example, *The Lovers* or *A Village in Heaven* don't. If we are denied – or are uncertain of – the significance of the images in a picture then the only way we can respond to it is either through some purely private correspondence – a fortuitous subjective recognition – or else by traditional methods of evaluation. This is the case with many of Spencer's pictures, and they suffer thereby. The same disadvantage besets the religious paintings. Suffused as they are with Spencer's highly individual sacramental vision, the odds on chiming with it naturally and spontaneously are small. Hence the almost inevitable accusations of whimsy (the British disease) or facetiousness. No such occlusion conditions our response to the portraits.

Not everyone would agree with Frank Auerbach's conviction that the only lasting and valid test of an artist's worth is how he or she treats the posed human figure. Mind you, they might not agree because it is such an exacting yardstick, before which many a lesser or vainglorious talent has its inadequacies brutally exposed. However, in a slightly wider context the assertion does have a real bearing on Spencer and his corpus of work. The great problem for artists of narrative, allegorical, ideological or symbolic subjects is that, more often than not, it is the story, the allegory, the politics, or the symbol itself, which fascinate, far more than the medium through which they are rendered. Form, as the cliché has it, is sacrificed to content. Hence the enduring presence of those great eternals in an artist's repertoire – the posed figure, the nude, the self-portrait, the interior, the still life, the landscape. Because the nature of the subject is so timeless, the balance between form and content remains in equilibrium. And it takes a real, not to say great, artist to raise the subject from the humdrum to the sublime.

The very nature of the religious and allegorical sequences, the *faux naïf* Beatitudes, and the domestic scenes place them in a different category. Here are the products of a highly personalized and maverick imagination, in the line of William Blake and Samuel Palmer. It is their very strangeness, their self-contained and self-assured idiosyncrasy that either enchants – or not at all. But in the astonishing portraits and double portraits of himself and his wives and a handful of other pictures Spencer reveals himself as an artist of major and enduring stature. All great art is unsentimental, and this is art of an honesty that is transcendent and magisterial in its formal accomplishments.

1991

Robert Hughes

Looking at the 'by the same author' list on the fly leaf of Robert Hughes's latest book, *Barcelona*, published a few months ago, it is clear that we have been the happy recipients of an explosion of productivity. It began in 1987 with the expansive and masterly history of the discovery and colonization of Australia, *The Fatal Shore*, and has continued apace. It was followed by two monographs – one on Lucian Freud (1988) and one on Frank Auerbach (1990) – a new edition of *The Shock of the New* (1991), his survey of twentieth-century art, and a weighty collection of his articles, *Nothing If Not Critical* (1991). Six substantial publications in five years represents an output of Ackroydian prolixity, a veritable torrent of creative juices all the more impressive when one notes that, apart from *The Shock of the New*, the publication listed before *The Fatal Shore*'s appearance in 1987 was *Heaven and Hell in Western Art*, published in 1969. What had Hughes been doing during all those years between? The answer is: writing art criticism (and, doubtless, researching and writing *The Fatal Shore*). Hughes has been art critic for *Time* magazine since 1970; notching up a near quarter century as the art world's most acute and uncompromising observer and interpreter. His position is pre-eminent and unchallenged: he is far and away the best art critic of his generation.

The reissue of the *The Shock of the New* provides a handy opportunity to reassess Hughes's achievements. A swift random collation between the two books threw up no examples of editorial doctoring, except, as might be expected, in the final chapter, 'The Future that Was', which has been significantly altered. The first edition signed off in 1980 and, a decade and more further on, the scene had changed dramatically. Hughes's conclusion in 1980 was gloomy, but one could detect an undertone that was cautiously upbeat. In the new edition his despair, not to say contempt, is conspicuous. That the worst excesses of the art market, with its obscene inflation of value, along with a frenzied hyping of reputation and image-mongering, have been played out in his own backyard, so to speak, probably explains Hughes's dismay, but his savage indignation makes a potent fuel for his criticism. Hughes is an exceptionally fine writer and, as with many great critics, it is scorn and vituperation which set his pen bulging with spleen, but, in castigating the minor talents and ego-driven poseurs, he negatively defines what he regards as positive and estimable. As he excoriates the prancings and posturings of the contemporary art world, a credo emerges and, so I contend, sets standards of evaluation, creates parameters of excellence, which are very hard to refute. (Interestingly enough, his approbatory gaze has crossed the Atlantic and heavily favours figuration. The expanded final chapter makes it clear that Hughes regards certain British artists as repositories of those qualities he admires. As well as Freud and Auerbach the list includes Hockney, Hodgkin, Bacon, Kitaj and Kossoff.)

If the fundamental function of criticism is to make a value judgement, to establish a system of ranking, to say why this is good and that is mediocre, and in so doing to explain and justify why the critic believes this to be the case, then Hughes's work over the years is as consistent and thorough as any. Of course all criticism is subjective, and of course it is just an expression of opinion, but in any argument the best arguer wins, other opinions are altered thereby and a consensus emerges. It is not set in cement, true, but broadly speaking, as a result of informed and intelligent critical discourse, standards are laid down and ideals are established which, if they are to be overturned by alternative criteria, have to be equally convincingly propounded and defended in their own right. This is the essence of the critical dance, if you like, and no one trips the light fantastic more effectively than Hughes.

Consider this statement, for example, which comes from Hughes's terrifyingly effective critical demolition of Julian Schnabel:

Every significant artist of the last hundred years, from Seurat to Matisse, from Picasso to Mondrian, from Beckmann to de Kooning was drilled (or drilled himself) in 'academic' drawing – the long tussle with the unforgiving and real motif which, in the end, proved to be the only basis on which the great formal achievements of modernism could be raised. Only in this way was the right to radical distortion within a continuous tradition earned, and its results raised above the level of improvisory play.

As a critical yardstick this seems to me unimprovable. Set this to work and see what it does for you. What winnowing! What wheat separated from chaff! Suddenly it feels like a window has been flung open in a hot and foetid room to admit a cool and vital breeze. Clear-eyed, refreshed, we can now see artist X and artist Y for what they truly are; stripped of obfuscation and meretricious jargon, they can be safely consigned to the crowded *spielraum* of fraudsters and hacks, no-talents and airheads. This is the function of good criticism; this is the crucial purpose of evaluation, and this is what Hughes has been doing for the last couple of decades with commendable rigour and unflagging energy.

It is not enough merely to expose failings and denigrate, even though, by extension, an alternative canon will inevitably emerge. But Hughes also writes with genuine enthusiasm and his tastes are eclectic and range throughout art history, as a glance at the contents page of *Nothing If Not Critical* will attest. But even in an area where you would expect his critical Geiger counter to be bleeping violently he seeks to extract whatever merit he can. The case of 'Land Art' – the physical shaping of a terrain, the arrangement and manipulation of natural phenomena *in situ* – is instructive. Hughes writes of *Complex One* by Michael Heizer, a large geometrical hill of rammed earth, bookended by triangles of reinforced concrete set in the Nevada desert:

Seen in isolation on the desert floor, under the pale burning blue skin of the sky, with the low sagebrush stretching away to the sun-charred and eroded rocks of the girdling range, *Complex One* is a magnificent and gratuitous spectacle . . . Even its minatory look, suggesting a bunker or an abandoned installation, seems proper to the site – the edge of the Nevada nuclear proving grounds.

Whatever you may feel about 'Land Art' as an aesthetic concept, you must admit that Hughes's refusal to sneer at this Ozymandian gesture, and instead to try and capture what is impressive about *Complex One*, is admirable – and entirely successful. It helps, of course, if you can write as well as that. Intriguingly, in the 1991 edition, these lines have been subtly altered. The skin of the sky is no longer 'pale' though it is still 'burning blue', and the sun-charred rocks have gone also, leaving only the 'eroded girdling range'. 'Le style est l'homme même' – Buffon's old saw is very apposite when contemplating Hughes's achievement. His style is not flowing and limpid, it has a knotted, intense quality, heavily adjectival and adverbial, with a large and precise vocabulary and a powerful forensic spin to his sentences. There is nothing evanescent or moody in Hughes's writing. His approach reminds me of those lines of Seamus Heaney in his early poem *Digging*:

> Between my finger and thumb
> The squat pen rests.
> I'll dig with it.

There is something irreducibly Heaneyesque – its heft, its palpable physicality – about Hughes's 'digging' that his editorial pruning won't ever
disguise. In a fine and recent essay (a reprint of a lecture delivered at
the New York Public Library, published in *The New York Review of Books*)
about Robert Mapplethorpe (that, incidentally, fixes Mapplethorpe's
reputation once and for all as a modestly talented photographer), Hughes
reveals that he is a part-time carpenter. And there is in Hughes's writing
a true craftsman's love of technique and precision. 'I can make a drawer
that slides . . . I love the tools, the smell of shavings, the rhythm of
work,' Hughes says with justifiable pride, and I'll bet he knows the
difference between a haunched tenon and a double-lapped dovetail joint
as well. Everything has its own name, and for a writer there is a magical
pleasure to be gained in using it correctly. From a reader's point of view
one of the delights of Hughes's criticism is in encountering just this
facility. At random from *The Shock of the New*: the boat in the background of a Matisse seascape is 'lateen rigged'; Bonnard is described
sitting 'quiet as an old tabby'; colours are 'rose, madder, lilac, chrome
yellow, viridian'; about Sullivan's Guaranty Building in Buffalo we learn
that 'Sullivan underplayed his horizontals by recessing the face of the
spandrels from the face of the piers.' We may not know exactly what it
means, but it sounds wonderful and possesses the unmistakable frisson
of authority.

   Naturally, Homer nods from time to time, and Hughes, like any critic
who is obliged to write about stuff he would never choose to see as a
member of the public or art lover, occasionally falls back on tried and
tested routines. Thus Sean Scully's abstracts

fairly breathe deliberation and earnestness. Their light and colour relate to the
Old Masters, in particular to Velázquez's silvery greys and ochres over a dark
ground. Their *gravitas* is real.

Sorry, no sale. But these moments are exceptionally rare, which is why
they draw one up short, and, by and large, Hughes copes extremely well
when writing about abstract painting. What more is there to say, really,
in front of a Rothko or a Jackson Pollock other than record colour

tones and the textures of the paint surface? It has always seemed to me one of the more telling and covert arguments against abstract painting that abstraction so reduces analytical discourse. The critic, the viewer, is left nearly wordless, like an amateur oenophile trying to describe the taste of a St Emilion. 'Nice, blackcurranty, metallic . . . er . . .' Stand in front of a colour-field painting – however big and imposing, with however much gravitas – or a slashed Lucio Fontana, or an Yves Klein monochrome square, and try and analyse your feelings and thoughts in more than three sentences. Great art, good art, in any medium should stimulate complex responses. An impoverished vocabulary indicates – if not a corresponding shallowness – then a simplicity that somewhat vitiates its claims to be taken so seriously.

Two other virtues in Hughes's critical persona need to be highlighted. First he is a phrase-maker of fine pithiness and wit. An aphoristic twang characterizes many of his judgements that, unusually, seems entirely natural and unforced. Hockney is summarized as the Cole Porter of figurative painting, not its Mozart; 'Fischl country is suburban Long Island. It smells of unwashed dog, barbecue lighter fluid, sperm'; now that communism has been defeated, the rise of the American Right's homophobia is explained thus: 'having lost the barbarian at the gates, they went for the fairy at the bottom of the garden'; 'for all its draw-backs, onanism was the one kind of sex that could not be controlled by the State or the Parent', Hughes remarks on the masturbatory fantasy that underpins Duchamp's *The Bride Stripped Bare by her Bachelors*; Caravaggio 'thrashed about in the etiquette of early seicento cultivation like a shark in a net'. The wit, the temerity, the sense of humour that inform Hughes's criticism are a marvellously rich seam in his prose, and it can be malignantly efficient when it comes to attacking pretension or vainglory. But Hughes's strictures are never delivered lightly, merely to break a butterfly on a wheel, and here we can acknowledge the second facet of his criticism that makes it so valuable. Hughes is a historian, and one of the highest scholarship as well, judging from the exegetical thoroughness of *The Fatal Shore*. All his writings are buttressed by a marked consciousness of the traditions out of which art springs, and his criticism is liberally seasoned with historical asides and cultural references from all disciplines. Like Ruskin, too – and it is a just comparison – Hughes is signally aware of the socio-political dimensions of art and the art world. Indeed it could be claimed that his art criticism during the eighties gives a clearer sense of the blight of the Reagan

years and of the various educational and cultural disasters afflicting the
USA in particular and the West in general than many an op-ed columnist or professorial pundit. The Mapplethorpe essay is exemplary in this
regard. Stimulated by the storm that arose over a publicly funded exhibition of Mapplethorpe's erotic photographs, Hughes not only shows
Mapplethorpe the exit door from the Pantheon but also analyses the
cultural malaise that produces both phenomena: a misplaced radical-chic
veneration and a complementary right-wing fundamentalist witch-
hunting. In addition, he outlines a defence of quality in art – as opposed
to a catch-all relativism – that is as eloquent in its simplicity as in its
passion. Expanding on his own fair skills as a carpenter Hughes remarks
that

. . . when I see the level of woodworking in a Japanese structure like the great
temple of Horyu-ji, the precision of the complex joints, the understanding of
hinoki cypress as a live substance, I know that I couldn't do anything like that
if I had my own life to live over. People who can make such things are an
élite; they have earned the right to be. Does this fill me . . . with resentment?
Absolutely not. Reverence and pleasure, more like. *Mutatis mutandis*, it's the
same in writing and the visual arts. Not all cats are the same in the light . . .
[but] these differences of intensity, meaning, grace can't be set forth in a cate-
chism or a recipe book. They can only be experienced and argued and then
seen in relation to a history that includes a social history.

As a justification of a critical modus operandi this seems to me to be
hard to better. And, moreover, it is one that Robert Hughes has been
practising for almost thirty years: as artists and critics, aficionados and
enthusiasts, writers and readers, we are all the richer for it.

1992

American Art

(Review of *American Visions: The Epic History of
Art in America* by Robert Hughes)

During the composition of this mightily impressive, beautifully written,
astute and capacious book, Robert Hughes found himself describing it
to others as 'a love letter to America' – a description which he now
qualifies with the reminder that 'different stages of an affair produce
different letters and some are not free of reproach to their brazen, abundant, horizon-filling subject'.

Pursuing the analogy, we might observe that the relationship starts
off with some cautious flirtation, is duly consummated, enjoys a passionate
middle phase and then, as doubts and suspicions crowd in, turns acridly
sour. By the book's end Hughes's love has turned, if not to hate, to
something close to contempt.

If *American Visions* is the history of a love affair gone bad, it is also
the history of a nation. Hughes, as well as being the doyen of art critics,
is also a historian of the first rank (as *The Fatal Shore*, his history of the
founding of his native Australia, and *Barcelona* testify). One of the extra
pleasures of this richly pleasurable book is that on its completion one
has read, almost by accident, a learned and succinct account of the last
300 years or so of America's existence, taking in and placing in context
all the familiar milestones, from discovery to colony to revolution, to
republic, civil war, industrialization, depression and eventual world dominance. Hughes does this effortlessly, it seems (which means the vast
scholarship and writerly skill are implicit), braiding his cultural exegesis
with his historian's, giving us the history not only of the development
of the visual arts in America but also of its multiform, energetic, striving
and troubled people.

As far as the art is concerned, it was a slowish beginning. Pueblo architecture and Amish quilts apart, the painting produced in pre-revolutionary
America is naive and on the quaint side. Tardily, artists of merit evolve
as the eighteenth century turns into the nineteenth: Copley, the brothers
Peale (Rembrandt and Raphaelle – clearly their parents had ambitions
for the boys); but the one dominant figure of this period is Thomas
Jefferson, brimful of prodigious talents – statesman, writer, farmer,

inventor, collector and architect of real note. Hughes's mini-essay on Jefferson is a gem; the book is studded with such glinting nuggets, models of concision and insight.

The first artist of real status to emerge, and one who seems quintessentially American, is Frederick Church, the Caspar David Friedrich of American art, whose vast apocalyptic canvases drew huge crowds. But the interest we have in the painters of the nineteenth century (Eakins and Winslow Homer aside) is largely topographical (Thomas Cole, Audubon), or cultural-historical (Remington), rather than aesthetic. Hughes is wisely cautious about making grand assertions (one is always aware, behind one's back as it were, of the muted roar of Europe's contemporaneous artistic achievements). For example, he posits Whistler as America's first great painter, but with the rider that it is 'absurd to class him with Degas or Manet'.

Indeed one is always conscious, because of the historical context into which the art history is woven, of America's other claims to fame as the twentieth century begins and advances – the industrial might, the innovations in architecture and consumerism, its increasing hegemony in the world – to such an extent that the accomplishments in the visual arts seem nugatory.

There are two exceptions. Hughes uses the word 'genius' only once in the book and applies it to Frank Lloyd Wright. I think he could also have appended it to Edward Hopper. Hughes's admiration for Hopper is of the highest, but it strikes me, inspired by Hughes's long view of the twentieth century, that Hopper emerges as the indisputable great modern American artist: painterly diligent, visionary, unique (Europe has produced nothing like him). And as the artistic efforts of this century end in a wet fart of faddery, flim-flam and self-indulgence, one wonders if we shall ever see his like again.

The long view puts everything in perspective. Even the golden years of American painting – the 1950s and 1960s – when New York was the demonstrable capital of the art world, now require some careful reassessment. Here Hughes is at his most incisively authoritative. While authentic geniuses may be thin on the ground, twentieth-century American art produced its fair share of legends and icon-makers, notably Georgia O'Keeffe, Jackson Pollock and Andy Warhol. There were artists of real talent – Davis, de Kooning, Diebenkorn, Kelly, Johns and Rauschenberg perhaps – and talents that flickered brightly for a moment (Kline, Lichtenstein, Rivers and Guston), but now the fuss has died down true merit will out and a lot of it looks thin stuff.

Hughes's thesis is subtle and persuasive and I apologize if my summary makes it seem all crude, broad strokes. Much of the blame for the decline in American art in the last half of the century is laid at the door of the art critic Clement Greenberg, champion of Abstract Expressionism and later of movements dubbed Post-Painterly Abstraction and Colour Field Abstraction. Greenberg's disastrous 'triumph', Hughes avers, was to suppress the evidence of skill – pictorial skill in an artist's repertoire being deemed a snare and a delusion. As a result of Greenberg's baleful influence (unparalleled in any critic before or since), America evolved a system of art education 'that has repealed its own standards', that destroyed a whole tradition in a generation or two by not teaching its skills, 'and that was what happened to figure painting in the United States between 1960 and 1980'. NO ONE CAN DRAW ANY MORE is the stark and frightening message. The art world is now reaping that whirlwind, and the stiff breeze is being felt on these shores also.

Hughes has plenty of positive things to say about contemporary American art, though it is clear that the current scene and its swarming Varps (Vaguely Art Related Persons) fill him with despair. He writes superbly, of course, and indignation often brings the best from his pen; for example, when he describes the art world of the eighties:

pumped by its own fetishism, by billionaires competing in the auction room like mountain goats clashing horns over possession of a crag or a mate.

What has made his criticism so trenchant over the last four decades is that it has always been based on sound and immovable principles: namely a firm belief that the bedrock of all serious art is technical prowess, a graphic literacy. Only that virtuosity coupled with 'the long tussle with the real motif' justifies the experimentation and horizon-expanding efforts of modernist art. Without this we are left with 'imps and goblins', their whimsical games and silly, talentless daubings: 'the sleep of reason' duly producing its monsters.

1997

Graham Sutherland

Ingres said it takes thirty years to learn to draw and three days to learn to paint. That may be putting it a little strongly, but one can understand the fundamental thrust of his argument: it is to do with delineation, with establishing the primacy of the line in art. And if there is one area of artistic practice where this primacy holds incontrovertibly it is etching, once defined as 'drawing at its most expressive'. In etching, the abstract and suggestive qualities of the line dominate and are given a further authority through the medium of printing. Graham Sutherland began his artistic life as an etcher, and it is in that fascinating and meticulous craft, it seems to me, that some of the clues to his artistic personality reside.

In etching there is a freedom denied the engraver, the freedom of the needle running easily over a grounded plate, whereas the engraved line – the burin cutting into the copper – has a necessary precision and discipline, a pondered finality. But every etching is an original drawing. The plate is prepared, the edge bevelled and the surface cleaned, the ground – beeswax and bitumen – is applied. The needle is poised. The implement held in your hand is closer to a nail or a knife than anything else. No pliant brush, no blurriness or shading of graphite or chalk, just a point. And the gesture it makes, its signature, however fluid, however graphic, is still a kind of cutting, a scratch, an incising. There are many variations of technique to be learned, many tricks of the trade to suggest distance and tone and differing effects of light, but etching is, in the end, purely a matter of expressive line.

Those early Palmeresque etchings of Sutherland, with the whole frame filled, dark with the precise scribble of cross-hatching, possess an assurance and mastery of technique that are mightily impressive. Inch by square inch the trees and the hills and the sky are rendered with the needle. The plate is immersed in the acid bath and the exposed metal eroded – 'bitten' – according to the artist's judgement: just a scratch here, the merest graze, here biting deeper, a scar, a furrow formed to hold the ink in a darker seam. But in the final process of etching, luck and experience apply: too many factors are at work – temperature, acid strength, character of the lines – to make for certainty. It is a job to be done indoors in an atmosphere redolent of the workshop rather than the studio. Perhaps this was something Sutherland responded to or even welcomed? He left school at sixteen and was apprenticed to the Midland Railway Works in Derby, where he worked with lathes and rivets, and welded plates to boilers for steam engines, before he quit the industrial world for Goldsmiths School of Art to specialize in printmaking.

Imagine, then, the almost terrifying freedom and immediacy of outdoors after the deliberate procedures of the print room – from the acid bath to the messy application of watercolour, from the permanency of the etched line to the rapid transit of pencil over a sketch pad balanced on your knee. Sutherland clearly responded to nature, as the faintly cod and cosy pastoral of those early etchings demonstrates, but the evident passion of the Pembrokeshire gouaches and oils in the mid 1930s testifies to a deeper liberation. This was not simply a numinous identification with landscape. There is – paradoxically – in that uncertain tremulous line of Sutherland, a liberation of technique. It is as if he cannot believe that the horizons have receded, that the light in the atmosphere is not produced by an electric bulb. Just as the lifer, once released, once through the prison gates, is more likely to savour the demotic pleasures of a coffee in a greasy spoon rather than embark on a holiday in Bali, so too Sutherland's new freedom never goes all out for the full Romantic orgasm. The focus is precise: the entrance to a lane, the stark contortions of a blasted tree, the prickly grip of gorse on a sea wall. This is not a Turneresque visitation of the egotistical sublime, it is an altogether more cautious feeling-out, a tentative survey of new possibilities, new geometries, new worlds.

The artistic process reflects this exactly. First comes the raw exposure to the subject matter: the roving eye waits to alight on something, anything, that holds it – stone, rock, fissure, fall of water, bole of tree – and the sketch is made on the spot. Then possibly a series of sketches from different angles. A colour wash is added. Back in the studio a selection is made and is then squared up for copying and placing in the frame of the finished canvas. Wordsworth defined poetry as 'emotion recollected in tranquillity', and Sutherland's working practice partially replicates this. But there is something dogged about the way the initial serendipitous *coup d'oeil* is worked up and worked on until its fitness as the subject of a painting is deemed suitable. Patience, thoroughness, endless practice, precision . . . These are the virtues of the etcher's craft,

and Sutherland transported them to his painting. Keith Vaughan testifies to the example Sutherland presented to a younger painter – the
sheer number of hours he spent at work, its relentless daily routine. For
those artists who rely on easy afflatus, or a facile or natural talent, or
happy accident, a painter such as Sutherland can seem dauntingly intense
and an almost shaming rebuke. Everyone else begins to look lazy, an
amateur.

Sutherland was born in Streatham in 1903, his family and upbringing
redoubtably middle class. He was a day boy at Epsom College (as was
John Piper, by uncanny coincidence) which he left early – not deemed
intelligent enough to continue to tertiary education – and was pointed
at that dependable middle-class career, engineering. Whatever it was that
made him want to go to art school and chuck his engineering apprenticeship was probably the saving of him, for there was no precocious
talent on offer, no bohemian role model that made him hanker for life
as an artist. He was handsome and polite, with a diffident charm, and
he married his first girlfriend, Kathleen, a sustaining and vitally important union that was to last to his death. In short, or in superficial terms,
there was nothing extraordinary about Graham Sutherland except his
vocation. Looking at the life and at the work one can see it as a series
of unfoldings, of revelations. The apprentice engineer discovers he can
draw, the student masters the technicalities of printmaking, then responds
to the vision of Samuel Palmer, which leads him in turn to landscape,
where his own vision supersedes and a new style and way of seeing are
created.

Even with portrait painting this process repeats itself. An excellent
rather than naturally brilliant draughtsman, Sutherland was reluctant to
attempt a likeness, yet in relenting to pressure and undertaking a commission to paint Somerset Maugham he produced one of the great portraits
of the twentieth century. And continued to do so in subsequent commissions. There is no braggadocio, no easy profligacy in the Picasso manner,
no bludgeoning personality, saturnine or sensational. Simply, the work
exists, a half century of extraordinary effort.

And at its back, at its root, is that evocative line, the Sutherland line,
his style, worth considering in more detail. It is idiosyncratic, unflowing,
full of pauses, changes of angle. Not feathery, not sinuous, but quite
strong, supplemented by little dashes, dots, squiggles, overlays, hatchings.
In the studies for the landscapes the broad ovals and rectangles of black
or colour are embellished or bordered with a fritter of pencil or pen

marks, small circles, a series of curves to suggest the contoured bark of a tree, nervy shadings or meticulous renderings of the texture of lichen, or the rutted imprints of a country road. These leaves from the sketch pads are heavily worked between the broader, smoother swathes of colour. The swift scratches of a pen – a suggestion of a furrowed field – fringe a wash of green; a freckling of leaf shapes separates two aqueous crescents of ochre; feathery strata, veins in rock, worm between rough squares of umber and aquamarine.

Who can say what it is about an artist's style that engages? What it is precisely that one responds to? How it pleasures the eye? How does that particular hand wield its brush or pencil or stick of charcoal, and what causes it to make its marks upon the surface in that singular way? With Sutherland I would say that it is this contrast of fiddly penmanship – of the black, the ink or the paint – with the smoother mass of the colour-field. The worrying, jaggy, suggestive line sits against empty calmer surfaces of colour, the tension of the one counterposed by the translucency or the opacity of the other. I am almost convinced this is a matter of instinct – this is unlearned, this is simply how you do it – and it is in these manipulations of pigment that the artist's quiddity resides. In Sutherland's case a quick skim through the oeuvre reveals this trope, this strophe, again and again. It is there in *Mountain Road with Boulder*, 1940, in the thorn trees and thorn heads half a decade later, in the Standing Forms of the 1950s, and the insects and corn cobs of the sixties and seventies. Any sketch, any gouache reveals that this tension, this contrast, is what his eye and his imagination respond to. Even the portraits are a variation of the same theme. The details of the face and clothing set against the broad empty panels of colour that form the background play with the same fecund juxtapositions.

It is not, however, a mere matter of busy line versus tranquil vacancy. With the move from the monochrome world of the print Sutherland's palette multiplied dramatically, with the result that there are few better colourists in twentieth-century painting, it seems to me. Sutherland could exploit the exquisite harmonies of greens – from apple to moss to bottle – with the same exhilarating subtlety as Braque handled his browns, greys and blues. But his range was never sombre or confined to tastefully complementing shades, and he never allowed the slubby, rainsodden tones of the British landscape to dominate. Sutherland could look at a Welsh estuary on a dull, drizzling day through the refulgent, sunfilled eyes of a Fauve or a Gauguin. True, his pictures took on a more evident mineral brilliance once he was exposed to the glare of the Mediterranean light, but his work was always boldly hued. Terracotta skies, corn-yellow clouds and magenta fields were part of his pictorial world from the thirties onwards, and it was his temerity in this area that perhaps most influenced his contemporaries and is another justification of claims for his eminence. Sutherland produced great paintings from humdrum, readily available material. Fields, trees, rocks, plants, animals. It is not through any heaped-on numinous import that his subject matter is special; it is that peculiar alchemy of line, form, colour and composition that combines on that square of canvas to give it a significance and import.

I want to resist, I suppose, too much neo-romantic baggage when it comes to an assessment of Sutherland. His imagination responded to forms in the natural world in the way that, say, Bonnard's was fired by domestic interiors or Morandi's by arrangements of vases and bottles on a table top. In each case it is what that artist does with the material selected that is important, rather than any subtext, philosophy or ideology that might be tacked on later. In any event, dogma or intellectual ambition are almost the first things that a great painting sloughs off on its journey through posterity. If we admire a Boccioni or a Marinetti today, for example, it has precious little to do with the Futurist Manifesto. The power that Sutherland's work has to enthral or move, disturb or enchant, is a tribute to his particular skill and talent and, occasionally, genius. It fluctuates, as it does in any oeuvre; there are great pictures and interesting ones, some enduringly powerful and some manifestly tired and slipshod (the Standing Form obsession of the fifties and sixties was a very overmined seam), but the qualities that make Sutherland a major artist are there to be seen in the pictures rather than read about later.

In the late forties and early fifties Graham Sutherland was the most famous living British painter. He was not only esteemed by his artistic peers, he also had a renown that prompted one critic to claim that he existed on the same level of public awareness as Brigitte Bardot and Ernest Hemingway. While the public never lost its interest in him – the Churchill portrait controversy, the Coventry Cathedral tapestry, kept him always close to centre stage – his critical reputation began to suffer in the sixties, and Sutherland never really managed to reverse its slow but steady diminution. It is a savage, unfair and inaccurate measure of any artist's standing, but it does indicate some degree of value to record that, today, a good, late-1940s Sutherland is probably one tenth the price of a good, late-1940s Bacon. Sutherland and Bacon . . . We will return to them in due course.

The problem with Sutherland's career is both instructive and minatory and I think goes a considerable way to explain this imbalance and injustice. Any twentieth-century artist's life is not simply a record of work done, there is also the question of the life led as an 'artist', how the personality is perceived and the extent to which it bolsters or detracts from the work. In a perfect world this would not be the case, and it is true that some artists do manage to maintain a reclusive non-presence and still be highly regarded. But it is difficult, and when the great and the good come calling and the seductions of acclaim beckon, only the toughest egos or the most taciturn spirits can spurn them.

Sutherland charmed people, he was an attractive man, and with his arrival on the scene in the late thirties he was also plainly a major talent, a British artist of international stature painting significant pictures among which were several enduring masterpieces. He attracted powerful patrons: Kenneth Clark, director of the National Gallery, Douglas Cooper, an opinionated and influential art critic, Lord Beaverbrook, and various others. They championed him, and he succeeded and thrived, but, in the way these well-meaning associations can turn into Faustian pacts, his familiarity with a powerful elite came to be a positive disadvantage, especially in Britain. His move to Menton did not help, and neither did his portrait commissions. Maugham, Beaverbrook, Churchill, Adenauer, Helena Rubinstein, and assorted industrialists and foreign aristocrats, however brilliant they were (and his 1957 portrait of Helena Rubinstein is as close to Velázquez as you can get in the twentieth century), gave off too rich a whiff of grandeur and plutocratic influence. There were too many exhibitions, too rapid an execution of canvases to fill up the shows. The public demand, not for the first time, served the artist badly. It is not hard to see why the critical wind shifted so uncompromisingly: changing the terms of reference, any artist today who found himself championed loudly and simultaneously by, say, Nick Serota, Robert Hughes and Rupert Murdoch might also feel that was too much of a good thing. And this was what happened to Sutherland, who, I feel, had unwittingly broken a key rule of British public life that applies to its artists as much as it does to other personalities, whether in show-business, politics or sport: if you've got it, don't flaunt it. A series of critical savagings in the sixties speeded up the undermining of his artistic reputation.

Sutherland grew richer (he was charging £20,000 for a full-length portrait in the 1970s), but he was not to enjoy the unrivalled estimation he had experienced in the years following World War Two. Interestingly enough, his greatest acclaim in the last decade of his life came from Italy, where he was widely collected and admired, his reputation as one of the leading artists of the century secure and undiminished.

And the loss is ours, and the shame that we are cursed with pusillanimous critics. The work of the last two decades of Sutherland's life is wonderfully full and ambitious, the colours richer, the scale larger, a mature extension of the themes and styles first shown to the world in the thirties and forties. The same spiky, intricate, organic forms set against glowing colour-fields, haunting and brooding interiors, marvellous luminescent landscapes that hark back to the charged Pembrokeshire canvases of thirty years previously, and an exemplary body of portraiture that has never really had its due.

As the century nears its end and we survey the past decades of British painting, two figures, I believe, will emerge as dominant influences, major talents who have produced a corpus of work that gives modern British art its true weight and significance in the international arena. One of them is Francis Bacon; the other should be Graham Sutherland. The canonization of Bacon is already under way, and it is hard to argue that this should be otherwise. But when we set Bacon alongside Sutherland, contemplate the oeuvres and assess the respective achievements, the comparison between the two artists is highly illuminating. In many respects the two men were complete opposites, not only in terms of their personality but also in many facets of their art. And in many ways they represent twin poles of artistic endeavour, twin touchstones of taste and evaluation. They seem to have met first in the mid 1930s, and became friends. Sutherland's star was in the ascendant, but he genuinely admired Bacon's talent and did a great deal to advance his career during the war. By the mid 1940s they were seeing a good deal of each other socially. In 1946 Bacon based himself in Monte Carlo and suggested Sutherland (and his wife Kathleen) join him there, which they duly did. It was his introduction to the Mediterranean littoral and to the pleasures of the roulette table; both were to prove lasting obsessions.

During the next few years the two men were at their closest, and it was inevitable that a certain amount of cross-fertilization would emerge. On the vexed question of who influenced whom Bacon is commonly granted the upper hand, but attempts to document the exchange precisely are fruitless. Baconian elements appear in some of Sutherland's works; but there are also elements of Sutherland in some of Bacon's canvases. Indeed, one could mount a very convincing argument that such major Sutherland paintings as *Gorse on Sea Wall*, 1939, or *Green Tree Form*, 1940, completely prefigure the classic Baconian composition – a twisted, tortured, organic form set more or less centrally against bold opaque panels of colour. But such point-scoring is redundant: it is in their dissimilarities that our interest lies.

The list of oppositions is fascinating and extends to their personalities. Sutherland charming and well mannered; Bacon the extrovert roué. Sutherland the devoted husband; Bacon the promiscuous homosexual. The paramount place of line in Sutherland's work; with Bacon the plasticity of the painted surface. Sutherland making study after study, laboriously squaring up and striving for perfection; Bacon relying on the adventitious moment, destroying everything that hadn't worked. Sutherland face to face with landscape and nature; Bacon confined to interiors. Sutherland's passionate response to the natural world in all its forms; Bacon's brutal obsession with the human condition. Sutherland the master etcher, the portrait painter, technically accomplished; Bacon who claimed 'I know nothing about technique'. And so on.

I am reminded here of Archilocus' ancient and somewhat baffling adage: 'The fox knows many things – the hedgehog knows one *big* thing.' If Bacon is the hedgehog of twentieth-century British painting – and any survey of his oeuvre will illustrate the 'one big thing' he knew, the relentless single-mindedness of his art, the one furrow he ploughed almost without deviation from the 1944 *Figures at the Base of a Crucifixion* – then Graham Sutherland is the fox. And one's response to both these artists will, in the end, be determined by one's affiliation to either the 'Fox' school of painting or the 'Hedgehog', if I can extend the metaphor. For those who judge that all great painting springs from a fundamental mastery of line, that it is the absolute bedrock upon which all other forms of expression, however free, rest, then Sutherland, the 'Fox', will claim their adherence. For those who like their emotions raw and unadulterated, then the 'Hedgehog' Bacon will win the day. From my point of view, I find Sutherland's achievement the more impressive. Much as I admire Bacon's single-mindedness, much as I acknowledge the sheer heft of his presence in the history of twentieth-century British art and respond to the visceral force of his canvases, I find the paucity of graphic skill a weakness at the centre of his work. A worry.

Bacon liked to sneer at Picasso and Matisse – the great modern masters of the line – and their talent for 'decoration' as he put it. So too did he dismiss Sutherland as their friendship cooled in the fifties and the sixties and as his own stature grew. He likened Sutherland's great portraits to '*Time* magazine covers', a peevish slur in any event, but one that might have more weight if there were any evidence that Bacon himself was his equal, or even near equal, when it came to sheer ability to draw. All artists set out to create a taste by which they may be appreciated, and Bacon's denigration of those artists who possess this immense graphic gift is highly revealing. Sutherland, who was blessed in this way, was a more generous spirit towards his former friend. But then foxes can always afford to be kind to hedgehogs.

1993

Pablo Picasso

(Review of *A Life of Picasso: 1907–1917:*
The Painter of Modern Life by John Richardson)

'Down with style!' Picasso once said, elaborating the exhortation with the further comment: 'Does God have a style? He made the guitar, the harlequin, the dachshund, the cat, the owl and the dove. Like me . . . He made what didn't exist. So did I.' I suppose if you are going to compare yourself to anyone you might as well aim high. But behind the vainglory is a shrewder understanding, as John Richardson discerns in this consistently fascinating biography. Picasso's genius was protean, that was its *raison d'être*. Style was 'beside the point', Richardson declares, making Picasso's Godlike analogy more lucid, in that as far as Picasso was concerned 'nobody would pay attention if one always said the same thing in the same words and in the same tone of voice'.

Insofar as this applies to Picasso it makes perfect sense, it seems to me, particularly when one considers what actually took place during the decade treated by this second volume of a projected four-volume biography. The year 1907 is one of the great watershed dates in the history of modern art and modernism, seeing as it did the painting of Picasso's huge, stylized brothel scene, *Les Demoiselles d'Avignon*. Along with, for example, Schoenberg's String Quartet in D minor in 1905 and the publication of T. S. Eliot's *The Love Song of J. Alfred Prufrock* in 1915, the painting of *Les Demoiselles* in 1907 becomes one of those 'significant moments' in an art form when, from then on, everything changes irrevocably.

Richardson makes very clear that Picasso deliberately cast himself in this role of innovator, iconoclast and boundary-breaker. *Les Demoiselles* was intended to be (and indeed remains) a shocking picture. It shocked Braque, but he (as well as every other serious artist who saw it) was instantly aware of its implications. Braque voluntarily yoked himself to Picasso as they began that assault on perspective and spatial representation that became Cubism. These two painters set about initiating the greatest revolution in the painted image since the Renaissance.

Richardson covers these momentous eleven years from 1907 to the end of the First World War with great elegance and quiet authority. All the familiar figures of modernism pass by: Gertrude Stein, Apollinaire, Matisse, Derain, Satie, Cocteau, Diaghilev et al. We move effortlessly from scholarly art history through Picasso's turbulent relationships with his friends, dealers and mistresses to, for example, a perfect distillation of the differences in ambiance between Montparnasse and Montmartre. Richardson is blessed by the fact that he knew Picasso well in the last two decades of the painter's life and also lived alongside one of the greatest private collections of Cubist paintings ever assembled. His tone, however, can be both intimate and dispassionate: there is no sense at all of undue reverence clouding judgement, and indeed what makes the two published volumes so outstanding is the sense of Picasso the man emerging – in all his complexity – alongside the superb analysis of Picasso the artist. When a druggy acquaintance of Picasso committed suicide, Fernande, Picasso's mistress, is quoted as stating 'no one ever smoked a pipe of opium again'. 'Nonsense,' Richardson says, robustly; 'virtually all the friends, except Picasso and herself, continued to do so.' He writes frequently with the unreflecting confidence of an eye-witness – and makes us believe in him completely.

Pre-First World War Paris is vividly alive in these pages, as is the community of friends and associates – whores, boxers, art dealers, conmen, poets, patrons, collectors and braggarts – amongst whom the painter lived and worked. So too are the country villages they summered in – Horta, Cadaquès, Ceret and Sorgues – forgotten hamlets then, but resonant now owing to the great paintings in whose titles they figure. Despite such a wealth of material there is no sense of being overburdened with the dogged citation of facts, dates and itineraries – the organization of the book is masterly. One fascinating and recurring theme – almost more fascinating than the collaboration with Braque – is the watchful rivalry between Matisse and Picasso as they vied for pre-eminence. Richardson is particularly astute here in his analysis, not just in human terms (the two men 'were friends but were enemies') but also in the reciprocal exchange of technique and inspiration that covertly went on between the two artists at this crucial stage in their developments. Richardson, in one succinct page, charts the similarities between the two masterpieces, Picasso's *Harlequin* of 1915 and Matisse's *Interior with Goldfish* (1914), and exposes the contrapuntal echoings and discreet gestures of *hommage* between them and, also, with Cézanne's *Self-Portrait with Palette* (1885–7). I am not aware if these buried similarities have ever been remarked on before but, in any event, it is art-historical commentary and connoisseurship of the very highest order and as much a testament to this massive work's exemplary status as, for example, the scrupulous delineation of the torrid ins-and-outs of Picasso's passionate affair with the eerily alluring, bisexual Irène Lagut.

Cézanne died in 1906; his torch was seized simultaneously by Picasso and Matisse as modern painting moved on from his astounding achievements and example. Three geniuses (and I use the word advisedly) working in the same art form so closely linked in time were bound to provoke potent change. But Picasso, it seems to me, was a genius of a different order. Cézanne and Matisse are similar types, but Picasso belongs not so much to that group of artists who represent the 'infinite capacity for taking pains' as with those artists whose Promethean energy dominates their work: multi-talented, prodigal, generous, wildly fluctuating. You could place, say, Brahms and Klee alongside Cézanne and Matisse and also Chekhov and George Herbert. Picasso belongs in the other group with Leonardo, Shakespeare, Mozart, Dickens and Wagner. And he was no exception: with them all you can find alongside the sustained and incomparable brilliance lapses and moments of almost vulgarity and mediocrity. In the ten years from 1907 (when he was twenty-six) Picasso had moved from the groundbreaking *Les Demoiselles* through Cubism, synthetic Cubism (reinventing modern sculpture on the way), and by 1917 was contemplating a return to classical figuration. Such huge talents, of course, attract mean-spirited criticism and debate about their true status and genius is always being reinitiated (it is not so very long ago that Mozart was denigrated for his 'horrid little tunes'). But Picasso is the giant figure bestriding the art of the twentieth century, as time and John Richardson's biography are steadily establishing. Such types, and such massively dominating figures, seem to attract more controversy (even in the Cubist years Picasso was regularly accused of plagiarism). Chekhov made a wise comment about this phenomenon: critics are like flies, he said, buzzing around the flanks of a horse ploughing a field. 'What does the fly buzz about?' Chekhov asks sadly. 'It scarcely knows itself; simply because it is restless and wants to proclaim: "Look, I too am living on this earth. See, I can buzz too, buzz about anything."' Artists will always be irritated by these buzzing flies – buzz, buzz, buzz – and Picasso's reputation is still dogged by them. John Richardson's wonderful biography should prove an excellent pesticide.

1996

Sarah Raphael (1)

When she was thirteen years old, Sarah Raphael received a cogent piece of advice from Michael Ayrton: 'Draw your own hand,' he said. 'If you can draw your own hand well you can draw anything.' The counsel is both sage and valid, then and now, and it was not ignored. In fact, the more one reflects on Sarah Raphael's exemplary skill and technique, the more one is prompted to wonder, in a spirit of idle speculation, just how many of her contemporaries and near-contemporaries, however lauded and fêted, could meet Michael Ayrton's simple yet demanding test and draw their own hand well? Good question . . . Embarrassing question . . . And one well worth posing in the light of this striking and impressive show of Sarah Raphael's paintings and drawings from the last three years. For the first thing that confronts one on viewing the work is the absolute confidence of Raphael's sheer ability. She draws exceptionally well. There is a bedrock of technical expertise, a meticulousness of observation that underpins both the smallest sketches and the large acrylics. This not only allows her to relax, I guess, but it permits us to breathe more easily as well. We all know that moment when an artist, in whatever medium, allows his or her ambition to expose his or her incompetence: when that top C isn't quite hit, or that *fouetté* looks distinctly dodgy, or the sonnet sequence drags on for ever. There is embarrassment on both sides, for the spectator, too, experiences an awful sense of why are you trying this when you can't even do *that*? As if, to extend the metaphor, a tennis player attempts the Wimbledon title in certain knowledge that his serve and volley game will let him down. Time and again, when one considers the claims made for our younger artists, listens to the brouhaha and the razzmatazz and hears about the prices and the prizes, a similar sense of embarrassed realization creeps in. While the emperor may not be buck-naked, he is certainly scantily clothed. Faced by the work itself, you find a still small insidious voice in your ear saying, 'I don't think he/she can actually draw . . .', 'I don't think he/she has heard of composition . . .', and so on.

The kind of facility which Raphael so abundantly possesses is the opposite to facile. Part gift and part hard graft, the ability to draw well is the result of relentless practice and strenuous application. It is, to my mind, the *sine qua non* of an artistic reputation, but it is never enough on its own. As they say in philosophy, it is a necessary condition but not a sufficient one. You cannot achieve great things without it, but sheer technical proficiency on its own, while it may dazzle and beguile, will always remain the summit of the craftsman's ambition rather than the artist's. The many small drawings and portraits in this show are mightily and enviably impressive, but it is in the larger works, the big allusive landscapes and the dense and dark charcoal drawings that we can really see this artist's imagination, raw and exposed and ready to be judged.

The large landscapes are the most obvious new departure in a continually evolving oeuvre. Raphael has always painted landscapes – three delightful small ones feature in this show, delicate and precise – but these big, darkly luminous panoramas, with their small figures and discreet symbols, represent something different. Here the scene appears charged and portentous, at once beautiful and yet gravid with unease – a lot of black mixed with the green.

The mood, in fact, is hard to pin down more precisely than that. In *A Member of the Family*, two stylized female figures seem to point something out on a distant hillside to a man. A little child looks away, huddling close to one of the women's skirts, arms oddly spread. They stand in shadow, yet the sky is blue, and the hillside facing them is lush and refulgent and traversed by many small criss-crossing paths. Quite what this signifies remains something of a mystery, but the ambiguity is not only powerful but oddly pleasing. The scene has its own beauty and its own potent secrets; any attempt to unravel them would seem heavy-handed and crude, not to say banal.

In many of her paintings and drawings Raphael introduces a few private, arcane references which recur. A goat, a tin helmet, an anxious child, a violin, a square of meshed wire fence. Curiously, this paucity of symbols and their repetition seem to guarantee their authenticity. Nothing is easier in painting, in art, in literature, than to encode or baffle. An easy surrealism, a profligate scattering of symbols and obscure private allusions all have the same effect: sense retreats, evaluation is redundant – 'You don't understand so how can you criticize?' – this method is the refuge of the charlatan, the pseud and the modestly talented.

But Raphael's few images have been emerging slowly, and pre-date the years covered by this exhibition. They congregate most noticeably in a series of drawings she made to accompany a text written by her father Frederic Raphael, published as *The Hidden I*. The drawings are small, densely worked, blurry with erasure, shading and scoring. As with her large charcoal works, Raphael leaves very little of the white paper to shine through. The drawings are not linear in that sense – nothing could be further from the naked meandering line of, say, a Hockney or a Schiele – they possess instead the texture and manifold tonal qualities of a painting. She brings that same density to her portraits – in pencil and oil – creating an indelible impression of reworking and then reworking again and again. The surfaces of the small oils are ridged and grainy from the earlier versions that exist, layer upon layer, buried beneath. This is not impasto; it is evidence instead of a dogged and indomitable patience.

Perhaps it is this aspect that concentrates the mood of stillness in the work. There is nothing sketchy or flurried about the painting, nothing suggested or dashed off. The forms are solid and irresistibly there – the bison in *The Villager II*, the stylized massy shapes of the trees and the vineyard in *Whilst Attempting to Escape*, for example. Even a picture as dramatic and disturbing as *Boys Chasing a Squirrel IV* seems suspended in time, a small atrocity captured in freeze frame (an image somehow more powerful and disturbing in its superb monochrome version). And pictures of this size do not sacrifice detail: highlights on individual blades of grass in *Whilst Attempting to Escape* are sedulously picked out, as is every pebble in the shingle beach sweeping across the big brown expanse of the *Three Families*. This last painting is the most unusual in the collection, and not just because it is a brown canvas set amongst others so glowingly green. Three small figures, men, raise their hands in greeting as they walk in single file towards three distant, seated women – all pregnant. And here too, it seems to me, the influence of Stanley Spencer becomes most apparent. It is not merely a question of mood – the picture seems to celebrate some private epiphany – but also one of technique: Spencer would have lavished similar care on the pebbles in that shingle bank. Indeed, one can catch an echo of Spencer in many of the canvases, and, if we want to place Sarah Raphael in a tradition of English painting, then that maverick line of visionaries which also includes Blake and Samuel Palmer is a more profitable area of investigation than, say, the neo-Romantics. There is nothing in Raphael's landscapes that sees the countryside *in itself* as numinous or animate in some way. The pictures derive their force from the human dramas played out against the rural scene. Remove the figures, and the panorama becomes as neutral as a Cézanne (the one exception to this rule is *David's Dream*, where the empty sunlit cornfield with its dark woods beyond commemorates a human absence). Raphael's work is reminiscent of W. H. Auden's comment, 'To me landscape is the background to a torso'; it is the arena she has chosen in which her human dramas, with their doubts, hopes, fears, desires and helpless longings, are played out.

This is what makes her work so fascinating and so rewarding: its redoubtable painterly qualities are there to buttress and enshrine a content and meaning which fascinate and unsettle, but whose precise significance just eludes us. These qualities are to be applauded all the more in a day and age when it seems that all it takes to become a 'successful' young artist is to develop a style of overweening boldness that can be recognized at a range of a hundred yards, and never deviate from it. This talent – and some of these painters are talented – is more suited to the billboard painter or the caricaturist. Nothing could be more different from the steady development that can be discerned in Sarah Raphael's work over the last ten years. And in this exhibition, it seems to me, she has found her voice, and it rings out with clarity and admirable confidence. The pleasures and satisfactions it provides are intense and various, from the dense small drawings with their fastidious technique (the brilliant gleams of light on the diamond wire mesh in one charcoal drawing are in fact the white pith of the paper, picked out with the point of a Stanley knife), to the big disturbing landscapes with their ambiguous shifting moods. All these qualities cohere particularly in one picture, *A Member of the Family*, which seems to me to be a superb contemporary painting, a judgement I make solely because I kept returning to it again and again to peer at and contemplate. It has a scale and ambition combined with a technical excellence which, in the peculiar alchemy of art, generates a singular but unmistakable profundity, enough to satisfy and enthuse, stimulate and beguile on all manner of levels. This is concrete evidence of what Sarah Raphael is achieving now, and one waits with immense anticipation for the work she is going to do in the coming years. We may expect great things of her.

1992

Sarah Raphael (2)

'Andacht zum Kleinen' – devotion to small things – was how Paul Klee tried to define one of the key components of his art and the phrase came strongly to my mind when faced with Sarah Raphael's new work. Looking at these large refulgent canvases – all bricky ochres, bleached yellows, burnt siennas – you may think the notion seems, at first glance, almost spectacularly invalid. Writers like to reach for a succinct authoritative quote to encourage and buttress the thrust of their argument and the last time I wrote about Sarah Raphael's work I embellished the text with Auden's line about landscape being but 'the background to a torso'. And now in this new show we are faced with a bold and signal absence of torsos; landscape – nature red in tooth and claw – faces us unadulterated by the human form or figures, the mothers and children, sometimes caricatured, sometimes doll-like, that had seemed to me such a Raphaelesque signature.

But, at the risk of getting it wrong again, Klee's dictum still seems to me particularly, if paradoxically, apt. Sarah Raphael has always been happy with a confined scale, particularly in her portraits, some of which are very small, and she brings to them an accuracy of line and a fiendish delicacy of touch that illustrate in exemplary fashion the miniaturist's poised and rapt precision. And the new portraits in this show reproduce this finesse with, if anything, even more aplomb. Peer closely and marvel how Sarah Raphael wields what must surely be the finest single-haired brush in the world; marvel also at the hours of patience and dedication implicit in such painstaking effort. Here, surely, is one aspect of the devotion that Klee was talking about.

But the idea of 'devotion' can carry more freight than that and it is when we turn to the large canvases inspired by the Australian desert that we begin to understand how charged the word can be. Sarah Raphael confesses how shocking and daunting these lurid and arid vistas were when she first found herself faced with them. An artist whose technical skills had always been the trustiest of allies suddenly discovered that these new configurations of rock, sand, shale and scrub left her feeling bizarrely helpless, almost bereft. One can see – one can deduce – from the smaller studies in the show, how salvation was arrived at, and how the large canvases were born.

And the lesson is salutary. If, like me, you agree with the critic Robert Hughes's asseveration that it is, in the end, 'only the long tussle with the real motif' that allows the radical distortions of abstraction and modernism then Sarah Raphael's development, as enshrined in this new work, bears this out admirably. To move from the stark figurative clarity of the two Greek landscapes (which to my mind recall the best landscapes of Stanley Spencer) to the massy nuanced colour tones of the desert paintings is to experience a palpable frisson of excitement. The temerity and the bravery of initiating such a change in style are emotions experienced no less by the spectator as by, I should imagine, the artist. It is a tribute to Sarah Raphael's 'long tussle with the real motif' that such an audacious formal shift delivers such sheer aesthetic pleasure (and, it should properly be added, it is also a tribute to the efficient catalyst of the Villiers David Travel Award).

The big desert landscapes seem to me to be a felicitous congruence of many forceful currents, blending the real strengths and resources of Sarah Raphael's gifts as a draughtsman and painter with the resources of art, or more particularly twentieth-century art. Like her small portraits these large pictures are *worked* to an astonishingly meticulous degree – the minute brushstrokes, the tiny pointillist flecks (recalling Aborigine stick paintings), the manipulation of colour and texture (raw pigment has been laid down on the canvas, red oxide and yellow ochre, some actually dug by the artist from local ochre pits) – and with phenomenal diligence have been transmuted into something greater. One hesitates to employ words like 'transcendent' but I do think these paintings transcend or transfigure the multitudinous sum of their parts. They are, on one level, works of brilliant hyperrealism: every pebble-shadow, every seam of frangible rock or desiccated twig has been precisely rendered. But the eye almost refuses to register these details, such is their profusion. And, on another level, the paintings take on the eerie and quasi-mystical properties of colour field abstraction. It is as if Georges Seurat met Mark Rothko in the Australian outback and this luminescent offspring was the astonishing result.

The desert paintings explore other possibilities of vision too. In some we are given a point of view to cling on to – tufty clumps of grass or scrub – a field of anthills – that appears to promise a perspective, that hints at a panorama or an aerial view. Other pictures, though, provide no conceptual handholds. Is that a cliff face? Is that a vision of migrating dunes? Songlines curving through micaed fields of blazing sand? The warmth and patina of the graded colour tones, the complex textures, the evanescent forms defeat our attempts at ranging and sorting them into ideas of order and we are left literally mesmerized.

Which is no bad state to be in before a modern painting. What makes these works different, what makes them remarkable, is that they manage to exploit the grandeur, the elemental aspects of abstraction but without resort to the aleatoric dribble or smear or the moody hypnosis of swathes of blended colour or the brute vigour of the gestural brush slash. The particular method Sarah Raphael has evolved to reproduce the inspiration of the Australian desert is to combine her 'devotion to small things' with a weighty and due reverence to the awe-inspiring contemplation of nature in a place on earth at its strangest and purest. Pascal looked into the night sky and testified to the mortal fear instilled by the 'silence éternel de ces espaces infinis'. The Australian desert, it seems to me, has worked a similar spiritual shrivening on Sarah Raphael, has provoked a similar re-evaluation of the human condition (is this why these land-scapes are unpeopled?), and her art has more than risen to the chal-lenge.

1993

Sarah Raphael (3)

'Draw your own hand. If you can draw your own hand well you can draw anything.' Such was the advice given to the thirteen-year-old Sarah Raphael by the sculptor, painter and all-round polymath Michael Ayrton. According to his biographer, Ayrton recognized Sarah's seriousness of purpose even at this early age. She wanted to be an artist – she was going to be an artist – and Ayrton gave her this significant tip. It was perceptive of Ayrton to spot this aspect of Sarah – and it has to be said she eclipsed him, artistically – but the counsel was wise, all the same, however unfashionable it may now seem. At the very root of all signif-icant art is the notion of virtuosity: good artists are better than mediocre artists – they can draw better, they can paint better, their sense of compo-sition is better, they can do everything better. Inept artists have become very successful, in a worldly sense, but there is no disguising this basic gift when you come across it: skill, ability, touch, instinct, feeling, a sense of colour, of line, of shapeliness and so on. It shines out; it is inescapable. Those who have it are blessed, quite simply – those who can't, bluster and bluff.

I met Sarah a couple of years after Ayrton when I went to interview her father, Frederic Raphael, for an Oxford University magazine. I remember, even then, there was a clear straightforwardness about her personality, a slightly daunting candour that impressed – as if you your-self were also being quietly weighed up on some private scale – perhaps this is what struck Ayrton, too? But, anyway, it's strange for me to consider now that there is no other artist, in whatever medium, that I have known for the full period of their working life. I have been, I think, to every significant exhibition Sarah had – from her first at the Christopher Hull Gallery to her last at the Marlborough. I write this far from my collection of her catalogues but I can mentally walk myself through her oeuvre with a familiarity that is only paralleled by the all-time greats. As time went by, I came to know Sarah better (and the Raphael family), bought some of her paintings, wrote about her work for *Modern Painters* magazine and also wrote an introduction to one of her shows. It's only now – now that she's no longer with us – that I realize I was privileged to witness the development of an artist in a unique way.

I remember particular paintings. An early, tall, thin interior with a face in an oval mirror. A group of stylized figures in front of a grassy hill. I remember also the big refulgent Australian paintings – this show being the moment where Sarah's ambitions and mastery really cohered in a dramatic way – but the one I wanted to buy was an immaculate two-foot-square unfinished landscape of jungle and palm trees. And I remember vividly the 'Strip' paintings – Sarah's audacious venturing into a kind of abstraction. At the time, my initial response was that this was a mistake but I wonder now if the Strip paintings will become her signature work. They were, for those who loved Sarah's confident, rich figuration, a swerve of huge temerity, but in their strident colours and frenetically busy surfaces they exhibited all her multifarious gifts: her patience, her draughtsmanship, her minute attention to detail. Unlike most abstract painting, Sarah's 'Strips' must have been fantastically hard to paint. Stand close to one and look at the work that has gone into six square inches. Stand back and look at the finished canvas. 'Art isn't easy,' Stephen Sondheim once wrote: Sarah exemplified that marriage of hard graft to nurtured ability. I don't know where she was heading but I feel that the Strip paintings heralded all manner of new directions.

And yet she always painted portraits. Like Graham Sutherland and Michael Andrews – artists who, more and more, remind me of Sarah – she could turn out a pencil sketch or a rapid oil that not only captured a likeness but were individual works in their own right. And here we come back to this idea of virtuosity. The art market, one might say, procreates the artists it deserves, but in a world where owning a video camera, or having a 'smart' idea, or instructing a team to install your installation is all that is required to merit the appellation 'artist', the notion that you might sit down with a pencil and sketch pad for a couple of hours to draw your child, or try to capture the essence of a beach in Greece with some watercolours, seems positively antediluvian. No matter – all this will pass, and faddy ephemera faster than most. Criteria of judgement do apply in all artistic endeavours, I'm happy to say, insofar as what is bad can be demonstrably singled out as third-rate or inferior and arguments about its third-ratedness and inferiority can be mooted and analysed – whether the work in question is a novel, a film, a play or a painting, etc. (What is not *understood* is another more complex matter, however.) It could be argued, in fact, that much of the nature of contemporary art is an attempt to evade or marginalize these criteria. If you never draw, for example, your drawing skills will never be judged. Yet it is no surprise, I feel, that the pantheon of great twentieth-century British artists is almost entirely dominated by (a) painters and (b) figurative painters. The reason why is that you can tell how good they are, yourself: you don't need the imprimatur of a gallery or a dealer or a patron. A Lucian Freud, a Michael Andrews, a Frank Auerbach, a David Hockney, a Francis Bacon or a Graham Sutherland is replete with the absolute confidence of its making. You may like some better than others but you cannot deny their individual integrity.

Looking at Sarah's work provokes the same response in me. How to define it? A kind of relaxation, a sense of calmness? Perhaps all forms of tremendous expertise, of great giftedness, signal this recognition. This person, this artist, knows what she is doing, you feel, and you want to share that discovery, to see where it takes you. The great sadness of Sarah's tragically short life is that our future voyages with her have been curtailed. She could draw her own hand. She could do anything.

2003

Franz Kline

A novelist, who had done his time in the screenplay salt mines of Hollywood, was asked once to define the difference between novel writing and script writing. The answer came in the form of this useful analogy: writing a novel is like swimming in the sea; writing a screenplay is like swimming in a swimming pool. The comparison is worth bearing in mind whenever one has to distinguish between radically different forms of activity within the same art form. Different satisfactions are in play, different resources are drawn upon and, it has to be said, one activity is going to be more rewarding than the other.

The analogy is particularly germane, it seems to me, when one comes to analysing the respective merits of figurative and non-figurative painting. I want to concentrate, as far as the last category is concerned, on what one might call pure abstract art, namely one where all attempt at representation has been eschewed, where, in the terms of one definition, 'neither the work itself, or any of its parts represents nor symbolises objects in the visible world'.

It is worth raking over the coals of this debate as one of the great exemplars of this form of abstraction has just had a major exhibition in London. Franz Kline and the loosely associated members of the New York School (Jackson Pollock, Mark Rothko, Robert Motherwell, William Baziotes, Clifford Still, Barnett Newman and others) initiated what one might call the second great wave of abstract painting in the late 1940s and 1950s (I am taking the work of Kandinsky and the Blaue Reiter group to be the groundbreakers in pure abstract painting, a trend that culminated in Mondrian's primary-coloured grid paintings in the late 1930s). However, nothing in this corner of European modernism matched the brouhaha that erupted in New York with the advent of Abstract Expressionism. 'The death of figuration' was loudly bruited about by both artists and critics, such was the influence and excitement generated by this group of painters.

Today, contemplating the pronouncements issued at the time, and the extravagant claims made for the artists themselves, a curious, not to say incredulous, distancing takes place. Can people *really* have believed that the arrival on the scene of Kline, Pollock, de Kooning, Rothko, Motherwell and the others signalled a watershed of such magnitude in the history of art? What does it say, half a century on from those days, about the kinds of critical judgement on offer? Can we really blame it all on Clement Greenberg?

As the twentieth century draws to its close, one of the most intriguing intellectual exercises will be the retrospective reassessment of 'Modernism' (by which I mean that generation of revolution against formal traditions in all the arts that started, one might claim, with Schoenberg's D minor quartet in 1905 and Picasso's *Les Desmoiselles d'Avignon* in 1907, and ended, let's say, with the publication of *Finnegans Wake* and the outbreak of World War II in 1939). As time relentlessly intercedes between then and now, it will be all the easier to chart Modernism's rise and fall, and analyse its application and transmogrification in the art forms of this particular 100 years. And it will be seen – it is already evident – that the archetypal, fundamental characteristics of the seven arts have absorbed and adapted themselves both to the serious currents of theory and innovation and also to the countless *bouleversements* of taste and wilful modishness that have swirled busily around them. Like mountains they are eroded somewhat, somewhat altered here and there, some cliff faces are more seamed and haggard, in some places the tree line has advanced or receded, but their elemental character remains the same. They have not, to extend the metaphor, suddenly become ox-bow lakes, or salt flats: for all the upheavals of their recent history they resolutely remain mountains. The novel, for example, has taken on board the lessons of Proust and Joyce, has filleted what little it likes from Virginia Woolf and decided to spit out much of what, say, B. S. Johnson and Alain Robbe-Grillet served up. Similarly with the theatre and the cinema – our diet is not pure Beckett and Brecht or Jean-Luc Godard and Ozu. Dance and music, too, have recognized where the culs-de-sac lie and have changed and reflected the upheavals in taste and aesthetics that have come and gone. One would like to say the same about painting and sculpture, and to a significant degree that is the case: the necessary lessons of the Modernist generation have been learned and have been exploited by most of our great artists. But to another, more worrying, extent it often seems to me that many artists – and critics and curators and dealers – still behave as if the Modernist iconoclasms of the 1920s and 1930s are as valid as they ever were. Here and there in the art world people still seem possessed of the desire to *épater les bourgeois* (as if they haven't been thoroughly routed), to be outrageous, to break the mould, to 'push the envelope', as they say in Hollywood, as if this were something new, as if it hadn't already been done for us before, many many times. In some areas Art at the end of the twentieth century – and this is not meant to be glib – seems the only art form that has not learned the lessons that the beginning of the century provided. It has not outgrown Modernism. It has not, in other words, grown up.

Franz Kline was a modestly talented American artist, born in Pennsylvania in 1910, who up until the late 1940s was painting figuratively in a style of sombre neo-Impressionism. There is some dispute about the source of the influence that caused him to turn so dramatically to abstract painting (possibly de Kooning's black and white abstracts of 1948, possibly Arshile Gorky's work), but whatever it was the change in artistic direction was marked and memorable. The first indications of the new style occur in the late forties in a series of small ink on paper sketches, clearly done almost spontaneously, in a manner of slashed doodling, sometimes one or two strokes of the brush, sometimes more squiggly and cursive. The key word often employed here is 'gestural', and it is by and large apt, suggesting as it does the vague arm movements one might make in conversation, the way one might render visually with one's hands the random geometry of a car crash. Kline's early black and white sketches reproduce this sparse but effective vocabulary. If a spread palm-down hand juddering through the air delineates succinctly the idea of a car skidding to a halt, then the smear and spotting of ink on paper also has a stylistic validity: one is conjuring up, suggesting, implying – in the same way as a raised fist implies a more complicated act of violence.

But – and there is always a 'but' with Kline, as there is with all the Abstract Expressionists – Kline's work is both enhanced and betrayed by reproduction. On the page an 11 x 8 inch sketch such as *Study for Buried Reds* can assume the massive gravitas of *Four Square*, which is 6½ x 4½ feet. In the museum, however, a collection of sketches known as the 'Telephone Page Series' turns out to be less than nugatory. Loose watery bands of black ink on torn out, yellowing pages of Manhattan's telephone directory, they are nothing more than a tribute to the framer's art. They are certainly beautifully framed.

Kline's work needs the large scale in order for it to function in its singular, solid, charged way. Even medium-sized canvases such as *Third Avenue* don't deliver the visual impact that the big pictures do, even though the ingredients and the manner of their execution are virtually identical. I don't want to suggest that Kline's work only succeeds by virtue of what one might term the skyscraper effect (a skyscraper is the same shape as an upended match box – which is the more impressive?), as there are other forces operating in addition to sheer size and graphic shock value, but I think that the disappointment, the banality, of the smaller work is due to the fact that the brushstroking is too evident. Too evident and too simple. The aleatoric dominates: one begins to think of the arrangement of volumes, of the painting's design, as merely serendipitous rather than consciously artistic. In a huge painting like *Wanamaker Block*, although the effect is of, let's say, a dozen great slashes on the canvas with a loaded housepainter's brush, there must in fact have been carefully considered dozens more. The big canvases are more worked, in other words, the black derives its density from more thoughtful application than a simple backhand sweep or haphazard doodle. And so is the white, too. One of the pleasant revelations of the Kline show is to observe how different the whites can be: sometimes a thick impasto, or sometimes a watery shading with the canvas showing through. There is a distinct textural quality to a successful Kline that reproduction again does not convey.

One is searching for instances of the painterly in work that seems deliberately to shun such values. But it is significant that the black and white pictures are not simply a stark contrasting of opposites. The painterliness is again more evident when Kline begins to introduce small notes of colour. In pictures such as *To Win* or *Lehigh V Span*, the note of purply maroon in the former and small streaks of blue and pistachio green in the latter function ideally with the dominant black and white – minor chords that set off the major themes. Curiously – or perhaps significantly – the less monochrome the pictures become, the more Kline's palette enlarges, the less memorable and effective they are. Kline's large colour pictures – exactly as 'gestural' and fervid as the black and white – seem mere angry discordancies. Pictures such as *Yellow, Orange and Purple* or *Head for Saturn* seem strangely un-Klinean, routine Abstract Expressionism exploiting some vague idea of energy or rage. Kline is a victim of his own success, a fate that often befalls abstract painters. Once your style is established and recognized (better still: if it can be recognized at fifty yards), then it is very hard to make a change. Kline's black and white paintings are as much a signature of the New York School as Pollock's luminous dribblings. Kline is not about colour in the same way that Pollock is not about draughtsmanship. To put it cruelly, they had both found their 'gimmick' and that was what the world wanted of them.

Kline died in 1962, aged fifty-one, of a heart attack, having wilfully, perhaps deliberately, ignored doctors' warnings to cut down his potent appetite for nicotine and alcohol. He was concentrating on colour in the last year or so of his life, wanting colour, as he phrased it, to behave structurally like black and white. It was a new direction, but, on the evidence of the works left behind, it might not have proved a fecund one. It is a measure of Kline's gift, his singular talent, that with such a reduced vocabulary – black and white, the ragged brushstroke, and the limits these factors impose on form and composition – he was able to produce abstract paintings that are so memorable. (I was about to say 'haunt', but I feel that is a misnomer: let us say that some of Kline's big simple paintings stay doggedly in the mind.) I think particularly of *Thorpe*, *Yellow Square*, *Lehigh V Span*, *Wanamaker Block*, *Accent Grave* and, to my mind his best painting, *Hazelton*.

What is it about *Hazelton* that makes it worthy of this distinction? It is large (41 x 78 inches) and the characteristic beamy slabs of black are painted with unusual confidence. There is less blurriness on the edges, less evidence of second thoughts or soft options, the black and white contrast is more austere, denser. It is also weighted heavily towards the right side, the volumes of black congregating in one half of the picture. One automatically scans a picture left to right, as one reads a book, the eye instinctively moves rightwards, and the massiness of the swathes of black in the right-hand segment seems gravid and packed, in powerful opposition to the two big white planes of the left-hand side, which are marred only by three or four tiny flecks. The flecks inevitably give a sense of scale, albeit arbitrary, small and scratchy beside the huge horizontal bar and the great tapered columnar vertical that almost divides the painting in half. There is an inevitable sense, too, of a horizon – a feeling that the top left rectangle of the picture recedes, is unpenned by the edge of the canvas.

Further comment becomes more subjective. The title of the painting suggests a place, the idea of a place implies a landscape, and one starts to imbue this dispersal of black and white pigment with attributes from our human world. Factors like 'winter', 'woods', 'snowfields', 'sky' intrude, possibly all quite wrongly, as Kline claimed only to add his titles after the picture was painted as a means of identifying them, of distinguishing them from the mass of *Untitleds* that confuse critics and perplex curators. I feel this explanation is somewhat disingenuous as there is no doubt that calling a picture *Wotan* rather than *Untitled 1957* inevitably adds something to the totality of response to that picture. Like it or not, one's reaction to an abstract painting is always bound up with one's human nature; it is virtually impossible (outside of an academic exercise) to confine it to the three essential judgements on colour, form and composition. People, human beings, who like art bring a whole complexity of sentiments – hard and soft, positive and negative – to the study of paint on canvas. By calling his picture *Hazelton* Kline slyly taps into that infinitely variegated richness, and thereby adds something to the picture's greatness. It is naive, not to say dishonest, to pretend that it doesn't matter.

I use the word 'greatness', but I use it advisedly. Much as I like and admire Franz Kline's work, I would never use the word 'masterpiece' about any of his paintings. Indeed I would never use the word about any purely abstract painting. This is what baffles and frustrates me about abstract painting in general, and not just the Abstract Expressionists of the New York School. When I consider the abstract paintings that I possess (by William Scott, Keith Vaughan, Sandra Blow and John Hoyland) and consider the pleasure I derive from them, it is of exactly the same order as my response to Franz Kline's best work. Yet for all the pleasure taken, there is something lacking, something fundamentally indifferent. Pure abstraction, in denying the human context, denies itself true greatness.

Two factors lead me towards this conclusion, and the presence of both of them is essential if a painting is to be deemed 'great' or the artist acclaimed as a 'master'. In 1928 Paul Valéry reviewed a book on Veronese's frescoes, during which he bemoaned the quality and calibre of the art of his time (this in 1928! One wonders how he would have felt today). He further commented that it was taken for granted in Veronese's time that there would be in any artist

a combination of ability and technique, that is currently extremely rare: it was assumed that any artist was in full command of the science of his art to a degree that it was second nature. The utmost virtuosity [in the practising of his art] was absolutely indispensable.

This is a working definition of an artist – an artist of stature – that seems to me to be timelessly valid. Would we rather require that an

artist have only a partial knowledge of the science of his art and be fair
to middling in the practice of it? Franz Kline could draw passably well,
certainly considerably better than Jackson Pollock, or Mark Rothko,
which is a plus, but the 'utmost virtuosity' was probably far beyond his
reach. It may be argued that by the different standards of Abstract
Expressionism Kline was indeed in full command of the science of his
art, but there is still the second factor to be considered before we crown
him with laurels.

I want to borrow and somewhat adapt a theory put forward by
Richard Wollheim in the conclusion to his wise and remarkable book
Painting as an Art. There, he offers an evolutionary argument for the
objective intelligibility of painting. He argues that painting is intelli-
gible – that painting conveys meaning – simply and precisely because
it has survived over the centuries as an art in human societies. If it did
not 'work', in other words, it would not have survived in these societies – 'societies in which a common human nature manifests itself'. In
my opinion, an art of pure abstraction reduces our ability to see our
common human nature in the work of art. (Wollheim would not agree
with me: he considers, for example, some late, purely abstract de Koonings
as masterpieces. We part company here.) I am not saying that our
common human nature is absent or degraded, I am merely saying it is
much reduced and severely simplified and, in so far as this is the case,
purely abstract art cannot function as art of the highest level and greatest
profundity. I feel this when I confront the work of Franz Kline, and it
prompts me to ask the old question: why swim in a swimming pool
when you can swim in the sea?

1994

Frank Auerbach

The difficulty of Frank Auerbach's uncompromising art has many antecedents and parallels in the twentieth century. Auerbach is difficult, it seems to me, in the way that, for example, Mallarmé is difficult, or Schoenberg is difficult. First encounters with artists of this calibre can be dismayingly unproductive, posing enormous challenges of interpretation, and seemingly denying pleasures of a more genial aesthetic sort. This difficulty, however, is at the very core of their artistic nature, is in a way defining and necessary. Citing this complexity, this intractability, is meant to be in no way pejorative and, as I hope the comparisons make clear, it is not intended to imply anything derogatory about Auerbach's artistic status.

This has always been the 'problem' with Auerbach and was one noted from the outset of his career. He is one of those artists who exerts a hefty *quid pro quo* from his admirers. He offers work of unstinting and dogged integrity and in return demands a serious response, a serious effort of contemplation before his canvases. Of all the artists in the notional School of London – Kitaj, Kossoff, Freud and even Bacon – Auerbach's work is the most rigorously stringent and obdurate: you have to come back at it again and again; you have to ignore the instinct to confess to bafflement or lack of empathy. The work demands a total and not always pleasant engagement with many sets of aesthetic criteria that have to be assessed and judged, weighed up and then reconsidered. You may not come away with the visceral shock that a big Lucian Freud nude provides, or the frisson of sheer delight that, say, a refulgent Hockney confers, but, uncertain or troubled, enlightened or engaged, you will be impressed. The huge seriousness of purpose implicit in the small loaded canvases radiates a sense of almost brutal artistic endeavour. It is a struggle to develop a taste for Auerbach's work, especially the portraits and the posed figures, but the effort is richly rewarded.

The same struggle applies, I think even more forcefully, to the large set of drawings from pictures in the National Gallery shortly on show in the Bernard Sunley Room there. Auerbach has used the National Gallery since he was a student in the fifties – and 'used' is the *mot juste*:

'visited' seems entirely insufficient and does no justice to the kind of artistic succour that the Gallery provides for him. As Auerbach himself has admitted, the great pictures in the Gallery act both as inspiration and, almost literally, as a kind of rejuvenating drug, an injection of new vigour. 'Towards the end of a new painting,' Auerbach has said, 'I actually go and draw from pictures more to remind myself of what quality is and what's actually demanded of paintings. Without these touchstones we'd be floundering. Painting is a cultured activity – it's not like spitting, one can't kid oneself.'

The exhibition is also showing six larger pictures that were painted in Auerbach's studio, worked up from drawings, that he describes as 'portraits' of certain National Gallery masterpieces. There are two of Rembrandt's *Belshazzar's Feast*, two of Rubens's *Samson and Delilah*, one of Rembrandt's *Deposition* and one of Titian's *Bacchus and Ariadne*. The *Bacchus and Ariadne* best illustrates what Auerbach means by 'portrait'. It is a dramatic transmogrification of an almost over-familiar picture into a work that is pure Auerbach, luminescent and fizzing with energy. At first glance it seems to bear almost no resemblance to the original, but on patient contemplation it slowly yields its correspondences, its reduction to particularly Auerbachian painterly tropes: the vivid colours recalling some of his Primrose Hill landscapes, the slashing gestural bars of paint, the cramming of force and dynamism into the canvas rectangle. This sort of transfiguration has a respectable recent history. One thinks immediately of Picasso's version of *Las Meninas*, or Bacon's screaming popes. It seems to me an artistic version of the literary concept of 'anxiety of influence' – the modern artist, dwarfed and burdened by the huge achievements of the past masters (as was Shelley by Milton, as was Yeats in turn by Shelley), reworks the great classics in his own image, creatively reinterprets (or misinterprets) them, thereby making 'space' for himself, and thereby making his art new. In this tradition Auerbach's 'portraits' ably hold their own, and his *Bacchus and Ariadne* is an exemplary illustration of what the exercise is designed to achieve.

But in many ways it is the mass of drawings done on the spot before the pictures that proves to be the most fascinating aspect of this exhibition and raises many intriguing questions about Auerbach's art. Here the analogy that seems most apt is not a literary one, but musical. The idea of 'variations on a theme' is a fecund source of inspiration in music, composers using – in the same way as Auerbach 'uses' certain paintings – other works as inspiration. Brahms, for example, wrote variations on

Schumann, Paganini, Handel and, most famously, Haydn. In the Haydn set there are eight variations, but Brahms freely develops melodic versions that are only distantly related to the original theme. Similarly Auerbach, seated before Gainsborough's *The Market Cart*, has produced seven small sketches directly inspired by what he is seeing. Some of these are instantly recognizable, but others are most obscurely linked to the original landscape, some almost wholly unrecognizable.

I saw the Auerbach sketches before the exhibition was hung and it was a diverting experience to see them emerge at random from the crates in which they were packed. The two National Gallery picture handlers who were with me in the store and showing me the drawings possessed a knowledge of the Gallery's pictures that possibly rivalled Auerbach's own, and, as the drawings were placed on the table, we would guess at the original inspiration. As an impromptu artistic quiz it was both intriguing and revealing. We would easily spot, say, *The Market Cart* or Philippe de Champaigne's *Vision of St Joseph*. Then, faced by another, I would say, 'Ah, the *Roqueby Venus*.' 'No,' would come the response, '*The Fighting Temeraire*.' 'Wrong,' the other handler would say, 'El Greco, *View of Toledo*.' We would turn the picture over to read the Gallery label: Poussin, *Landscape with Man Killed by a Snake*.

I use the anecdote to illustrate just how dramatically transformed are some of Auerbach's versions. The medium varies: pencil, coloured crayon, a rare watercolour wash and, more often than not, black felt-tip pen. Sometimes the marks on the paper are sparse: the familiar zigzag squiggle of crayon, a few bold slashes of felt-tip, recalling the studies for the Primrose Hill landscapes. Others are dense with cross-hatching and vigorous shading executed freely and spontaneously. The schematic ones prove the hardest to recognize – a *Naked Maja* after Goya, a version of Franz Hals's *Young Man Holding a Skull* – are almost idiogrammatic in their simplicity. The same opacity, though, sometimes occurs with the more heavily worked drawings. There are versions of *View of Toledo* and Constable's *The Cornfield* that defy recognition. On first examination, that is. What is remarkable about these occluded sketches is that, once the identification is made, the resemblances emerge, as if by magic, as if a code has been broken.

What remains harder to grasp is exactly what Auerbach himself gleans from these repeated studies and why they alter so much. Auerbach has confessed that they are inspirational touchstones, so it is possible that merely by sketching the vaguest details of, say, Tiepolo's *Allegory of Venus and Time* some sort of physical contact with the painting is enough to provide a vicarious sense of its greatness. This is merely a hunch, a guess, of course, but it seems psychologically plausible. It is common for all artists to turn to the great exemplars for some free tuition whenever a dilemma or knotty problem is encountered, but Auerbach, it seems to me, is not so much studying these paintings but attempting to capture some of their power. In the way New Guinea cannibals are reputed to eat the brains of their enemies to make them twice as cunning, so Auerbach, similarly, in his momentary, extemporized versions of these great paintings is creating an almost mystical fusing that transcends time, establishing in that brief replication a circuitry of talent or, to recast the metaphor, hacking into the mainframe of post-Renaissance European art.

As I say, this is mere speculation. Auerbach, as far as I am aware, has never *fully* explained what processes are involved. Yet he has affirmed that the core concern of his art is that his painting must 'awaken a sense of physicality'. Everything Auerbach has done in his artistic career is an effort to provoke that elemental sensation – his use of impasto emphatically bears this out. To a man with such concerns, then, merely to stand before a painting and stare at it will never be sufficient: there must be a physical engagement with the painting's own forces, its vectors and composition – there must be an eye, brain, hand, implement, paper connection, otherwise these energies, this physicality, will remain inert.

Perhaps it is something entirely subjective that reproduces such differing responses. Some of the drawings have been squared up, as if Auerbach were concerned to reproduce, albeit diagrammatically, the composition as accurately as possible. On other occasions something more fluid and improvisatory has sufficed. For Auerbach, clearly, his choice of painting is governed by this notion of physicality, of something palpable in that particular subject, in that particular arrangement of pigment. And the way to unlock this, to decode and capture the painting's secret, is to draw it.

Other questions are provoked by this remarkable series of drawings. Is there a difference for Auerbach when he is drawing a landscape or a portrait from a painter who has concentrated almost without exception on these two genres? Does a different response ensue whether he is drawing from, for example, *The Market Cart* or from Rembrandt's two great portraits of *Margaretha de Geer*?

The various versions of *The Market Cart* provide some sort of clue.

As they become progressively more distant from the original so too does Auerbach's jaggy cross-hatching become ever more frenzied. The ostensible focus of the landscape – the cart and the pool – becomes subsumed in the darkness of scribbled felt-tip as Auerbach's instinct and interest appear drawn by the two looming masses of the overarching trees. It is as if the density and volume of the trees in Gainsborough's landscape – their mass and bulk – provide a key to understanding the painting's architectonics. It is no longer a simple matter of composition, of balance and perspective, sightlines and vanishing points – the way the view is arranged: Auerbach's rapid sketches appear to vector in on something altogether more fundamental, pointing to the painting's very quiddity. Or so one supposes. We are left in the end with supposition, because it seems to me that these sketches are an essentially private enterprise – of which we are fortunate to have a privileged view – but whose meaning and purpose we cannot really plumb.

The *Margaretha de Geer* sketches, however, may indicate a link closer to home. Something about the old woman's desiccated, bony face recalls many of Auerbach's own portraits – the heavily impastoed face reduced to an emblematic death's head almost, the skull beneath the skin revealed – particularly the portraits of his first model, EOW, that he made through the 1950s and 60s. It is intriguing too, looking at the Rembrandt itself, to observe just how much impasto the painter has used. If one could separate the face from its collar of filigree lace it would possess all the lineaments of a proto-Auerbach portrait, in my opinion – suggesting perhaps that what Auerbach is doing in these highly intense sketches is searching for common factors, the roots that bind, elements in the great art of the past that coincide with the painter's own work.

Auerbach has reminded us that painting – serious painting – is a 'cultured activity – it's not like spitting . . .' These sketches illustrate one painter's relentless search through the culture of the past for the qualities that make great and enduring art new. Auerbach looks for, as he once put it, 'individuality, independence, fulness and perpetual motion', and he looks not just with his eye, but with his moving hand drawing on the paper.

1995

Howard Hodgkin

1906. February.

Paul Klee writes in his diary:

My work in the studio will grow considerably more lively. I have succeeded in directly transposing 'nature' into my style. The notion of 'study' shall be a thing of the past. Everything shall be Klee, regardless of whether impression and representation are separated by days or moments.

I wonder if a similar revelation was ever experienced by Howard Hodgkin round about 1975; if he suddenly knew, instinctively, as Klee knew sixty-nine years earlier, that henceforth 'everything shall be Hodgkin'. Certainly the marvellous exhibition that was in New York and moves to Fort Worth and then Düsseldorf later this year seems to imply that 1975 was the watershed.

I was, serendipitously, reading Klee's diaries as I was visiting the exhibition and generally thinking about Hodgkin and his work. This happy accident provoked a series of parallel reactions and cross-fertilizations that wouldn't necessarily have been made otherwise. Klee and Hodgkin are not yoked together in the way that, say, Vuillard–Hodgkin and Bonnard–Hodgkin more commonly are. It proved an interesting way of looking at Hodgkin's work from a different angle, and in the light of a different exemplar. For simple instance, the idea Klee floats in the extract quoted above of 'impression and representation' being separated by days or moments seems a succinct definition of the modus operandi that Hodgkin also avows. The impression – the private event, the memory – is transfigured in paint on wood as representation, although its final 'representation' may take years, rather than days or moments, to be finalized. In Hodgkin's case the original afflatus may be entirely lost on the viewer, or is so enigmatic as to have an identical effect, or may – simply – have been rendered in shapes and colour tones. Klee can often be quite as oblique as Hodgkin and, set beside his, Klee's titles possess a similar hazy allusiveness – are oddly Hodgkinian – and hint at a hidden meaning rather than describing the painted image. Klee: (examples taken at random) *Contemplating, Blossoming, Uplift and Direction (Glider Flight)*. Hodgkin: *Self-pity, Writing, Talking about Art*.

Klee's remarkable diaries prove salutary and humbling reading in this the day and age of the artist on fast track, the artist as snake-oil salesman, the hype-master with limited or undeveloped formal skills, the one-smart-idea pedlar. We see in these candid and beguiling pages the fascinating record of a great artist's growth: its almost unbearable deliberation, full of struggle, laborious self-education, moments of despair and doubt, of inspiration provided by other arts – literature and music – and we are reminded of the old definition of 'genius' as being the infinite capacity for taking pains. Klee's sheer diligence, his doggedness, his search for that moment when 'everything shall be Klee', are powerfully reminiscent of Hodgkin's own slow and steady development, of its learned and scholarly undertones; there is a further parallel in Hodgkin's comparatively late flowering.

That it has indeed flowered is clearly evidenced in this collection of paintings spanning two decades. Two decades of work, moreover, that display an astonishing homogeneity and occupy a near-perfect plateau of success. The nature and extent of this consistency is quite clearly revealed in two similar paintings: *The Hopes at Home* and *Patrick Caulfield in Italy*. The first was painted in 1973–7, the second in 1987–92. In both pictures we see gathered together what we might call Hodgkin's painterly vocabulary, the key Hodgkinian tropes. Two things strike the viewer immediately: the framing effect, a dark inky green in *The Hopes*, black in *Caulfield*, and the glowing lambency of the colours the frames surround. The frame, of course, achieves several ends. It 'offers' the painting; it defines its edges; its colour offsets and complements the colours in the framed space. It creates, too, a *trompe l'oeil* effect of, as it were, setting back the painted area. These visual consequences are commonplace and were doubtless understood by the first artist who painted a border round his picture or set it within a wooden frame. Hodgkin, however, has made it almost his trademark: the painted frame itself and the painted framed surface are integral to the whole effect of the composition and not a decorative afterthought. Almost without exception we view Hodgkin's pictures through a painted framing device.

Klee too, interestingly enough, was very conscious of where his picture ended – took pains pointedly to establish the picture edge (often achieved in his case by a form of mounting). In both Klee and Hodgkin the rationale behind this practice can be summed up thus: the more evident the frame – the more 'edged' the picture – so the more discrete the image becomes. The concomitant idea of a cinema frame is entirely wrong here. These pictures are resolutely bounded, hemmed in. Nothing is implicit beyond the picture's border. The gaze may not wander, it is precisely focused.

And within that frame Hodgkin spreads or stipples his refulgent colour tones. The effect, it has to be said, is highly seductive. These are paintings you covet, that boldly change your mood, that – to put it very crudely – you want to steal (no higher praise?). Many artists achieve this effect from time to time, but few can sustain it over a whole body of work: Matisse, Braque, Sam Francis are some modern artists that come to mind, but it is a tribute to Hodgkin's mastery of colour that time and again one finds oneself entranced, ravished by the intensity of contrast, of counterposing and harmonizing colour and hue.

This is, I would claim, the initial response to a Hodgkin painting: immediate and instinctive, almost physical, I find, provoking an interior shout or laugh of recognition that this sorcery has worked so swiftly upon you. It is not simply a question of electric ultramarines offset by Naples yellows. Hodgkin can work his magic with a limited palette too. A picture like *After Degas* is completely beguiling, playing with a pistachio green and a chestnut brown and yet managing to glow as if it were lit from within.

The paint is applied in certain basic modes. There is the splodge, or dotted, or stippled effect and then there is what might be termed the smear, or swathe, often a gentle ogee or section of a curve in which the history of the painted gesture can be read. The loaded brush passing over the wooden ground, releasing its thinning paint to reveal colours beneath. This apparent spontaneity is, we now know, the product of possible years of reflection and afterthought and is far removed from the aleatoric frenzy of the abstract expressionist. However, like the abstract expressionist, Hodgkin's painting can often be described as 'gestural', but it is important to establish that the individual gesture has been studied, rejected and reapplied many times and is not the impromptu slashing of some tormented id.

Klee, 1908:

By using patches of colour and tone it is possible to capture every natural impression in the simplest way, freshly and immediately.

This was Klee documenting his slow shift from a heavy reliance on the graphic to a greater confidence with colour. By 1975, the graphic element in Hodgkin's work is almost entirely subsumed by the process Klee describes above. The drawn object – a figure, a window, a tree – is at most blurrily present or is hugely stylized in the paintings of the last two decades. But Hodgkin does not rely only on colour and tone to achieve all his ends. There is no doubt – whatever protestations to the contrary – that the titles he appends to his paintings are designed to have an effect on the whole. Otherwise why not call them *Composition no. 168* or some such, if it were simply a matter of designation? But in almost every Hodgkin the totality of the 'impression' the painting conveys is adulterated, sometimes significantly, sometimes in a minor way, by the title the artist gives to it. (Again, this is an old trick – even the banal can be rendered portentous by a suitable title, as both Marcel Duchamp and Joseph Beuys were aware.) Hodgkin has consistently individualized his paintings by the titles he bestows on them. Sometimes this has the effect of a lens twitched into focus. In *Red Bermudas*, for example, crude columns of beige and red suddenly become the bottom half of a sunbather. The title *In Bed in Venice* makes the painting immediately semi-figurative. Whereas *Haven't We Met? Of Course We Have* or *Burning the Candle at Both Ends* remain impenetrably private references. This form of titling can also, it must be said, be an irritating affectation. The innocently ignorant viewer is stymied, redoubtably bogged down in his ignorance, denied the significance that the painting clearly holds for the artist and a few privileged others. A sense of exclusion is fostered, and nobody likes to be left out.

The late Bruce Chatwin was the subject of a Hodgkin painting (of the 1960s and not exhibited) and explained its genesis and key *points de repère*. The inspiration was a dinner in Chatwin's minimalist flat decorated only by a Japanese screen and 'the arse of an archaic Greek marble kouros'. Mr and Mrs Hodgkin and a couple called the Welches were the other guests. 'The result of that dinner,' Chatwin wrote,

was a painting called *Japanese Screen* in which the screen itself appears as a rectangle of pointillist dots; the Welches as a pair of gun turrets, while I am the acid green smear on the left, turning away in disgust.

Chatwin gives a further insight into Hodgkin's approach:

I remember Howard shambling round the room, fixing it in his memory with the stare I came to know so well.

Chatwin also elucidates another painting called *Tea*, which he explains as 'a seedy flat in Paddington where a male hustler is telling the story of his life'.

Hodgkin may not encourage us to attempt an interpretation or to try to seek out a figurative element in his paintings, but there is no doubt that an important side effect of the titles is to make us do exactly this. In fact I think this tendency is a distinct advantage even though we are frequently balked and defeated. There is a figurative undercurrent in Hodgkin's work, sometimes strong, sometimes subtle, and the paintings, even the most seemingly abstract, benefit from this potential urge to investigate and decode.

It is an instinctive and natural process in any event. The eye and the mind unconsciously seek to arrange and interpret the phenomena they encounter, and particularly those things deliberately presented to them, a category that includes abstract paintings hanging in art galleries. This natural human urge has to be curbed voluntarily or by some formal element in the painting, if we are to respond to it, judge and appreciate it solely, purely, in terms of shape, colour and composition. Hodgkin's paintings – with their knowing allusiveness, their *taquineries*, and their representational shadowings – encourage us to look deeper, to go beyond the initial aesthetic thrill and try to see if there are more profound chords to be struck.

What we are talking about here is a particular stimulus common to certain works of art where visceral delight cohabits with analytical curiosity or even analytical imperatives. The two responses are not mutually exclusive, they can exist separately and can be present *fortissimo* or *piano*. But in Hodgkin's case I find that what I have described as the aesthetic thrill generates a potent need to understand how this thrill was brought about. Vladimir Nabokov said that the first response to a work of art should be with the nape of the neck, but there is more going on in a Hodgkin painting than mere spine tingling. There is a complexity of reaction that functions on deeper, more cerebral levels too, and that demands further deliberation. The best of Hodgkin's paintings, and there are many of them, provoke this response, and this explains, I think, both the unique frisson his work delivers – its sheer pleasure quotient – and its ultimate seriousness.

Klee's art functions in the same way, it seems to me: it both delights on a simple level and reveals complexities of more profound and complex tenor. I don't want to push the Klee–Hodgkin thesis too far – I'm reluctant to posit Hodgkin as a late twentieth-century Klee; there are marked differences on the graphic level, for example – but time and again the correspondences illuminate and odd affinities elide harmoniously: reasons for admiring Klee will be found to be similar to the reasons for admiring Hodgkin.

For example, Klee, in 1915:

I have long had this war inside me . . . And to work my way out of my ruins, I had to fly. And I flew. I remain in this ruined world only in memory, as one occasionally does in retrospect. Thus, I am 'abstract with memories'.

Abstract mit Erinnerungen: it could be the cipher to unlock almost all of Hodgkin's work. That combination of private event, recalled and eventually transfigured (with words, with music, with paint), is the deep source of much artistic endeavour in many art forms. One thinks of Wordsworth's definition of poetry as 'emotion recollected in tranquillity', and, indeed, it is to poetry that one can go, in my opinion, to find a key to Hodgkin's particular alchemy.

Klee and Hodgkin choose memory as that function of the mind which provides the motor for their art. The American poet Wallace Stevens was obsessed with another transforming power of the human mind – imagination – and, in many respects, his entire oeuvre is a sustained meditation of this unique power and how it reshapes, irradiates and adds value to the world of appearance. Stevens's poetry is a combination of a highly seductive word-mongering and manipulation ('the aesthetic thrill') coupled with this basic concern, this serious contemplation of the faculty that lies behind all art and, as Stevens would have it, all meaningful human existence.

There is a short, not very well known Stevens poem called 'Bouquet of Roses in Sunlight' (it is one of many that could be chosen) which analyses the emotional charge that comes with seeing something beautiful, that tries to establish 'what exactly is going on' in that moment (his 'Ode to a Grecian Urn', if you like). Taking the sunlit vision of the roses as its starting point it begins:

> Say that it is a crude effect, blacks, reds,
> Pink yellows, orange whites, too much as they are
> To be anything else in the sunlight of the room . . .

> And yet this effect is a consequence of the way
> We feel and, therefore, is not real except
> In our sense of it, our sense of the fertilest red,
>
> Of yellow as first colour and of white,
> In which the sense lies still . . .

I can't think of a better description of the effect of looking at a Howard Hodgkin painting – one can almost imagine the Hodgkin version of 'Bouquet of Roses in Sunlight' – but what lifts the poem beyond mere apt description is the awareness of the defining interaction of the human mind. And of course the very experience itself has in turn been distilled and reconstructed in a work of art. Life, Stevens says – to put it very straightforwardly – is not truly real 'except in our sense of it'. And this is what great art both understands and acknowledges when it tries to make sense of our sense of life. A similar process to the one that Stevens elucidates – a highly conscious one, it seems to me – is going on in Howard Hodgkin's work: an attempt to fix the quiddity of an event – or a view or a moment or an emotion – rendered significant by 'a consequence of the way we feel' through the manipulation of pigment upon a flat ground. (The move, as Klee describes it, from 'impression to representation'.) The finished result, when it works, provides an elemental and intense pleasure but is also, as Stevens says later in the poem,

> Like a flow of meanings with no speech
> And of as many meanings as of men . . .
> . . . this is what makes them seem
> So far beyond the rhetorician's touch.

At the risk of sounding like a rhetorician I would claim that Hodgkin's paintings are, in their own way, a contemplation of what it is to be human – a celebration of all the complexities accruing in the act of being alive, sentient and conscious. Of course these are ancient – not to say timeless – concerns of all serious artists, but art that can do this is exceptionally rare: it deserves to be richly celebrated.

1996

Curating an Exhibition

In 1928, introducing a book of Veronese's frescoes, Paul Valéry wrote that 'contemporary artists have their merits, but one has to admit that they rarely attempt great work; they seem uneasy . . . they no longer like to invent. If they do invent, it is often to do with detail . . . bits and pieces absorb them. Today our art seems created only in a spirit of exhaustion.' This is 1928. What would he have said today? Probably exactly the same, and doubtless the identical sentiments could have been reiterated in 1828 or 1728 and so on. It's important to remember, it seems to me, that in any society at any given time over the last 2,000 years most of the art produced was, at best, mediocre or banal; at worst, below consideration. Genuine talent has always been a scarce commodity, genius unbelievably rare. What has come down to us from preceding centuries is the *crème de la crème*, posterity's judgement sifting nuggets of excellence from tons of indifferent ore.

Some of those working on posterity's behalf are art critics, much maligned, but whom we might see as the shock troops, the first wave over the top, if you like, in the complex business that is the forming of a consensus – however vague, however shifting – about which work has merit, which has value, which artist is worth celebrating and, perhaps, which art is worth preserving. This endless effort of evaluation is not confined to them alone, however: many others participate, worldwide, and it is constantly going on (this journal is a tiny cog in that huge machine) and its effects – like erosion, like a tree growing – are hard to discern in the short or even medium term. But it is happening all the same, constantly – one might say that this is what culture is about – and we all, in one way or another, when we bid for a picture, go to an exhibition, read a catalogue, buy a poster or a postcard reproduction – play some part, however infinitesimal, in the process.

I had the opportunity in June of this year, along with five other *confrères*, of participating in a vastly accelerated and concentrated version of this, for want of another expression, universal exercise of taste. 'The Discerning Eye' is an annual exhibition of a particular and beguiling nature (this is its fifth year). It is for work of small scale – no painting may be larger than 20 x 20 inches. Six selectors are invited to choose approximately sixty paintings that they are happy to declare are a fair representation of their taste, pictures that enshrine the selector's artistic credo, that represent, put most simply, 'the sort of painting they like'. The sixty pictures are chosen from three categories. From an open selection; from invited, 'lesser known' artists; and from invited 'well-known' artists ('well-known' meaning having had a solo exhibition in an established London gallery). The last two categories are the easiest filled. Each selector has already made up his mind (there were no 'hers' this year) about whom he admires and respects. The invited artists submit a small selection and a choice is made.

However, the most fascinating aspect of the exercise is the open selection. This year the response was huge: over 2,500 pictures were submitted, and several hundred pieces of sculpture. We had two days to boil this mass down to approximately 120 pictures – let's say twenty or so from each selector. The exhibition's title suddenly became all too apposite.

The selectors, too, are notionally divided: two critics, two artists, two collectors. This year the critics were William Packer and Martin Gayford, and the artists were Leslie Worth and Dr Derek Hill. The collectors category has always been the most loosely applied and this year was no exception. I do own a fair number of paintings but would hesitate to describe myself as a collector; and Jonathan Watkins, fellow occupier of the category, is a curator at the Serpentine Gallery. Anyway, there we were, the six of us, in the basement of the Federation of British Artists in Carlton House Terrace, about to put our artistic standards through a gruelling test of fitness and endurance. (In fact, there were occasionally seven of us: Dr Derek Hill, who couldn't make the initial selection, had a 'short list' drawn up by two proxies, the painter Michael Reynolds and the critic Brian Sewell, from which he eventually made his own choice.)

The process of selecting for the open exhibition goes like this: a team of tireless and good-natured handlers (under the supervision of the exhibition organizers – the equally tireless and good natured Annabel Elton and Sheridan McLardy) presents, in total anonymity, the work of each artist who has submitted for the 'open' category to the six selectors, who sit in a row facing a counter upon which the works are held or displayed. Sometimes it is one solitary painting, sometimes as many as eight. If any selector wants one or more set aside for later consideration, he makes this fact known; the other paintings are then 'rejected'

and we move on to the next submission. The decisions can be unbelievably rapid – an instantaneous, groaning chorus of noes – or slightly
lengthily pondered. Speed, however, was of the essence if we were not
still to be there a fortnight on. So, by and large, the paintings flash
before your eyes and you make your judgement within, on average, ten
seconds. Ideally, five to six artists a minute, 300–350 an hour. We probably managed 250 an hour. To those who submit their paintings in good
faith and high hopes, this breakneck speed may appear risible, not to
say downright insulting, but these are the rules of the game and this is
pragmatically and physically the only way it can be played.

Such a concentrated, accelerated and relentless method of evaluation
was both oddly exhilarating and highly intriguing. There was no time
for musing, no humming and hawing, no 'yes maybes' or 'what ifs'. Your
critical standards – the benchmarks and touchstones of your taste – had
to operate almost instantly and completely independently. I cannot speak
for my fellow selectors, but this is what was going on in my head. As
the paintings whizzed by, I scrutinized them first for any sign of expertise
or virtuosity, second, for any evidence of integrity and honesty, and
third, for any manifestation of thought (wit, audacity, originality). One
hopes, of course, to encounter all these facets in the individual work of
art, but this is, inevitably, very rare. I would say that technical skill –
whether graphic, tonal, compositional or in the handling of paint or
other media – was what gained a picture its initial high estimation and
ensured its selection. Sad though it is to admit, so much of the work
was so ineptly done that simple evidence of an ability to draw blazed
like a beacon. As the two days wore on, it seemed to me that amongst
the selectors – six individuals with strong opinions and entrenched and
sometimes differing tastes – our demands, our criteria for selection,
steadily converged. Occasionally we disagreed; occasionally our differing
agendas were plain to see, and occasionally all of us wanted to select
one artist's work. In these instances, what produced this unanimity was
clear and unmistakable evidence of skill, of finesse, of graphic or painterly
flair. Not all the pictures we finally chose were 'wonderful' or 'exceptional', but most of them, I feel, have something of merit about them.

More controversially, I would say further – but this is only my opinion
– that our basic standards of judgement over the many hours of selection were on the whole pretty objective. This may seem a strange observation to make in this day and age where subjectivity rules, but I have
to say that contemplating an endless stream of the undistinguished, the

unachieved and the unequivocally appalling made the old verities glow like jewels.

The experience of being a selector for the exhibition was profoundly thought provoking. Did this totally unnatural process of judging and choosing, I wondered, reveal in concentrated microcosm what in fact is going on and has always gone on – at a fundamental level – in the world of art and its evaluation? I came to feel that our experience over the two days showed that, despite the hype, the market, the flim-flam and the faddery, there are still certain deep-rooted criteria of judgement about art that we instinctively turn to and that will always apply. It was only because we put ourselves – and our taste-engendering faculties – under such stress and strain that these core values emerged as the only ones that would really, truly and in the end, do the job. Just as in moments of danger and crisis your own strength of personality and qualities of character are all you have to rely on, so too during these long hours of evaluation certain quintessential ideas of what is good art – and what is bad art – emerged as crucial. I found the experience both unexpectedly exciting and curiously reassuring, and I like to think, perhaps fondly, that we all shared this feeling. Our discerning eyes – our personal aesthetics – had been put to the test and had survived.

1996

Michael Andrews:

An A–Z

A. Ayers Rock

In the biggest of the Ayers Rock paintings, *The Cathedral, the North East Face* the blue of the sky is so intense that the rock itself appears to stand out against it almost as a *trompe l'oeil* 3-D effect. It is most disconcerting. This effect is achieved because of the contrast between the sky (painted absolutely flat, the cirrus clouds that speckle it so hazily, filmily rendered that they look miles up) and the shadow-edged fissures and irregularities of the crags and cliff faces. Solidity, mass and eroded frangibility set against infinite depth.

B. Blur

There is an effect of blurriness often present in much of Andrews's painting. In some Ayers Rock paintings the rock seems almost to swim and deliquesce, to soften into quasi-fleshy contours. One thinks also of the folds of the hills in the background of the deer-stalking series. Perhaps this ability to capture evanescence explains the uncanny ability he has of painting – in whatever medium – that most elusive and shifting of substances, water.

C. Contemporaries

Freud, Auerbach, Bacon, Hockney. Add Michael Andrews to that list (and he has every right to be up there in the pantheon beside them) then post-war British painting begins to seem, as time remorselessly passes, almost a nonpareil. To think of the quality and integrity of the work – of the painting – that this congregation of British artists has produced in the second half of the twentieth century makes one wonder when we will see their like again. All, it's worth reiterating, are to be found situated here and there within the generous and capacious tradition of figuration. Funnily enough, one catches glimpses of these and other artists in Andrews's own work: Freud in *Portrait of Tim Behrens*; Peter Blake in *All Night Long*; Euan Uglow in *The Family in the Garden*; Bacon in the small portrait sketches (*Study of a Head with Green Turban*, for example); Hockney in the middle panel of *Good and Bad at Games*.

D. Dogma

At the Slade in the early 1950s Andrews came heavily under the influence of William Coldstream and the almost dogmatic faith Coldstream possessed in 'the criterion of figurative quality'. Andrews was, owing to his clear talent, the perfect disciple, but much of his early work, one can now see, is an attempt to escape the anxiety of influence that Coldstream imposed. Hence the deliberate distortions of *Four People Sunbathing* and the heavy impasto and unfinished look of the Colony Room paintings and sketches. When Andrews found his own style, his abundant graphic gifts returned with fresh confidence. Lawrence Gowing's introduction to the 1980 Hayward Gallery retrospective is particularly good on the Coldstream effect, as is Colin St John Wilson's *The Artist at Work*, a fascinating study of the working methods of both Coldstream and Andrews.

E. Early Work

Andrews was acclaimed as a student. The two paintings *August for the People* and *A Man who Suddenly Fell Over* were hailed as evidence of his tremendous promise. I don't think they really prepare you for the later work (which is another way of saying I don't like them that much). So which painting marked the turning point? The huge *Late Evening on a Summer Day* (1957)? Possibly, but it seems unresolved – the parts greater than the whole. I think it must be the equally large (2 x 3 metres) *The Family in the Garden* (1960–2), an ostensibly run-of-the-mill subject but on this scale a formidably ambitious undertaking for a young painter. You see here a fusion of the Slade, Coldstream-inspired 'criterion of figurative quality' but – because of the size of the canvas – many of the preoccupations of the later work are in evidence: the cohesiveness (or not) of the social group, the precise delineation of atmosphere, the quiddity of the moment. It goes without saying that it is exceptionally well painted, but there's a compositional audacity that makes the grouping so memorable (the fact that this is the artist's family is irrelevant: this painting is not fundamentally about portraiture). What is it about the position of the woman's legs in the centre that is so arresting? Anyone looking at this painting would not be surprised that the same artist could go on to paint 'Lights', 'School', or the Ayers Rock and deer-stalking series. In this painting Michael Andrews sets his stall out.

F Fish

The 'School' series. These (and the studies for them) are perhaps the most simply hedonistic of Andrews's paintings. They are limpid, luminescent works and they show off his skills as a colourist to an almost Hodgkinian degree. There is a level of interpretation that one can impose on them – ideas of social order, of uniformity, of predator and prey – but my feeling is that such an attempt at reading these beautiful paintings is burdensome.

G. Good and Bad at Games

I borrowed this title for the first film I wrote. Which must date my initial acquaintance with Andrews's work fairly precisely, I suppose. I wrote *Good and Bad at Games* in 1982. The first big Andrews retrospective had been at the Hayward in 1980, ending early in 1981. I didn't go to the exhibition but I knew of Andrews's work – but only the 'Lights' series – which takes us back to the 70s. But *Good and Bad at Games* was when I first made my real connection with the man and the work. I liked the ring of the title and applied it literally to my story of hearty public schoolboys and their brutal persecution of an unsporty junior. Andrews's 'games', however, are social – to do with the games people play at parties. (My film was shown on Channel 4 in 1983 – I wonder if Michael Andrews ever saw it?) The gallery of distorted portraits that make up the painting – people squeezed thin or expanding according to the state of their social confidence – has a loose, coincidental connection with my fictional characters and their respective neuroses or swaggering self-assurance. Andrews was a shy man, by all accounts. Shy people often relish the anonymity that a large and noisy party provides.

H. Heads

Andrews's small portrait heads – studies for uncompleted pictures – or more formal portraits are exemplary. Some of them look like miniature Bacons. Others (*Portrait of June, Portrait of Colin St John Wilson*) are as good as Graham Sutherland. You wouldn't think of Andrews as a portraitist of the first rank: his reputation is to do with the large-scale landscapes and series. Yet he is, and the portraits show the complete range of his formidable gifts, the full extent of his prodigious artistic arsenal.

I. Impasto

Andrews associated the use of impasto as an illustration of effort – of a layered, scored and thickly furrowed surface as being somehow an analogue of intensity and concentration. Impasto preserved the record of change in the painted surface. Yet he is criticized as a painter of flat surfaces. Indeed, perhaps this is the most serious criticism levelled at Andrews as a major artist. Namely that his use of the spray gun (the airbrush) and of stencils renders his work lifeless in some way – the surface 'dead'. And it's true, to a certain, minor extent. With some paintings (*Lights V: The Pier Pavilion*, say) you can have your eye two inches from the canvas surface and discover that the paint is applied as evenly and neutrally as household emulsion. But everything Andrews did with paint is highly deliberate, and the use of the spray gun with its implication of industrial effortlessness was essential for the mood and ambience of certain paintings. The same is true for the argument over acrylic paint versus oil. Acrylic is made for the flat surface. But anyone who thinks Andrews avoided oil paint because it was too difficult to manipulate need only look at his little Scottish oil sketches (*Mist Clearing, Glenartney, Glenartney, 19 October '89*, for example) to see his absolute, confident mastery of this medium: oil sketches with all the verve and freshness of a Constable. And later Andrews would use impasto to provide telling contrast: in the huge landscape, *A View from Uamh Mhor* (1990–91), for example, or the slightly smaller *Oare, the Vale of Pewsey* (1989–91), Here, in these technically superb oil paintings, the paint is often thinned to near-transparency and the unpainted canvas is allowed to show through. But they also illustrate the way a heavily loaded brush is used to brilliant effect in the details. A smear or thick squiggle of oil and, hey presto, you have a hawthorn hedge or a gorse-filled ravine, or a stream shining silver in a gulley.

J. June

Andrews's wife, June Keeley, whom he met in 1963. She is present in the first *Good and Bad at Games* painting – the second ball-like figure on the left. In 1970 their daughter Melanie was born. The postcard reproduction of Andrews's painting, *Melanie and Me Swimming* (1978–9), is reputedly the most purchased postcard in Tate Britain.

K. Klee

Paul Klee – not an artist one would instantly associate with Andrews – two different senses of scale, for a start. But they have a lot in common. Both men read widely and thought profoundly about their art, and Klee was an accomplished musician. Andrews was always writing his thoughts down and one wishes he had kept a diary as Klee did. One example. Klee, October 1901: 'In the evening there were subdued and serious colour effects of a sombreness and subtlety that one would never believe possible in Italy . . . There is a moral strength in such colour. I see it just as much as others do. I too shall be able to create it one day. When?' I suspect this was similar to the Ayers Rock effect.

L. 'Lights'

The critical consensus would probably regard this series of seven paintings at the centre of Andrews's working life as his greatest monument. (As I write this I can see out of my study window – with eerie synchronicity – a child's silver helium balloon flying up into the sky over Radnor Walk, SW3.) Anyway, looking at the series together – as one did at last year's astounding, never-to-be-forgotten Tate Britain retrospective – both cemented its reputation and exposed its weaknesses. Without the overarching concept – the voyage of the ego (the balloon) – to bind the individual canvases together, some of the paintings might seem less significant. That the series ends with *Lights VII: A Shadow* is its great strength and advantage. *A Shadow* – the shadow of the balloon on a stretch of sand, with the sea and the horizon and the sky beyond – is one of the great paintings of the twentieth century, and part of its greatness lies in the difficulty of explaining precisely why this should be so. It's much bigger than you would expect – which was the first shock I received on seeing it. (An aside: what other modern figurative artist has painted such really large paintings throughout his or her career with such consistent aplomb and authority?) *A Shadow* is as flat as any of the other paintings in the series – acrylic paint, spray gun – but I think its power lies somewhere in the tension between the serenity of the moment – balloon shadow, sand, sea, sky – and the confused tangle of sea-wrack to the left of the balloon shadow. Andrews apparently created this with tape, dipped in black paint, and draped on the canvas. This juxtaposition of the aleatory and the measured, the messy and the serene seems to me the key to this painting's quiescent and mesmerizing power.

M. Masterpiece

This is a word that should be used with huge discretion and extremely rarely. Vladimir Nabokov was continually outraged by the way American critics would casually bandy about the word 'genius' – as if such people were a dime a dozen. The same caution applies to the appellation of 'masterpiece'. In fact, only posterity should be the real judge here but Andrews is often described as a painter who 'only painted masterpieces', probably because his output was comparatively small and possibly because so many of his paintings were on a large scale: their ambition and their near-faultless execution tend to stake a big claim – as well as having the side-effect of scaling down the less well-achieved work of other painters. However, it is true that seeing Andrews's work over the period of his lifetime one is struck by how memorable so many of his paintings are. Or, to put it another way, how few comparative failures there are. Andrews died seven years ago and we have only had one posthumous retrospective but, as one starts ranking the paintings in order of eminence and importance, one realizes just how many exceptional paintings there are in the oeuvre.

N. *Narrative*

Not so much narrative painting, as we would commonly understand it, but a vague concept of story emerging, tying the individual paintings together, however loosely. Andrews's practice was to work out a concept or an idea over a series of canvases: the party paintings, 'Lights', 'School', the deerstalking paintings, Ayers Rock, the final Thames paintings. One can't easily trace the exact connections, but the ghost of a narrative line is teasingly there (from the Colony Room paintings to *All Night Long*, for example), begging the questions of interrelationships, of sequence, of deciphering. Biographical details help (for example, in the deerstalking sequence, we know that Andrews was not a natural deerstalker – his days out on the hill were fraught) but in the end the links between the paintings remain tenuous. Trying to tell the exact 'story' of the progression of 'Lights', for example, is an open invitation to pretentiousness.

O. *Odd Ones Out*

I don't like Andrews's painting *Cabin*. The perspective of the plane is wrong, yet the perspective of the coastal city below it is perfect. I know there were meant to be faces at the windows, and that he abandoned the idea of placing them there, but any one of the small portrait studies that he prepared for this is better than the finished painting. I also don't like his landscape *Daylesford*, a grand house seen in its manicured park (a commission?). It is expertly painted but it seems dead – the oil paint managing somehow to reproduce here the dull flatness of acrylic.

P. *Photography*

Andrews used photography extensively in his painting, either as a spur to invention or else as a precise model for the finished canvas. The deerstalking pictures, for example, are almost identical to photographs that Andrews had taken of himself and the gamekeeper during the stalk. Working this way from photographs seems to me to be entirely acceptable. To see both the paintings and the photographic originals (as one did at the Tate Britain retrospective) serves only to remind you of the artistic gulf between a photograph and a painting.

Q. *Q-tip*

Andrews often used Q-tips when painting. To blur? To smear? To lift off? It is a useful symbol of his fastidiousness, it seems to me, a sign of his precision. He also used to bang the canvas: ball up tightly a piece of rag, grip the canvas edge with his left hand and bang the rag-ball firmly on the painted surface, four or five times. This would randomly disperse the paint but it would also drive the pigment deep into the weave of the canvas.

R. *Rimbaud*

Arthur Rimbaud appears in the middle of *The Deer Park* – the title taken from Norman Mailer's novel. William Feaver has taken a photograph of some bookshelves in Andrews's studio. They make interesting reading – other people's books tell you as much about them as do the paintings hanging on their walls. In this selection there is a diverse group of writers: Jung, R. D. Laing, de Sade, William Burroughs, *Opium and the Romantic Imagination*, lots of Mailer, Paul Scott, Isherwood, Sylvia Plath and other poetry. We know enough about Andrews to see this reading matter as typical of his tastes and interests. But it is the fact that he was an avid reader (by no means true of all painters) that is intriguing – especially to a writer. Rimbaud gave the title to 'Lights' (a free translation of *Les Illuminations*). And Auden is present too in the title of Andrews's prize-winning painting at the Slade, *August for the People* (1952). 'August for the people and their favourite islands' – to give the line in full. I've always thought another line of Auden could serve very well for the 'Lights' series: 'As the hawk sees it, or the helmeted airman'. Early Auden was obsessed with the view from above – unemotional, objective, clear-eyed. This is the point of view of the balloonist too: silent, often unnoticed by those on the ground, drifting high above the earth.

S. *Silk-screen*

The portraits in the three *Good and Bad at Games* paintings are set against a silk-screened photograph of an office block. Andrews had this done by an industrial silk-screener. There is something about the process of silk-screening that is very typical of the look of an Andrews painting. It seems to me he often strove to paint in a way that made the finished result look silk-screened (the spray gun). And of course he used stencils extensively, particularly in the 'School' series. I think he must have used stencils in the deerstalking pictures also. The tiny running deer are so exquisitely done, the outline of their antlers so perfectly set against the misty hills in the background that I feel sure he must have stencilled them on. This doesn't matter at all, of course. Even in the fish paintings, where the stencil was a way of (a) saving him from having to paint the same fish twenty times and (b) allowing him to achieve the blurry complexities of dark and light pigmentation of fish scales (the pike, for instance), there are examples of precise and beautiful brush-work – stippling, slashing, shading. Look at the foreground grass in the painting *Running with the Deer*. Can that tough, tussocky, windlashed highland grass ever have been painted better?

T. Thames

Andrews's last series of paintings, the three Thames paintings, are a fitting conclusion to his life and work. Everything tried before seems to come together here. This is both a real place and a symbol with a great freight of allusion (Sweet Thames, the Styx, the flux of life). The innovation in these canvases is in the use of an almost tidal manipulation of paint and turpentine to replicate the daily ebb and flow of the river itself. Andrews would lay his painting flat on the floor, pour on his mix of turps and oil and push the fluid around with the help of a powerful hairdryer. The effect is astonishing. The accumulation of grit (sand and sediment were added to the colour) and the way the mix happened to swirl and settle on the canvas mean that the effect of light on the finished painting, and the viewer's position, make the pictures endlessly changeable. Both *The Thames at Low Tide* and *Thames Painting: The Estuary* are great, dark, brooding, moving paintings – late Beethoven quartet paintings; 'Four Last Songs' paintings.

U. Unfinished

Andrews often left his paintings with an unfinished look to them (*The Deer Park*, for example). But his death in 1995 meant that his last painting in the Thames series, *Source of the Thames*, was unfinishable. We know from photographs he took how to interpret the possible final form the painting might have taken: a stream flowing out of a dense clump of undergrowth, widening and thickening, the water surface reflecting a blue sky with clouds. But as it stands now it is the most abstract of all his work, and the paint surface is, here and there, clotted with grass stems and seeds gathered from the banks of the river. If the other two paintings are reliable guides, the fluid image would have been fixed somehow with the addition of recognizable branches or leafage. But one sees all the same, in this forcibly arrested work, all the natural atavistic energies of a painter who would later bring his calculating, sophisticated, painterly mind to bear on the subject. He would have given scale – which is lacking at the moment. Look at the figures in *The Estuary* or *In Shade, Foot of Olga Gorge* (perhaps my favourite Ayers Rock painting) to get a glimmering of where *Source of the Thames* might have gone.

V. A View from Uamh Mhor

This huge landscape is another *tour de force*. Anyone who knows the wilder parts of Scotland will testify to its refulgent veracity. Andrews, reputedly overdosed on the mineral brilliances of Ayers Rock and the palette of rusts, reds, ochres and yellows it compelled, longed for the sopping, airy greenness of remote Perthshire, and this picture is painted with a freedom and brio that are the opposite of the Ayers Rock paintings. Paint dribbles, canvas shows through, the confident rapid passage of the brush is everywhere in evidence. Scotland inspired Andrews – not just in the deerstalking series but also in the bravura oil sketches of the views around Glenartney where he holidayed each summer. His *Edinburgh (Old Town)* captures that city's ancient, dour, unique atmosphere with perfect palpability. You can feel the cold scowthering rain coming in off the Firth of Forth.

W. Watercolour

Is it surprising that Michael Andrews was a watercolour painter of the very highest rank? One of the phenomenal bonuses of the Tate Britain show was to see a selection of the small watercolours of a river near Andrews's house in Norfolk. Technically, they are breathtaking: a painting like *Angler: Geldeston* makes you marvel about how these effects are achieved. You feel there is something almost magical going on here. Take a box of watercolours: with your paint reproduce the effect of brilliant sunlight glinting on turbid water.

X. The X-shape at the Centre of the Parterre at Drummond Castle

Seen from the air, 'as the hawk sees it'. And in *Drummond: the Multicoloured Parterre* he leaves the unpainted canvas to mark out the huge Saltire cross of the gravel paths. Is it because it is so precisely formal? Here we see the shaping hand of man working on and controlling nature. The parterre at Drummond is the very antithesis of a phenomenon like Ayers Rock – but perhaps its creation is not so far removed from the process of an artist trying to capture the look and spirit of Ayers Rock by manipulating coloured pigment on a rectangle of canvas. And what do the strange carnival figures marching across the foreground represent? Jolly clowns or anarchic ghouls? Benign jesters or Lords of Misrule?

Y. W. B. Yeats

'Like a long-legged fly upon the stream/His mind moves upon silence.' For some reason, these lines always remind me of Michael Andrews (whom I never met).

Z. Zen

Andrews was very preoccupied with the teachings of Zen – the whole 'Lights' series, it can be argued, is analogous to the progress of the soul

towards transcendence. And you could further argue that the fastidiousness of Andrews's eye, his searching for the numinous, transfiguring
moment, has a Zen-like quality to it. But this knowledge, though interesting (as interesting as Andrews's reading, say), doesn't significantly help
one's response to the paintings, particularly the greatest. (Andrews himself
said, 'You can't paint ideas.') To put it at its most simple – and banal –
Andrews was a wonderful, astonishingly gifted painter and a man of
intelligence and feeling. He could do anything – oil, acrylic, landscape,
portrait, watercolour, vast canvas or tiny sketch – with absolute confidence in the mastery of his powers. This is a blessing to an artist – to
know how formidably accomplished you are, and it is very rare. Andrews
is without doubt one of the finest virtuoso painters British painting has
seen this century – and I believe the claim could be extended back
through time without being seriously gainsaid. But what makes him
great – and this is what makes all great artists great – is, as Lawrence
Gowing noted in 1980, his ability to yoke his prodigious technical
capacity to an uncommon imaginative spirit. There is one other necessary factor I would add to the other two, one which is out of anyone's
control – luck. In Michael Andrews all three cohered. His achievement
stands there – inspiring, incontrovertible, immutable. In artistic terms a
veritable Ayers Rock.

2002

Thirteen Ways of Looking at a Photograph

(Introduction to *Anonymous: Enigmatic Images from
Unknown Photographers* by Robert Flynn Johnson)

> I know noble accents
> And lucid, inescapable rhythms;
> But I know, too,
> That the blackbird is involved
> In what I know.

'Thirteen Ways of Looking at a Blackbird', Wallace Stevens

We go to photography for images of reality, but images that are more
immediately real than the more contingently intimate, adroit and nuanced
versions that other art forms provide. This is both photography's blessing
and its curse: it appears to bear irrefutable witness to the nature and
content of our world yet it is achieved mechanically. In theory, anyone
with a camera can do it: hence its ambiguously freighted appellation –
the 'artless art'.

The first photographic image I purchased was in 1967 when I was
fifteen. I bought – for £5 (a vast sum to me then) – one sheet from
the 1965 Pirelli calendar (the month was November) owned by a boy
at my school. It was only the exorbitant price I offered that made him
part with it and the picture was pinned for many months on the wall
above my desk until it was lost in some end-of-term packing fiasco.
Doubtless there was some now-forgotten adolescent sexual fascination
that drove my determination to buy this picture but this does not explain
why, over the thirty-seven years since I first saw it, I have been able to
summon this image to mind effortlessly. A young blonde sunglassed
woman, in a white T-shirt embroidered with a small anchor, sits at a
cafe table in some seaside location. She has a cigarette in her mouth
and is caught by the photographer in the very act of lighting it (from
a book of matches), her lips are slightly pursed to hold the cigarette
steady, the match is flaring at the cigarette's tip. I had no idea who this
woman was and I had no interest in the name of the photographer.
But something about that image made me covet it and urged me to

spend so much money to make it mine. Even though I lost it some months later its place is secure in the small but select image-bank in my memory. For the first time in my life a photograph had worked on me. Why? What happens on these occasions? How can a seemingly run-of-the-mill image stir one so?

That photograph was to all intents and purposes anonymous and, the more you come to think about it, in photography anonymity is the norm. When you consider the thousands – perhaps the tens of thou-sands – of photographic images each one of us encounters in a given year the vast majority – 99 per cent I would venture – is anonymous. In newspapers, magazines, colour supplements, advertisements, in-store promotions, posters, manuals, part works, CD covers, mailshots, travel brochures, textbooks, knitting catalogues, and so on, the photographer's byline – if by chance there is one – is irrelevant. When it comes to the way we consume photographs we are like sperm whales, jaws wide, cruising through an ocean of swarming images, unreflectingly scooping up those that our eyes alight on.

The only times we are consciously aware of the authorship of a photograph, I would argue, are when we contemplate the photographs we ourselves have taken (or those of friends and family) or when we go deliberately to the photographer's monograph or exhibition. The signed image – the appropriated, the owned image – is by far the rarest in this pullulating world of pictures.

Therefore to isolate and pointedly categorize the anonymous, as *Anonymous* does here, is to postulate something both unusual and intriguing. In our twenty-first-century world of millions upon millions of anonymous images what does the selection of a couple of hundred or so, enshrined in a beautifully produced book, say both about our response to the photograph and the practice of photography and, perhaps more importantly, to its status as an art?

The anonymous photograph, thus selected and presented, makes us ask, with new concentration, what it is about a photograph that elevates it above the casual and banal. What criteria do we bring to our evalu-ation of a photograph, what makes one memorable, another not? What, in short, makes a photograph good? We have become so accustomed to *not* seeing photographs, through their omnipresence, that now here is a chance to try and determine (without the bubble reputation) why some images move and enthral and remain in our memories – like paintings, like pieces of music.

It's for this reason that I've appropriated the title of Wallace Stevens's famous poem, 'Thirteen Ways of Looking at a Blackbird'. Looking at anonymous photographs and trying to analyse them, without a famous name attached, has the effect of sifting out a variety of responses to the photographic image. It seems to me that we look at photographs in ways that are far more varied and multifarious than the ways we look at other works of art. Sometimes these different responses complement each other, sometimes they cancel each other out, but when the photographer's name is absent (and thus the photo's historical-cultural-biographical context) we can, with better precision, more exactly investigate what assumptions and prejudices we bring to the photograph and how the photograph works on us.

Therefore I've tried to isolate, for harmonic poetic neatness, thirteen different ways we look at photographs. Perhaps there are more: perhaps some of my categories overlap somewhat, but I think the exercise – the thought-experiment – is valid because at the end of the process, if I am right, then what conclusions we draw about the anonymous photograph will bear intriguingly on the so-called 'artless art' of photography itself.

Aide-memoire

Is this not why most of us take photographs? We use a camera to provide a visual analogue of a potential memory. We take photographs of places, people, pets, cars, houses, and so on, to store away. How many photographs are kept in boxes and not displayed in frames or mounted in albums (or, in this digital age, on hard disks)? Many of the anonymous photographs in this book inevitably fall into this category: here a little boy is snapped in front of a car; there, a housewife on a lounger looks up from her newspaper. Photographs of pets are of interest only to the owner (and possibly win the prize for the most boring photographs ever). The memory referent in these and other examples is lost to us now but in so many cases this must have been the motivation: the photograph functions simply as a way of recalling, a way of summoning up the past.

Reportage

This is the public face of the previous private category, in a sense. Often these images – of wars, of natural disasters, of historic events, of famous people, of gathered crowds – provide some of the most memorable images in the history of photography. Here the photograph is testimony, often of a shocking and harrowing order. Occasionally the horror gives way to more disturbing responses. The picture of the decapitated head moves beyond the initial shock of the image to something more surreal and unsettling. The juxtaposition of crashed car, empty country road and the victim's head, seemingly carefully placed fifteen feet away from the body, looks like a scene from a Buñuel film. The camera is fortuitously present – or else, especially in combat zones, the photographer chooses to go where most of us would dare not. The great war photographers – Robert Capa, Don McCullin, Philip Jones Griffiths, Larry Burrows – come to mind

Work of Art

Sometimes the photograph tries to replicate the classic images of painting or sculpture. Think of the nude, the still life, the portrait. Here the photograph presents itself as a quasi-painting, a pseudo-canvas – with mixed results, in my opinion. Photos such as these – a corn cob or a vase of roses – seem vaguely ashamed of their mechanical reproductive nature and, by copying a genre, try to buy some aesthetic respectability. What's the point of these images, one wonders (*pace* Mapplethorpe)? Only rarely can they outshine their equivalents in the plastic arts.

Topography

This category is related to the former, where the photograph tries to reproduce the effect of painted landscape, or a refulgent sunset. Or else the photograph is taken to register some natural phenomenon – mountain ranges, canyons, gorges, cataracts. As a means of recording a topographical situation the precision of photography is unrivalled. But is anyone as moved by the image of a photographed landscape as they are of a painted one?

Erotica and Pornography

This is perhaps a field that photography can claim as its own, having vanquished all rivals except, perhaps, the cartoon. The massive proliferation of sexual images (soft and hard) in our world exhibits something of the sheer range of photography's power and effect – the gamut is extensive, the nuances of erotica are manifold. The naked women flourishing their suspender belts and baring their plump buttocks is frank titillation. The before-and-after images of three women, clothed and unclothed, make, perhaps guilelessly, a more intriguing social point. But the picture of a man and a prostitute in a darkened room with the shadow of a blind fanning over the cut-out pinups on the wall is interested purely in creating a fine photograph. Any erotic subtext is subliminal.

Advertisement

Subjects of erotic or pornographic images are selling their sexual frisson, such as it may be. But this category of photograph – the advertisement – is as ubiquitous as porn. These are photos that are programmed to function wholly as a form of allurement, as bait, as temptation. It is something photography does extremely well – better than any other form of image, conceivably. The whole huge world of fashion photography, for example, can be subsumed in this category.

Abstract Image

Here is another subclass that links with painting but in which photography has carved out a niche for itself. Something photographed in extreme close-up, for example, loses its quiddity and becomes near or wholly abstract. Two pairs of spectacles or the pistons and driving wheels of a locomotive are presented arrangements of shape and mass. A strange angle or extreme cropping can produce the same effect. The photograph functions simply and purely, being judged, like an abstract painting, in terms of form, pattern, texture and composition.

Literature

Again and again we are tempted to 'read' a photograph, as if it were part
of a narrative or a short story. This is particularly the case in anonymous
photographs as we have so little to go on. Who are these masked women
in their identical dresses? Or the odd trio in the bar (almost like a Brassaï)
– the two card-playing women and the young man with the glass and
bottle. Is he with them? Perhaps he's the true subject of the photograph.
Does he know the photographer? (He's looking into the lens.) We want
to supply a 'story' to the image, we want to find a narrative frame – or
a series of frames – into which we can slot this image, and, as we bring
our deduced or inferred narrative to the picture, attempt to understand
it. This is a potent impulse in all photography and again it comes to
the foreground when the image is anonymous. Walker Evans said: 'Fine
photography is literature, and it should be.'

Text

Why are there so many photographs of signs? There is a whole sub-
division, throughout the history of photography, that concerns itself with
the photography of writing or printed signs, running from an image
like the photograph of a diner where its signs are what attracts –
'Bohemian Lunch Café' – to the sophisticated work of someone such
as Lee Friedlander. I find it hard fully to comprehend this impulse but
it is clearly near-universal and one the anonymous photographer is
equally prone to adopt. The entrance to a town, the hand-painted advertisement, the comic misspelling or the absent letter – something about
words seems to provoke the desire to photograph them, as if the verbal
joke needs to be visibly enshrined.

Autobiography

Every photograph, if we knew enough about the circumstances of its
taking, will contain some biographical information about the photographer. A photograph such as that of the little black boy with the dummy
in his mouth and the toy rifle in his hand is a form of biographical
signifier of the man or woman who took the picture. This is a wonderful

photograph (very Diane Arbus in its calm eeriness) but is the juxtaposition of symbols deliberate or a result of chance? Is this child the photographer's son? What's trying to be conveyed here about the photographer's attitude to innocence and experience? Can we move on from there to ask if every photograph, therefore, is an unconscious fragment of the photographer's autobiography? Will all the photographs a person takes in his or her life be as much a record of that individual as anything written down?

Composition

One could argue this is a subclass of the 'work of art' category but I feel that the traditional fine-art concept and rules of composition particularly apply to photography. Many of the most memorable photographs, in my opinion, are also beautifully composed. The picture of two Nazi storm troopers hand in hand with their identically uniformed toddlers is, apart from anything else, a perfect composition: it could almost be a Cartier-Bresson. The photograph of two boys fishing works precisely because of the inadvertent mirror-imaging of their pose. Of course the classical elements of composition – balance or asymmetry, grouping of forms, the placing of light and dark etc., etc. – apply to a photograph as well. But I find in a well-composed black and white photograph – and perhaps this is something to do with a combination of depth of field and the photo's monochrome nature – an element that is absent from painting. One is more intensely aware of composition in black and white photographs. I think, for example, that this idea of composition is behind the unanalysable appeal of some of Cartier-Bresson's photographs. Why are they so tenaciously memorable? It's not simply a question of subject matter: the ones I remember best also tend to be the best composed.

A Means to an End / Tool

Photography cannot be separated from its pragmatic advantages. The huge subclass of anonymous photography as pedagogical illustration (in text books and encyclopaedias, for instance) bears this out. There are interesting ramifications, however: a photograph, for example, of James

Dean's wrecked Porsche will fall under the category of 'reportage'. A similar photograph, but taken by the insurance loss adjuster investigating the accident, will have an entirely different import. Crime scene photographs also vacillate between these two designations, at once helping to solve the crime but also with their own curious aesthetic effect. Or, to put it another way, once the pragmatic task of the photograph has been satisfied it may transmogrify into something else. The professional photographer's Polaroid is an exemplary instance. As someone who has been photographed many times by professional photographers, I often find the most pleasing image is the one they discard after the shoot. Professional accessory eliding into serendipitous portrait.

Snapshot

The photographer Nan Goldin has gone on record claiming that the snapshot is one of the highest forms of photography. I would like to go one step further and say that in the snapshot we distil the very essence of photography and find in this concept an explanation of this artless art's idiosyncratic and enduring power. All photographs and all the types of photographs that are outlined above borrow from or share in the nature of the snapshot to a greater or lesser degree. For what distinguishes photography from all the other visual arts is its particularly intense relation to time. That mechanically retrieved image is the record of a split second of the world's history. A photograph is a stop-time device and this is what makes every photograph, however sophisticated, however humdrum, unique. And because our mortality and our lives are so bound up with the sense of our time passing – or with the sense of our lives heading on remorselessly to their end – then the artificial ability to stop time yourself with your own photographs, or to witness time stopped in the photographs of others, is profoundly, atavistically appealing. I would argue that it is this feature of photography (and not, for example, Roland Barthes's concept of the *punctum*, the 'detail') that explains the individual response to the strange enticement of an individual photograph. One of the great images in this collection (it could have been taken by Henri Lartigue) is a photo of a group of wealthy, well-dressed people, holding umbrellas high against the rain, dashing across a wet road through advancing traffic. The women's feet are blurred in their hurry, defying the speed of the camera shutter. The ambience is all energy and momentary alarm. The composition of the group is near-perfect: the diagonal swerve of the tyre track imprinted on the glossy tarmac (and how it draws us back into the picture); the vertical shafts of the umbrellas beginning to cant forward in the direction of the rush. Yet what, finally, 'makes' this photograph – why it *works*, I would claim – is the women's feet frozen in the air in mid dash. This is the pure element of snapshot (our rosebud, our blackbird): we see it plain – time is halted, time stands still.

I think this same notion underscores the allure of the November image in the 1965 Pirelli calendar for my fifteen-year-old self (and thereafter: I have it now – again – in a Pirelli album). There are agreeable associations in the picture – of sea, of sun, of summer – and the girl is pretty enough, in a very 1960s way, but – crucially – the image is unposed, candid, snapped. Time has stopped: that match will for ever flare, her lips will be for ever slightly pursed.

This crucial, elemental aspect of photography could not be better enshrined than in the image on the title page of this book. In the middle distance a man, silhouetted against the sky, leaps from one towering column of rock to another. The unknown photographer captures him in mid-air, in mid-leap, poised above the significant abyss. This is a great and memorable photograph. All sorts of potential readings and interpretations crowd around it – was it a dare? What was the man trying to prove? Who was this leap designed to impress? How dangerous was it? We will never know, the facts of the photograph are lost to us: and because we can never know therefore all explanations are equally valid. But that moment of time has been recorded and held and the symbolic resonance around the split-second happenstance of its taking is rich. It could stand as a synecdoche for all photography. The great photographs – anonymous or otherwise, the photographs we love and remember – must have a snapshot of the human enterprise, of our human condition, about them, somewhere.

2004

Pierre Bonnard

An artist's antipathies can often be as revealing as his enthusiasms. Picasso, for example, loathed Bonnard, describing his painting as a 'pot pourri of indecision'. Mind you, Picasso also purported to loathe Monet, which is not bad company to keep, I suppose. One can understand why it was necessary for Picasso to react against these painters – their evanescence, their seductive powers, their refulgence represented everything he himself didn't want to do. Too soft, too representational, too retrospective, too harmonious and finally, for him, too safe. But like many antipathies such hostility often tells us more about the hater than the target. Such a dismissal of an artist of Bonnard's rank is a brutal and deliberate misunderstanding. Bonnard's work is far more disciplined and dogged, more modern and integrity-filled than Picasso's aspersions would imply – indeed, as this superb exhibition at the Tate amply demonstrates – and it is both intriguing and telling to note that Matisse – the other giant of twentieth-century painting – was a lifelong and close friend of Bonnard and, as their wonderful correspondence illustrates, they were almost co-theorists in painterly matters. Matisse's world could encompass Bonnard's, but for an artist like Picasso Bonnard *had* to be removed far beyond the pale.

There is another problem with Bonnard, and not just his refusal to 'go modern': his pictures are simply too beautiful, too sensuous, too flooded with the most delicious light and colour. Any art – however high, however serious – that is hard to resist, that provokes immediate, almost unreflective pleasure, makes people (critics, historians, curators, academics) illogically suspicious. It is this reaction that prompts the classification of Bonnard as a kind of lazy post-post-Impressionist, a hangover from the nineteenth century, still basking in the creative afterglow of Monet, Renoir, Pissaro, Sisley et al. In fact Bonnard (born in 1867) first made his name at the end of the nineteenth century as an innovative, ultra-modern graphic designer, designing posters and making coloured lithographs. It is worth remembering that underneath the shimmering, feathery brushstrokes and the blurry juxtaposition of pigment there is a tried and robust graphic talent. In 1915 (when Bonnard was forty) he told his nephew that he had resolved a profound artistic crisis in this efficacious and straightfoward manner: 'I drew ceaselessly.' And, as the studies for his big landscapes reveal, every painting had its beginnings in a series of highly detailed drawings.

The 1915 crisis had arisen from a fear that colour alone was beginning to rule and overwhelm his art. So Bonnard reapplied himself, quite consciously and with no small pain, relearning the fundamentals behind painting, namely drawing and composition. This was the second crisis of his life that had redirected and corrected his artistic course. The earlier one had occurred in 1905 when he saw the work that Matisse was doing and realized that modernism and everything it implied − all its iconoclasm, its uncompromising decorative side and potential abstraction − was not for him. He voluntarily left that field to others and pursued his own lonely course, a factor that both explains the remarkable homogeneity of Bonnard's work and also accounts for the marked decline in his reputation between the wars.

Bonnard stayed faithfully with figuration and remained *sui generis*: his subject matter was classical − the nude, the landscape, the interior, the still life. His development and stylistic divagations were consequently undramatic, often marked by nothing more significant than looser brushstroking, a more severe flattening of the picture plane, a brilliant and daring use of composition, some mannerist distortion and, of course, one of the most rich and beguiling palettes of the twentieth century.

His reputation and his popularity have recovered, unequivocally, from the inter-war slump. Bonnard is now rightly considered one of the great painters of the nude − an equal of Degas and Modigliani. This was an obsession that began early in his life, particularly after his meeting with his muse, a working-class woman called, simply, Marthe, who was his model and companion for most of his life. They met in 1893 and Marthe died in 1942 − immortalized in a sequence of paintings covering five decades, ranging from the erotically charged *L'Indolente* (1898) to the disturbing and celebrated *Nu à la Baignoire* (1930).

But it is Bonnard's domestic interiors that remain the quintessential Bonnardian subject, a form of 'intimisme', as the genre is so called, that he made his own. These pictures are in fact highly sophisticated and respond to the most stringent analysis (indeed this is where it can be convincingly established that Bonnard directly inspired Matisse). Yet for all their artistry, their bold coloration, their 'flatness', their use of a form of *faux-naïf* style, they exert an appeal that extends beyond the

painterly. Bonnard's interiors are pictures that we should and do
unashamedly love because – effortlessly, inevitably – they conjure up
and provoke memories, experiences and associations of ideas that we
can all share and verify. The opening lines of Wallace Stevens's great
poem 'Sunday Morning' summon up exactly this ambience and these
universal emotions:

> Complacencies of the peignoir, and late
> Coffee and oranges in a sunny chair,
> And the green freedom of a cockatoo . . .

Stevens's poem could be the text behind any number of Bonnard's
magical pictures – and 'magic' is the right word, I feel. Trying to analyse
one's response to these luminous, quotidian, yet timeless images is almost
redundant, a waste of effort. As Vladimir Nabokov observed: art of this
order is experienced in the nape of the neck. They are intimate, they
are domestic, there is not much *sturm und drang* about them, but Bonnard's
paintings – very much like Edward Hopper's, I would claim – possess
an allure that is almost defiantly anti-intellectual – to their eternal and
enduring credit. William Blake offered to show us the world in a grain
of sand; Bonnard chooses to show us the world in a sunlit breakfast
room, with a coffee pot on a gingham tablecloth, and a view through
wind-stirred curtains of a green, dew-drenched garden with a distant
glimpse of the sea beyond . . . Who is to say which is the more valid
and enticing?

1998

Georges Braque

The Late Works

Braque and Picasso. Picasso and Braque. The two names will be for ever yoked together in the history of twentieth-century art – a fact that is, curiously, to Braque's detriment. Picasso's reputation is so reful-gent that his partner in what was the greatest revolution in painting since the Renaissance is inevitably somewhat obscured. Braque is the Shelley to Picasso's Keats; the Gene Kelly to Picasso's Fred Astaire; the McCartney to Picasso's Lennon. The comparisons are not wholly fa-cetious – they illustrate a genuine anomaly that often arises in the vexed and complex question of Reputation. The work that Braque accomplished after Cubism is, broadly speaking, almost unknown. The odd image of a bird, a still life or two may linger in the memory. But, outside the circles of connoisseurship, who is familiar with the great sequence of studio interiors painted through the late forties and the fifties? Or the small, charged, late landscapes whose intensity rivals that of Van Gogh? This superb show at the Royal Academy should, at the least, do something to rectify that ignorance; at best it will reconfirm Braque as an artist of the very first rank, with a character and adaman-tine integrity that are unique.

The show concentrates on the work of the last two decades of Braque's life (he died in 1963) but it is worth considering Cubism as a starting point. In the few years after 1909, as Picasso and Braque simultaneously assaulted the north face of pictorial representation. It is fair to say that each had his period as trailblazer, but it can be fairly convincingly argued that it was Braque who made the most significant contribution, that Picasso seized on ideas that Braque introduced – *papier collé*, wood-graining techniques, the introduction of lettering, say – and gave them his own special spin. What this show makes absolutely clear, however, is that the revolution they both inaugurated in those few momentous years provided the aesthetic that was to drive Braque's work from then on until the end of his life. Picasso returned in 1918 to classical figu-ration, but for Braque the essential Cubist principles of representation – the still life the dominant subject, use of multi-view perspective, the 'celebration' of two dimensionality, analysis of space and relationship between objects within that frame – remained his artistic touchstones. They were elaborated, transformed and developed with a dogged consistency throughout the work that followed in the decades after the end of the First World War and Cubism's great phase.

This doggedness, this singlemindedness in Braque reminds me of another genius and near contemporary, Paul Klee. Like Braque, Klee spent his life perfecting and refining his art with a concentration and devotion that is almost heroic. It is their attitude of mind that is similar rather than their output (though both were amongst the century's greatest colourists). Intriguingly, they both found a form of epiphanic serenity in that fervent and solitary focus. Braque said in an interview late in his life that 'objects don't exist for me except insofar as a rapport exists between them or between them and me. When one attains this harmony one reaches a sort of intellectual non-existence . . . Life then becomes a perpetual revelation.' Klee wrote in his journal: 'Everything we see is a proposal, a possibility, an expedient . . . the world [is] my subject even though it [is] not the visible world.'

The genuineness of this sort of transcendence is only established by the quality of the work that it produces. There is a profound beauty in Braque's canvases as well as a distinct gravitas. This last note is often struck by the extraordinary way he uses black – a facility matched only by Matisse. Black becomes, paradoxically, a rich colour amidst the other hues. In a painting such as *Le Chaudron* the canvas is almost 50 per cent black. But its sombreness is offset by the palest of blues and lemony creams. I cannot think of any other artist who can modulate such extremes of colour tone with such seductively harmonious results.

Towards the end of his life Braque's work came full circle. His career started as a Fauvist – with vivid, astonishing landscapes – and his final period sees him quit the interiors he so loved – the secular cathedral of the artist's studio – returning to *en plein air* representation. These small, often horizontally elongated landscapes of extreme simplicity are loaded with powerful emotion. Heavy with impasto, frequently painted with a palette knife rather than a brush, the paintings of flat Normandy fields or beach scenes carry an astonishing freight of foreboding, and *memento mori* – though it is hard exactly to pinpoint why. Unlike Van Gogh's tormented cypresses or swirling skies there is no one element here that can be designated disturbing. But disturb they do, with remarkable force, but in a way that is stoical rather than demented, resigned rather than terrified or despairing. As a coda to a life's work of remarkable consistency and artistic excellence they serve to underwrite both this artist's greatness and his humility.

1997

Claude Monet

Bathers at La Grenouillère

Picasso, it is intriguing to note, did not like Monet's work, particularly the famous water lily sequences, the *Nymphéas*, painted towards the end of his life. He found it insubstantial, flimsy, perhaps even pretentious. Picasso was clearly reacting against Monet in order to find and determine a place for his own work, to create a taste by which *he* might be appreciated (just as Monet and the other Impressionists had reacted against the confining Beaux-Arts classicism that preceded them).

Of course, it is possible, if you are determined to be prejudiced, to be 'against' almost anything, however universally admired, and, if one adopts Picasso's standpoint and considers his own contribution to twentieth-century art, one can understand the thrust of his reservations. For a painter obsessed with structure and physicality the suggestibility and sheer airiness of Impressionism, with its concentration on the fleeting and iridescent, might indeed make it seem somewhat incorporeal and vacuous. However, I have always thought that Monet's painting *Bathers at La Grenouillère* can stand as a particularly redoubtable response to this line of attack.

First of all, while the painting seems to be prototypically Impressionist in subject matter, two factors make it less obviously generic. First it is a painting of shadow rather than sunlight – deep shadow too, its dominant tones are blues, browns and greens, not yellows, lemons or creams – and, second, it is anything but ethereal in treatment. Although more than half the painting is water it is rendered with a solidity and plasticity that, I dare say, Cézanne would have been proud of. True, the painting is a sketch, a study, presumably for a larger more 'finished' painting that was never completed, and the boldness of the individual brushstrokes might not have survived in anything more worked up, but the thick smears of paint, the broad slashes of impasto recall the uncompromising way the Fauves applied pigment to their canvases – and Fauvism was still three decades or so away from 1869 when Monet's painting was executed. That such thick, dark oil paint can look like rippling light-freckled water is part of the individual magic of this painting; and that a palette so subdued, so positively sombre, can summon up all the luminous ambience of a riverine scene is testimony to a talent and a painterliness that are remarkable. Even a pusillanimous Picasso might have had grudgingly to concede that, sometimes, Monet could do no wrong.

1998

Edward Hopper

Notes towards a Definition of Edward Hopper

1. In December 1946 Edward Hopper showed a picture in the Whitney Annual Exhibition at the Whitney Museum in New York. The show was reviewed by Clement Greenberg – champion of Jackson Pollock and Abstract Expressionism – and he had this to say: 'A special category of art should be devised for the kind of thing Hopper does. He is not a painter in the full sense; his means are second hand, shabby and impersonal . . . Hopper's painting is essentially photography and it is literary in the way the best photography is . . . Hopper simply happens to be a bad painter. But if he were a better painter, he would, most likely, not be so superior an artist.' Greenberg's facile nonsense is almost entertaining here – a fine example, as Chekhov saw it, of the critic as horse-fly bothering the quietly labouring artist – 'buzzing', Chekhov called the irritating noise, as if the critic were saying: 'See, I can buzz too, buzz about anything.' But in the midst of Greenberg's self-satisfied buzzing he is actually on to something. Hopper is, as anybody can see who has looked closely at the body of his work, a superb painter. He was also an excellent draughtsman, a dramatically innovative etcher and a water-colourist of fantastic ability. Compared to Jackson Pollock, for example – whose draughtsmanship is awesomely inept – Hopper's talent is out of sight. Hopper was such a good painter that he deliberately decided to make his paintings look as if he were a bad painter.

2. There is a Hopper chalk drawing of his wife, Jo Nevinson Hopper, sitting on a bed, her knees raised with her arms loosely folded around them. It is a study for the painting *Morning Sun* (1952). The figure is surrounded by little scribbled notes that Hopper has written to himself. 'Legs cooler than arms', 'cool reflections from sheets', 'cool blue–gray shadows', 'very light reflected light', 'warm shadows in ear', 'thighs cooler', 'light against wall shadow', 'brownish warm against cool', 'cool half-tone', and so on. Light, cool, shadow: conceivably the absolute verbal reduction of a Hopper painting. But on this small drawing there are over twenty such memoranda: powerful evidence of the acuteness of his eye, his awareness of minute nuance. The painting itself is of a woman

in a pink peignoir sitting on a sheeted bed staring out of a window on to a truncated cityscape. Only the top of a small terraced row of brownstones is visible and above them is a large expanse of washed-out blue sky. Through the open window morning sunlight streams, casting a wide panel of light on the featureless wall to the side of the bed and illuminating the pensive woman. Yet the finished painting is virtually without detail, its illusionary three-dimensionality (its depth-of-field) more notional than precise, giving the picture its trademark Hopperian stage-scenery feel.

3. A few random facts. Edward Hopper was an avid reader: according to his wife he 'drank print'. He suffered from 'chronic boredom' which often prevented him from working. He was also six feet five inches tall. Hopper was born in 1882 so by the time he left art school in 1905 he would have been fully grown. In the early twentieth century a man who was six foot five would be regarded as freakishly tall. For a self-conscious, shy individual such marked loftiness would have a significant effect on one's comportment, on one's self-consciousness and one's attitude to fellow human beings. Some of Hopper's reclusive, taciturn nature must be due to this fact: nobody likes to be stared at in the street, after all. Few artists have spoken less about their work but it's significant, I think, that Hopper painted a picture of an isolated multi-storeyed apartment building and entitled it for a while as a 'self-portrait'. He also strongly identified himself with the lighthouses he painted so often.

4. As a young man Hopper made three trips to Europe. In 1906/7 he spent some time in Paris (from October to August) and also visited London, Amsterdam, Berlin and Brussels. In 1909 he spent another four months in Paris (April–July). In 1910 he went to Paris, Madrid and Toledo during a short trip that began in May and ended on 1 July. When he returned to New York in 1910 it marked the end of his transatlantic voyages and he never left the USA (apart from the odd trip to Mexico) again. All in all he spent just over a year in Europe, most of it in Paris, but he was also drawn to Spain. Paris is a beautiful and memorable city and while he was there Hopper painted in what might be termed a recognizable post-Impressionist style. Yet his most remarkable painting of this early period is *Soir Bleu* (1914). A painted clown, unlit cigarette dangling from his mouth, sits on a cafe terrace

attracting no curious stares from the other recognizably French drinkers around him. An American in Paris? A portrait of the artist? Whether it is or not, this painting is linked to the mature style both in mood and method. Hopper was a late developer: he sold his first painting at the age of thirty-one. His name was made with a retrospective at the Museum of Modern Art in New York in 1933. He developed his visual style and manner in his early forties and for the next four decades nothing really changed.

Hopper died in 1967 when he was two months short of his eighty-fifth birthday. He was born in a small town called Nyack some forty miles up the Hudson River from New York and almost all his life was lived in Manhattan (in Greenwich Village) or in Truro in Cape Cod. In his eighty-five years he spent approximately fifteen months in Europe, showing, after 1910, no serious inclination to return there. In these circumstances, to try to position him as somehow European in spirit takes tendentious effort. It would be more appropriate to reconfigure Augie March's proud boast: 'I am American, Nyack-born.' It seems the natural claim for Edward Hopper.

5. Hopper liked to paint buildings. The more angled the sunlight, at the beginning or the end of the day, the more obvious the building's form and decoration – entablatures, friezes and architraves were picked out and defined by the longer shadows. His many watercolours of houses and Cape Cod street scenes are testimony to this straightforward aesthetic delight. In the composition it is the blockiness and mass of the houses that attract him and he uses the pigment as if it is poster paint, with a bold impasto effect that almost seems to fight against the medium. In his oils, however, buildings take on vaguer, more symbolic freight – their isolation in the landscape being the resonating feature. Unlike the water-colours, these buildings are not rendered with an architect's knowing eye: they become simpler, cruder and sometimes the perspective of their walls and roof planes is deliberately slightly skewed.

6. Hopper was a realist, squarely positioned in the capacious and all-embracing tradition of figuration. But to claim, as Clement Greenberg does, that his work is 'photographic' in some way is absurd. In his poem 'Lines on a Young Lady's Photograph Album' Philip Larkin precisely describes what a photograph does:

> But o, photography! As no art is,
> Faithful and disappointing! That records
> Dull days as dull, and hold-it smiles as frauds,
> And will not censor blemishes . . .

'As no *art* is,/Faithful and disappointing' (my emphasis). Gail Levin, Hopper's exemplary biographer, first wrote about him in a small book called *Hopper's Places* (1985) where she juxtaposes, with as much exactitude as possible, photographs of the houses, landscapes and buildings with Hopper's finished paintings. The book is a brilliant elucidation of Hopper's working practice: it tells you so much about his purpose and ambition for his paintings and at the same time provides the most succinct and telling refutation of the photographic comparison. Hopper's discerning, transforming eye – his stern aesthetic of simplification and reduction (Levin calls it: 'his relentless parsimony of exclusions') – is everywhere in evidence. Being 'faithful' to what he sees is the last thing on his mind.

7. Our intellect is hard-wired to seek explanations and understanding. As the critic Frank Kermode commented, 'We are programmed to prefer fulfilment to disappointment; the closed to the open.' When you look at a Hopper painting, particularly his peopled paintings, the urge to supply a narrative, to link a causal chain together, to place the image into a context – to 'close' the picture – is very powerful. But all serious artists know that in reality life isn't like that: at best we can interpret, not explain, and our interpretation will be subjective, not final. The plots in our lives never thin, they relentlessly thicken. There are any number of possible interpretations of *Nighthawks* for example, each one of them perfectly valid. Hopper knew that because he was painting realistic people in realistic settings – hotel lobbies, motel rooms, apartment buildings – the viewer would instinctively and inevitably attempt an interpretation of what they were doing there and what was going on. But to signal the impossibility of arriving at a true explanation he chose the blandest of titles: *Office at Night*, *Office in a Small City*, *Automat*. A rare exception to this rule is the late painting *Excursion into Philosophy* (1959) – a very un-Hopperian title. This painting, soused in sexual conflict, repression and disappointment prompted Jo Hopper to write to a friend: 'It may be that Edward won't stand for naming the new picture "Excursion into Philosophy". You know E. Hopper. He'll call

it "Sunlight on the Floor" or something equally non-committal. But "Excursion into Philosophy" is its true name, that's how he referred to it himself & I grabbed right on to it as perfect.' Hopper knew exactly what he was doing with his scenes of isolated and alienated people and what emotions and feelings would be aroused by them but his titles were deliberately chosen to defeat the idea of any final interpretation. His great paintings remain fully 'open'.

8. In 1948 during one of Hopper's artistic blocks he and his wife went driving around Cape Cod looking for subjects to paint – in vain, as it turned out. 'Nothing seemed to crystallize into a picture,' Jo Hopper wrote in her diary. Looking back over previous canvasses searching for inspiration, she added, 'Only a few of them had been done from the fact. The fact is so much easier – than digging it out of one's inner consciousness. It's such a struggle.'

9. For the last six years I have probably looked more closely at actual Edward Hopper paintings than the work of any other artist. In New York, the Whitney Museum regularly displays about half a dozen of its large Hopper holding in its permanent collection. When I'm in New York, about three to four times a year, I walk past the Whitney at least twice a day: on several of those days I pop in and look at the Hoppers. Their allure never dulls and their integrity shines with iconic force in that institution.

What you immediately notice when you look at a Hopper oil up close (say six inches) is how laboriously the paint is applied and worked. There is nothing free-flowing, no agile brushstroking. There is a dogged-ness and flatness about the painted surface, a patient air of covering the canvas diligently. The effect, as I've mentioned above, is to make the paintings look almost amateurish in technique. If you look at how the grass is painted in *Four-Lane Road* no effort is made to render the blades of grass, to convey any tuftiness or differentiation in light and shade. He might as well be painting Astroturf. Similarly the trees in *Gas* are an amorphous lumpy mass with a lot of black mixed with the near uniform green. Time and again the great paintings illustrate this homogenizing, low-rent effect – the bleached grass in *South Carolina Morning*, the slab buildings in *Approaching a City*, the cow-pat hills in *Western Motel*. The technique looks clumsy, heavy-handed and homespun. It's not quite paint-by-numbers but there is something automatic about the look: 'grass is green', 'paint walls beige', 'shadows are purply-blue'. Hopper used a great deal of turpentine when he painted in oil. This simple parsimonious texture of his actual canvases explains why they reproduce so exceptionally well – nothing is really lost in the process apart from the evidence of how it is achieved.

The same qualities apply to his figures. His wife posed for all the women in his paintings but there is no sense that a portrait of Jo is ever being attempted. The raddled stripper in *Girlie-Show*, the buxom secretary in *Office at Night*, the woman reading in *Chair Car* barely register as individuals – they are more mannequins than people.

Why did Hopper subdue his manifest skills in this way? A glance at his preparatory sketches shows his tremendous facility, his confidence, his natural sense of composition. But everything in the finished painting seems designed to remove any indication of talent and ability. Faces are cartoonishly hybrid, poses are awkward, hands are badly rendered. It's as if he wanted to be seen as a very average, not particularly gifted painter (he certainly convinced Clement Greenberg). He did not want his virtuosity to get in the way of the picture's effect.

10. The late painting *Rooms by the Sea* (1951) exhibits this tendency at its most emphatic. The sea looks like it's bad *trompe l'oeil*. The door of the room seems to open directly and impossibly on to the water. There is no sense of receding distance in the sky or of the horizon. Through another door we glimpse some furniture as featureless as a dentist's waiting room. A wedge-shaped block of sunlight lights the floor and wall, and in the room beyond another lucent parallelogram mimics the first. The plaster wall is roughly, almost carelessly painted, short brushstrokes clearly visible. Such mundanity, such absence of brio. Sun, sea and shadow are all we have to go on. So how do we explain this painting's enduring power to move and affect us? What abstract nouns brew in this refulgent atmosphere? Eternity? Solitude? Bliss? Transience? Emptiness? I suspect the answer lies in the individual viewer, but nothing in the painting, or its title, makes any overt effort to provoke portentousness.

11. One of the few remarks Hopper made about his work is very telling. Asked what made him choose a particular subject – a hotel lobby, a house in the dunes, a cinema usherette – Hopper said: 'I do not exactly know, unless it is that I believe them to be the best mediums for a

synthesis of my inner experience.' This is another way of saying that his paintings are all about mood.

12. Wallace Stevens is a great American poet. He is 'American' in the same sense that Hopper is 'American': they are both in their own way unique and uniquely a product of their country. No European poet is like Stevens even though Stevens's work is replete with references to European civilization. Stevens, a deeply educated man who loved European culture, was even more stay-at-home than Hopper. He never left the USA at all.

Stevens wrote an essay entitled: 'The Relations between Poetry and Painting'. In it, he states, 'No poet can fail to recognize how often a detail, a propos or remark, in respect to painting, applies also to poetry.' A few pages further on he says, 'The world about us would be desolate except for the world within us.' This, it seems to me, is what is going on when we look at a Hopper painting. The 'world about us' of the subject matter – the couple in a hotel room, a group of people in a night-time diner, the secretary in the office – is pervaded and invaded by the 'world within us'. Hopper's simple paintings encourage that interchange, what Stevens calls the 'migratory passings to and fro, quickenings, Promethean liberations and discoveries'. Strong stuff with powerful after-effects. To provoke such Promethean liberations and discoveries with such studious, careful artlessness makes Hopper the great American painter of the twentieth century. Perhaps it makes him the Great American Painter, full stop.

2004

Nat Tate

The True Story

The origins of 'Nat Tate' go back a fair distance. In 1987 I published my novel *The New Confessions* which took the form of a fictional auto-biography. Reviewing it, Bernard Levin said, 'hypnotised by its autobi-ographical form I found myself riffling through the pages for the photographs'. 'Photographs . . . ?' I thought, 'I've missed a trick there.' Then some years later I was invited to contribute to a book called *David Hockney's Alphabet*, in which twenty-six writers were asked to provide a short text – of any sort – to accompany Hockney's graphic depic-tions of each letter. I was given the letter 'N' and wrote a biographical memoir of a wholly fictional francophone Laotian writer called Nguyen N, who had briefly flourished in Paris between the wars. I quoted a letter from N to André Gide and I cited his celebrated work of apho-ristic philosophy, *Les Analects de Nguyen N* (Monnier, Toulon, 1928). At the launch party for the book I was engaged in protracted conversation with a guest who claimed to remember reading about N, and indeed had a French bookseller searching for a first edition of *Les Analects*. It was an awkward few minutes and I thought it best to leave enlighten-ment for another day.

In both cases it was not the idea of a hoax that intrigued me so much as the ability to make something entirely invented seem aston-ishingly real. I began vaguely to formulate the idea of taking the fictional biography mode even further into the area of verisimilitude and, some years ago, started collecting discarded photographs – from junk shops, house-clearance sales, *brocantes* in France – with a view to one day writing a 'life' tricked out with all the artefacts of a real biography – illustrations, notes, bibliography, index and so on.

Thus when, last year, Karen Wright, the editor of *Modern Painters* magazine (on whose editorial board I sit), started talking to me about the forthcoming New York issue – and was wondering if there was a way of getting fiction into the magazine – I realized immediately that here was the perfect opportunity. 'Why don't I invent a painter?' I said, knowing I already had the raw materials to hand. And so I duly did and so Nat Tate was born, lived for three decades and died.

I placed Tate in a period of twentieth-century artistic history that I was already fascinated by – namely the 1950s in New York, which saw the emergence of the New York School of artists and the birth of Abstract Expressionism. This was the era of Jackson Pollock and Action Painting, of de Kooning, Kline and Motherwell. It was the first time that the full glare of hype and media interest transformed a group of impoverished, unknown artists almost overnight into national and inter-national celebrities, and with that renown came the more destructive elements of sudden wealth, notoriety, groupies, drugs, booze, jealousies, acrimony and premature death. This background had everything I needed for Nat and as I began to evolve the details of his brief life I began to invent characters – his foster parents, fellow artists, gallery owners – whose personalities would fit the photographs I had collected.

It was a complex process – but hugely enjoyable – and as it enlarged I started factoring real people into the Nat Tate story – the poet Frank O'Hara, Georges Braque, Franz Kline, Picasso and Larry Rivers amongst others. I began to feel like Dr Frankenstein. Nat Tate became my benign, doomed monster: I had his photo in front of me, I had put together all the ingredients of his short, tragic life; he seemed, even in manuscript stage, almost to live and breathe. The search for authenticity went further – some of Nat Tate's drawings were created, and a large abstract oil. I approached Gore Vidal and John Richardson (Picasso's friend and biog-rapher), both of whom I knew, and asked them to 'reminisce' about meeting Nat in the 1950s – which they sportingly and readily agreed to do.

But at the same time as I worked to provoke immediate credulity I knew that the story could not withstand sustained analysis – far too much was invented. Indeed one of the key witnesses to Nat's life – an English writer called Logan Mountstuart – was a character taken from one of my short stories published in *The Destiny of Nathalie X* in 1995. The book was, in the end, studded with covert and cryptic clues and hints as to its real, fictive status. For me, the author, this was part of the pleasure – a form of Nabokovian relish in the sheer play and artifice – and the fundamental aim of the book, it became clear to me, was to destabilize, to challenge our notions of authenticity. First would come belief – the thing looked so wonderfully genuine, beautifully produced, full of photographs – then doubts would set in, alarm bells begin distantly to ring. But then the reader would come across – say – Gore Vidal's recollections, and there would be a picture of Frank O'Hara and a Frank

O'Hara poem mentioning Tate and credulity would be established again for a while – before suspicions crept back in. What was created was a form of reverse propaganda. Not truth disguised by lies, but 'Truth' peeled away to reveal the true lie at the centre.

But we – the key conspirators and 21 Publishing – decided to present the book absolutely straight, deadpan. People had to be seduced – deluded – at first in order for the plan to work. The *Sunday Telegraph* joined the inner circle – an extract would be published, again in deadpan, orthodox manner, on the arts pages. Launch parties were planned, a week apart, in New York and London. We synchronized our responses and waited to see what would happen.

My own expectations were that we would experience a form of slowly mounting scepticism ending, on our part, in candid confession. But in fact the projected slow burn became a loud detonation when a journalist on the *Independent*, who had overheard two conspirators' loose tongues wagging, decided to blow the whole thing wide open.

I wasn't there. When the 'hoax' was exposed I was in Paris promoting the French edition of my new novel, *Armadillo*, hearing everything at second hand. The unspooling of the Nat Tate story was always intended to be something far more subtle and intriguing, but I must confess to a strange frisson when I read, in Paris, an account of the affair in the *Herald Tribune*. There was the name 'Nat Tate' printed in bold alongside other celebrities – Eva Perón, Jimmy Stewart, the Rolling Stones. Perhaps, I thought, poor Nat would, in a curious way, endure – and Nat Tate would have a sort of life, after all.

1998

AFRICA

I was born in Africa (in Ghana) and for the first twenty years of my life regarded it unreflectingly as my home. I felt far more at ease in Ibadan, for example, the regional capital of western Nigeria, than I did in Edinburgh, the city nearest my family's home in Scotland, where we went on two months' leave each year – as the rainy season drenched equatorial Africa – to enjoy a showery Scottish summer. So, as I started to write fiction, it seemed entirely natural for me to set that fiction in the continent that, in a way, had both nurtured and fired my imagination.

As a result of this I have found myself perceived as an expert or potential commentator on all things African and have been asked to review books on subjects as varied as the Fashoda Incident, the exploration of the Sahara, the apartheid regime in South Africa and the civil war in Sierra Leone. By and large I have readily complied, and in the process have learned a lot.

But Ghana and Nigeria are the only countries I can claim to know well at first hand and Nigeria, where I spent my teens, provided me with most of the raw African material that I transmuted into my novels and short stories. It also provided me with a friend in the shape of the Nigerian writer, Ken Saro-Wiwa, and through him, inadvertently, to a saddening connection with ruthless Nigerian politics that I had never expected or sought.

I wrote a great deal about Ken Saro-Wiwa over the years and the articles selected here reproduce the bitter trajectory of his life from contented and successful writer to inspiring political activist, to stubborn prisoner, to condemned man, to the executed victim of a repressive regime.

Ken Saro-Wiwa (1)

Nigeria is the most populous country in Africa. The latest population estimate is 100 million and rising. Yet every Wednesday evening at 8.30, about a third of that vast population sits down in front of its television sets to watch a particular soap opera.

They are enthralled, they are obsessed with it, and they laugh. This is a comedy, pointed and unsparing, scabrous and overtly moral. What makes the whole phenomenon singular and bizarre is that the audience is laughing at itself. This is not some sanitized, deodorized version of family or community life, or some farcical ad-man's sitcom; this is a soap opera about corruption and graft, about idleness and self-delusion, about futile dreams and impossible aspirations. It is a soap opera about what not to do with your life.

The man who created this is a forty-nine-year-old Nigerian writer called Ken Saro-Wiwa. When I mention the viewing figures he smiles wryly. 'You wouldn't think it an unreasonable conclusion to draw . . . that as the writer and producer of a television programme that has run to 156 episodes with an average audience of 30 million, I would have made a fortune,' he says.

'Well, yes.'

'Well, you'd be wrong.'

'But you do break even?' I venture, somewhat amazed.

'Not yet.' He shrugs, and smiles again. 'Maybe one day.'

Perhaps this is the most extraordinary feature of a most extraordinary enterprise: Mr Saro-Wiwa is not in this for the money. Mr Saro-Wiwa, and I say this with genuine admiration, is not bothered by being in the red. The forces that impel him to make and pay for his soap opera have nothing to do with the profit motive.

The programme in question is called *Basi & Co.*, and although there has never been an official assessment, viewing figures of that size must make it a contender for the world's most watched television serial.

The idea itself stemmed from a radio play Mr Saro-Wiwa wrote in the early seventies called *The Transistor Radio*, about an inept conman in

Lagos who tries to rip people off by posing as a collector of fees for transistor radio licences.

He was invited by the director of programmes of Nigerian Television to produce a television series of thirteen episodes. He took the characters from his radio play and assembled a troupe of actors to perform his scripts and went into production.

The first episodes were screened in October 1985. Since then, Mr Saro-Wiwa has written the series, produced it, paid the salaries of the cast and crew and has sold the finished programmes to Nigerian Television and the thirty-five local television stations.

Five years later, *Basi & Co.* has established a place in the national Nigerian consciousness as firmly and redoubtably as *Coronation Street* or *Dallas* in other countries. As with any soap opera or sitcom, the central cast of characters inhabit a precise location, in this case Adetola Street in Lagos. The series features half a dozen key personalities, but the eponymous hero is Basi, or Mr B, as he refers to himself. Mr B is an idle, likeable rogue who is powerfully convinced that the world most definitely owes him a living. His personal motto which he has printed on the red T-shirt he invariably wears is, 'To be a millionaire, think like a millionaire.' Basi's dreams are always almost about to be realized.

Almost, but not quite. True, Basi's vulgar aspirations are timeless and perennial, shared by all lovable rogues, from Barry Lyndon to Basil Seal, but Mr Saro-Wiwa's objective is not solely to entertain. For it seems clear that the series has succeeded so emphatically precisely because it holds a mirror up to Nigerian society. It is a soap opera fuelled and driven by vehement satire and moral indignation rather than the usual lures of vapid wish fulfilment, folksy low-life homilies or squeaky-clean fantasies of impossible communities. In five years, *Basi & Co.* has become a Nigerian phenomenon, as, indeed, has its only begetter.

Mr Saro-Wiwa was born in 1941 in the River State in the southeast of Nigeria, near the Niger delta. He won scholarships to a respected secondary school and to the University of Ibadan, where he read English literature. He was a post-graduate when the Nigerian civil war broke out. As the Biafran rebel enclave steadily shrank, Mr Saro-Wiwa escaped to the federal side and was appointed civilian administrator of the crucial oil port of Bonny, a post he held for the rest of the war. (His most recent book, *On a Darkling Plain*, deals with this portion of his life.)

After the war he stayed in government for a number of years before he abandoned politics and went into business in 1973.

'I was writing before that,' he says, 'and I had published two books of poetry, but in 1973 I decided to stop writing and turn to commerce.' He became a general merchant and ran a grocery store, selling imported foodstuffs and kitchen equipment. He worked hard and his business grew. The profits he made were invested in property. After ten years he was a wealthy man with a comfortable income. 'You have no idea how hard I worked in those years,' he says, a flicker of retrospective exhaustion crossing his face. The money was in the bank; it was time to return to his writing career.

The efforts of the seventeen years since then have been no less prodigious. In addition to *Basi & Co.*, Mr Saro-Wiwa has written three novels, two volumes of short stories, a volume of autobiography and six children's books.

They are all published, moreover, by himself, with Saros International Publishers, head office in Ewell, Surrey. Mr Saro-Wiwa prints and publishes the books in England and exports them to Nigeria. The entrepreneurial drive has not been entirely abandoned. 'How many copies do you sell?' I ask. He laughs. 'That's a trade secret.'

Mr Saro-Wiwa is a spry man who does not look his age. His demeanour is genial and amused, quietly self-assured. He does not appear driven or manically energetic, yet his workload is astonishing. On top of his business, television and publishing interests, he also has a reputation as one of Nigeria's fiercest political journalists, writing a weekly column in the local *Daily Times*. I ask him how he sees himself now, how he would describe himself. 'A publisher, I suppose,' he says.

Mr Saro-Wiwa's most extraordinary novel, which he published in 1985, is called *Sozaboy: A Novel in Rotten English*. It is a story told by a young conscript caught up in the horrors of the Biafran war and is written in a blend of Nigerian pidgin English, broken English and occasional limpid passages of correct idiomatic English. It has no rules and no syntax and, as Mr Saro-Wiwa observes, it thrives on lawlessness.

The effect at first seems too complex and discordant, but gradually the rhythms and expressive potential of this 'rotten English' begin to take hold with remarkable force and impact. In this book, the demotic soul is given a unique literary voice.

Somehow, Mr Saro-Wiwa keeps all these various literary balls up in the air. His energy is fuelled by two extra ingredients not normally associated with writers, let alone soap opera producers.

The first is a strong pedagogic inclination: Mr Saro-Wiwa wants to show his audience and readers how to improve themselves. The implication is clear: African writers today rarely write for their own populations. 'They're published in London or New York.'

Mr Saro-Wiwa loves Nigeria and enjoys his life there. He makes it sound an extraordinary place. This is a country where anything is possible, he claims, however he is not sanguine about the return to civilian rule in 1992. 'There will be a short civilian period, then the military will take over again,' he says. 'We need an enlightened despot.' What about Nigeria's bad image abroad? 'It's just lousy PR by the government.' He enthuses further about the astonishing freedoms in the country; anything can be done, he says, anything is possible and at the same time claims that it is the Nigerian people who actively encourage the military to take over when things get out of hand. Hearing him talking so enthusiastically about Lagos, say, he makes the place sound like Barcelona or pre-Castro Havana.

'Oh, Lagos is not so bad,' he says with a smile. 'Things go wrong, sure. But there's a lot of fun to be had there, too. A lot of fun.'

1990

Ken Saro-Wiwa (2)

'Although, everybody in Dukana was happy at first' is the wonderful and audacious opening line of a wonderful and audacious novel. By the novel's conclusion, however, this sentence's disarming grammar and its minatory simplicity (what does that 'at first' portend?) have taken on more sinister and melancholy hues. One has learned that this is the beginning of a story about innocence brutally lost and of a consolatory wisdom only fleetingly and partially grasped. The incomprehension – and the profound sadness – are gathered there in those few words; the inspired, odd displacement of 'Although' carries a new poignancy.

Sozaboy is a war novel, the narrative of one young man's helpless and hapless journey through a terrifying African war. Although – it is curious how the word has changed, somehow, charged with its *Sozaboy* freight – Ken Saro-Wiwa does not specify it is in fact set during a particular and precise conflict, namely the Nigerian civil war of 1967–70, also known as the Biafran war. Unusually for an African conflict, it was one that figured prominently on British television screens. Nigeria was a former colony (independence had been granted seven years previously) and Britain had powerful vested interests there. The British government's support – material and diplomatic – was firmly behind the Federal Government, led by General Gowon, and against the secessionist eastern states, known as Biafra, led by Colonel Ojukwu. There were no clear-cut heroes or villains in this conflict, and culpability can be equally distributed; but with hindsight one can see that the decision of the eastern states to secede made war – and also eventual defeat – inevitable. That the war lasted as long as it did, and that it caused as much misery and suffering (over a million died, mostly civilians, mostly from disease and starvation in the shrinking, blockaded heartland that was Biafra), is a result of many familiar factors: heroic tenacity, woeful stupidity, tactical blunders, difficult terrain, muddle and confusion, extended supply lines and so on. Anyone who requires an overview of this almost forgotten war should read *The Struggle for Secession* by N. U. Akpan, the best account that I know. Histories of the war are very thin on the ground or otherwise ponderously, not to say ludicrously, partisan; Nigerian novelists have been swifter off the mark and truer to this bleak chapter in their country's history, and there are fine and moving works of fiction by Chinua Achebe and Ben Okri (among others) which treat of the conflict. But in my opinion *Sozaboy* remains the war's enduring literary monument.

Ken Saro-Wiwa is from eastern Nigeria, a member of the Ogoni tribe. The outbreak of war in 1967 trapped him within the new boundaries of the Biafran state. It is important to establish that not all easterners wanted to secede from the Nigerian federation. Colonel Ojukwu was an Ibo, the dominant tribe in eastern Nigeria. When he declared Biafra independent, 'Ibo' and 'Biafra' were not at all synonymous: like it or not, some thirty or so other ethnic groups were included in the new country. Like it or not, these other tribes found themselves at war against Nigeria.

This fact explains much that is intentionally fuzzy about the novel. No one seems to understand why war is impending or why it breaks out. No one seems really sure why they are fighting or against whom: they are designated simply as 'the enemy'. To many eastern Nigerians caught up in the Biafran net, the motives for war and the nature of their adversaries must have seemed equally vague. Sozaboy – as the hero, Mene, is dubbed ('Soza' means 'soldier') – is one such uncertain conscript and he meanders through the novel in an almost permanent state of ignorance; clarity beckoning from time to time only to be occluded promptly. This is a state of mind familiar to all front-line soldiers, but to the many non-Ibos dragooned into the Biafran army there must have been an extra degree of obfuscation.

Ken Saro-Wiwa was one who perceived the absurdity and injustice of fighting another man's secessionist war. He escaped through the front lines to the federal side and was appointed civilian administrator of the crucial oil-port of Bonny on the Niger River Delta (he has written of his own experiences in the civil war in his fine autobiography, *On a Darkling Plain*), where he served until the final collapse of the secessionist forces, marked by the flight of Colonel Ojukwu to the Ivory Coast in January 1970. I lived in Nigeria during the Biafran war and can testify to the novel's authentic feel. The war did seem that crazy, that surreal and haphazard. But any reader will experience the same undeniable reek of life as it comes off the page. *Sozaboy* is vivid with the special authority of personal experience.

It is also vivid with a language of uncommon idiosyncrasy and character. Saro-Wiwa subtitles the novel as 'A Novel in Rotten English'.

Rotten English, as he explains, is a blend of pidgin English (the lingua franca of the West African ex-colonies), corrupted English and 'occasional flashes of good, even idiomatic English'. In other words, the language of the novel is a unique literary construct. No one in Nigeria actually speaks or writes like this but the style functions in the novel extraordinarily well. Sozaboy's narration is at times raunchily funny as well as lyrical and moving, and as the terror of his predicament steadily manifests itself, the small but colourful vocabulary of his idiolect paradoxically manages to capture all the numbing ghastliness of war far more effectively than a more expansive eloquence. It helps to hear the rhythms of a Nigerian accent in your ear as you read, but even if that cannot be reproduced, the cadences of the prose take over after a few lines or so and this remarkable tone of voice holds the reader's attention absolutely. Some obscure words or phrases are explained in a glossary, but one is never in any doubt about what is going on, and the sheer freshness and immediacy of the subjective point of view are exhilarating. Here Sozaboy visits a local dive:

So, one night, after I have finished bathing, I put powder and scent and went to African Upwine Bar. This African Upwine Bar is in interior part of Diobu. Inside inside. We used to call this Diobu New York. I think you know New York. In America. As people plenty for am, na so dem plenty for Diobu too. Like cockroach. And true true cockroach plenty for Diobu too. Everywhere, like the men. And if you go inside the African Upwine Bar you will see plenty cockroach man and proper cockroach too. Myself, I like the African Upwine Bar. Because you fit drink better palmy there. Fine palmy of three or four days old.

This mode of literary demotic is a highly impressive achievement. Saro-Wiwa has both invented and captured a voice here, one not only bracingly authentic but also capable of many fluent and telling registers. I cannot think of another example where the English language has been so engagingly and skilfully hijacked – or perhaps 'colonized' would be a better word. Indeed, throughout the novel, Saro-Wiwa exploits Rotten English with delicate and consummate skill. We see everything through Sozaboy's naive eyes, and his hampered vision – even in the face of the most shocking sights – is reproduced through inevitable understatement. Sozaboy's vocabulary simply cannot encompass the strange concepts he encounters or the fearful enormity of what he is undergoing. Yet these silences, these occlusions and fumblings for expression exert a marvellous power. Here a fifth-columnist has been undermining the new recruits' shaky morale:

So that night Manmuswak did not spend long time with us. After some time he told us that we must be careful because nobody can know when the war will come reach our front. So we told him goodnight, and he began to go away, small small like tall snake passing through the bush, making small noise.

The threat of impending disaster has never been more economically or chillingly conveyed.

Sozaboy's nightmare picaresque begins when, full of zeal to impress his new wife Agnes, he decides to join up and become a 'Soza'. It is the uniform he is really after, hungry for the esteem it will confer on him in his village, where he is only an apprentice lorry driver. The downward spiral of his fortunes in the army – boredom, mutiny, punishment, battle and capture – depresses and mortifies him, but he somehow never loses his fundamental ebullience, his innocent *joie de vivre*. He reminds me of another classic of African literature, Mr Johnson in Joyce Cary's novel of the same name. Like Mr Johnson, Sozaboy knows shame and humiliation, and like Mr Johnson it is his resilient spirit and the thought of his young wife that spur him on to greater endeavours no matter what desperate straits he finds himself in. But Sozaboy is also an African Candide and this is where Ken Saro-Wiwa's novel takes on dimensions that are absent in Joyce Cary's. Mr Johnson is a great character, as is Sozaboy, but – like Voltaire's Candide – Sozaboy is also an archetype and a victim in a way that Mr Johnson is not. Malign forces pluck up Sozaboy, whirl him around and deposit him in a heap, his spirit almost crushed, his village ruined, his family slaughtered, his prospects negligible. One needs only to glance at the recent history of Africa to see how paradigmatic Sozaboy's story is: young men in uniforms, clutching their AK47s, spread fear and desolation, march and die all over the continent.

At the novel's end, Sozaboy contemplates the destruction that has been wreaked on his life and reflects:

I was thinking how I was prouding before to go to soza and call myself Sozaboy. But now if anybody say anything about war or even fight, I will just run and run and run and run and run. Believe me yours sincerely.

Heartfelt and timeless thoughts, any simple bathos undercut by the astute final sentence, where the half-remembered formal valediction (the words are vapid and empty at the end of a letter) takes on an unfamiliar fervency and gravitas in its new and bitter context.

Sozaboy is a novel born out of harsh personal experience, but shaped with a masterful and sophisticated artistry despite its apparent rough-hewn guilelessness. With equal skill and deftness, it also carries a profound moral message that extends beyond its particular time and setting. Sozaboys are legion, and their lives are being destroyed everywhere on the planet. *Sozaboy* is not simply a great African novel, it is also a great anti-war novel, among the very best the twentieth century has produced.

1994

Ken Saro-Wiwa (3)

Ken Saro-Wiwa was a friend of mine. At eleven thirty in the morning on 10 November 1995, he was hanged in a prison in Port Harcourt, in eastern Nigeria, on the orders of General Sani Abacha, the military leader of Nigeria. Ken Saro-Wiwa was fifty-four years old, and an innocent man.

I first met Ken in the summer of 1986 at a British Council seminar at Cambridge University. He had come to England from Nigeria in his capacity as a publisher and had asked the British Council to arrange a meeting with me. He had read my first novel, *A Good Man in Africa*, and had recognized, despite fictional names and thin disguises, that it was set in Nigeria, the country that had been my home when I was in my teens and early twenties.

Ken had been a student at the University of Ibadan, in western Nigeria, in the mid sixties. My late father, Dr Alexander Boyd, had run the university health services there, and had treated Ken and come to know him. Ken recognized that the Dr Murray in my novel was a portrait of Dr Boyd and was curious to meet his son.

I remember that it was a sunny summer day, one of those days that are really too hot for England. In shirt-sleeves, we strolled about the immaculate quadrangle of a Cambridge college, talking about Nigeria. Ken was a small man, probably no more than five feet two or three. He was stocky and energetic – in fact, brimful of energy – and had a big, wide smile. He smoked a pipe with a curved stem. I learned later that the pipe was virtually a logo: in Nigeria people recognized him by it. In newsreel pictures that the Nigerian military released of the final days of Ken's show trial, there's a shot of him walking towards the courthouse, leaning on a stick, thinner and aged as a result of eighteen months' incarceration, the familiar pipe still clenched between his teeth.

Ken was not only a publisher but a businessman (in the grocery trade); a celebrated political journalist, with a particularly trenchant and swingeing style; and, I discovered, a prolific writer of novels, plays, poems and children's books (mostly published by him). He was, in addition, the highly successful writer and producer of Nigeria's most popular TV soap opera, *Basi & Co.*, which ran for 150-odd episodes in the mid eighties and was reputedly Africa's most watched soap opera, with an audience of up to 30 million. Basi and his cronies were a bunch of feckless Lagos wide-boys who, indigent and lazy, did nothing but hatch inept schemes for becoming rich. Although funny and wincingly accurate, the show was also unashamedly pedagogic. What was wrong with Basi and his chums was wrong with Nigeria: none of them wanted to work, and they all acted as though the world owed them a living; if that couldn't be acquired by fair means foul ones would do just as well. This was soap opera as a form of civic education.

Whenever Ken passed through London, we'd meet for lunch, usually in the Chelsea Arts Club. His wife and four children lived in England – the children attended school there – so he was a regular visitor. And, though I wrote a profile of him for the London *Times* (Ken was trying to get his books distributed in Britain), our encounters were mainly those of two writers with a lot in common, hanging out for a highly agreeable, bibulous hour or three.

Ken's writing was remarkably various, covering almost all genres. *Sozaboy*, in my opinion his greatest work, is subtitled *A Novel in Rotten English* and is written in a unique combination of pidgin English, the lingua franca of the former West African British colonies, and an English that is, in its phrases and sentences, altogether more classical and lyrical. The language is a form of literary demotic, a benign hijacking of English, and a perfect vehicle for the story it tells, of a simple village boy recruited into the Biafran army during the Nigerian civil war. The boy has dreamed of being a soldier (a *soza*), but the harsh realities of this brutal conflict send him into a dizzying spiral of cruel disillusion. *Sozaboy* is not simply a great African novel but also a great antiwar novel – among the very best of the twentieth century.

Sozaboy was born of Ken's personal experience of the conflict – the Biafran war, as it came to be known – and, indeed, so were many of his other writings. Biafra was the name given to a loose ethnic grouping in eastern Nigeria, dominated by the Ibo tribe. The Ibo leader, Colonel Chukwuemeka Odumegwu Ojukwu, decided to secede from the Nigerian Federation, taking most of the country's oil reserves with him. In the war that was then waged against the secessionist state, perhaps a million people died, mainly of starvation in the shrinking heartland.

Not all the ethnic groups caught up in Ojukwu's secessionist dream were willing participants. Ken's tribe, the Ogoni, for one. When the war broke out, in 1967, Ken was on vacation and found himself trapped within the new borders of Biafra. He saw at once the absurdity of being forced to fight in another man's war, and he escaped through the front lines to the Federal side. He was appointed civilian administrator of the crucial oil port of Bonny on the Niger River Delta, and he served there until the final collapse of the Biafran forces in 1970. Ken wrote about his experiences of the civil war in his fine memoir, *On a Darkling Plain*.

Ken's later fight against the Nigerian military, as it turned out, was oddly prefigured in those years of the Biafran war: the helplessness of an ethnic minority in the face of an overpowering military dictatorship; oil and oil wealth as a destructive and corrupting catalyst in society, the need to be true to one's conscience.

This moral rigour was especially apparent in Ken's satirical political journalism (he was, over the years, a columnist on the Lagos daily newspapers *Punch*, *Vanguard* and *Daily Times*), much of which was charged with a Swiftian *saeva indignatio* at what he saw as the persistent ills of Nigerian life: tribalism, ignorance of the rights of minorities, rampant materialism, inefficiency and general graft. Apart from *Basi & Co.*, his journalism was what brought him his greatest renown among the population at large.

In the late eighties, I remember, Ken's conversations turned more and more frequently to the topic of his tribal homeland. The Ogoni are a small tribe (there are 250 tribes in Nigeria) of about half a million people living in a small area of the fertile Niger River Delta. The Ogoni's great misfortune is that their homeland happens to lie above a significant portion of Nigeria's oil reserves. Since the mid 1950s, Ogoniland has been devastated by the industrial pollution caused by the extraction of oil. What was once a placid rural community of prosperous farmers and fishermen is now an ecological wasteland reeking of sulphur, its creeks and water holes poisoned by indiscriminate oil spillage and ghoulishly lit at night by the orange flames of gas flares.

As Ken's concern for his homeland grew, he effectively abandoned his vocation and devoted himself to lobbying for the Ogoni cause at home and abroad. He was instrumental in setting up the Movement for the Survival of the Ogoni People (MOSOP) and soon became its figurehead. That struggle for survival was an ecological more than a political one: his people, he said, were being subjected to a 'slow genocide'. Ken protested against the despoliation of his homeland and demanded compensation from the Nigerian government and from the international oil companies – Shell in particular. (He resented Shell profoundly and held the company responsible for the ecological calamity in Ogoniland.) But from the outset Ken made sure that the movement's protest was peaceful and non-violent. Nigeria today is a corrupt and dangerously violent nation: it was enormously to the credit of the Ogoni movement that it stayed true to its principles. Mass demonstrations were organized and passed off without incident. Abroad, Greenpeace and other environmental groups allied themselves with the Ogoni cause, but, ironically, the real measure of the success of Ken's agitation came when, in 1992, he was arrested by the Nigerian military and held in prison for some months without a trial. The next year, Shell Oil ceased its operations in the Ogoni region.

At that time, the Nigerian military was led by General Ibrahim Babangida. Ken was eventually released (after a campaign in the British media), and Babangida voluntarily yielded power to General Abacha, a crony, who was meant to supervise the transition of power to a civilian government after a general election, which was duly held in 1993. The nation went to the polls and democratically elected Chief Moshood Abiola as President. General Abacha then declared the election null and void and later imprisoned the victor. Nigeria entered a new era of near anarchy and despotism. Things looked bad for Nigeria, but they looked worse for the Ogoni and their leaders.

Over these years, Ken and I continued to meet for our Chelsea Arts Club lunches whenever he was in London. In 1992 he suffered a personal tragedy when his youngest son, aged fourteen, who was at Eton, died suddenly of heart failure during a rugby game. Strangely, Ken's awful grief gave a new force to his fight for his people's rights.

We met just before he returned to Nigeria. From my own experience of Nigeria, I knew of the uncompromising ruthlessness of political life there. Ken was not young, nor was he in the best of health (he too had a heart condition). As we said goodbye, I shook his hand and said, 'Be careful, Ken, OK?' And he laughed – his dry, delighted laugh – and replied, 'Oh, I'll be very careful, don't worry.' But I knew he wouldn't.

A succession of Nigerian military governments have survived as a result of the huge revenues generated by oil, and the military leaders themselves have routinely benefited from the oil revenues, making millions and millions of dollars. Any movement that threatened this flow of money was bound to be silenced – extinguished. With the ascendance of Abacha and his brazenly greedy junta, Ken was now squarely in harm's way. Even so, he returned to Nigeria to continue his protests. These protests were now conducted in a more sinister country than the one I had known – a country where rapes, murders and the burning of villages were being carried out as a deliberate policy of state terrorism. There have been 2,000 Ogoni deaths thus far.

In May of last year Ken was on his way to address a rally in an Ogoni town but was turned back at a military roadblock and headed, reluctantly, for home. The rally took place, a riot ensued, and in the general mayhem four Ogoni elders – believed to be sympathetic to the military – were killed.

Ken was arrested and, with fifteen others, was accused of incitement to murder. The fact that he was in a car some miles away and going in the opposite direction made no difference. He was imprisoned for more than a year and then was tried before a specially convened tribunal. There was no right of appeal. This 'judicial process' has been internationally condemned as a sham. It was a show trial in a kangaroo court designed to procure the verdict required by the government.

On Thursday, 2 November, Ken and eight co-defendants were found guilty and sentenced to death. Suddenly the world acknowledged the nature of Nigeria's degeneracy.

Things did not augur well. But, instinctively wanting to make the best of a bad situation, I hoped that the publicity surrounding Ken's case, along with the timely coincidence of the Commonwealth Conference in New Zealand (the biennial gathering of the former members of the British Empire), would prevent the very worst from happening. Surely, I reasoned, the heads of state congregating in Auckland would not allow one of their members to flout their own human rights principles so callously and blatantly? General Abacha, however, did not dare leave his benighted country, which was represented by his Foreign Minister instead.

The presence of Nelson Mandela at the conference was especially encouraging, not only for me but also for all the people who had spent the last months fighting to free Ken. (We were a loosely knit organization, including International PEN, the Ogoni Foundation, Amnesty International, Greenpeace and others.) We felt that if anything could persuade the Nigerians to think again it would be Mandela's moral authority. We were baffled and confused, though, when Mandela did little more than persistently advocate that we should all be patient, that the problem would be resolved through an easy, low-key diplomacy.

Despite Mandela's advice, there was a clamorous condemnation in the media of the Nigerian military. In response, Abacha's junta released newsreel pictures of Ken's trial to establish the legality of the 'judicial process'. One saw a row of prisoners, still, faces drawn, heads bowed, confronting three stout officers, swagged with gold braid, ostentatiously passing pieces of paper to each other. In the background, a soldier strolled back and forth. Then Ken addressed the court. His voice was strong: he was redoubtably defiant; he seemed without fear, utterly convinced.

These images both defied belief and profoundly disturbed. If Abacha thought that this would make his tribunals look acceptable, then the level of naivety, or blind ignorance, implied was astonishing. But a keening note of worry was also sounded: someone who could do something this damaging, I thought, was beyond the reach of reason. World opinion, international outrage, appeals for clemency seemed to me now to be nugatory. Abacha had painted himself into a corner. For him it had become a question of saving face, of loud bluster, of maintaining some sort of martial pride. I slept very badly that night.

The next day, 10 November, just after lunch, I received a call from the Writers in Prison Committee of International PEN. I was told that a source in Port Harcourt had seen the prisoners arrive at the gaol at dawn that day, in leg irons. Then the executioners had presented themselves, only to be turned away, because – it was a moment of grimmest, darkest farce – their papers were not in order. This source, however, was '110 per cent certain' that the executions had eventually occurred. Some hours later, this certainty was confirmed by the Nigerian military.

So now Ken was dead, along with eight co-defendants: hanged in a mass execution just as the Commonwealth Conference got under way.

I am bitter and I am dreadfully sad. Ken Saro-Wiwa, the bravest man I have known, is no more. From time to time, Ken managed to smuggle a letter out of prison. One of the last letters I received ended this way: 'I'm in good spirits . . . There's no doubt that my idea will succeed in time, but I'll have to bear the pain of the moment . . . the most important thing for me is that I've used my talents as a writer to enable the

Ogoni people to confront their tormentors. I was not able to do it as a politician or a businessman. My writing did it. And it sure makes me feel good! I'm mentally prepared for the worst, but hopeful for the best. I think I have the moral victory.' You have, Ken. Rest in peace.

1995

Cecil Rhodes

(Review of *The Randlords* by Geoffrey Wheatcroft)

The story of the South African gold and diamond fields and of the men who rose to wealth and notoriety as a result of their exploitation has stimulated writers since the 1870s, when diamonds were first discovered there. And yet amongst the millions of words there are curious lacunae, particularly in the area of biography. The key figures are Cecil Rhodes, Barney Barnato, Alfred Beit, J. B. Robinson, Solly Joel and Julius Wernher. None has a definitive biography, and on someone such as Beit there is an almost complete silence. This is even more true of the minor figures, such as Rhodes's henchman Rutherfoord Harris, his partner Charles Rudd or even Leander Starr Jameson. Paradoxically, there exists a first-rate scholarly account of Rhodes's involvement with the annexation of Bechuanaland – yet no similar treatment of his life. Even the most recent biography (by J. Flint, 1976) is inadequate on certain areas of his life. If one wants to learn about Neville Pickering, his first private secretary and the great love of his life (Rhodes, in his second will, left his estate to Pickering), one must turn to Brian Roberts's *Cecil Rhodes and the Princess*, where, for the first and only time, Pickering's early life and background are accurately delineated. Other murky areas – Rhodes's dealings with Lobengula and the Matabele, the formation of the British South Africa Company, the widespread concession racketeering – still await their chroniclers.

As a result, no study of the period or of its protagonists can do without a process of assiduous weeding and winnowing of all manner of sources, from rambunctious Victorian travel books to dry works of Bantu topography. Wheatcroft is particularly good on the financial machinations that went into the making of the vast fortunes achieved at Kimberley and on the Rand. For the history of the gold and diamond fields – superficially a glamorous, adventurous one of strikes and rushes, booms and slumps – is, at a more profound level, a chilly illustration of the working of monopoly capitalism at its most forthright and ruthless. The early diggers were drawn by the lure of quick wealth for a little hard work; those that survived and stayed on were concerned with consolidation. They were essentially financiers and speculators interested solely in profit. What distinguished the men of Kimberley and Johannesburg from the grey souls who populated the world's stock exchanges was a robust, frontier insouciance – no veneer of bland decorum had yet had time to form.

People like Beit and Wernher devoted their lives to making phenomenal amounts of money for themselves and after a while this process ceases to be interesting. I had expected that Wheatcroft's book would fill in the gaps, particularly on Beit, but there is nothing about him in *The Randlords* that we cannot find elsewhere. This now seems to me not so much a deficiency in Wheatcroft's research as a shallowness in Beit's character. He was a timid, portly, extraordinarily hard-working man with superb financial acumen. He associated himself with Rhodes early on in his career and Rhodes came to rely heavily on his judgement. Perhaps there is nothing more to say. Others, such as Barney Barnato and J. B. Robinson, were more flamboyant – almost Gogolian – characters. Barnato was a Cockney Jew who arrived in the early days of the diamond fields with assets consisting of forty rather bad cigars. He became a multi-millionaire with – almost obligatory for the South African magnates – a Park Lane mansion. He never lost his accent and was never truly accepted by the high society of the day. Towards the end of his life he became afflicted by paranoias and depressions, and committed suicide by jumping overboard from an Atlantic liner. One story about Barney, which Wheatcroft doesn't mention, occurred in his heyday. He bought a Millais called *Joseph and the Sheep* which he hung with due prominence in his Park Lane house. At a reception Barney was loudly asked by an aristocratic society *grande dame* (presumably to effect some social discomfiture) why he had bought the picture and what was it that made it appealing to him. Barney, goaded and irritated, replied with equal volume: 'I bought it, madam, because one of the poor fuckin' sheep looks just like me.'

Barney Barnato, sometimes accused of being a shady operator, was nevertheless a popular figure in the minefields. J. B. Robinson, on the other hand, inspired nothing but hate. After his death in 1929, the *Cape Times* published an obituary which must rank as one of the most vitriolic ever written. His will, the obituary said, was 'scandalously repugnant . . . it stinks, too, against public decency'. What provoked the ire was the fact that Robinson's will set up no trust funds nor benefited the country in any way. Robinson, the *Cape Times* went on, should serve as a warning: 'those who in future may acquire great wealth in this country will shudder lest their memories should come within possible risk of rivalling the loathsomeness of the thing that is the memory of Sir Joseph Robinson.' It is ironic now to reflect that when Rhodes died he was regarded as a national hero. His funeral train passed through the solemn and mourning country as if he were some great monarch being laid to rest. Robinson's legacy was one of personal bitterness and repugnance. Rhodes's bequest to his adopted country was altogether more complex and damaging. Rhodes was not only a corrupt and ruthless capitalist who used his ostensible imperialist aims to win large fortunes for himself (he made at least a million pounds out of the creation of Rhodesia): he also laid the foundations of apartheid with his racial legislation when he was Prime Minister of the Cape; and he was directly responsible for the Boer War and all its repercussions, thanks to the fiasco of the Jameson Raid. It is harder to calculate the long-term effects of his actions on the Matabele tribe, and the results of his colonization north of the Zambezi. It is perhaps sufficient to observe that he and his agents (the good Dr Jameson again) adopted methods no less severe than the United States did in their wars against the Plains Indians in the 1870s: the smallpox weapon, the reservation policy, found an echo in Rhodesia.

And yet this man died an imperial hero. If ever there was a case for a revisionist biography, Rhodes positively cries out for one. Wheatcroft makes no attempt to rehabilitate, but holds back from attempting a full analysis. Speculating about the absence of a satisfactory 'Life of Rhodes', he asks: 'Is it because, as hinted in Chapter Nine, and to borrow Gertrude Stein's words in another context, "there is no there there"? The looming gap between his deeds and his unfathomable personality remains.' That 'hinted in' is revealing, and I think that to preserve ideas of 'mystery' and 'unfathomableness' does Rhodes too great a favour and lends him an air of glamorous potency. There were, it is true, baffling sides to Rhodes, but in many crucial respects he seems to me entirely transparent.

Wheatcroft illuminates one significant fact early on. 'Even in a rough age,' he observes, 'standards of financial morality on the diamond fields were low.' This is almost a euphemism. The key to Rhodes's character lies in the fact that his education — unusually for a boy of his class — was in the polyglot graft and corruption of the diggings. Rhodes left school at sixteen, moreover; unlike the other Englishmen of his class, he was not a public schoolboy. He did not possess that protective veneer which years in a single-sex boarding school provide. When he finally entered the English educational system – Oxford – it was as a mature young man with several years in the diggings behind him. He had, in fact, more in common with the working-class financiers – Barnato, Joel – than with the English 'gents' he messed with. We are inclined to see Rhodes as typically middle class (father a vicar, brothers at Eton and Winchester, Oxford education), but it is more instructive to see him as an East End wide-boy in disguise. He was streetwise. The history of his career is of a man who gets what he wants by whatever means is most effective. Sometimes it was charm, sometimes guile, sometimes main force, sometimes bribery and corruption. 'Tell me a man's ambitions,' he said, 'and I will tell you his price.'

Wheatcroft refers to a bribery case of 1876. The facts are more complex than he has space to make them. At that time, the diamond fields were in one of their slumps. Rhodes and his partner Rudd were very nearly broke, and they diversified into ancillary professions. The price of diamonds was low, mining was often impossible for months on end because of massive mud slides and cave-ins. Diggers were leaving Kimberley in their hundreds. Rhodes hung on, selling ice cream in the market square. Then he decided to attempt to gain pumping contracts from the various mining boards. First he needed a pump. He used charm. He spent a week persuading a Boer farmer to part with a new pump he had just installed on his farm. The man refused to sell, but through bull-headed persistence and by promising more and more money (which he did not have) Rhodes got his way. Again and again he was to persuade people into courses of action to which they were implacably opposed. It was his greatest skill.

Having secured his pump, he got a contract in one of the smaller mines. He then bribed a mining engineer in charge of the pumps in De Beer's mine to damage them – thereby allowing Rhodes and Rudd to come to the rescue. This skulduggery came inadvertently to light during the deliberations of an official committee of inquiry into miners' grievances. At the time it made a huge scandal, Rhodes effectively silenced it by suing the engineer (a Mauritian called Heuteau) for perjury. The case was called in court, then the charge was suddenly dropped. As Wheatcroft implies, this was achieved by collusion between Rhodes and the public prosecutor, Sidney Shippard – later, significantly, executor of Rhodes's will. At the time of the trial, Rhodes and Shippard were living in the same mess. Heuteau's allegation had been neutered by being transferred from a court of inquiry to a court of law. There, with Shippard conniving, the matter was swiftly settled. Rhodes dropped his case against the hapless Mauritian (who never raised the matter again). Shippard was well rewarded for his aid. Rhodes was tarnished, but free to operate, and, eventually, got the De Beers pumping contract. The same modus operandi appears again and again in his short but very busy life. To take an example not generally known: when Rhodes was negotiating with Lobengula, king of the Matabele, for a mining concession and the king was proving intractable, Rhodes drew up a contract with one Frank Johnson (an adventurer who was to lead the pioneer column to found Rhodesia) for the killing of Lobengula. Johnson revealed this in his autobiography, *Great Days*, and reproduced the contract. But the relevant chapter was withdrawn from the published manuscript, though the typescript still resides in a state archive in Harare. It is an astonishing document and reads like something from a CIA covert-operations file. (One has constantly to remember that this was the beginning of the British South Africa Company – lengthy negotiations with the Colonial Office eventually secured Rhodes a Royal Charter.) Johnson writes in the chapter:

I had an open mind as to the procedure after securing the king and his entourage. We might make a complete job of it by killing Lobengula *and* smashing each military kraal . . . The contract went on to promise me the sum of £150,000 [a vast sum – multiply by 25 to get some idea of its contemporary value] if I succeeded. If I failed [and presumably was killed] I got nothing but provision for my widow. I was also to have my BE shares exchanged for Chartered company shares . . . I still believe the coup would have succeeded – I had the support of such splendid men – but, alas!, it had to be dropped like a hot potato.

Because news of it leaked out and Rhodes (who was Prime Minister at the time) was arraigned before the Governor of the Cape. Rhodes denied everything, and Johnson adds: 'I was then taken to Government house to confirm Rhodes's innocence.' And so, he concludes, the 'scheme for the forcible occupation of Rhodesia failed, but only for a short time. It was not long before once more, and this time successfully, I became involved in a fresh attempt to capture Rhodes's hinterland.'

Here we see the thought-processes behind the Jameson Raid. We might indeed have had a Johnson's raid to capture Matabeleland had

Rhodes not been pre-empted. It must have seemed like a good idea, and he saved it up for another time. Notice, too, Johnson's references to shares. Shares were the currency with which Rhodes bought men. Dr Jameson left his lucrative practice (£5,000 p.a.) in Kimberley to work for Rhodes, first as negotiator with Lobengula, then as Governor of Rhodesia. Why? For shares in Rhodes's company, not for any imperialist's dream. Wheatcroft is very good at illuminating the somewhat arcane workings of the various stock markets and the financial scams that went on. The most common method was insider dealing – what was known as the 'ground-floor issue'. Stock of a new company was allocated to friends – the 'vendor's allocation' – the shares were floated, and in the bullish conditions that surrounded South African shares they could be sold again within days for enormous profits.

Rhodes himself was a past master at this. When he eventually secured the mining concession from Lobengula – known as 'the Rudd Concession' after Rhodes's partner – he knew he could gain the Royal Charter he so desperately needed, both to finance his pioneer expedition and to give him the administrative power and licence he required. Delicate negotiations ensued between the British South Africa Company, as Rhodes called his new venture, and the British Government in the form of the Colonial Office. Rhodes lied constantly throughout. He assured the Colonial Office that the BSA owned the Rudd Concession. Without this assurance the Charter would not have been granted. The BSA was a public company, with shares publicly quoted, and the value of those shares consisted precisely in the fact that the BSA owned the Rudd Concession. But it didn't. The Rudd Concession was owned by a company called the Central Search Company who *leased* the concession to the BSA in return for 50 per cent of BSA's profits. Who were the directors of Central Search? Rhodes, Rudd, Beit, Rochefort MacGuire (an Oxford friend who worked for Rhodes), and two men called Cawston and Gifford (rival concession hunters who had been, in Rhodes's favourite phrase, 'squared'). Surreptitiously, Central Search became the United Concessions Company. Two years later United Concessions sold the Rudd Concession to BSA for £1 million (Wheatcroft says £2 million – either way multiply by twenty-five). It was a blatant and unscrupulous sequence of frauds: first, and fatally, on Lobengula and the Matabele, second on the City of London Stock Exchange, third on the shareholders of BSA, and finally on the Government of the United Kingdom. Rhodes painted another part of the map red and made a vast profit for himself and his cronies.

His career was a catalogue of similar delinquencies: some of them notorious, as with the collusion with Chamberlain over the Jameson Raid (they both brazenly lied under oath to a Parliamentary Committee), some of them less well-known, such as the falsifications of a smallpox epidemic in Kimberley in 1883 where a diagnosed smallpox epidemic was rediagnosed (on Rhodes's instructions) by a committee of doctors led by, yes, the good Jameson as a 'bulbous disease allied to pemphigus' (no such disease exists). The quarantine camps were taken down: inoculation more or less ceased, and black labour continued to flow into the mines (they would never have come if there was smallpox). There were hundreds of deaths, black and white, before health inspectors managed to have quarantine and inoculation reintroduced.

Some people did see Rhodes as he really was. One was Henry Labouchère, who described Rhodes as 'a vulgar promoter masquerading as a patriot and the figurehead of a gang of financiers with whom he divided the profits'. Yet there is no denying there was something phenomenal about him that distinguishes him from the other Randlords and which accounts for the horrible fascination he exerts. In the 1890s he could claim to be the richest man in the world. Quite apart from his assets (De Beers had the virtual monopoly of the world's diamonds), his salary from the company was £200,000 a year, while from his Gold Fields of South Africa Company he earned £300–400,000 a year. Share dealings and directorships would have brought his annual *income* up to a million. Multiply by twenty-five.

After the Jameson Raid, Chamberlain had occasion to reflect on his lucky escape. His heartfelt words still possess an eerie aptness: 'What is there in South Africa, I wonder, that makes blackguards of all who get involved in its politics?'

1985

White Mischief

(Review of *White Mischief* by James Fox)

In 1941 a murder case drove the news of the war from the front pages of British newspapers. The crime was committed in Nairobi, Kenya. The victim was Josslyn Hay, the Earl of Errol. The alleged murderer was Sir 'Jock' Delves Broughton. The motive, the prosecution claimed, was jealousy: Errol had been having a passionate affair with Broughton's beautiful young wife, Diana.

These are the broad outlines of one of the most intriguing and fascinating cases of this century. Its ingredients are almost too rich, too classically apt to be credible. It draws in and illuminates certain quintessential British preoccupations – aristocracy, colonialism, privilege – as well as certain quintessential human ones – love, betrayal, jealousy and revenge. As an added twist to the tale we can add injustice: the guilty man was acquitted.

It all began and ended in a remarkably short span of time. Delves Broughton arrived in Kenya in mid November 1940 with his young wife Diana. Broughton was fifty-seven, Diana twenty-seven. They had just been married in South Africa and had come to Kenya to escape the rigours of blitz-damaged Britain. In Kenya the war had made few inroads into the social lives of the aristocratic settlers and remittance men who lived in and around Nairobi. Indeed there is little that the most decadent socialite of contemporary Manhattan could have taught the denizens of 'Happy Valley' when it came to having a good time.

It was this small and select community that Broughton and Diana joined. Almost immediately she began to have an affair with Joss Errol, a handsome though somewhat debauched figure with already a considerable reputation as a womanizer. What is remarkable is the extent to which it soon became public knowledge. Broughton, too, was soon fully in the know, yet he continued to see Errol socially; indeed they were so friendly (Broughton, the cuckold, often dined with his wife and the adulterer) that it was generally assumed he had resigned all claims on Diana and had tacitly given his blessing to the liaison. By now, however, Diana was planning to leave Broughton for her lover.

And then in the very early morning of 24 January Errol's car was found nose-down in a gravel pit not far from the Broughtons' house. The headlights were still on and, hunched in a curious foetal position beneath the dashboard, was the body of Joss Errol with a bullet in his head. After some short delays Delves Broughton was charged with the murder and the trial ensued.

But was Broughton guilty? Fox has organized the book in two distinct parts. Part one presents the facts of the murder and the social backgrounds of the major characters. Part two details the more recent attempts to come up with a conclusive answer to the various puzzles and problems still associated with the case. These researches were initiated by Cyril Connolly, who was obsessed with the Errol murder, and arose in connection with an article which Connolly wrote with Fox for the *Sunday Times* magazine. Part two makes as fascinating reading as part one with Connolly and Fox – a somewhat unlikely pair of sleuths – digging up the past, tapping reluctant memories and seeking out long forgotten crucial witnesses. After Connolly's death Fox continued to investigate alone.

The evidence they uncover seems to me to be conclusive. Broughton murdered Joss Errol and got away with it more by luck than judgement, and with the help of a clever defence lawyer. Just how he did it remains a matter for conjecture which goes a long way towards explaining the abiding fascination of the case. But not all the way. What makes the Errol murder so different is the extraordinary characters that are associated with it and the bizarre lives they led in Kenya: the eccentric settlers and shady aristos, the neurotic wives and sad drunks, the *morphineuses* and lounge-lizards. The cast and the setting are unique. It's a measure of James Fox's remarkable achievement that in *White Mischief* he not only produces an impeccably researched and lucidly written 'last word' on this notorious case but also brings these astonishing people and their perplexed and tormented lives so vividly and compellingly to life.

1983

Liberia

(Review of *Monrovia Mon Amour:*
A Visit to Liberia by Anthony Daniels)

The title is ironic, of course, as is the tone almost completely throughout this exiguous and pricey book. Anthony Daniels visited Liberia in Easter of 1991 shortly after the end of the Liberian civil war, that shocking, surreal, and thoroughly nasty little conflict that illuminated our news bulletins for a while before it was superseded by that far greater conflagration in the Gulf. Certain images of that civil war, certain personalities, certain atrocities will linger on in the mind, however, as the twentieth century limps towards its conclusion: pyjama-clad, Disney-mask-wearing, AK47-toting 'boys'; the various strutting warlords – Prince Johnson, Samuel Doe and Charles Taylor; the massacre of 600 refugees in a church . . . The list is not very long, but then this little flare-up in West Africa only fleetingly attracted the attention of the Western media.

We should be grateful, then, for Daniels's visit, and his alternatingly irritating and fascinating account, insofar as it will prevent us forgetting, for a brief while, yet another bloodsoaked and shameful episode in Africa's history. All the same, his motives for going there are never explicitly revealed. Judging solely from the tone of his observations he seems to have been drawn to Liberia by a kind of ghoulish misanthropy, a sinister *schadenfreude*. He looks at the Liberians and their appalling plight with all the empathy of a scientist examining bacteria through a microscope. 'I am a controversialist,' he avers at one stage, 'I am not emotional,' he confesses at another, so perhaps the pose of mildly amused disdain and contempt for Africa and all things African is meant merely to provoke.

If so, then in the event the aim is misguided. For, as Daniels guides us through the short, crazy history of the war, tours innumerable ruins, visits Prince Johnson and other personages surviving in the uneasy peace that prevailed, his voice – veering from fair Evelyn Waugh pastiche, to knee-jerk Conservatism (too many poor jokes about lefties, arties and liberals) – stimulates lassitude rather than outrage. But, occasionally, there is a passage of bracing Swiftian rage at humankind and its manifest follies that suddenly moves the book on to another plane. It is at these moments too that Daniels allows his fastidious objectivity to drop and we can believe for a moment that, despite the mad farce of the war and the madder farceurs, he possesses a sense of basic fellow feeling for the dead and devastated. Without these rare glimpses (particularly evident when he visits the site of the church massacre, and when he writes about Venice in the book's envoi) the relentless, mannered cynicism becomes enervating. The great contemporary commentator on Africa and its calamities is the celebrated Polish foreign correspondent Ryszard Kapuscinski – someone who is just as honest and scathing about Africa's corruption and stupidity as Daniels, but who never forgets, as he lists the ghastly atrocities and evils he has witnessed, that there is a human cost that must be acknowledged and that sympathy for those who have suffered and endured is not an emotion of which one should be ashamed.

So, as the voice changes, then, so does one's reaction to the book. At one moment, Daniels presents himself as a languid flâneur: 'There is one thing to be said in favour of a sacked city: afterwards it is very quiet,' and the archness of the forced aphorism has one squirming. And then there is an account of Daniels watching a videotape of the torturing and death of Samuel Doe (both of Doe's ears are cut off) that is utterly chilling and the measure of anything Kapuscinski might relate. In Venice, too, the mask slips and Daniels allows himself to confess that: 'Since my greatest desire is to write, I have come almost to fear the beauty and wordlessness [the city] provokes in me; but Venice is so completely without parallel, so hauntingly exquisite, that its spell is irresistible *even to me*' (my italics). What? Even to that latter-day Diogenes Anthony Daniels? Never! D. H. Lawrence said, 'Trust the teller, not the tale.' It was a piece of advice designed to help the reader, but in the case of *Monrovia Mon Amour* its counsel might profitably be reversed: the best sequences of the book occur when the teller forgets what pose he should currently be striking and trusts himself and his capacity for human feeling for a moment or two.

1992

African Wars

(Review of *Marching Over Africa* by Frank Emery)

Queen Victoria certainly kept her armies busy. There were the big wars – Crimea, the Indian Mutiny, the Boer War – but almost every year seemed to initiate another campaign: the Opium War, the invasion of Afghanistan, fighting in Burma. And Africa, of course. Between 1868 and 1898 there were major military confrontations with the Ashanti in West Africa; the Xhosa, Pedi, Sotho and Zulu nations in South Africa; wars against Egyptian loyalists, and latter-day Moslem fundamentalists in the Sudan; the first Boer War (1880–81) against the Afrikaners of the Transvaal and the Orange Free State, not to mention a host of bloody skirmishes and punitive expeditions throughout the colonies and protectorates. Indeed, from one angle the history of Africa in the nineteenth century can be viewed almost exclusively in terms of military activity – a vast continental Beirut, as it were, riven with the bloody strife of warring factions provoked or encouraged by vastly more powerful interested parties.

In his fine and interesting book Frank Emery concentrates on those major conflicts listed above which provide the familiar roll-call of British Imperial History – Rorke's Drift, Tel El Kebir, Majuba Hill, Omdurman, etc. My one reservation here is that the net might have been cast a little wider. There are less well-known corners of African military history that could profit from some illumination. The Matabele Rebellion, for example, or the Uganda Mutiny of 1898 or the fascinating and disastrous punitive expedition to Benin in 1897. It's perhaps a little unfair to Emery to mention these as his book is not intended to be a history of African colonial wars and the areas he does cover are largely dictated by the source material he has at his disposal. Emery provides us with a brief historical context to the wars but his main aim is to acquaint us as directly as possible with the experience of soldiering in nineteenth-century Africa. He does this predominantly through the use of contemporary letters home, written, in the main, by other ranks. One hears, then, the voice of Tommy Atkins in person, addressing an intimate private audience with no eye on posterity. Emery has done his research assiduously and many of the letters he reproduces are extraordinary documents, not only for

what they reveal about the day-to-day business of being a Victorian
soldier but also for the high degree of democracy they exhibit. The
tone, indeed, is surprisingly modern and direct, freed as it is from the
posturing hindsight of the military 'memoir' and the smug complacen-
cies of jingoism. Here is a cavalryman telling his parents about the charge
of the 21st Lancers at Omdurman.

It festered, and I had a funny hand for about three days but it is healed up
now and I am ready for another man-killing job. It is nice to put a sword or
a lance through a man; they are just like old hens, they just say 'quar'.

From the dozens of voices and personalities that are revealed to us
through the collection of letters a sort of photofit portrait of the
nineteenth-century British soldier emerges: tough, stoical, with a meagre
vein of sentiment (for 'poor chaps' who get killed, horses shot out from
under him, and grudging admiration for the suicidal bravery of his
enemy), a scant interest in the reasons for his presence in Africa, and
absolutely no compunction when it comes to killing as many of the
continent's inhabitants as possible. Perhaps this is true of all soldiers at
all times (one is reminded of paratroopers in the Falklands who kept
insisting they were only 'doing a job of work') but the almost total
absence of moans, complaints and criticism in these letters home is quite
intriguing. Conditions on most of these campaigns were so harsh:
Scottish regiments in kilts and spats, a twenty-hour march on empty
stomachs to find fouled wells at the end of it, for example (to say nothing
of disease and climate), that one would imagine a few more notes of
dissent.

This, I suppose, is the result of relying so heavily on source material. Emery found many of these letters reprinted in contemporary local
newspapers where one would be unlikely to discover much outspoken
criticism or general bitching. It is in this area that I think the book
could have benefited from more editorial comment and instruction.
For example, when a naval surgeon tending the seriously wounded at
Majuba Hill says, 'All we had to give them was water and a little opium,'
I would like to know something more about this treatment. How was
it administered? Was this a common anaesthetic on the battlefield? And
perhaps the account would benefit from some more general information about the care and survival prospects of casualties in those days?
Again, one correspondent says 'it would be too sickening' to give details

of the way the Zulus mutilated dead bodies. Emery then implies that he knows what went on but does not tell us. One's interest in the details, the 'nuts and bolts' of soldiering, is quickened not from pedantry or ghoulishness but because increasingly – especially in the field of military history – this kind of precise specification is the norm. Historians such as John Keegan and Richard Holmes led the way and have transformed the way war and battle are written about. Emery's reticence here is disappointing if only because of the very intimacy of much of his material. One feels something of an opportunity has been lost, that *Marching Over Africa* had the potential to become a minor classic, of the order of, say, Evan S. Connell's brilliant book about Custer's final campaign against the Plains Indians, *Son of the Morning Star*. It is exactly contemporary with some of Emery's campaigns (1876) and it employs the same method of extensive use of original source material. It's true that from time to time Emery achieves this same vividness, especially in the chapters on the wars in the Sudan, but too often one wants to know more or one has to fall back on imagination and reading between the lines.

About one aspect of Victorian soldiers in Africa, however, Emery is wholly candid: their brutal and unreflecting racism.

We repassed the battlefield on our right, where our dead were still lying unburied and came across some wounded niggers whom we shot at once. I got some breakfast and lunch, and all started again at 3.30 p.m. for the Nile . . .

The utterly casual slaughter of wounded enemy on the battlefields of Africa is perhaps the most important revelation in the book. It was widespread and effected with enthusiastic diligence. These Victorian soldiers regarded their African enemies as subhuman, and would think no more of bayoneting a wounded Dervish than they would of swatting a fly.

O tempora! O mores! No doubt Victorian soldiers could offer our century the same rebuke, and more, but there is something particularly rebarbative about that brand of sanctimonious Victorian hypocrisy, especially when it is couched in the terms Sir Garnet Wolseley employed when exhorting one of his commanders about to go on the warpath in Africa:

I envy you the good fortune of being once more upon the warpath, the only path upon which it is worth travelling in these degenerate days of cant, puffed-up philosophical cosmopolitanism and maudlin humanitarianism. I know that wherever you go you will do well and maintain our national reputation for hard straight hitting and gentle humanity of a manly nature.

1986

Ryszard Kapuscinski

(Review of *The Soccer War*)

The Soccer War broke out in 1970 between El Salvador and Honduras. The catalyst was a qualifying match for the World Cup of that year, which El Salvador won three–nil. The hapless Honduran fans not only had to watch their team being beaten but then had to run the gauntlet of jubilant and violently hostile El Salvadoreans. Two were beaten to death, dozens wound up in hospital and 150 cars were torched. A few hours later El Salvador invaded Honduras and the Honduran air force commenced a retaliatory bombardment of Salvadorean industrial and strategic targets. Ryszard Kapuscinski, acting on a tip-off, was the sole foreign journalist there, busily wiring back reports to the Polish Press Agency about the sudden and increasingly savage conflict. A small Third World war, a bizarre footnote in twentieth-century history, needless human suffering, observed by a humane, unflinching eye – these are the familiar ingredients, the stock in trade of Kapuscinski's exemplary reportage, a thirty-year-long record of folly, despair, danger and black humour which makes him the doyen of foreign correspondents, and, latterly, with the publication in English of his books – *The Emperor, Shah of Shahs* and *Another Day of Life* – a writer of genuine authority and distinctive, idiosyncratic vision. *The Soccer War* is a collection of his journalism from the sixties and the seventies, interspersed with fragments of reflection and autobiography. And although the book takes its title from an article written about Latin America most of its concerns are African and to do with various disasters that have afflicted that continent since the independence of Ghana in 1957. The book begins and ends in Ghana and in between voyages far and wide: to the Congo at the time of Lumumba's assassination, Algeria during the abduction of Ben Bella, Nigeria in turmoil with the factional strife preceding the Biafran War and the Ogaden in the midst of one of its endless famines.

The Third World is Kapuscinski's personal 'beat'; he has worked in Islamic Russia and the Far East as well as Iran and Latin America but there is something about the quality and feeling of his African reports that seems to set them apart. Or at least so it seems to me, and I don't think this is simply a reader's imputation or fond prejudice operating here. Kapuscinski, on his own evidence, appears to have lived more intensely, suffered more grievously, exposed himself to more danger in the African countries he has reported from than anywhere else on earth. No one writes more effectively of the sweaty cafard, the brutal contingencies, the hilarious and terrifying randomness of events, of the blithe, cruel anarchy of African countries in chaos. But at the same time no one conveys better that seductive allure of the continent, the captivating, tenacious fascination for the place that is always present despite the irritation and despair, and no one better testifies to the stoicism and the dignity that prevail despite the most shocking and casual atrocities.

Kapuscinski remarks in this book that foreign correspondents are not only witnesses to events on behalf of the rest of the world but that they also function as the world's vicarious consciences. The foreign correspondent goes where we are not permitted or would not dare to venture. It is not simply a job or a vocation: the urge to bear witness, to record and report the world's conflicts and conflagrations seems to be an urge, a need, that is impossible to resist. Kapuscinski refers to it as a 'fever' – and the diagnosis appears accurate, for nothing else could explain the extraordinary risks the man takes with his own life other than a temporary dislocation of the senses, a dysfunctioning of normal rational procedures. And here lies a danger: there can be something ghoulish in the need to observe human suffering, to confront the worst excesses of depravity and self-destruction. In eighteenth-century London it was regarded as a fashionable afternoon's diversion to spend an hour or two at Bedlam, the city's asylum, and watch the poor naked lunatics rant and rave. There can be something of the Bedlam-watcher in the foreign correspondent too, particularly where wars are concerned. Here the lethal technology of the twentieth century can add a spurious glamour to the sordid business of people trying to kill each other and the correspondent in this arena can all too easily see himself as a heroic, semi-mythic figure, a pseudo-warrior, one who has been through hell and back, with his sweat-stained fatigues and grim countenance, trudging through the earth's trouble spots with a world-weary, yet indisputably macho swagger. In 1979, James Fenton, a highly distinguished foreign correspondent himself, who had reported the Vietnam War and witnessed the fall of Saigon, rounded on this breed in the *New Statesman*, calling them 'war-freaks', describing them as journalists more interested in the unique and heady sensations of the war-zone – where war is seen and experienced as the 'ultimate trip' – indifferent to its context or conclusion, exulting in its crude power and rabid energy, heedless of the awful human damage being wreaked. All this is by way of defining negatively what Kapuscinski resolutely is not. What makes his work remarkable, it seems to me, is its persistent humanity and concern, and his steadfast refusal to judge or condemn others even when he himself is the potential victim.

In November 1965 Kapuscinski drove from Ghana to Nigeria, passing through Togo and Dahomey. It was a 520-kilometre drive through a West Africa seemingly in a terminal stage of collapse. In each country there was a state of emergency, coups were being hatched, parliaments dissolved, governments falling, heads of state being deposed, all taking place in an atmosphere that was a bizarre amalgam of mad farce and terrible danger. The easy responses in such conditions are either those of disdain or despair but both are shunned by Kapuscinski: no judgement is passed, no facile observation is made. Perhaps this reserve, this effort to understand, exists because Kapuscinski is a Pole. As he reiterates throughout the book his own country's history is as troubled as any African state's: colonized, invaded, subjugated and partitioned. And from this angle, unusual in the West, nothing about Africa's problems and difficulties seems exceptionally perverse or untoward. As a Pole observing Africa Kapuscinski's first inclination is to empathize, not condemn or mock. The effect of this on his writing is to produce its entirely distinctive and beguiling tone, at once cool and detached, self-effacing and sagacious.

This is nowhere more evident than in one of the most extraordinary episodes he relates, in a piece entitled 'The Burning Roadblocks', that took place in Nigeria in 1966. The roadblocks in question were in western Nigeria, Yoruba land, constructed by the members of a political party called UPGA which had won recent elections but, through the trickery of the central government, had been denied power. In its place another party, the NNPD, ruled, courtesy of the central government. UPGA supporters went on the rampage. Roadblocks were set up throughout the country as supporters of the puppet NNPD were sought out and, invariably, killed.

In this terrifying atmosphere Kapuscinski took it upon himself to drive up a minor road to see what was going on. Some would say it was foolhardy; some would say Kapuscinski had a death wish. Kapuscinski explains it thus, quite simply: 'I had to experience everything for myself . . . I had to do it myself because I knew no one could describe it to me.'

I was a teenager living in Nigeria during those years and I still remember the atmosphere of alarm and fear that any long journey by road engendered. As I recall, the way to indicate you were an UPGA supporter was to stick a palm frond or other type of greenery in the radiator grille of your car. This way, it was hoped, you would be waved through any roadblock. You never drove after dark. Then, so terrified rumour had it, political pressure gave way to general banditry and extortion. Burning logs would be placed across the road, when your car stopped the tyres would be slashed by machetes to prevent you escaping, then the gang would gather round . . .

On this particular drive Kapuscinski was halted at three road blocks. At the first he was clubbed with a rifle butt and paid five pounds to join the UPGA. At the second he was hauled from his car, beaten up, robbed of his remaining money and soaked in benzene preparatory to being burned alive. Benzene guarantees complete incineration. But for some reason the mood changed abruptly from manic aggression to wild hilarity. Unbelievably he was allowed back into his car and waved on his way. At the third roadblock he knew he had no option: he put his foot flat down on the accelerator and blasted his way through the flaming barrier.

I smashed into the fire, the car jumped, there was a hammering against the belly pan, sparks showered against the windshield. And suddenly – the roadblock, the fire and the shouting were behind me . . . Hounded by terror, I drove another kilometre and then I stopped to make sure the car wasn't on fire . . . I was all wet. All my strength had left me; I was incapable of fighting; I was wide open, defenceless. I sat down on the sand and felt sick to my stomach.

As indeed does the reader. Kapuscinski's simple, direct style is admirably gripping and powerful and the authenticity of the eye-witness account is stomach-churningly effective. You are in total awe at the astonishing lengths Kapuscinski will go to simply to get a story and at the same time impressed at the modest refusal to capitalize on his temerity. And this particular piece encapsulates the essence of the Kapuscinski approach. It is not about historical analysis, it is about feelings, sensations, the vividity of the singular moment. No one will read 'The Burning Roadblocks' in search of enlightenment regarding political in-fighting amongst Nigerian regional parties in the mid 1960s, but if you want to know what the country was actually like at that time, what the mood was, what particular tensions and anxieties, animosities and fears were in the air, then Kapuscinski is unparalleled.

Indeed this quality applies to all the pieces collected in this fine book. Kapuscinski gallops through the history of the Algerian war but paints a portrait of Ben Bella that is highly individual and immediate. The complexities of Congolese politics are sketched in as background to an article on Lumumba but what lingers in the memory is a wonderful description of a bar in Leopoldville.

And so on. Again and again it is Kapuscinski's feeling for the quiddity of a place, a person or a moment that emerges as trenchant and moving. For a man so widely travelled, who must have seen enough of the world's injustice and misery to last several lifetimes, Kapuscinski's essential magnanimity and sympathy remain a constant behind his writing and irradiate it with a kind of tough, clear-sighted integrity. In one of his personal reflections that punctuate the book (having once more come close to death) he reflects on an unknown official in Leopoldville whose act of kindness, whose selflessness, has saved his life. 'There is so much crap in the world,' Kapuscinski concludes bluntly, 'and then, suddenly, there is honesty and humanity.' True of the world. And true of Africa.

1990

The Sahara

(Review of *The Sword and the Cross* by Fergus Fleming)

The Sahara desert is bigger than the USA. I have flown over it dozens of times – travelling to and from Europe and West Africa in the first half of my life – and so have an abiding sense of its monstrous size and, even from the air, a clear impression of its arid beauty and of the fear it can inspire (truly terrifying turbulence in my case). The other memory it conjures up is of absolute emptiness – perhaps only polar wastes can rival this sense of tracklessness, of human absence. The Sahara seems like the great unpeopled void at the heart of Africa and it's perhaps Fergus Fleming's great achievement that, in this beguiling and fascinating book, he has managed to populate it so thoroughly and substantially.

In the so-called Scramble for Africa that began at the end of the nineteenth century, when the European powers tried to snaffle the toothsome bits of the continent for themselves, nobody was interested in the vast desert that lay between the Mediterranean and the Niger River. Nobody except the French, that is. The Sahara eventually became theirs but almost by accident. They were very reluctant to claim it and, as Fleming shows, the fact that they eventually ended up colonizing the desert – in the shape of southern Algeria and what was then known as the Soudan (today's Mali, Niger and Chad, more or less) – was, astonishingly, largely through the efforts of two men, two of the most unlikely figures in the crowded annals of African exploration.

They were Charles de Foucauld and Henri Laperrine, both of whom seem almost figures from a comic opera: the first a monk, devout to the point of mania, and the second an obsessive martinet soldier. Foucauld is perhaps the most extraordinary, a man who began his career (in the final decades of the nineteenth century) as an obese, dissolute cavalry officer and who transformed himself into an almost caricatured hermit – bearded, emaciated, barefoot and pitilessly ascetic. And it was the Sahara that provoked this astonishing metamorphosis. Stationed with his cavalry regiment in the struggling colony of Algeria, Foucauld became literally smitten with the desert, victim of its potent allure. It is an interesting syndrome, this – somehow the desert enters your soul or else it afflicts you like a toxic drug (as T. E. Lawrence and many others would testify). In Foucauld's case it drove him out of the army and into the arms of God.

Foucauld wanted severity, discipline and relentless mortification of the flesh and thought that the Trappist monks would supply enough dutiful hardship. Having become a Trappist, he found the order simply wasn't tough enough for him (Fleming is very good on the comic implications of all this) so he decided to found an even more severe order for himself. He named it the Little Brothers of the Sacred Heart of Jesus and during his lifetime he was, not surprisingly, its only adherent, though the movement lives on today around the world.

Henri Laperrine also seems straight from central casting: a hard-boiled, emotionless, career soldier for whom the army was everything. He too fell in love with the Sahara and ended up serving there in the loneliest military outpost on earth – Fort McMahon. Laperrine's achievement was to make the military arm of France's colonial expansion south actually function. In the early years of the twentieth century he created a camel corps that could rival the native Tuareg. His fiercely disciplined troops rode fine-boned racing camels, *méharis*, and all the officers had to be fluent Arabic speakers. It was almost a proto-Special Forces unit, capable of travelling immense distances through the desert on minimum rations.

It was Laperrine's idea to bring Foucauld back to the Sahara (they had known each other in the army). He established Foucauld as a benign anchorite figure in Tamanrasset, a forsaken spot sixty days' travel from the nearest French garrison. Foucauld's vaguely defined role was to reassure the bellicose Tuareg that France's interests were not purely territorial. The reputation of the French holy man soon spread and duly had the effect of ameliorating the war-like posture of Laperrine and his dashing *méharistes* as they subdued the Tuareg heartland. The sword and the cross worked effectively together and within a few years France's transSaharan dream – Africa colonized from Algeria to the Congo – was realized.

This summary does little justice to the scale of Fleming's enterprise here. He has written, effectively, a history of French colonization in Africa that runs from the early forays into Algeria (the mid nineteenth century) to the present day, pegging the complex chronicle of events around the lives of these two exemplary men. And it is complex: the arcana of French ambitions and setbacks, annexations and legislations, punitive columns, missions, expeditions and all manner of desperate measures are sometimes hard to grasp (I wouldn't have minded a few more illustrations, either). But Fleming has a sure narrative skill, as well as a prose style of ideal limpidity, and this forgotten corner of African colonial history is perfectly illuminated.

And what of our two heroes? The desert claimed them in the end as, perhaps, they would have wished. Foucauld was killed during a bungled raid by Senoussi tribesmen from neighbouring Tripolitania during the First World War and Laperrine died as a result of injuries received during a plane crash in the depths of the Sahara in 1920. Fittingly, the two men ended up being buried side by side.

Fleming concludes his book with the minatory envoi that the only endemic disease of the Sahara is madness, and there is a deal of insanity in the lives of Charles de Foucauld and Henri Laperrine. The desert does seduce but its realities are harsh and unforgiving and you venture into it at your peril. As we witness current events in another desert on another continent there has never been a more salutary and sobering reminder.

2003

Carving Up Africa

(Review of *The Scramble for Africa* by Thomas Pakenham)

The 'Scramble for Africa' began, according to Thomas Pakenham, in 1876. The Germans had a handy word that summed it up more succinctly – the *Torschlusspanik* – the 'door-closing panic'. There the continent lay, ripe for exploitation, and nobody wanted to miss out. Europeans had been there for many years, of course, but only on the fringes – in Lagos, Zanzibar and Alexandria, for instance – where trade and climate had made a settlement necessary and possible, but, as the last quarter of the nineteenth century approached, they queued up, in an unseemly turmoil, like avid shoppers on the opening day of a sale, to see what they could lay their hands on. The 'shopaholic' analogy is worth pursuing a little further: some of the would-be colonists had vaguely justifiable reasons to be in the race, but others were there fortuitously, simply to partici-pate. There was land to be grabbed, vast tracts of it, and, so they believed, unimaginably large amounts of money to be made, and in their train came the added bonuses of strategic and political influence, of setting the agenda for the power struggles of the new century. And so they moved in on Africa: Britain, France, Belgium, Spain, Portugal, Italy and Germany all at once found themselves involved in an extraordinary 'Sale of the Century'. A whole continent was available – and surely everyone would be able to claim a piece of the action. But the avid metaphors of commerce can only be sustained so far: this was no real sale, there were no real 'vendors'. The multitudinous populations of Africa were not consulted about the identity of their new landlords. Heavy and powerful fists were beating at the door and property was going to be sequestered, like it or not. Suddenly the image of a smash-and-grab raid appears more apposite, and it would take another half century to set that particular injustice right. After a fashion.

A glance at a map of Africa, around about 1912, is a daunting testi-monial to the sheer efficacy and uncompromising nature of that over-whelming urge to stake a claim. We now see that the entire continent, this vast unexplored landmass, most of which, fifty years before, had been *terra incognita*, has been parcelled up. Only two independent states exist: the empire of Ethiopia and the state of Liberia. All the rest belongs to Europe. Thomas Pakenham's fine book tells the story of this particular gold rush with admirable and judicious poise. These four decades of European colonization contain some of the best-known episodes of nineteenth-century history as well as some of the most mythologized and colourful characters the world has ever seen. Pakenham steers us through the familiar and less familiar chapters lucidly and expertly. He is particularly good on the famous battles and short, brutal wars that characterized this period of history – notably Isandhlwana, Tell el-Kebir and the savage genocide of the Herero uprising. We encounter Livingstone and Stanley, Brazza and Rhodes, Kitchener and Gordon, Lugard and Jameson. We relive the seige of Khartoum and the Boer War, the relief of Emin Pasha and the Fashoda incident, and investigate the sinister manipulations of that most malign of colonists, Leopold II, the king of the Belgians.

Inevitably, any attempt to provide a conspectus of these tumultuous decades, however detailed, is bound to be accused of sins of omission. In the last year, for example, I have reviewed a massive life of Cecil Rhodes and a hefty biography of Stanley, both books considerably longer than *The Scramble for Africa*. In order to subsume this type of exhaustive documentation Pakenham has had to condense, summarize and elide constantly, yet there is never any sense of sketchiness or corner-cutting – and the fact that he has brought the book in under 800 pages is a phenomenal achievement. To take one small instance: the annexation of Bechuanaland in 1885 is both a key episode in the career of Cecil Rhodes and also of major importance in the subsequent evolution and history of southern Africa. The bibliography of this forgotten but highly complex episode is considerable – shelves of learned articles and doctorates and at least one highly documented, and excellent, scholarly monograph. Pakenham manages to summarize the whole affair, identify the key players and outline the vital consequences in little more than two highly readable and comprehendable pages. His ability to ingest libraries of primary source material and transform them into a clear, authoritative and compelling narrative is a remarkable talent and one that this book bears witness to again and again.

There was another scramble, of course, this time *out* of Africa, in the eleven years between 1957 and 1968 when the former European colonies emerged as the forty-seven independent nations of contemporary Africa. We may marvel at the pace of change in Eastern Europe today but the speed of transformation that Africa has undergone in just under a century appears, with only a little hindsight, to be even more breathtaking. The twentieth century arrived in Africa with astonishing and devastating pace. For example, the French explorer Brazza (founder of Brazzaville on the Congo) reached that mighty river in 1880 after one of the most arduous and debilitating cross-country treks ever undertaken – he was sick, exhausted, his clothes in tatters. A mere twenty-five years later he passed the same spot sitting on the deck of a double-storeyed steam-powered river boat with an ice-making machine on board. In the light of this incredible velocity – no continent has ever 'fast-forwarded' through history in this way before – Pakenham asks at the end of his book (clearly expecting the answer 'no') whether the Africans of today 'would wish to turn the clock back to the 1880s'. It is a fantastical notion, of course, but I have a feeling that rather more of the continent's inhabitants would like to indulge in that hypothesis than he suspects. The Scramble for Africa, whatever zealous gloss might have been put on it by missionaries such as David Livingstone (by all accounts a thoroughly unpleasant individual) with his idealistic vision of the 'three Cs' that he was bringing to Africa – Commerce, Civilization and Christianity – was at the end of the day far more to do with plain avarice and chauvinistic ambition, and it would be revisionist, not to say wrong, to infer otherwise. It was all about the greater greed and glory of Britain and France, Germany and Belgium and the other Europeans participating in the carve-up. The Africans did not feature in the equation at all.

1992

The African Hundred Years War

(Review of *Frontiers* by Noel Mostert)

This is the epic narration of a war in Africa that lasted one hundred years. It was fought in fits and starts from its first tentative skirmishes in the eighteenth century until it reached its full-blown military denouement in 1877. It took place at the continent's southern tip and embroiled all of southern Africa's tribes and peoples: white and black, coloured and Boer, settler and nomad, English redcoat and Xhosa impi. In the footnotes of imperial history books these bush conflicts were dubbed the 'Kaffir wars' – inglorious, violent, muddled affairs, that brought no particular honour to the British Army (no Victoria Crosses were won) and reflected rather the attentuated, sweaty struggle involved in administering the *pax Britannica*. There were nine of these wars altogether, punctuating the century with savage and absurd regularity, but they have been overshadowed in the popular imagination – in the historian's imagination too – by the more dramatic and compelling Zulu wars of the 1870s and Cecil Rhodes's annexation of Matabeleland.

All this will change now, I should imagine, as a result of this massive, extraordinary and fascinating book. All histories of colonization shame the colonizers and this one is no exception. But *Frontiers'* ambitions are prodigious. Over 1,300 pages, weighing as much as a car battery, its sheer heft and palpable scale provide a daunting objective correlative of its historical claims and scholarly revisionism. For Noel Mostert's grand aspirations are cogently and confidently set down from the outset. Forget other imperial struggles in Africa, he states, the nineteenth-century wars in South Africa's Cape are 'central to the experience of the Atlantic community, or the Western world as it is usually referred to . . .' and, moreover, he will also demonstrate how these wars, this interminable conflict, are 'integral to the confused moral debate about human conscience and the values of empire that arose in the post-abolition world of the nineteenth century.'

These are large claims, but Mostert makes his case not only exhaustively but with skill and passion. They arise from events that took place in a comparatively small area of land around the coast, eastwards from the Cape, on territory demarcated and irrigated by two rivers, the Great

Fish River and the Great Kei River. It was here, more or less, that the crucial frontier was variously to be found between white and black, between the colonists of the Cape and one of the indigenous black peoples of southern Africa, the Xhosa nation. This was the line of confrontation where the battles and skirmishes ensued, the volatile border where colonial expansion met local intransigence and brutal warfare proved to be the only solution to the impasse.

Mostert begins his history some five centuries earlier, however, with a vivid and extensive account of the first visitors to the Cape, the Portuguese, who arrived in 1488. This was a small fleet of three ships commanded by one Bartolomeu Dias. A two-week gale blew them round the Cape and they landed to replenish their water barrels. Natives approached and began hurling stones. Dias picked up a crossbow and shot one of the stone throwers dead. This was the first indigene to be killed by a white man in southern Africa. It hadn't taken long. (Indeed one of the many satisfactions in this book is the way hindsight provides such ghoulish and baleful ironies – the breezes of discord that presage the whirlwind we are reaping today.)

After the Portuguese came the Dutch who planned to use the Cape as a provisioning port-of-call for ships making the long voyage to the East Indies. The little plantation (first established in 1615) did not thrive and the colonizers were reluctant settlers. As they struggled to survive and slowly establish themselves they encountered three distinct native groups: the Bushmen (whose few successors still roam the Kalahari desert), the Khoikhoi (known disparagingly as Hottentots) and, a little further north, the handsome, prosperous and peaceful Xhosa, leisurely following their vast herds of cattle from grazing ground to grazing ground.

As with all incipient colonies at first some sort of coexistence appeared possible. There were occasional flare-ups and hostilities but by and large this curious new white tribe posed no real threat, even when pastoralist Boers began to move out of the Cape settlement into the hinterland during the 'long quietude of the eighteenth century'. In fact at this stage there was little to separate Boer and Xhosa in terms of way of life. It centred round their beasts and their needs; it was tough, secular, communal and distinctly un-European in character. Families slept together in crude huts, miscegenation was frequent and unstigmatized. The Boers, like the Xhosa, wanted only to lead their own lives, free from external influence and control.

All this changed at the end of the eighteenth century, more or less when the British arrived, and took over from the Dutch as the colonial power in the Cape Colony. After 'a century and a quarter of slothful and haphazard presence in South Africa' the remorseless northward drift of the whites had begun to penetrate the traditional Xhosa grazing lands. Cattle-raiding, farm-burning and skirmishes forced the government of the day to try and determine where the colony ended and a rudimentary frontier was posited. What this meant, of course, was that the Xhosa had to yield. They were to be encouraged to move north of the Great Fish River. If they wouldn't move they would be 'dislodged'. The hundred years war had begun.

The story of the nine 'Kaffir' wars between the whites and the Xhosa is the main burden of Mostert's history. Essentially, all the wars followed the same pattern. As a result of repeated provocation and encroachment the Xhosa would take to arms and attack white settlements. Commandos – groups of armed horsemen – would be raised (in the early days) in reprisal and Xhosa kraals would be attacked and their cattle driven off and seized. There would follow some terrifying ambuscades and hand-to-hand fighting in the bush before exhaustion set in and some sort of peace would be made and the frontier redrawn, inevitably to the Xhosa's disadvantage.

By 1828 the Cape had become a fully-fledged British colony and the subsequent wars and the subsequent destruction of the Xhosa people take on a different character. Now professional British soldiers marched against black insurgents and the violence and blood-letting remorselessly escalated on both sides.

No summary can do justice to the vividness and detail of Mostert's patient documentation of this tragic crescendo, nor can one do more than indicate the wealth of character and incident that this turbulent period of history throws up. Certain personalities emerge, on both sides, as key players in the drama. Harry Smith, a coarse, stupid and colourful British soldier determined 'to put the kaffir in his place'. Andries Stockenstrom, a wise and humane Dutchman endlessly trying to mediate between settler and Xhosa. The Xhosa chiefs themselves, Maqoma, Ngqika and Hintsa, shrewd and proud. And the missionaries, the soldiers, the farmers and their families all trammelled up in the endless cycle of war and pillage.

In retrospect we can now see that the penultimate frontier war, the eighth, proved to be the most significant. It lasted twenty-eight months, the longest war in South Africa's history (longer than the Boer War), and was its most bloody and devastating. It cost the British government £2–3 million to prosecute and 16,000 Xhosa died compared to 1,400 on the colonial side. The carnage and turmoil were to have a more bizarre and terrible side-effect on the Xhosa people. As if in response to the virtual disintegration of their way of life a millennial fervour arose en masse amongst a majority of the tribe. A young girl called Nongquwuse claimed to have seen a vision that promised the resurrection of the Xhosa and their eventual triumph. The British would be swept into the sea and new cattle would replace the old herds. The great day was proclaimed as 18 February 1857. Two suns would rise that day as a signal that the new order was about to begin. In preparation the Xhosa began killing their cattle and ceased to sow and reap grain. As an example of mass hypnosis this shocking self-immolation of the Xhosa is virtually unparalleled in human history. With the cattle slaughtered and the grain stores empty the Xhosa gathered on hilltops to watch two suns rise. As the day dawned, bright and completely orthodox, and the solitary sun marked its regular trajectory across the African sky the Xhosa nation knew that its time was over. Appalling famine and fatalities completed the job that one hundred years of frontier warfare had only partially achieved. Forty thousand are believed to have died in the famine and the survivors were dispersed about the colony as menial labourers. The first and most tenacious frontier to the north had been breached. The white tribe was moving on. Now it was the turn of the Zulus and the Matabele.

1992

FILM

As I began to write and publish my novels I always hoped that this would encourage a door to open to the world of cinema. And it did, relatively quickly, thanks to the arrival of Channel 4 and their decision in their first season of 'Film on Four' to ask non-film writers to write a film for their new channel. I was duly commissioned and the first film to be made from one of my scripts was Good and Bad at Games in 1982. Since then twelve of my scripts have made it to the screen, one of which — The Trench — I also directed. I suppose I must have written some three dozen scripts in total over the years since Good and Bad at Games. A success ratio of one-in-three is actually not bad going for a screenwriter. The debilitating aspect of the job is that so much of the work you do goes both unseen and unpublished, therefore the key thing, from my point of view, is that films must be made from time to time: otherwise all the effort and frustration that inevitably comes with the job begins to take its toll. Luckily enough — and a lot of luck is involved — I seem to have been able to keep that sporadic momentum going. An added bonus for a moonlighting novelist is that the film world provides a refreshing sense of collegiate mutual endeavour. After the long solitary work required on a novel it is a pleasure to collaborate. Equally, after collaboration, it is a pleasure to return to the closed study.

This section opens with a long interview I did for Alistair Owen's book Story and Character (2003) in which he interviewed some ten British screen-writers. I think all of us were delighted with the rare opportunity he provided to make our voices heard.

Making Films

(Interview with *Alistair Owen*)

Do you consider yourself as much a screenwriter as a novelist?
No, I consider myself a novelist, but after spending a year alone writing
a novel I find it tremendously refreshing to hang out on a filmset for
a while. I've always loved movies, and after I'd published my first novel
and a collection of short stories – and my second novel was in the
works – I hoped that this would open the doors to film or television,
but of course they say, 'Have you written a script?' and you say, 'No,
that's what I *want* to do.' I did write a couple of trial scripts which my
agent could show people, but then came a lucky break: Channel 4 started
up and approached non-screenwriters to write scripts, and their remit
was that it had to be British and it had to be contemporary and that
was it.

Why did you choose the subject of public school?
The original plan was to write a series of short stories – I wrote one
called 'Hardly Ever', about putting on a Gilbert and Sullivan operetta,
which was in my first collection – but I decided that I would use some
of my ideas for a film, *Good and Bad at Games*, a very dark piece about
revenge and torture and madness. After that I was approached by an
independent producer, Sue Birtwistle, to do a comedy about public
school, so I wrote a lighthearted look at sexual conditioning, *Dutch Girls*,
and that used up the rest of my material. I published the two scripts,
wrote a long memoir about my own schooldays and discovered that I'd
done what I'd set out to achieve: a completely honest account of what
it's like to be in a single-sex boarding school. Having spent nine and a
half years in one of these institutions, an experience common to a huge
number of writers, it was astonishing to me that if you looked for
anything remotely true or realistic about them in literature, let alone in
film or television, you could count them on the fingers of one hand.
With the exception of *If . . .* , and a TV film which Frederic Raphael
wrote, called *School Play*, everything was a bit Victorian or romanticized.
It's very odd, this absence, a sort of collective act of unremembering by

British artists who will not look closely at these incredibly powerful institutions. My schooldays are a long time ago now, but they still have a resonance – nothing has changed that much. The public life of these schools has changed, in that the kids are more sophisticated and they go home at weekends, but the private life of every closed society is by definition not available for scrutiny and can be a particularly nasty and unpleasant place. It doesn't have to be 1965, it could be 2001.

Your early fiction was compared to the work of Evelyn Waugh, some of which you later adapted into the television dramas Scoop *and* Sword of Honour, *and he also wrote about public school in* Decline and Fall. *Did you want to bring something of his satirical style to these scripts?*
Decline and Fall *is about prep school, which is a sub-category of the genre. Waugh's own diaries, which he kept as a schoolboy, are a harrowing and realistic portrait, and the same savage indignation is at work in *Good and Bad at Games*. It was based on a boy I remember who was hideously persecuted for five years. I always wondered what had become of him, so I invented a fate for this character: he goes mad and exacts revenge. I know quite a few very successful, apparently well-balanced, adults who are still tormented by their schooldays. It does have a profound effect on you, and it was quite a controversial film when it came out. I was actually attacked for it – like a class traitor. *Dutch Girls*, though, is a comedy, and is meant to make you laugh and say how ridiculous it is to bring up boys with this attitude. There are satirical elements in it, but I want all my work to be grounded in the real. However dark or absurd it is, I don't want it to take off into fantasy or magic realism. I'm very pleased with the films. They're still requested by schools, and I go and talk about them.

What did you learn from working with directors Jack Gold and Giles Foster?
I learned how the industrial process of film-making can influence the way it turns out on-screen. Because they were television films – and because I've always worked with people I've got on well with – my role was far more respected than if I'd started out writing for the movies. I was a welcome presence, as involved as I wanted to be, and in fact on both films I was on set almost every day. They were original scripts, so I was the source of all wisdom, and they're very close to what was written. But once you know how a film is physically made that shapes

a lot of your thinking, especially if you're working on a low-budget independent movie.

Scoop *was your first experience of adapting a classic. How did you find it?*
When I saw the finished film, I said to Sue Birtwistle and the director, Gavin Millar, 'You can relax. Not even the most dyed-in-the-wool Waugh pedant is going to object to this.' And boy was I wrong. It got a real hammering. It's never been repeated, unfortunately, but I still think it's a good adaptation: lavish, brilliantly acted, faithful to the narrative shape of the book and true to the spirit of Waugh. One of the only things I left out was a literary joke. William Boot writes his country column about the badger, and his sister changes the word 'badger' to 'great-crested grebe'. It's hilariously funny, but the only way it can work on-screen is if you show the words – which is manifestly not filmic. But there seems to be something about Evelyn Waugh which gets the most jaded hack asking to write a piece for their editor. Having been a TV critic for two years with the *New Statesman*, I know the thought processes that go on, and when we were really pleased with *Sword of Honour*, I said, 'Beware!'

In fact, you were one of the few critics who disliked the TV adaptation of Brideshead Revisited.
I was teaching at Oxford at the time and knew the novel inside out, so I was probably a bit self-righteous. It was a memorable event in television history and was compelling in its own way. It was nine hours long, which seems extraordinary today. Again, the problem is one of adaptation. It's a first-person novel, so everything is in the voice of Charles Ryder, which is why there was masses of voiceover.

What do you think of voiceover, by and large?
Voiceover is one of the tools in your toolkit and should be employed whenever it works well. I remember having an argument with someone who put money into *The Mission*. He said, 'I didn't have the faintest idea where this country was.' I said, 'Why didn't they use a map?' Shock! Horror! I'm a great believer in maps or captions if they do the job, otherwise you have to explain it all with dialogue. 'Of course, you used to be the ambassador to Indo-China and then you were fired. What

was it for, now? Yes, it was because of . . .' That's classic bad screen-writing, and you can cut through that nonsense by putting, say, 'The Libyan Desert – 1942'. Captions are very succinct and very effective. With voiceover, however, I think there are certain ground-rules. It should be present from the start: often it's a rescue attempt, bolted on here and there, and usually that doesn't work. I've been guilty of this myself, so I know what's involved. And it should have nothing to do with what's happening in the scene: there's nothing worse than seeing a man going into a house and hearing him say, 'When I went into my house . . . All this is to do with the problems of adapting for film. No one goes to see Verdi's *Falstaff*, then comes home to compare it to *The Merry Wives of Windsor*. No one goes to see the ballet of *Eugene Onegin* then comes home and compares it to Pushkin's epic poem. The two art forms are allowed to coexist. But the first thing people say about a film adapta-tion of a novel is, 'Why did you leave out the bit about . . . ?' It's a mistake, a complete category error. 'Did it work as a film?' is the ques-tion you should be asking, and if you say, 'Yes, I enjoyed myself and I was engaged,' end of story. Having been a victim on numerous occa-sions of that sort of critical misunderstanding, I feel this can't be said often enough. You have to make it work as a film, not as a simulacrum of the novel. The two forms are quite distinct, and there are different aesthetic pleasures to be derived from each.

Scoop *was adapted from a single novel into a single drama.* Sword of Honour *was adapted from three novels into two parts totalling four hours, with adverts, yet a trilogy would seem to lend itself to three parts. Whose decision was that?* It was Channel 4's decision. Initially they asked for six times one hour – it was going to be weekly – but then there was a change of thinking: 'Channel 4 audiences do not tune in every Sunday night to watch the classic serial, so could we do it as two film-length episodes back to back on consecutive nights?' For me, having written my six-hour version, moving the goalposts in this way was something of a kick in the teeth, but in fact I think it was the right decision. I said to the director, Bill Anderson, 'This is the David Lean version. Think of it as *Lawrence of Arabia*.' And, of course, when you think of it like that you can strip away all the stuff which you'd normally do in a leisurely TV way and concentrate on the essence of the story. The novels are wonderful but incredibly uneven, full of longueurs. Guy Crouchback's war is essentially Evelyn Waugh's, and when Waugh was bored rigid from 1942 to 1944 there's an enormous sag in the books. He left a seven-year gap after writing Volume Two, and was jaded and embittered and close to the end of his life when he wrote Volume Three, but because we had our new format we were able to make the narrative lines more graceful and more telling. But there's a lot left out.

Whether it's six hours or four hours it's still a difficult story to tell because it's about lives intersecting randomly, one of your favourite themes.
To a certain extent that's my interpretation of it. Evelyn Waugh might disagree with me. What makes the books endure, I think, is that they're like an English *Catch-22*. War is horrifying. Armies can't function. You think something is going to happen and the opposite will happen. You try to be brave but you're forced to be a coward. These are very cynical, disenchanted, Joseph Helleresque points of view. Waugh would argue, as he did in the preface to the novels, that he was actually writing about the collapse of Roman Catholic values in contemporary Britain, but what you take away from the trilogy now is its modernity, its sense of the cruel and absurd, its dark and ruthless observation of human beings in a war zone. I stressed that angle because as a devout atheist I wasn't remotely interested in Evelyn Waugh's tormented workings-out of a Catholic gentleman attempting to cling on to his faith when the hideous modern world was trying to trample it underfoot.

Did you tailor the script to suit the budget?
I don't think you really do tailor your first draft because these decisions often come later on, but you know you're not making *Gladiator*, and you don't have $185 million to spend, so you save your bravura shots for things you can actually deliver. The Battle for Crete was going to be our big set-piece and would need a cast of thousands, so there was no point in writing earlier, 'A convoy steams over the horizon and we see it from the coast of Africa.' That's just common sense. But because of special effects you can now do stuff which looks fantastic. We had two Dakotas, one with American markings and one with RAF markings, but we couldn't get a Stuka in Majorca because Spanish air-traffic control wouldn't allow us to fly one into their airspace. So we did the Stuka attack with CGI and it actually looks better, because we had *three* Stukas coming out of the sky. These decisions are often taken on the

hoof. You don't really think about them when you're writing. But there is a scene on board a destroyer off the coast of Africa, and I knew that could be done on a blue screen, so the whole scene was written shooting out, as it were, from two men leaning on a railing. It works well, it looks great, it didn't cost a lot and it's underpinned in the writing by a sense of, 'What's the best way of shooting this that will give us the biggest bang for our buck?'

Do you prefer writing for the big screen or the small screen?
I would never say, 'I'll only write movies,' like certain actors say, 'I don't do television.' It's really a question of what works best – and what's available – although for me that choice is a luxury because I'm primarily a novelist: that satisfies so many urges and needs.

Mister Johnson *and* Aunt Julia and the Scriptwriter *were based on novels by Joyce Cary and Mario Vargas Llosa which both feature highly exotic settings, something they share with your own fiction. Is that why you were approached?*
Commissioned work is often very attractive because the book appeals to your tastes or chimes with your interests. *Mister Johnson* is set in Nigeria, and I'd lived in Nigeria and written an introduction to the Penguin World Classics edition of the book, so it was an easy decision. *Aunt Julia* came about as a result of my relationship with David Puttnam, because the adaptation of my novel *Stars and Bars* was with his company, Enigma, before he went off to run Columbia Pictures. It was suggested that I might be the person to adapt it, so I read it and loved it but knew it was going to be a bold adaptation. By then it was no longer at Columbia but with an independent company, and they said it could be set anywhere in America but not in Peru, so it seemed to me that New Orleans delivered the same polyglot mix as Lima. That was one of those nice jobs which comes your way, and the relationships I built up at that time endure to this day. Mark Tarlov, who produced *Aunt Julia*, also produced *A Good Man in Africa*, and we have any number of irons in the fire.

I believe you actually discussed the changes to Aunt Julia *with Vargas Llosa.*
Yes, I did. There's a character in the novel who writes soap operas for the radio, about fifteen different stories which get progressively more

surreal and outlandish, and there was no way the film could cope with that. Vargas Llosa, who had approved the Americanization of the novel, just said, 'Go for it. Do the best you can.' He knew the book would be respected and he was very pleased with the film. What got him furious was that the American distributor changed the title to *Tune In Tomorrow*. It was a real no-brainer, but they thought that they had a comic hit on their hands and they felt that the original title was a bit too arthouse. I protested vehemently; Vargas Llosa refused to have anything to do with it; the film did no business at all; and every review started with, 'What idiot changed the title?' But it's good work and I'm proud of it. I've got a full-page ad for the film from *The New York Times* which is chock-a-block with raves. We got across-the-board raves for *Mister Johnson*, as well – Bruce Beresford said he's never had such good reviews – but it didn't even do a million dollars' business in the US. It did nothing here. It played for just four weeks in one cinema. If you looked up *Mister Johnson* on some database of US critics you'd say, 'Why didn't this film do better?' Well, because of the financial precariousness of the distributor, and the fact that the guy at Fox who commissioned the movie had been fired. The main achievement was to get the films made, so I'm quite philosophical about these things.

Three of your novels have been filmed: Stars and Bars, A Good Man in Africa *and* Armadillo. *Are you able to take more or less licence with your own work?*
More licence. Because the book is always there, the adaptation is a wonderful bonus and I can authorize myself to strike a pencil through this or that character and this or that episode. I also find that as soon as a character becomes flesh and blood, once you see the contribution of a talented actor in the role, all sorts of beneficial and productive things can suggest themselves. A minor character can bloom with the right casting, and you might exploit that by bringing them into a scene and giving them lines to say. In *A Good Man in Africa*, Sean Connery brought something to the role of Dr Murray which simply wasn't there on the page. So we worked on his part together, and wrote a few more gags for Dr Murray, because it would have been a terrible shame not to exploit that acerbic and laconic sense of humour.

How did you stay philosophical when Stars and Bars *and* A Good Man in
Africa *failed both critically and commercially?*
They were not great critical or commercial successes, but I don't think
of them as films which have failed. Bits of them don't work, but they
both have tremendous casts and they're both really entertaining, which
is not bad given the vagaries of the business. Again, getting the films
made was probably the great achievement. We had hellish problems
setting up *Stars and Bars*, then it was flushed down the toilet by Columbia,
post-Puttnam, so it never had a chance. It might have been ahead of
its time. If a quirky comedy about an Englishman abroad had been
released in 1999 instead of 1988, it might have been seen in the context
of all these British films which play to their strengths in the same way.
Lots of works of art are perceived not to have delivered at the time of
their presentation to the marketplace but can be savoured later on, when
all the fuss has died down. The effect of criticism is transient and
ephemeral, but these films pop up on television in their post-release life
and are watched and appreciated. You want everything you do to be as
big a success as possible, but you should also be trying to make the best
film that you can. If you try to second-guess the market and write a
sub-Hannibal Lecter film and it bombs, then you must feel like a
complete whore, but if you've done your best and you're pleased with
the film, then it has to take its chances. *The Trench* didn't get a US
distributor, but there's nothing I can do about that. It's the film I wanted
to make and if it's too dark and sad to play commercially then so be
it. You're striving all the time – I think this is true of every artist – to
be popular *and* preserve your integrity: 'Can I have both, please?'

*That aspiration was certainly true of Charlie Chaplin, whose life you tackled
for Richard Attenborough. What attracted you to that project?*
It came at a very good time for me because I'd just finished writing
Brazzaville Beach, my brain was empty and I literally had nothing to do.
Everybody knows a bit about Chaplin – about 'The Tramp' and United
Artists – but the true story is unbelievably dark and intense. 'The Tramp'
was not Charlie Chaplin. He was very left wing but ran his studio like
a fascist dictator. He was vastly wealthy and became obsessed with young
girls. Having written *The New Confessions* by then, I found that whole
period of American film-making fascinating. Also I really, really liked
Dickie. You think, 'I get to work with Richard Attenborough. How

fantastic is that?' He has this habit of saying, 'Steve used to say to me
. . .' and you think, 'Who's Steve?' and after a while you realize it's Steve
McQueen. He has a phenomenal history, he's known everybody and is
an amazing man.

In The New Confessions, *you had several hundred pages to explore the life
of its fictitious director. In* Chaplin, *you only had three hours or so.*
The biopic is the hardest genre to pull off without it ending up as some
sort of documentary. Again, it's an adapting problem, but instead of
having a book to adapt you have a life, so it becomes a question of
choosing key moments or filmically interesting moments and somehow
alluding to the rest. The studio executive on the project, Barry Isaacson,
came over here and we thought, 'Let's choose a template, given what
we know about the man.' We decided to choose *Raging Bull* – which
sounds silly, but that film also covers a long period and is very dark and
intense. To a degree, it distorts Chaplin's life just to look at his neuroses,
but that's what's really interesting about the man.

*Presumably the character played by Anthony Hopkins, a book editor going over
Chaplin's autobiography with its elderly author, was invented as the means of
'alluding to the rest'?*
The scenes of Chaplin as an old man were exclusively the work of
William Goldman. I didn't write a single word of them. My first draft
started with Chaplin as a boy of seven, and ended in his late sixties
when he was banished from America. My thinking was that his banishment was the end of the story: 'We made you, so we can throw you
out.' After that he lived in Switzerland and had lots of kids. We thought
that Robert Downey Jr could pick it up at seventeen and age up to
about seventy, but taking it to eighty and having him wear twenty
pounds of prosthetic make-up was stretching credulity a bit far, in my
opinion. The history of the film was fraught, because it collapsed and
Attenborough had to set the whole thing up again. It was ready to go,
but Universal were unhappy with the budget. Tom Stoppard did a pass
at it before they put it in turnaround, then a year later it went to Carolco
and his revisions were lifted out and William Goldman was brought in
to write the extra scenes.

Including the scenes where Chaplin accepts a Lifetime Achievement Oscar?
We always envisaged that as a bookend device: Hollywood admitted that they were wrong and welcomed him back. We showed him preparing for the ceremony, then had a huge flashback, and right at the end he picks up the award.

Were you present while the film was being shot?
I flew out to LA with Dickie to look at the locations, I got to know Robert during the making of it and I went to see it being filmed here. In spite of its terrible ups and downs, a very happy group worked on the film, and what emerged is a really intriguing portrait. It's possibly Attenborough's darkest film, and Downey is absolutely brilliant, but powerful men just wanted to get their fingerprints on it. Look at the first version of *Blade Runner.* 'Let's stick in a voiceover.' Look at the director's cut: you don't need a voiceover. These things happen.

The screenplay credit actually reads . . .
Me, Bryan Forbes and William Goldman. It was decided in arbitration. In theory the first writer should get the first credit, but in fact I was the second writer.

Can you explain how a Writers' Guild credit arbitration works?
There can't be more than three writers credited, unless two of the writers scrabbling for those three credits are a writing team, so if you're claiming a credit you have to write a declaration of why you think you earned it. You never write to claim a shared credit, you always write to demand sole credit, however unjust that may be. And you have to do it, because if you opt out, your credit is gone. You then submit all the drafts of the script you've written, and it goes before a kind of secret Star Chamber court.

Comprising other screenwriters?
The Writers' Guild publish a list. Any member of the Guild could be called upon, but there seem to be about 200 or 300 writers who make up these committees. You don't know who they are, and there's no right of appeal, but certain things usually apply. The first writer nearly always gets a credit, even if there's not a comma of theirs in the script, then

the subsequent writers need to have changed something like thirty per cent of the script to even qualify for consideration. But, by definition, the last writer on the script is going to have more of his work in the film, so if there have been seven or eight writers before him the whole process can be very unfair. There are instances where a well-known writer has written an entire film and not got a credit, and the credited writer has picked up an Oscar or a Golden Globe. It's a source of great bitterness, this tendency to rewrite, and is one of the besetting sins of Hollywood. It pits writer against writer and involves an unseemly scrabble for prominence. I was subsequently asked to rewrite a script – a comedy called *Hot Water*, which has never been made – and I decided to meet the original writer to clear the air and make it non-adversarial. His advice was, 'Tear it apart.' The time when I was rewritten, in the case of *Diabolique*, I withdrew from the arbitration, and they gave sole credit to a very interesting writer, Don Roos. I'd probably have got a credit because I was the first writer on the film, but I didn't want my name associated with it in any way and just thought, 'To hell with this!'

Why is there this tendency to rewrite in Hollywood?
Hollywood is governed by a fear of failure, and what happens is that as a film is being greenlit the studio hires another writer at vast expense – a quarter of a million dollars, half a million dollars, paid by the week – to put in some more gags or to look at the beginnings and endings of scenes, to 'put it through their machine', as the saying goes. Most celebratedly, Robert Towne was called in to polish *The Godfather*, and wrote the scene before Brando keels over in the garden. I won't name any names, but when *Kindergarten Cop* was being greenlit the studio hired a very well-known screenwriter to put in a few more one-liners. The work came in and it was utterly useless, but if you've paid a celebrated screenwriter hundreds of thousands of dollars, what could be wrong with that? I call it the 'only a fool' syndrome. If you've got a really crap script, but Brad Pitt and Julia Roberts will accept huge sums of money to be in it, then, well, only a fool wouldn't make that film. It takes the curse off the decision. And sometimes it pays dividends. If you're a hugely intelligent person, like Tom Stoppard, you can tinker with anything and improve it: come out of this scene a bit earlier, start the next scene a bit later. A script is endlessly malleable. But the process

is driven by a fear of failure, it seems to me, rather than a genuine search for excellence.

In the case of Diabolique, *there was already a classic adaptation of the novel by Boileau and Narcejac, so why did you agree to give it another shot?*
I knew the film well; I didn't go back to the novel. The brief was very clear: update it from fifties France to contemporary America. Again, it was a good moment; I can't remember what I'd just finished. And it was for Warner, who I hadn't worked for. When you take on these studio jobs you look for something challenging. *Chaplin*, *Diabolique* and *The Gunpowder Plot* are all very interesting assignments. In updating an old film all sorts of things had to be considerably altered, while at the same time delivering the mood and the menace of the original. The headmaster's wife dying of fright has to be made ultra-plausible today, so you have to lay in her medical history. And, in contemporary mores, would you tolerate your husband openly sleeping with another teacher at the school? The updating was really quite complex. I did a lot of hard work and wrote a script which everybody seemed pleased with, then the studio put it in turnaround and it was picked up by a large independent company – who brought in Don Roos. I was sent the shooting script when the credit arbitration approached, as I was obliged to be, and it was apparent that they had basically remade the old film. All my stuff, the modernity, the plausibility, had gone, so I said, 'It's all yours.'

How long did it take you to write?
I worked on it for several months, made two trips to LA and did a lot of free work because I liked the producer. You're contracted to do a first draft, a set of revisions and a polish – three passes – but I must have done at least another three polishes to try and get it right. This is another thing the Writers' Guild is up in arms about. Writers want a film to work, and it's very easy for producers to say, 'Maybe if we just fiddle with those scenes in the middle,' so you do the extra, unpaid work in good faith and it turns out to be a waste of time. I now resist polishing and polishing because there will always be more work to do when a director comes on board. It would seem sensible to wait before you say, 'This is the finished script.'

We've talked about the film adaptations of your novels, but you've also written a couple of unproduced adaptations of your short stories. 'Cork', first of all.

In a lot of my short stories, I take real characters and write something fictional about them. 'Cork' was inspired by a Portuguese poet called Fernando Pessoa, who led an extraordinarily schizoid life. He wrote under different pseudonyms – he called them 'heteronyms' – and took on different identities. He'd take on the personality of a rustic pagan poet, for example, and then a tortured intellectual poet, and he'd write in that particular style. It's unapologetically complex, intensely erotic, has an unhappy ending and requires two brave actors. Various directors have been attached to it, and in the course of its life one of the actors we saw was Catherine McCormack. When the project languished, Catherine rang up and said, 'Could I option the script?' I think she was sick to death of the kind of movie roles she was being offered and thought, 'I must find interesting work which I can have some sort of influence over.' I'm often asked to option my short stories and always say no, because you never get them back, but I said, 'Let's see if my producing team, with you added, can put it together.' The more we talked about it, the more we realized she had very strong opinions about it, so Mark Tarlov said to her, '*You* should direct this film.' Of course, I think she was hoping for someone to offer her that, and without a second thought she went for it. The current state of play is that she's going to direct and star in it, which is unusual because not many women do that. It's not unprecedented, but it's a tall order for your first movie as a director. So we now have a script, a producer, a director and a leading actor; we just need to cast the other role and get some money. I've also adapted another of my short stories as a short film, a ten-page script, which in a funny way was more challenging than taking a short story and expanding it.

What was that?

Two young film-makers approached me and asked if they could option a story of mine, 'The Care and Attention of Swimming Pools', about a mad pool-cleaner in LA. I thought the producer wanted to do it as a feature film, but she said she wanted to do it as a short, so I said, 'Why don't I write it for nothing and let's see how we go?' I wrote it, we got it financed, they spent six weeks out in LA setting it up and then it all fell apart. There was a Screen Actors' Guild strike at the time, so the cast and crew were all sitting around, prepared to work for scale, then overnight the strike ended and everybody was working again. Rather than blow the money – there was a lot of private equity involved – the producer thought, 'Let's come back and fight another day.' They were young and very enthusiastic, and I thought, 'I can move this process forward a huge amount by not insisting they pay me to option the story or write the script.' It was just an interesting experiment.

Do you find it more or less satisfying, adapting a story rather than a novel?
More satisfying, in a way, because you tend to add on rather than cut out. If you're looking to literature for inspiration for a film, a short story is better than a novel because you have the germ but there's often not enough material to fill 90 or 100 minutes, so you're forced to open it out and think about other elements which can work filmically. It's more creative expanding something than boiling it down, which is what happens with novel to film adaptations.

Presumably 'Cork' *is a full-length script, ninety pages or so?*
Cork is actually very tight, about eighty pages, but because of the nature of the material it will run to a full-length feature. I used to think 120 pages was about right, but now I think all scripts should be between 90 and 100 pages, because any film which crosses the two-hour barrier brings all sorts of industrial problems in its train. A film will always expand from the script. *The Trench*, which was a ninety-page screenplay, is a ninety-seven-minute film. *The Gunpowder Plot* would be a long film – two hours fifteen, two hours thirty – but the script was only 105 pages, because I knew the film would balloon if it got to 115 or 120. All our scripts for *Armadillo*, which is three one-hour chunks, were fifty-four or fifty-five pages, and as a result we have no length problem. It's better to make these tough decisions on the page than in the cutting room. Of course, there's usually a chunk you can lift out during editing if you have that problem, but it's always soul-destroying to lose a sequence which cost hundreds of thousands and took nine days to shoot – and you can usually spot the joins and have to do a bit of reshooting to smooth things out. In some ways, length depends on the genre. *Chaplin* was always going to be two hours-plus, but a comedy or a thriller which is much over an hour and forty minutes is asking a lot of itself.

Why do you think the scripts you write for yourself to direct are less exotic and more confined than the scripts you write for other people?
It's knowing my own strengths and, by definition, weaknesses. *The Trench* minimized the hassles for me as a first-time director. We shot a lot of it in the studio and it was fantastic working on a set. You started work at eight and knocked off at seven. You didn't have to worry about rain or aeroplanes flying overhead. Offices were there. Cutting rooms were there. It was a great experience and, so, planning my second film, I thought, 'Softly, softly.' This one will be maybe seventy-five per cent studio-based and twenty-five per cent location-based. I won't be going to live in a hotel for six weeks, so I'll be able to do the work without all that endless hanging around involved in film-making. And having cut my teeth on the war movie, I thought that the kind of film I'd like to do next would be a complicated and sophisticated thriller. *Chinatown*, *Body Heat*, *The Parallax View* and *Three Days of the Condor* are films which made a big impression on me. Film does genre really well: that's where it seems to excel and is particularly true to its own art form. I've also got this hankering to make a film about Billy the Kid, which again is genre, but nobody wants to make Westerns these days. I wrote about the Kid in *The New Confessions*, where the hero makes a film about him, and I've read a lot about the real Billy, revolting little scumbag of a human being that he was.

Many screenwriters try their hand at directing in an effort to exercise greater control over their work, but your screenwriting experiences have mostly been very positive – so what drew you to become a director?
I originally wanted to be a painter, so this desire to direct may be satisfying the painterly side of my nature, reflected in the compositional and choreographical elements of film-making. I remember seeing *The Conformist* when I was nineteen, and being struck as much by the look of the film as by the story it was telling. One of my favourite films is *Electra Glide in Blue*, which is beautifully shot and blew me away when I saw it in my early twenties. I think that aspect was drawing me towards being a director rather than thinking, 'I must have more control' – although, of course, directing a film as well as writing it is very alluring. I would never abandon writing novels to become a film director, but, as time has gone by and yet another director drops out of a project, friends have said, 'You should direct this,' and I realized that one day I would direct, but I wanted to do something tailor-made for me. And,

in the end, I enjoyed it so much that I want to do it again. But because I'm a novelist, and have the ultimate creative control there, I don't mind sharing the burden sometimes. I enjoyed the making of *Armadillo*. Howard Davies is a brilliant director, and I've learned a lot from him and other directors. I enjoy being a benign presence behind the scenes and I'll always write scripts for other people to direct, but I would never direct an adaptation of one of my novels and I would never direct a script by anybody else. I would only direct an original script of mine.

Why would you never direct an adaptation of one of your novels? An adaptation of your second novel, An Ice-Cream War, *has spent many years in development hell, for example. Why not take the director's chair for that film?*
Because I know what's involved in adapting. For me, creatively, it's truer and fairer to the art form to write something which is purely a film. *The Trench* can sit on the shelf with any of my novels because, although it's a huge collaboration, it's exactly as I hoped it would be. I couldn't say that a film version of *An Ice-Cream War* would be part of my body of work in the same way.

You could direct The Galapagos Affair, *too. What prompted you to option such dark and difficult material yourself?*
I have a desert-island obsession. These myths are buried deep within us: *Robinson Crusoe*, *Swiss Family Robinson* and so on. I read a review of John Treherne's book and thought, 'What an extraordinary story.' A nymphomaniac baroness, an American millionaire in his white yacht, the mad German philosopher who swaps partners; the ingredients intrigued me. And at this stage in my screenwriting, I was thinking about optioning books to give myself more independence. The book had in fact been optioned by Nic Roeg and the option had lapsed, so I took it over and wrote a script, then set about seeing if I could find a producer and director. It eventually wound up at Working Title, and Tim Bevan and Mel Smith were hugely taken with it. We worked on it for a long time and they spent a lot of money – Mel had even done location recces in Australia – and then it all fell apart because of the nature of the material. It revived with Sarah Radclyffe as producer, but by then the PolyGram writing was on the wall, and because I'd signed no contract and received no money, I was able to take the book and script away and live to fight another day. I occasionally think about directing it, because

it's been on the go since 1985, but again it's an adaptation, and something makes me think that any films I direct will be original.

Have you learned anything from writing these original screenplays for yourself to direct which you can bring to bear on writing adaptations for other people?
I really don't know. I'm reluctant to create rules like, 'If you're writing a scene and it's seven pages long and it isn't over yet then you're in trouble,' because in fact you may not be. Or to insist, 'Don't put in any camera moves,' because camera moves might actually be useful. But I'm now much more aware of the issue, 'Is this going to be a problem to shoot?' When I was writing for other people, that was their problem not mine. Take a dinner-party scene, for example, with ten people chattering away around a table. There's really only a bog-standard way of filming that kind of scene, and because I know how long it takes and how much coverage you have to shoot and how it still looks like a bunch of people talking at a table, I now think, 'Maybe this scene shouldn't take place at a dinner party after all. Maybe it would be more interesting if they were walking through a park.' It's not going to justify the sheer effort of shooting it, because you can do it in a more elegant or intriguing way. If you look at the opening of *Reservoir Dogs*, Tarantino set himself exactly that problem and obviously thought, 'To hell with this', and got someone to walk round and round with a steadicam. If you weren't in shot when you were talking and he didn't have coverage for it, so what? It's actually quite a good way of shooting a lot of people talking at a table, although you may find when you come to cut it that a really crucial line is masked by somebody's head, whereas if you'd storyboarded it and shot it from five or six different static positions you'd have got your coverage. The directorial influence makes itself felt more in the details than the big picture. Some establishing shots are key, for example, but do you really need to see people arriving in their cars and unlocking their front doors? You know you'll cut that during editing, so why write it in the first place? Unless you happen to be Michael Mann and have seven cameras running simultaneously, there's no interesting way of shooting someone arriving home. So maybe a better way of writing a scene like that is to have someone inside the house hearing the car pull up, followed by the driver bursting through the front door. Everyone will be able to envisage what happened outside. That sort of writing decision is all as a result of having stood behind a camera.

The vast majority of your scripts are adaptations. Do you think that Hollywood somehow perceives British screenwriters as more literary?
I think that's a fair point. Maybe the classic serial generates that feeling. *Masterpiece Theatre* is hugely popular in America. But I also think it's an industry-wide taste – or problem. For every original script commissioned there are four or five adaptations. Again, it's driven by this fear of failure: 'It's a really successful book. Let's make it into a movie.' The art of film is not best served by constantly doing adaptations, because of the problems inherent in shifting from one form to the other. It's like putting pop songs on soundtracks. Isn't it better to have a proper score? Isn't that what film music is all about? It's not about taking ten hit records and sticking them on so you get a great CD. Similarly, I feel, in a vaguely purist way, that film is best served if the script was always destined to be a film.

Which, looking at your filmography, is rather ironic.
That's my point. That's the nature of the beast. I bet most screenwriters would rather write something based on their own ideas than on this best-selling novel or that work of non-fiction. It's not just books; they're adapting TV shows, comic strips, other films. *Traffic* is an adaptation of a British television series. That's why, in any scriptography, there will always be three to one in favour of adaptations. I was quite lucky that the first two scripts I did were original scripts. I think you have to separate adaptations and original scripts, because there are totally different sets of mental gears engaged in producing them.

How quickly did you adapt to writing scripts?
You can learn the grammar of a screenplay incredibly quickly. That's why there are so many screenwriters out there. Any resting actor can produce a screenplay which looks exactly like a Robert Towne screenplay in terms of format but ultimately you have to fall back on whatever storytelling ability you have. You also have to understand what you can do with film and what you can't. You'd have to be a very talented director, for example, to make a forty-five-page dialogue scene work. My advice to aspiring screenwriters is that if you see a film you really like, get hold of the screenplay and read it watching the movie simultaneously, with the remote control close at hand. You begin to understand the rhythms and cadences of film. Why is this scene so arresting?

Stop. Rewind. Look again. Because you're hearing this person talking, but you're actually seeing the other person listening. And you realize it's much more powerful that way. You learn.

Though that might not be written down.
It's surprising how much is written down. I know, having directed myself, that you do a master shot and close-ups and reverses so that you can cut it any way you want. But if, for example, one character is announcing the news of the other character's wife's infidelity, then you will often write in the script, 'Hold on a big close-up of John.' That's simple storytelling. It's more important to see John's reaction than it is to see Fred speaking the words. And if you, the writer, think the moment should be played that way, then you haven't even got a chance of getting it done like that if you don't write it down. The rule of thumb is: if you want it in the film, make sure it's in the script. Of course, stuff that's in the script often doesn't get shot, which is particularly galling for the writer. You come to the editing stage and say, 'Where's that close shot of Sally turning round as he walks off?' 'Oh, we never did it.' 'But it's on page forty-three.' 'Well, we were pressed for time.' But a good film writer will put these shots in, all the same.

Or not, depending on the advice you listen to. Aspiring screenwriters are often told precisely the opposite: the fewer camera directions the better.
In fact, the first screenplays I read were by Harold Pinter, who's extremely sparing with directions, so my first screenplays were similarly spare. I don't think William Goldman even puts scene headings in, it's just 'Cut to . . .' But there are moments where a scene has no dialogue so you have to write directions, and you would be better off writing them in a way that you think they would be well shot.

Of course, a script – particularly a spec script – isn't simply a blueprint for a film, it's also a sales tool for a project, so it has to be as readable as it is shootable. For example, directions in parentheses to indicate how the dialogue should be spoken.
It's called 'grandstanding' in Hollywood. When I was writing for Universal and Warner it was understood that this kind of thing would go in. It makes an easier read for overtaxed executives, because you're

telling them what the emotion is and they don't have to deduce whether a character is happy or sad. Now, because I've worked more with actors and I understand an actor's take on a script, I tend to strip that stuff away. Actors hate things like, 'Ted (with a thin smile)', because you're saying, 'This is how I want you to act it.' But if you're writing a film for a Hollywood studio you write it in a different way. A script has to be so many things in its life, and is going to be read by so many people who have a vested interest in saying no, that you want to give it your best shot – and there are all sorts of ways you can garnish it so it seems user-friendly. Hollywood is very conventional, in its own way. They want the script to be presented in the right typeface – Courier – to be printed on the right paper – American letter-size is not the same as our A4 – and to be bound with three clips – brass not silver – else they'll say, 'Foreign', and throw it away. British screenwriters who take their scripts down to Kall Kwik and get a plastic binding are handicapping themselves. When I was writing a lot in Hollywood, I used to buy great stacks of American paper and brass clips precisely so that it 'looked right'.

You also get the impression from screenwriting manuals that if the spec writer doesn't place the heroine in jeopardy on page twenty then the executives aren't going to read any more of the script. Or even that much.

And not just spec writers. As a gun-for-hire screenwriter you can find yourself having to do things which you regard as mind-bogglingly stupid to satisfy some berk at the studio. In my opinion, these screenwriting courses are designed so executives can come back from them and say knowing things to writers about 'character arcs' and 'three-act structure'. It's just jargon, really. Why not have a five-act structure, like Shakespeare? I don't know any screenwriter who doesn't regard these courses as laughable, but they have to take the jargon on board because they know they'll go into meetings with people who'll be spouting it. Fundamentally, all these decisions are to do with telling a story. Does the story demand that the heroine should be in jeopardy after twenty minutes? That's the only true criterion.

Do you have a rigid writing routine?

I do for writing novels. I have the same approach for screenwriting, to a degree, in that I spend a long time figuring everything out before I start. That's true whether it's an adaptation or an original. As a rule, I make notes and draw diagrams and do scene lists, so that when I sit down to write the script I have the whole thing planned. From page one, I know exactly how it's going to end. Then I write the first draft as quickly as possible, which may only take two or three weeks, because compared to a novel a screenplay is so short. There are maybe 10,000 words in a screenplay: a couple of chapters, if that. And then I can look at the 110 pages and reorder them and fiddle around with them. That's where the similarity ends, in a way, because the script is now at a stage to show people and talk about. It's unfinished in the sense of, 'Who's going to direct it?' or, 'Who's going to put money into it?' You know that there's going to be more changes required, so you consciously don't make it word perfect.

Though you have said that the first draft should be fairly close to the final draft.
I think so. You shouldn't submit a first draft which wouldn't make a perfectly good film. There are always changes – often nothing to do with the story but to do with the input you get from the producer and the director and the actors – but if in a parallel universe the film company said, 'We'll make this,' the draft which you present should be the film which you want, not just something 'along the right lines'. Then, if you're going to make changes, they're usually not substantial. One of my working maxims is, 'All intelligent suggestions gratefully received,' but if you present something which is polished then it has to be really quite a bright idea for you to say, 'Actually, you're right.' If somebody says, 'I don't like the ending,' you say, 'Why? Come up with a better one.' That sort of script note drives you mad: 'I just feel the character of Julie isn't sufficiently developed.' 'Really? In what particular areas? Because I think she's pretty damn developed.' There's an endless process of tinkering required as the various investors are given notes by their script readers, and one of the main attractions of being a writer–director is that you can say, 'The director is very happy with this script as it stands.' But if you're working with people you're sympathetic with, that process is mostly beneficial. We did a lot of work on *Armadillo* before we submitted it to the BBC, so the notes which came back were pretty valid – or else we had cogent counter-arguments if we thought that some suggestion was a mistake.

When you choose to adapt something or are offered something to adapt, do you respond to the material in an emotional or an intellectual way?

I suspect the two are related. If a story appeals to me, it's bound to have things in common with the stories I write myself, to a greater or lesser degree. As a novelist you always write the books that you would like to read yourself, so that feeling probably governs your choice of commissioned work too: 'I wouldn't mind seeing this movie.' I don't think I would write a horror film, for example, because I don't particularly enjoy that genre, but there are all sorts of other genres I *would* tackle. You might not think I'd like to write a Western, but I've got this very dark Western in mind. Your choice is shaped by your own tastes and inclinations, and if you're not intrigued or stimulated then sure as hell the work you do is going to be similarly lacklustre.

2001

The Trench

The First-time Film Director: An A–Z

Anxiety. No, let's not beat about the bush, high anxiety. It is 6.30 in the morning, early in November 1998, and I am being driven down the M4 towards Bray Studios, near Windsor, where, in an hour or so, we will begin filming my first film as director, *The Trench*. What am I thinking about? The first shot? No. I spent two months last summer storyboarding the entire film. I have planned every single shot – from the bravura to the minuscule – the film demands. So why am I so nervous? Maybe because I am starting, the new boy, and everybody else, who is hugely experienced, will be watching to see what I do and how I perform. I feel the indigestion mount and suck on a mint. I sense the worry in me course through my body like a bacillus, curdling my blood.

Blood is one of the easiest things to arrange on a filmset. *The Trench* is a war movie, about forty-eight hours in the life of very young soldiers waiting to go over the top before the Battle of the Somme in 1916. Despite this we don't have much call on blood. Annie Buchanan, our make-up supremo, has gallons. Sometimes we just need a dribble but for one scene we need masses. Annie and her assistants come in with a lapping baby bath full of the stuff and buckets of what looks like the sweepings from an abattoir. I want this particular scene to shock, I want to see, literally, blood and guts. As the butcher meat begins to be strewn around I wonder if I have gone too far. Too late. The die is cast.

The cast is very young, eighteen-, nineteen-year-olds, most in their early twenties. We forget how young soldiers are and there is no disguising a genuinely youthful face, that innocent incongruity beneath a tin helmet. I ask one actor what he is doing after the film and he tells me he is going back to school. At rehearsals they are polite but guarded, as if curious to see how I will set about directing.

Directing struck me as a major challenge, despite the fact that I had written eight scripts that were turned into films and had hung around a lot, asking questions and undergoing, I suppose, a kind of education.

David Mamet said that all the first-time director has to do is show up
and be civil. I think it's a little more stressful than that. The key thing,
it seems to me, is to know exactly what you want (even if it is hugely
ambitious). If you know what you want to do, then at least you can
answer the several hundred questions that come your way each day. I
was massively, preposterously overprepared: working on the theory that
in order to catch me out you'd have to get up exceptionally early.

Early rises are a nightmare, especially for the lazy, spoilt, self-indulgent
novelist. I used to wake up at 5.30 each morning, go through the day
ahead, and record into a dictaphone the events of the day before (this
turned out to be the most turgidly boring journal ever). At about 6.15,
the car was there and I was ready for some food.

Food is another filming problem. The key aim is to keep your weight-
gain under a stone. Food is constantly available: bacon butties, sausage
butties, biscuits, coffee for days, lunch, sandwiches, Mars bars, more coffee,
more sandwiches. I had the same lunch every day for six weeks – baked
potato and baked beans – it was the only way I could keep control of
the waistline (it's a very high-fibre meal), the only way I could keep a
grip.

Our grip was called Dave Appleby, whom everyone called Applebox,
for some reason. The grip pushes the dolly – a little wheeled cart-thing
– that the camera is mounted on. Our dolly, however, had a socking
great crane and a remote control camera dangling from it so we could
weave through the trenches as if a disembodied spirit. We asked Dave
Applebox to do some highly complicated manoeuvres. He didn't turn
a hair.

Haircuts in 1916, by one of the cyclical accidents of history, bore a
remarkable resemblance to haircuts in 1998: very short back and sides,
very short on top. I have a photograph of a World War One soldier
with a mohican – he could be in Vietnam. We had our actors' hair cut
to the bone every week. They looked good in their uniforms; in their
civilian clothes the shorn look gave them a kind of innocence.

Innocence seems to me the abiding feature of the Battle of the Somme,
and its sibling, Ignorance. The war had been going on for two years yet

everyone – from the generals to the private soldiers – thought the battle would be a walkover. They thought the week-long barrage before it started would kill every German soldier opposite. They didn't know the Germans could descend to deep concrete dugouts and sit the barrage out. If you had said to a British Tommy, on the eve of the battle, that the Germans were just sitting there, waiting, he'd have thought you were joking.

Joking is vital, even in the direst circumstances. Gallows humour keeps you sane. The British soldiers joked all the time. Like surgeons in an operating theatre – or chefs in a kitchen.

Kitchener's Army was the name given to the hundreds of thousands of volunteers who joined up in 1914 eager to 'have a bash at the Hun'. And it was Kitchener's Army, by and large, which went over the top at seven thirty in the morning on 1 July 1916, and had the soul ripped out of it. Sixty thousand killed and wounded in the first day alone. Casualties like that defeat our attempts to describe them, a figure beyond language.

Language – bad language. Soldiers swear, vilely, all the time – swear like troopers, in fact. Anyone who wants to know how soldiers swore in 1916 should read *Her Privates We* (published in 1930), a magnificent novel by Frederic Manning, a writer who served at the Somme as a private soldier. Manning's fellow soldiers swear vigorously and colourfully. They craft their own profane music.

Music in film, I believe, should be music written for the film in question. I know there are lots of successful exceptions but a proper film score is so much part of the art form that it seems a missed opportunity just to tag on something from the classics or the greatest hits of the seventies. I wrote out of the blue to Evelyn Glennie asking her to write the music for *The Trench*. To my amazement she agreed. She and her husband, Greg Malcangi – just the two of them – came up with a film score which fulfilled every ambition I had. It works like a clever drug, subtly, covertly getting to you, like arsenic or nicotine.

Nicotine is what the army marched on, not on their stomachs. World War One saw a massive increase in smoking. Luckily for us, of our thirteen key actors, ten were hardened smokers. But even they found the authentic Woodbines we provided for them a little too much. No filters and high, high tar. On one scene we had many takes, each requiring a fresh fag. One actor begged a five-minute respiratory rest. 'Seven Woodbines an hour is about my limit,' he gasped, his face a pale shade of ochre.

Ochre, sepia, chocolate, mud, burnt sienna, charcoal. All the shades of brown and its related colours delineate the world of the trench. Khaki is equally various. No one uniform looks the same. We think of World War One as a monochrome event but it was exceptionally vivid within its limited range. During filming, our world of browns seemed an unusually rich palette. It was only when we had a colonel come into the trench, his breast ablaze with medal ribbons, that we realized how confined our Technicolor spectrum was. The reds and the yellows, the vivid blues and greens, hit our eyes with particular power.

Powerful explosions can make men disappear, atomize them. We had one powerful explosion in which two men are blown to smithereens and only half of one is left. Our prosthetics expert constructed a bit of shattered torso which we strapped on to the back of an actor. When we laid him in the shell crater and the blood and the bits and pieces were added, suddenly only the top half of him was there. We all went a bit quiet.

QUIET! is the most common cry on a filmset. We had horrific problems – not with overflying aeroplanes but with hobnail boots. In the interests of authenticity we had every soldier issued with World War One standard hobnails. Crunch crunch crunch, they went. They drove our sound recordist, Chris Munro, if not over the edge, at least to its very rim.

The rim of a 1916-style tin helmet – and this was the first time in the war that tin helmets were issued – is razor sharp. So many injuries were caused by men bumping into them that an extra, protective, blunter rim was added. This later model is the only kind you can find nowadays. Our costume department had a tiring time painstakingly removing this extra rim with pliers. If they were wearied by their task they showed no sign.

Signs were everywhere in the trenches. After all, the Western Front was a labyrinth some 600 miles long and it was very easy to get lost. Battalions had specialized sign-writers so all the boards and signposts were very neatly painted. It became something of an obsession with me and the props department to get as many signs as possible somewhere in the background. Only that way would they seem, somehow, real trenches.

The trenches at the Somme were solidly constructed, deep, well revetted and duckboarded. The Somme Valley had been a quiet sector until the decision to have a battle there in 1916. People tend to forget that it took place in the middle of the summer. Wildlife abounded. No man's land was unmown, uncropped pasture. Summer was everywhere except in the earthy confines of the trench, its only evidence in the strip of blue sky above your head. Otherwise, your world was as confined as a World War Two U-boat.

U-boats and trenches seem an unlikely corollary until you consider they share the same cramped, dangerous claustrophobia. I had the idea for *The Trench* after seeing Wolfgang Petersen's U-boat movie, *Das Boot*. The same filthy proximity, the same absence of horizons, the war confined to a few dozen men in a few dozen yards. No escape from the tedium or the smell of fear, from the tea and bully beef or the shit and the vomit.

Vomit, in a movie, is a kind of soup. As chunky or as runny as you want. Annie Buchanan cooked up a beauty. She also does something with egg white when the actors have to spit – ordinary spit doesn't show up, apparently. Our central character, Billy MacFarlane, vomits when he sees something horrible when he goes for a walk.

Walking across no man's land into a hurricane of machine-gun bullets seems a stupid thing to do. But the British soldiers who went over the top on 1 July 1916 had little choice. They were trained to advance at a steady walk but they were also burdened with 70–80 pounds of equipment. Think of it as the heaviest, biggest suitcase you would take on holiday. You can't run, anyway, for more than a few paces with that kind of weight on you. It was like a noose around their necks.

X-certificate is really the only category that applies to warfare. It is the most disgusting, random, horrific experience that we humans visit on each other. Whether one writes about it or makes a film about it one's prime duty, it seems to me, is to refuse to idealize, excuse or glorify what goes on. When you are young there is a tendency to see the glory and the glamour – which is why, perhaps, armies like their soldiers young.

Young men fight our wars, very young men. At the Battle of the Somme there were boys of sixteen (who had lied about their age) in the army. Think of yourself as a teenager and think what those boys had to live through and endure. It cuts at the soul like an adze.

ZZZZ. Sleep. Catch some zees, as the Americans say. We spent eight weeks making *The Trench*. There is no getting away from the fact that film-making is exhausting. When we finished I was tired. I went home and slept for three days.

1999

Adaptations

One of the funniest and best loved jokes in Evelyn Waugh's *Scoop* occurs when the innocent hero, William Boot, who is nature correspondent for the *Daily Beast*, has his copy tampered with by his sister. William had written his weekly piece about badgers and wherever the word 'badger' occurred his sister Priscilla had replaced it with 'great crested grebe'. The copy had been filed with the mischief uncorrected and the outcry was predictable. 'The mail had been prodigious. Some correspondents were sceptical, others derisive . . . A major in Wales challenged him categorically to produce a single authenticated case of a great crested grebe attacking young rabbits. It had been exceedingly painful.'

It was an equally painful decision for me, when I came to adapt *Scoop* for the screen, that I decided to leave the 'badger' joke out. It is succinct and very funny on the page but I felt that it simply could not work on the screen. The only way for it to function at all was the laborious one of presenting a close-up of William's badger article, hold on it long enough for audiences to read enough of it to get the drift, then hold on it still further as Priscilla crossed out 'badger' and wrote in 'great crested grebe'. Pause to allow people to read the new copy and savour its absurdity. Cut to printed newspaper containing the vandalized article, and so on.

I use the story to illustrate just one of the many problems faced by a screenwriter adapting a much loved classic. The only way film could serve the novel in this case was to turn it into a visual 'book'. This is a joke that works *only* when it is read. And it would have to be read on the screen too. It seemed to me to be a negation of what film was all about to ask people to read screeds of text from a screen to try and reproduce a joke that would, in any event, fall flat, so ponderous was its execution. When *Scoop* was broadcast critics predictably bayed for blood – how could anyone be so crass as to leave out the 'badger' joke?

The adaptor is really on a hiding to nothing. The novel confers a near total writing freedom, the form is unbelievably generous and capacious. Screenwriting, by consequence, and adapting even more so, offers only a collection of handicaps and constraints. If novel writing is like swimming in the sea, then adapting is like swimming in a bath.

The first and most daunting constraint is one of length. When you write a film the rule-of-thumb calculation is: one page equals one minute. Consequently, very few screenplays exceed 120 pages. By my calculation between 60 to 70 per cent of a novel is left out when it makes the transfer to the screen. Your first task as a screenwriter when your chosen text is presented to you is to reread the novel, pencil in hand, crossing out as much as possible.

In the recent adaptation of *Martin Chuzzlewit*, for example, David Lodge made the wise decision to refer only obliquely to the American scenes (time has not served them well, they read desperately unfunnily today). He thereby excised a significant chunk of the novel and saved the production huge sums of money. For, as well as length, two other curbs crowd round the tormented adaptor – logistics and budget, though often the two coincide. When I came to adapt Mario Vargas Llosa's wonderful novel *Aunt Julia and the Scriptwriter* the very first thing I was told was that this film of the Peruvian novel would *not* be set in Peru. Similarly, anything in a novel that requires a cast of thousands or period detail or complex special effects takes on the lineaments of a sacrificial lamb. It either goes out or is drastically transformed: the battalion becomes a platoon, the Champs Elysées becomes a side street, a surreal nightmare becomes a sweat-drenched man tossing and turning in bed. Boil down, edit, reduce, discard, cut back, conflate – these are the hectoring instructions that echo in the adaptor's increasingly frustrated head.

And it is a job that any screenwriter finds very hard to escape from. I would reckon that three quarters of all films made are adaptations of some sort – certainly that proportion conforms to my own career. Cinema loves literature for two main reasons. First, world literature is a vast warehouse of ready-made stories, a great many of which are absolutely free. And, second, in most cases the public has already declared its taste. Any producer suggesting an adaptation of *Anna Karenina*, for example, is unlikely to be regarded as a vulgarian. Studios and producers are cautious animals, and there's nothing they like better than climbing aboard a bandwagon or gravy train. A successful or much loved book is perceived as already being on a roll.

So call in a screenwriter and set him or her to work. It is a peculiar craft, demanding particular skills. There is an injunction often presented to learner sculptors confronted with their first block of marble which is to 'try to find the statue in the stone'. The adaptor, to extend the analogy, is like a sculptor presented with a finished statue, let's say Michelangelo's *David*, and enjoined to fashion another *David* from the original. The key to the adaptor's job, then, is to try and find 'the statue in the statue'. You have your mallet and chisel in hand and you have to chip away at the much venerated, not to say iconic, original and make another *David*. The new statue will certainly be smaller and no doubt cruder, and inevitably, in the chipping away process, it will have lost an arm or other appendages, but if all has gone well the original statue will be called to mind. But it is never going to be a faithful or slavish copy, the very nature of the job rules that out.

Vladimir Nabokov, contemplating Stanley Kubrick's film of his novel *Lolita*, diplomatically professed himself well pleased. If ever there was a novel that would radically alter and diminish in its transition to the screen, then *Lolita* was that novel. But Nabokov, who had tried to adapt the novel himself, and whose script had been turned down, understood the problems inherent in the adaptor's dogged and difficult task. Film versions of novels, Nabokov said, should not strive to reproduce exactly what was on the printed page, they should aim to be 'vivacious variants' of the original. The creating of 'vivacious variants' is fundamentally what screen adapting is all about, and with that in mind one should never judge the film by the book, but let the film stand on its own.

1995

Three-Act Structure

At the foot of the greasy pole that is the Hollywood power structure toil the D-boys and the D-girls. The 'D' stands for Development and what these minions do is provide 'coverage', in other words write reports on the hundreds of filmscripts that are submitted routinely day in day out to the studios and independent film companies in the hope that someone somewhere will like them.

Almost without exception this script analysis utilizes the concept of three-act structure to construe the merits and demerits of the screenplay in question. '. . . the conclusion of act one is weak and does not prefigure the emotional highs in act two . . .'; '. . . acts one and two work well but there are real problems of pacing in act three . . .' and so on. There are other buzz- or nonce-words that figure in Hollywood script analysis – 'character arcs', 'backstory', 'beats', 'gracenotes', 'pushing the envelope', etc. – but none – none – has such a pernicious hold as three-act structure.

Now this notion may be a handy device for writing coverage (by and large American filmscripts do not number scenes), but the use of three acts has become widespread in the teaching of screenplay writing and, inevitably, in the writing of screenplays also, and there its use is far less felicitous. No one ever determined that a screenplay should have three acts – why not five? why not two? – and there is no reason on earth why the 120-page screenplay, and therefore the ninety minutes to two-hour film, should have these segments imposed on it. The fact of the matter is that film is a narrative art form, a particularly straightforward narrative art form too, compared to the novel, and the rhythms and cadences of that narrative, its rise and fall, its crises and denouements should be determined, not by some arbitrary matrix, but by the demands of the story (how compelling is it, how entertaining, how suspenseful, etc.) and the characters it is dealing with (how real are they, how sympathetic, how dramatically effective, etc.). Any shape, any structure will do if it works narratively. There is no predetermined mould into which a story should be poured: its justification is provided solely by its success. If there is one area of a film where a strong sense of form may be relevant then that is its ending, but that is because it is the end of that particular *story*, and not of act three.

1996

The Cannes Film Festival

'It's Cannes, Baby,' James D'Arcy whispers in my ear as we wait outside the Olympia Cinema on the rue d'Antibes in Cannes on a hot, sultry afternoon. James is an actor in *The Trench*, a film I have written and directed, and which is about to be screened in Olympia 2. He is here with two other of the film's actors – Daniel Craig and Paul Nicholls – and we are all, all four of us, a little apprehensive, I think, as we stand here watching the audience of studio executives, international film buyers and assorted journalists from around the world file, stony-faced, into the cinema. One of Paul Nicholls's lines from the film comes, unbidden, unwelcome, into my head: 'They don't look too happy, do they?' I reflect that this screening is, in effect, the world premiere of *The Trench*. No audience has ever seen it before. I wonder vaguely, far too late, of course, if this audience is the ideal one to test it on.

I first came to the Cannes Film Festival in 1971 when I was nineteen. I was studying along the coast at the University of Nice and one evening, with a German girl, hitchhiked the few miles to Cannes and strolled up and down the Croisette for a few hours, rubbernecking, looking for stars. I'm pretty sure I saw John Lennon and Yoko Ono on the terrace of the Carlton Hotel – but this may be a fantasy that I'm reluctant to let go. I remember little else about the visit but here I am, twenty-eight years later, back again.

In Nice, we quondam Niçois were somewhat disparaging about Cannes. Nice was the real city on the Côte d'Azur, Cannes was a kind of erstatz artefact, a pseudo city, all show and bravura, not worth the bother of visiting. Even Monte Carlo had more heft, more life to it. And certainly, walking up and down the Croisette – as one does, endlessly – all these years later I reflect that film festival time does not show the place in its best light. There are posters for movies everywhere – big expensive posters – stuck on the façades of buildings, specially designed to fit on lamp-posts, even the porte-cochères and the balustraded ramps of the driveways and terraces of the luxury hotels are artlessly remodelled to promote this film or that. The place is permanently mobbed too, great crowds of people aimlessly wandering, day and night. Nothing reminds you more forcibly that Cannes is, let's say, 5 per cent glamour, 95 per cent market. It's a convention, an American friend of ours reminded us: think of it as a town invaded by sales representatives.

There are many different Cannes, depending on your needs and your function. There is the buyers' Cannes: men and women scurrying from cinema to cinema burdened with press kits and synopses, sometimes watching only minutes of one film before they furtively leave to watch another few minutes of the next. There is the velvet-roped, red-carpeted razzamatazz of the Official Selection screenings – movie stars, the great and the would-be-great, pausing to wave to the paparazzi before they enter the concrete blockhouse that is the Palais des Festivals. However, one slowly but surely gets the impression, overwhelmingly, that Cannes is an Anglocentric event. Nothing but English spoken, it seems to me, in the cafes and bars and streets – American, English, Australian, European-English accents abound. Where are the French, one asks? All in our hotel, as it turns out.

We are staying at the Martinez, a huge art deco construct at the far end of the Croisette from the Palais and the Majestic. On the beach opposite a substantial open-sided TV studio has been built by Canal Plus to house their amazingly popular chat show, *Nulle Part Ailleurs*. As it happens I have been on *Nulle Part Ailleurs* once, in Paris – its usual home – and I know its power and its terror. It decamps to Cannes for the two weeks of the festival. It is live and unique – a combination, if that can be imagined, of, let's say, *Parkinson*, *TGI Friday*, *Spitting Image*, the *South Bank Show* with a little bit of alternative comedy and soft porn thrown in for good measure. Everybody who is anybody in France obeys the *Nulle Part Ailleurs* summons. And Everybody is staying in the Martinez, or at least is temporarily present at the Martinez waiting to go on the show – which seems to last about three hours.

Which explains, I quickly realize, why there are several hundred young people corralled around the hotel's entrance screaming their lungs out. For the serious French punter the Cannes Film Festival actually takes place here, occupying the fifty yards it takes to get from the Martinez lobby to the Canal Plus studio. The rest of the town can be left to the rest of the film industry.

I call a French friend of mine, an eminent film director, to see when he will be arriving. Oh no, he says, I'm not coming. He tells me he took special precautions to ensure his new film would *not* be ready for Cannes. It's terrible what they do, the French press, he says. Look how they have massacred Carax and *Pola X*. 'Already?' I say, sceptical. The film was screened on day one and this is only day three. 'Le film est mort,' he says in a sober voice.

And it is true that the French are hardest on the French here. No reputation is immune and the attacks can be and are unremittingly savage. Catherine Deneuve – braving the firestorm in several films this year – said that for French film-makers the Cannes Film Festival is a 'douloureux et dangereux' experience. Blood on the Croisette. It's not all parties.

Thank God – because the parties are awful, appalling, a total waste of time. And yet we all go to them. We went to two in the two nights we had available: the MTV party, a modest affair of 1,200 on the Carlton Beach, and the Austin Powers party, in a deserted casino miles away. Rumours had it that there were 7,000 invitations issued for this one. We finally fought our way in, through crowds of desperate liggers, thankful our special invitations allowed us access to the exclusive VIP area where a mere 2,000 privileged guests drank free drinks and chatted sweatily to each other. Actually, the Austin Powers party was worth it, if only for the sight of a grinning, aged, squamous Hugh Hefner, sitting on a sofa, surrounded by four impossibly pert Bunnies, living tribute to the properties and potentials of Viagra and silicone, respectively.

On the morning after our screening, Daniel Craig, Paul Nicholls, James D'Arcy and I reported for duty on the Majestic Hotel beach. We were all – how shall I put it? – a little fragile and unanimously decided a round of Bloody Marys was the best way to get our press call off to a good start.

The Trench is a film about the forty-eight hours before the Battle of the Somme in 1916, concentrating on a group of very young soldiers waiting to go over the top to what is almost certain death. The first day of the Battle of the Somme was the bloodiest day of slaughter – 60,000 killed and wounded – in the entire history of the British Army. Daniel Craig drily made the point to me, as we were whizzing between TV crews and journalists, the sun shining, people sunbathing, yachts in the bay, drink-toting waiters running around, that there was a certain baleful incongruity about where we were and what we were talking about. He was right, of course, but at the same time in that realization all the absurdity and the craziness of the festival coalesced. Boys trying to come to terms with the prospect of their imminent death in 1916; young actors trying to explain the import of all this to a Brazilian film crew on a jetty in the sun on the Mediterranean shore in 1999. It was good to note the farcical nature of the juxtaposition. But we carried on. We were in high spirits. The screening had gone well: people clapped, people cried, people stumbled out wordless. That was Cannes, Baby.

1999

The Bonfire of the Vanities

(Review of *The Devil's Candy* by Julie Salamon)

Amongst the many gobbets of received wisdom that make up what purports to be the lore and logic of the desperately unscientific business that is making a movie is the adage that 'good books make bad films, and bad books make good films'. The exceptions to this rule are so numerous that one might have thought this was one old saw that could decently be retired. My own version of it is somewhat different (born of bitter experience, needless to say) and runs along these lines: 'Well-known and much loved books are always perceived to be unfilmable no matter how brilliantly they are adapted for the screen, whereas nobody worries unduly about what you do to little-known books.' It lacks a certain aphoristic pithiness, I admit, but I cling to it as valid and true.

It has a particular bearing on *The Devil's Candy*, the story about the filming of Tom Wolfe's novel *The Bonfire of the Vanities*, probably one of the best-known and most enthusiastically read books of the eighties. The film starred Tom Hanks, Bruce Willis and Melanie Griffiths and was directed by Brian de Palma and paid for by Warner Bros. It cost somewhere in the region of $50 million and was one of the biggest flops of 1990. There is no reason on earth why the novel couldn't have been well filmed but I could have told Brian de Palma, had he enquired, citing my rambling apophthegm, that no matter what he did he was on a hiding to nothing with this one. It was too soon, it was too controversial, it was too high profile, it was too prestigious, too many reputations were on the line, and so on.

Julie Salamon doggedly charts the downward slide of the making of the film in a more or less studiously neutral manner and a more or less turgid style. The book is both fascinating and irritating in the extreme: fascinating for what her privileged status as observer reveals (de Palma's weight problems, Bruce Willis's ego problems, Melanie Griffiths's breast enlargement problems, among others) and irritating for what it omits. Salamon's story starts in pre-production but tells us next to nothing about the scriptwriting process. Now, there are those in the film industry (and not just film writers) who will confidently aver that this is the area where every film's success or failure is actually determined, that if it isn't right in the script then it will *never* be right on screen, whatever the allure of the stars, the skill of the director or the hype of the marketing. Whether *Bonfire* was doomed from the outset because of what was done in the scriptwriting stage, or what brief the writer was given, is still a matter for debate, a debate, however, that is not one jot better informed as a result of this long and detailed book.

Another omission is that Salamon declines to blame anyone for the debacle. Indeed it is rare that she allows critical faculties free rein at all. Who was responsible for this failure, in the end? What can we learn from this sorry story of warring egos, profligacy and hubris? The answer in this case, it seems to me, is the system and mood that prevail in Hollywood at the moment, factors that affected all the key players and key decisions in this particular drama. To put it very simply, when a studio makes an expensive, high-profile film what you might call the feel-good factor inevitably ends up controlling the content. Rough edges are inexorably softened, dark moments are irradiated with light, unhappy endings are ruthlessly transformed into happy ones, characters have to be likeable, empathized with. The whole process is to make the film more bland, more happy, less offensive, in other words, SAFE. This mood, this tone, applies to all major Hollywood films, and clearly it will not affect some mindless teen romp, or romantic comedy. But when you take as the source for your movie one of the most bile-driven, savage, satirical novels of recent years then applying the feel-good factor is going to be little short of disastrous. Reading through the book with this in mind one sees again and again that the crucial decisions, the vital mistakes were initiated and compounded by this enervating spirit of relentless compromise. It's a tenacious and pervasive virus in contemporary Hollywood and exceptionally hard to avoid. The result is everywhere to see: a film culture playing very very safe, making fewer and fewer films that are *not afraid of their own subject matter*. And it is precisely that temerity, that hard-nosed confidence and self-belief, that was and is required, not only for *Bonfire*, but for any film that wants both to entertain and challenge, to beguile and stimulate and generally try to raise itself out of the slough of mediocrity and aspire to the status of art.

1992

Hollywood Excess

(Review of *High Concept* by Charles Fleming)

Recently, a wily old producer told me in all seriousness that, in his opinion, Hollywood should be looked at purely and simply as a river of gold, endlessly flowing; all one has to do is, from time to time, stroll down to the river bank, reach in and grab a handful of money. In its single-mindedness, its brutal candour, this theory seems reasonably astute. And it is true that, for a small minority, Hollywood and the movie business are indeed a source of endless, profligate wealth. Of course, this theory only functions if you have already succeeded, and it could be said to be true of any successful person in any successful enterprise (banking, plastic surgery, hamburger franchises, undertaking). But it is worth recalling that what takes place in Hollywood is the creation of an art form, not, as might reasonably be thought, drug-dealing or trading pork-belly futures – yet, of the seven arts, only the cinema proffers the alluring, tantalizing prospect of a permanent Klondike.

There is another, related theory of Hollywood: 'Anyone can be a film producer.' All it requires is the assertion, 'I am a film producer' and – bingo – you are one. All you really need is a business card, a telephone and the vaguest idea of the film you plan to 'produce' and a degree of self-confidence coupled with social plausibility. Which brings us to Don Simpson and Charles Fleming's book about him and the environment that allowed him first to flourish and then to self-destruct.

Simpson was the co-producer of a series of loud, action-packed, mind-numbingly simple Hollywood films that made vast sums of money: *Flashdance*, *Beverly Hills Cop* (and *BHC II*), *Top Gun*, *Days of Thunder*, *Crimson Tide* and a few others which will inevitably slide into movie oblivion. In the 1980s, together with his partner Jerry Bruckheimer, he was regarded as the most successful independent producer in town, and was royally rewarded (formidable perks aside, they each received, at the apex of their careers, a fee of $9 million per film). Simpson was a small, aggressive man with a tendency to obesity, who played the 'bad cop' in the partnership. Bruckheimer produced the films (did the work) while Don hogged the limelight. What is remarkable about Fleming's racily written, but diligent, account of Simpson's short life is that, try as one might, one can perceive nothing remarkable about it. You don't have to live in Hollywood to be a scumbag; you don't have to be a film producer to be a cocaine addict and an S&M enthusiast; you don't have to have untold millions in the bank to be consumed with self-loathing and behave like a spoilt child (Simpson, staying in a hotel in Hawaii, would call his assistant in Los Angeles and get her to order room service for him). The world is full of such people and sometimes, unfortunately, such tendencies congregate in one body. But, if they do, is it necessary to chronicle their inadequacies over 300 pages?

Flashdance, Beverly Hills Cop, Top Gun . . . money and power seemed mainly to fuel Simpson's vices: for cocaine, for expensive call girls, for boozing, bingeing and bad behaviour and, inevitably, more and more rehab. When *Days of Thunder* (Tom Cruise in racing cars) went massively over-budget, the magic seemed to leave the Simpson-Bruckheimer formula. They moved their deal to Disney. There was still a ton of money swilling around but no films got made. What's a guy to do? Some plastic surgery, more hookers, massive weight gain, buy a Ferrari, porn videos, three jars of peanut butter a day, rehab, cocaine, more hookers . . . The litany of Simpson's relentless over-indulgence gets boring. Even when, at the end of his life, in an effort to alleviate his addiction to illegal drugs, Simpson became addicted instead to prescription drugs (he was spending $75,000 a month in pharmacies), the ironies accruing around his sad, over-privileged existence provoke a kind of weary pity rather than moral outrage.

High Concept is the book's title and it is suggested that Simpson (and Bruckheimer) invented the genre – if that is not too grandiose a label for what the veteran producer Dick Sylbert has called extended MTV videos: 'It's "rock and roll in a steel mill", or "rock and roll in a jet airplane", or "rock and roll in a race car".' The 'high-concept' film is one where the 'idea is king', as Simpson once eloquently phrased it. One of his champions put it this way: 'Don made up this logarithm [*sic*]. There is the hot first act with an exciting incident and the second act with the crisis and the dark bad moments in which our hero is challenged, and the third act with the triumphant moment and the redemption and the freeze frame ending.' Although Simpson claimed to be the only begetter of this category of film he had, and has, a host of angry rivals who say they got there first.

There are many wealthy, powerful people in Hollywood, far more famous than Simpson ever was, who behave just as badly as he did, who have the same bizarre sexual proclivities and consume equal amounts of drugs. Charles Fleming's wider point in this book is that there is something inherent in the culture of Hollywood which makes such excesses tolerable, inevitable or even encouraged. My own hunch – my theory – is that it is not so much the fault of Hollywood as that of human nature. Put vulnerable, dysfunctional people in positions of immense power, provide them with every available venal temptation, give them more money than they know what to do with and there's a fair chance they will go off the rails. But, despite the horror stories, it should be stated that the Hollywood film business is also populated by many hardworking, intelligent, honourable souls who don't do drugs, and whose idea of an evening out does not include weird sex with a $10,000-a-night call girl. Simpson was not one of these, but his story is ultimately banal because he personally achieved nothing concrete – in his life or his work – and, crucially, in a creative world filled with creative people, he did nothing creative. I suspect it was this sense of fraudulence, of worthlessness, that provoked the demons that drove him. He died in 1996 of a heart attack brought on by massive drug-abuse, at the age of fifty-two.

'He had everything, but he had nothing,' as one ex-girlfriend reflected on hearing of his death. Perhaps such a contrary figure deserves two epitaphs. One of his cronies said, 'For all his drug derangement [Don] was adamant about not being full of shit.' Another less partial acquaintance, who encountered him at Simpson's favourite rehab ranch, described him as 'the epitome – as a successful man, as a representative of Hollywood, as a male animal – of the kind of person who made your skin crawl'. Take your pick.

1999

Basquiat

The bio-pic is a difficult genre, perhaps as difficult as it comes in the film world, and the longer and more familiar the life to be filmed, the tougher the challenge. Films are rarely over two hours long; at two and a half hours you are probably at the maximum length for these times of ours, stretching the tolerance of studio, exhibitor and – possibly – audience as well; and to encompass an entire life, public and private, and do it some justice (let alone produce an interesting or watchable or memorable film) within that frame is a daunting challenge.

The modern exemplar of the bio-pic – in my opinion – is Martin Scorsese's *Raging Bull*. Scorsese was initially fortunate in that his subject was virtually unknown outside the fight game. Secondly, the area of Jake La Motta's life that he chose to treat was comparatively short – the rise and fall of a professional boxer, a decade or so. And third, Scorsese showed real astuteness in opting to eschew traditional narrative chronology. The film is a series of vignettes, punctuated by flash-forwards to the bloated, ageing Jake in his premature dotage as a nightclub raconteur. The style of the film is fractured and eclectic: sometimes naturalistic, almost *cinéma-vérité*, sometimes stylized (particularly the fights), but as a portrait of a man and his life it is remarkably successful. It could only have been bettered in that most fluid, capacious and malleable of art forms, the novel, but, in Scorsese's hands, film – and I don't mean this as faint praise – takes on a rare depth and texture (Robert de Niro has a lot to do with this, it goes without saying). It is nuanced, it resonates, it is both banal and passionate, it is full of complexities and ambiguities – we do not understand everything. It resembles, in short, life.

All this is by way of preamble to Julian Schnabel's film *Basquiat*. A bio-pic also, and one that shares many features with – however paradoxical this may seem – *Raging Bull*. Basquiat is comparatively unknown: certainly, outside of an art-world coterie, the details of his life are unfamiliar territory. Furthermore, his life was short, dramatic and controversial. Schnabel's film needs only to concentrate on the few years – approximately 1981 to 1987 – that chart his discovery, sudden fame, exploitation and ultimate drug-propelled downfall and death. Wisely, too, the style of the film is fractured and impressionistic. Basquiat's story is presented in a series of episodes, often concentrating around encounters with friends, or girlfriends, artists, dealers, etc., who move in and out of the story at random. One of the film's most memorable shots is visionary: Basquiat, contemplating Manhattan's vast roofscape, sees the sky replaced by sea, with a solitary surfer riding a creaming breaker, high above the skyscrapers. Is this a vision of happiness? Of mere wishful thinking? Or simply the kind of aesthetic epiphany that can visit any artist, however down and out?

These ambiguities complement the film's tone and atmosphere well, and Schnabel is excellently served by his cast too. Jeffrey Wright is superb as Basquiat: understated, befuddled, endearing, he can move effortlessly through the range of emotions from sweetness and charm to the manic, spoilt selfishness of the drug-dependent. One's sympathy is thoroughly engaged, rarely the case with addicts, and Wright's fraught depiction of a desperate soul on self-destruct rivals Ray Milland's great portrayal of an alcoholic in *The Lost Weekend*.

The supporting cast solidly buttresses Wright's central position. The luminously beautiful Claire Forlani as Basquiat's girlfriend is touchingly, edgily vulnerable. Benicio del Toro for once keeps his mannerisms under control as Basquiat's friend from his graffiti-spraying days. Christopher Walken, playing a journalist, manages to invest a two-minute interview with such an amazing freight of off-beat menace and downright weirdness that it almost steals the show. Dennis Hopper and Gary Oldman, old reliables, do not let the side down. Special mention must be made of David Bowie as Andy Warhol. This expertly pitched performance is kept well this side of caricature (very hard to do with a white frightwig on your head). More importantly, you see a version of Warhol that for once makes sense. Warhol emerges, not as some spaced-out partyanimal, but as Basquiat's only real, unconditional friend in the sea of sharks that is the New York art world. The friendship is played as manifestly genuine, without a trace of *quid pro quo*. And Warhol's death, when it comes, provokes a vicarious sense of loss. And one understands vividly why this may well have been the factor that pushed Basquiat over the edge.

The film further benefits from an easy, unforced authenticity. Julian Schnabel knew Basquiat well, and has thrived and suffered (to a degree) in the same world. Tellingly, in the production notes to the film, Schnabel describes that world as an 'arena'. In which artists as gladiators are pitted against a succession of wild beasts, perhaps?

As an oblique demonstration of biting the hand that feeds you, or of fouling your own nest, Schnabel's take on the art scene of the eighties is unsparingly harsh. One wonders if it is fuelled by a personal bitterness, or perhaps a retrospective wisdom, but whatever the motivation, his portrayal of the gang of asset strippers that gathered round the frail personality and modest talent of Jean-Michel Basquiat makes other sinks of iniquity – Hollywood, the music business, oriental sweat shops – seem positively perfumed.

And this provides the material for the searching subtext that runs beneath the film. At another level it can be seen as a Hogarthian satire, a dire moral warning to the unsuspecting artist. And here we encounter the vexed question of Basquiat's reputation, both while he was alive and posthumously. Basquiat died at the age of twenty-seven, a year older than Keats was when he died, but Basquiat is no Keatsian figure. Basquiat's own idols were doomed, drugged musicians like Jimi Hendrix and Charlie Parker, and perhaps there the parallels are more valid, but not entirely. One would hesitate to call Charlie Parker the Basquiat of the jazz world. The inversion is revealing – it tends to diminish Charlie Parker – for what it tells us, both about Basquiat's 'gift', whatever that may have been, and the world he moved in, where it became a commodity of huge value.

The fact is that Basquiat belonged to that category of artist who traded in, for want of a better term, one smart idea. It is a recent phenomenon, this, perhaps only prevalent in the last four decades or so, and posterity is already marking down the dividends sharply. Artists of this category offer a quick fix of appreciation and that quick fix can be relied upon to pack many a gallery and fuel many column inches for a limited period of time. I do not deny that the frisson such work generates may be genuine, but it is like a firework rocket, refulgently, gloriously *there* for a short time, and then darkness, and then the faint distant thump of the wooden stick and scorched cardboard falling back to earth.

Scenes in the film of Basquiat frenziedly producing his huge, vivid, scribbled upon canvases are excellently done and fascinatingly revealing (canvases on the floor, paint slapped on, scribbled words and phrases randomly added). Basquiat was unusual – young and black in a white, highbrow world. He would have liked to claim to have come up from the street, but his origins were bourgeois. He had a certain wit, a certain worldly cynicism and an artful enough *faux-naïf* style. And that was it. But it was enough to provoke an engineered feeding frenzy amongst the dealers and their patrons, the critics and the gallery crowd.

In his notes on the film Schnabel happily bandies about the term 'genius' as applied to Basquiat, but the idea is utterly risible. Basquiat was not a modern snake-oil salesman, not quite; but the currency of his talent, his ability, his 'knack', was on the lightweight side, and I suspect – and Wright's deeply sensitive performance encourages this conclusion – that amongst the demons that hurried him on his way to his premature death were those that were whispering 'fraud' and 'sham' in his ear. One of the loudest messages this film broadcasts is that there is no medium- or long-term substitute for talent, hard work, elaboration and exploration of technique, intelligence, hard work, empathy, thought, virtuosity, hard work and so on. This is the serious artist's lot – his or her via dolorosa, if you like – and the froth and spume of celebrity, of radical-chic acclaim and lots of easy money cannot drag you away from it. One smart idea may buy you all this, for a while, but unless you cultivate a redoubtable cynicism (and bank your loot) it will not stand you in any further stead. Plenty of other flim-flam men and women are coming along behind you with all their smart ideas. Soon you will be old hat.

Perhaps Basquiat saw old-hatdom beckoning, perhaps he couldn't think of anything else to do apart from his graffiti stuff? But, in any event, the indictment is not his to bear alone, but must rather be the burden of the world and its denizens who fell upon him and pushed him into the lucrative glare of the limelight.

Basquiat was vulnerable from the start because he held the wrong concept of what an artist was, believing that 'Your life was the price you paid for your talent.' Such ideas of 'being an artist', a poet *maudit*, a tormented genius, or whatever, demonstrate a fanciful romanticism of the most puerile sort (which is why they are more often found amongst very young rock musicians, or very deluded actors). No serious artist can afford to believe in this notion of afflatus, whether God-given, spontaneous or drug-induced. The art world may be indifferent, or reluctant to make such a judgement, but the world of the real artist is ruthlessly self-regulating. The Stoics' famous rejoinder, 'Be silent – unless what you have to say is better than silence,' casts a long, minatory and humbling shadow over all artists' endeavours.

Julian Schnabel has made a fine film and he can be proud of his debut as a director, but it seems to me that what emerges is something different from what he may have set out to achieve. Schnabel has said that 'Jean-Michel's work mocks categorization. It wasn't enough for him to be a great black artist, or a graffiti artist or even a young artist. He placed himself among the great artists of all time.' Good God. Well, if he did, he paid a heavy price for his hubris. But this is not what the film conveys: there is a marked absence of vainglory, of preening self-congratulation. As Basquiat is fêted and wooed by his well-heeled acolytes and hangers-on, his mood appears rather to start as one of gratified bafflement, shading swiftly into cynicism, self-disgust and ultimate despair. Basquiat, it seems to me, is not so much Icarus or Narcissus but a sort of latter-day, low grade, Manhattan Faust. Too young, too gullible, too insecure, too easily led, he made his own Faustian pact with the art world – he did the Faust deal – and got royally burned.

1996

Woody Allen

I have seen Woody Allen in the flesh three times in my life. I've never actually met him but the encounters remain vividly memorable, not to say poignant. I regard myself as a committed fan, though not an uncritical one, and my acquaintance with his work began with his very first film as a writer and director, *Take the Money and Run* (1969).

I saw this film as a teenager in an open-air cinema one evening in Ibadan, Nigeria, in 1970. I'd gone to the cinema – casually, uninformed – expecting vaguely to catch some American thriller. Instead I was presented with a wry, knowing, absurdist, comic vision of life that seems to have emerged fully formed and that has really hardly changed over the subsequent thirty-odd years. As the moths and other night insects dipped and dived through the projector's beam, scattering their ephemeral shadows across the screen, I found myself laughing, first incredulously, then out loud, then painfully, at the Allen persona – nerdy, intellectual, inept, randily heterosexual, angst-ridden. I was eighteen and such first encounters with an artist you come to revere and admire remain embedded in the memory, anchored there by something close to shock: a shock of recognition – the pure thrill of finding your own sense of humour, your own view of the world, replicated by an artist in an art form. At that age empathy and identification are the shortest route to aesthetic pleasure. Who is this Woody Allen? I wondered. Where can I see more of his stuff?

As it happened I didn't have to wait long, nor have any of us. By my count he has made thirty-four feature films as writer/director and (mostly) actor since that debut. A Woody Allen film is as predictable as spring or autumn – every year sees a new launch, new debate about its quality, new speculation about the stellar cast. Until this year, that is. Woody Allen's latest film, *Anything Else*, was released in the US in August, indeed it's available for purchase there on DVD and video from the end of this month. You can currently see it in cinemas in France but not in the UK. A British distributor, it appears, may or may not be imminent, but why the delay? It is some sort of ominous signal when the new Woody Allen film, as far as his UK fans are concerned, risks going straight to video. One reluctantly starts to wonder: have audiences begun to fall out of love with the Woodman?

The first time I actually *saw* Woody Allen was in New York. It was 1981 and it was my first visit to the city. I stepped out of my hotel and wandered north up Park Avenue gawping at the skyscrapers and the other New York clichés that were on display. Then the biggest cliché of them all came sauntering down the avenue towards me: Woody Allen in trademark baggy chinos and combat jacket. Even better – he was arm in arm with Diane Keaton. I stopped still and tried not to stare too intently. They were laughing and chatting freely, apparently unaware of the ripples of interest and rubbernecking their passage provoked. They passed close by me. Was I rocked slightly by the turbulent wake of their renown and charisma? Yes: it was an epiphanic moment and in a way I now expect to see Woody Allen every time I go to New York. It was almost as if the sighting had been arranged for first-time visitors by the New York tourist board, so synonymous is Allen with the city. And to see him strolling its streets within hours of my arriving there, with his co-star and lover to boot, seemed both a serendipitous blessing and unbelievably appropriate.

This sighting occurred only a few years after *Annie Hall* (1977), remember, and I suppose that film still survives as his trademark, signature work. So many Woody Allen tropes were established there, and to such an extent, that later films that have gone back to the source suffer badly in comparison. This is all too true of the latest: *Anything Else* is a kind of poor man's *Annie Hall* but without its freshness. Two other actors – Jason Biggs and Christina Ricci – replicate the Allen and Keaton roles but are hopelessly handicapped by our knowledge of their forerunners. Biggs (of *American Pie* fame) is seriously miscast and Christina Ricci (a wonderful actress) seems strangely lost, out of sorts – as if she were too aware of the ghostly redolence of the earlier film and of her vain efforts to recapture its allure. I loved *Annie Hall* when it first came out and decided to re-watch it last year. I stopped after five minutes, not wanting to spoil the memories of those earlier viewings. Age has not been kind to it. Furthermore it has had a baleful influence on American comic acting – what you could call the *Friends* school of acting. Allen's furrowed-brow, hesitant, stuttering, self-regarding delivery and Keaton's ditsy, kooky, stuttering, self-regarding delivery have spread like a pestilence through American drama schools. Pale shadows of Allen and Keaton throng American TV sitcoms (*Friends* being the most culpable in my opinion – but the disease is spreading over here too – fast). *Anything Else* is a ghastly depiction of the malady. Jason Biggs can't get out three words without a pause, a 'mmm', a 'huh', a twitch, an 'I mean'. 'No' emerges as 'N-n-n-n-n-no'. Beside him even Woody Allen himself sounds as sonorous and articulate as John Gielgud.

But I don't think Allen minds his occasional turkeys and flops. His working practice is simply to work and work again and carry on working and he seems indifferent to criticism, positive or adverse. Like old-school film-makers he is concentrating on producing an oeuvre, a body of work. Out of the thirty-plus films he has made so far there might be six comic classics: a success rate most artists would kill for (think of *Manhattan*, *Stardust Memories*, *The Purple Rose of Cairo*, *Hannah and her Sisters*, *Husbands and Wives* and *Bullets over Broadway* to name the first half dozen that spring to mind – there are another six that could also be contenders). But such a relentless output has a built-in fault mechanism: it's impossible to maintain excellence with that level of productivity – whatever the art form you are working in. Allen's yearly film prescribes that some will inevitably disappoint and fail. But something else has happened recently. I find myself less intrigued by the recent movies: I haven't seen *Celebrity* (1998), *The Curse of the Jade Scorpion* (2001) or *Hollywood Ending* (2002). It's not just a question of over-production. I worry that it's a question of over-familiarity – with the man himself.

The second time I saw Woody Allen was in 1995. I walked into a Madison Avenue bookshop and there at the rear I could see there was a small book-launch party going on, twenty or so people with glasses of wine and canapés in their hands. Customers were still allowed to browse, so I did and after a minute or two looked up to see that I was browsing beside Woody Allen. A little way off Soon-Yi Previn was standing. The whole Soon-Yi scandal, Allen's humiliation and Mia Farrow's despair and outrage, has changed our perception of Allen in a disastrous way, I feel. The confusion between the man and the roles he played in his films was one he deliberately allowed to take place – and it was creatively very effective: whatever the name of his character you felt you were watching, in essence, Woody Allen. But it was funny and ambiguous and self-deprecating. And then we found out it wasn't: the court appearances, the memoirs, the suits and counter-suits provided us with too much unsavoury information – we came to know too much about the man and that knowledge has begun retrospectively to shadow the work. It's very hard now to watch a film like *Manhattan*, for instance, or *Husbands and Wives*, and watch Allen lust after his young co-stars and remain in the state of benign, amused ignorance you were in when they first came out. As I stood beside him in that bookstore that day he looked much older and frailer than I expected. Then Soon-Yi called him over and he rejoined the guests.

In the latest film, *Anything Else*, Allen permits himself no unseemly sexual dalliances with much younger women. He's a wiseacre, wannabe comedy writer dispensing laconic aphorisms about the human condition and worldly advice to his younger alter-ego. On a scale of ten the movie probably rates a four: it doesn't really work – the dialogue seems strangely clunky, the situations appear reheated and mannered and we never engage with the central couple. I suspect Allen will chalk it down to experience. His next film, the *Untitled Woody Allen Fall Project (2003)*, is in post-production (awaiting a title) and will be released in 2004. And then he'll make another.

The third time I saw Woody Allen was in the spring of last year. I was in Manhattan, sitting in Bemelmans bar in the Carlyle Hotel one evening having a drink. On my way out to dinner I paused in the corridor between the bar and the Café Carlyle and squinted into the cafe through the glass door at the live show that was performing. A small jazz orchestra was on stage and there, in the second row, was Woody Allen playing his clarinet. I watched him for a minute or two. He seemed a contented man.

2003

Electra Glide in Blue

I have loved movies for as long as I can remember. One of my earliest memories – I must have been about six years old – is of being so terrified by *The Wizard of Oz* that I covered my eyes for most of the film. Another is of a bizarre Disney film called *The Three Caballeros*, a mixture of animation and live action, which I saw in a cinema in Accra, Ghana, in the late 1950s, and of being bafflingly but erotically stirred by a sultry flamenco dancer who was flirting with the cartoon characters. These moments are the start of a long catalogue of subconscious influences that the cinema has had on my imagination and, no doubt, my personality. When I was at school I was a member of the film society and was profoundly affected (for some reason) by *Juliet of the Spirits*. In 1971 I lived in France for a year and went to the movies three or four times a week. I recall vividly oddities like *Le Voyou*, *Bof*, *Le Beau Monstre* – films I will probably never see again – as well as modern classics like *The Conformist* and *Little Big Man*. But none of these films, although they left indelible imprints on my mind, can really be described as crucially influential. The first film that had this effect on me, that for ever altered the way I responded to film, was *Electra Glide in Blue*.

There is a moment in every writer's life when he or she consciously starts to think of himself or herself as a writer. It can happen early or late but as soon as that moment has arrived everything changes. That self-consciousness then mediates all experience. *Electra Glide* provided something similar for me which is why I select it as important. Up until I saw *Electra Glide* (in 1973) I had gone to the cinema as, if you like, a simple consumer, happy to be amused, thrilled, shocked or whatever. But when I saw *Electra Glide* I was no longer content with these unreflecting emotional responses. It was the first film I saw where I began actually to analyse how it worked; the first film I saw where I became excited by the process of movie-making, the manipulation of image and mood, rather than responding to it as a straightforward intellectual and sensual stimulant.

The film itself is an odd amalgam of thriller and road movie, of nihilism and wry humour, of action-adventure and morality tale. It tells the story of a motorcycle cop who wants to be a detective, who becomes one and, in the process of investigating a murder, discovers his ideals and standards are corrupted or misguided. It was written by Robert Boris and directed by James William Guercio, a former record producer, and as far as I know it is the only film he ever made. But for a debut it is extraordinary. There is a tremendous central performance by Robert Blake as the diminutive but tough motorcycle cop and the photography, by Conrad Hall, is audacious as well as sensational. I think it is the look of the film that is initially haunting – Monument Valley and the Arizona desert have always made great cinema – and on the wide screen the vast landscape with its lonely ribbon of road becomes a potent symbol. In fact I think that there lies the explanation of *Electra Glide*'s special allure: as the story unfolds the film subtly plays with key metaphors and icons of Americana and American film and refashions them for a modern audience. You have the elemental and essential loneliness of the American West; the one brave man; violent death and raw carnality (there is a bravura performance of white-trash sexuality from Jeannine Riley); you have the eternal appeal of the road movie – the transitoriness of experience, the possibilities of freedom – and an ending of shocking and absurd tragedy.

Electra Glide in Blue is not a great movie but it understands, I think, what movies can do best (and other art forms can't) at a visceral and unconscious level, and exploits these particular strengths with seductive skill and brio. It certainly changed – irrevocably – the way I went to the cinema and it is a measure of how much it affected me that I still find myself thinking about it over twenty years later.

1998

Adapting *Armadillo*

When I told people that my novel *Armadillo* was being filmed for the BBC the first question I was inevitably asked was: 'Are you adapting it yourself?' Yes, I would reply, instinctively, and then a part of me would shout 'No! I'm not *adapting* it. What I'm doing to it is far more complicated than that: I'm writing it again, which is something entirely different.' I think the first thing we have to do is get rid of the word 'adaptation' – the problem lies in the image conjured up by that innocuous noun. And the verb 'to adapt' sounds too easy: 'I'll adapt it' implies something anyone could do – just hand me my tool kit and give me half an hour and I'll adapt it. But in actual fact turning a novel into a TV series or a film – or an opera, or a musical, or a radio play – is a far more complex and radical act than one might think. By changing the art form the rules are completely rewritten. Turning a novel into a TV series isn't a simple matter of 'adaptation' – what we're actually talking about is 'transformation'.

Let's try a thought-experiment. Let's imagine the novel *Armadillo* as a house, a standard three-bedroom detached house with a garden. Now you want to turn it into a three-hour series for BBC1. The way you do this is to demolish the existing house and rebuild it using the same materials. As everyone knows when you knock something down and try to put it together again it's not going to look exactly the same. Some of the bricks will have been smashed, windows broken, pipes burst, tiles cracked, joists given way and so on. As you assemble your materials and try to conform to the original plan certain compromises and alterations will have to be made: the sitting room will be smaller, the attic bedroom will have gone. You find that you can only make the central heating work downstairs, the new windows won't quite fit their embrasures, you can only get into the kitchen through the downstairs loo and the garden has been ruined by all the heavy machinery. This image is not meant to be flippant or facetious: in my opinion and experience it genuinely reflects the process that is undergone when a novel is rejigged, reshaped and reformed for the screen. When you've rebuilt your demolished house it will look similar to the original but the building itself will have been through a process of death and rebirth and in so doing will be utterly transformed. Something different – something new – has been created.

Transforming a novel into a series brings about two fundamental changes, one challenging, the second often wonderfully exciting. First of all, when you move from the page to the screen, you move from a world of almost total liberty – where anything is allowed and anything can be achieved – to a world of boundaries, of peripheries, of no-go areas. In this world we have schedules, budgets, problems of availability, issues of length and timing. But, more dramatically than that, we find ourselves in a world where there is basically only one point of view – that of the camera and its lens. As a novelist who writes for the screen (large and small), I have to say this is the greatest change you encounter. In a novel you can spend the entire time effortlessly occupying the subconscious of one or as many characters as you like. On screen, however, it is astonishingly difficult to be subjective for any length of time. *Armadillo* is a novel where we are provided almost total access to the thoughts and dreams and fantasies of the central character, Lorimer Black. To reproduce that subjectivity on screen, to get to know Lorimer as well as we do in the novel, required special efforts – and very special acting.

This is the second feature of the film transformation, and one that often provides the happiest bonus – casting. As a reader of a novel you are in effect a one-man or one-woman casting director. You, the reader, flesh out the character on the page; you can imagine what he or she looks like, sounds like and so on. And it's an intensely private process: each reader will have their own version. But once the film is cast, however, that specificity disappears – the look becomes universal. James Frain is for ever 'Lorimer Black', Catherine McCormack will be the eternal 'Flavia Malinverno', Stephen Rae is 'George Hogg' and so on.

For the writer this particular identification is not, as some might feel, a source of worry. In fact it is one of the wonderful pleasures of seeing your work turned into a film or series to witness the word made flesh in this way. A TV series is drama but it is also photography and to see these creatures of your imagination as living, breathing human beings can be a magical experience.

Having adapted several novels for the screen (including three of my own) it seems to me that film and television adaptations of novels are handicapped by certain misguided expectations – more so than adaptations that occur in any other art form. Commentators too seem to have no real, practical idea of what is involved in turning prose fiction into filmed drama. I think the problem arises from the assumption that the processes of film-making are in some way close to novel writing, whereas in fact, as I've tried to show, the two forms are quite distinct – as distinct as a radio play is from a stage play, or a stage play from an opera. No one, for example, goes to see Verdi's *Falstaff* and then comes home to read Shakespeare's *The Merry Wives of Windsor* and then berates Verdi for the audacious changes he has made. Similarly, no one in his right mind would say that Benjamin Britten's *Billy Budd* is *better* than Herman Melville's. You might as well say an apple is a better fruit than an orange. Yet such comparisons and judgements are routinely and unthinkingly made when a novel is filmed.

I think, however, there is some instinctive understanding of this funda-mental alteration that occurs in book-to-film adaptation – for why else would people, having seen and enjoyed the film or the TV series, want to read the novel? All adaptations actively encourage readings of the original source not because people want to see what's been changed or left out but because the aesthetic pleasures involved are entirely different. The pleasures you derive from seeing, for example, the film of *One Flew Over the Cuckoo's Nest* are quite different from those prompted by reading Ken Kesey's novel. And we don't need to rank those respective pleas-ures in a notional hierarchy – each has its own validity. The house of fiction has many windows, Henry James said, and that applies to all the seven arts: we want to keep as many open as possible. And, having taken *Armadillo* apart, brick by brick, timber by timber (with the help of a few old friends), and then (with the help of dozens of new friends) put it back together again, I can say that the transformed house stands proudly on its re-landscaped plot. The lights are on, people are wandering from room to room, I can hear laughter and conversation. I like my new house very much indeed. Come on in.

2001

The Screenwriter's Lot

Last week in Hollywood a small but significant victory was won by screenwriters. In the course of their negotiations with the Studios the Writers' Guild gained a provision that affected the credits in the 'end-titles' of a film. Hitherto the last three titles you see on every film have always gone – WRITER, then PRODUCER, then DIRECTOR. As a result of the new deal with the Studios they will now read – PRODUCER, WRITER, DIRECTOR. From being 'Shmucks with Underwoods' we now *officially* rank second to the director in the creative pecking order.

There is a conspiracy theory bandied about amongst screenwriters that runs along these lines. The writer – the script – is so vitally important, is so crucial in the making of a film that if writers had artistic and industrial influence commensurate with that importance then they would effectively be running the show. So, keep the writers down at all costs, pay them peanuts, set them against each other, denigrate their creative role, grant others the title of 'auteur', anything, *anything* to prevent them realizing that the real power lies in their hands.

Paranoia? Well, a year or so ago, Robert King, a screenwriter in Hollywood, had the bright idea of analysing the Fall/Christmas Movie Preview in the *Los Angeles Times*. Of the 114 movies cited in the preview the screenwriters were credited six times. The directors were mentioned 114 times. King also studied six months of film reviews in the *Los Angeles Times* and discovered the following fascinating statistics. Where a film received a bad review the screenwriters were blamed 61 per cent of the time; directors only 21 per cent of the time. Where a film was deemed a success, however, screenwriters were praised 33 per cent of the time, directors received the plaudits 45 per cent of the time. Bad movies, the conclusion would appear to be, are the results of bad scripts – brickbats to the screenwriter. A good film, however, is down to the director.

When the Oscar nominations were announced this year a deal of British attention was focused, naturally enough, on *Four Weddings and a Funeral*. I did my own straw poll, à la Robert King, of how the nominations were covered on the news that evening. Now, the one and only and undisputable begetter of *Four Weddings* is the screenwriter, Richard Curtis. It was his idea, he invented the story, he created the characters long before his fellow collaborators came together to make the finished film. And quite rightly Richard Curtis was nominated for an Oscar for Best Original Screenplay. However, this fact was not mentioned on any of the early or late evening news coverage on BBC or ITV. It did not make it on to the Teletext or Ceefax list of nominations. Here was a great British success story, trumpeted and bruited abroad for months, for which its creator had received the ultimate accolade. Anyone interested? *News at Ten*, Trevor MacDonald, saw the day's sole mention of Curtis's achievement. Amidst all the *Forrest Gump* fanfares and Hugh Grant's bitter disappointment some editor at ITN had finally decided it was worth reporting. *Four Weddings* was 'also nominated in the category of Best Original Screenplay'. Were we to hear the writer's name? No. As far as my researches revealed the name of the man who created the most successful British film ever, never even rated a mention on the day he was nominated for an Oscar.

Am I overreacting? A little. This is standard stuff, and screenwriters are wryly and reluctantly accustomed to this level of routine neglect. But it is symptomatic of a wider attitude, it seems to me, and that is why writers everywhere, in whatever medium, can derive a little satisfaction from the Writers' Guild's negotiating savvy last week. Shortly after the day of the Oscar nominations I went into one of London's best bookshops to buy a published screenplay. In the film section I read the sign on the bookshelf. 'SCREENPLAYS LISTED A–Z UNDER DIRECTOR'. There is more work to be done.

1993

TELEVISION

Can there be any other form of criticism more ephemeral than television criticism? Even the basic function of encouraging or discouraging the punter is denied the critic as the view is always a backward one and the programme has already vanished into the ether.

Yet I was very pleased indeed, in 1981, to be offered the job of writing the television column of the New Statesman, taking over from Julian Barnes, who was moving on to be the Observer's TV critic. Not only was I joining the staff of a magazine I revered but I was also to be paid a sum of £80 per week and provided with a free television and video recorder. I started on 1 May 1981 and lasted until 25 February 1983. It is the only regular column I have ever written and the most sustained work of journalism I have ever attempted. When I left I calculated I had written some 80,000 words of television criticism — a reasonably sized novel's-worth.

When it came to compiling Bamboo, I wondered if there was anything worth salvaging and to my vague surprise discovered that there was. Amongst the reviews of plays and soap operas, sporting events and chat shows were, amongst others, pieces on Chekhov, Evelyn Waugh, the Falklands War, the work of Mike Leigh and Ken Loach. Also, when I was writing my weekly column I was hard at work at the beginning of my novel-writing career: clearly a lot of what was going on in my head that had to do with fiction was finding its way into my animadversions on television. The only slightly alarming thing about rereading these columns, given the time that has passed since then, is just how many of the people I so blithely judged, analysed and commented on then, I have later come to know really quite well.

Stalky & Co.

Kipling's novel *Stalky & Co.* relates the adventures of three public schoolboys during the 1880s. The three are independently minded, anti-authoritarian rebels, but there's never the slightest doubt – a crucial point – that they're *good*. Between the ages of nine and thirteen I must have read *Stalky & Co.* two or three times a year. It's hard to explain the grip on the imagination the book had then. It's even harder now since seeing BBC1's adaptation: Alexander Baron's script is faithful to the text and the mood as far as I remember, and so the blame for the general feebleness of the whole thing must lie with Kipling.

The central triumvirate look right, as do the sets. The acting, though, is somewhat self-conscious and unnatural; the voices pitched a couple of registers above normal, slightly pedantic over-articulation, and an insistence on saying 'do not' instead of 'don't' – as if contraction were somehow modern and anachronistic. The tone throughout is one of high jinks and wheezes.

But this is nothing new. Almost the entire genre of the public school novel and its various film and TV adaptations seems locked in a jejune world of cads and decent chaps, where moral behaviour is either shining white or pitch black. What's surprising about this is that a largish proportion of English writers must have been through the public school system and yet we're still living with the ethos of the dated classics of the genre: *Tom Brown's Schooldays*, Hugh Walpole's *Jeremy at Crale* and *Stalky & Co.*

In his piece about the series in *Radio Times* Benny Green comments on the ruthlessness with which the boys inflict retribution on those who cross them. We saw nothing of this in episode one. Stalky and Co., who are in King's House, are called 'stinkers' by the members of Prout's House. Revenge is effected by hiding a dead cat in the ceiling above Prout's main dormitory. Who are the stinkers now? Such was the delicacy of feeling on display that we didn't even get to see the dead cat: it was always decently shrouded in a sack.

A little more visible harshness in this series wouldn't go amiss, as it's fairly well established that the Victorian public school was an extremely

nasty place to be educated. But one suspects that the unshakeable consistency of the form will survive. Only Lindsay Anderson's *If* and Frederic
Raphael's excellent *School Play* have done anything to show the other
side of the coin. But why this pervasive blandness? One explanation
might lie in the nature of the powerful appeal these fictional versions
of public school life hold for the young reader. They appeal because
the world they describe – regardless of the age of the protagonists – is
essentially a pre-pubertal one. These are prep school novels, not public
school. Stalky and Co. are well into their teens – sixth formers – yet
they manifest none of the signs or symptoms of adolescence. These boys
– even taking the book's period into account – don't view the world
from the perspective of adolescence; they're still confined in their pre-
teen years. This is why their values are so simple and unreflecting, why
the emphasis is on fun. But it's not very real.

'Don't mix with the makers' is a good piece of advice for a critic, and
one formulated – if I recall – by a former Literary Editor of the *New
Statesman*. Too much fraternization in the end leads either to appalling
embarrassment – barbed exchanges, insults, fist fights – or else a prudent,
and fatal, dulling of critical edge. It might, then, be seen as foolhardy of
Sylvia Clayton – TV critic of the *Telegraph* – to have written a TV play,
Preview (BBC2), but it was clever of her to make it about TV critics, a
rarely explored topic and one she, perforce, will know very well.

Four TV critics gather in a seedy basement preview theatre to watch
a documentary called *The World of Work*. But the documentary's arrival
is delayed and while they're waiting for the director to turn up with
the film a sinister projectionist offers to run one of his own. The critics
scoffingly settle down, but to their amazement find themselves watching
a bizarre fantasy in which they themselves are featured and in which
their relationships with each other are cruelly parodied and caricatured.

At the end the oldest hack, Val (Anton Rodgers), is found dead of a
stroke. Some ambulance men are called and cart him off. The others
compose themselves and settle down to the documentary which has
now arrived. All except Babs who can't stomach any more TV. As she
leaves, the world beyond the exit doors is revealed as a bright whistling
void.

'Very *Last Year in Marienbad*,' one of the critics sneers about the film
within the play, thereby pre-empting remarks about *Preview*. In fact the
surrealism was very well handled until the return to reality at the end

with the arrival of extra bodies (policemen, ambulance men, apologetic director) in the enclosed world of the theatre, all of which had the effect of swiftly undermining the mystery and begging questions of an annoyingly causal and pragmatic sort. If there had been regular traffic between theatre and street (cop, ambulance man etc.), whence the sudden echoing void? Why, too, did the projectionist want to humiliate the critics? What were his motives? To answer 'it's surreal', isn't enough. The problem with surrealism is that although it readily imparts a kind of eerie portentousness, it needs to be handled carefully – and, paradoxically, with its own brand of consistency – otherwise the suspicion lingers that all those compelling and unsettling effects are being bought just a little too cheaply.

1981

Brideshead Revisited (1)

'This novel,' Evelyn Waugh said about *Brideshead Revisited*, 'lost me such esteem as I once enjoyed among my contemporaries and led me into the unfamiliar world of fan-mail and press photographers.' It's not difficult to understand the novel's abiding popularity: nostalgia for a vanished era, deep sentimentality, saccharine romance among aristocratic types – many of the ingredients of the contemporary best-seller. It's Waugh's best-known book, but in many respects it's his worst, and problems arise when it's seen in the context of his work as a whole. How could Evelyn Waugh, one of the great English novelists of this century, write this sort of rubbish?

> The languor of Youth – how unique and quintessential it is! How quickly, how irrecoverably, lost! The zest, the generous affections, the illusions, the despair, all the traditional attributes of Youth – all save this – come and go with us through life.

How also could he construct such a broken-backed plot; labour so clumsily with the techniques of first-person narration; abandon an excellent leading character for one of the most lifeless heroines in modern fiction?

Waugh himself, when he came to revise the book in 1959, was not unaware of its deficiencies, and the preface he wrote for the new edition represents an unmistakable demotion. The Magnum Opus, as it was known in the writing, becomes just a souvenir of the Second World War. But *Brideshead Revisited* can't be dismissed as an aberration. It's too large a book and its central position in Waugh's career means it can't be ignored.

Waugh's novels divide themselves fairly neatly into two groups. On the one hand there are the comedies – with their naive or roguish protagonists – such as *Decline and Fall, Scoop, Black Mischief* and *The Loved One*. On the other are *A Handful of Dust, Work Suspended, Brideshead Revisited, The Ordeal of Gilbert Pinfold* and *The Sword of Honour* trilogy. It's on this last category of novels that Waugh's status as a major novelist rests. They all contain examples of his comic genius but they are supplemented by an element which is best, though simply, described as autobiographical.

Waugh drew heavily on events in his own life to furnish himself with the necessary raw material for his fiction. In almost all his novels, even the most outrageously comic, this transposition can be detected with little effort – a procedure considerably aided by the publication of his letters and diaries. The egregious Captain Grimes in *Decline and Fall* is a faithful portrait of a master at the prep school where Waugh taught. The bizarre evangelist Mrs Melrose Ape in *Vile Bodies* is Amy Semple McPherson. *Scoop* is a thinly fictionalized version of his travel book *Remote People*. Most famously, *The Ordeal of Gilbert Pinfold* is a case history of his own paranoia. And so on. The image of Waugh as a beleaguered Tory squire tends to obscure the modernity of his fictional approach. In almost all cases the fiction remains very close to the source.

This is not to deprecate Waugh's genuine imagination or great talent. All novelists – all realistic novelists – make the same transference, but some rely on it more heavily than others. In Waugh's case, it seems to me, there is less pure *invention* than we might normally have supposed. The kind of world he described in his fiction wasn't one he had to experience imaginatively: its elements lay dispersed all around him.

If this premise is acceptable it allows a more precise idea of the kind of novelist Waugh was (he is not like Dickens, for example) and it also makes a reading of *Brideshead Revisited* a little easier to achieve.

To summarize as briefly as possible, the novel consists of a sustained recollection on the part of the narrator, Captain Charles Ryder. It opens during the Second World War. Charles's battalion is billeted in the grounds of Brideshead Castle and his arrival there prompts a long reconsideration of the relationships he enjoyed with its one-time occupants – the aristocratic, Catholic Flyte family – during the 1920s.

At Oxford Charles meets and is taken up by the dreamily eccentric Lord Sebastian Flyte, the younger son of the family. Charles is soon introduced to its other members and spends increasing amounts of his time at Brideshead. He is utterly captivated both by Sebastian and by the house itself. But, as Charles is drawn closer into the family, he and Sebastian drift apart. Sebastian evolves into a self-destructive alcoholic, finds life at home impossible and moves abroad.

Some years later, Charles – now a successful artist – meets Sebastian's sister Julia again while on a transatlantic liner. They soon become lovers and plan to marry. This course of action is impeded because they both have to divorce their respective partners and also because of the return to England of Julia's father Lord Marchmain. Lord Marchmain had scandalized society by openly taking a mistress and had abandoned his wife, family and religion to live abroad in self-imposed exile. He returns home to die, still a resolute apostate. The climax of the novel is a death-bed scene where, at the very last moment, Lord Marchmain acknowledges his faith. This gesture compels Julia to remain true to hers also, and she refuses to live with or marry Charles – even though Lord Marchmain had altered his will to leave Brideshead to them both. Charles accepts her decision and they part for ever.

The novel's epilogue sees Charles wandering through the deserted and decrepit Brideshead contemplating the past. He is a sad and melancholy man but the experience has provided him with a faith of his own and, it's strongly implied, he has converted to Catholicism.

The novel, Waugh said in a letter to Nancy Mitford, 'is all about God'. This is only part of the truth. The events in Waugh's life which made an appearance in his fiction were treated with an unremitting honesty, as *Gilbert Pinfold* makes abundantly clear. This is also true of the theme of betrayal and the faithless wife in *A Handful of Dust*, and his experience of war in the excellent and often underrated *Sword of Honour*. *Brideshead* belongs to this line of Waugh's fiction but it's the one book where the area of personal revelation and exploration is obscured by the unsatisfactory 'story' surrounding it. The lingering over meals and wine, the implausible destinies of most of the characters, the meandering sprawl of the narrative are distractions and obfuscations. Beneath this Waugh's real intentions can with some effort be made out. To put it crudely, *Brideshead Revisited* is not, as he would have it, about 'the operation of divine grace on a group of diverse but closely related characters'; it's about, first, the nature of a love that can exist between two young men and, second, the particular character of Waugh's own religious faith.

The first part of *Brideshead Revisited* is an evocation of Oxford in the twenties and of a class of friendship which would now be recognized as homosexual. Waugh clouds the issue but the homosexual references are so numerous that only a wilful stubbornness could ignore their implication. When Charles's relationship with Sebastian ends, the love interest is sustained in the person of Julia. However, although her similarity to Sebastian is continually stressed, the description of Charles's love affair with her is almost wholly lifeless. It's the character of Sebastian which attracts our interest, but his exit from the novel is clumsily abrupt and his ultimate fate – as a tame drunk in a monastery somewhere – is a feeble stab at plausibility.

After the Sebastian–Charles relationship the second theme of the novel engages Waugh's remaining serious attention. As the family prepares for Lord Marchmain's death, Charles systematically attacks, with devastating rationality, the tenets of the Catholic faith. To the agnostic or atheist reader – perhaps to the non-Catholic reader – everything about the book's conclusion is maddeningly unsatisfying. And Waugh encourages this reaction with grim perversity. The reader is cajoled into condemning the Flyte family's destructive faith. We cannot understand and must deplore Lord Marchmain's death-bed recantation. We find it impossible to comprehend the reasons why Julia rejects Charles and we earnestly hope Charles will curse her for an ignorant fool. Finally, it becomes inconceivable that – at the novel's end – Charles too should adopt their faith. But Waugh has no wish to provide a comforting or remotely rational explanation for his faith. It does not partake of reason or logic. Its sustaining power would be of no account if it did. It functions, for him at least, as the most severe and uncompromising of challenges, and it's this aspect that Waugh so ruthlessly illustrates in the final pages.

This disharmony between the two themes of the novel and much of the narrative which is meant to reveal them may be one way of explaining the many dissatisfactions arising from this curious novel. Essentially it comes down to this: Waugh fudges the issue on the first theme and takes up the second halfway through the book, encumbered by having to work through a narrative in which he has only a superficial interest.

A television adaptation, I surmised, might seize the opportunity of focusing the emphasis on these subtextual obsessions. To a very limited extent this has been attempted.

I've seen the first five episodes – six hours – of Granada's forthcoming adaptation of the novel. It is scrupulously faithful to the original. John Mortimer's script uses Waugh's own dialogue and vocabulary at every opportunity. Even the 'feel' of the novel has been maintained through the extensive use of voiceover narration.

These episodes cover the relationship between Charles and Sebastian and take in their Oxford careers, a visit to Lord Marchmain in Venice, and several holidays at Brideshead. One of the defects of the novel, and where television actually improves on the original, is in the character of Charles. In the book his personality is – frankly – dull and boring. It's hard to imagine why someone as intriguing as Sebastian should want to have anything to do with him. On film we have Jeremy Irons as Charles, fleshing out the 'I' figure admirably. At least we can *see* why Sebastian and the preening aesthete Anthony Blanche (excellently rendered by Nicholas Grace) should be fascinated: simply he's good-looking and they clearly fancy him. This implication is more heavily emphasized than in the novel but doesn't move much beyond this. Sebastian puts his arms round Charles's shoulders but otherwise their affection remains chaste. (Mortimer does get Charles on some occasions to light his cigarette from Sebastian's. A code?)

This policy decision to follow the book at all costs is commendable (it extends to set decorations, costumes, even – with one important exception – hairstyles) though I should imagine it's going to be progressively hard to maintain in the second half. However, it does mean that the faults of the book are carried over to the film. Certain explanations are not forthcoming – notably in the case of Sebastian's self-loathing and his mysterious shame 'of being unhappy'. A charge of tedium is sure to be levelled, as it can be at the book. A lot more could have been cut with little damage, and, as it is, it's going to have to be spread fairly thin to cover twelve hours of viewing time.

There is one slip-up, though, which seems, in the midst of so much attention to detail, curious. In the novel both Sebastian and Julia are dark. Their extreme likeness to one another is regularly referred to – a fact which is intended to make Julia an obvious Sebastian surrogate. But in the series Sebastian (Anthony Andrews) is blond and Julia (Diana Quick) is dark. Why, I wonder. It seems a stupid oversight.

Otherwise one can only applaud. The acting is of a uniformly high standard. Anthony Andrews gives the performance of his life as Sebastian, the locations – Oxford, Venice, Castle Howard – are superb, and there's a classic John Gielgud cameo as Charles's eccentric father. The first episode is being shown on Monday 12 October. Despite all the problems, well worth watching.

1981

Brideshead Revisited (2)

In the final episode of *Brideshead Revisited* Charles Ryder and Julia sit on the steps in the enormous house and agree to part. They're both weeping and generally inarticulate, but one of the 'broken sentences' Charles manages to mutter between stifled sobs is 'So long to say so little.' It could serve quite nicely for the last word on this paradoxically compelling serial. Rather like the book itself, I suspect that it was the first half that got us watching the second. The departure of Sebastian, leaving centre stage to Charles Ryder, consigned most of the final episodes to a level of infuriating dullness. It's a foreseeable defect, but one which scriptwriter John Mortimer seemed reluctant to avoid.

There's been much talk of Mortimer's faithfulness to the text, but in changing medium – from novel to TV series – such commendable rectitude can often be technically inept if not wrong-headed. This was particularly evident in episode six, where Julia is finally led on stage. Almost the entire episode was a sepia flashback of the courtship of Rex Mottram. In the book this largely takes the form of straightforward reported speech, but there are also some pages of direct conversation – *post facto* reminiscence by Julia and Charles. This is a clumsy device in the novel, but on the screen it comes across as sheer thoughtlessness. The voiceover renditions of this dialogue, and the clear intimacy that the interlocutors share, effectively deprive the forthcoming Charles/Julia romance of any vestige of suspense. We know from the very outset of Julia's appearance, while we're still in the process of learning about her and Rex, that she and Charles will end up together. One minute Charles is an art student in Paris, then suddenly we're presented with a view of him on an ocean liner arm in arm with Julia. To someone who doesn't know the book such methods of moving the story on must appear bafflingly amateurish.

Mortimer, of course, is simply reproducing Waugh's own struggles with the plot, and to that extent is blameless. But, while Mortimer's adaptation is by and large unobtrusive, he can't entirely escape responsibility as he does occasionally contribute material of his own.

The most notable expansion has been of the General Strike episode.

The strike, and the party Charles and Boy Mulcaster go to while it's on, occupy some five and a half pages in the novel. In the serial these peripheral events took up an entire episode. The party scenes in particular had to be supplied almost entirely by Mortimer. This isn't a bad thing; in fact these scenes were amusing and entertaining. The point is that if you can take these sort of liberties with the text on one occasion, then there are no grounds for not taking them on others, and the excuse of 'scrupulous adherence' is no longer viable.

This takes us on to another area where Mortimer's script has to bear some of the blame: dialogue. Because, in the novel, Waugh has selected first person narration, he finds himself having to get other characters to tell Charles various facts in order to fill in gaps in his – the narrator's – knowledge. Waugh does this by allowing these other characters very lengthy uninterrupted monologues. A good example is provided by Cordelia telling Charles, over several pages, of Sebastian's fate. Now, this only just works on the page. On the screen it seems almost a wilful breach of the conventions of realism. Film is an omniscient style of narration, the technical requirements of restricted point-of-view don't apply, we're not – in other words – inhabiting Charles Ryder's consciousness. Where the whole thing broke down was in maintaining these monologues on the screen. Just because Charles doesn't interject in the book didn't mean that, in the realistic world of the TV serial, he had to keep a similar silence. He never said a word. Never said 'Mmmm' or 'I see' or 'You've got a point there.' The camera frequently cut to him but all you got was a soulful look.

This had a further consequence as well as the irritation it gave rise to. Jeremy Irons as Charles had a difficult task. Charles Ryder is a typically dull Waugh narrator figure, like Tony Last in *A Handful of Dust* and Guy Crouchback in *The Sword of Honour* trilogy. But, somehow, Irons has contrived to make him more pompous and unlikeable than he is in the book. This is partly to do with his persistent non-participation in conversations but it's also to do with Irons's interpretation of Charles's character, his repertoire of weak smiles and pursed lips. By the end of the serial I found Charles intensely off-putting, a sidling, supercilious creep, his cigarette daintily poised between thumb and forefinger. This may have been deliberate; it certainly makes Julia's rejection of him at the end eminently comprehensible. But it also had more ironic side effects. In comparison to Irons's Charles, Waugh's villains – Julia (his wife), Rex Mottram and even Hooper – appear warm and sympathetic.

Julia may be silly and materialistic but it's very hard to sanction Charles's treatment of her, let alone his callous disregard for his children. Even in the book this comes across as something of a puzzle, but in the serial it looks almost like a deliberate attempt to alienate the audience from Charles.

Curiously, though, the vast amount of criticism the serial has generated is a tribute to the overall success of the venture. It has provoked persistent debate and controversy at all levels and on all manner of topics, which is no mean achievement after all, and should be a source of genuine satisfaction to those who participated in the project.

It's most lasting effect is a comprehensive and timely reassessment of the novel itself and the position it occupies in the Waugh canon. It's surely clear now that *Brideshead Revisited* represents an aberration, a lapse. More kindly, perhaps, it can be seen as an unsuccessful prototype, a false start on themes tackled more skilfully in Waugh's greatest achievement *The Sword of Honour*. The next challenge?

1981

The Cherry Orchard

All the speculation about and reaction to *Brideshead Revisited* drew attention to a fascinating similarity that exists between it and Chekhov's *The Cherry Orchard*, screened last week on BBC1. Chekhov's play is, in many ways, his *Brideshead*: an ancient country estate enshrining certain traditional and aristocratic values, threatened by a new order of a proletarian or *arriviste* class, whose standards (materialism, philistinism) ultimately take possession of the house and cherry orchard – a multifaceted symbol, but one which, like Brideshead Castle, represents entirely different potentialities to the opposing parties.

Admittedly, Waugh's concern in *Brideshead* is more disgruntled and minatory than documentary. The egregious Hooper and his ilk represent a possible future for the new England. At the end of the book the desecration of the ornamental fountain in front of the house – it becomes a repository for cigarette ends and half-eaten sandwiches – was only intended to be a prophetic utterance.

Of course, there is a strongly prophetic note in Chekhov's play (written in 1903) though it's hard to tell just how much this has been amplified by hindsight. However, I don't think Chekhov viewed Lopakhin with the same fear and loathing with which Waugh regarded Hooper. Certainly, the Lopakhin in this production – the excellent Bill Paterson – was a more sympathetic figure. His desire to turn the cherry orchard into plots for holiday homes may be unfeeling and misguided but one never feels it's malicious. He is, after all, trying to do the impoverished Mme Ranevsky (Judi Dench) a favour.

Richard Eyre's direction of the play was magnificent. I'm not qualified to judge Trevor Griffiths's 'version' of the text, but it seemed admirably unstilted and plausible. The production was crammed with felicities. One very subtle one, perhaps not immediately apparent, was the imaginative use of Scottish accents – possessed, by and large, by those of ex-serf or peasant background. But the identification went even further than that. The old serf Firs (Paul Curran) spoke broad Scots. The oily dandy Yasha (David Rintoul) was Edinburgh public school. Socially mobile Lopakhin, who's made a fortune from his business ventures, had the nasal, faintly mid-Atlantic twang that some Scottish professional footballers – and managers – acquire after a career in English clubs. No names, no pack drill. They were all spot on, naturally, because the actors were themselves Scots, which seems a good time to make a plea for similar worthy typecasting.

Most exciting, though, was the visual quality of the play. Future studio work will be judged by the standards set here. Quite simply, it looked as though it had been shot on location. There was a clean, pastel quality to the lighting, beautiful and thoughtful set design too, creating a sensation of the other, partly glimpsed rooms of the house extending capaciously beyond the one in which the action was taking place.

I can go on. The acting was first-class all round, and Richard Eyre's direction showed expert manipulation of composition and depth. It's very hard to get more than four characters in the 'frame' of a TV screen without making it look like they're standing in a crowded lift. In the final scenes, when Mme Ranevsky leaves the house, there were, at one point, nine people comfortably in view. Overall, Eyre's use of the space available to him was exemplary. The property developer in Lopakhin makes him say to Mme Ranevsky that 'the only remarkable thing about your cherry orchard is its dimensions'. The dimensions of Eyre's *Cherry Orchard* were remarkable too; but then so was everything about this production.

1982

How Many Miles to Babylon?

E. M. Forster's famous dictum about hoping he had the guts to betray his country rather than a friend turned out to be unusually applicable this week. Most notably to the excellent *How Many Miles to Babylon?* (BBC2), a subtle and visually entrancing film about two Irish friends caught up in the First World War, based on Jennifer Johnston's novel of the same name, and benefiting from a masterly adaptation by the *New Statesman*'s Derek Mahon.

The film opened some years before the war. Alex (Daniel Day-Lewis) is the weedy scion of an aristocratic Irish family. An only child, he makes friends with a boy from the local village, Jerry (Christopher Fairbank). The friendship continues through adolescence to young manhood, even though it is forcefully proscribed by Alex's frosty and heartless mother (virtuoso stuff from Siân Phillips).

The war comes and Alex – a reluctant soldier – is bullied into joining up by his mother, partly to keep her end up socially in the neighbourhood and partly to thwart Alex's ineffectual father. Alex duly becomes a subaltern in the regiment that Jerry has also joined. In France their bond strengthens, overcoming the barriers of army discipline and hierarchy. However, Jerry goes AWOL to look for his father, missing in action in another sector of the front. He returns in secret and is caught sheltering with Alex in his billet. He's sentenced to death and Alex's blimpish major (Barry Foster) – who despises the 'bog Irish' under his charge – orders Alex to command the firing squad. Establishing that there's no possibility of a reprieve, Alex cheats military justice by acting as executioner himself.

It seems a simple and affecting story, saved from sentimentality by extremely good acting all round and commendable restraint in direction (Moira Armstrong) and scripting. The measured pace of the film – a positive advantage here – allowed the resonances and sub-themes to assert themselves unobtrusively: Alex's loveless family background, the tension experienced by the Irish fighting in a British war, the resilience and survival of personal loyalties. Even the Yeatsian echoes – more easily established in a text – were cleverly alluded to.

Interestingly enough, the film has drawn some accusations of implausibility, not in terms of its period detail – which seemed immaculate – but rather in the relationships on show. Would this intense friendship across widely separated classes ever have existed in the first place? Could it conceivably have continued in the army? Would Alex's company commander have been quite so mad? All these objections are irrelevant. If the scenes have an imaginative veracity, then that's all that's required. It's a curious fact, but in fiction we tend to generalize about the past in a way that would be inconceivable about the present. Very broad truths about human nature, social mores and customs are unquestioningly accepted and assumed to be wholly and entirely applicable: 'This couldn't have happened'; 'People never said that sort of thing'; 'No one would ever behave in such a way.' How can anyone know for sure? The answer is they can't, and everyone treating of the past in a fictional way should do their utmost to resist these orthodoxies of interpretation of human nature wherever possible, while – and it's an essential qualification – scrupulously avoiding any documentary vagueness or anachronisms. *How Many Miles to Babylon?* succeeded admirably on both counts.

In a fascinating way the film's fiction highlighted certain factual events of the Second World War which were aired in a remarkable *40 Minutes* (BBC2) called *Mutiny*. This concerned the mutiny of 191 British soldiers at Salerno in 1943. Fifteen hundred veterans of the 8th Army were shipped from their transit camp in North Africa to Italy. The men believed they were being sent to rejoin their own units in Sicily. On the voyage they were told that in fact they were going to be used as reinforcements for the 5th Army at Salerno. Unit pride being unusually fierce in the 8th Army, the men felt they had been deliberately conned by the army staff. In fact they were victims of a classic army balls-up. The message for reinforcements had gone to the wrong transit camp. Their disgruntlement reached a peak when they were finally ordered into the lines. Thirteen hundred marched off, 191 refused. The men were sent back to North Africa and tried as mutineers and all found guilty. Heavy sentences of penal servitude were passed and three sergeants were condemned to death.

The men all pleaded not guilty. As much-decorated veterans they felt that *they* had been let down by the army and refused to concede that in any way they had impugned their honour. The mystery is that shortly afterwards *all* the sentences were suspended and the men returned to the front line, where strong evidence exists to show that they were to be deliberately exposed to the fiercest fighting.

On *Newsnight* (BBC2) one of the condemned sergeants was confronted with one of the army judges who had sentenced him to death. Both were unrepentant. The one refused to admit that a mutiny had occurred, and the ex-judge – in a quite astonishing display of patrician aloofness – maintained that the man sitting opposite him deserved to have been shot and that he would still sentence him to death if the case came before him today.

Both men were victims of the institution they served in. The 8th Army veterans should have known that their entirely reasonable request to fight with their own units could never justify refusing to obey such an order. Equally, the judge, hide-bound by his conceptions of 'honour' and 'the need to maintain absolute discipline', could never admit he was wrong without undermining his entire military ethos. It's chastening to reflect that had those veterans been returned to their 8th Army units they would have willingly sacrificed their lives in battle. A sad and bitter confusion of misplaced loyalties, from which the army proves to be emerging with absolutely no credit.

1982

Ken Loach and Barry Hines

Events in the South Atlantic have lent a telling and naturally unsought for irony to the latest Ken Loach/Barry Hines collaboration *Looks and Smiles* (Central). The opening sequence shows a sergeant presenting a recruiting film to a group of school leavers. 'Things have changed,' he avers. 'There are no John Waynes in the Army now.' This line is meant to encourage youngsters to join up, dangling the lure of a secure job, valuable apprenticeship and little risk of danger: propositions which seem highly attractive to the film's central duo, Mick Walsh (Graham Green) and Alan Wright (Tony Pitts), both on the point of leaving school, but faced with the prospect of an interminable place in the dole queue rather than any avenue of bright tomorrows.

Alan succumbs to the temptation, and so too would Mick, except that his father forbids him. The rest of the film concerns itself with what life on the dole is like for Mick, charting the steady decline of his hopes and aspirations, his casual involvement in petty crime and, most movingly and convincingly, his relationship with his girlfriend Karen (Carolyn Nicholson).

The narrative is episodic and leisurely as we follow the mundane events that compose Mick and Karen's life. We witness their courtship, their falling-out, their reconciliation. Mick goes through several interview stages for a job, gets involved in a fight in a pub, makes futile visits to a job centre. Such drama as exists is provided by Karen's stormy relationship with her mother. Karen's parents are separated and her mother is involved with another man. A blazing row, triggered by Mick and Karen being caught *in flagrante*, prompts Karen to leave home and run away to her father in Bristol, whither Mick transports her on his motorbike. That venture, too, ends with disappointment, compromise and resignation – the only qualities life seems to offer – when Karen discovers that her father has set up another home with girlfriend and new baby – too cramped and intimate to admit a fourth. The film ends with Alan talking to the pair about life in the Army, extolling its virtues which include participating in snatch squads in Belfast and ransacking Catholic households in the Falls Road. Mick, confronted by the same vista of dead ends, is still tempted. But Karen issues an ultimatum: it's either her or the Army, he can't have both. The last shot of the film sees Mick joining the queue to pick up his giro cheque.

This is an excellent, sombre film – with few moments of light-heartedness – made all the more so by being shot in black and white, which, against the familiar north of England industrial background, recalled various 'working-class' movies of the fifties – *Room at the Top, Saturday Night and Sunday Morning*, etc. It reflects the by now familiar, but continually remarkable, Loach/Hines hyperrealism with excellent performances from the entire cast. This, one feels, must get very close to what life is like for unemployed youngsters in the north – or anywhere come to that. One reservation, though, is that it seems on this occasion that the documentary impulse is stronger than the dramatic one, saving the Mick and Karen romance, that Loach and Hines are more concerned to reproduce than to tell and this conceivably lessens the overall effect somewhat. It's in the combination of documentary truth and dramatic sympathy that this type of film makes its most powerful impact, as *Kes* and *Family Life* testify, and where *Looks and Smiles* falls a little short.

The incomplete meshing of the two strands makes itself most evident on at least two occasions when polemic takes over. One happens when Mick lambasts the lady at the job centre with an attack on the waste and illogicality of mass unemployment and another when Alan produces a plastic bullet in the pub at the film's conclusion, initiating his account of a soldier's life in Northern Ireland. The points made on each occasion are entirely worthy but bring about the only pauses in the easy flow of the film's naturalism.

It goes without saying that neither Loach nor Hines is interested in remaining impassionate or neutral. All their work makes broad and commendable social points as, indeed, did *Looks and Smiles*, and with these exceptions, it did so subtly and apparently effortlessly, gaining instant sympathetic engagement from the viewer. The two instances referred to departed from this method and thereby drew attention to themselves, alerting us to the contrivances employed in the weaving of any fiction, and seemed in the context of the film clumsy and ill-composed. They were, clearly, attitudes that Barry Hines was concerned to express, but that they ended up being done in this way illustrates the inferior place the drama – the storytelling – took to the documentary.

This is a minor quibble about an otherwise wholly absorbing film, but it's one that's worth airing. Highlighting certain truths is a vital part of any fictional enterprise but if the medium is imaginative – creating characters and a narrative – then doing it through *story* rather than *statement* will always be the most effective way of getting those truths across.

1982

The Falklands War (1)

The compelling drama surrounding the 'War of the Falkland Islands', or whatever it will come to be known as, made most of the week's television seem nugatory – or, to put it in a more charitable way, highlighted its essentially artificial and fictive nature. Radio won the day, however, with its live transmission of the emergency parliamentary debate on Saturday morning. If there was ever a time when one wished TV cameras had been allowed into the House of Commons, this was surely it. Equally astonishing was the blare of xenophobic, jingoistic sentiment that erupted. It was an unsettling experience seeing the bellicose clichés being dusted off and reading the trumpeting headlines and leaders in the national press. This must have been what it was like before the Crimea, the Boer War or 1914, one thought bemusedly. Edward Du Cann's absurd but surely to be immortalized assertion about the impossibly stretched lines of communication summed it all up: 'I don't remember Wellington whining on about Torres Vedras,' he said with no trace of irony. Yet we were whizzing further back through time by Monday morning as an *ITN Special Report* brought us the departure of the *Invincible* and the *Hermes* for the South Atlantic. 'There's a curiously seventeenth-century atmosphere about Portsmouth today,' the reporter opined. Sir Francis Drake and the Armada were regularly alluded to. However, the irate gung-ho spirit seemed to have subsided to a degree. The analyses offered by various experts were in a tone that seemed to imply a faintly unreal air about the whole undertaking. Were we really sailing off to wage war against the Argentinians? Were these prognoses about the superiority of the British Fleet, for once, not part of some hypothetical war game?

And yet the crowds packed the quayside, there was cheering and flag-waving as our gallant boys sailed off to do battle with the foe. The most alarming aspect of all the multitude of words so far expended is that comparatively few of them have been concerned with the actual fate that may greet these servicemen. 'People will get hurt' appears at the moment to be the favourite euphemism for 'killed and maimed'. 'I'm afraid people get hurt in war,' was John Nott's variation during a commendably vigorous and aggressive interview by Brian Walden on *Weekend World* (LWT), as if he were talking about pulled muscles or tennis elbow. Once again the bleak sense of déjà vu descended: images of chateau-dwelling, claret-swilling generals during the First World War, staff officers planning strategy hundreds of miles from the front line. The front line in this particular case looks like being halfway round the world. If I were a naval rating on HMS *Invincible* I would feel very uneasy about what I was being asked to do.

But then that's not a characteristic response from people who *volunteer* to join the armed forces. This fact was made evident by a coincidental repeat of *The Woolridge View* (BBC2) about the Navy fieldgun teams which participate in the Royal Tournament. Here men volunteered to 'learn to withstand unreasonable physical pain' within a training regime whose working conditions were blind obedience to the unbelievably tyrannical discipline of the NCO coaches. These men mercilessly knock their teams into shape. 'Once fit,' a coach boasted, 'they become beasts.' I suppose at this point one should growl 'Look out Argentina', but on reflection – not much required – it seems demeaning and sad. Clearly there's nothing terribly sinister about it being applied to sport, but, equally clearly, one knows that these same values on display are intended to function on the battlefield as well.

1982

The Falklands War (2)

Shortly after the Falklands War I made two predictions in this column. One was right and the other was wrong. The first was that the journalists would have large axes to grind and deep grudges to settle over the treatment they had received. The second was that when the reels of film finally came back with the cameramen and reporters the visual record of the war would be transformed, that, finally rid of the MOD minders and government censorship, we'd get to see the pictures that had been denied us. 'There should be,' I said, 'some fascinating documentaries.'

Well, I was wrong. The Falklands documentaries and videos have established that what we saw at the time – albeit two weeks late – is all we're going to get. That it was a naive assumption to think otherwise was made clear on *Panorama* (BBC1) in an excellent and informative programme on the astonishing hamstringing that the media experienced.

The main argument against unrestricted reporting of a war is that any information made available to the public is of value to the enemy. This is manifestly true in the case of military operations. 'Eisenhower announces date of D-Day invasion' would not have been the kind of headline calculated to win friends among the armed forces, and no one, not even the most passionate advocate of a free press, would expect this sort of information to be made open. On the *Panorama* programme various top brass and the editor of the *Daily Telegraph* made exactly this point. This would have been fair and just if the practice at the time had been even approximate to this ground rule. But the mare's nest of crossed lines, ambivalences, duplicities, disinformation and plain lying made the excuse of preserving military secrets a ludicrous sham.

The best example of this was the Goose Green leak when the World Service announced that the paratroops were advancing on the settlement, as indeed they were. The understandable wrath of the men on the ground was directed at the quislings of the BBC when in actual fact the information had been provided by a 'senior government official' keen to provide some 'good news'. Not, in any event, that it would have been difficult for the Argentinians to have drawn the conclusion that Goose Green was a key target. One of the more curious assumptions of the MOD's case is that the enemy is extremely stupid and can only base his strategic and tactical decisions on what he happens to read in the newspapers.

It was Churchill who coined the phrase 'in war the truth is so important that it must be protected by a bodyguard of lies'. The aptness of this saw is very confined. Give it a general frame of reference and its aphoristic certainties conceal a more sinister import. As one of the news editors perceptively remarked, this sort of media manipulation possesses only short-term advantages, but in the longer term its consequences can be far from beneficial for the perpetrators. It's clear that from now on a deep cynicism and profound suspicion will colour the relationship between the press and the MOD. It won't be a bad thing if some of that rubs off on the public.

But will it? Most of the truth about the Falklands will emerge eventually. Some books are already telling us facts we didn't know before, certain reporters are re-filing the 'missing' dispatches. But they will be read by only a fraction of those who were tuned in to the news and reading the newspapers at the time.

And the MOD and the government will no doubt claim that this *Panorama* programme was biased. Of course it was and correctly so. The gags have been removed and the media have made a convincing case against the government's manipulation of the news to suit its ad hoc political motives and ambitions. The ball is now in its court. But I suspect that the response will be 'not available for comment'.

1982

The Falklands War (3)

Those Tory MPs dismayed by Archbishop Runcie's lack of gung-ho spirit over our Great Victory in the Falklands will be able to console themselves with reruns of the first major documentary to have emerged from the conflict: BBC1's eight-part *Task Force South*. Here was a chance, one thought, to get things straight, to produce an account of the war under conditions where accusations of aiding and abetting the enemy and lowering national morale need no longer apply. And, what's more, under circumstances that should be a gift to your average documentary maker, namely an eager public who sensed there was more to be told and, perhaps most valuable, a public who, if not well informed, was at least cognizant of all the major facts, geography, names of key personalities, etc.

So why was *Task Force South* – or at least the two episodes we saw last week – so wretchedly bland, almost insultingly simple in its tone and approach? It was as if a decision had been taken not to make the thing too complicated, as if it were aimed at an intermediate class of foreign language students – a teaching aid in an 'O' level course on contemporary British history. There was a lot of skilful editing on show and for much of the time the pictures were allowed to tell their own story, but the narration – supplied by Richard Baker and Brian Hanrahan – and the editorial approach seemed studiously inoffensive and pussy-footing. There was a notable absence of comment over the Carrington resignation and the merest nod at Al Haig's furious shuttling. Both those topics, I'll concede, are particularly gamey cans of worms, and I dare say that it could be argued that even lifting the lid for a second or two could eat into time that could be more profitably used elsewhere: but some indication of the complexities and controversies surrounding them was definitely required. Thus far at least, it doesn't seem to be forthcoming.

The first two programmes dealt with the initial days of the crisis and the dispatch of the fleet and here, it seemed to me, was another manifest lapse. The fact that there was a deal of jubilant unreflecting patriotism in the air at the time was incontrovertible and was clearly established by the pictures. But the narration failed to comment on the illusory nature of this elation or display any of the sobering but necessary ironies with which hindsight has now provided us. The most remarkable phenomenon of the early days of the crisis was exactly this dangerous self-delusion about the nature of war that appeared to have almost the entire country in its chilling grip. The prime function of any programme dealing with those heady days in April should be first to point out and highlight the cruel absurdities of the 'Stick it up your junta' spirit and then do its utmost to eradicate any residual traces. There is no sign of that happening at the moment in *Task Force South*.

1982

Mike Leigh (1)

What's the difference between Realism and Naturalism? The concepts are bandied about as if they are interchangeable, but there is a distinction and one worth trying to pin down, I think, especially as last week saw the start of a Mike Leigh season, the writer with whom the two terms are most frequently associated. In an enjoyable *Arena* (BBC2) that heralded the start of the 'season' or 'festival', Leigh himself claimed that he wasn't a Naturalist, on the grounds that his plays were structured and distilled from a mass of material and weren't simply random and contingent. By this token, then, the paradigm of Naturalism on film is something like Andy Warhol's *Sleep*, where for a beguiling eight hours you can watch a man do just that. But, that reservation aside, the *Arena* profile contained many references to a striving for reality which informs and motivates all Leigh's plays and films. He 'confronted the viewer with reality'; 'a reality starts to grow' in the improvisation techniques; the ultimate object was 'to be real' and so on. So, strictly speaking, Leigh isn't a Naturalist, in that he doesn't simply set up his camera and let it run; but much of the strength of his work, I think, derives from an illusion of Naturalism, a *cinéma-vérité* or documentary approach that, in short segments, is almost indistinguishable from anything that a hidden and free-associating camera might pick up.

One could quibble endlessly about the extent to which the two terms overlap but Realism seems to me a much more general term, with a broad referential base to be compared with a category like fantasy or science fiction. *Coronation Street* is Realistic in this sense but is a long way from a Leigh play like *Grown Ups*. Perhaps we should call Leigh's work Hyperrealism in the manner of those American artists who spend six months painting sunflash and gleam in the chrome guts of a ton-up motorbike. The point is worth labouring – and I don't usually bother about categories – because the efforts Leigh goes to recall those painstaking artists, and because in his passion to mimic reality – real life – Leigh has discovered a way of making television function more effectively for him than it does for any other dramatist currently at work.

The *Arena* profile – 'Mike Leigh: Making Plays' – wove conversation with Leigh, and some of the actors who've worked with him, with clips from the plays and filmed a workshop – specially set up for the programme – showing the celebrated improvisational approach in practice. Leigh went to RADA and from there to Camberwell Art College. Much was made here of the life class as a source of inspiration, and indeed it seems a fair analogy to make with the television work. The same pernickety observation is required, the models are not glamorous, the line drawing is faithful to every flaw and fold and the end result, though nothing like a photographic record, is precise and unflinching. The little play Leigh devised for the workshop – a spoof about a trendy theatrical director with a yen for improvisational techniques – actually didn't seem that good, but it provided an efficient vehicle for displaying the methods. The actors were isolated, invented names for themselves, personalities, biographies, and so on, all under the careful tutelage of Leigh.

In fact, although Leigh claimed to be placing the onus on the actor, what became apparent – if the workshop was any guide – was the extent to which Leigh is in control. He coaxes and suggests all the time, guiding the personality that is being invented in directions that *he* wants and in which the actor seems only too content to follow. As Leigh stressed – and now we're obliged to agree with him – 'it's not a committee job'. One omission though, and a surprising one, was that we only saw the process go so far. Nothing was shown of the way the script was evolved. Is it a distilled and edited transcript of the actors' ad-libs recorded during improvisations? Or is it something Leigh himself writes once the various personalities and contexts have been established? Perhaps it's a trade secret.

This season is very welcome indeed. Leigh is a major television dramatist whose output deserves dissemination and celebration. What makes him most intriguing is that he has not only evolved a unique method but that he also puts it to traditional use: 'In the end it's about telling a story.' So much for the man. Next week: the work.

1982

Mike Leigh (2)

Mike Leigh's films are so good because he understands the medium that he's working in so well. Last week I discussed the differences between Realism and Naturalism, whether Leigh was a realist or not, whether his films borrowed from both modes and so on. The distinctions to be made are fine ones, but perhaps only come down to academic niceties because in the end we are talking about a property common to almost anything we see on television. Something about the medium, something about its ubiquity in contemporary life, confers on every dramatized or fictional work an overriding air of verisimilitude. Indeed, perhaps that's the best word to stick with. Things look real, pictures borrow an illusion of reality irrespective of their content, style or whatever editorial or directorial trickery has gone into the making of them.

And yet few forms are as unrealistic as television or film when one thinks of the way they're put together: cross-cutting, fades, mixing, editing – all the 'tools' of the trade, so to speak – scarcely parallel the kind of visual world we all possess. Yet this artificiality doesn't work against the feeling of verisimilitude. We are all – we feel – spectators gaining privileged access to a sequence of other worlds, all by virtue of the medium, imbued with a sense of reality so powerful that, I would suggest, it's well nigh unshakeable. At the back of it lies a notion perhaps best expressed as 'the camera never lies'. Words, paint or marble are manifestly *not* the things they claim to be presenting. Photographic images are a different matter. Ocular proof – 'I saw it with my own eyes' – has always been the most convincing testimony. And it's exactly this quality that television and film trade on so effectively. Some artists in the medium quite naturally find this a constraint and seek to tamper with the form. But Mike Leigh, I would surmise, is entirely happy with this state of affairs. He sees verisimilitude as a powerful ally.

The three films we saw in last week's extremely welcome and enjoyable season on BBC2 were a good illustration of the work. (I'm excluding *Abigail's Party*: conceived as a stage play it can't fairly be included with the films.) *Nuts in May* was the most light-hearted, *Who's Who* the most unstructured and episodic. They both brought about the uncanny sense of being invisible watchers of other people's private lives but didn't have the impact and shapeliness of the impressive *Grown Ups* where all the Mike Leigh ingredients – superb acting, gimlet-eyed observation, cringing embarrassment *and* comment – came together with wonderful fidelity.

Leigh is often criticized for appealing to our worst instincts: it is suggested that residual snobbery and a sense of superiority are responsible for the laughs or the frisson the plays produce. The charge can be denied on one count at least by pointing to the range of targets he's selected. Leigh has, as the three films demonstrated, turned his gaze on all classes and types, from vegetarians to PE teachers, from young stockbrokers to sales assistants. His even-handedness thus established, he's surely free to concentrate on whatever social stratum his inclination or his story demands. But in many respects it is the very existence of this sort of criticism – along the 'We don't want to know about such people' school – that shows his films are achieving the desired effect. As Leigh himself stated in the *Arena* profile, his films are 'morality plays'. He is interested in making statements about the kind of lives people lead and the way they behave towards each other. Like Thoreau, Leigh is of the opinion that most lives are characterized by 'quiet desperation' rather than by anything more uplifting or homely. It seems to be a conclusion that latterly he is becoming more inclined to underscore if *Grown Ups* and the bleak *Home Sweet Home* are any guide. Any edginess or unease prompted by his observations can only be a sign that certain truths are too uncomfortable for some critics to acknowledge. Ostrich-complexes are easily fostered; complacency is a very tolerable state of mind. Leigh's telling rejoinders to the opposite effect are immensely valuable in a medium that has done its share to promote the bland, the neutral and the inconsequential.

But it's as well to remind ourselves of the other facets of the plays: the marvellous performances Leigh gets from his actors; his consummate exploitation of the comedy of embarrassment. This is something else that television aids: because we feel like invisible watchers in a Mike Leigh film, when we see something performed as though it were unobserved, we squirm all the more guiltily and enjoyably. Certain images from this all too short season (repeats of *Hard Labour* and *Home Sweet Home*, please) will live on in my memory: Keith Pratt, in *Nuts in May*, bullying the diffident PE teacher Ray to sing along with him and Candice Marie; the wonderfully awful dinner party given by the young stockbrokers in *Who's Who*; the grim sullenness of the Faggs' home life in *Grown Ups*. Very funny and very sad: a comic vision of the world at its most effective and profound.

Another attack against ostrich-complexes was mounted by *Living in Styal* (Granada), a four-part documentary filmed in the women's prison of that name and grim evidence that the desperation of some lives isn't always suffered with stoic resignation. The first two programmes followed the arrival and first weeks of three new inmates. One, Jenny, related a catalogue of misfortunes that make Mike Leigh's various worlds look like a rose-tinted fantasy. She had arrived in Styal leaving a three-and-a-half-month premature baby (weight 1lb 12oz) in hospital and four other kids in the care of her estranged husband. Her eldest daughter, aged eight, had been raped the year previously. Even the Deputy Governor seemed overwhelmed by this tale of woe, but Jenny – up for shoplifting – appeared remarkably unbowed.

Styal is run like a fairly strict girls' boarding school: the tone is firm but friendly rather than authoritarian and repressive. Once again, as with the *Police* documentary, one wonders just how influential the presence of the cameras is on behaviour and attitudes. Certainly in these two programmes everyone's demeanour seemed formal and unnatural. Even when one inmate was informed of her father's death (something of an invasion of privacy, surely?), she seemed unable to take in the news, her eyes constantly darting towards the lens. It was certainly depressing viewing. We've had a glimpse under the lid, but the feeling remains that the truth isn't going to be visible. It may be that documentary, with all its paraphernalia, can gain only limited access into this kind of private, enclosed world. Paradoxically – with the example of Mike Leigh fresh in our minds – perhaps fiction remains the best way of getting to the reality.

1982

The Human Brain

Brains taste nice. Foreign menus are dangerously misleading. These two unrelated propositions were forcibly conjoined when I happily tucked in to what I mistakenly thought was a wood-pigeon casserole in Italy a while ago. To my faintly nauseated horror I later discovered that the literal translation of the quaintly named menu item was 'Brain Stew'. All this is by way of preamble to stating that I won't be eating grey matter again, now that I've watched *Human Brain* (BBC2). This is largely as a result of a particularly eye-watering session of cranial surgery that was on offer, but also – given the validity of the programme's conclusions – out of some vague vegetarian respect for the organ.

Human Brain, lucidly written by Robin Brightwell, presented in this first episode the three main schools of thought on how the brain works. Put extremely simply these are: first, the old-fashioned dualists, who believe in the actual existence of mind, a nugget of psyche, so to speak. Second there are the materialists, who see it as an extremely complicated machine. And thirdly, what one might call the 'sociologists', who see the brain as composed of competing 'cells', all of them controlled and dominated by the language centre in the left hemisphere. This last interpretation was illustrated by the case of an American woman who, as a cure for chronic epilepsy, had the nerve circuits – the *corpus callosum* – which join the two hemispheres of the brain, severed. As a result she possesses, in certain circumstances, two distinct personalities, the separate hemispheres, for example, each simultaneously choosing with either hand clothes from her wardrobe.

Such abnormalities are well known to logicians and philosophers, and have been gleefully used by them in knotty arguments about the precise nature of truth, questions about reality and so on. The logicians call such cases 'bizarre situations' and one of the intriguing aspects of the programme was to see the scientists finally getting round to the hoary old epistemological problems that have been bedevilling philosophers for centuries. By the end of this first episode it was clear that Robin Brightwell was plumping for the 'sociological' theory. The tag comes from the idea of the brain as a kind of society, a group of cognitive systems all with their own emotions and memories but, with the exception of the left hemisphere, lacking the crucial benefit of a language system. They do, however, control muscles and behaviour patterns and seek to express themselves through these. This throws fascinating light on all those acts we commit which seem inexplicable or out of character and the furious efforts we subsequently make somehow to comprehend, justify and explain them to ourselves. Why you bought the car you couldn't afford; why X has fallen for Y; why, even, on this week's *South Bank Show*, Melvyn Bragg's left sideburn was an inch and a half longer than his right. What mute but Bolshie cells are operating here?

Future programmes promise to look at vision, memory, language, movement and fear. There seems a vital omission. All these categories are behavioural to a major extent, closely linked to the way we operate in the world. What about the higher realms of abstract thought: algebra and the purer forms of maths, say? What about, more pertinently, art, creativity and the imagination? One needn't be religious to have a notion of a separate controlling mind. It was the creative imagination, after all, that got the Romantic poets so excited, convinced them of the preeminence and autonomous role of the mind in shaping experience, and prompted Shelley's confident bellow at Mont Blanc:

> And what wert thou, and earth, and stars, and sea,
> If to the human mind's imagining
> Silence and solitude were vacancy?

He may have been wrong, but at least his case deserves a hearing.

1982

PEOPLE AND PLACES

This is a catch-all title to enable me to include articles I've written that often have a bearing — sometimes remote — on books I have published or the release of films I have written. Both my essays on the British 'Caff' and minicabs, for example, were designed to promote, first, my novel Armadillo *and then the broadcast of my three-part adaptation of it on the BBC. More and more the publication of a book seems to involve the author in all manner of ancillary journalism. The advantage of this, however, is that the article can be more uncompromising, and to the point: the necessary finesse involved in slipping hard facts into a work of fiction is not required. In this kind of journalism polemic overrules disinterestedness: a case has to be made as entertainingly as possible and sometimes that motive is exhilarating.*

'Stars at Tallapoosa'

It turned out to be a 150-mile detour. Shortly before one o'clock in the afternoon I saw the first sign. 'Welcome to Tallapoosa'. It had an unreal familiarity: Tallapoosa revisited, almost. Then there was another sign. 'Lions Club of Tallapoosa welcomes you. Meets every Thursday at Tally Mt. Country Club.' And then, a little way up the road, 'Tallapoosa city limit. Welcome. City of Tallapoosa. Please obey all ordinances. Population 2,869. Drive carefully.' The familiarity, I realized, was a poetic one: 'Stars at Tallapoosa' by Wallace Stevens:

> The lines are straight and swift between the stars.
> The night is not the cradle that they cry,
> The criers, undulating the deep-oceaned phrase.
> The lines are much too dark and much too sharp.
>
> The mind herein attains simplicity.
> There is no moon, on single, silvered leaf.
> The body is no body to be seen
> But is an eye that studies its black lid.

'Stars at Tallapoosa' was published in Wallace Stevens's first collection of poems, *Harmonium*, in 1923. It's a perfect example of how he manages to be at once opaque and entrancing. I had read the poem many times and for some reason, when I knew I was going to the South, I looked up Tallapoosa on my Rand McNally road atlas and was disappointed to discover that it was on the Alabama–Georgia border, some considerable distance away from the rough circle of contacts that was going to take me from Atlanta to Augusta, to Charleston, South Carolina, Beaufort, Savannah and back to Atlanta again. My disappointment was mitigated by the consideration that, if I didn't ever get to Tallapoosa, then at least it could be preserved intact in my imagination; that the Tallapoosa Stevens's poem had conjured up for me – the quintessential hick town, but also somehow magic and potent – would never be undermined by reality.

★

To drive from Savannah to Atlanta you take Interstate 16. It speeds you directly through the rather monotonous countryside that prevails in this corner of Georgia, monotonous because all the trees seem to be of one type – a rather tough-looking average-sized pine. The only relief from this homogeneous landscape comes with each junction or intersection. Here there are gathered the fast-food franchises, the twenty-four-hour supermarkets, the motels, the gas stations. Steak 'n' Ale, Starvin' Marvin, Econo-Lodge, Scottish Inns (the cheapest), Bi-Lo, Wife-Saver, Wife's Nite Off. These huge plastic signs tower high over the countryside, a hundred feet tall, like giant cocktail-stirrers stuck in the earth.

In the big car, a chill cell thanks to the air-conditioning, there's nothing to do apart from listen to the radio. Every town has its radio station. You pass them from time to time, a concrete blockhouse below a teetering aerial. I search the wavebands, trying to escape the plangent moralizing of country and western music, but in vain. If the station isn't broadcasting keening guitars and sobbing voices telling of adultery, divorce, alcoholism, mental and physical cruelty, then it's pumping out religious homilies, sermons and hymns interspersed with advertisements for waterproof Bibles 'for poolside reading' or the Bible on tape 'while you're travelling, working or relaxing at home'.

Macon, Georgia, marks the halfway stage. After the pine forest I was looking forward to Macon – reputedly a grim, featureless industrial town – but Interstate 16 whisked me around it promptly. I was due in Atlanta that evening but had wildly overestimated how long it would take me to get there. By late morning I found I'd covered most of the ground and needed to kill some time. I turned off the highway and drove to a small town called Jackson.

Jackson was nondescript, a typical long, thin town that straggled along the road for a mile or so. A red sandstone courthouse stood in the middle. A notice warned that 'anyone using this building as a comfort station will be prosecuted'. Outside was a cement statue of a soldier. 'Our Confederate Heroes', it said on the plinth.

I went into a cafe, ordered a coke and a doughnut and wondered what to do for the rest of the day. I was meandering through the South – Georgia and South Carolina – looking for hick towns, one-horse towns off the beaten track with no touristic allure. I had seen dozens – Smyrna, Bamberg, Denmark, Crawfordville, Madison, Smokes, Apalachee, Walnut Grove, Tyrone. I stopped long enough to mooch around, take some photographs or have a bite to eat. Some were beautiful places, the azaleas blooming fiercely outside immaculate ante-bellum frame-houses, the lawns in front of the courthouse and post office cropped like cricket squares, the shops in the malls bright and fresh with new paint. Others were mean and forgotten, consigned to a slow decay and oblivion now that the network of interstate highways so efficiently linked the main centres of population.

In many ways the rural South fulfilled all my expectations. People were poor, attitudes were confined or frozen, and yet I've never encountered such candid friendliness. The first old woman I talked to said 'Ah do declare', and the Civil War lived on in people's memories as if it had happened only a decade before. But the towns had disappointed me. They were either too frothily perfect – porches, rocking-chairs, coruscating flowers – or drab and banal, lacking any frisson or atmosphere. One caught it occasionally – a group of old black men sitting motionless outside a store in Madison, a shop in Beaufort with a display of trophies from the Little Miss Teenage South Carolina pageant – but it was fleeting or too localized. I wanted something more. I wanted to go to Tallapoosa.

I took out my map and spread it on the table. I was a somewhat alien presence in the cafe, filled now with Jackson ladies who had interrupted their shopping for a chat. I told myself, not tempting fate, that Tallapoosa would now surely be a smug dormitory for Birmingham or Montgomery, or else have been transformed from what it was in Stevens's day by the erection of some steel mill or sprawling chemical plant, but the urge to see it for myself was too strong to resist. I left Jackson, with its 'comfort station' ban and chattering ladies, with a feeling of elation.

'Tallapoosa city limit. Welcome. City of Tallapoosa. Please obey all ordinances. Population 2,869. Drive carefully.' *City* of Tallapoosa?

The day was hot and the sky cloudless. Soon, on either side of the road, were small wooden bungalows with porches carrying the usual freight of azaleas. At first it all looked too pretty. Then there was a grain silo – a silver cigar – and the houses seemed to fall away as the road climbed quite steeply. Then you hit the brow of the hill and it turns into the main street.

The road is straight. For a hundred yards it runs alongside railway-tracks. A railroad running smack through the centre of town, freight trains passing cars in the main street. It looked very strange. I parked the car and got out. Across the tracks was a wide tarmacked area that fronted a modest mall of shops – flat-fronted, two-storey, flat-roofed buildings. Black cable power-lines, that ubiquitous feature of all American townscapes, looped haphazardly here and there. 'Tallapoosa Drugs' said a big sign above one store. A Coke machine stood outside. The plate-glass window of the shop seemed to contain no items for sale. On the other side of the road were rutted lanes leading to more shops: Tallapoosa Auto, Electrical Goods, Dr Tire, Tallapoosa Seed Merchants, Tallapoosa Home Center. The name was everywhere. Tallapoosa Baptist Church.

It was hot and the sun spangled off the railway-tracks and off the windscreens of the large matt and battered cars and pickups parked in front of the mall of shops. There were very few people out and about. Occasionally a car roared through on the way to Bremen down the road, but it was generally very quiet. The town sat low and squat beneath the sun, the pavements were cracked and weeds sprouted freely from the cracks. The fat cars stood squarely on their patches of shadow. I felt no foreboding, only a sense of relief and pleasure.

> The mind herein attains simplicity . . .
> The body is no body to be seen
> But is an eye that studies its black lid.
>
> Let these be your delight, secretive hunter . . .

There certainly was no body to be seen. I stepped up on to the raised wooden sidewalk. On this side of the road, opposite the mall and the railway-tracks, there was a bar. Standing in the doorway behind a mosquito-proofed screen was a man holding a can of beer, wearing dusty denim overalls and a wide, manic smile on his face. I walked by, following the sidewalk to its end. Beyond that there were some sheds, a gas station and an auto shop. Beyond them stretched Alabama and a whole dry country.

The gas station had a small cafe that operated a drive-thru window. Three cars were parked outside. In each, two women sat in the front and children lounged in the back. Everybody was eating. A girl hung out of the drive-thru window, talking to the women in one of the cars.

As I approached, they stopped talking and turned and looked at me. I changed course, crossed the street, stepped tentatively over the thick, burnished railway-tracks, through a strip of knee-high, sun-bleached grass and weeds, and on to the broiling parking-lot in front of the mall.

Dusting my trouser legs free of seeds and grass burrs, I saw the red neon rosette of a Budweiser sign glowing palely in the sunlight. Bars at Tallapoosa. I went in.

It was very dark. And full of men – white men. Drunk men.

A long bar stretched back into the depths of the room where there was an antiquated mechanical skittle-machine. Dusty plastic beer signs advertised Millers, Budweiser, Pabst. There were racks of old bottles of what I took to be country wines. A hand-printed sign said 'No credit. No personal checks', but some drunken good ol' boy was loudly trying to persuade the taciturn, impassive barman to break his own house rules.

I asked politely for a beer and was given one in the can. Looking around, I saw that everyone drank direct from the bottle or the can. There wasn't a glass in sight. I stood there, one hand in one pocket, and tried to drink my beer as fast as possible. No one spoke to me or showed the slightest curiosity. They were just waiting patiently for me to get my drinking done and get out. I didn't belong here, I was an irritant in the melancholy life of the bar. When I put my empty can down, the barman muttered the obligatory Southern valediction, 'Y'all come back and see us again some time, heah?' but his heart wasn't in it.

Outside I was dazzled by the glare of the sun. Then I saw a big maroon car cruising very slowly through the mall. A girl was driving and another sat beside her in the front. It slowed to a crawl as it passed the bar. The girls – eighteen going on thirty – were smoking and had dyed blonde hair. The car had a hubcap missing. It looked too big for the girls to drive. I let it pass and walked across the car park, stepped back over the railway-lines and across the main street. The car pulled out of the mall, bumped across the tracks and accelerated away in the direction of Bremen. The girls were laughing at something.

> Their pleasure that is all bright-edged and cold . . .
> Making recoveries of young nakedness . . .

The town seemed stuck in its hot midday stupor. Where was everybody? I wondered. In the bars? I walked down towards the white Baptist church, wooden, painted white. The Baptists have Georgia sewn up. I saw a pawn shop and next door another drugstore. I went in, hoping to find a soda fountain or some kind of snack-bar but with no luck. Instead, I bought another reel of film from the little mustachioed man who worked inside. He asked me where I was from. I told him. He said, maybe to make me feel less of a stranger, that there were two or three European girls who lived in Tallapoosa; German girls who had married Tallapoosa men serving in Germany and who had been brought back to the States to live. I wondered what the German girls must have made of their new home. The promise of a new life in the USA. The reality of a lifetime in Tallapoosa.

I asked the little man if there was a nice restaurant in town where I could get a bite to eat. He thought for a while – it was clearly something of a poser – and said that I should head out of town on the road to Bremen; then turn left, following the signs for Interstate 20. There was 'quite a decent little place' about two miles down that road.

I followed his instructions. Turning off the Tallapoosa–Bremen road, I saw a large factory: the Tallapoosa Rubber Company. Perhaps its presence explained the paucity of men on the streets. I drove on, looking for the restaurant. Then I saw it: the 'Big O' hamburger house, on the Tallapoosa exit of Interstate 20. So this was the best restaurant in town.

Inside it was empty, not a solitary trucker. Greasy formica, battered, chipped chairs, drab curtains. The 'Big O' offers that day were Mountain Man stew and steak sandwiches. I chose a steak sandwich.

Two bored girls took my order. They looked like younger sisters of the girls in the car: heavy make-up, streak jobs, glinting jewellery. My sandwich came – a small steak fried in batter, a leaf of iceberg lettuce and a squirt of mayonnaise. I hankered vaguely for Mountain Man stew.

I ate my sandwich and thought about Tallapoosa. It had been the evocativeness of the poem that had lured me here. But in my reading I had imagined something entirely different from the banalities of small-town America. Now the lines between the stars were merely the haphazard loopings of electric cable spanning the street and alleyways. The stars themselves were reduced to sunbursts off windscreens and dusty chrome. To a significant extent the topography of the poem is redundant – no doubt Stevens never expected any reader to check it out. Its power resides in the potency of its phrase-making: 'secretive hunter', 'recoveries of young nakedness', 'the lost vehemence the midnights hold'. And yet it wasn't all disappointment. Even though I had no idea what Wallace Stevens was doing in the place, I sensed an understanding, some sixty years or more later, of the entrancement he seemed to have felt, or at least a rendered-down, displaced 1980s version. Tallapoosa was so tawdry and down-at-heel and yet here, undeniably, I had found the very frisson I was after, that formed a bridge, albeit a flimsy one, between the experience of the poem and the reality of the present. The atmosphere on the main street had been a kind of brazenness, a flashiness, a self-confidence manifested in the constant reiteration of the name: Tallapoosa this, Tallapoosa that. Perhaps it was the name alone that had attracted Stevens – some incantation in its utterance that infected the citizens and the environment. Or was I merely wishful-thinking, investing the place with my personal designs on it, my eye studying its own black lid?

I left the 'Big O' and drove back to take some more photographs. I wandered uneasily around, snapping shots covertly. The girls in the maroon car were back, parked at the drive-thru, eating something, but the streets were as quiet as ever.

> Let these be your delight, secretive hunter,
> Wading the sea-lines, moist and ever-mingling,
> Mounting the earth-lines, long and lax, lethargic.
> These lines are swift and fall without diverging.
>
> The melon-flower nor dew nor web of either
> Is like to these. But in yourself is like:
> A sheaf of brilliant arrows flying straight,
> Flying and falling straightway for their pleasure,
>
> Their pleasure that is all bright-edged and cold;
> Or, if not arrows, then the nimblest motions,
> Making recoveries of young nakedness
> And the lost vehemence the midnights hold.

I didn't stay to see the stars at Tallapoosa. I left for Atlanta long before night fell.

1984

The Wright Brothers

Ninety years ago this week, on a cold blustery Thursday morning on 17 December 1903, Wilbur and Orville Wright carried their flying machine – the Flyer – from its wooden shed and set it carefully on the forty-foot launchway of pine two-by-four planks and prepared it for take off. Their camp was on the Outer Banks, long thin islands, 90 per cent sand dunes, off the coast of North Carolina. The nearest hamlet was Kitty Hawk, a small cluster of clapboard houses that sheltered the seasonal fishermen and the crew of the coastguard station. If you didn't fish or work for the coastguard there was nothing much to bring you to Kitty Hawk. All around them was sand and a few huge dune hills, the Kill Devil Hills, thrown up by the scouring winds that blew in off the wintry Atlantic. It was the winds – their constant presence, their reliable force – that had drawn the Wright brothers from Dayton, Ohio to Kitty Hawk where, over the previous three years, they had spent the autumn and early winter months testing their big man-carrying soaring gliders and perfecting the controlling mechanisms that allowed them to steer.

The wind that December day was gusting between twenty-two and twenty-seven miles an hour, a little too strong for their purposes but, as both the brothers were determined to be back in Dayton in time for Christmas, they decided to press on. So they hung out a signal on their wooden shack to alert the men in the coastguard station at Kitty Hawk some four miles away. They needed witnesses for what they hoped was about to ensue. Three surfmen duly strolled down the beach from the station: John Daniels, Adam Etheridge and Will Dough. Two curious hangers-on accompanied them, a lumber merchant called W. D. Brinkley and a teenage boy, Johnny Moore.

Orville Wright set up his glass-plate camera on a tripod some way off aiming at a point towards the end of the launching rail. John Daniels was invited to take the photograph, a simple matter of squeezing the rubber bulb that activated the shutter. The small four-cylinder petrol engine that powered the two pushing propellors on the Flyer was started and was run for a while to allow the motor to warm up.

The honour of piloting the Flyer had been decided by a toss of a coin and it was Orville, dressed in his usual business suit, with stiff collar and tie, who lay down beside the motor on the bottom wing and hooked his shoes behind a strut on the trailing edge. His hips were fixed in a wooden cradle that could slide laterally to and fro, a movement that activated the 'wing-warping' devices that allowed the pilot to control the direction of the Flyer. His hands were on the control lever that operated the front horizontal elevator. The whole 600-pound flying machine rested on a plank which in turn was supported by a small wheeled trolley (with wheels made from bicycle hubcaps) which ran along the launching rail, which was pointed in the direction of the prevailing wind.

At 10.35 the restraining wire was slipped and the Flyer began to clatter slowly along the launching rail. It was moving so slowly that Wilbur – who was holding the struts on the right-hand wing tip to keep the machine level – had no difficulty jogging alongside. As the Flyer reached the end of the track Orville pulled the control lever to turn the big front elevator up and the machine rose abruptly into the air, the plank on its trolley falling away from the skids into the sand. The Flyer's speed was approximately thirty miles an hour at this stage but, because of the stiff headwind, was actually moving through the air at about seven mph. Wilbur, loping alongside, easily kept pace with the machine's undulating progress through the air. Orville, now some ten to fifteen feet above the ground, was having difficulty controlling the big elevator. He would raise it, and the Flyer would surge upwards, he would lower it and then it would dip suddenly towards the sand. This sinuous vermiculate course was maintained for about twelve seconds until an oblique gust of wind coinciding with a downward dip caused one of the skids beneath the machine to hit the sand and the Flyer came suddenly to earth with a severe jolt some 120 feet along the beach from the point where it had risen from the launching rail.

One small miracle, besides the larger one that was achieved that day at Kill Devil Hills, was that John Daniels, the big surfman from the coastguard station, had remembered to press the rubber bulb that activated the shutter release of the camera as the Flyer took to the air, thereby inadvertently producing one of the most famous photographs of the twentieth century. It's not just that the camera recorded one of those moments that changed the world irrevocably but it is also, or so it seems to me, a wonderful photograph in its own right: perfectly exposed, wonderfully sharp, and a poignant and moving tribute to the human spirit; values enshrined not so much in the fragile beautiful white machine lifting itself slowly into the air but rather in Wilbur's figure to the side – tautly poised, legs apart, staring at his younger brother prone on the lower wing, his arms half crooked, expectant, almost willing the machine into its new element. Of all the many photographs the Wright brothers took of their flying machines in their months at Kill Devil Hills, and some of them are superb, this adventitious snapshot by John Daniels must rank as one of the most memorable images of all time.

One wonders, also, what Wilbur would be thinking at that moment, at the culmination of this intense but comparatively brief interest in powered, heavier-than-air flight. It is hard to say: neither Wilbur nor Orville Wright seemed to be expressive or forthcoming men; there is no trace in their writings of much exhilaration or indeed of any romantic notion of being the first men to fly. They were a redoubtably practical pair, modest, capable and dogged, and it seems almost as if they were drawn to the challenge of powered flight out of a sense of whim rather than adventure, of a need to find some beguiling way of passing their time rather than being driven by obsession.

They were members of a large family: there were two other older brothers and a younger sister, and Wilbur's birth, in 1867, the third child, preceded Orville's by four years. Their father was a bishop of a non-conformist Protestant sect called the Church of the United Brethren in Christ, but neither Wilbur nor Orville 'got' religion, their only concession to their father's faith was that they would not fly on a Sunday. The atmosphere in the family home was close and folksily fun. Wilbur and Orville, neither of whom married, appeared to have a twin-like communication and understanding with each other. Neither drank or smoked. Both were averagely tall and lean, Wilbur was quite bald by his thirties, Orville was balding but wore a bold moustache that caused some to liken him to Edgar Allan Poe. He had a reputation in the family of being something of a dandy, though by any other standards than those of the Wrights such foppishness is hard to detect, though it is true that in one photograph of the two of them Orville is wearing a pair of snazzily checked socks.

When the cycling craze hit America in the 1890s the two brothers, who had initially gone into printing as a profession, opened a bicycle shop in downtown Dayton that was soon a flourishing business where they manufactured and sold their own brand of bicycle. It seems that the ease with which they had triumphed in this area of transportation caused them to look elsewhere for another challenge. And aerial navigation, as it was then referred to, was what took their fancy.

The myth has it that it was newspaper reports of the death in 1896 of Otto Lilienthal, the famous German glider, that concentrated the brothers' minds on flying machines. Lilienthal did indeed do much to pave the way for powered flight with his scientific formulations of surface pressures and wing construction but powered flight, by the end of the nineteenth century, seemed as remote a possibility then as turning base metal into gold was in medieval Europe. H. G. Wells however, in a celebrated essay in 1901, predicted that the first aeroplanes would take to the air *long* before the year 2000: 1950 was his educated guess.

So the Wright brothers applied their minds to the problem of powered flight and sent off to the Smithsonian Institution for whatever literature on the subject was available in May 1899. The Smithsonian duly responded and sent along four slim pamphlets, free of charge. In this context of almost total ignorance the fact that just four and a half years later the Wright brothers' own powered flying machine took off from the sands of Kitty Hawk almost defies belief and is perhaps the most effective testimony to the cool practicality, the commonsensical thoroughness of their unique cast of mind.

For they were not alone: in France, Germany, England and the USA would-be aviators were all trying to make the next step from manned gliders. Lilienthal had made over 2,000 glides; Englishman Percy Pilcher had glided 750 feet from the top of one hill to another, in the States Samuel Langley had successfully flown thirty-pound steam-powered model aeroplanes and Octave Chanute was developing manned gliders to carry on from where Lilienthal's premature death had left the science.

Broadly speaking, all these experimenters were making a conceptual error about the prospect of flight. They tended to view the air much as they would the sea: something to be ridden much as a boat rides the waves. Langley hoped his flying machines would harness the 'internal work of the wind' and even be able to circumnavigate the globe without landing. Chanute built a six-wing glider with wings that could move as the air currents buffeted them. The pragmatic Wrights, however, approached matters differently. They saw everything as a fundamental problem of control, that there was little purpose in providing any kind of glider with power if you didn't know what to do if and when you suddenly found you were flying. The first models they made in 1900 were large kites and then they quickly evolved into building unmanned gliders which they flew with ropes attached and finally manned gliders, taking to the air on the dunes of Kitty Hawk, making many glides of over 200 yards and staying aloft for half a minute at a time. Back in their bicycle workshop in Dayton they analysed the information they had gleaned and, as they built a new flying machine each year, steadily modified its design.

Because they concentrated on controlling the flying machine the brothers quickly encountered the key inherent problems of sustained flight. Control has to be organized around three axes, lateral, vertical and longitudinal, or, put in nautical terms, the pilot has to be able to control pitch, yaw and roll. What the Wright brothers achieved, to simplify drastically, during their gliding experiments in 1901 and 1902 at Kitty Hawk was a method of controlling movement in these three dimensions. Only by controlling all three dimensions, for example, is it possible to make a banked turn in a flying machine. In the gliders of Lilienthal, Pilcher and Chanute the only way of exercising control was for the pilot to hang by his arms and thrash his body around to disturb the centre of equilibrium. A dangerous manoeuvre in any event as both Pilcher and Lilienthal died in gliding crashes. In the powered 'hops' – where the flying machine left the ground for a second or two – of such pioneers as Langley and Maxim there was simply no time to demonstrate control.

But in 1902 in the dunes of Kill Devil Hills Orville and Wilbur Wright were turning and banking their big glider right and left with remarkable consistency. They were able to do this through the process they called 'wing-warping', a precursor of the modern aileron, where cables controlled by lateral movements of the hip cradle twisted the ends of the wings, pulling one into a positive angle and the other into a negative, or vice versa, with wind pressure then causing the wing with the positive angle to lift, and the wing with the negative to dip – and so the turn begins.

In the course of their four years of work the brothers made many discoveries about the mystery of flight, and, amongst other achievements, built their own four-cylinder engine and tested wing cross-sections in their own wind tunnel, but it was their development of the three-dimensional system of aeroplane control – the basic system that still operates all winged transportation today – that really marks them out as the great progenitors, the first true flyers.

*

The epochal day of 17 December 1903 did not end with Orville's sinuous 120-foot flight. In true Wright fashion the damaged skid was swiftly repaired and the Flyer carried back to the launching rail for another attempt. Three more flights were completed, the third being the most remarkable. This time Wilbur piloted the Flyer and by now he had become more accustomed to the sensitive front elevator. The Flyer took off, its course through the air less undulating, and puttered off across the sandy plain at a speed of no more than ten miles an hour. Wilbur had flown nearly 300 yards when, once again, a slightly over-enthusiastic adjustment of the controls brought the machine down to earth, badly damaging the front struts that held the elevator. That was that for the day, and for 1903, as it turned out, for the Flyer was further damaged when, as the men were replacing it in its shed, a powerful gust of wind flipped it over on its back.

In many ways the fourth flight of that December day deserves the real prominence in the history of aviation. It lasted fifty-nine seconds and covered 852 feet and if anyone ever doubted that the Flyer was capable of sustained flight then Wilbur's effort at the end of that memorable day would have quashed them completely.

Of course the 1903 flights were only the beginning of the Wright brothers' story. New Flyers were built and tested and by 1905 the Flyer III was capable of staying aloft for half an hour at a time and flying many miles. As news of the brothers' achievements began to be broadcast to an incredulous world so too did the atmosphere of envy, malice, bad faith and cupidity that attends most great innovators begin to gather round round them. Sceptics at home and abroad refused to believe these taciturn bicycle makers from Ohio had conquered the air; former colleagues strove to hog the limelight; less successful aviators stole their ideas. Lawsuits, patent battles, controversy, claim and counter-claim continued to dog their lives for many years. Even in the 1930s there was a systematic effort to discredit their achievements when the so-called 'lost' flights of Gustave Whitehead (it was suggested, quite fraudulently, that he had flown half a mile in 1901) were advanced as the true precursors of aviation history. But the Wright brothers, true to their natures, worked on relentlessly, steadily perfecting their flying machines until the technology they had initiated eventually superseded them. Wilbur died in 1912 of typhoid fever. Orville lived on until 1948, the grand old man of American aviation, surviving long enough to see the astonishing progress of his invention and see what contribution – good and bad – it had made to the history of the twentieth century.

Such speculation risks entering the realm of banality and sentiment, but, as we idly cruise the upper atmosphere in our jumbo jets pondering the wisdom of a second Bloody Mary before lunch, and, elsewhere, Stealth bombers wreak pinpoint destruction by laser beam, it is worth reflecting on that winter day at Kill Devil Hills when the five men from Kitty Hawk watched the two brothers in their white muslin flying machine lift off the ground and chug erratically through the air over the chilly sand dunes. It was *such* a short time ago and feverish hindsight makes one want to invest the occasion with monumental significance. But, reportedly, John Daniels, Will Dough, Adam Etheridge, W. D. Brinkley and Johnny Moore were not overly impressed – they had seen the brothers make much longer and more graceful flights in their gliders in previous years. Even the brothers, when they cabled the news that evening to the family that the flights had been successful, seemed more concerned to let them know that they would be home in time for Christmas. However there was an eyewitness the following year when a new Flyer made the first ever circling flight and with a little effort of imagination one can gain some vicarious sense of the sheer strangeness of the phenomenon, as it must have seemed then, and share a little of the moment, a sense that the world would never be the same again:

The machine is held until ready to start . . . then with a tremendous flapping and snapping of the four cylinder engine, the huge machine springs aloft. When it first turned that circle, and came near the starting point, I was right in front of it; and I said then, and I believe still it was one of the grandest sights, if not the grandest sight of my life. Imagine a locomotive that has left its track, and is climbing up in the air toward you – a locomotive without any wheels, we will say, but with white wings instead . . . coming right toward you with the tremendous flap of its propellors, and you will have something like what I saw. The younger brother bade me move aside for fear that it might come down suddenly; but I tell you friends, the sensation one feels in such a crisis is something hard to describe.

1993

Anthony Burgess 1917–93

About eleven months ago in Edinburgh, so I have just been told by a friend who was there, Anthony Burgess turned to the audience he was addressing and said quite calmly, 'I have only a year left to live.' There was a shocked silence and then Anthony, apparently, carried on without a care in the world.

I knew, we knew, that he was not in good health latterly, but the last time I saw him he did not seem much changed. He was smoking, inevitably, and we had a drink or three. He was participating in what-ever book business had brought him to London with his usual heroic energy and benign composure, and, for all I know, was writing a novel, a book review and a concerto in his idler moments. All the same, the news of his death comes as a huge shock perhaps because one always thought that, having cheated the grim reaper once, Anthony's prodigious energy would continue to defy mortality as long as he felt it was worth it.

I refer, of course, to the now legendary moment in 1959 when Anthony was diagnosed as suffering from an inoperable brain tumour and was told he would be dead before a year had run its course. In the time he had left remaining to him, or so he tells it, to provide some sort of legacy for his soon-to-be widow, he wrote four novels, non-stop, one after the other. And when the diagnosis blessedly proved to have been false he carried on working with that same restless creativity. From the outside it seemed as if Anthony's artistic momentum was indeed a kind of life force, sustaining and vivifying, and that as long as he was there working he would outlive the lot of us.

He was an exemplary writer in many senses. He was the towering example, for instance, to all late starters, not writing his first novel until he was in his forties. He was an intellectual, a polymath, at home in many languages, with a cultural sweep that was awe-inspiring, but at the same time he avoided all pretension and elitism, equally happy to let frivolity and fun – in the form of movies, soap operas, TV, chat shows, beach blanket best sellers or whatever – benefit from his shrewd and enthusiastic evaluation. And he worked hard, worked hard for his living, writing novels and criticism, screenplays and libretti, almost anything he wanted to do and could turn his pen to.

In this sense he seems to me to be a very British writer. If there is one thing that characterizes the British writer, from the eighteenth century onwards, it is that by and large he or she writes a *lot*, is very productive, is professional. Writing is both a serious calling and a serious career, and Anthony, in the twentieth century, embodied that attitude with more style and panache and consistent high standards than anyone else I can think of. But in many other senses he regarded himself as something of an outsider. A cradle Catholic, a northerner, non-Oxbridge, with a working life spent largely abroad, he considered himself, I believe, beyond the pale of the metropolitan literary world. And so much the better for him: he is the perfect example of the non-parochial in British literature. If ever the British novel is described as being cramped and confined by this cramped and confined little island Anthony Burgess can provide the flourishing counterpoise.

I remember on the occasion of his seventieth birthday celebrations him saying cheerfully on television that he never expected to be honoured by his native country. 'You have to be a footballer or a jockey to be recognized by the establishment in Britain,' he said. And of course it is the usual matter of shame and a sad reflection on our inherent philistinism that someone as special and worth celebrating as Anthony should have been ignored. But he would know, as would any person of sense, that what matters in the end is the work done rather than any bauble conferred, and the work will continue to fascinate and beguile in all its multitudinous facets. Amongst the thirty-odd novels he wrote the consensus would probably be that *Earthly Powers* is his masterpiece and it is hard to argue against its huge and confident sweep. But my own particular favourites, the ones I re-read, are the Enderby novels, *Inside Mr Enderby* and *Enderby Outside*, which are about the life and extraordinary times of a minor English poet – wonderfully rich and funny novels. I first read these books twenty years ago at university and read them again when I had the chance to meet Anthony many years later. Enderby, eccentric, unworldly, insouciant, obsessed by his art, but fully caught up in the physical pleasures of this world, brings Anthony's unique and vital spirit forcefully to mind. I shall go and read them again now, and think how lucky I was – how lucky we all were – to meet and know their remarkable creator.

1993

Meyer Lansky

(Review of *Little Man: Meyer Lansky
and the Gangster Life* by Robert Lacey)

Jackie Mason, the American comedian, has a joke about the Mafia. Those
Italians, he would ask, those Guinea goombahs with their padded shoulders and dark glasses – how could they possibly have created something
like the Mafia? No way . . . Unless they had a Jew to show them how.
Well they did, as it happens, and the Jew in question was Meyer Lansky,
the 'Little Man' (only five foot three without his lifts), and the subject
of Robert Lacey's fascinating and exemplary biography.

Lansky's eponyms were various: 'the thinking man's gangster', the
Henry Kissinger of organized crime, the only man on the FBI's 'most
wanted' list who had a subscription to the Book-of-the-Month Club.
They all indicate similar propensities: brain power and respectability.
Lansky was the least likely criminal mastermind you could imagine;
towards the end of his life he strove resolutely to be ordinary, to blend
in with the retired accountants, dentists and cosmetic surgeons in Miami
Beach. He was just another businessman enjoying the sun and his coffee
and Danish at the local deli – except his business just had happened to
be running an illegal gambling empire turning over billions of dollars
a year.

Throughout this book Lacey's admirable motive is to debunk and
demythologize. American society derives its image of hoodlums and
gangsters from their archetypes in the entertainment industry. The reality
is something altogether different and no one exemplified this better than
Meyer Lansky. The Godfather of Godfathers, the Chairman of the Board
of the National Crime Syndicate was no demonic monster corrupting
the soul of the nation but a smart Jewish numbers man who knew a
profitable business when he saw one. As Lacey observes, when Meyer
Lansky described himself as a 'common gambler' he spoke as a man
who had attained a certain status in the world.

And yet it is easy to understand how Lansky attained this mythic
status. From one angle his career – which Lacey tracks with scholarly
thoroughness – possesses all the classic ingredients of the cinema
mobster. Starting out as a strong arm man for petty criminals in New

York he soon moved on to bootlegging, in tandem with his notorious colleagues Lucky Luciano and Bugsy Siegel. But illegal gambling quickly became the metier in which Lansky's intellect and numerical gifts flourished. In the forties he provided the financing for Bugsy Siegel to get started in Las Vegas, and it was Lansky who organized the establishment of big-time gambling in Batista's Havana, where he owned and ran his own hugely successful hotel-casino, the Riviera. At the height of his career Lansky's worth was said to be in the region of 300 million dollars and he achieved a particularly American apotheosis when he was portrayed by Lee Strasberg as the gangster Hyman Roth in *Godfather II*.

The fall of Batista signalled the beginning of the decline of Lansky's own fortunes but his attempts to 'retire' or to seek some form of respectability were thwarted by his increasing notoriety, a process that began in 1951 when Senator Estes Kefauver's Senate Crime Committee named him as one of the three syndicate bosses on the East Coast. Indeed, Lacey makes a convincing case for seeing Kefauver's misguided obsession with the Mafia – and the inevitable distortions of its influence and pervasiveness – as initiating America's current and seemingly insatiable fascination for its gangster underworld. In the light of this there was no way that the 'Biggest Damn Crook in the Whole Wide World' could be allowed to retreat to his south Florida condo to live off his ill-gotten gains. And as a result, for the last thirty years of his life, Lansky was the subject of dogged but essentially fruitless persecution by the Immigration Department, the FBI and the IRS. It was some measure of revenge.

The compelling nature of Meyer Lansky's story is not to do with any sinister glamour that movies and television have conferred on racketeering and gangsterism but rather with Robert Lacey's thorough and diligent removal of all that gloss and glitter. The truth, as always, is vastly more complex and more banal. There was no great showdown, no brilliant trial, no incarceration, no violent death in some pasta joint in Little Italy. Lansky lived on into relatively comfortable old age, frugal, beset with family problems and the misspent lives of his unhappy children, trying always to back out of the baleful limelight that the American media had beamed down on him. Eventually a lifetime's heavy smoking took its toll and, succumbing to a privation experienced by many of Florida's senior citizens, he underwent a course of radiation treatment for cancer. Progressively weaker, he was admitted to hospital at the end of 1982. Distresssed and sedated, he would pluck fretfully at the tubes and drips feeding his wasting body, attempting to remove them. He died on 15 January 1983. His last coherent words were 'Let me go!'

1991

Paris

(Review of *Around and about Paris*,
Volumes I–III by Thirza Vallois)

I first went to Paris in 1969, when I was seventeen, with my best friend, Charlie Bell. We were two callow sixth-formers determined to hitch-hike through France to the fleshpots of the Côte d'Azur. We went to Paris only because we were given a lift there from London by a mutual friend, Rick, who duly dropped us at the access road of the main autoroute south. I think there were probably 200 other hitchhikers waiting there already and after three hours, during which time the queue had barely diminished, we decided to give up.

As luck would have it, Rick was staying in a large apartment on the Ile St Louis with a fine view of Notre Dame, and a spare room was found for us as we plotted other means of getting out of the place and heading for the Mediterranean. It took us a week to decide that we should pool our meagre savings and catch a train, but in that week, wandering around aimlessly, we made our acquaintance with a small section of the city – St Germain, Boul' Mich, the southern *quais* of the Seine (and a small park near Notre Dame where we would lunch frugally, daily, on a baguette and sliced tomatoes) – which, twenty-nine years later, still maps out my personal geography of the place. I am an irre-deemable Left-Banker (as I suspect most non-Parisians are); the 5th, 6th and 7th arrondissements seem to contain all and more than I will ever need. Of course I venture elsewhere – the Marais, Montmartre, the 4th – but it is as if the city was defined for me by those indigent, fretful, peripatetic days we spent there in 1969.

I started returning to Paris regularly in the early eighties when my novels began to be published in France. I suppose I have been going there four or five times a year ever since but I still never stray far from my usual haunts. Which is to confess that of these superb guides written by Thirza Vallois the only volume I have any qualification to assess is Volume I (1st–7th arrondissements). But if the other two volumes match the sheer mass of detail and anecdotal and scholarly information of the first, then I think we can safely toss all other Paris guidebooks aside.

I tried to catch her out. My publisher, Le Seuil, has its offices in an elegant building in the rue Jacob (6th) whose façade is used as its colophon; an eminent and venerable firm, but it is not mentioned (fair enough; in fact, neither are the firms of Gallimard and Grasset, its great rivals). Not far away is a cafe I often visit, a little self-consciously artistic, but undeniably *authentique* all the same, called La Palette. This is what Thirza Vallois has to say:

At no. 43, on the corner of rue Jacques-Callot, La Palette is a stronghold of arty bohemia. The café has some exquisite ceramic decorations (signed Fouji: is it Foujita?) and it certainly has atmosphere, but it should only be visited by those who can tolerate a heavy veil of cigarette smoke and a surly welcome.

Couldn't agree more. What could I add, having visited the establishment for more than a decade? They do a nice line in *tartines* – an open sandwich of *pain poilâne* with cheese or ham or pâté – and the loo is a genuine old-fashioned squatter, a ceramic-framed black hole picturesquely redolent of ancient sewers.

But this is to nit-pick with inexcusable pedantry. Thirza Vallois writes about her city with passion and, more importantly, the unmistakable authority of first-hand knowledge. No visitor to the city (and, I suspect, more than a few Parisians could benefit also) who seriously wishes to venture beyond the mere *touristique* could do better than follow the numerous walks Thirza Vallois has devised through the city's twenty arrondissements.

Paris is a small city, certainly compared to London. During the public transport strikes of last year a friend of mine told me he used to walk regularly from Montparnasse to his apartment in Montmartre – effectively traversing two-thirds of Paris – in forty-five minutes. Paris is made for walking and Thirza Vallois's guides are made for Paris. There can be no higher praise than if I say they come close to the standard set by the world's greatest guidebook, J. G. Links's *Venice for Pleasure*. All that is required is that the publishers reformat them (they are heftyish volumes) in handy, pocket-size paperbacks of maybe three arrondissements per book and they should soon achieve similar legendary status.

1998

The Galapagos Affair

One lucent September morning in 1928, two Germans, a man and a woman, and their worldly possessions, were landed on the beach of Floreana, an uninhabited island in the Galapagos archipelago. The man, Friedrich Ritter, was small, blond and wiry, a doctor and an amateur philosopher with a bent for bizarre, male-supremacist metaphysics. The woman was his lover, Dore Strauch, equally small, dark and somewhat self-consciously bohemian in dress and manner. She adored and venerated Friedrich.

Friedrich and Dore had planned their new life with Teutonic thoroughness. In Berlin during the course of their affair they accumulated a vast supply of stores and provisions and, when the time came for them to leave, they arranged a dinner party and introduced their astonished, respective spouses to each other and told them of their plans. Friedrich suggested to Herr Strauch that, as he was being deprived of a wife, perhaps it might soften the blow if *his* wife, Mrs Ritter, came to live and work for Herr Strauch as his housekeeper. This completely bizarre proposal was deemed a very satisfactory arrangement by all parties and so Friedrich's wife duly moved in with Dore's husband.

Having sorted out their abandoned spouses, Friedrich and Dore travelled halfway round the globe to this small island in the Pacific, their tropical Eden, where they planned to live out their days, far from the corruption and clamour of Europe.

Beyond the jagged lava beach Floreana was and is a lush and plentiful tropical island. Friedrich and Dore struggled up from the shore through the thickly forested slopes of the dominant mountain (Dore with some difficulty, her arthritis had left her with a pronounced limp but Friedrich's stern philosophy forbade him from giving her a helping hand) until they found a clearing by a stream where they decided to build a house and a garden (designed and laid out upon strictly philosophical lines). They called the house, rather sweetly, 'Friedo' and soon they had a rather ramshackle dwelling erected and a garden that was producing sufficient vegetables and fruit for their complicated diet. All, so far, was well.

The mistake Friedrich and Dore had made was to talk about their plans to journalists while they were waiting in Ecuador for passage to the Galapagos. Their story inspired and inflamed other troubled souls who, spurred on by Friedrich and Dore's example, decided that there was room to spare in this particular earthly Paradise. Soon the first of a series of new arrivals on Floreana took place.

The first to come were an innocuous petit bourgeois family, also German, the Wittmers – Heinz and Margret with their young son Rolf. The Wittmers built their camp a mile away from Friedo and, although there was candid resentment between the two women, the Floreana settlers seemed to coexist with reasonable harmony.

But that equilibrium was soon to be seriously and fatally disturbed by the arrival of the third party of settlers to the island. The Baroness Eloïse Wagner de Bosquet could have stepped straight out of a film noir thriller directed by Erich von Stroheim. Sexually licentious, a peroxide blonde, gun-toting and with a murky and dubious past, the Baroness spoke French and German with an Austrian accent and claimed her great uncles were Liszt and Wagner. She had with her two lovers, a Frenchman, Rudolf Lorenz, and a well-built young American called Robert Philippson. She too had been inspired by Friedrich and Dore's Edenic dreams but she planned to imbue them with a more practical thrust. She set about constructing what she described as a luxury hotel, to be known as the 'Hacienda Paradiso'. Its clientele was to be the many millionaires cruising the Pacific in their yachts. It never really got beyond planning stages and Lorenz appeared to be the one paying for everything. He was completely in thrall to the Baroness and had sold his shop in Paris in order to finance the venture. Initially all three of them slept together in a large bed, but Lorenz soon became the victim of sadistic games played upon him by the Baroness and Philippson and took to spending more time visiting the Wittmers or up at Friedo with Dore and Friedrich. Dore felt particularly sorry for the young man and grew close to him. Lorenz's abuse provoked in her a violent hatred for the Baroness, who she was convinced was entirely evil.

It was by now 1932 and the main protagonists in the Galapagos Affair were assembled. And in the event the mix proved too rich for one small Pacific atoll. Enmities grew and animosities deepened. The three groups of settlers withdrew increasingly into their own camps.

There was one benign and regular visitor to the island who tried to keep the peace. This was an American multi-millionaire and amateur botanist called Alan Hancock who every year cruised the Galapagos in his luxury yacht collecting specimens of marine life. Friedrich and Dore, who had met him first, regarded him as their special ally.

The bad feeling between the three groups of settlers was fairly generalized – petty squabbles and jealousies, arguments over minor thefts and water sources, and slights and snubs arising over important visitors to the island (the settlers had become remarkably famous, many yachts called in and cruise ships changed course to pass by Floreana in the hope of glimpsing them). But soon the ill nature began to be concentrated around the Friedo/Hacienda Paradiso axis.

What set events moving towards the bloody and mysterious final act is hard to gauge. It seems to have been the frequency with which Lorenz left the Hacienda to seek solace with the Wittmers and Friedrich and Dore but the feuding was also stimulated by the increasing egomania of the Baroness. She claimed to visiting journalists that she was now 'The Empress of the Galapagos', an assertion that particularly enraged Friedrich, and adopted high-minded and imperious manners that went with the self-conferred title. Furthermore the summer of 1934 was particularly hot – there was a serious drought – and Lorenz appeared to be growing weaker as a result of the constant physical abuse he received at the hands of the Baroness and Philippson. Philippson regularly beat him up, with the Baroness occasionally lending a hand with a riding crop. Also, they locked away Lorenz's few possessions and denied him access to his money.

One day, the date is not clear, in late March of 1934, as the Galapagos Islands suffered their fifth month of broiling, desiccating heat, Lorenz appeared at the Wittmer house and announced that the Baroness and Philippson had 'gone away' with some friends who were passing in a yacht en route for Tahiti. He told the same story to Friedrich and Dore, who accompanied him to the Hacienda Paradiso to see for themselves. Dore remembered that the place was like the *Marie Celeste*, perfectly neat and tidy, with family photographs still in their frames, and, sitting on a table, the Baroness's most treasured possession, her copy of *The Picture of Dorian Gray*. Dore found it hard to believe that the Baroness would have gone to Tahiti and left this behind.

But nothing happened; suspicions remained unvoiced and no one investigated further. The drought broke, the rains came in April, visitors and journalists still arived, and life seemed to go on as normal. Then in July, Lorenz decided finally to leave, taking advantage of the visit of a Norwegian fisherman called Nuggerud – who lived on a nearby island called Santa Cruz. Lorenz had become an increasingly morose and haggard figure since the Baroness's mysterious disappearance, often observed weeping. But he managed to persuade Nuggerud to take him to Chatham Island where he could catch a ship bound for Ecuador. The Wittmers and Friedrich and Dore said farewell with mixed feelings. Dore reassured him that in time his miserable years on Floreana would appear merely as a bad dream.

The Baroness and Philippson gone, and now Lorenz. Three months later the startled Wittmers were surprised one morning by a distraught Dore at the door of their house. Friedrich, she said, was terribly ill, poisoned as a result of eating some potted chicken that had gone off. Dore too, so she claimed, had been sick after eating the meat, but Friedrich's condition had seriously degenerated.

They found Friedrich in an appalling state, wracked with stomach cramps and his tongue so swollen he was unable to speak. The ever-practical Margret Wittmer rigged up an impromptu stomach pump but found it impossible to operate. Friedrich refused to allow her to inject him with morphine. According to Margret he scribbled a few words on a piece of paper and handed them to Dore. They read: 'I curse you with my dying breath.' Friedrich died in the night, his body writhing with convulsions. When he was lifted up they found his back was a livid bluish red. Thick dark blood oozed from his nose. He was buried under a pile of stones in his philosophical garden.

Friedrich died on 21 November 1934. Four days earlier the captain of a tuna clipper, cruising near an uninhabited island in the north of the archipelago called Marchena, saw the beached remains of a small skiff and on going to investigate found the mummified bodies of the Norwegian Nuggerud and Lorenz. It was obvious that they had been shipwrecked weeks earlier and had died of thirst. The news of Friedrich's death and the discovery of Lorenz's body reached Alan Hancock in Los Angeles as he prepared another of his Pacific cruises. He sailed straight to Floreana to comfort and ultimately take Dore away. She returned to Berlin, leaving Floreana to the Wittmer family, where their descendants still live today. The final victim of the Galapagos Affair had been accounted for.

No one knows what really happened to the Baroness and Philippson, certainly they were never seen in Tahiti or anywhere else. But the consensus on the island, even at the time, was that Lorenz killed the

Baroness and Philippson and dumped their bodies in the ocean for the sharks to dispose of. However it is most unlikely that such a weak-willed and physically wasted man could have overpowered them both single-handedly. His most likely accomplice was Friedrich, whose loathing of the Baroness was intense and who publicly exulted in her 'departure'. Moreover, he regarded his relationship with Dore as effectively over and, for the last few months before his death, had been urging her to leave the island. With the Baroness gone, and Dore banished, and the Wittmers no challenge, he could resume his self-appointed role as solitary philosopher king of Floreana.

And Friedrich? In a book Dore wrote some years later she said he died of a stroke but the symptoms all point to botulin poisoning. The Wittmers claimed that Friedrich had told them earlier that the poisoned chicken meat would be safe to eat after it was boiled, and Dore told Alan Hancock she had given the meat 'a good boiling'. Did Dore, either through malice or carelessness, not boil the meat enough? My own hunch is that she may have wanted to 'punish' Friedrich for his suggestion that she leave him (after all, she had eaten the chicken herself, or so she claimed, and a sick Friedrich might have appreciated the ministrations of a dutiful Dore) but the punishment had gone hideously out of control.

Whatever the truth, the brute facts of the matter are that what began as an idealistic utopian experiment degenerated under the strain of the predictable human emotions of envy, pride, greed, lust and resentment – and a mix of atavistic territoriality and sexual threat – into a mystery that has fascinated and intrigued for over sixty years. Of the original settlers four died: one accidentally, one a victim of a possible crime of passion and the two others almost certainly as a result of cold-blooded murders motivated by fear and hatred. But who *really* did what to whom and why? The Galapagos Affair continues to enthral and beguile.

1995

Alan Ross

(Address Given at Alan Ross's Memorial Service)

I first met Alan about twenty-five years ago and, although I can't claim to be an old or a close friend, I owe him a great deal – as do many of the other writers here today. 'Mentor' is a word that I think Alan would shrug off and say 'nonsense' or 'ridiculous' if you tried to associate it with him. But I, and many other writers that he published over the years, came to think of him as a mentor, albeit an exceptionally kindly and diffident one. It's a question of taste, I think, and Alan's taste was as well-rounded and inclusive and eclectic as anyone's I've ever met – so that if you wrote something, and he liked it, or better still, published it, you felt that his approval was a form of artistic imprimatur. It was exceptionally valuable, his approval of your work: it was something to strive to earn.

In my own case – which I suspect is typical of all the writers linked with Alan and the *London Magazine* – that first sign of approval was unforgettable. I was twenty-four years old, unpublished, dreaming of becoming a writer, and had sent, on spec, a story to the *London Magazine*. And then one morning the never-to-be-forgotten reply came: 'Thank you for your story. Yes, we would like to publish it. The title must be changed. Yours, Alan Ross.'

I think it was written on notepaper from the Hyatt Regency Hotel in Manila, or the Mandarin Oriental in San Francisco. He was a great recycler of hotel stationery, was Alan – and a great recycler of postcards, too.

But the great thing about Alan was that the connection didn't end there. Shortly after the story was published, I was asked if I would like to drop by the office for a spot of lunch. I remember climbing the stairs in South Kensington to find Alan sitting behind a desk covered in books and manuscripts, with a couple of dogs (I think) lying on the carpet. On the walls were big oil paintings. Alan greeted me with his habitual polite, hesitant manner and asked me if I'd like to review some books. Yes, thank you very much, I said. He gave me a handful of hardback novels and then we went for lunch at an Italian restaurant across the street. 'I'm having a Negroni,' he said, 'What about you?' I'll have one too, I said, though I had no idea what a Negroni was. I quickly discovered it was amongst the most powerful pre-lunch drinks known to man.

I can't remember what we talked about at lunch – books and writers, probably – we drank a bottle of wine as well, of course – but I remember saying to myself: so this is the literary life . . . Can I have some more, please?

I think that's what Alan came to exemplify for me: he was living a kind of life that, from the outside, seemed almost impossibly ideal – the literary magazine, the racehorses, the modern art, the foreign travel, cricket, poetry, drink, sun . . . and all the rest. And he'd known everybody, from Evelyn Waugh to Cyril Connolly to Ian Fleming, from Keith Vaughan to John Minton. And he never changed, either – even the last time I saw him, at a party a few months before he died, he looked incredibly like the man who had greeted me twenty five-years earlier.

Anyway, this was what Alan seemed like to a young writer. And of course it's only a small part of the big picture that goes to make up the man, a picture gracefully and movingly delineated by himself in his two volumes of autobiography, *Blindfold Games* and *Coastwise Lights*. But to my generation the man was always associated with the magazine and in celebrating Alan's life we must also celebrate *London Magazine* and the forty years that Alan 'helmed' it, as they say in Hollywood. Which is not a bad metaphor, when you come to think of it, as applied to an ex-naval officer. *London Magazine* is a tremendous monument to him and to the taste that informed it. Alan was, I suppose, very English, in some respects, but the magazine was fantastically wide-ranging, the very opposite of parochial. Before I came here today I reached down a few of my back issues at random and came across writers and artists and photographers from India, Greece, Peru, Egypt and Poland.

Dickens said, towards the end of his life, that, 'I rest my claims to the remembrance of my country, upon my published works – and to the remembrance of my friends, upon their experience of me.' The magazine stands as an exemplary memorial and so do the poems, the travel writing and the exceptional autobiography. But I feel, because Alan touched so many hundreds, if not thousands, of lives – through the forty years he edited the magazine – that his circle of friends is vast – and that our collective 'experience of Alan' is far greater than is the norm with any other writer, almost without exception. It is that feeling that so resonates here today – his remembrance is assured – and will endure.

2001

Richard Meinertzhagen

(Review of *Richard Meinertzhagen:*
Soldier, Scientist and Spy by Mark Cocker)

Richard Meinertzhagen died, aged eighty-nine, in 1967. In the course of his long and astonishingly diverse life he had, among many other achievements, shaken the hand of Charles Darwin, evacuated troops from Dunkirk in a small boat, dined with Cecil Rhodes, written standard works on ornithology, killed dozens of human beings, hunted tigers in Burma, met and admired Hitler and been the confidant of T. E. Lawrence.

These facts we can be sure of, but Meinertzhagen, in addition, claimed also to have rescued one of the Tsar's daughters and flown her to safety; to have wiped out in a savage gun battle a cell of fifteen Bolshevik spies in Spain in 1930 and, at the age of seventy, to have slipped ashore from a boat anchored at Haifa, joined up with a gang of Israeli Haganah and killed five Arabs.

About these episodes, however, there are genuine grounds for scepticism. And yet, in tone at least, they appear entirely plausible, given the extraordinary colour and richness of Meinertzhagen's life.

He was born into a large, eccentric and well-off extended family, one of those typically English dynasties, such as the Huxleys and Darwins, whose various members seem able to incorporate almost every facet of cultural and political life – from merchant bankers to suffragettes, from dotty naturalists to apoplectic brigadiers, or any other category you care to think of.

Richard, though no fool, always tended to the man-of-action branch and, after the obligatory molestation and savage beatings at prep school, an uneventful time at Harrow and a few miserable months in the City, he joined the Army, the Royal Fusiliers, and was posted to India.

Thus began the most interesting segment of his life as a very unorthodox but professional soldier, which was to last from 1899 to 1924. His first posting after India was to British East Africa, and it was in that young colony that his large tally of human lives commenced.

He was a firm believer in the short sharp shock theory of colonial administration, especially so far as rebellious tribes were concerned. On one occasion he had an entire village razed and its inhabitants – men, women and children – executed as a reprisal for the death of a single white man.

A brief period of spying in the Crimea followed his removal from East Africa after his controversial killing of a local witch doctor in an ambush, but he was back there at the outbreak of the First World War as chief intelligence officer to the British Empire Forces in their fight against Lettow-Vorbeck in German East Africa.

In fact, Meinertzhagen's story in his *Army Diary*, of the first eighteen months of that bizarre and fascinating conflict, is unsurpassed; far and away the most vivid historical account that we possess. He witnessed the debacle of the Battle of Tanga in 1914 – possibly the most ineptly fought battle in the entire annals of the British Army – and was scathing in his condemnation of the uniquely farcical events of that day. His outrage did not prevent him, however, from executing a few hapless Indian sepoys in the field when they refused his order to advance.

After Africa came Palestine with General Allenby, and Meinertzhagen's dramatic and original intelligence work there is generally credited as contributing significantly to the capture of Jerusalem. It also initiated an involvement in the affairs of the Middle East – he was an early and convinced Zionist – that was to preoccupy him for most of his life.

With his departure from the Army in the early twenties, after a stormy period as military advisor to Churchill's Middle East Department, he concentrated on his parallel career as a natural historian and ornithologist. Inevitably, the account of his life loses some of its zest and vigour from here on.

He married and had three children. His wife died in 1928 as a result of a shooting accident and his eldest son was killed at Arnhem. Over the next decades Meinertzhagen came to be perceived as the Grand Old Man of British ornithology. His last years were dominated by various wrangles with ornithological institutions and individuals, and by the publication of his scientific texts and three volumes of the enormous diary he had kept almost all his life.

The clutter and detail of such a packed and busy existence can only be hinted at here. But what makes Meinertzhagen's life so unusual, and thus far more fascinating than those of, say, contemporary diplomats, private secretaries, generals or fringe political figures, is the man's own perplexing character.

At first, he appears a familiar type: the scholar/soldier – killing Huns and then sitting down to read some Virgil (or, in Meinertzhagen's case indulge in a spot of birdwatching) – but the many contradictions in his personality deny this too facile identification.

He was, clearly, a stubborn, single-minded man, brave and outspoken, and a notoriously difficult colleague. But the more one learns about him the more contrasting categories he seems to fit: bumptious subaltern and naive romantic; strict moralist and gleeful killer; admirer of Hitler and passionate Zionist; sexual innocent and worldly, perspicacious politician. The contradictions mount and the final assessment retreats into a labyrinth of antitheses.

Mark Cocker lucidly and honestly tries to pin the man down, and succeeds admirably insofar as such an attempt is possible. The problem with Meinertzhagen, and therefore the problem with any biography of him, is that the chief witness and key source is the man himself. Cocker has unearthed in the diaries patent elaborations, exaggerations and falsehoods and there is evidence too that in his scientific career Meinertzhagen indulged in practices that would be considered highly fraudulent.

Consequently, a life that reads anyway like an aggregate of Kipling, Buchan, Rider Haggard and Henty begins to reek, here and there, of the distinctly fictional. But with that reservation it is a compelling story and Meinertzhagen, however bizarre or preposterous or sinister or admirable we may think him, is one of those genuinely fascinating mavericks of twentieth-century history.

Malcolm Muggeridge described him as a 'legendary figure without a legend' and that seems to me to be a fair judgement, even though – as a result of Cocker's researches – we can now see that there is a touch of the Baron Munchausen *de nos jours* about him too.

1989

The Missing

(Review of *The Living Unknown Soldier* by Jean-Yves Le Naour)

In this time of war it is both useful and sobering to consider earlier conflicts. Often the battlefield statistics we are presented with, if they can be believed, or even if they're forthcoming (how many Iraqi dead for example?), tell only a tiny portion of the story they encode. At the end of the First World War, to give one instance, there were 630,000 widows in France. A million and a half young Frenchmen died between 1914 and 1918 (more than the British, fewer than the Germans) but the fate of these hundreds of thousands of widows – the personal and social consequences of their loss, of their mass grief – has gone untold beyond the brute fact of their enumeration.

Another brute fact is revealed in *The Living Unknown Soldier*, a fascinating and moving footnote to the Great War. Among France's 1.5 million dead, we learn that there were some 400,000 categorized as 'missing'. 'Missing' because no body could be found, nor any identity disc, nor witness to that soldier's demise. Both the pulverizing potency of twentieth-century weaponry and the indifference that advancing or retreating armies paid to the corpses they encountered meant that a huge proportion of battlefield deaths was simply not logged, particularly in the early years of the war.

It doesn't take a great act of imagination to consider that many of these hundreds of thousands of widows, whose husbands had been posted as missing, might harbour the hope that they were still alive – in a camp or in a hospital somewhere in Germany. And at the war's end, when the prisoners came home, there were some amazing reunions but for most it was a bleak reality check.

But there was a category of returned combatant that proved that hope did live eternal. These were the deranged or the amnesiacs. Soldiers who had no idea of their identity but were shipped home from Germany to France to survive as best they could. One such man was called Anthelme Mangin, and it is his story that Jean-Yves Le Naour tells here with judicious precision and admirable lack of sensation and sentiment.

Mangin was part of a transport of diseased and mentally ill prisoners shipped back to France in the last months of the war. He had no distinguishing marks on his filthy uniform and could remember nothing apart from his muttered name. He was suffering from total amnesia and dementia praecox and was duly incarcerated in an asylum in Rodez in central France.

It was rare for these men not to be eventually identified and the authorities made every strenuous bureaucratic effort. By 1920, there remained only six of these unfortunates left unnamed, and the decision was taken to publish their photographs in national newspapers in the hope that some family member would come forward. In the case of Mangin, though, there seemed only mounting confusion. Thousands of people suddenly claimed him as a son, husband, uncle or brother. He became a *cause célèbre* and the hordes of people wanting to visit him in his Rodez asylum became almost impossible to administer.

The urge to claim Mangin was a symptom of France's post-war grief and trauma. Families exhibited a form of pathological delusion and would identify Mangin in the face of all evidence to the contrary, so desperate were they to believe their loved one was still alive. Mangin submitted to these visits and profoundly emotional importunings with catatonic blankness. But for the man charged with sorting out the validity of the competing families – the asylum director, Feynarou – the task was thankless, obliging him to perform several judgements of Solomon per day. Feynarou emerges from this account with great credit: doggedly refusing to be swayed by tears and emotional blackmail, calmly interviewing claimants and pointedly evaluating their evidence (distinguishing marks, photos, measurements, etc.) and, inevitably, politely and firmly turning them down.

The Mangin case, however, refused to go away. Families took the administrators of the Rodez asylum to the courts insisting their loved one was being wrongly incarcerated. Things rumbled on until the 1930s, but by this time only two contenders had the stamina and conviction to carry on the fight. One had been there from the outset: Lucie Lemay was convinced that Mangin was her missing husband Marcel. Pierre Manjoin, on the other hand, claimed Mangin was his son Octave. In the various court cases that followed (running on right up to the outset of the Second World War) it became obvious that the Manjoin case was the right one. Finally, Mangin was identified as Octave, the long-lost son of Manjoin.

Only the next war put a stop to the litigation, however. Lemay appealed the case, but Manjoin died in 1939 before things were finally settled. Sadder still, Octave/Manjoin never left the asylum: he died of illness associated with starvation in 1942 (another forgotten scandal: according to Le Naour, mental defectives in asylums were deprived of food during the war in a covert euthanasia project).

Le Naour recounts the details of the Mangin case with impressive and unobtrusive scholarship and exemplary lucidity (in which he has been well served by his translator, Penny Allen). The case illuminates much about the complex psychology of mourning, and the real problems posed by the absence of a body – what Le Naour calls 'the drama of the missing', neither officially dead nor physically present. In closing the book, however, one is left with a feeling of great sadness and an abiding, useless rage against warfare. True, Mangin was the real victim, but the deluded grief of those who claimed him as a loved one is even more poignant and distressing. As we note that the American fatalities of the second Iraq war have now passed 1,000, it requires a prodigious, near-impossible mental effort to imagine what coping with 1.5 million would be like. The potency of Le Naour's narrow focus is to individualize one man's suffering in the First World War – and in that one man to see a nation's awful suffering also. Yet we should remember that this was a nation that won. What was true of France must have been true of Britain and its empire – and perhaps more so of vanquished Germany, too.

Mythologized as the 'living unknown soldier', Mangin, and his lonely half-life in the asylum and the symbol he came to represent for hundreds of bereaved, baffled and miserable families, opens a baleful window on to the aftermath of war and exposes the long dark shadow that it casts for decades, far beyond its conclusion.

2004

Charlie Chaplin (1)

In 1943, in open court, an American lawyer described Charlie Chaplin as 'a little runt of a Svengali', a 'lecherous hound who lied like a cheap cockney cad'. The lawyer went on to call upon 'American mothers and wives to stop this gray-headed buzzard dead in his tracks'. The world was at war and Charlie Chaplin was being hauled through the courts in a highly publicized, bitter and vituperative paternity suit. It was a low point in the extraordinary life of the world's most popular entertainer, arguably the most famous film star in the history of the movies, but worse was to come.

Charlie Chaplin was born in south London, probably Walworth, in 1889. Both his father, Charles Chaplin senior, and his mother, Hannah, were moderately talented minor artistes in the Victorian music hall. Charles wrote and published a few songs but his modest career soon foundered on his chronic alcoholism. Hannah's life in the theatre was cursed too, but this time by her mental instability. Legend has it that young Charlie's first stage appearance occurred when his mother 'dried' on stage in the middle of a song and her little son – he was five years old at the time – took over to the audience's unequivocal delight and rousing acclaim.

By then, however, the Chaplin marriage was already over and, what with Charles senior's descent into drunkenness, and Hannah's religious dementia, Charlie and his half-brother Sydney's early life was one of signal poverty and hardship. The family home was now located in a couple of rooms in a foetid Lambeth tenement where Hannah took in piece work and Charlie combed the mudflats of the Thames at low tide for anything salvageable that could be sold. Hannah's indigence meant spells in the workhouse for both her children and on occasion the entire family. And there the routine humiliations of Victorian welfare were never forgotten by Chaplin: he was beaten and bullied and his head was shaved and daubed with iodine against ringworm. Sometimes Hannah was confined to the workhouse as well but her bouts of insanity saw her more and more often incarcerated in Cane Hill asylum, where her violent hysteria was treated by periods of isolation in a padded cell.

Sydney Chaplin, four years older than Charlie, made his escape from this distressing world by joining the merchant navy as an apprentice steward. Charlie, meanwhile, at the age of nine, embarked on a stage career – clog dancing with a variety troupe called 'The Eight Lancashire Lads'. From now on he was to support his mother from his earnings as an actor and performer. Charles Chaplin senior died, aged only thirty-seven, from cirrhosis of the liver, and Hannah's intermittent periods of delusion and dementia meant ever longer spells in the bleak precincts of Cane Hill.

Chaplin's early stage career proved reasonably successful, occupying juvenile roles in long-running touring plays, but his first real break came when Sydney left off seafaring and found a job with one of the greatest impresarios of the music hall age – Fred Karno. Before long, Charlie Chaplin was also on the Karno bill, as a comedian and mimic, and thus began a rise in his fortunes that would only terminate half a century later.

Chaplin soon moved into the elite of Fred Karno's Army – as the travelling vaudevillians were known – where he won particular acclaim for his drunk act – playing an 'inebriated swell' who pretends to interrupt the show. Chaplin worked with Karno's troupe for eight years and it was during this period that he acquired and perfected the comic skills – the timing, the gags, the pratfalls and slapstick – that he was to put to such innovative use in the early silent movies. By the time Chaplin left for a tour of America in 1913 he was a thorough professional. He was earning £8 a week and had prominent billing on the company's posters. He was a small man – about five feet four – but dark and handsome, and a dapper and fastidious dresser. His first serious love affair occurred about this time, with a young dancer called Hetty Kelly, but was cut short by his embarkation for the American tour. However, Chaplin invested this short-lived, unconsummated teenage romance with tremendous romanticism. The love he felt for Hetty became exalted and transcendent and Hetty substitutes were to figure in many of his movies. Whenever he was with Hetty, he said, he 'was walking in paradise with inner blissful excitement'. Something about her purity and youth (she was fifteen when he met her) obsessed Chaplin – 'it was but a childish infatuation to her, but to me it was the beginnings of a spiritual development, a reaching out for beauty'. – and his retrospective fascination for her and what she represented (she died of influenza in 1919) may well have influenced his own sexual tastes and nature throughout the rest of his life.

The trip to America with the Karno company proved to be the watershed in Chaplin's life. His stage act was watched one night by Mack Sennett, founder and producer of the Keystone Kops, and at the end of 1913 Chaplin was offered a job in the then embryonic world of the movies, at a salary of $150 a week (a multiple of twenty will give an approximation of what Chaplin's salary is worth in today's terms).

In 1914 Hollywood was nothing more than farmland – miles of orange and lemon groves – far from the outskirts of Los Angeles. The first studios were reconstituted farms and barns where short films were churned out at the rate of one every three days or so. The medium was not highly regarded and was seen as a modern 'fad' being exploited by a bunch of get-rich-quick entrepreneurs. Chaplin went to work for the doyen of comedy film-makers and just as he had cut his music hall teeth with Fred Karno so Chaplin learned the film business from the loud-mouthed, tobacco-chewing braggart that was Mack Sennett. In 1914 thirty-five films starring Charlie Chaplin were released. By the end of the year Chaplin signed a new contract with a new company, Essanay. His salary had climbed to $1,250 a week.

In one year everything had changed; in one year the nature of film comedy had been irrevocably altered and the twentieth century had acquired a new icon. And all because of the Tramp. No one really knows how the Tramp was created, and Chaplin himself provided several contradictory versions over the years, but the fact remains that at some stage in February 1914, during the shooting of a Sennett one-reeler called *Mabel's Strange Predicament*, Chaplin went down to the wardrobe shed at Keystone and emerged carrying a cane walking stick and wearing a bowler hat, a toothbrush moustache, a tight jacket, baggy trousers and oversized shoes. The Little Tramp was born.

And was an almost immediate and enormous success. Chaplin began to write and direct his own films as well as star in them. He moved into an apartment in the fashionable Athletic Club and acquired a valet as well as opened several bank accounts. He wrote to his brother Sydney, in his inimitable style, urging him to come over. 'I have made a heap of good friends hear and go to all the partys etc . . . I am still saving my money and I have 4000 dollars in one bank, 1200 in another, 1500 in London not so bad for 25 and still going strong thank God. Sid, we will be millionaires before long.'

And he was. At the age of twenty-five, while Europe was embarking on the long agony of World War One, Charlie Chaplin from the slums of Lambeth set about mining one of the most lucrative seams in show business. Given the privations and suffering of his early life the money Chaplin made was always of vital importance to him and he was never in any doubt about what he was worth. Sydney duly came over and became his manager, and between the two of them they negotiated some of the shrewdest and most remunerative contracts in Hollywood's history. One New York journalist observed, after Chaplin had spent a month in the city, that he 'kept his bankroll exclusively to himself . . . never has Broadway known a more frugal celebrity.'

Chaplin could have contented himself with cranking out Keystone-style comedies, amassing his personal fortune and living the good life in the lotusland that was Hollywood, but his artistic ambitions were there from the start and always drove him on to greater challenges. He saw the huge potential of the movies at once, both as a means of mass entertainment on an international scale and also as an art form in their own right. Very soon after his initial success with the short comedies he tried his hand at a film of greater length and polemical heft – *The Immigrant* – the first of the series of comedies with a marked social comment that was to establish him as one of the founding geniuses of the movie industry.

Coexistent with the inexorable rise of his fame and fortune (his salary in 1918 was over a million dollars a year) his emotional life by contrast proved a far rockier business. After an affair with his leading lady in *The Immigrant* – Edna Purviance – Chaplin became infatuated with a small-time teenage actress called Mildred Harris (she was sixteen years old and, as Chaplin put it, 'no mental heavyweight'). This was the first of a series of disastrous liaisons with very young girls, a sexual obsession that was to dog Chaplin well into middle age, and was to provide his enemies with powerful ammunition.

Mildred became pregnant and to avoid the prospective scandal Chaplin married her. It was hardly a *grand amour* and what little affection Chaplin had for his bride evaporated when the pregnancy turned out to be a false alarm. As always, when his emotional life distressed him, Chaplin turned to his work. *Shoulder Arms* was made to boost the war effort and, in association with his old friends Douglas Fairbanks and Mary Pickford, United Artists was formed – the novel idea of a film studio controlled and run by actors that gave rise to the phrase, spoken by a disenchanted producer, that 'the lunatics have taken over the asylum'. United Artists was to be another phenomenal money-spinner for

Chaplin, but in the meantime the war was ending and his marriage was in ruins. Chaplin was editing his next film, *The Kid*, when Mildred Harris sued for divorce on the grounds of mental cruelty. It was finally granted in 1920.

In the celebrated dream sequence in *The Kid* a twelve-year-old child actress called Lita Grey played the part of an angel. Something about her fascinated Chaplin and he put her under contract. However, a more celebrated dalliance with the spectacularly beautiful actress Pola Negri dominated the gossip columns and there was a farcical series of on-off engagements that had more to do with enlarging Pola Negri's public profile than any great infatuation. Chaplin was deeply embarrassed by this public speculation about his private life, and in fact Pola was not his type. It is hard to say exactly when his affair with Lita Grey began but by 1924, when she was fifteen, she had been signed up – to the dismay of his colleagues – as leading lady on Chaplin's next big film *The Gold Rush*. When she signed the contract it was reported that she jumped up and down clapping her hands and crying 'Goody, goody!' Lita was no star, and not much of a beauty – she was described by one journalist as a 'peculiarly shy, reticent and far from loquacious girl. She seemed phlegmatic.' Chaplin's folly was compounded in September of that year when Lita announced she was pregnant. Sexual relations with an under-age girl were regarded as *de facto* rape in California, a crime that carried up to thirty years' imprisonment. The arranged marriage that followed took place covertly in Mexico. Press releases gave Lita's age as nineteen.

Chaplin's marriage to Lita Grey brought him two sons and a degree of misery and personal torment that almost drove him insane. In his autobiography he devotes no more than a couple of lines to the whole episode: 'For two years we were married and tried to make a go of it, but it was hopeless and ended in a great deal of bitterness.' In typical consolation he concentrated on his work with demonic intensity. As soon as he finished the arduous shoot of *The Gold Rush* he embarked on *The Circus* and shortly after the completion of that film, Lita walked out with her two children. The acrimony and publicity of the subsequent divorce action – its sexual innuendo and scurrility – drove Chaplin to a nervous breakdown. His hair turned grey overnight, he would bathe repeatedly and compulsively wash his hands dozens of times a day, and at night, paranoid and suspicious, he would patrol his empty house with a shotgun. As Lita prepared to announce to the world the names of five prominent women she alleged Chaplin had slept with during their short marriage (they included Marion Davies, newspaper magnate Randolph Hearst's mistress) Chaplin agreed to a cash settlement of $600,000. It was the largest such settlement in American legal history.

While Chaplin's personal life reached its nadir his films and popularity seemed ever on the ascendant. After the acrimonious divorce one headline read simply: 'CHARLIE IS A REAL HERO'. But at about this time, unknown to him, a new factor had entered his life that was to have profound consequences later. The FBI, under its director J. Edgar Hoover, had, since its inception, been convinced that Hollywood and the film community were a nest of vipers, of corrupt and seditious Communist degenerates who were undermining the moral fabric of the United States. The first file the FBI opened on Chaplin was in 1922, recording the fact that Chaplin had hosted a reception for a prominent labour leader. At the end of his life the full dossier was discovered to be 1,900 pages long. One report was titled 'Affiliation of Charles Chaplin with Groups Declared to be Communist Subversive Groups'. Chaplin's politics were broadly, if idiosyncratically, left wing, and he made no secret of them. But something about the FBI's diligence in singling him out from the other 'parlor Bolshevists' of Hollywood suggests a more malign vendetta, one probably inspired by Hoover himself. Chaplin and Hoover had met at a dinner early in Hoover's career and whatever took place that night initiated a dislike and distrust that were corrosive. Chaplin, moreover, did his cause no favour, in the eyes of the righteous, by never taking up American citizenship, by being regularly engaged in tax disputes with the IRS, and in making films with a pointed humanist-socialist message. They were also convinced he was Jewish (which he was not: faced with the accusation once Chaplin replied, 'I'm afraid I do not have that honour.' This did not stop the FBI from labelling his files: 'Charlie Chaplin alias Israel Thonstein.') His Achilles heel, however, proved to be the sexual scandals he became embroiled in. Lita Grey's bitter muck-raking set a tone of derogation and abuse that was finally to bring him down.

In the thirties, during the Depression and beyond, the crescendo of red-baiting and witch-hunting provided a hysterical and shrill backdrop to Chaplin's film career. After *The Circus* came *City Lights* (1931) – a remarkable silent movie success in the first heyday of the talkies – and then *Modern Times* (1936), that brilliant satire on the machine age and its complementary dehumanization of the worker. Chaplin's fame was worldwide and he fraternized with the Great and the Good – Winston Churchill, Gandhi, H. G. Wells and the Mountbattens among others – on many continents. In the thirties too, perhaps the most adult and emotionally fulfilling of his relationships thus far occurred. He had a long affair with Paulette Goddard (whom he persuaded to change her peroxide blonde hair back to her natural brunette) and to whom he was briefly married. The rise of fascism in Europe pushed Chaplin further to the left and was responsible for his reluctant conversion to sound. His trenchant satire of Adolf Hitler in *The Great Dictator* (1940) was courageously prescient, as well as being the last appearance on film of the Little Tramp.

To Hoover and the FBI Chaplin's films and his support of the Soviet Union were nothing short of an arrogant betrayal of American values, and although more and more voices were orchestrated to speak out against him Chaplin's popularity appeared impervious to such slanders. Part of this was explained by Chaplin's shrewdness in portraying himself as a humanitarian, an artist above partisan politics, and part of it was due to the fact that he was obligated to no man or system. Chaplin's great wealth not only ensured his financial independence, it also meant he could not be leaned on. He had his own studio, he paid for his own films, he could do what he liked without fear or favour. There seemed no way the FBI could bring him down. Until . . .

In 1941 he had a short affair with a buxom twenty-two-year-old actress called Joan Barry. Chaplin described her as 'a big handsome woman, well built, with upper regional domes immensely expansive'. Another very young girl – Chaplin was fifty-two – another colossal error of judgement. Barry was mentally unstable and began to drink heavily. After a series of incidents – a car crash, a break-in at Chaplin's house where she threatened him with a gun – he broke off the relationship, settled Barry's debts and provided her with a one-way ticket back to New York.

At around this time Chaplin – with a coincidental neatness that no novelist would be permitted – met another young actress who turned out to be the great love of his life, the seventeen-year-old Oona O'Neill. While Oona's beauty and extreme youth were as always a potent allure, there is no doubt of the sincerity of their mutual adoration – and this time, for once, he had made no mistake.

Chaplin's wooing of Oona and their eventual marriage took place against a turmoil of controversy that was as distressing as it was damaging. Joan Barry reappeared on the scene, six months pregnant, claiming Chaplin as the father of her unborn child. A series of court cases then took place, covertly organized by the FBI, with the sole purpose of blackening Chaplin's reputation beyond repair. First he was arraigned under the Mann Act, legislation designed to entrap pimps and brothel-keepers, and accused of paying Joan Barry to cross state boundaries for the purpose of having sex with him. When he was acquitted of this charge the FBI encouraged Barry to bring a paternity suit against him. Chaplin submitted to a blood test which proved negative but, in the subsequent trial, it emerged that blood tests were not recognized in Californian courts. Under a barrage of vilification and contempt that makes today's gutter press look positively restrained Chaplin was condemned in court as a vile seducer and corrupter of American woman-hood. He was declared the father of Barry's child and ordered to pay maintenance.

And this time the character assassination seemed to work. After the war Chaplin continued to make films – *Monsieur Verdoux* and *Limelight* – but he was increasingly under attack, especially as the McCarthyite anti-Communist purges were now running at full maniacal stretch, and his once indestructible popularity began to crumble and wane. A leading article in the *Herald Express* criticized his 'complacent self-worship' and described him as 'a moral nonentity'. The final move by the FBI came in 1952. Chaplin set sail from New York for Britain for the premiere of *Limelight*. Once he had quit territorial waters a telegram was sent: Chaplin's re-entry permit to the United States was rescinded under legislation which permitted banning on the grounds of 'morals, health or insanity, or for advocating Communism'. He was effectively *persona non grata*. Ahead of him stretched the long years of exile.

And here too the dramatic story of Charlie Chaplin, his rise and fall, ends. The boy from the slums of Lambeth had triumphed beyond measure amongst the freedoms and opportunities America offered. He had achieved astounding fame, vast riches, was acknowledged as one of the abiding geniuses of the cinema but in spite of all this something in him – hubris, moral fervour, arrogance, guilt, some curious self-destructive urge? – something had contrived to bring about his down-fall and his banishment from the promised land. Chaplin went to live in Switzerland with his beloved Oona where they raised a large family of eight children. Other films were made – *A King in New York* (1957),

The Countess from Hong Kong (1967) – other milestones were passed, many honours were conferred, but the twenty years of his exile from Hollywood have a flatness about them, and, inevitably, lack the excitement and energy and passion of the ones that preceded them. In 1972 he was welcomed back to Hollywood and presented with an Academy Award (a belated apology) and in 1975 he was knighted by the Queen. In 1977, on Christmas Day, he died quietly in his sleep. He was eighty-eight years old.

1991

Ian Fleming

In October 1963, Evelyn Waugh spent the weekend with Ian and Ann Fleming in their new house near Sevenhampton. Waugh wrote up the occasion in his journal: 'A two day visit to see what Ann has been up to. The full horror of her edifice did not appear until the next day . . . Ian Fleming, near death, in a woollen sweater drinking heavily the whisky forbidden him by his doctor.' Fleming was only fifty-five and suffering from a chronic heart condition. Waugh continued in the same vein a few days later in a letter to Nancy Mitford: '[Ian Fleming] looks and speaks as though he may drop dead any minute. His medical advisors confirm the apprehension.'

Fleming carried on disobeying doctors' orders for another ten months, enduring ever-increasing ill-health. In his drawn-out demise Fleming managed to sum up much of the character of his life: contrary, foolhardy, perverse and – somehow – very English. He was looking forward to dying and didn't see why, until that moment arrived, he should be denied his booze, cigarettes and games of golf. Interestingly enough, Fleming's key companions in his last months were other writers: William Plomer, Alan Ross and Cyril Connolly. He and Waugh were cordial but one senses that they didn't much like each other. Waugh – another eccentric Englishman who drank, smoked and drugged himself to an early grave – was much friendlier with Fleming's wife, Ann, a vivacious and somewhat terrifying society hostess. I once met a female contemporary of hers and asked what Ann Fleming had been like: 'One of those women who didn't much like women,' came the reply.

Ann Fleming was the great love of Fleming's life but by the 1960s the passion had long gone. Fleming was having an affair with a divorcée in Jamaica and Ann was dallying indiscreetly with the Leader of the Opposition, Hugh Gaitskell, but in their brittle, wealthy, worldly way she and Fleming kept up appearances. But Waugh and Ann Fleming were disdainful of Fleming in their letters and conversation, referring to him as 'Thunderbird', Waugh, as ever, choosing to mock someone he probably would naturally envy.

For, on paper, Fleming seemed to possess everything that Waugh felt he lacked. Fleming was born (in 1908) into a rich and famous Scottish banking family. He went to Eton where he excelled as a sportsman, and then Sandhurst. He was tall, dark and vaguely handsome. After Sandhurst he followed family tradition and went into the City, becoming, in his terms, 'the world's worst stockbroker' and led a stereotypical playboy life – pretty girls, fast cars, foreign holidays. He then had a 'good war' in the celebrated Naval Intelligence Division, where he was perhaps at his happiest, at the centre of a highly efficient espionage network, with the power to plot and scheme, to travel on clandestine business, to flirt with genuine danger (he accompanied the Canadians on the disastrous Dieppe raid in 1942, for example). The war ended and he became a senior executive and occasional journalist on the *Sunday Times*. And finally came the invention of James Bond, the huge sales, the money and the movies.

Like most people, I first encountered Fleming through his famous creation. I remember, aged eleven or twelve, reading *From Russia with Love* with a real illicit thrill. The book was passed around my pre-adolescent coevals as if it were some form of rare samizdat pornography. So this was what the adult world was like, we remarked to each other, utterly captivated by the now familiar blend of snobbery, sex, ludicrous violence, exotic travel and superior consumer goods.

The scales fall from your eyes pretty quickly but the allure of Bond and Bondiana is potent while it lasts. Bond's world was Fleming's fantasy: a comic strip version of a life he almost lived. But when, after his death, Fleming the man began to crop up in the memoirs and biographies of his contemporaries I found my attention began to focus more on the author himself than his works. As a case study he provided rich material. To such an extent, in fact, that I have now inserted him as a minor character in my latest novel.

It's hard to say what fascinates and intrigues about Ian Fleming. My own hunch is that it has something to do with his torments, his personal demons. At first glance he appears to be the man who has everything but who, in some way, is simultaneously fundamentally unhappy. The Fleming I write about is the Fleming of the late thirties and the war years, when the useless stockbroker turned into the avid spymaster. Notwithstanding his business ineptitude, Fleming, thanks to his inherited wealth, was able to live in some style before the war: with his specially decorated apartment, his red sportscar, his regular orders of 1,000 custom-made monogrammed Morland cigarettes (he was a dogged sixty-a-day man). When he joined the Naval Intelligence Division in 1939 he became the assistant to its chief, Admiral John Godfrey. He was awarded an honorary rank in the Royal Navy Volunteer Reserve and had a uniform made by his tailor. Yet when he was teased by his raffish friends about being a 'chocolate sailor' he took real offence and sulked. It's a telling anecdote, and it testifies to his insecurities, his vanity and childishness. His behaviour displays the very opposite of Bondian cool self-esteem.

And the more one reads about Fleming, as he appears in the two biographies thus far written, in his wife's published letters and in the comments and observations made by his friends and associates, the more complex and flawed he appears. He seems to be one of those emotionally closed Englishmen, incapable of fully engaging with the women he took up with. Time and again his girlfriends complain of being used and then discarded. His seduction technique rarely varied. First the girlfriend would be invited to peruse his collection of erotica (heavy on flagellation), then a Viennese waltz would be played on the gramophone while dinner was served – kedgeree or sausages with copious alcohol – then to bed. The common complaint was that Fleming was clearly far more interested in himself than his companion.

Fleming described himself thus: 'I've always had one foot not wanting to leave the cradle, and the other in a hurry to get to the grave. It makes rather painful splits of one's life.' And, one might add, provides a field day for the amateur psychologist. Am I wrong in thinking that this curious blend of the infantile and the world-weary is most commonly found in a certain type of upper class Englishman? One can mention any number of soldiers and explorers, industrialists, aristocrats and politicians who all too easily fit this peculiar bill. James Bond now seems a kind of hopelessly remote role model, a Platonic dream – the juvenile defects replaced by expensive hobbies, the emotional failings by carnal ruthlessness: the ultimate form of wishful thinking.

The 'hurry to get to the grave' recalls Waugh again, another man eager to meet his maker. What was it about Fleming's gilded life that prompted this death wish? My own supposition, for what it's worth, is that it is fostered by a sense of the bogus and the sham. 'To thine own self be true' is not a bad aphorism to guide you through your life but neither Fleming nor Waugh adhered to it, creating elaborate personas to shore up the bundle of neuroses and fraught contradictions that made up their innate selves. Their *taedium vitae* is just that: the urge to quit this world being a sign of the huge fatigue that maintaining the pretence engenders.

So it comes as no surprise that, at the end of his life, Fleming so cavalierly disregarded his doctors' orders: he knew he hadn't long to go – his heart was failing, there were blood clots forming on his lungs – his clock was rapidly ticking down, so why not carry on eating and drinking and smoking as if he were a young man again? And this knowledge perhaps explains the new serenity that his writer friends observed in his last months, whether watching cricket with Alan Ross at Brighton or reminiscing with Cyril Connolly about pre-war dalliances in Kitzbühel. Connolly found him altogether 'sadder, gentler, and wiser'. According to his wife, however, 'he stared from his bedroom window at the sea in total misery'. Relief and release came on 11 August 1964. He was fifty-six.

2002

Charlie Chaplin (2)

(Review of *Charlie Chaplin and His Times* by Kenneth S. Lynn)

In 1925 Charlie Chaplin was at the absolute apogee of his renown. He was, arguably, the most famous man in the world, his latest film *The Gold Rush* had just been released to enormous acclaim, he was massively wealthy and unhappily married to his second wife, a sixteen-year-old actress named Lita Grey. In New York he embarked on a passionate two-month affair with the incandescent Louise Brooks, yet to achieve her own lasting celebrity as the quintessential Lulu in G. W. Pabst's *Pandora's Box*. Louise Brooks was not a typical Chaplin conquest. Shrewd and self-confident, she was entirely her own woman and her assessment of her temporary lover is worth bearing in mind. She described Chaplin as 'the most bafflingly complex man who ever lived'. It is as succinct an epitaph as can be imagined and – who knows? – one that Chaplin might have wryly conceded was accurate. Certainly, this exceptionally thorough but somewhat disingenuous biography underlines the contradictions in his nature again and again: the multi-millionaire who was a Communist sympathizer; the social charmer who suffered from profound self-doubt; the coy sentimentalizer of womanhood whose sexual appetite makes your average movie-star stud seem like a sadsack dweeb; the working-class boy who ran his studio like a demagogic plutocrat; the passionate anti-fascist who defended Stalin's purges – the antitheses march on to the crack of doom.

Much of the Chaplin story is familiar to us through numerous retellings, not least David Robinson's fine authorized biography of 1985, which tactfully corrected the obfuscations and blatant omissions of Chaplin's own reinvention of himself in *My Autobiography*. And here, again, is the Dickensian poverty of his early life in Kennington and Lambeth, the music hall beginnings with Fred Karno's circus, the tour to the USA, the summons to Hollywood by Mack Sennett in 1914, the creation of the Tramp, the extraordinary success of the first series of two-reelers, the mounting fame and the massive pay cheques ($650,000 in 1916 – multiply by fourteen to get some idea of current values). And then came the unprecedented run of silent movie masterpieces released between 1920 and 1936 – *The Kid*, *The Gold Rush*, *The Circus*, *City Lights* and *Modern Times* – followed by the audacious and astonishing *The Great Dictator* in 1940.

But behind the glittering career, the society hobnobbing and international plaudits, Chaplin's private life repeatedly hit the ropes. His first wife, Mildred Harris, was sixteen years old when they married; he met his second wife, Lita Grey, when she was just twelve; Paulette Goddard – whom it appears he never actually wed – was the only one of his long-term consorts who stood up to him – and he reverted to type again when, aged fifty-three, he married the eighteen-year-old Oona O'Neill. And along the way there were innumerable couplings and liaisons of varying duration and intensity. There is no doubt that Chaplin has a sexual fixation on very young women – add this to unprecedented access to such women, coupled with huge wealth and fame, plus a deep personal insecurity, and it is little surprise that, with monotonous regularity, his private life degenerated into the proverbial can of worms.

Our image of the 'Little Tramp' and the sentimentality and genius of the films tend nowadays to make us forget that Chaplin's life was almost continually dogged with scandals – either sexual, financial or political. Kenneth Lynn diligently catalogues these, though at times the implicit gleefulness makes one suspect he has fallen victim to the biographer's disease (also known as the Alfred Goldman syndrome after its most notorious sufferer) – namely an abiding loathing for the subject of the biography. Lynn claims a clear-eyed neutrality but the mask slips from time to time and a snide relish at the evidence of our hero's feet of clay makes its all-too-obvious appearance.

This is particularly relevant in the third act of Chaplin's life when his Communist sympathies and his idealistic socialism ran so counter to the zealotry of McCarthyite America in the forties and early fifties. Chaplin experienced an organized campaign of vilification and character assassination in the press that is almost inconceivable to imagine – even nowadays. For example, it was regarded as completely above board for a US senator to demand, in the US senate, how a 'man like Charlie Chaplin, with his communistic leanings, with his unsavory record of law breaking, or rape, or the debauchery of American girls of 16 and 17 years of age' could remain in the USA. It is here that one senses Lynn's judiciousness fraying. His own value judgements are telling: Brando's *The Wild One* is described as 'a piece of trash'; Warren Beatty's

Shampoo dismissed as 'unrelievedly tawdry satire'; and he comments disparagingly on the 'grotesqueries' of Kubrick's *Dr Strangelove*. Kenneth S. Lynn is no bleeding-heart liberal, one senses, and the gloves come off when he tackles Chaplin's public and critical rehabilitation in the 1970s, culminating with the 1972 presentation of an honorary Oscar: 'The anti-Vietnam war politics of the group that clustered round Chaplin were defined most clearly by three figures: Jane Fonda . . . (recipient of her father's gratitude for heeding his plea not to turn her acceptance remarks into a pro-Hanoi harangue) . . . Jack Nicholson, wearing a print shirt and a McGovern button; and emcee Sammy Davis junior who had pleased the crowd a few hours earlier by flashing a peace sign and whose main item of jewelry was a peace-symbol necklace.' Good God, a 'print shirt', 'a peace-symbol necklace' – clearly the most dangerous type of subversives.

More pertinently, though, Lynn argues the case that Chaplin calculatedly used media hostility in the late 1940s to turn himself into a political martyr – that the eventual denial of a re-entry permit to the USA suited him fine and, indeed, that he had made elaborate preparations for such an eventuality. In my opinion he seriously underestimates the role played by the FBI in the systematic smearing of Chaplin over the Joan Barry case, a paternity suit brought against him in 1943, just after he had married Oona. It was a case that Chaplin won – he was not the father of her child, as the actress claimed – but the mud slung in the trials and hearings was suitably besmirching.

The point is that Chaplin was not at risk from McCarthyite blacklisting because he owned and ran his own studio and in that sense was untouchable. The only way for the anti-Communist organizations to 'get' him was the moral turpitude route. And it is highly significant that Chaplin's re-entry permit was denied – not for political reasons of pro-Communist sympathies – but on the more loaded one of 'morals'.

Charlie Chaplin the man – aside from the artist – was a bizarre and baffling case. Given his nature as an individual, his particular demons – his abject start in life, his abiding fear of madness (at the age of fourteen he had to incarcerate his mother in an asylum) – and the enormous fame and wealth that arrived suddenly when he was only twenty-one, we should not be too surprised that he turned out the way he did. We are, perhaps, in this age of excess and neurosis, more understanding now. Let us leave the last word with another bizarre and baffling case – Marlon Brando – who, after a stormy working partnership with Chaplin on *A Countess from Hong Kong*, remarked: 'I don't think anyone had the talent he did: he made everyone else look Lilliputian. But as a man he was a mixed bag, just like all of us.'

1998

The Duchess of Windsor

17 August 1940. Does this date mark the lowest level in the fortunes of Wallis, Duchess of Windsor? On 17 August 1940, a day of humid, relentless heat, the Canadian cargo ship MV *Lady Somers* docked at Nassau harbour, in the Bahamas. On board was the colony's new governor, accompanied by his wife: the Duke and Duchess of Windsor. At the end of the gangway the Duke paused, allowing the Duchess to pass by, ensuring that she set foot on Bahamian soil before he did: neither of them had any idea that this tiny colony was to be their home for the next five years. They were being sent into a form of exile – one might even say a form of penal servitude – for Nassau, in those days, was a shabby colonial town with one main street, Bay Street, and a shifting population of around 20,000 – made up of tax exiles, American tourists and, of course, the indigenous Bahamians. Government House was dilapidated and the swimming pool was empty. For the Duke and Duchess, after the life they had been used to living, it was an unequivocal tropical hell (albeit one peopled with servants). They were far away, constrained (they had to ask Churchill's permission to leave the island) and gainfully employed. If you interpret the Duke's posting as an act of revenge by the Royal Family it was a particularly shrewd and malicious one. Since the abdication and their marriage in 1937 the Duke and Duchess had led an idle, wealthy life in Paris and the Côte d'Azur (with a certain amount of foreign travel thrown in). But now war had broken out in Europe they had to go somewhere, and whoever thought of the Bahamas ensured that the biggest of bigwigs now found themselves in the smallest of small towns: the Duke and Duchess must have looked around them in dismay and incredulity.

For once, I feel I can say 'must have' with some justification. Because, bizarre and presumptuous claim though it may seem, I feel I know the Duke and Duchess of Windsor in a peculiarly intimate way. This is because I placed them in my latest novel, *Any Human Heart*, as significant characters with whom the hero has, for some weeks, a close and fraught relationship. I undertook the usual research into their lives, spending months reading about them, poring over photographs and memoirs and generally trying to get inside their heads. But in a case like this the novelist's task is different from the historian's or the biographer's. Having never encountered the Duke and Duchess, I had to imagine them into life, as I would do with the fictional characters I usually create. The better and more fully you can imagine a character the more they will live on the page – so I set about imagining the personalities of the Duke and Duchess buttressed by all the documentary evidence I could muster. Paradoxically, in the strange process that is the creation of a fiction, authenticity and plausibility are among your most powerful assets. So I had to imagine, for example, what it would be like to sit beside the Duchess of Windsor at a private supper party in Government House in Nassau in 1943. I had to imagine how it would be to play a round of golf with the Duke of Windsor in Portugal in 1940. And in the course of this exercise the couple began to flesh themselves out and become real – to such an extent that I was able to create fictitious conversations and encounters that seemed to me to have the ring of authenticity. The Duke and Duchess became as familiar to me as the other fictional characters in my novel and that strange familiarity now colours everything I read about them.

Their Bahamian exile was particularly interesting because I had visited the islands many times in the 1980s and had become highly intrigued by the Duke's suspicious role in the investigation of a notorious murder (in 1943) of a local millionaire called Sir Harry Oakes. In my novel I try to make a convincing case – and the evidence is damning – that the Duke of Windsor conspired with corrupt detectives to pervert the course of justice and would have happily seen an innocent man hang for Harry Oakes's murder. The more I came to learn about the Duke the more I came to dislike him. But the Duchess – subject of so much obloquy over the decades – was different. I wasn't so much charmed by her as came to understand her better, somehow. The fact is that in the hell of their Bahamian exile – she called the place 'this moron paradise' – the Duchess actually behaved extremely well – with patience, decorum and graciousness. The image of her as a spoilt, grasping harridan, manipulating the ineffectual Duke, doesn't chime with the serene public face of the woman who was in fact loathing every minute of her life in Nassau. One could argue that almost everything that the Duchess aspired to in marrying the Duke was now absent from her life in the Bahamas. Position, high society, renown, glamour, haute couture and all the fine things money could buy were absent – or rather were replaced by farcically reduced simulacra. She had position – she was the governor's wife – but that was a joke in this tinpot colony. High society was composed of dreary official receptions for visiting minor dignitaries and the unsavoury local politicians. Renown didn't exist – during the war they were virtually forgotten – and as for haute couture, copious perspiration will make a mess of the most elegant outfit. And so on.

What makes the Duchess's compliance more remarkable is that this role-playing, this tolerance of circumstances that she could never have imagined she was destined for, was not inspired by great love. The relationship between the Duke and Duchess was heavily one-sided. He adored her abjectly, slavishly, caninely. She was fond of him: the 'great love' flowed only in one direction. It says something about the Duchess's own sense of duty that she didn't crack up under the strain. Her health was bad, she suffered from ulcers, but she didn't let the side down. During the Bahamian years, 1940–5, she behaved, it has to be said, in an exemplary manner: just like a true royal.

But in fact the Duchess did crack – the mask slipped – but not until six years later. In 1951 she met a young man called Jimmy Donahue. He was good-looking, good company, very wealthy and homosexual. And the Duchess became obsessed by him. What is fascinating about the relationship between the Duchess and Jimmy Donahue is that such a fall from grace took so long in arriving. The suspicion remains that it was an after-effect of those years of drudgery during the war. Jimmy Donahue – a gossip, a joker, outrageously camp – offered the Duchess something that had been absent from her life and still was: fun and frivolity.

The Duchess was fifty-five, Donahue was twenty years younger. He was an heir to the huge Woolworth fortune and initially the Duke and Duchess's interest in him was purely mercenary: Donahue's even wealthier mother was lavish in her gifts to the royal couple and they did very well by her. In 1951 the Duke was a lugubrious, fussy, hollow man. The empty life he and the Duchess now led was well established and for the Duchess the prospect of the years ahead was daunting. She set out to win Jimmy Donahue and quickly did so. The Duke and Duchess and Jimmy Donahue became an unusual trio in the *beau monde* of Paris and New York and Mediterranean cruises where the Duchess's torrid embroilment with her new young friend was rarely concealed. They were observed kissing passionately in a Parisian night club; one of Jimmy's friends provided him with the use of an apartment so they could meet when the Duke was away. There was a sexual relationship between the Duchess and Jimmy Donahue but what precisely went on behind the bedroom door will only be informed guesswork. Donahue himself later claimed that it was mutually bestowed oral sex but by then he had been ousted from the royal circle and consequently his testimony has to be weighed up in that light.

But something carnal did go on and the relationship lasted just over four years. It ended with a row in a restaurant in Baden-Baden. Jimmy was growing bored trailing around Europe with the elderly couple. One evening he got drunk, became angry at some remark the Duke made and kicked the Duchess under the table, drawing blood on her shin. The Duke ordered him out and the end of the affair was finally achieved.

It's not hard to imagine what the Duchess took from this association. In the kind of life they led – of peripatetic, well-heeled idleness that took them on a seasonal round to Paris, New York, Palm Beach, Biarritz, Monte Carlo, Portofino and back again – the great enemy is boredom. Jimmy Donahue was a gossip and a prankster and his own wealth and social connections made him unimpressed by the faux-regal aura around the Duke and Duchess. He made the Duchess laugh and passed the time, and the fact that he was handsome and prepared to put his own sexual proclivities on one side in order to pleasure her was an added bonus. As for the Duke, he became a public cuckold, a subject of whispered jokes and condescending tittle-tattle, but he bore the humiliation, until the final row, with glum stoicism. Nothing, it seemed, could dull the edge of his total devotion.

The Duchess, it has to be said, behaved badly and seemed unperturbed by her betrayal of her husband. As one of her friends later told her, Jimmy Donahue had destroyed her reputation and indeed it is the Duchess's post-war incarnation – the mask-faced, immaculate, society hostess and permanent house guest of the vastly wealthy – that has coloured the world's perception of her, subsequently. It is interesting to contrast her behaviour with Jimmy Donahue with the recent revelations of her so-called affair with Guy Trundle in 1935, before the abdication. But, thinking of the Duchess I 'know', I find I'm highly sceptical about the Trundle relationship. I can easily understand why she became infatuated with Donahue in the 1950s but I cannot imagine she would ever risk betraying the Prince of Wales, as the Duke then was, for a brief fling in a Mayfair flat with a man from the motor trade. Too much was at stake in 1935 for her to risk even a whisper of scandal: the prize was too big and her own affair with the Prince of Wales was by now fully established and at its most intense. I would argue that her behaviour in the Bahamas during the war underlines that she had as clear a sense of protocol and duty as any royal. That punctiliousness would have been at its most acute while the Duke was wooing her and the prospects of a royal marriage one day were not some impossible fantasy.

Picture the situation. It is 1935: you are an ageing, not particularly attractive American woman in a loveless marriage to a portly and dull businessman. You are having a passionate love affair with the world's most eligible bachelor, the Prince of Wales, the future King of England. You have just been on a luxurious Mediterranean cruise and holiday with your lover. You are at the very pinnacle of high society: the prince's terribly smart and aristocratic friends are suddenly your friends. After a difficult and rackety life and two husbands you find yourself breathing the rarefied air of a world you could only have dreamed about. Outside royal and political circles no one in Britain knows of the affair nor of the Prince of Wales's obsession for you (you have helped him overcome his 'sexual difficulty'). So do you pop off to Bruton Street, W1 for some clandestine sex with a Ford Motor Company salesman, however handsome and dashing? Whatever Mrs Simpson was doing when she visited Guy Trundle – if indeed she ever did – it wasn't to have sex with him. Duff Cooper – one of the Prince's inner circle and one who had no axe to grind – came up with an assessment that seems to me to be completely valid and true: Wallis Simpson, he thought, 'is a nice woman and a sensible woman', and he concluded, 'but she is as hard as nails and doesn't love him'. She didn't love him but I believe she remained true to him, in her way, and lived up to the demands her role as his wife required of her – until, that is, she met Jimmy Donahue.

2003

Edward VII and Frederick Treves

On 13 June 1902 Edward VII had under a fortnight to wait until his coronation. On that day the King travelled from Buckingham Palace to Aldershot to review a parade of troops. He did not feel well and it was observed that his normally florid complexion was blanched and drawn. By the 14th he was complaining of pains in the abdomen and nausea. Edward was a prodigious eater and drinker and his personal physician, Sir Francis Laking, suspected that these symptoms were the familiar ones brought on by His Majesty's compulsive over-indulgence. He prescribed a laxative and confidently expected matters to resolve themselves naturally. It was not to be. On the night of the 14th the King suffered violent spasms of abdominal pain and repeated vomiting. Laking called in an eminent surgeon for consultation, Sir Thomas Barlow. The two men feared the worst: King Edward VII was afflicted with perityphlitis.

Perityphlitis is one of the forgotten names in the medical lexicon. It was used to refer to the mysterious and inevitably fatal 'abdominal affections of the right side' that had been killing people for thousands of years. The cause was obscure but the symptoms were remorseless: abdominal pain, followed by vomiting, fever, intestinal inflammation and ultimately death from general peritonitis – the inflammation and corruption of the serous membrane which lines the stomach cavity. The disease was a potent killer: in 1856 one study showed that out of forty-seven cases of perityphlitis only one survived. Over the years countless victims' corpses had been dissected and their innards poked about and pored over but it wasn't until 1812 that a surgeon suggested that this fatal inflammation of the stomach cavity may be caused by an initial inflammation of the vermiform appendix, a small worm-shaped attachment of the blind gut.

'Appendicitis', as the disease came to be known towards the end of the nineteenth century, was very much an American appellation. American surgeons, in particular McBurney and Fitz, were in the vanguard of the treatment of the disease. Unlike surgeons in Europe, they advocated the earliest possible removal of the appendix as soon as the symptoms appeared. In Europe this was regarded as modish, not to say perverse, nonsense. If, in the nineteenth century, as a European, you were afflicted with appendicitis you would be dosed with opium and purgatives and it would be hoped the problem would disappear of its own accord. If not, and if an abscess appeared around the appendix and grew as it filled with pus, it would be hoped that a natural process of capsulation would then occur that would seal off the abscess from the abdominal cavity. The argument ran that the American method of early intervention created greater risks of general infection: it was too precipitate, better to wait until capsulation had occurred and then drain off the offensive matter. There was no greater advocate of this procedure, and no greater sceptic of the American way, than Britain's most eminent surgeon, Frederick Treves, and it was he who was now called to the King's bedside.

Frederick Treves (1853–1923) was a self-made man, the son of a cabinet maker who had risen to the heights of the medical profession. In 1902 he was internationally recognized as a brilliant surgeon and the authority on diseases of the abdomen and gut. He was a prolific writer and his medical textbooks were in standard use. More than this, he was a friend and confidant of King Edward and Queen Alexandra and was sergeant-surgeon to the monarch from 1901. Additional renown had accrued in the 1880s over his care and handling of Joseph Merrick, the so-called 'Elephant Man'. It was Treves who formulated the adage that a good surgeon needs 'a lacemaker's fingers and a seaman's grip'. He might have added that, in what we now recognize as the dawn of modern surgery, a good surgeon also required an adamantine ego and an unswervable ambition. Treves possessed all these attributes and in the small world of Edwardian medicine he guarded his pre-eminence jealously.

Treves was called to Windsor on the 18th where he confirmed the earlier diagnosis of perityphlitis. True to his own methods he proposed waiting a while before operating to ensure that the capsulation should be completed. Treves visited the King daily and then, on the 21st, an improvement was observed. The King's temperature dropped and the abdominal swelling appeared to go down and he felt well enough to travel to London. The coronation, set for the 26th, seemed likely to take place as planned, the abdominal pains apparently cured by the traditional doses of opium. But on the afternoon of the 23rd the pain returned and with it fever and repeated vomiting. The remission had been short and it was decided that an operation should take place on the morning of the 24th. Treves was to act as surgeon; also present were Laking, Lord Lister and surgeons Barlow and Smith.

Edward VII was grossly corpulent – his waist measurement was forty-eight inches – and Treves had to cut to a depth of almost five inches before he found the abscess, fortunately still encapsulated, surrounding the remains of an almost completely destroyed appendix. Treves then cut into the abscess and the pus was discharged. The resulting cavity was cleaned and two rubber drainage tubes were inserted. The wound was dressed with ideoform gauze. As Treves's biographer Stephen Trombley* comments, 'Contrary to contemporary reports and current misinformation, Treves did not remove the King's appendix. The belief that Treves and the King combined to make appendicitis "fashionable" is ill-founded.'

Treves deliberately did not remove the appendix and he would have been appalled to think that he had done anything to popularize 'appendicitis'. But the fact is that Treves took a massive risk in proceeding the way he did and in not removing the appendix. It was now vital that the wound cavity close of its own accord, but from the bottom up, as it were. Any other form of healing might give rise to a sinus which could provoke other complications. The few days or so after the operation were anxious ones as the surgeons and doctors waited apprehensively for any sign of the symptoms of general peritonitis. Luckily for them King Edward made a good recovery and by mid July was fit enough to convalesce for three weeks on the royal yacht. The coronation eventually took place on 9 August.

Treves was credited with saving the King's life (and was duly made a baronet) yet there is a school of thought which would allege that in fact he needlessly endangered it. His insistence on waiting for some days before operating, his surgical intervention occurring finally when the King was *in extremis* and then his decision not to remove the appendix and only to drain the abscess were in line with prevailing medical orthodoxies. But they were far from being unchallenged orthodoxies, even in 1902. Indeed there was a consensus of well-informed medical opinion and overwhelming evidence that indicated that the swift removal of the appendix was the only truly successful method of

---

* *Sir Frederick Treves* by Stephen Trombley (1989). Treves's wife destroyed all her husband's private papers and this is the only biography of Treves. I am indebted to Trombley's fine book for many of the facts recorded here. All suppositions, however, are my own.

treating these abdominal inflammations. Each of Treves's decisions could have resulted in King Edward's death: the delay and the reliance on opium could have caused the abscess to rupture; the tendency to operate only at the last minute often provoked peritonitis rather than relieved it, or was so late as to be redundant; and to leave the remains of the ulcerated appendix in the wound and to rely on chance that it would heal properly can be argued, with even a little hindsight, to be instances of malpractice.

Why was Treves, who throughout his career was such an innovator, such an advancer of surgical practice, so remiss when it came to the saving of his sovereign's life? The answer lies, I would suggest, in a curious blend of xenophobia, vanity and shameful remorse.

In 1888 Frederick Treves removed a vermiform appendix and laid claim to be the first man in Britain to do so. However there is no doubt that the honour in discovering that the appendix was the root of so many abdominal inflammations went to American surgeons. Treves, for all his pioneering work, was an also-ran and his substantial ego was unhappy with this state of affairs. He then sought repeatedly to denigrate all the American advances in this field using every resource of patronizing mockery and pompous cynicism at his disposal. His disappointed vanity led him uncharacteristically to adopt the most conservative of approaches in this area of his expertise. Most surprisingly for a surgeon, as Trombley observes, Treves did not advocate surgery. His preferred method of treating 'perityphlitis' was by medical means – bed rest and opiates. His wilfulness was to have tragic consequences.

In 1900, Treves's daughter Hetty, aged eighteen, fell ill with abdominal pain. Treves did not diagnose appendicitis. Hetty became iller and iller, feverish and vomiting. For some reason Treves refused to see what was happening. Eventually, inexorably, other symptoms appeared that indicated that, as a result of her father's delay, Hetty had contracted peritonitis. Treves decided to operate but two colleagues persuaded him that it was pointless. Hetty died in great physical distress.

It is almost impossible to imagine Treves's feelings at this time and he never spoke of the enormous grief and guilt he must have felt. Yet he did write about it, obliquely. In 1923, the year he died, Treves published a curious story called 'The Idol with Hands of Clay'. It tells the story of a young surgeon who, so convinced of his own mastery of his craft, decides to operate on his own wife when she falls ill with appendicitis. During the operation he makes a fatal mistake and his wife falls into a coma, the surgeon struggles to save her and yet is unable to do so and she dies in his arms. Some glimpse of Treves's response to his own tragedy is made available here:

[The surgeon] caught a sight of himself in the glass. His face was smeared with blood. He looked inhuman and unrecognizable. It was not himself he saw: it was a murderer with the mark of Cain upon his brow. He looked again at her handkerchief on the ground. It was the last thing her hand had closed upon. It was a piece of her lying amidst this scene of unspeakable horror. It was like some ghastly item of evidence in a murder story. He could not touch it. He could not look at it. He covered it with a towel.

And yet this terrifying object lesson made him an even stauncher opponent of the new advances being made in America. By ironic happenstance, a few days before he operated on Edward VII, Treves gave a lecture on appendicitis in Hammersmith Town Hall, a talk which was a sneering exemplar of his contempt for the American surgeons as well as being both patently wrong and purblind about medical matters. He stated with arrogant confidence that 'The very great majority of all cases of appendicitis get well spontaneously . . . [another fact] which I think should be emphasised as strongly as the last one, is this: operation during an acute attack of appendicitis is attended with great risk to life.'

Four days later, the man who held these opinions had to operate on his king.

Treves was very lucky. Edward VII was even luckier, and no thanks to his sergeant-surgeon. Treves's hubris, negligence or wilful obstinacy had caused the death of his daughter. That same wilful obstinacy could easily have caused the death of Edward VII. It is intriguing to speculate what the course of the nation's history, and perhaps Europe's history, might have been if George V had come to the throne in 1902 instead of 1910.

In Treves's case, however, the analysis is not so speculative. The death of his daughter, as the story demonstrates, shocked him terribly. In such a situation what could he have done? To admit all his thinking and public statements about appendicitis were wrong would be to compound the guilt unbearably. The only way I can understand this aberrant behaviour in an otherwise innovatory and brilliant surgeon is that for Treves so doggedly to persist with his old discredited theories, to continue to think he was right and the Americans were wrong, allowed him to live with himself more easily; the more he scoffed and sneered the more it allowed him to see his daughter's death as a tragedy and not as something of which he was directly culpable. More relevantly, when the same set of symptoms recurred in his monarch, for Treves then to advocate the swift removal of the royal appendix would also have been a tacit admission of the fatal misdiagnosis of his daughter, just two years earlier. Because of his personal grief, the barely admitted guilt he felt, Treves had to recommend bed rest and opiates to his dangerously ill king. He nearly got away with it. The remission of 21, 22 and 23 June seemed to bear out everything he had said in the Hammersmith lecture. But when the pain and the vomiting returned Treves had to contradict his own best medical advice and undertake an operation during an acute attack of appendicitis. But even then he could not go all the way and remove Edward's appendix. The ruined vestigial organ was left in the King's body, almost, one might say, as a small symbolic gesture of medical defiance – the final act of a man who could not admit he had been wrong.

1994

The Duke of Windsor and Sir Harry Oakes

During a stormy night in the middle of World War Two – Wednesday, 7 July 1943 – in Nassau, in the Bahamas, a multi-millionaire called Sir Harry Oakes was murdered in his bedroom. The cause of death was a blow to the head by some sort of spiked weapon or club causing four circular wounds an inch deep and a quarter inch in diameter. Shortly after, an attempt was made to set the victim on fire. Petrol was doused on the body and bedclothes and lit. The murderer – or murderers – then left, but the fire did not take. A house guest discovered the badly scorched corpse before breakfast the next day.

During the 1980s I visited the Bahamas on many occasions and heard all sorts of lurid tales about the Oakes murder – tales embellished with rumours of currency speculation, sexual innuendo, Mafia gangsters and millionaire Nazi sympathizers. I decided to feature the murder as an episode in a new novel to see if I could elucidate the mystery and began to read everything I could find on the subject. The truth, as far as I can determine, is more banal, but, in a way, no less sinister.

Harry Oakes had made his fortune prospecting for gold in Canada and had come to live in the Bahamas to avoid paying tax on his millions. However, he involved himself in the community, forming partnerships with local businessmen, and philanthropically encouraging the islands' industries. It would be fair to say that Sir Harry Oakes was the colony's most important citizen – after the governor of the Bahamas himself.

And that governor of the Bahamas was the ex-King of England, Edward VIII, now the Duke of Windsor.

The Duke and Duchess of Windsor had been sent to the Bahamas in 1940, after the fall of France, in a deliberate attempt to keep them out of the public eye and under control. Both of them were infuriated by the appointment, seeing it as an insulting act of royal spite, and detested the place (the Duchess referred to it as 'this moron paradise'). However, they both pursued their official duties with conspicuous diligence and no visible signs of bad grace – even though the Duke made every effort to have himself transferred away. He wanted desperately to be a kind of roving ambassador for Britain in the United States.

The death of Sir Harry Oakes came as shocking news to the Duke. He had known Sir Harry well but the last thing he wanted now was the scandal and notoriety that such a prominent murder was bound to encourage. The case had to be solved – and fast.

This can be the only explanation for the Duke's next move. Instead of calling on the Bahamas' perfectly competent CID force (headed by Police Commissioner Colonel Erskine-Lindop) he asked two Miami homicide detectives (one of whom had acted as his bodyguard on a trip to Florida) to fly immediately to Nassau and take over the investigation. The Miami police force at this time was one of the most corrupt in the USA: there is no reason to assume the Duke was aware of this.

The two detectives – Captains Melchen and Barker – arrived on Thursday after lunch and went to work. In the small, febrile and somewhat decadent community that was the wartime Bahamas speculation about the identity of the murderer was loud. Common gossip centred immediately on one Alfred de Marigny, Sir Harry's son-in-law, as the likely culprit. De Marigny, an indigent playboy figure straight from central casting, had eloped two years earlier with Sir Harry's eighteen-year-old daughter, Nancy, and they had married. Sir Harry's death would see a significant amount of his fortune devolve on her.

Like most of Nassau's white community, the Duke was convinced de Marigny was prime suspect. Melchen and Barker swiftly interviewed de Marigny and took away samples of his clothing for investigation. De Marigny had given a dinner party on the night of the murder but had driven some guests home, not far from Sir Harry's house, Westbourne, and there was a damaging thirty-minute hole in his alibi. De Marigny had motive and means: if he could be placed in the house the case would look watertight.

Melchen and Barker summoned de Marigny to Westbourne for further interrogation. In the course of being questioned de Marigny was asked to pour a glass of water from a carafe and was made to handle a cellophane-wrapped packet of Lucky Strike cigarettes. He was then allowed to leave.

The next day, Friday, 9 July, the Duke came to Westbourne where he had an unwitnessed, confidential twenty-minute discussion with Melchen and Barker. This is the crucial moment in the investigation. In all their inquiries the Miami detectives had been accompanied by Erskine-Lindop or other members of the Bahamian police. But now the Duke wished to talk to Melchen and Barker alone. Two hours later de Marigny was arrested and accused of the murder. A perfect finger-print – from the little finger of his right hand – had been found on a piece of furniture (a folding screen) in the murder room. De Marigny had been caught: it was almost as good as a smoking gun.

When de Marigny came to trial in October 1943 the prosecution case against him was demolished with brutal thoroughness by his counsel, Godfrey Higgs. Captains Melchen and Barker, the fingerprint experts, were rapidly exposed both as incompetents and liars. De Marigny's fingerprint had been 'lifted' (with a piece of Sellotape, probably from the cigarette pack) and placed on the screen. It was established beyond doubt that the print could not have been genuine. The case against de Marigny was a clear set-up and he was found not guilty and acquitted.

Now it was vital to keep a lid on the stench rising from the Oakes affair. The Duke was conveniently absent (in the USA) during the trial; he had not been interviewed and was not called as a witness. Neither he nor the detectives were ever asked about the substance of their Friday, 9 July conversation. Why? Simply because royal prestige and royal sway were still very potent in those days. Huge efforts were made to spare the Duke any embarrassment. He never explained why he had bypassed his own CID. More curiously still, after the trial the case was closed. Yet de Marigny was innocent: therefore, by definition, the killer was still at large. The Duke refused ever to talk about the subject of Sir Harry Oakes and his death and forbade the matter to be raised in his presence.

Why was the Duke so sensitive? What did he know? I now don't believe the theory that he was speculating in wartime currencies – with Sir Harry Oakes's help – for vast profits through Mexican banks (a trea-sonable offence); nor do I believe this murder was anything to do with American Mafia bosses wanting to build a casino in Nassau. The Duke called in Melchen and Barker because he wanted the affair solved quickly: he reasoned that the Americans would work faster than the local CID. And he was right. By planting a fingerprint Melchen and Barker had incriminated and arrested de Marigny in just over twenty-four hours. De Marigny was duly locked up in jail until the trial and everyone assumed he was guilty. Only the brilliance of the cross-examination saved him and exposed the detectives' culpability.

But what about the Duke's role in all this?

My theory goes like this. The planting of the fingerprint, in the context of Miami 1943, was routine work for Melchen and Barker. The carafe and the cigarette pack ploy testify to this. In their unwitnessed twenty-minute conversation with the Duke on Friday, 9 July, I believe they would have hinted that they had conclusive proof, or could manufacture the conclusive proof, that would put de Marigny in the murder room. Language would have been veiled and euphemistic on both sides. But the Duke – however covertly – would have to authorize them to go ahead. It is inconceivable that, having been summoned by the Duke himself, the two American detectives would have corrupted the evidence in a high-profile murder case on British colonial soil without, at the very least, a royal nod and a wink.

The governor of the Bahamas was a weak and worried man in 1943 but even the most charitable interpretation of his actions tends inexorably to the conclusion that the Duke of Windsor colluded with Melchen and Barker to pervert the course of justice. I deliberately don't use the word 'conspiracy' – that requires too much malice aforethought. The Duke would always be able to deny that he knew what the detectives planned, but he was no fool. De Marigny, thanks to his lawyer's skills, was acquitted and the false evidence exposed. But what if he had not been? If de Marigny had been found guilty then he almost certainly would have been hanged. One wonders if the Duke's conscience would have been unduly troubled. I suspect not.

So who killed Sir Harry Oakes, and why? That, as they say, is another story. But the Duke's duplicitous role in the investigation and the incrimination of an innocent man is hard to gainsay. In 1943 the Duke wrote to the Foreign Office saying, 'The whole circumstances of the case are sordid beyond description.' No one else was better placed to know.

2002

Charles Lindbergh

(Review of *Loss of Eden: a Biography of
Charles and Anne Morrow Lindbergh* by Joyce Milton)

It is almost impossible now, in these days of cheap global air travel, laser-guided weaponry and routine trips to outer space and back, to conjure up the astonishing glamour and fascination of aviation when it first began. Hard too, when thousands of airline pilots are being made redundant around the world, to envisage the aloof, almost superhuman allure of the figure of the aviator. Part demigods, part daredevils, the first flyers achieved a renown and provoked an awestruck reverence in the public that now seem almost incredible. These were real men and women who risked their lives in a medium previously denied human endeavour and in machines that seemed to counter every natural law. And the fact that they were the first truly *modern* heroes, with the ancient values of fortitude and temerity yoked to the very latest technology the twentieth century could produce, perhaps explains why the mix was so potent and the idolatry so febrile and impassioned. Not until the first astronauts came along would the aviator as modern hero be displaced from his pedestal, but even then it was only by another form of pilot.

The most famous aviator of the early decades of the century, and arguably the most famous aviator of all time, was Charles Lindbergh who, in 1927 at the age of twenty-five flew his single-engined plane *The Spirit of St. Louis* non-stop from New York to Paris. This considerable feat, while impressive, does not however fully explain why Lindbergh should become one of the great, iconic figures of his time. The answer – and this intriguing biography attempts to delineate it – must lie in a curious combination of historical circumstance and individual personality. The world has a way of creating the heroes it wants that has little to do with rationality and more to do with collective intuition – why Charlie Chaplin and not Buster Keaton, for example, why James Dean and not Montgomery Clift? – and there was something about the gauche youthfulness of Lindbergh that sent crowds wild. Here was a tall thin Minnesotan barnstormer who didn't smoke and didn't drink and loved his domineering mother. There was no vainglory, no false modesty and, apparently, no undue cupidity either.

Whatever the blend was – a combination of naivety and technolog-ical skill, a kind of 'aw, shucks' mentality coupled with massive deter-mination – it worked, and after his historic flight Lindbergh ascended to a plateau of international fame enjoyed by very few this century. Fortune, honours, reputation, personal happiness followed. The young man married a shy, pretty heiress, Anne Morrow, and the couple became the focus of media attention in the Western world and seemed perma-nently at home among the great and the good.

But of course if that was all there was to it the Lindbergh name would eventually have dimmed and his celebrityhood would have occu-pied its due niche in aviation history. But along with clouds of glory, great fame trails more noxious vapours. When Lindbergh's baby son was kidnapped and held to ransom he was plunged into the dark side of the Faustian contract that all who become famous unwittingly sign.

Lindbergh himself supervised the various agencies – police, FBI, private sleuths – involved in the hunt for his baby son and in the farcical negotiations with the kidnappers. The discovery of the baby's decom-posing body a few hundred yards from the Lindbergh home brought no end to the trauma. The ransom money had been paid and it was only by chance that a sequence of marked notes turned up and led the police to the prime suspect, an immigrant German called Richard Hauptmann.

Joyce Milton devotes much space to the details of the kidnapping and its ramifications and, inevitably, it proves to be the most compelling episode in this joint biography. Somewhat against recent trends she firmly and very effectively makes the case that Hauptmann was in fact guilty of the kidnap and murder and was not, as some commentators have suggested, a convenient scapegoat. She suspects that he did not work alone and, more tentatively, suggests possible accomplices.

The exemplary drama that was Charles Lindbergh's life still had a few acts to play out, however. Having come from obscurity to huge fame, having known scandal and tragedy (all carried on in a blaze of publicity), Lindbergh now seemed wilfully to court opprobrium and disgrace. A long-time believer in 'air-mindedness' (a vague philosophy that air travel could foster peace and international understanding) Lindbergh saw those values enshrined in the new Nazi state in Germany. Throughout the 1930s various visits to Germany, coupled with a disen-chantment with life in the USA and a growing Anglophobia, pushed Lindbergh ever further to the right. He became a leading figure of the isolationist America First movement and his public pronouncements became ever more shrill and anti-Semitic. By the time America entered the war Lindbergh's reputation was at an all time low, and to that generation of Americans it never really recovered. However, the new obscurity he found himself in allowed him covertly to participate in combat operations in the Pacific theatre (where he worked as a consultant for defence contractors, testing aeroplanes) and after the war his rehabilitation was completed when Eisenhower restored his commission and promoted him to brigadier general in 1954.

Lindbergh continued his work as a consultant in the airline industry but the triumphs of the post-war years belonged to Anne who had real success as a best-selling author – an experience Lindbergh was to share himself in his surprisingly accomplished autobiography *The Spirit of St. Louis*, published in 1954. The later years provide less diverting copy as the Lindberghs grew old, more or less gracefully, educating their four children, prosperous and comfortable, with homes in Geneva and Hawaii, still travelling the world and still dabbling in various half-baked spiritual philosophies. Lindbergh died of cancer in Hawaii in 1974. His widow still survives him.

There is no doubt that there is something totemic or emblematic about the Lindbergh life. Such huge and sudden fame, followed by personal tragedy of such a shocking and disturbing nature, seems almost mythic in its retribution, as if Lindbergh was another Icarus who had flown too near the sun. And at the centre of the story resides the curious, oblique and complex personality of Charles Lindbergh himself (Anne Lindbergh, for all that this is a joint biography, essentially plays second fiddle). Joyce Milton too appears to have problems pinning it down. In a lucid biography of otherwise scholarly and professional qualities she refers to her subject haphazardly as Lindbergh, Charles, Slim (a nickname), Slim Lindbergh, Lindy and Charles Lindbergh – sometimes using three different appellations in one paragraph. It is as if this baffling persona is still ducking and weaving, evading the biographer's scalpel. Was he an innocent who had fame thrust upon him and couldn't cope with its pressures? Was he a bigot and a fool? Or a hopeless idealist suckered by more unscrupulous forces? Was there, to paraphrase Gertrude Stein 'no there, there'? Each reader will make his or her judgement but one of the shrewdest comments on Charles Lindbergh comes from Harold Nicolson, the diplomat and writer, who befriended Lindbergh at the time of the kidnapping but who turned away from him in the crypto-fascist, America First years. Nicolson described the great aviator thus:'he is and always will be not only a schoolboy hero, but a schoolboy.' It explains a great deal.

1993

Newham

An A–Z

Aeroplanes announce Newham to the approaching traveller as they steeply climb and bank above this distant and forgotten borough of London. The STOL-jets and prop-planes from the City Airport strain skyward. Nobody looks up: people pay as much attention to these soaring aircraft as they would to a dog barking.

Barking Road, Newham's old commercial spine, built early in the nineteenth century to connect the East and West India Docks with the river port of Barking. Now it wears the familiar garb of every urban high street: franchise chains and letting agencies, car salesrooms, pubs and shuttered shops. Here and there the odd sixties high-rise. Rows of two-storey terraced houses lead off on either side. The Boer War lingers here in pockets – Mafeking Road, Kimberley Road – as do little bits of Scotland – Glasgow Road, Tweedmouth Road, Perth Road. Bright doors speak of stubborn house-pride: cerise, mauve, moss green, canary.

Canary Wharf's solid blunt obelisk looms everywhere, over house gables, dominating the western horizon, confronting you as you turn corners. Margaret Thatcher's real lasting monument, a concrete and glass hymn to commerce, capitalism and market forces rising heftily, beefily, out of the Isle of Dogs.

Dogs shit freely on Newham's streets as they do throughout London, in Chelsea and Mayfair as well as in Barnet and Peckham. And dogs run free around the estates behind the Barking Road. The few dogs on leashes look at their free-ranging brothers enviously, longing to be released.

East London goes on for ever, the great 'other city' within the vast spreading mass of London. Cut off from the west by the office towers of the Square Mile, it runs from Stepney to Dagenham, onwards and onwards. The sluggish flow of traffic on the arterial roads glints in the afternoon sun like the scales of fish.

Fish still swim in Roding Creek, I suppose. One hundred and fifty years ago Barking was a fishing port with over 200 Barking smacks and 1,000 men and boys to man them. Now the northern outfall of London's main drainage decants here at the mouth of Roding Creek where it joins the Thames. The air is rank with the smell of gas.

Gasworks can provide a kind of immortality. Beckton Gasworks are so called after Simon Adams Beck, governor of the Gas Light and Coke Co., who bought the site at East Ham in 1867. Beck-town grew and grew and became the largest gasworks in the world. On the map all colours cease at Beckton: it remains white, the gasometers, the tanks and the filterbeds marked as neat rows of circles – strange hieroglyphics.

Hieroglyphics badge Newham's walls today, the graffiti and the tags of the urban young, a form of writing that can be found replicated in Paris, Rio and Manhattan. Tribal markings that defy the local – all seemingly written in the same crazed hand – which are, bizarrely, truly international.

'International cheap phonecalls' proclaims the sign above a shop window, an audacious oxymoron. Indeed, 'International' appears to be a favoured adjective in Newham. 'International hair styling', says another shop window. There is 'International rowing', also, at the regatta centre, and you can pray for your misbegotten soul at the Amazing Grace International Worship Centre on the Barking Road. Two senses of 'international' operate here: one is about inclusion – come one, come all – one is about keeping up with the Joneses.

Jones Scrap Metal, at the beginning of Barking Road, is reputedly the biggest in London, which is a not-to-be-sneezed-at claim-to-fame for Canning Town. Another feather in Newham's cap is the City Airport. Amongst London boroughs only Hounslow can boast a fully fledged international (that word again) airport. You can fly all over Europe from Newham, to Rotterdam and Amsterdam, Paris and Brussels – which is not bad from a borough generally regarded to be on the skids.

Kids mooch around in tatty recreational areas, kids with bikes and skateboards, all colours, all nationalities. The walls and sheds and garage roofs around them are all crowned with barbed wire or razor wire or more complicated revolving impediments. Keep kids out, these hostile barriers seem to say, indications of deeper suspicions, no innocence here, a want of love.

Lovage Approach is the new Newham, south of Tollgate Road. Dinky, villagey lanes, with small, clustered brick houses, leaded diamond-paned glass in the windows, porches and dormer windows, a hotch-potch of domestic styles. Architects creating a 'community', here, reaching back to their notional roots – a reckless pillaging from a catalogue of olde-worlde vernacular styles – as we approach the millennium.

Millennium Mills still stands, built decades before the Millennium Dome, not so far away. A monument to the borough's industrial past when the 'offensive trades' were ordered out of metropolitan London and were obliged to set up shop in the east along the Thames. An industrial base almost vanished now, impossible to rebuild or renew.

New City Road turns off Barking Road. A long run of terraced houses. On either side are other identical streets, Kingsland Road, Patrick Road . . . Avenues of neatly pollarded plane trees, houses built in the nine-teenth century for clerks working in the City. This could be Fulham or Battersea twenty years ago. Now with the new 'villages' proliferating perhaps this is all there is in Newham that is really old.

'Old' Newham never really existed, however. The borough was created in 1965. The county boroughs of East Ham and West Ham brought together with bits of Plaistow and Woolwich and Upton. 'Ham' means low-lying pasture.

Pasture is hard to find today. There are angular bits of waste ground, thick with buddleia and rosebay willow herb, abandoned tracts of land between spur roads and the wire-mesh walls of tyre depots and scrap metal merchants. Strangely, along the Royal Albert Dock Spine Road there is a sudden profusion of allotments, well tended. Things are growing here: runner beans and potatoes, lettuce and cabbages. Prince Albert would be pleased, I think, to see such husbandry and enterprise, and so would his queen.

Queen Victoria's presence still leaves a marked trace. All the royal docks are in the borough. Her own Victoria Dock, her husband's Albert Dock and her grandson's dock, George V. The City Airport sits between Albert and George like an aircraft carrier moored in a wide placid river.

River views are distant ones in Newham. The docks dominate the river here: huge wind-flurried rectangles of water reflecting the turbulent skyscape. And the sewage jetties and the sludge piers of Beckton hog the river bank at Galleons Reach as the Thames' northern meander turns east again. From a spine road you can catch a glimpse of the scalloped towers of the Thames Flood Barrier, shining like burnished steel.

Steel shutters on modest shops – newsagents, electrical goods – tell you something about a place. Many shops selling second-hand furniture tell you something about a place. But just when you think you have Newham sited in its demographic circle of hell you see the dry-ski run – the Beckton Alps Ski Centre – and the Asda superstore. The contrasts abound: pie and mash for sale and McDonald's Drive-Thru; boarded-up, torched flats and bijou pseudo-villages. And everywhere streets bulging with traffic.

Traffic lights in Newham seem set longer than anywhere else in London. 'The borough doesn't like motorists,' a minicab driver confides. The wait seems to go on for ever. And look at all the speed-bumps. Yet most people's view of the place is from a car – passing through, heading east or west, on a spine road or a flyover – or from the tall gantries of the Docklands Light Railway. Rare names appear that ring a distinct bell – West Ham, of course – and others that provoke fainter recognitions – Custom House, Silvertown (can there be a place in London called Silvertown?), Canning Town and Upton.

Upton Park, it is hard to believe, had – in the eighteenth century – a botanic garden second only to Kew, hence its name. It is famous now for being home to West Ham FC, for some of the worst housing in Europe and for The Spotted Dog, the oldest pub in the borough, which dates from the sixteenth century. The Spotted Dog – *ave atque vale*.

Valediction forbidding mourning. Can there be a stranger borough in London? Can there be images of the city more dramatically bleak and excitingly futuristic? The wind seems keener and fiercer in Newham than elsewhere in London, tugging at you as it rushes from across the

North Sea and the Thames estuary, hurrying on its giant flotilla of dark rain clouds, spinnakering westwards. Stand on the dockside at the city airport and watch the planes lift off for Frankfurt and Bruges, your eye momentarily held by the flashing light at the tip of Canary Wharf, your ear catching the rumble of a train on the elevated trackways of the DLR – as you turn you note the precisely angled slope of the dry-ski run and the bright stacked apartments of a new village-cluster and, behind you, the fuming steel ziggurat that is the Tate and Lyle sugar factory. Some sort of weird rejuvenation is happening here out in the east of London, however surreal. The mineral rain spits on your face, abrading your cheeks gently, as with a fine steel wool.

Woolwich, or to be more precise, North Woolwich, forms the south-ernmost portion of the borough, and, because the rest of Woolwich was south of the river – in Kent – it was known, until it was amalgamated into Newham, as 'Kent in Essex'.

Xeroxing a map of Newham and noticing how it is composed of so many real places with real histories made me realize how artificial a construct it is. So I suggest we should abandon its current pronuncia-tion, the apologetic, half-swallowed mumble of 'newum', and boldly rechristen it New Ham, which, along with the ancient low-lying meadows of East and West Ham, might give the place a sense of conti-nuity and a kind of validity – make it seem less young.

Young boroughs lack traditions, lack a sense of community. Newham has existed for only thirty-five years. West Ham, by contrast, is an ancient parish and was even a parliamentary borough in 1855 and, moreover, one that played a significant role in the history of socialism. Keir Hardie was elected Labour MP for West Ham South in 1892. Neville Chamberlain suspended its Board of Guardians in 1926 for what the government regarded as over-generous poor relief. What can youthful Newham offer in terms of history and tradition that won't seem wholly ersatz?

Zoroastrianism may seem an unlikely notion, even a facetious one, but Newham and its agglomeration of parishes and county boroughs have always been a home to nonconformity and pluralism. There were over a hundred nonconformist chapels of all denominations at the turn of the century; there were Quaker meeting houses in Plaistow in the seventeenth century and the borough still boasts two convents and two friaries. I'm sure that today any passing Zoroastrian would receive a warm welcome in the Amazing Grace's International Worship Centre on the Barking Road. You look around at all the contrasts and contradictions of the place and have to conclude that, whatever its difficulties, its transformations and its deprivations, the real and enduring spice in Newham's life has always been its ineffable, unrivalled and bewildering variety.

2000

France 1940–44

(Review of *Occupation: The Ordeal of France
1940–1944* by Ian Ousby)

In France the great sacrifices of the First World War are proudly and
visibly commemorated: the smallest village has its obelisk or icon with
its sad list of its sons who paid the ultimate price; every town square
has its monument, usually a heroic bronze *poilu* 'mort pour la Patrie'.
However the fallen of World War Two seldom merit a separate ceno-
taph, their names carved into the existing plinths as a kind of faintly
embarrassed postscript. For the French the actual fighting was short-
lived and the casualties consequently few: the war against Germany ended
in 1940 with the armistice of 22 June. What happened subsequently was
not a 'war' as we commonly understand it but a heavy price was exacted
all the same – the scar tissue is still raw and, as the unfolding trial of
Maurice Papon in Bordeaux reminds us, the wounds can still bleed.

Not a war, then, but certainly an ordeal, as Ian Ousby's subtitle empha-
sizes in this compelling and lucid account of France's four-year occupation. It takes a real effort of historical imagination to conceive what
it must have been like for the French in 1940 as the Wehrmacht swept
across the Belgian border. For a notional eighty-year-old living in 1940
it must have seemed the worst possible nightmare: the third successful
German invasion in a lifetime. For the British in particular, last invaded
in 1066, such an act of empathy presents some obstacles – but, as Ousby
warns, any sense of smugness or superiority is highly dangerous. National
catastrophes – and the June 1940 surrender was indubitably that – do
not necessarily bring out the best in any nation's peoples.

Ousby starts the story early, with the First World War, in fact, and
effectively demonstrates how the long shadow of 1914–18 was still dark-
ening the French psyche. Defeatism married to stunned incredulity
dominated the national mood. There was a real sense – and one has to
banish hindsight here – that the country could not experience or survive
another trauma so profound as the First World War. So peace was made
and the recriminations began, a lot of it taking the shape of a potent
Anglophobia – especially after Churchill ordered the sinking of the
French fleet at Mers el Kébir. There was a corresponding humanization

of the victors: the Germans were not arrogantly triumphalist; they were well-behaved, polite – 'ils sont correct' – was the surprised observation and the word 'collaboration' (entirely neutral in 1940) was enshrined in the very terms of the armistice itself.

As time goes by it seems to me more and more that the attitudes struck and convulsions experienced in France during the four years of occupation reflect psychological moods that any person can recognize. Ousby charts the progress from humiliation to guilt, to recrimination and the searching for scapegoats (as well as citing the British, Vichy France was swift to initiate its own anti-Semitic policies), to sullen resignation and then, somewhere around 1942, something more stubborn and hostile beginning to be born, a realization that quietistic acceptance was all wrong. Ousby makes the telling point that,

It takes a great deal to make the French ashamed of being French. Even the defeat of 1940 had not quite managed to do that, however loud the clamour of mutual recrimination it had provoked. But the years that followed did. They created a sense of disgrace more subtle yet far more disturbing than anything that had happened on the battlefield.

That sense of disgrace (and increasing brutality from the occupiers) in the end saved the nation from itself and the Resistance was born. Ousby guides us through its modest beginnings, its frustrations and de Gaulle's fraught and problematic task of casting himself as national saviour. It had its dark side too: one bitter consequence of some French people starting to fight back was that they initiated a form of civil war, of French *Maquis* against French *Milice*, the legacy of which is still being painfully played out.

It is easy to be cynical, to point to the deliberate mythologizing of the Resistance, to log their small numbers and modest contribution to the Allies' actual liberation of France, but Ousby's perspective is always wise and candid.

For the British consideration of what it meant for France to be occupied has always involved covert self-questioning. If we had been occupied too, what would have happened to us? How would we have behaved?

Good questions. And if our former king, Edward VIII, is any guide (perfectly happy, in 1943, to launder his British pounds through a German bank in Mexico) they might provoke disturbing answers. Perhaps Wallis Simpson did us an even bigger favour than we could have ever realized. In the event, and lucky for us, it is all hypothetical.

1997

Evelyn Waugh (1)

Evelyn Waugh died on Easter Sunday, 10 April 1966, at the age of sixty-three. I was at boarding school and had just turned fourteen but I remember the occasion of his death. One of the more rebellious intellectuals in the sixth form had pinned a notice to the main notice board deploring the fact that the philistine school authorities had made not a single announcement, had urged not a solitary act of remembrance, about the passing away of one of the greatest English novelists. This ardent Waugh fan urged that individual boys make donations so that flowers could be sent to the family. A small list of names, with modest sums of money beside them, was scrawled below. I don't know whether some bouquet or other eventually made its way from the school to Waugh's home in Somerset – but I do remember pointedly logging away the unfamiliar name of this author. Evelyn Waugh? . . . Wonder if he's any good?

Thirty-five years later I now know the answer to that question but I could never have foreseen just how intense my relationship with the works and the man would become. Its latest manifestation is the four-hour adaptation of Waugh's *Sword of Honour* trilogy and for which I wrote the script. This is the second time I have adapted Waugh's work for the screen. The first was *Scoop*, a two-hour film for LWT, made in 1987. In 1982 I was TV critic for the *New Statesman* and wrote at length about John Mortimer's epic adaptation of *Brideshead Revisited*. But by then the embroilment was well underway: I had read all the novels, of course, and had even taught them to undergraduates at Oxford. I had started searching second-hand bookshops for first editions. My Waugh obsession was fully developed.

Waugh, more than any of his peers, provokes this level of interest. The obvious reason for this is that the works endure so well and provide such great rewards. But the other explanation must be that we know so much about the man himself. I own four biographies, not to mention several other memoirs by family, friends and acquaintances. The juvenilia have been published and so have the travel books and the complete journalism; then there are the notorious journals and the collected letters and other additional volumes of correspondence between Waugh and Nancy Mitford, Waugh and Diana Cooper. Almost every public and private word the man wrote has been published and he's not been dead forty years – we have all the information on Evelyn Waugh we could possibly want.

And this is what informs and charges our reading. Waugh is the most autobiographical of writers – even the grotesque and outlandish comedies – *Vile Bodies*, *Black Mischief* – are solidly rooted in the details of his life. This tendency to recycle his own experience is nowhere more evident than the trilogy of novels Waugh wrote about the Second World War – *Men at Arms* (1952), *Officers and Gentlemen* (1955) and *Unconditional Surrender* (1961) – which he collected together, somewhat revised, under the general title of *Sword of Honour*, first published in a single volume in 1965.

The central figure of the trilogy is Guy Crouchback who, at the outbreak of war in 1939, is thirty-five years old, almost the same age as Waugh at the time. There all similarity breaks down: Guy is, in effect, an almost fantasy alter ego for the author – a cradle Catholic from an ancient aristocratic family, an independently wealthy single man living in Italy. Everything, so the uncharitable view would go, that Waugh himself aspired to and yearned for in his life.

But the course that Guy Crouchback's war follows is, in almost every degree, that of Waugh's. Waugh eventually managed to secure a commission in the Marines and was later transferred to the Commandos. The glamorous resonance of these names belies the mundanity and relentless frustration of Waugh's military experience. Like Guy, Waugh's first brush with action was a mission to Dakar in West Africa. Then in 1941 he was sent to Crete with the Commandos to try and repel the German invasion, just managing to escape before the British forces surrendered. Then, after a period of inactivity (during which he wrote *Brideshead Revisited*), Waugh was dispatched to Yugoslavia in 1944 to be part of a military mission liaising with Tito's partisans.

Waugh was hugely discontented as a soldier. He was a brave man (quite fearless under fire during the Crete debacle) but he was difficult and unpopular. No commanding officer wanted Waugh in his force and he was routinely shunted from command to command as patience ran out and tempers erupted. He was rude and truculent: a wealthy and famous novelist, he was a malign and prickly presence in the officers' mess. I remember once meeting Fitzroy Maclean – with whom Waugh served in Yugoslavia – and I asked him what he thought of Waugh. Maclean said he had never known an officer more loathed and detested by the men who served under him. Maclean and Waugh cordially disliked each other so the opinion has to be treated with some caution. But, after Crete, Waugh's disillusion with the army and its values was profound.

The section of *Sword of Honour* that deals with Crete is a magnificent and chilling tour de force. As a chronicle of military incompetence and absurdity it rivals *Catch 22* as a bitter indictment of men at war. It is also a fascinating example of Waugh's method, of how he turned his experience into fiction.

Waugh, like Guy Crouchback, arrived in Crete as the British and Empire forces were in full and shambolic retreat from the invading German army. The Commandos were ordered to provide the rearguard to protect the embarking men on the beach head. Under almost constant air attack somehow large numbers of the army were taken off by the navy. Waugh and the Commandos watched with alarm. As the clock ticked down it was apparent that there was not enough room on the boats and many would have to surrender.

Waugh's commanding officer – whom he revered – Colonel Robert Laycock, dictated a false statement and had Waugh write in the war diary that he had ordered his men to evacuate Crete, 'in view of the fact that . . . there was no enemy contact'. This was patently false: serious fighting was still going on in the hills, but Laycock ordered his men to abandon the rearguard positions, embark and thereby escape. After their departure many hundreds of soldiers were captured by the Germans. Waugh was complicit in this blatant disregard of orders and he felt the shame deeply, talking of 'my ignominious flight', and 'my bunk from Crete'.

In the novel everything is subtly different. First, the character based on Laycock – Colonel Tommy Blackhouse – conveniently breaks his leg on a destroyer approaching Crete and never even lands on the island. Instead the man who ignominiously flees is the idealized, aristocratic warrior, Ivor Claire, whom Guy idolizes. Guy refuses to disobey orders and escapes in a small boat rather than surrender. But learning later of Ivor Claire's desertion brings about Guy's potent disillusion with the army. Ivor Claire bears all the guilt that Waugh felt himself at his duplicitous escape from Crete. Guy behaves with honour throughout but, when he learns of Ivor's cowardice, his love affair with the army and all things military is effectively over.

As always with Waugh, he was brutally honest with himself. When *Officers and Gentlemen* was first published Guy's last day on Crete is described as 'fatal' – the day on which he resigned 'an immeasurable piece of his manhood'. This makes no sense: Guy has done nothing wrong, but the words represent the true measure of Waugh's own feelings about the incident. The sentence was excised from the later omnibus edition.

When *Officers and Gentlemen* was published (dedicated to Laycock) Waugh's inner circle knew the facts. Ann Fleming, a close friend, waspishly telegrammed to Waugh 'Presume Ivor Claire based Laycock dedication ironical.' Waugh denied this absolutely: 'if you suggest such a thing anywhere,' he wrote back, 'it will be the end of our beautiful friendship . . . Just shut up about Laycock. Fuck you. E. Waugh.'

The autobiographical facts – and Waugh's personal agony – underpin the fiction and explain its particular power and vehemence. Guy Crouchback, like Waugh, wanted to go to war – it was a just war and he was zealous for battle – but everything he experienced resulted in bitter disillusion and disappointment.

It is this element in Waugh – his fundamental and unsparing honesty – that I find so compelling and admirable. The various poses and images of himself that Waugh presented to the world were deliberately provocative, not to say deliberately preposterous. Whether he is acting the choleric Tory squire, or the Victorian paterfamilias, or the Pall Mall clubman; whether he is expounding on his hatred of all things modern or displaying his near-manic adherence to the Catholic Church and the aristocratic values of county house life – almost everything is calculated to challenge and offend, to draw down, it would seem, the inevitable accusations of social-climbing, class-hatred, snobbery and affectation.

But nobody was more aware of the sham and the bogus than Waugh. His late self-portrait in *The Ordeal of Gilbert Pinfold* proves beyond doubt that he knew himself better than anyone. And the same unblinking candour informs his dark, comic vision also. He saw the world and its denizens with absolute clarity and devastating unsentimentality – nowhere more so than in *Sword of Honour* – and displayed the nature of the human condition with almost gleeful ruthlessness. This is what makes him, I think, an enduringly modern spirit – however paradoxical that adjective might seem – and explains why his books have lasted so well and will continue to survive.

2001

The British Caff

There's a fine, near-classic example behind King's Cross Station, and there's a particularly austere – brutally austere – one in Hounslow. If you're looking for down and out seedy there's a beauty on the Old Kent Road, guaranteed to set the soul in a slow slide of despair. For pure grease, however, the air peppery and astringent with fat fumes, there's one I frequent in Notting Hill and on the Gray's Inn Road there's a monster – London's version of *La Coupole*, as it were – with a venerable history of some few decades.

I'm talking, of course, about that great, possibly obsolescent British institution – the Caff. 'Cafe' seems far too classy an appellation, too foreign. 'Greasy spoon' somehow recalls the 1930s American Depression to me, or a truckers' halt – the semantics is not quite right. We say, don't we, 'I'm off down to the caff,' or 'See you in the caff in half an hour' and the word seems just about perfect – bluntly anglicized, demotic, accentless, unpretentious, apt. Whether you're in Aberdeen or Guildford, Norwich or Durham, you know exactly, precisely what you're going to get – in terms of ambience and nourishment – when you call a place a 'caff'.

Forget pubs, the British caff is our true and enduring culinary landmark. You can find a flawless replica pub in Prague or Barcelona, these days. Pubs have gone up-market, are franchised, themed. The caff resists this gentrification doggedly and triumphantly. They exist nowhere else, indeed no other country in the world would want them. They remain irreducibly ours. Ignored, despised, avoided, unrecorded, unclassified, guide-free, the caff clings on in all corners of our cities and towns, an enduring testimonial to our indifference to comfort, our bad taste, our appalling eating habits and our complete lack of *savoir-vivre*.

When I was researching my latest novel, *Armadillo*, which is set entirely in London, my travels around the city took me to many of these bleak estaminets, these gloomy watering holes, and I spent long hours in them, observing the traffic of customers, gingerly eating and drinking, making notes. I went into them initially in a spirit of anthropological curiosity, but the more time I spent, caff-dwelling, the more a form of creeping affection for them grew in me. Feelings of hygienic distaste, of mild shame, gave way to sneaking admiration, of almost pride. Who else could have evolved such a dauntingly rebarbative institution? What did it say about us as a people, a nation? Surely, I reasoned, here was some form of pure objective correlative for us, the British, one untouched by hand of marketing man, design team, tourist board or whatever. Here lay – in gustatory terms at least – a small quintessence of our national psyche.

This increasing familiarity with and affection for the caff grew into a near-obsession. I started seeking out more and more examples, sub-species and hybrid types, started pestering my friends for their local variations. I even gave my central character in the novel – who also spent a lot of time caff-bound – a similar fixation. He started – let's be honest, I started – to evolve a crude taxonomy, writing prime exemplars down in a notebook under the rubric 'Great British Caffs'. Like some latter-day Linnaeus, my protagonist set about distinguishing the true from the bogus, steadily evolving criteria for a more exact classification, beginning to understand what fitted the bill – what was an *echt*-caff, an *über*-caff – and what fell short of the archetype.

Months of experience, of diligent patronage, have led me to some basic definition of the key constituents. I think I can now describe what I would term the exemplary British caff – the Platonic Ideal – with some accuracy.

First of all the question of location – irrelevant. Some of the most authentic caffs thrive in the trendiest purlieus, indifferent to the modish frenzy around them, but, in truth, the real aficionado prefers mean streets. Litter, graffiti, urban decay, gasometers, a palpable sense of fear – a rubbish-clogged canal or railway marshalling yards nearby add a certain *je ne sais quoi*. That the caff flourishes in such an inhospitable domain is part of its essential appeal.

Second: size. The smaller the better. One room contains all – food and drink preparation, counter, tables and chairs together in the same rectangle. There is an argument to be made for a rear area – dingier, darker, redolent of the lavatory – but one room remains a key criterion.

Third: decor. The essential factor here is absence of decor. Charm lies in charmlessness. Lino, Formica, plastic cladding, melamine, stainless steel, aluminium, glass, styrofoam tiles, cork (at a pinch) – these are the materials out of which the Platonic caff is constructed. The only exception to this austerity is kitsch. Extreme kitsch is self-justifying – bad murals, clashing paint schemes, bric-a-brac and the rest. There is one caff I know whose decor revolves around a Union Jack theme (the owners are very patriotic). The flag motif overwhelms, is overabundantly in your face – no one in their right mind would want to see so many Union Jacks in one small room – which is why it works. We will allow also the odd calendar, a poster or two, a stray bit of never-to-be-removed Christmas bunting, an occasional pot of struggling moribund greenery – spider plants or parched geraniums, preferably. Otherwise an almost total Bauhausian form-and-function, abhorrence-of-the-decorative ethos should prevail.

Fourth: food. Again, the idea of a few central ingredients endlessly re-combined is the dominant concept. Eggs, bacon, sausage, beans, chips, bread, mushrooms, peas, black pudding, gammon, tomato sauce, brown sauce, vinegar and so on. Quality is irrelevant. Indeed, the true connoisseur wants bad food – high gristle quotient in the sausage, nothing but margarine, over-generous salting everywhere, maximum water content in any cooked veg – but in fact it is fine if the food is tasty: no problem. The crucial factor, nutritionally, is the unhealthiness package. Baked beans are the only fibre admissible; a high saturated-fat content is a *sine qua non*, massive cholesterol intake is vital. Soft white sliced bread, everything pan- or deep-fried rather than grilled, a mix of carbohydrates that would defeat the training programme of an olympic athlete – bread and fried bread and chips *and* a pie, say, to accompany bacon and sausage and black pudding. The list is not long and any attempt to add something exotic (curried baked beans just pass muster) excludes the place from true caff classification. Any spaghetti, lasagne, any fish, chops, etc. – any *salad*, for heaven's sake – move it into the sphere of pseudo-restaurant. Sandwiches are allowed but again must be strictly controlled – we want no hint of Marks & Sparks or Pret à Manger, no sesame seed baps or wholemeal baguettes. The bread is white – period – the whiter and more taste-free the better. The fillings are limited – ham, cheese, roast beef (just), chicken or turkey roll (nothing off the bone) and tomatoes and cucumbers which must be sliced transparently thin. One caff I know offers – year round – only egg, tomato, ham and cheese. On no occasion must the filling even approach the thickness of the bread slice. Tuna is allowed as long as it is mashed with vinegar to achieve a near-fluid state. Egg can be rendered similarly deliquescent with the addition of salad cream – never mayonnaise.

Drink. Firm rules apply here. Tea or coffee, milk – a glass of milk, an almost vanished drink these days, is regularly consumed in caffs – tins of cheap gassy colas (unrefrigerated) and that's it. You might get a carton of juice and no caff is ever licensed to sell alcohol. Refinements on the hot drink agenda include tea being served from the pot (a real bonus) and, amazingly, there are some caffs still using Camp Coffee (the liquid mix, for those with long memories) but normally the coffee must be instant and unbranded. As soon as there is a Cona machine or a Gaggia then we are in espresso bar territory and caffdom is lost, irretrievably.

These are, I think, the essential defining factors of the Platonic caff. There are variations and some enthusiasts may argue for alternative necessities. But, as any regular caff-goer realizes, there are other more elusive, harder to define qualities that make the places and the experience of being in them so distinct and memorable. Think of pre-eminent factors such as condensation and cigarette smoke. To have a plate-glass window that one can see through seems entirely wrong (indeed, ideally one wants condensation *and* a diamond mesh security grille). Also, a non-smoking caff seems oxymoronic. A purist would insist on roll-up cigarettes only. A badly tuned transistor radio (Radio 1, Capital Gold) also adds to the ambience as, of course, do the *patron* and his staff and their various attitude problems (whether raucous or sullen, suicidally depressed or irredeemably sloppy). All these elements contribute immeasurably to the aggregate of features that makes the places unique.

But there is something higher, more intellectual and philosophical that makes caff-life so addictive in its special way. I think it is because caffs are not, fundamentally, social places. They tend to favour the solitary or the untalkative; indeed, they have to be uncrowded in order to function best. You sit there in a corner alone with two or three others. The old geezer with his tightly folded tabloid; the seventeen-year-old mother-of-two smoking herself to death; the tattooed youth with his face full of iron. You don't want to share a table, you don't want to talk, you're not (unless you happen to be a novelist) even curious about these strange folk and they in turn are deeply incurious about you. There is something wonderfully solipsistic about being in these places, provoking a mood of melancholy reflection, of indulgent soul-searching, of eschatological ponderings. You feel in a kind of social and moral limbo – you can't even see the outside world because of the condensation and you can't imagine what sort of a city contains these curious denizens eating their extraordinary food. But then, you ask yourself, what are you doing here, caff-haunter? Eating, drinking, hanging out. What does that say about *you*? . . .

Solipsistic, egalitarian, existential, democratic, esoteric, insouciant, disinterested, cheap – what kind of establishment offers you all this, plus baked beans, chips, fried bread, sausage, bacon, fried eggs, mushrooms, black pudding, bread and margarine, HP and tomato sauce and a chipped Pyrex cup of stewed tea? We should preserve these singular, beguiling places before they disappear but – and this is what adds the bizarre magic – how could you possibly achieve that? The very attempt to cherish and enshrine or consecrate removes everything special, destroys the quiddity of the establishment at once. It is as if there is a built-in, anti-tamper, self-destruct device designed to counteract our best arty-liberal-bourgeois intentions. The caff has evolved in these islands of its own accord – organically, mysteriously, almost unnoticed – and if one day it becomes extinct it will have been something self-willed, a kind of benign suicide, not driven out, not victim of an enforced, unnatural transformation, part radical chic, part heritage industry. All we can do is watch and contemplate these remarkable loci of our urban lives carefully, see how they adapt and change or die away, log and note them for posterity – and make sure to go in from time to time.

1998

Evelyn Waugh (2)

In 1971 Cyril Connolly flew to the University of Austin, Texas, to view an exhibition of first editions of key twentieth-century works of literature inspired by his book *The Modern Movement*. Immodestly, Connolly had asked that one of his own books be included and suggested his 'word-cycle' *The Unquiet Grave*, published in 1944. The university duly agreed and, having purchased Evelyn Waugh's library on his death, decided to display Waugh's own heavily annotated copy of *The Unquiet Grave*, sent to him on publication by Nancy Mitford. Connolly read the copious marginalia with horrid fascination: he was shocked and appalled at the cold dismissiveness and abuse they contained. Amongst the aspersions were 'Irish corner boy', 'hack highbrow', 'drivelling woman novelist'. Writing about the experience later Connolly commented: 'What I minded most was the contempt that emerged from a writer for whom for twenty years I had looked on as a friend.' He conjured up a demonic image of Waugh, contemplating the 'bloated, puffed-up face of my old club-mate, the beady eyes red with wine and anger, the cigar jabbing as he went in for the attack'. Friends rallied, contrary and consoling alternative judgements were proffered. Waugh, it was generally agreed, was a venomous parvenu consumed by envy and snobbery.

I cite this anecdote because this portrait of Waugh still rings true, and it continues to represent for many the abiding image of the writer, born a hundred years ago on 28 October 1903. The fact that it does is in large part down to Waugh himself. The persona he created for himself in the later stages of his life was an elaborate construct – full of contradictions – but calculated to stir up derision, confusion and animosity amongst his perceived enemies. It was at times so close to the absurd, to the caricature (the bookie's tweeds, the hearing trumpet, the brandished cigars) that its very artifice seemed to be designed to be exposed. Anthony Powell – who was always acutely perceptive about his peers – wrote about Connolly and Waugh, saying that both men were 'mesmerised by *beau monde* mystique, both in their different ways fundamentally ill-at-ease there, unless in a position to perform his own individual act, put on a turn, in fact'.

'Putting on a turn' is what Evelyn Waugh did for most of his adult life and it had many manifestations: country squire, iconoclastic Tory, devout Catholic, fearless soldier, virulent anti-modernist, stern pater-familias, rural anchorite, senile patrician and so on. Why he did this, and why he did it so assiduously, is a matter for endless debate (we all have our theories) but the consequences have not helped his posthumous reputation: the man, I feel, has in recent years shouldered the work aside – the life has become more compelling than the fiction.

The problem is that we know an enormous amount about Evelyn Waugh – we have the letters, the diaries, the collected journalism, five large biographies, let alone the memoirs of friends and neighbours – perhaps only Virginia Woolf of twentieth-century English writers has been more compendiously documented. This is a genuine shame because, however diverting the show might be, the spectacle of Evelyn Waugh guying or exploiting various forms of eccentric Englishness detracts serious attention from a fascinating and enduring body of work. Waugh's debut was assured and precocious. His first novel, *Decline and Fall* (1928), published when the author was twenty-five years old set the style and the tone for the string of great comedies that followed: *Vile Bodies* (1930), *Black Mischief* (1932) and *Scoop* (1938). In between *Black Mischief* and *Scoop*, however, came *A Handful of Dust* (1934), considered by many to be Waugh's 'best' novel. I don't agree: I see the novel as an uneven and semi-disguised act of revenge against Waugh's first wife, whom he divorced after a year of marriage in 1928. Despite its modishly nihilistic superstructure (the title coming from T. S. Eliot's *The Waste Land*) it is essentially a society novel about an adulterous wife and the bleak conse-quences of that betrayal. It also heralded the concerns of his later work – a building religious dimension, a hatred of the new, a fawning admi-ration of the aristocratic past – that reached an early apotheosis in *Brideshead Revisited* (1945, considered by many to be his worst novel) and was continued and refined in the *Sword of Honour* trilogy. *Scoop* is, in my opinion, his real masterwork. It has a classical and deeply satis-fying shapeliness but also contains sequences of hilarious comic writing unrivalled in English literature. As it turned out it was to be his final, sustained essay in the comic form. *The Ordeal of Gilbert Pinfold* (1957) forms a strange coda to these four great comedies but is really too idio-syncratic to be truly cognate with them.

A hundred years on from Waugh's birth and thirty-seven from his death it is perhaps timely to assess the measure of his achievement, to see how the work has survived. The 'Brideshead myth' will, I suppose, always be the first aspect of Waugh's output that seems the most visible if not the most significant. Yet a moment's reflection – or a few pages of rereading – will expose the book as flawed and self-serving. It was conceived in wartime as an act of nostalgic recall, of rose-tinted reveries of a never-never-land Oxford (Waugh himself admitted as much). In a later edition he tried to curb the excesses and strip away as much as he could of what was lush and verbose but with little success. The subsequent television version in the 1980s only served to reinforce the sentimental romance. The book's huge success was always rather embarrassing to Waugh: he was grateful for the revenue but vaguely ashamed of the way it was acquired. He never attempted such panting excesses again. *Brideshead*'s love affair with aristocratic virtues was dramatically honed down in the *Sword of Honour* trilogy. Claret, teddy bears and stately homes devolve into Mr Crouchback's austere injunction 'not to repine'. Lyrical upper-class hedonism gives way to an unbending and stoical faith in God's edict and man's duty to God on earth. To a non-believing or even agnostic reader the trilogy's moral underpinnings appear close to mumbo-jumbo, but to anyone familiar with Waugh's life they reflect his almost manic piety: he clung to his demanding faith with the tenacity of a drowning man to a piece of driftwood.

The contrast with the later novels and the early comedies is acute. What makes the four novels of 1928–38 so continuously readable is their tone of voice. Waugh sees the world as fundamentally absurd and indifferent to mankind's fate. With this in mind the comedy is triumphantly dark and pitiless: the evil thrive, the innocent are punished. Happiness is transitory or delusional; hopes, dreams and ambitions are redundant in the face of an uncaring, cruel and arbitrary universe. Waugh didn't invent this point of view: one could argue that it first received its full fictional expression in the mature short stories of Anton Chekhov. The great follower of Chekhov at the time Waugh was beginning his writing career was the now forgotten William Gerhardie. Later in life Waugh admitted his debt to Gerhardie's early novels – *Futility*, *The Polyglots*, *Jazz and Jasper* (published to huge acclaim in the early twenties). It was not so much a question of borrowing (though a lot of *Jazz and Jasper* has slipped into *Vile Bodies* and *Scoop*) but of seizing on an authorial point of view that Waugh found entirely congenial. Gerhardie did not have Waugh's talent as a writer but he saw the world in the same absurdist, amoral way and, like Chekhov, refused to pass judgement on his characters and their actions. For the young Evelyn Waugh it must have come both as a recognition and a revelation: the tone of voice in *Decline and Fall* is so assured because it had already been aired and developed by Gerhardie. Waugh applied it to his own fictional ends and hit the ground running.

Waugh was received into the Catholic Church in 1930 after the humiliation of the collapse of his first marriage. He was, by all accounts, a diligent and sincere neophyte but the religiosity that makes its first pronounced appearance in *Brideshead* is absent from the three comedies he published in the decade following his conversion. The world of the comedies is, in effect, Godless. Indeed one might claim that it is a precondition of comedy that it is, covertly or not, atheistical: based on the premise that no omnipotent god could possibly have created or be responsible for the ghastly and rebarbative world we live in. However, Waugh's developing obsession with his faith meant that the comedy in his work becomes intermittent and less successful: it lacks the cool, gimlet-eyed dispassion of the earlier works. As Waugh's novels became more self-consciously serious – as God entered the frame – so they began to creak and sag.

Perhaps this was inevitable. Waugh is the most autobiographical of fiction writers and as he reached middle age so he began to be afflicted by melancholia and *taedium vitae*. Only his unbending religious beliefs offered him any kind of support. His son Auberon speculated that perhaps his father might actually have been clinically depressed – though he would never have admitted it and indeed the only medication he permitted himself for his condition was regular large measures of gin and lemon barley water.

In his writing life a similar zeal attached itself to the concept of style. Waugh saw himself as a craftsman whose medium was the English language: someone responsible for shaping a coherent sentence, choosing the exact words to convey the exact meaning the author implied. No language was richer and more suited to the task than English – 'The most lavish and delicate which mankind has ever known.' And Waugh is a consummate artist but within a particularly confined manner of English prose – he strove to write in an almost mock-Augustan idiom, sometimes beautiful and classically severe but sometimes verging on parody where too many Latinate orotundities tend to bleed the life from the fiction. As Thomas Hardy once tellingly remarked, 'If you want to have a living style then it's important not to have too much style.'

In this centenary year of Waugh's birth, therefore, I feel it's necessary to push to one side the image of Waugh the tweeded, social-climbing bully, and even Waugh the self-appointed guardian of the English language. Why we continue to read Waugh is why we are drawn to all great novelists: namely that in their fiction they tell us truths about our human nature and the human condition. Waugh's perfect medium in this endeavour was comedy and what made his comedy so alluring in the 1930s is as true in 2003 as it was then. Reflecting on his father's life and its litany of hostilities and antagonisms, Auberon Waugh wrote how sad that it should have been so when 'one reflects that all he really wanted to do . . . was to make jokes, to turn the world upside down and laugh at it and enliven this vale of tears with a little fantasy'. This would also pass muster as a fair summation of the effect of his comic novels. But, fantastical though they are, the fantasy is founded on a bedrock of precise observation and unflinching honesty. And it is this element in Waugh – his fundamental and unsparing honesty – that I find so compelling and admirable. The various poses and images of himself that he presented to the world were deliberately provocative, not to say deliberately preposterous. But this honesty meant that nobody was more aware of the sham and the bogus than Waugh himself. And there is no better proof than his late self-portrait in *The Ordeal of Gilbert Pinfold*: he knew himself better than anyone. *Gilbert Pinfold* is the record of an actual attack of dementia that Waugh suffered but it is also a merciless depiction of the author in middle age. All criticisms of the man are pre-empted because the most devastating come from the man himself. And the same unblinking candour informs his dark, comic vision also. He saw the world and its denizens with absolute clarity and absolute unsentimentality – nowhere more so than in the great comedies where he displayed the nature of our short lives on this small planet with gleeful ruthlessness. This is what makes him, I think, an enduringly *modern* spirit (however paradoxical that adjective might seem when applied to Evelyn Waugh) and explains why the comic novels continue to beguile readers – provoking both laughter and serious reflection – and will continue to survive.

2003

Minicabs

Picture the scene. It is late at night, two or three in the morning and I am almost the last guest at a bibulous dinner party in north London. I need to get back home to Chelsea. I turn to the host: 'I'd better call a cab,' I say. 'Don't worry,' he replies, 'we have a local firm. Here in five minutes.' True enough, five minutes later there is a peremptory honking in the street. I make my farewells and go out to find my minicab. The car is not difficult to locate – double-parked and throbbing with muffled techno-pop. I slide into the back seat – apparently springless. Indeed the car, an indeterminate, currently unrecognizable model, appears to sit surprisingly low on its haunches, a real road-scraper.

The driver is smoking; the tearing, harsh voice of the dispatcher fizzles from the radio. 'Where to?' the driver asks. The accent is foreign, foreign to London, anyway – the accents tend to come from far and wide, from Leeds, Aberdeen, Belgrade, Lagos, Kingston, Larnaca, Islamabad, Kiev. 'Chelsea,' I reply. The set of the shoulders betokens no familiarity with this destination. 'South-west London,' I add. 'Embankment?' says the driver. 'Get me to the Embankment and I can give you directions,' I say breezily, and settle back, noticing for the first time the curious smell – frowsty, farinaceous – here in the rear of this unclassifiable saloon, as if someone had cooked a spicy meal in the back of the car last week. Indeed, the material – the carpet – beneath my feet feels moist and tacky. I keep my hands in my lap and we pull away.

'POB,' the driver says into the handset of his radio. I know this means 'passenger on board' – everybody knows this, so why the coy acronym? Then there is a fair bit of 'Chelsea, yeah, Chelsea. Roger, Rog,' and the mike is rehung.

We drive crazily south, at high, reckless speed. I vaguely recognize the North Circular, Islington Green, then the Barbican, then the towers of Canary Wharf begin to loom closer. 'Where are you going?' I ask, baffled. 'Embankment,' comes the reply. 'This is the wrong way,' I advise.

So, we turn and make our zig-zag way back to the West End, Parliament Square, Big Ben – now I know where I am and give confident instructions from the rear seat. The car is still being driven with adolescent disregard – exaggerated wheel-turn, heavy braking, muttered oaths. We pull up outside my house, a preposterous sum of money is demanded as the fare and a hostile altercation ensues. I see lights going on in my neighbours' windows as the rhythmic thud of techno-pop rouses them from their beds. A compromise, but still-too-high figure is agreed (no tip) and no pen or paper is present either to furnish me with a receipt. I leave the car exhausted, frazzled, nervy, angry. I have just been minicabbed.

Admittedly, this scenario is an aggregate of several bad minicab journeys I've made – a nightmare amalgam of fear, irritation and noisome frustration – but aspects of this experience will ring true to almost everyone, I would claim. At some stage in their lives every Briton has been or will be minicabbed in a similar way. This, of course, is the downside of the minicab experience: there's an upside too which we mustn't forget (handy, cheapish, friendly, nearly always available). And 'forget' is the key word, because the minicab, as we love and loathe it, will not be around for much longer: another quintessentially British phenomenon is about to be legislated – not out of existence – but into something safer, surer, more user-friendly. The minicab is going to become a pseudo-taxi.

From this time next year (approximately September 2002) all minicabs will have to be licensed (in fact minicab firms are meant to have had their licence applications in by now but there has been some foot-dragging). But, within a year, as far as I understand it, all the new licensed minicabs will have to display a plate on the rear bumper; it will be permissible to hail them in the street; insurance will be checked and verified by the local council; there will be possibly two mandatory MOTs a year (at least one) and there may even be a meter to regulate fares. It will not be the same thing at all.

I came to live in London in 1983, in Fulham, and there was a minicab office at the end of our street. I'm a non-driver and so this firm (let's call them Ferret Cars) became one of my principal modes of transport around London. I opened an account with them (I still have an account with them). I came to know the drivers well – it was quite a small firm in the eighties (it's rather flash and grand now, with a huge fleet) – and, equally, they came to know me. I learned of their many travails and woes – whose marriage was on the ropes, who was gambling away his wages, who was drinking too much, who was going to get fired and so on. The drivers became familiar to me almost as friends are: Tommy, with his shocking emphysema; Jeremy, the redundant City trader, working a twenty-hour day to repay his debts; Trevor, who as I approached his car would greet me with a stiff-armed salute and a shout 'Heil Hitler'; Ben the worldly and cynical ex-police sergeant from Antigua . . . because I used minicabs so frequently I grew to know them all. Ferret Cars and their drivers inexorably became part of my life.

As the years went by, unconsciously, almost by a process of symbiosis, I learned a great deal about the minicabbing life – indeed, short of becoming a minicab driver myself, I couldn't have been more familiar with their world. I knew how much you could earn; I knew when car insurance went up; I knew why the old-model Ford Granada was the minicabbers' dream car; I knew all sorts of shortcuts and back-doubles in London; I knew how to avoid a traffic jam on the M4 (duck through a particular filling station on to a road unmarked on maps). Sometimes I felt I lived in a minicab – whereas, in fact, I almost died in one.

Well, if not death, then I risked fairly serious injury. I had ordered a Ferret car to take me to some 'do' in central London one evening, and was picked up by Colin, a genial man but the most compulsive liar I have ever met. He was telling me about some vast house he was building in Majorca (the week before it had been in County Cork) when he drove through a junction without looking and we were hit broadside on by – irony of ironies – a black cab. Luckily the black cab hit the central door jamb. A foot to the right and I would have been in the way. Colin's car was badly staved in but the superstructure held (was it a Saab? I can't remember). I was thrown across the interior (a few bruises) but was otherwise fine.

I staggered out of the good door, adrenalin fizzing, and sat on the kerb for a moment to calm down and check the damage. I seemed fine but Colin was in a state. However, his mind was working fast. He asked me to leave the scene as soon as possible and said I would not be charged for the ride (I was grateful but I suspect there was an insurance issue going on here), the only other stipulation was a plea that I breathe not a word of the incident to Ferret Cars. I promised I wouldn't and went groggily on my way, looking for a tube station, leaving Colin and the irate cabby to sort things out.

So it was not surprising, given my intimate association with Ferret Cars, that minicabs duly found their way into my fiction – the seam was too rich not to be mined at some stage. And a minicab firm is very central in my novel, *Armadillo*, where the hero's brother, Slobodan 'Lobby' Blocj runs the family firm, 'B&B mini-cabs and International Couriers' with his dodgy partner Phil Beazley. B&B are at the low end of the minicab food chain (nothing like Ferret Cars who proceeded to go from strength to strength) and it was one of the enduring pleasures of seeing the book adapted for television to witness B&B come to vivid and appalling life.

This sort of firm in a way presents the inverse of the Platonic Ideal: B&B mini-cabs, in a pure and idealized way, is as bad as it gets – and we have all hired cabs from a B&B at some stage. First of all, the premises have to be condemnable and very small – a tiny dispatcher's office (soft-porn calendars obligatory) and a slightly larger bull-pen adjacent to it where the waiting drivers sit, smoke and talk (what do minicab drivers talk about? They talk about cars) which is furnished with laboratory standard fluorescent lighting, a carpetless floor, a couple of winded sofas and overflowing ashtrays. And the more pretentious the name of the firm, the better: 'Elite', 'Transcontinental', 'Platinum', 'International', 'Exclusive' – these are the adjectives that tend to be associated with the meanest congregation of clapped-out motors.

The cars themselves are a vital adjunct to the picture: the older and dirtier the better. One of the Ferret Car drivers (in the early days) drove an ancient Ford Cortina, through whose floor the road could be glimpsed. This driver, moreover, was the angriest man in London. I remember getting off transatlantic flights and seeing him waiting to take me home, scowling, wordless, full of hate for the world – and my spirits would wilt at the thought of the M4 waiting for us and the gush of abuse that would spout from him on the endless drive to Chelsea.

Seeing the road through the floor is good; having dangling wires hanging from the dashboard is good; very loud music is good; joss sticks burning by the gearstick is good. Eventually you become an aficionado of all the archetypically bad aspects to the *echt* minicab. Perversely, you don't want the glossy Merc picking you up, you want the 1978 Toyota Corolla with the rusted chrome and the driver with Tourette's Syndrome. You want rap music and chain smoking, you want the monoglot Serb with his new *A–Z*. Rather like greasy-spoon cafes (the caff, that uniquely great British contribution to culinary matters) it is what is awful that delivers the real aesthetic frisson. We want furry dice hanging from the rear-view mirror; we want photos of the kids sellotaped to the dashboard; we want a boot full of junk with no room for your suitcase; we want a car that won't move out of second gear; we want the driver-as-bore, the driver-as-kamikaze-pilot, the driver-with-terminal-halitosis.

This is what makes the experience special, gives the journey its own frisson and texture – takes it out of the run-of-the-mill.

But it's all going to disappear: clean, well-maintained cars, healthy, polite, heavily insured drivers will be the minicab norm – soon they'll have to do the 'knowledge'. But picture the scene: it's 2005 or 2006, very late in the evening and you are almost the last to leave a dinner party far from your home. You turn to your host: 'I'd better get a cab.' He says he'll call a licensed local firm. Then he turns to you: 'Or would you rather go unlicensed?' Ancient, uninsured cars, he says, all the drivers are asylum seekers. The hairs on the nape of your neck prickle. You realize how you've missed the authentic minicab experience. You decide to go unlicensed. Five minutes later you hear that old familiar peremptory honking outside. You leave; you locate your car. Strange music emanates from it, your driver speaks to you but you can't understand what he says. The static from the radio cuts through your brain. You slide into the back seat, there is dampness under the soles of your shoes and an unfamiliar odour fills your nostrils. 'Drive,' you say, a catch in your voice – it may be illicit, but it's real.

This is a fantasy, of course, but it is a fond one. And I suspect it contains an element of truth: however they legislate, however they seek to root out the old-style minicab it will linger on in secret parts of London, tenacious and ineradicable – like an arctic lichen, a Coelacanth, a Tasmanian devil – a little bit of England that refuses to lie down and die.

2001

Montevideo

Montevideo, Uruguay . . . Why did I want to go there? I had never been, but there was one very good reason why I shouldn't have planned a visit: the opening pages of my last novel are set in the place and I have found it's a very bad idea to check out the validity of your research – your assumed knowledge – *after* the book has been published. I have written novels set in the Philippines, Kenya and Berlin, for example, and have still to visit these places. I had travelled there in my imagination and my imagination had enjoyed the experience – it seemed somehow unnecessary, or risky, to have to verify if it knew what it was talking about.

But I found myself, this July, in Argentina, in Buenos Aires, and was due to move on from there to Rio de Janeiro. Across the vast estuary of the Río Plata lay Uruguay and Montevideo – this strange South American city that my imagination had inhabited for some months. I knew the layout of its streets, I knew where to find the cathedral, I knew about its solitary hill with a fort on top, I knew the name of the street where the hero of my novel had been born. So close – two hours away by speedy hydrofoil – it would have been a crime not to have checked it out.

Novelists travel – or don't travel – for all sorts of perverse reasons. And as I boarded the sleek *buquebus* (the hydrofoil) at Puerto Madera in Buenos Aires I started to wonder what had made me select Montevideo as the starting point for my last novel. These decisions are, more often than not, made almost unconsciously. My novel, *Any Human Heart*, was the story of one man's progression through the twentieth century narrated via the medium of his intimate journals. For some reason I wanted this man, this Englishman, to be born abroad, to be somewhat deracinated, and I chose Montevideo as his birthplace and the locus of the first few years of his tumultuous life. For 'some reason'. The first reason was simple: corned beef. Everyone older than me, everyone of my generation and perhaps younger, for all I know, has heard of Fray Bentos corned beef. But not many people know that Fray Bentos is not a brand name but a city in Uruguay. A city built in the late nineteenth century around beef and its processed variants. Corned beef, 'bully beef', that staple of our national diet for well over a hundred years, originated in large part from *frigoríficos* – vast abattoirs and canning factories in Uruguay. Corned beef – iconic food of the British nation – came from Uruguay. Where better to start an Englishman's life story?

But this wasn't the complete explanation. I recently reread Graham Greene's novel *The Honorary Consul*, which is set in Paraguay. It starts like this, in a mood of classic Greenean evocativeness.

Doctor Eduardo Plarr stood in the small port on the Paraná, among the rails and yellow cranes, watching where a horizontal plume of smoke stretched over the Chaco. It lay between the red bars of sunset like a stripe on a national flag . . . It was an evening which, by some mysterious combination of failing light and the smell of an unrecognised plant, brings back to some men the sense of childhood and of future hope and to others the sense of something which has been lost and nearly forgotten.

I realized that when I had first read the novel on its publication (in 1973) I had conjured up from these few sentences an abiding image in my mind of South America – however factitious and romantic. Dusk, a broad river, a certain world-weariness. I knew that something that had lingered with me from Greene's novel had, decades later, made me start my own in Montevideo.

The *buquebus* headed off from Puerto Madera at high speed, judging from the fountaining spume of its impressive wake. The Río Plata was ideally calm but there was no possibility of going on deck – forbidden. Crossing the huge refulgent river as the sun set was almost like being in a plane. As we travelled towards Uruguay I realized there was another personal connection that was urging me on to Montevideo. When I was very young, I was best friend at school with the son of the famous film director Michael Powell. The one film of his that we saw in those days was his (now virtually forgotten) version of the hunting and destruction of the German battle-cruiser, the *Graf Spee*, in 1939 – *The Battle of the River Plate* (1956). The *Graf Spee*, pursued by the British fleet, made for the safety of Montevideo harbour. Uruguay was neutral and the *Graf Spee* was allowed only forty-eight hours in port. Rather than face the British ships waiting offshore the captain scuttled the ship in the river and committed suicide. Something of this connection – Michael Powell, this forgotten film, my early schooldays – had suggested

Montevideo to me, also. Such is the strange congruence of sources that combine and cohere in the writing of a novel: corned beef, Graham Greene, an old black and white war movie. And now I was going to see the place for myself.

It was in the final fading light of sunset that we pulled into Montevideo's harbour – light enough for me to recognize (as if it was familiar somehow) the low conic hill that signalled Montevideo to so many visitors over the centuries. It was a strange moment. I had written in my novel (some two years earlier): 'Did I weep when I looked back at my beautiful city beneath its small, fort-topped conic hill as we left the yellow waters of the Río Plata behind?' Now I was arriving in this very city – and the hill was duly there, but the waters of the Río Plata were black with the oncoming darkness, reflecting the dancing lights of the custom house. Moreover, I had been writing about a Montevideo that existed in 1914 – would it still be beautiful?

The short, brutal answer is 'no'. But the city, as I explored it over the next two days, was no less fascinating for that. I was there, I should say, for only two days in the middle of the Uruguayan winter – nowhere looks its best in winter (unless it's a ski resort). Montevideo was the thin sliver of corned beef in my South American sandwich: Argentina and Brazil being the thick slices of bread. I was really doing the city – let alone the country – no justice and my motives for being there were both arcane and personal. The sandwich analogy is apt in other ways, however. Uruguay's export economy has suffered greatly in recent years: first from Brazil's devaluation of its currency in the late nineties and second (how unlucky can you get with these two neighbours?) with the Argentinian financial crash of 2001. While Buenos Aires and Rio both show healthy signs of recovery and some evident civic pride, Montevideo is still clearly reeling from this double whammy.

Geographically, Montevideo is easily grasped. The bay forms a natural harbour and it was on the western side that the old walled city was first established. In the nineteenth century the new city was constructed, spreading further westwards and built in a style, common to most South American cities of the period, that was vaguely Parisian – broad boulevards, tree-lined avenues, important squares and so on. This move westwards continued in the twentieth century along the coast road – the various *ramblas* – so that modern Montevideo is amazingly attenuated and, great boon to the citizens, the beach is only ever a few blocks away. The beaches were empty while I was there but I was assured that the river and its riverine life were what made Montevideo such a nice place to live in. Strong contrast to Buenos Aires, interestingly enough, in which city one is rarely aware of the vast river at its doorstep. Montevideo, in this respect, is more like Rio but without Rio's tropical élan. In fact it's élan that's most conspicuously missing as the city struggles to recover from its economic woes.

Paradoxically, if you're not looking for a deluxe tourist-brochure time (i.e. if you happen to be a novelist), its air of decrepitude makes the city all the more atmospheric and intriguing. For reasons which have now been explained I kept thinking of Graham Greene while I wandered around Montevideo. The streets are filled with ancient, noisy and noisome buses, constantly revving their engines, changing gears, belching blue diesel fumes. I was almost coughing blood after a couple of hours and I understood the weary sallowness of the inhabitants' faces. Signs of disrepair are all around. Outside the city's grand hotel the doorman's coat is worn and greasy. Litter fringes the puddles in the gutters. Shops display poor, low-grade wares. The pavements are buckled and crumbling. The public buildings have an over-ornate Soviet-style kitsch. The main square, the Plaza Independencia, is graced with possibly the ugliest 1920s skyscraper you will ever see. I kept wondering why I was thinking of Russia and I realized that the tower of the building (the Palacio Salvo) looks like a Russian space rocket and the makeshift, malfunctioning air of space-station Mir seems the right metaphor for the town. The opera house, the Teatro Solis, was closed for renovations, and no one was sure when it would reopen. The former grand boulevard of the new town, the Avenida 18 de Julio, has been ruined by unrestrained shopping malls and gimcrack developments. I found the whole place absolutely fascinating. The peculiar friable, melancholic atmosphere of Montevideo is strangely beguiling even though unsought for and no doubt deplored by its more upright citizens. You itch to write a novel set here.

There is money and moneyed folk in Montevideo, of course. They tend to live in Carrasco, in big modern houses with security guards, to the west of the city and have summer homes in Punta del Este – the St Tropez of southern South America. But a wander round the old town gives the impression of a city struggling to rise up but still resolutely on its knees. But there are surprises – fruit shops ablaze with super-abundant produce, a wonderful old bar (straight from the 1920s) called the Bar Bresilia, and – the key reason why everyone should go to Montevideo at least once in their lives – the Mercado del Puerto.

This is an old covered market down by the docks opposite the defunct railway station (built by the British). It is full of bars and restaurants – *parrillas* (grills) – serving meat of stupendous quality grilled in front of your eyes over great pans of glowing coals, pans fed from an upright flaming cage into which logs are regularly thrown. The heat is clearly intense and the meat is cooked with amazing speed. It's very cheap and in no sense exclusive – working men sit at the bar having their lunchtime steak or chorizos or spare ribs. Lunch for four at the classiest *parrilla*, El Palenque, cost £20 (with lashings of wine). The Mercado is only open at lunchtime and even in winter was packed. I've never seen anything like it in my life and have never eaten anywhere similar: at once utterly simple, completely functional and efficient, wholly delicious and gratifyingly democratic.

I left Montevideo in darkness, just as I had arrived, but this time pre-dawn, to catch the early plane to Rio. In the airport people were having their luggage covered with industrial-strength sticky plastic. The day before I had stopped briefly at the naval museum on the *ramblas* where there was a gun on display recovered from the *Graf Spee*. I was told there were serious plans afoot to raise the ship from the river bed. Because the *Graf Spee* was scuttled it settled slowly in the water and was essentially undamaged. It would be an amazing tourist attraction: a World War Two German pocket battleship in perfect condition. I hope they do it: it would be a fine symbol of Montevideo's eventual recovery from its current state of enforced indigence. Just as long as it doesn't become too smart.

2004

Rio de Janeiro

Three Nights of Samba in Rio

Midwinter in Rio de Janeiro. It's late June, the temperature is a very agreeable 25°C (80°F) and the sun is shining in a cloudless ice-blue sky. Standing on the top of Corcovado mountain at the foot of the concrete Christ (actually an impressively austere art deco sculpture clad in mosaic), looking around at the unsurpassable view, you have to admit there is no more beautifully positioned city in the entire world. Cape Town, San Francisco, Vancouver, Hong Kong or Sydney don't even come close. It helps to be this high, of course – even the *favelas* look picturesque. Down at ground level things turn a little bit more Miami Beach.

Until the end of the Second World War, Rio was a splendid nine-teenth-century city with tree-lined boulevards, ornate apartment blocks and grand public buildings in the Parisian vein. Ruthless redevelopment in the 1950s and 60s has left few vestiges of the original urban plan. If they hadn't knocked almost everything down Rio would have easily outdone Buenos Aires for the 'Paris of South America' title. No matter, Rio still has its own unique magic: the sheer, forested mountains surging up here and there, the vast bay and the ocean beaches more than compensate – and everything costs approximately one tenth the price of Europe.

I went to Rio this year to see the city and experience something of Brazil. Or should I say Brazilians. Rio is as much Brazil as New York is the USA – it's almost impossible to grasp the vastness and diversity of the country. Yet something of Brazil's heterogeneity can be found in the city – its music. And here I have to confess to a long-term Brazilian obsession. Very early on in my writing career my books were published in Brazil and they continue to appear there regularly. But up until this year I had never managed a visit (for various frustrating reasons) and the measure of my frustration was expressed in a short story I wrote in 1996 called 'Never Saw Brazil', in which a London minicab driver redeems his sad, shabby life through his love of Brazilian music. I too love Brazilian music and play it constantly. I love it in an uncompli-cated, almost ignorant way. I listen with enthusiasm to the great singers and song writers of recent decades – Milton Nascimento, Elis Regina, Ivan Lins, Maria Bethania and so on – but as I don't speak Portuguese most of the content of the songs is lost to me: their potent allure becomes solely a question of rhythm and melody. So one of my ambitions when I went to Rio was to come to closer grips with Brazil's music. I decided I wanted the real thing. And the real thing had to be samba.

I made inquiries. Yes, you can hear authentic, wonderful samba in Rio but there is a problem. Most of the best clubs are in a district called Lapa – not a place for the innocent, music-loving tourist to venture alone. On this trip, however, I had a guide, who was not only a native of Rio (a *carioca*), an artist and an expert on the history and culture of the city but was also an accomplished musician. His name was Fabio Sombra. Over several days Fabio guided me safely through hidden and undiscovered Rio and he also educated me about samba. Thus, any pretensions to expertise in this account owe everything to him: I just kept my ears open.

Lapa is in the centre of Rio and, up until fairly recently, was one of its most seedy and dangerous quarters. Perhaps because of its reputation it has been spared the developers' bulldozers and its streets are still lined with crumbling nineteenth-century houses and warehouses of that era. In the past few years, however, it has begun a slow regeneration: theatres and clubs have opened; the drinking dens, the transvestite prostitutes and drug-dealers are less in evidence. Lapa is becoming the place in Rio where you go to hear music.

I went on three separate nights to three extraordinary clubs. The first was the Centro Culturel Carioca. The club itself was in an enormous first-floor room – a huge space that could happily accommodate 300 people. We were here to see Teresa Cristina, a new samba star – a singer – and her group, the Grupo Semente. Teresa Cristina – in her twenties – sings classic samba. As an introduction it was ideal because the Grupo Semente was a prototypical samba band. The instruments were heavy on percussion. A tambourine (forget all nursery school associations: in samba the tambourine is a dominant presence, played in an extemporized way you have never before witnessed), a small hand-drum, a big bass drum (the *surdo*) and a small conga drum. Then there is the *cavaquinho*, a tiny four-steel-stringed guitar that looks like a ukulele and which gives samba its inimitable melodic line, and, finally, a seven-string guitar. In a way this is all you need for a samba band. The assembled percussion produces a heavy, driving rhythm that is incredibly exciting, and above this, the icing on the percussive cake, you have the steely-shrill chords of the *cavaquinho* and the seven-string guitar providing a kind of rich semi-bass line. And then you have the singer's unique voice.

One factor that was quickly evident in samba is that there is no 'attitude'. Everybody dresses down. Even Teresa Cristina, a big emerging talent, does nothing pop-starry: she stands demurely at the microphone – wearing a dress, a frock – and sings. It's all about serious music-making. And dancing, of course. Almost everybody watching was dancing and some of them were amazing dancers.

Our second Lapa club, a few nights later, was the Café Musical Carioca da Gema. *Gema* means 'yolk' – a slang expression loosely translated as 'the genuine article'. The night we were there it was hosting a scratch band of session musicians under the aegis of a middle-aged samba legend called Paulo Seite-Cordas – a world expert on the seven-string guitar. It was his evening and he'd invited a few friends along to play. The club was a fair-sized, nineteenth-century house. The main room, with a mezzanine, had exposed brick walls hung with semi-abstract paintings.

Somewhere there must have been a kitchen because you could order food (and drink) as you watched the show. Paulo's band had even more percussion. The now familiar *surdo*, two tambourine players, a mini conga and a small snare drum. The guest singer was Rhichah – a massive Barry White figure, perspiring copiously, dressed in a cream linen suit. Another classic samba instrument was in evidence this night, the *cuica*. A piece of wet cotton is rubbed on a stick, which is attached to the underside of a drum. This somehow produces the intermittent eek-eek-eek sound that you hear among the aggregate of samba rhythm effects. Apparently, it takes great skill to play the *cuica* properly. The conga player would occasionally set aside his congas and pick up the *cuica*, drawing spontaneous applause. We were sitting very close to the band and I was aware of the palpable effect of the drums: you could feel the sound waves of the *surdo* reverberating through your body.

The third excursion was a perfect completion of my samba education. We went to a huge night club in Lapa – three floors, each opened up by a central atrium. By day it functions as a store for film production props, by night it transforms itself into a club called Rio Scenarium.

This is why you see ten ancient bicycles hanging on the wall, three dozen bird cages, telephone booths, cabinets full of dolls and antique umbrellas, papier mâché dinosaurs, many, many varieties of chandeliers, and so on. The walls are lined with great floor-to-ceiling swags and swathes of blue and red PVC. Huge vases hold enormous bouquets of lurid plastic flowers. Each floor, thanks to the central atrium, has its own view of the stage on which the band plays. On a busy Friday night it can take hundreds of people (its success has prompted the owners to buy the derelict building next door – this is the future of Lapa). It costs about $2 to get in. Fabio said this was a bit pricey for Rio.

In the event, the music we heard that night was sensational. We started off with a bossa nova band. Now, samba enthusiasts are contemptuous of bossa nova. They call it 'samba-lite'. It was a jazzy form of samba created for North American and European tastes by João Gilberto in the 1960s. In Brazil it is going out of favour with the resurgence of traditional samba (bossa nova is huge in Japan, intriguingly enough). The three-person band we saw was first class but, blooded now by real samba, I could sense immediately how bland and easy-listening the music was. And nobody was dancing. You chat while you listen to bossa nova. Samba urges you on to your feet.

The samba band that came on after the bossa novans, Nicolas Krassik, was named after its founder, a violin player (from France). This was a more eclectic samba band with elements of Bahian music from north-east Brazil (more African-influenced). There was an accordion player and a rare type of big drum called a *zabumba*. Apart from Krassik himself, the surprise was to find a young woman called Nilze on the *cavaquinho*. A child prodigy, she is a star in Brazil. Nilze sang, as did another girl, with a great deep, rich voice. The sound that Krassik produced was most unusual. This was modern samba: a classic samba foundation with new ingredients. With the violin and the accordion playing it could sound, from time to time, almost Celtic or bluegrass – as if country and western had travelled south to meet samba – but this note was endlessly coun-terposed by the familiar pounding rhythms of the *zabumba*, *surdo* and congas. Africa always dominated. Rhythm ruled.

After a two-hour set we went out into Lapa, ears ringing, stirred and exhilarated. It was late, and Lapa was buzzing. In a square we saw the cheap liquor stalls plying their trade and the 'cat' barbecues (nobody knows what the meat is) were sizzling away. Blazing neon lit the twenty-four-hour car-repair shops and incredibly young prostitutes were begin-ning to gather on street corners. We wandered off to look for a taxi. I was already contemplating my next trip back to Rio, but the next time I plan to detour north as well – to Bahia. Now I've seen Brazil, I have to go back.

2004

Index

(*Compiled by Christopher Hawtree*)

BLOOMSBURY

BLOOMSBURY

The Dream Lover
Includes a new introduction by the author

'Perfect ... Suffused with an understanding of love, desire and
emotional incompetence' *Guardian*

Funny, moving and sharply observed, these stories are confirmation
of Boyd's status as one of English fiction's finest writers. Here are
twenty-two gripping tales told in bold, distinct voices from Brazil to
Africa and from Nice to Hollywood. This eclectic omnibus, previously
published as the collections *On the Yankee Station* and *The Destiny of
Nathalie 'X'*, is a must-read for any lover of the short story.

'His eccentric wit and restless intelligence exert a powerful appeal'
New York Times Book Review

ISBN: 9 780 7475 9229 7 / Paperback / 7.99

Order your copy:
By phone: 01256 302 699
By email: direct@macmillan.co.uk
Online: www.bloomsbury.com/bookshop
Prices and availability subject to change without notice.

Visit Bloomsbury.com for more about William Boyd including a
downloadable reading guide for *Restless*

www.williamboyd.co.uk